400 BUDGET
BEST-EVER RECIPES

400 BUDGET BEST-EVER RECIPES

How to create fuss-free, economical and delicious dishes for all the family, with fabulous recipes shown step by step in more than 1800 beautiful photographs

Smart cooking on a budget – everything you need to know to make low-cost, healthy and tasty meals, plus hundreds of hints and clever cooking guidelines

EDITED BY LUCY DONCASTER

LORENZ BOOKS

NOTES

Bracketed terms are intended for American readers.

For all recipes, quantities are given in both metric and imperial measures and, where appropriate, in standard cups and spoons. Follow one set, but not a mixture, because they are not interchangeable.

Standard spoon and cup measures are level. 1 tsp = 5ml, 1 tbsp = 15ml, 1 cup = 250ml/8fl oz.

Australian standard tablespoons are 20ml. Australian readers should use 3 tsp in place of 1 tbsp for measuring small quantities of gelatine, flour, salt, etc.

American pints are 16fl oz/2 cups. American readers should use 20fl oz/ 2.5 cups in place of 1 pint when measuring liquids.

Electric oven temperatures in this book are for conventional ovens. When using a fan oven, the temperature will probably need to be reduced by about 10–20°C/ 20–40°F. Since ovens vary, you should check with your manufacturer's instruction book for guidance.

The nutritional analysis given for each recipe is calculated per portion (i.e. serving or item), unless otherwise stated. If the recipe gives a range, such as Serves 4–6, then the nutritional analysis will be for the smaller portion size, i.e. 6 servings. Measurements for sodium do not include salt added to taste.

Medium (US large) eggs are used unless otherwise stated.

This edition is published by Lorenz Books, an imprint of Anness Publishing Ltd, Hermes House, 88–89 Blackfriars Road, London SE1 8HA; tel. 020 7401 2077; fax 020 7633 9499

www.lorenzbooks.com; www.annesspublishing.com

If you like the images in this book and would like to investigate using them for publishing, promotions or advertising, please visit our website www.practicalpictures.com for more information.

UK agent: The Manning Partnership Ltd; tel. 01225 478444; fax 01225 478440; sales@manning-partnership.co.uk
UK distributor: Book Trade Services; tel. 0116 2759086; fax 0116 2759090; uksales@booktradeservices.com; exportsales@booktradeservices.com
North American agent/distributor: National Book Network; tel. 301 459 3366; fax 301 429 5746; www.nbnbooks.com
Australian agent/distributor: Pan Macmillan Australia; tel. 1300 135 113; fax 1300 135 103; customer.service@macmillan.com.au
New Zealand agent/distributor: David Bateman Ltd; tel. (09) 415 7664; fax (09) 415 8892

Publisher: Joanna Lorenz
Senior Managing Editor: Conor Kilgallon
Project Editor: Lucy Doncaster
Design: Paul Oakley Associates and Nigel Partridge
Production Controllers: Pedro Nelson and Steve Lang

ETHICAL TRADING POLICY
At Anness Publishing we believe that business should be conducted in an ethical and ecologically sustainable way, with respect for the environment and a proper regard to the replacement of the natural resources we employ.
As a publisher, we use a lot of wood pulp to make high-quality paper for printing, and that wood commonly comes from spruce trees. We are therefore currently growing more than 750,000 trees in three Scottish forest plantations: Berrymoss (130 hectares/320 acres), West Touxhill (125 hectares/305 acres) and Deveron Forest (75 hectares/185 acres). The forests we manage contain more than 3.5 times the number of trees employed each year in making paper for the books we manufacture.
Because of this ongoing ecological investment programme, you, as our customer, can have the pleasure and reassurance of knowing that a tree is being cultivated on your behalf to naturally replace the materials used to make the book you are holding.
Our forestry programme is run in accordance with the UK Woodland Assurance Scheme (UKWAS) and will be certified by the internationally recognized Forest Stewardship Council (FSC). The FSC is a non-government organization dedicated to promoting responsible management of the world's forests. Certification ensures forests are managed in an environmentally sustainable and socially responsible way. For further information about this scheme, go to www.annesspublishing.com/trees

A CIP catalogue record for this book is available from the British Library.

Previously published, in part, as *The Clever Cook*.

Main front cover image shows Sausage and Pepper Stew – for recipe, see page 346.

PUBLISHER'S NOTE
Although the advice and information in this book are believed to be accurate and true at the time of going to press, neither the authors nor the publisher can accept any legal responsibility or liability for any errors or omissions that may be made nor for any inaccuracies nor for any harm or injury that comes about from following instructions or advice in this book.

Contents

What is Clever Cooking?

Clever cooking is the notion of buying and using ingredients that will enable you to create a fabulous feast for less than it would cost to buy an ordinary sandwich from a store. Whatever your skill level or culinary preferences, with just a little common sense and planning you can produce a healthy, hearty and tasty two-course meal, complete with side dishes and accompaniments, for any occasion – from simple family suppers to dinner parties, barbecues and buffets.

About this book

Feeding a hungry family can be an expensive business, and with today's hectic lifestyle it is all too easy to disregard the importance of fresh, healthy home-made food. Lack of planning can result in huge amounts of food being thrown away, wasting both money and resources. However, with just a little bit of thought, some simple shopping tips and a wealth of inspiring recipes, you can create delicious meals without breaking the bank.

This book contains everything you need to know about what, when and where to buy the best value, best quality ingredients, and how to turn them into a wide range of healthy and delicious home-cooked meals. Detailed guidance on planning and preparation is given, covering everything from drawing up a weekly menu and managing a budget to shopping tips and buying in bulk. Techniques for storing and freezing raw ingredients, as well as inspiring ideas for converting leftovers into delicious dishes, make ingredients stretch further and will enable you to enjoy seasonal ingredients all year round.

Expert advice about growing your own herbs and foraging for free food, such as berries, nuts and mushrooms, is provided, as well as tips and techniques for easy ways to introduce flavour and texture to dishes using a range of herbs, spices and aromatics.

There then follows a comprehensive section outlining which foods are the best value for money, ranging from fresh fruit and vegetables to dairy, fish and meat, as well as pasta, beans, peas and grains. This invaluable directory provides essential information about when and where to buy ingredients so you get the most for your money.

Storecupboard staples – ranging from baking basics such as flour and sugar to stock (bouillon) cubes, oils and aromatics –are also listed in a separate directory, and arm the clever cook with the power to convert simple ingredients into stunning meals. Seasonality charts and sample menus make planning meals easy, although with over 400 mouth-watering recipes to choose from, you may well find that you are spoiled for choice!

Above: *A well-stocked storecupboard can save you time and money when cooking, and will encourage you to try your hand at more home baking.*

How recipes are costed

The cost of each recipe is based on average prices of ingredients at large supermarkets, and assumes the use of goods that are middle of the range rather than at either end of the price scale. Unless otherwise specified, all fruit, vegetables, dairy, fish and meat are fresh rather than canned or frozen, and all eggs are free-range. Fresh ingredients are priced when they are in season, and it is important that you bear in mind that the price of these foods may rise, and their availability may be limited, when they are out of season.

Many items may be cheaper to buy at wholesalers, markets or independent stores – such as butchers, fishmongers and greengrocers – and special offers and bulk-buying will also bring the cost of ingredients down: shopping around is vital.

Items that appear under the "From the storecupboard" heading in the ingredients list are not included in the final cost, since they should be part of the clever cook's storecupboard. Wherever possible, the use of home-made stocks, sauces, condiments, flavoured oils and pastries is encouraged, and there are recipes for a range of basics at the back of the book. Not only are home-made versions much cheaper, but they also taste better and contain no additives or preservatives.

How to use the key

Each recipe has been placed into one of three categories, depending on the overall cost of the dish per person. These categories are clearly illustrated by the symbols that appear beside each recipe name.

Below: *Choosing fresh, seasonal, good-quality ingredients will help you to create delicious dishes with the minimum effort and cost, as well as contributing to a healthy diet.*

The categories are:

✳	Bargain
✳ ✳	Very economical
✳ ✳ ✳	Economical

These price bands are a guide to the relative cost of each recipe, with one star representing the cheapest dishes and three stars denoting those that are slightly more expensive. All you have to do is work out how much you want to spend, which courses you want to serve, and then simply combine recipes to create your perfect meal. Suggestions for side dishes and accompaniments for each recipe are provided, as well as cook's tips and variations to allow you greater flexibility. Alternatively, you could use one of the menu plans provided – the possibilities are endless!

How to be a Clever Cook

BEING A CLEVER COOK INVOLVES THE APPLICATION
OF SEVERAL COMMONSENSE PRINCIPLES, INCLUDING:
PLANNING AHEAD; SHOPPING AROUND; BUYING GOOD
QUALITY FOODS WHEN THEY ARE IN SEASON; MAKING
THE MOST OF BARGAINS AND SPECIAL OFFERS; HAVING
A STORECUPBOARD THAT IS WELL STOCKED WITH
BASIC ESSENTIALS; KNOWING HOW TO STORE AND
FREEZE FRESH FOODS; AND, OF COURSE, BEING
EQUIPPED WITH THE NECESSARY KNOWLEDGE TO
TRANSFORM SIMPLE INGREDIENTS INTO A FEAST FOR
EVERY OCCASION.

Preparation and Planning

Proper prior planning helps to ensure that you eat a wide variety of foods and make the most of seasonal produce. If you know that you are going to be short of time in the evenings, then you should consider preparing make-ahead meals and stocking up the freezer, so that you avoid the temptation to buy an expensive store-bought meal or unhealthy fast foods.

Weekly planning

For many people, the thought of planning an evening meal simply never crosses their minds until dinner-time arrives. This lack of forethought often results in people eating out or buying ready meals, both of which can be very costly if indulged in on a regular basis. A little bit of planning not only saves money, but it also ensures greater variety in the diet and can save time at the end of a busy day.

Nutritional guidelines indicate that the main meal each day should include a balance of protein, carbohydrates and several portions of vegetables, which help us on our way to the recommended 5-a-day target. Planning a weekly menu ensures that this balance of food groups is covered every day, makes shopping easier, and gives us greater control over the variety of foods eaten. It also helps to prevent waste, as you can plan how and when to use fresh ingredients, ensuring that if necessary they are either eaten shortly after they are bought, or that they are incorporated into dishes that are then frozen.

The easiest way to plan a weekly menu is to fill in a simple chart that you create yourself at home. This shows at a glance which courses and dishes are going to be served, and makes sticking to a budget much easier. All the family can be involved in this planning process, making everyone feel that their food preferences are being acknowledged and that they are taking an active role in deciding what they eat. Below is a sample weekly menu planner with some ideas for different combinations of courses and dishes:

Left: *Writing a list of exactly what meals you plan to make and the ingredients that you need to buy is an excellent way to ensure that you don't go over budget.*

Day of the week	Appetizer	Main dish	Accompaniment	Dessert
Monday	Lentil Soup	Mexican Spicy Beef Tortilla	Steamed Seasonal Vegetables	
Tuesday		Barley Risotto With Roasted Squash and Leeks		Apple Pie
Wednesday	Mushrooms With Garlic and Chilli Sauce	Dublin Coddle	Champ Braised Red Cabbage	
Thursday		Tofu and Green Bean Thai Red Curry	Boiled Rice	Lemon Sorbet
Friday		Hake with Lemon Sauce	Boiled Potatoes Carrot and Parsnip Purée	Treacle Tart
Saturday	Summer Minestrone	Lamb and Carrot Casserole	Mashed Potatoes	Nut and Chocolate Chip Brownies
Sunday	Leek and Potato Soup	Roasted Duckling with Potatoes	Steamed Seasonal Green Vegetables	

Above: *Strip the tender roasted flesh from the carcass of a roast chicken and use the meat to make a casserole, pie or curry and the bones to make chicken stock.*

How to make the most of leftovers

Left-over food accounts for a large proportion of the food that is wasted every day. But this senseless waste is completely unnecessary, as left-over food can easily be transformed into a wide range of delicious new dishes. As part of the planning process you should take left-overs into account, and even make more than you need for one meal so that the leftovers can be converted into something else. Here are some budget-friendly ideas for ways in which you can make the most of the food you buy:

• A surprising amount of flesh can be stripped from a carcass after a roast meal, and this delicious cooked meat can be converted into a wide range of pies, curries, soups or even simply fried with onions to create a tasty and very quick supper. The stripped carcass can then be converted into home-made stock for use in any number of recipes. Left-over vegetables can be combined with the stock and flesh, if you like, to create a tasty soup, or fried up to make a variation on Bubble and Squeak.

• Cold roast beef, pork, chicken and turkey make excellent sandwich fillers, or can be served with a baked potato and salad for an easy supper dish.

• It is a good idea to make more Bolognese sauce than you actually need, as it freezes very well and forms the basis of many dishes, such as lasagne, moussaka, cottage pie and chilli con carne.

• The same applies for meat stews, which are easily made into pies with the addition of a potato or pastry topping.

• With the addition of a few ingredients, most left-over fish can be made into pies, tarts, salads or sandwich fillings, and the bones can be used to make fish stock.

• Boiled or steamed potatoes can be sliced and transformed into a Spanish omelette, or cubed and combined with corned beef, onions and tomato sauce.

• Other boiled or steamed vegetables make an almost instant ragu or curry when combined with a can of chopped tomatoes and a few storecupboard flavourings.

• Left-over pasta and rice is often thrown away because it is cheap. This is a waste, as it can be used to create a cold pasta salad, or to bulk out omelettes and soups.

• Cooked beans, peas and lentils can be readily incorporated into many meat and vegetable dishes, adding protein, texture and flavour as well as making more expensive ingredients stretch further.

• Cooked chickpeas can be puréed to make home-made hummus, and black beans are delicious when combined with chopped tomatoes, avocado, spring onions (scallions), coriander (cilantro) and lemon juice.

• Cold beans make a nutritious salad when combined with a little olive oil, lemon juice and seasoning.

• Stale bread has many uses: it can also be brushed with oil and grilled (broiled) or fried to make home-made croûtons, added to soups, dipped in egg and made into French toast, or used in recipes such as Autumn Pudding or Bread and Butter Pudding with Whiskey Sauce.

• Left-over stewed fruit makes a healthy and delicious topping for porridge (oatmeal), yogurt and ice cream, and can be added to fruit pies, cobblers and crumbles.

• You can use the hard rind from cheeses such as grano pedano to add flavour to soups and sauces. Simply add it at the start of cooking and remove before serving.

• Add left-over sauces and gravies to soups and pies, making sure that the flavours complement each other.

Above: *Making Autumn Pudding is an excellent way of converting a glut of fresh seasonal fruit and some stale bread into a truly stunning dessert.*

Clever Shopping

Before you go shopping, you should have a list of the items you want to buy. This list should be written when you are planning the weekly menu. Writing a list not only ensures that you don't forget anything, but it also helps to prevent you from impulse buying and going over budget.

Above: *Buying fresh produce to cook at home is not only cheaper than using ready-made meals, but it is also likely to be much healthier and taste better.*

Shopping around

The cost of produce varies from store to store, as well as from season to season, and it is important that you shop around to get the best deal and the best quality. Many of us get into the habit of visiting the same supermarket every week and don't explore other retailers. This is a bad habit to get in to, because while supermarkets are convenient and usually offer a good range of products all year round, other outlets such as farmer's markets, butchers, greengrocers and other independent shops may be cheaper, or stock a wider range of fresh seasonal or speciality ingredients.

Many stores have multi-buy offers, as well as bargain bins and reduced-to-clear items, and it is a good idea to find out when stores do their stock turn-over, as this is the time when they are most like to drastically reduce the cost of items in order to clear the stock. By finding out this information, you can pick up great bargains on a weekly basis and drastically reduce your overall shopping bill. It is important to note, however, that you should look at the quality of the produce that has been reduced, and only buy it if it is on your list and you are going to use it immediately or freeze it.

The internet is a very convenient way of doing the weekly shopping, and it can save you money as well as time. By buying online you can avoid the temptation to impulse buy, and by comparing the prices at different stores, you can ensure that you get the best deal. The drawback with internet shopping, however, is that you can't check the quality of the fresh produce, and although multi-buy deals apply, you usually can't get reduced-to-clear items. Smaller, independent retailers often have their own websites, too, and it is important to check both the price and range of produce that they offer, as well as delivery costs.

Specialist wholesale stores represent extremely good value for money if you are bulk-buying for a party or have the space to store large quantities of food. Some outlets require membership, which may only be granted to businesses, so it is worth checking this before travelling to the store. You should also check that there is not a minimum purchase requirement, or you may end up spending more than you budgeted for.

Getting the best deal

Buying in bulk, in conjunction with shopping around, is often the best way to reduce the relative cost of foods. It is, however, important to take several factors into consideration. If you are buying fresh produce, you will need to use it quickly, freeze it or preserve it as jams, pickles, chutneys or other long-lasting foodstuffs. If you are buying a large quantity of canned, bottled or packet goods, you will need space to store them, and you should be aware that they may have a limited shelf life.

Despite these factors, bulk-buying can save you money, as well as allowing you to stockpile seasonal produce so that it is available all year round. If you are short of space or have a small household, you could join forces with a friend or neighbour and split the cost and the produce. In this way you both benefit from the reduced cost but are not overwhelmed with more food than you can deal with.

Buying fresh produce when it is in season ensures that you get the best quality and value for your money. Almost all fresh food is most abundant at one particular time of the year, and it is a good idea to make the most of it when it is available. Eating seasonal meat, fish, fruit and vegetables also helps to ensure variety in your diet, and encourages experimentation in the kitchen.

Many supermarkets offer fresh produce all year round, whatever the season. It is worth considering that food that has been imported from abroad may have lost some of its taste and nutritional value, and may have been treated with preservatives. Imported food is also often more expensive than home-grown seasonal produce,

Picking your own fruit and vegetables, either from your own garden or from farms, is a fun way of gathering fresh produce. By taking children along to help, you will educate them about the food they eat as well as giving them a great day out in the fresh air. In rural areas you can often buy eggs directly from farms, which ensures that they are absolutely fresh, and they are often better value. Please note, you should always check that the eggs have both a use-by date and a mark to show that they have been produced to the highest standards of food safety. If in doubt, do not buy them.

Above: *Take children along to pick-your-own farms or to harvest home-grown produce from the garden – it is fun, and it will help them to understand how food is produced.*

Below: *Greengrocers and markets often offer a better range of locally grown seasonal produce than supermarkets, so shop around to get the best value, variety and quality.*

Free Food

As our lives have become busier and our gardens have grown smaller, we have for the most part forgotten the art of growing and gathering our own food. Yet nature's bounty knows no bounds, and the pleasure that can be derived from planting, tending and harvesting home-grown fruit and vegetables should not be underestimated. Open spaces and hedgerows are a rich source of fresh, free food – from blackberries, sloes and elderflowers to nettles, dandelions and mushrooms – and with a little know-how and patience you can gather all the ingredients required to create a feast.

Grow your own

Sowing, growing and harvesting your own food is not only much cheaper than buying it, but the produce is inevitably fresher. It is usually healthier, too, as you have total control over the amount of fertilizers and pesticides you use, and it often tastes better than store-bought goods. But despite the obvious benefits, growing your own food is neither possible nor desirable for everyone. To grow fruit and vegetables, you need access to a garden or an allotment, and for the large number of people who live in apartments in cities, this is simply not an option. Many people also simply do not have the necessary time that growing and cultivating fruit and vegetables requires.

Home-grown herbs, however, require very little attention or horticultural know-how, and they can usually be grown in pots, either outdoors or on a window ledge. Everyday culinary herbs, such as basil, rosemary, mint, thyme and sage can be bought in pots from gardening centres or at many supermarkets, and provide you with a ready supply of fresh herbs.

Below: *Growing herbs indoors is easy, and will fill your kitchen with their distinctive aroma.*

Growing leafy herbs in containers

Most herbs grow well in containers, and there is a wide variety to choose from. A collection of containers of different shapes makes an attractive display on the patio. Do not choose anything too large if you want to be able to move pots around, for example, when you want to bring them into a sheltered position during the winter.

For convenience, several different herbs can be grown in one container, but bear in mind that they are not all compatible. Mint and parsley do not grow well together and fennel does not mix with caraway, dill or coriander (cilantro). Mint, tarragon and chives are best grown in separate containers as they will stifle any other herbs they are mixed with. Some herbs, such as rosemary, thyme, marjoram and sage like a sunny spot, while mint, chervil and chives prefer more filtered light.

During the spring and summer months all container-grown herbs need daily watering, as they can dry out in a matter of hours. However, do not be tempted to overwater any herbs. The soil should never become waterlogged.

Whatever type of pot you choose, make sure there is a hole in the base for drainage. Fill the base with a layer of broken terracotta or stones and then a layer of grit or sand before filling with potting compost (soil mix). Once the herbs have been planted and watered, raise the container off the ground using wooden battens or clay pot supports to free the drainage holes and prevent clogging.

Growing herbs indoors

Most culinary herbs will thrive indoors provided they are sited in a light and sunny position and enjoy a fairly humid environment, away from central heating and severe temperature extremes. Indoor herbs benefit from being grown collectively because of the massed humidity. Basil is one of the most successful herbs to grow indoors as it is protected from garden pests which often decimate it outside. Care must be taken not to overuse indoor herbs, otherwise the plant will die from loss of foliage.

Nature's bounty

If you go for a walk in the countryside at the right time of the day and in the right season, you may be lucky enough to come across such treasures as a hedgerow groaning under the weight of plump, juicy blackberries, wild strawberries nestling in the long grass, or tender mushrooms that have sprung up, as if by magic, overnight. If you live on the coast, the sea is a particularly bountiful source of free food, ranging from tender mussels and nutritious seaweed to fabulous fish and shellfish. Knowing what foods are available in each season, as well as the sort of habitat in which they are likely to thrive is all the knowledge that is required to successfully find many of these and other wild foods, and there are many specialist books devoted to the subject.

Mushrooms are a particularly sought-after delicacy, but you should note that they require extremely careful identification, since many wild mushrooms are poisonous. The same applies to berries, and you should always carry detailed identification guides with you when out foraging. If in doubt, don't pick them. You should also always check that you are not trespassing, and you should ask the owner's permission before walking over land that is not clearly marked as being a public path.

Above: *The early morning is the best time to go foraging for nuts, berries and mushrooms.*

If you respect your surroundings and forage thoughtfully, you will discover a whole new world of possibility, with the added bonus that you know that the food is absolutely fresh as well as being free. By gathering your own food you will become more aware of the natural cycles of food, as well as how produce should really taste. Foraging is also fun and can make a great day out in the fresh air for all the family.

Below: *Wear suitable clothing, take a container to collect into and, above all, carry a guide book when collecting mushrooms.*

Storage and Freezing Techniques

Having spent time and money buying, growing or foraging for fresh produce, it is important that you do not allow it to go to waste. Correct storage and freezing techniques will help you to make the most of fresh ingredients as well as leftovers, and will provide you with a supply of food throughout the year.

Storing foods

All foods in the refrigerator or freezer, and particularly raw meat and poultry, should be well wrapped or stored in sealed containers. Perishable items, such as meat, poultry, fish and shellfish, eggs and dairy products must be kept refrigerated at a temperature of 1–5°C /35–40°F. For longer storage, many can also be frozen at −18°C/0°F. Cooked leftovers must be refrigerated or frozen.

Storing fresh fruits

Keep apricots, kiwi fruits, mangoes, nectarines, papayas (pawpaws), peaches, pears, pineapples and plums at room temperature until ripe, then refrigerate and eat in 2–3 days.

Apples can be kept at room temperature for a few days, dates for a few weeks, and grapefruit and oranges for up to a week; beyond that refrigerate them.

Unless you intend to eat them on the day of purchase, refrigerate fully ripe and perishable fruits such as berries, cherries, figs, grapes, lemons, melons, pomegranates and tangerines. They can be kept refrigerated for 2–3 days.

Storing fresh vegetables

Store garlic, onions, potatoes and sweet potatoes, swedes and pumpkins in a dark, cool place (about 10°C/50°F) with good ventilation. All can be kept for about 2 months.

Store tomatoes at room temperature until they are ripe. After that, refrigerate them. Other vegetables should be stored in the refrigerator.

Below: *Store potatoes in a dark place for up to 2 months.*

Above: *Medium, wide-necked jars with plastic coated screw-top lids are ideal for most preserves.*

Types of containers

It is useful to have a range of different types of receptacle – from small to large containers and from airtight to freezer-proof types. Think about what type of food you are storing when choosing a container; it is no use storing crisp items in a container that is not airtight, and large containers with only a small amount of food in them are a waste of space.

Ice cream tubs make ideal freezer-proof containers for fruit and vegetables, such as blackcurrants, after they have been frozen in a single layer. Some take-away (take-out) containers are microwave-proof, making them ideal for reheating food, but always check this before heating.

Jars and bottles are ideal containers for home-made preserves, sauces and salad dressings. Pickles or preserves made from whole or large pieces of fruit or vegetables should be packed into medium or large jars or bottles with a wide neck. Pourable sauces or relishes can be stored in narrow-necked bottles, but thicker, spoonable preserves should be packed in jars.

Before potting, it is essential to sterilize jars and bottles to destroy any micro-organisms. Check for cracks or damage, then wash in hot, soapy water, rinse and turn upside down to drain. Stand the containers, spaced slightly apart, on a baking sheet lined with kitchen paper. Rest any lids on top. Place in a cold oven, then heat to 110°C/225°F/Gas 1/4 and bake for 30 minutes.

Freezing techniques

Different foods can be frozen for different amounts of time and may require a variety of freezing methods. Below is a table of the freezer life of some of the most common foods that are suitable for freezing. Handling hints are included where applicable. Unless otherwise specified, items are raw prior to being frozen.

Freezing soft fruit

Place on a baking sheet in a single layer. Once frozen, transfer to a container.

Meat and poultry	Storage time	Handling hints
Bacon	1 month	
Burgers	2–3 months	Separate each burger with a layer of waxed paper before freezing
Casseroles and stews, cooked meat, fish and poultry	3 months	Allow a small space above the cooked food for expansion
Minced (ground) beef, lamb and veal	2–3 months	
Minced (ground) pork	1–2 months	
Joints:		Check that the packaging has no holes in it before freezing the joint
Beef	6–12 months	
Lamb, veal	6–9 months	
Pork	3–6 months	
Sausages	1–2 months	
Steaks and Chops:		
Beef	6–9 months	
Lamb, veal	3–4 months	
Pork	2–3 months	
Venison, game birds	8–12 months	
Chicken, cooked	3 months	
Chicken, whole or cut-up	10 months	
Chicken liver	3 months	
Duck, turkey	6 months	

Fish and shellfish	Storage time	Handling hints
Fillets and steaks from lean fish: Cod, flounder haddock, sole	6 months	Wrap fish in clear film (plastic wrap) and freeze as soon after purchase as possible
Fillets and steaks from oily fish: Trout, mackerel, salmon, sardines	2–3 months	Freeze small fish in one piece. Freeze larger fish in thick steaks or fillets
Breaded fish	3 months	
Clams	3 months	
Cooked fish or shellfish	3 months	
Crab	10 months	
Lobster tails	3 months	
Oysters	4 months	
Prawns (shrimp)	12 months	
Scallops	3 months	

Fruit, vegetables and herbs	Storage time	Handling hints
Soft fruits: Apricots, berries, cherries, peaches, pears, pineapples, plums, etc	12 months	Freeze in a single layer on a baking tray before transferring to a moisture-proof container once frozen
Citrus fruit and freshly-squeezed fruit juice	6 months	
Fruit juice concentrate	12 months	
Other fruits: Apples, bananas grapes, pears	Do not freeze	
Vegetables: All except celery, greens, salad leaves and tomatoes	10 months	Freeze quickly in small batches to prevent large ice crystals forming
Fresh herbs: Rosemary, thyme, oregano, sage		Freeze in bags, or chop, mix with water and freeze in ice cube trays

Baked goods	Storage time	Handling hints
Yeast bread and rolls, baked	3–6 months	Cool completely before freezing
Rolls, partially baked	2–3 months	
Cake, baked:		Freeze cakes in rigid containers to prevent them from being damaged. Frosting made from egg white does not freeze well
Chiffon, sponge	2 months	
Cheesecake	2–3 months	
Chocolate	4 months	
Fruit cake	12 months	
Iced (frosted)	8–12 months	
Pound cake	6 months	
Cookies, baked	8–12 months	
Pie, baked	1–2 months	

Dairy	Storage time	Handling hints
Butter	6–9 months	Store in moisture-proof wrap
Margarine	12 months	
Milk	1 month	Pour some out before freezing as it will expand
Buttermilk, sour cream and yogurt	Do not freeze	
Cheese	4 months	Defrost slowly in the refrigerator before use

Fuss-free Flavour

You don't need to spend a fortune on expensive ingredients to make delicious family food. A whole range of simple herbs, spices and aromatics can be used to complement and bring out the flavours of the main ingredient of the dish, without the need for lots of costly extra ingredients. Match the seasoning to the ingredient and try some of the simple techniques outlined below, which include stuffing, dry rubbing, marinating, glazing and infusing.

Flavours for fish

Classic aromatics used for flavouring fish and shellfish include lemon, lime, parsley, dill, fennel and bay leaves. These all have a fresh, intense quality that complements the delicate taste.

• To flavour whole fish, such as trout or mackerel, stuff a few lemon slices and some fresh parsley or basil into the body cavity before cooking. Season, then wrap the fish in foil or baking parchment, ensuring the packet is well sealed. Place the fish in an ovenproof dish or on a baking tray and bake until cooked through.

• To marinate chunky fillets of fish, such as cod or salmon, arrange the fish fillets in a dish in a single layer. Drizzle with olive oil, then sprinkle over crushed garlic and grated lime rind and squeeze over the lime juice. Cover and leave to marinate in the refrigerator for at least 30 minutes. Grill (broil) lightly until just cooked through.

• To make a delicious marinade for salmon, arrange the fillets in a single layer in an ovenproof dish. Drizzle with a little light olive oil and add a split vanilla pod. Cover and marinate for a couple of hours or overnight, if you have time. Remove the dish from the refrigerator, cover with foil and bake in the oven until cooked through. Remove the vanilla pod before serving.

Pepping up meat and poultry

Dry rubs, marinades and sticky glazes are all perfect ways to introduce flavour into meat and poultry. Marinating the tougher cuts of meat, such as stewing steak, also helps to tenderize it.

• To make a fragrant Cajun spice rub for pork chops, steaks and chicken, mix together 5ml/1 tsp each of dried thyme, dried oregano, finely crushed black peppercorns, salt, crushed cumin seeds and hot paprika. Rub the Cajun spice mix into the raw meat or poultry, then cook over a barbecue or bake until cooked through.

• To marinate red meat, such as beef, lamb or venison, prepare a mixture of two-thirds red wine to one-third olive oil in a shallow non-metallic dish. Stir in some chopped garlic and bruised fresh rosemary sprigs. Add the meat and turn to coat it in the marinade. Cover and chill for at least 2 hours or overnight before cooking.

• To make a mild-spiced sticky mustard glaze for chicken, pork or red meat, mix 45ml/3 tbsp each of Dijon mustard, clear honey and demerara (raw) sugar, 2.5ml/^{1}/$_2$ tsp chilli powder, 1.5ml/^{1}/$_4$ tsp ground cloves, and salt and ground black pepper. Cook over the barbecue or under the grill (broiler) and brush with the glaze about 10 minutes before the end of cooking time.

Vibrant vegetables

Most fresh vegetables have a subtle flavour that needs to be enhanced. When using delicate cooking methods such as steaming and stir-frying, go for light flavourings that will enhance the taste of the vegetables. When using more robust cooking methods, such as roasting, choose richer flavours such as garlic and spices.

• To add a rich flavour to stir-fried vegetables, add a splash of sesame oil just before the end of cooking time. (Do not use more than about 5ml/1 tsp, because it has a very strong flavour and can be overpowering.)

• To make fragrant, Asian-style steamed vegetables, bruise a couple of lemon grass stalks with a mortar and add to the steaming water, then cook vegetables such as pak choi (bok choy) over the water until just tender. Alternatively add a few kaffir lime leaves to the water. You could also place the aromatics in the steamer under the vegetables and steam as before until just tender.

• To enhance the taste of naturally sweet vegetables, such as parsnips and carrots, try glazing them with honey and mustard before roasting. Simply mix together 30ml/ 2 tbsp wholegrain mustard and 45ml/ 3 tbsp clear honey in a small bowl, and season with salt and ground black pepper to taste. Brush the glaze over the prepared vegetables to coat completely, then roast until they are sweet and tender. You could also use maple syrup and/or omit the mustard, if you prefer.

Fragrant rice and grains

Accompaniments to main course dishes, such as rice and couscous, can be enhanced by the addition of simple flavourings. Adding herbs, spices and aromatics can help to perk up the rice and grains' subtle flavour as well as adding a splash of colour. Choose flavourings that will complement the dish that the rice or grains will be served with.

• To make fragrant rice to serve with Asian-style stir-fries and braised dishes, add a whole star anise or a few cardamom pods to a pan of rice before cooking. The rice will absorb the flavour during cooking.

• To make zesty herb rice or couscous, heat a little chopped fresh tarragon and grated lemon rind in olive oil or melted butter until warm, then drizzle the flavoured oil and herbs over freshly cooked rice or couscous.

• To make simple herb rice or couscous, fork plenty of chopped fresh parsley and chives through the cooked grains and drizzle over a little oil just before serving.

Making a bouquet garni

This classic flavouring for stews, casseroles and soups is very easy to make. Using a piece of string, tie together a fresh bay leaf and a sprig each of parsley and thyme. Alternatively, tie the herbs in a square of muslin (cheesecloth). It can be added to dishes at the start of the cooking time, left to impart its flavour for the duration, and then removed before serving.

Fruit

Widely incorporated in both sweet and savoury dishes, fruit can be used either as a main ingredient or as a flavouring to complement the taste of other ingredients. Make the most of the different types of fruit when they are in season – they can be eaten on their own, in combination with other fruits, in pies, tarts and cakes, or made into delectable preserves that can be enjoyed throughout the year.

Orchard fruit

This family of fruit includes apples, pears and quinces, which, depending on the variety, are in season from early summer to late autumn. Choose firm, unblemished fruit and store in a cool dry place.

Apples There are two main categories of apple – eating and cooking, and although imported varieties are available all year, they are at their best in autumn. Eating apples have sweet flesh and taste good raw as a healthy snack or dessert. Many can also be used for making pies and open tarts. Cooking apples have a sour flavour and are too sharp to eat raw. They are ideal for baking, or for making into sauces and preserves.

Pears Most commercially available pears are dessert fruits, just as good for eating as for cooking. They can be pan-fried or used in tarts and pies. They are also excellent poached, especially in a wine syrup.

Quinces Related to the pear, quinces have hard, sour flesh. Cooking and sweetening brings out their delicious, scented flavour. They are worth buying when you find them, and are often used in jellies and sauces.

Below: *Crisp, fresh-tasting apples are great as an economical and healthy snack or dessert.*

Stone fruit

Peaches, nectarines, plums, apricots and cherries all belong to this family of fruit, and contain a stone (pit) in the middle. Most stone fruits are at their best through the summer months, but some, such as plums, are best through the autumn. Choose firm, smooth-skinned fruit without any blemishes and store in a cool, dry place.

Apricots With their slightly sweet-and-sour flavour, soft texture and downy skin, apricots are delicious eaten raw, or they can be poached, made into desserts or converted into delicious preserves. Pick those with the strongest colour.

Cherries These fruits are divided into two main groups: sweet cherries, which may be black (actually dark red) or white (usually yellow), and sour cherries. They only have a short season, so enjoy them while you can. Choose ones with green, flexible stems and that are firm and plump, but not hard. You need to remove the stone when eating them raw, and before adding them to pies, tarts and puddings or making into preserves.

Nectarines and peaches These fragrant, sweet fruits are the essence of the summer. They should be richly coloured, heavy for their size and have a strong aroma. They are at their best when eaten raw; cut around the middle of the fruit through the crease that runs from the stem to the tip, then twist the two halves in opposite directions to separate, and remove the stone with a knife.

Plums, damsons and greengages These stone fruits are in season in autumn, and are extremely versatile in cooking. Plums and greengages have a sweet, refreshing taste, while damsons are fairly sour.

Soft fruit

These delicate fruits, which include strawberries, raspberries, blackberries, blackcurrants, redcurrants and white currants, need careful handling and storing, and for the best price and quality only buy them when they are in season. Store in the refrigerator for up to 2 days.

Citrus fruit

Oranges, lemons, limes, grapefruit, mandarins and satsumas are popular citrus fruits; but there are also hybrids such as clementines. Citrus fruits are available all year round, with satsumas and clementines at their best in winter. Choose plump fruit that feels heavy. The skin should be bright and not shrivelled. Most citrus fruit is coated with wax to prevent moisture loss, so buy unwaxed fruit when using the rind in a recipe, or scrub the fruit well before use.

Exotic fruit

Once expensive and difficult to find, these wonderful fruits are now widely available in supermarkets throughout the year. Eat them fresh or use them in recipes.

Kiwi fruit The pale green flesh of kiwi fruit is good in various desserts and savoury cooking. Kiwi fruit are rich in vitamin C. Choose plump fruit with smooth skin and store in the refrigerator for up to 4 days.

Mangoes There are many varieties of this fleshy fruit available throughout the year. Choose strongly fragrant mangoes that give slightly when gently squeezed. Store in a cool place, but not the refrigerator, for up to a week.

Below: *Perfectly ripe pineapples have sweet, tangy flesh with a crisp bite and a fragrance that is quite irresistible.*

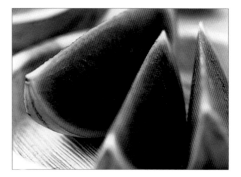

Above: *Watermelon has bright pink flesh and a light, delicate flavour that is sweet yet refreshing.*

Passion fruit This small round fruit has tough, wrinkled purple-brown skin. A passion fruit should feel heavy if it is nice and juicy. Store in the refrigerator.

Pineapple These sweet, tangy, juicy fruits are delicious in fruit salads and desserts. When choosing a pineapple, pull off one of the green leaves at the top – if it comes away easily, the pineapple should be ripe. Store in a cool place, but not the refrigerator, for up to a week.

Other fruit

There are a few fruits that are delicious and very versatile but that don't fit into any particular group. These include figs, grapes, melons and rhubarb.

Figs Available in summer, fresh figs require careful handling. Store in the refrigerator for up to 2 days. Fresh figs can be expensive, so buy them when they are on offer.

Grapes At their best in late summer, there are many varieties of grape. Handle with care.

Melons There are two types of melon – dessert melon and watermelon. Charentais, Ogen, cantaloupe, Galia and honeydew melon are all dessert melons, which are in season from summer to winter. Watermelons are in season from summer to autumn.

Rhubarb Rhubarb is available from early spring to mid-summer. Pale, finer-textured pink forced rhubarb is available in winter. It has a good colour and flavour, and is considered the best.

Vegetables

Used in salads and savoury dishes, vegetables are delicious served as the main ingredient in a vegetarian dish, as an accompaniment, or as a flavouring ingredient in a meat, poultry or fish dish. For maximum flavour, select healthy-looking specimens that are in season.

Root vegetables and potatoes

Grown underground, these vegetables include carrots, parsnips, beetroot (beets) and turnips and many varieties of potato. They are available throughout the year but are at their best in the winter months, when they are very good value for money. Choose firm specimens with unblemished skins. Store in a cool, dark place for up to 2 weeks.

Cabbages, broccoli and cauliflower

Members of the brassica family, these vegetables are packed with nutrients and good served in many ways.

Broccoli Packed with antioxidants and with a delicious flavour and crisp texture, broccoli and purple sprouting broccoli can be boiled, steamed and stir-fried. Choose specimens with bright heads and no sign of yellowing. Store in the refrigerator and use within 4–5 days.

Cabbage Regardless of variety, cabbage has a distinctive flavour and can be steamed, stir-fried or boiled. The white and red varieties are tight-leafed and ideal for shredding, and can be enjoyed raw in salads such as coleslaw. Green cabbage can be loose or close-leafed, smooth or crinkly and is best cooked. Buy fresh-looking specimens and store in the refrigerator for up to 10 days.

Cauliflower Good cut into florets and served raw with dips, cauliflower can also be boiled or steamed, and is delicious coated in cheese sauce. To ensure even cooking, remove the hard central core, or cut into florets. Choose densely packed heads, avoiding specimens with any black spots or marks, and store in the refrigerator for 5–10 days.

Left: Choose cauliflowers with firm, clean white florets.

Above: *Plump, juicy tomatoes have a rich, sweet flavour and are tasty used in salads or cooked in stews and sauces.*

Vegetable fruits

Tomatoes, aubergines, peppers and chillies are actually fruit, although they are generally used as vegetables. They all have a robust flavour and lovely texture, and although available all year, they are at their peak in the summer.

Aubergines/eggplants These can be fried, stewed, brushed with oil and grilled (broiled), or stuffed and baked. Choose firm, plump, smooth-skinned specimens and store in the refrigerator, where they will keep for 5–8 days.

Chillies There are many types of chilli, all with a different taste and heat. As a general rule, the bigger the chilli, the milder it is; green chillies tend to be hotter than red ones.

Peppers/bell peppers These may be red, yellow, orange or green, with the green specimens having a fresher, less sweet flavour. Peppers can be grilled, roasted, fried and stewed. Choose firm, unblemished specimens and store in the refrigerator for 5–8 days.

Tomatoes There are numerous varieties of tomato, including cherry, plum and beefsteak. They are eaten raw or cooked. Choose plump, bright-red specimens and store in the refrigerator for 5–8 days.

Leafy green vegetables

There is a wide selection of leafy greens available, which may be used raw in salads or cooked.

Salad leaves There are many different salad leaves, including various types of lettuce. They are delicate and need to be stored in the refrigerator, where most will keep for a few days. Avoid buying vacuum-packed ready-to-eat leaves as they will be costly and less nutritious.

Spinach Tender young spinach leaves are tasty raw. Mature spinach leaves can be fried, boiled or steamed until just wilted; they overcook very easily. Store spinach in the refrigerator for 2–3 days, and wash well before use.

Leafy Asian vegetables Asian vegetables, such as pak choi (bok choy), can be used raw in salads or cooked. Prepare in the same way as cabbage or spinach.

The onion family

This family includes onions, shallots, spring onions (scallions), leeks and garlic. Choose firm, unblemished specimens. Store onions in a cool, dry place for up to 2 weeks; store leeks and spring onions in the refrigerator for 2–3 days.

Corn, beans and peas

These are good boiled or steamed and served as a side dish, or used in braised dishes and stir-fries.

Corn Large corn cobs are good steamed and served with butter, while baby corn is better added to stir-fries. Buy only the freshest specimens when they are in season, because stale vegetables can be starchy.

Green beans Many varieties of green beans are available throughout the year. Choose firm, fresh-looking beans with a bright green colour. Store in the refrigerator for up to 5 days.

Below: *Corn cobs are delicious steamed and served with butter.*

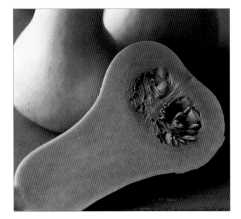

Above: *Butternut squash has orange flesh, a sweet taste and a smooth texture. Roasting brings out its flavour.*

Peas Fresh peas are generally only available in the summer and can be expensive. Frozen peas are often better than fresh ones because they are frozen within a short time of picking and retain all their natural sweetness. They are also much cheaper.

Squashes

These vegetables come in many different shapes and sizes and include courgettes (zucchini), and butternut, acorn and spaghetti squashes, and pumpkins and marrows (large zucchini). With the exception of courgettes, all need peeling and seeding before use. They can be cut up and boiled, or baked whole. Select smooth, unblemished vegetables with unbroken skin. Most squashes can be stored in a cool place for 1 week, although courgettes should be stored in the refrigerator for 4–5 days.

Mushrooms

Freshly picked mushrooms have a rich, earthy flavour, but are rarely available to most cooks. Brown cap (cremini) mushrooms are a good alternative; they have more flavour than cultivated mushrooms. Shiitake mushrooms are full-flavoured and delicious in Chinese- and Asian-style dishes.

There are many types of edible wild fungi or mushrooms of different flavours and textures. They tend to have a more intense taste than cultivated mushrooms and are also more expensive and more difficult to find. Wild mushrooms are seasonal and can generally be found in late summer, autumn and winter.

Dairy Produce and Eggs

Milk and milk products, such as yogurt, milk and cheese, are widely used in cooking and can add a delicious richness to many sweet and savoury dishes. Strong-tasting cheeses, such as Gorgonzola or Parmesan, not only contribute a wonderful texture, but also add real bite to many savoury dishes.

Milk, cream and yogurt
These products are widely used in both sweet and savoury cooked and uncooked dishes, adding a rich, creamy taste and texture. There are many varieties of each available in supermarkets, and most are reasonably priced, apart from double and clotted cream, which can be expensive.

Butter
There are two main types of butter – salted and unsalted (sweet). Unsalted is better for baking cakes and cookies.

Hard cheeses
These firm, tasty cheeses are good for cooking, and if you select stronger varieties you will not need to use as much to give a good flavour. Cheddar, Parmesan and Gruyère are the most popular, although grano pedano makes a very good economical alternative to Parmesan, which tends to be expensive. All should have a dry rind. Store wrapped in baking parchment in the refrigerator for up to 2 weeks.

Semi-hard cheeses
These vary in softness depending on the type. Choose cheeses that feel springy and have a firm rind. Wrap in waxed paper and store in the refrigerator for 1–2 weeks. Popular choices include fontina and halloumi.

Below: *It is worth paying a little extra to buy free-range or organic eggs; they will taste a lot better and even the most expensive varieties represent very good value for money.*

Above: *Stilton has a tangy flavour and creamy texture. It is good served on its own or used in salads and cooking.*

Blue cheese
These strong, often sharp, cheeses usually melt well and are good for cooking and flavouring sauces. Stilton is usually good value for money.

Soft and fresh cheeses
Store these unripened cheeses in a covered container in the refrigerator for up to 1 week. Mozzarella has a mild flavour and melts well. Feta is crumbly with a salty flavour and is good in salads. Marscapone is creamy and can be used in sweet or savoury dishes.

White rind cheeses
These creamy cheeses are delicious used fresh in salads or cooked. Brie is one of the best and its flavour ranges from mild to extremely strong. Goat's cheese has a distinctive flavour and can be used in a range of dishes.

Eggs
Widely used in sweet and savoury cooking, eggs are incredibly good value for money and are very versatile – they can be boiled, poached, fried, scrambled or baked. They are also widely used in baking. Buy the best you can afford – hens reared in better conditions produce better-tasting eggs.

Fish and Seafood

Always buy really fresh fish and seafood: look for bright-eyed fish with plump flesh and bright, undamaged skin; they should not smell "fishy" but should have a faint aroma of the sea. Store fish and shellfish, covered, towards the bottom of the refrigerator, and use within a day of purchase.

Above: *Sardines are very good value for money, as well as being nutritious, tasty and versatile for cooking.*

Oily fish
The rich flesh of oily fish is tasty and rich in omega-3 fatty acids, which are an essential part of a healthy diet. Oily fish are also usually cheaper than other fish.

Mackerel These very economical fish have iridescent skin and quite firm, brownish flesh.

Salmon Wild varieties tend to be very expensive, so only eat them occasionally. If you buy farmed salmon, check that it is from a reputable supplier. Canned salmon can be used in pasta and rice dishes.

Sardines These small fish are delicious fresh, cooked over a barbecue with lime or lemon juice and herbs.

Whitebait These are the small fry of herring and sprats, and taste excellent fried and eaten whole.

Rich, meaty fish
This group of firm-fleshed fish has a meaty texture, and includes monkfish, red mullet, seabass, swordfish and tuna. They are often expensive, so look out for special offers in the supermarket or fishmongers. Canned tuna makes a good, cheap alternative to fresh tuna and can be used in omelettes, salads and pasta dishes.

White fish
These fish have firm yet delicate white flesh and are excellent cooked simply with subtle or piquant flavouring.

Cod Stocks of cod are diminishing due to overfishing, so check where the fish comes from before buying. Hoki or pollard are much cheaper and make good alternatives.

Haddock This flaky fish can also be used instead of cod. Smoked haddock is delicious but avoid the bright yellow dyed variety and go for the paler, undyed version.

Halibut This flat fish is very good value and tastes a bit like turbot. Do not overcook it, or the flesh will become dry.

Seafood
This group includes molluscs, such as mussels, crustaceans, such as crabs and prawns (shrimp), and squid. Store in the refrigerator and use within 1–2 days.

Crab This is available raw, ready-cooked or in a can. Fresh crab is relatively expensive, so use canned crab in baked pasta or rice dishes as a cheaper alternative.

Prawns/shrimp There are many types of prawns of different sizes, cooked or raw, in the shell, or peeled. Frozen prawns are usually very good value for money.

Squid This economical seafood is available all year. It needs to be cooked either very quickly or very slowly.

Below: *Buy fresh prawns when they are on special offer.*

Meat and Poultry

It is important to choose good quality meat as well as watching the price, so look out for special offers on organic and free-range meat and poultry, and avoid buying really cheap, bottom-of-the range packaged meat. Offal and other less well-used cuts of meat, such as beef shank, chuck or brisket represent very good value for money. Bulk out expensive cuts of meat with vegetables and beans.

Above: *Roast Loin of Pork with Stuffing makes a delicious, satisfying and healthy main meal.*

Pork

Comparatively inexpensive and available all year round, pork is a very versatile meat that can be roasted, grilled (broiled) or cooked on a barbecue. It is generally tender and has an excellent flavour that has a natural affinity with apples. Look for firm, pale pink flesh, which is moist but not damp or oily. The fat should be white, and the bones should be tinged with red.

Shoulder, leg and loin The shoulder or leg is the best cut of pork for roasting, and is cheaper than many other joints of meat. To make good crackling, ensure that the rind is completely dry and rub it generously with sea salt. Stuff boneless loin joints with herbs and onion before roasting. Loin or shoulder chops are suited to pan-frying or braising.

Bacon Available smoked or unsmoked, bacon comes in a variety of different forms, from rashers and steaks to joints.Dry-cured bacon rashers, although more expensive than some other types, have the best flavour and do not shrink when they are cooked, so you won't need to use as much. Streaky (fatty) bacon can be cooked to a crisp-fried texture and is excellent for placing on the breasts of chicken and turkey before roasting. Back bacon is normally more expensive than streaky bacon but has larger rashers (strips) and a good balance of lean to fatty areas.

Beef

Popular all over the world, beef provides a full-flavoured ingredient for stewing, succulent joints for roasting and tender steaks for grilling (broiling). It is available all year, and there are cuts suitable for all types of dish and for every budget. Ideally beef should be hung for several weeks before being eaten, and will be brown rather than red.

Fillet/beef tenderloin, forerib, topside and silverside/pot roast These reasonably expensive cuts taste best roasted. To make the most of the flavour of the beef, serve medium, not well-done, and to make the joint feed more people, serve with plenty of vegetables.

Shin or leg/shank, chuck and brisket These cuts are very good value for money. They can be quite tough and are best stewed slowly to tenderize them and bring out their excellent flavour.

Mince/ground meat This is a very versatile ingredient for a whole range of dishes. Avoid cheap, bought frozen mince as it is usually of inferior quality.

Lamb

Tender young lamb is delicious in roasts and superb grilled (broiled), pan-fried and stewed. It can be quite expensive, so buy it when it is in season in spring, and go for cheaper cuts. Look for firm, pink meat with a fine-grained, velvety texture. The fat should be creamy white, firm and waxy.

Chump chops and leg steaks These have a full flavour and can be either grilled (broiled) or pan-fried.

Scrag end, middle neck, and fillet These are inexpensive and ideal for stewing, braising and casseroling. Fillet is good for grilling.

Shank or knuckle An economical yet flavoursome cut, it can be tough so it needs long-cooking, such as stewing, pot-roasting or braising.

Sausages and offal/variety meats

Offal refers to all offcuts from the carcass but in everyday use, this usually means liver and kidneys. Offal is very good value for money, tastes delicious and is packed with essential vitamins and minerals.

Sausages There are many types of fresh sausage from around the world. Depending on the variety, they may be fried, grilled (broiled) or baked. They are normally quick and easy to cook and a favourite with all the family.

Kidneys Lambs' kidneys are lighter in flavour than pigs'. They should be halved and the central core discarded before they are pan-fried or used in stews and pies.

Liver Pigs', lambs' or calves' liver has a strong flavour and tastes good pan-fried, with bacon and mashed potato.

Poultry

Many people prefer the lighter flavour of poultry to that of red meat, and it is incredibly versatile and easy to use. There is usually a range of options to choose from, and although organic birds taste better, they are normally considerably more expensive than intensively reared birds. It is often cheaper to buy a whole bird and joint it yourself at home than to buy ready-prepared joints.

Chicken Choose smooth-skinned, unblemished plump birds. You can use every part of the bird in cooking, including the carcass, which you can boil up to make stock. Chicken drumsticks, leg quarters, thighs and breast portions on the bone are usually better value than skinless chicken breast fillets. You can remove the skin yourself, if you wish, although the skin adds flavour and helps to keep the flesh moist.

Below (clockwise from top): If you choose to buy ready-jointed chicken portions, then economical options include the leg quarter, drumsticks and thighs.

Jointing a bird

1 Put the bird breast-side up on a chopping board. Use a sharp knife to remove the legs by cutting through the thigh joint.

2 Following the line of the breastbone and using poultry shears or kitchen scissors, cut the breast in half, making the cut as clean as possible.

3 Turn the bird over and cut out the backbone. Discard. Leave the wings attached to each breast half and turn over so the skin is uppermost.

4 Cut each breast in half crossways at the widest part. This will leave one portion attached to the wing. Cut off the wing tip at the first joint.

5 Using a sharp knife and firm pressure, cut each leg cleanly through the knee joint to separate the thigh and drumstick from each other.

Duck Traditionally, duck can be expensive and very fatty with a fairly small amount of meat on the carcass. An average duck will serve two or three people. Duck breasts and legs are a good choice for simple cooking. Buy when they are on offer and freeze until required.

Turkey This economical and versatile meat can be used in the same way as chicken and duck. When buying a whole bird, look for well-rounded breasts and legs, and soft and evenly coloured skin. Turkey mince (ground turkey) makes a good, cheap alternative to beef mince (ground beef).

Storecupboard Staples

A well-stocked storecupboard (pantry) is a must for the clever cook, and will help you to create delicious, economical dishes without the need for expensive ingredients or having to make a special trip to the supermarket. Staples range from flour, sugar, canned goods and oil to rice, pasta, dried herbs and stock (bouillon) cubes, and the following items have not been included when costing the recipes.

Above (clockwise from top): *Strong bread flour, self-raising flour, plain flour, and gluten-free flour.*

Flours

This is an essential ingredient in every kitchen. There are many different types, which serve many purposes in both sweet and savoury cooking – from baking cakes to thickening gravy and making cheese sauce.

Cornflour/cornstarch This very fine white flour is useful for thickening sauces and stabilizing egg mixtures, such as custard, to prevent them curdling.

Gluten-free flours For those with an allergy to gluten, which is found in wheat and other grains, gluten-free flour is an invaluable ingredient. It is widely available from most large supermarkets and health-food stores.

Wheat flours Plain (all-purpose) flour can be used in most recipes. Self-raising (self-rising) flour has a raising agent added and is useful for baking recipes. Wholemeal flour is available as plain (all-purpose) or self-raising (self-rising). Strong bread flour contains more gluten than plain flour, making it more suitable for making breads.

Raising agents You can add baking powder to plain flour to give a light texture to cakes and cookies. The powder reacts with liquids and heat during cooking and produces carbon-dioxide bubbles, which make the mixture rise.

Sugars

Refined and raw sugars can be used to sweeten and flavour many different types of dish, including cakes, bakes, pastries, cookies and desserts.

Brown sugars These dark, unrefined sugars have a rich, caramel flavour. There are several different types of brown sugar, including light and dark muscovado (brown) sugar and dark brown molasses sugar. As a general rule of thumb, the darker the sugar, the more intense its flavour. Always check that you are buying unrefined sugar, because "brown" sugars are often actually dyed white sugar.

Caster/superfine sugar This fine-grained white sugar is most frequently used in baking. Its fine texture is particularly well suited to making cakes and cookies.

Demerara/raw sugar This golden sugar consists of large crystals with a rich, slightly honeyish flavour. It is great for adding a crunchy texture to cookies.

Granulated sugar This refined white sugar has large crystals. It is used for sweetening drinks, and in everyday cooking; it can also be used as a crunchy cookie or cake topping, or stirred into crumble mixtures for extra texture.

Icing/confectioners' sugar The finest of all the refined sugars, this sugar has a powdery texture. It is used for making icing and sweetening flavoured creams. It is also excellent for dusting on cakes, desserts and cookies as a simple yet effective decoration.

Right: *Granulated sugar has larger crystals than caster sugar but both are good for making cakes and desserts.*

Pasta and noodles

These are invaluable storecupboard ingredients that can be used as the base of many hot and cold dishes.

Pasta Dried pasta keeps for months in an airtight container – check the packet for information on its keeping quality. There is a wide variety of pasta in all shapes and sizes. Egg pasta is enriched with egg yolks. It has a richer flavour than plain pasta and is often more expensive than dried varieties, which are very cheap. Generally, the choice depends on personal taste – use whichever type you have in the cupboard. Cook pasta at a rolling boil in plenty of water. Fresh pasta cooks very quickly and is available chilled. It can be stored in the refrigerator for several days, or in the freezer for several months.

Egg noodles Made from wheat flour and eggs, these may be thick, medium or thin. Use them for stir-fries or as a cheap accompaniment to Chinese and Asian dishes.

Rice noodles These transluscent white noodles are a good alternative to wheat noodles – particularly for those on a gluten-free diet. They are available as broad flat or thin noodles that can be added to stir-fries and soups as well as used cold as a base for salads. Rice noodles are easy to prepare, because they don't need to be cooked. Simply soak in boiling water for about 5 minutes, then stir-fry, add to soups or toss with salad ingredients.

Below: Tiny soup pasta is available in hundreds of different shapes – buy whichever shape you prefer, and use to make substantial soups that can be eaten for lunch, or as a light meal when served with bread.

Above: *Egg noodles have a nutty taste and are extremely good value for money, as well as being very versatile. They can be served hot in Asian-style stir-fries and soups, and cold in salads.*

Couscous and polenta

Like pasta and noodles, couscous and polenta are very cheap and can be served as an accompaniment or act as the base of many dishes. They have a mild flavour, and go particularly well with other, strongly flavoured ingredients, such as aromatics, herbs and spices.

Couscous Made from durum wheat, couscous is often regarded as a type of pasta. Traditional couscous needed long steaming before serving, but the majority of brands available in supermarkets today are "instant" and need only brief soaking in water. It is the classic accompaniment to Moroccan tagines, but also goes well with all kinds of meat, fish and vegetable stews. It makes an excellent base for salads and is very economical.

Polenta This is made from finely ground cornmeal. It is cooked with water and served either soft (rather like mashed potato) or left to set and then cut into pieces that can be grilled (broiled) or fried. Quick-cook and ready-made polenta are available in most supermarkets and can be made into simple, hearty dishes. It is best served with flavourful ingredients.

Above: *Canned beans are cheap and versatile and can be used in stews, healthy salads or tasty dips and pâtés.*

Rice

This great-value grain can be served as an accompaniment, or form the base of sweet and savoury dishes.

Basmati rice This long-grain rice is widely used in Indian cooking. It is aromatic and cooks to give separated, fluffy grains. Brown basmati rice is also available.

Long-grain rice The narrow grains of white rice cook to a light, fluffy texture and are generally served as an accompaniment to main dishes. They also make a perfect base for other dishes such as stir-fries and salads.

Risotto rice This rice has medium-length polished grains. The grains can absorb a great deal of liquid while still retaining their shape. There are several types of risotto rice, including the popular arborio and carnaroli. When cooking risotto rice, it is imperative to stir it regularly. Liquid or stock should be added periodically throughout cooking to prevent the rice sticking to the pan and burning, and spoiling the overall taste.

Short-grain rice There are several types of short, stubby, polished rice such as pudding rice and sushi rice. These usually have a high starch content and cook into tender grains that cling together and can be shaped easily.

Dried beans, lentils and peas

These staples are a fantastic resource for any cook and provide a very good low-fat source of protein. They are very good value, and can be used to help a meat dish go much further, thus reducing the overall cost.

Beans There are a wide variety of beans available in many stores, including red and white kidney beans, butter (lima) beans, haricot beans, flageolet beans and cannellini beans. To use, place the dried beans in a large bowl, cover with cold water and leave to soak overnight, then rinse under running water and drain. Kidney beans are poisonous unless they are properly cooked, so you need to boil the beans vigorously for 15 minutes, then change the water and simmer for about $1^3/_4$ hours until they are tender.

Lentils Red, green and brown lentils are all extremely versatile and do not require pre-soaking. Simply rinse under cold running water and add to a wide range of dishes.

Chickpeas These peas have a lovely creamy texture and hearty taste and can be used to make home-made hummus or to bulk out soups, stews and salads.

Canned goods

Although many foods taste best when they are fresh, there are some canned foods which are as good as or better than the fresh variety. These include canned tomatoes, which are usually cheaper and much more convenient to use than fresh tomatoes; canned beans, peas and lentils, which simply require rinsing before use; and some canned fish and shellfish, such as tuna and crab, which are significantly cheaper than the fresh varieties and make excellent additions to baked pasta dishes and salads.

Below: *Brown basmati rice.*

Left (from left to right): *Corn oil and vegetable oil are cheap and extremely versatile.*

Oils

Essential both for cooking and adding flavour, there are many different types of oil.

Corn oil Golden-coloured corn oil is inexpensive, has a strong flavour and can be used in most types of cooking.

Groundnut (peanut) oil This virtually flavourless oil is used for frying, baking and making dressings such as mayonnaise.

Olive oil Extra virgin olive oil is made from the first pressing of the olives. It has the best flavour but is the most expensive type, so it is best reserved for condiments or salad dressings. Ordinary olive oil is generally made from the third or fourth pressing of the olives, so it is cheaper and should be used for cooking.

Vegetable oil This is a blend of oils, usually including corn oil and other vegetable oils. It is cheap, flavourless and useful in most types of cooking.

Flavoured Oils

Herb-infused oil Half-fill a jar with washed and dried fresh herbs such as rosemary or basil. Pour over olive oil to cover, then seal the jar and place in a cool, dark place for 3 days. Strain the herb-flavoured oil into a clean jar or bottle and discard the herbs.

Chilli oil Add several dried chillies to a bottle of olive oil and leave to infuse for about 2 weeks before using. If the flavour is not sufficiently pronounced, leave for another week. The chillies can be left in the bottle and give a very decorative effect.

Garlic oil Add several whole garlic cloves to a bottle of olive oil and leave to infuse for about 2 weeks before using. If you like, you can strain the oil into a clean bottle and store in a cool, dark place.

Vinegars, sauces and condiments

Not only are vinegars, sauces and condiments perfect for serving with dishes at the table, they are also great for adding flavour and bite to simple dishes during cooking.

Vinegars It is worth buying a good-quality vinegar as it will keep better. White wine vinegar, cider vinegar, malt vinegar and balsamic vinegar are the most commonly used.

Soy sauce Made from fermented soy beans, soy sauce is salty and just a small amount adds a rich, rounded flavour to Asian-style stir-fries, glazes and sauces.

Tomato ketchup Add a splash of this strong table condiment to tomato sauces for a sweet-sour flavour.

Worcestershire sauce This brown, very spicy sauce brings a piquant flavour to casseroles, stews and soups.

Curry paste There are many ready-made curry pastes, including those for classic Indian and Thai curries. They can also be used to spice up burgers or meatballs.

Mustard Wholegrain mustard has a sweet taste and makes a mild salad dressing. French Dijon mustard has a piquant flavour which complements red meat. English mustard is excellent added to cheese dishes.

Passata/bottled strained tomatoes This Italian product, made of sieved tomatoes, has a fairly thin consistency and makes a good base for a tomato sauce.

Tomato purée/paste This concentrated purée is an essential in every storecupboard. It is great for adding flavour, and sometimes body, to sauces and stews.

Below: *Tomato purée (paste) can add extra flavour to tomato sauces, soups and stews of all types.*

Dried herbs and stock cubes

Cheap and very useful, dried herbs and stock (bouillon) cubes are convenient standbys when you don't have fresh herbs or stock to hand, although for some recipes you will only be able to use the fresh type. Dried herbs have a much more concentrated flavour than fresh, so be careful about how much you add or the flavour might be overpowering.

Basil This distinctive herb is the perfect partner to tomato-based dishes, and can be used in soups, stews and to make tomato sauces.

Bay Dried bay leaves are a perfectly satisfactory substitute for fresh bay leaves. They are used when making a bouquet garni and can be added to meat dishes, stews and casseroles before cooking. Remember to remove them from the dish before serving, as they are tough.

Oregano Dried oregano has a strong, pungent flavour that will permeate the whole dish, so use in moderation. It adds a distinctive aroma to Italian-style dishes, and is an integral part of a basic tomato sauce for spreading on pizzas or topping pasta dishes.

Rosemary This is another pungent herb that will enhance the flavour of many meat dishes, especially those made with lamb.

Below: *Store dried herbs, such as bay leaves, in airtight containers to help to preserve their flavour better.*

Above: *Rock or sea salt is generally regarded as the most superior type of salt available, and it is not treated with any chemicals. You will need to grind it in a mill or a mortar before adding to food.*

Sage Peppery-tasting sage has large, slightly furry leaves when fresh. Dried sage goes particularly well with pork, or in pasta sauces and in stuffings. It has a very strong flavour, so use in moderation or it will overpower the dish.

Tarragon This fragrant herb has a strong aniseed flavour, and is most often paired with fish and chicken dishes.

Stock (bouillon) cubes These handy cubes are an excellent way of adding flavour to a range of cooked meat and vegetable dishes, although if you are making soup, it is better to use home-made stock if you possibly can, because it is such a key ingredient and forms the basis of the dish. It is worth paying a little extra for good quality stock cubes because cheaper varieties tend to contain a lot of added salt and will give a less satisfactory result.

Salt

A key ingredient, salt can be used in moderation to add flavour and to bring out the taste of other foods. It also acts as a preservative when it is used in pickling and chutney-making, or when curing meats and fish, since it draws out the moisture and prevents decomposition. It is worth paying a little extra for rock or sea salt, since these types do not contain any added chemicals, which are often found in table salt. Sea salt has a stronger taste than table salt, so use it in moderation, and add a little at a time, tasting in between additions to prevent oversalting.

Spices

These flavourings play a very important role when cooking with relatively inexpensive ingredients, adding a warmth and roundness of flavour to simple dishes. It is difficult to have every spice to hand, but a few key spices will be enough to create culinary magic. Black pepper is an essential seasoning in every storecupboard; cumin seeds, coriander seeds, chilli flakes and turmeric are also good basics. Store spices in airtight containers in a cool, dark place. Buy small quantities that will be used up quickly, because flavours diminish with age.

Allspice This berry has a warm, slightly cinnamon-clove flavour. It is more readily available in its ground form and can be used in both savoury and sweet cooking.

Caraway seeds These small dark seeds have a fennel-like flavour and can be used in sweet and savoury dishes.

Cayenne pepper This fiery, piquant spice is made from dried hot red chillies, so use sparingly. It is excellent added to cheese dishes and creamy sauces and soups.

Chilli flakes Crushed dried red chillies can be added to, or sprinkled over, all kinds of dishes. You can easily make your own by drying fresh red chillies on a radiatior and then crumbling them with your fingers.

Chinese five-spice powder This is a mixture of ground spices, including anise pepper, cassia, fennel seeds, star anise and cloves. It is a powerful mixture, so use sparingly.

Cinnamon This warm spice is available in sticks and ground into powder, and has many uses. Add sticks to Moroccan stews, and use powder in baking.

Cloves Available whole or ground, these dried flower buds are used in savoury and sweet dishes. Ground cloves are strong, so use sparingly.

Coriander Available whole or ground, this warm, aromatic spice is delicious with most meats, particularly lamb.

Cumin This warm, pungent spice works well with meats and a variety of vegetables.

Fennel seeds These little green seeds have a sweet, aniseed-like flavour that pairs well with chicken and fish.

Garam masala This mixture of ground roasted spices is made from cumin, coriander, cardamom and black pepper and is used in many Asian dishes. Ready-mixed garam masala is widely available, although the flavour is better when the spices are freshly roasted and ground.

Ginger The ground, dried spice is useful for baking. For a fresher flavour, it is best to use fresh root ginger.

Green cardamom The papery green pods enclose little black seeds that are easily scraped out and can be crushed.

Nutmeg This large aromatic seed is available in a ground form, but the flavour is better when it is freshly grated.

Paprika Used in many Spanish dishes, paprika is available in a mild and hot form. It has a slightly sweet flavour.

Pepper Black pepper is one of the most commonly used spices, and should always be freshly ground or it will lose its flavour. Green peppercorns have a mild flavour. They are available dried or preserved in brine. White pepper is hotter than green, but less aromatic than black.

Turmeric Made from dried turmeric root, the ground spice is bright yellow with a peppery, slightly earthy flavour and is used in many Indian dishes.

Vanilla Dried vanilla pods (beans) are long and black, encasing hundreds of tiny black seeds. Natural vanilla extract is distilled from vanilla pods and is a useful alternative to pods.

Above: *For the best flavour, grate whole nutmeg as and when you need the spice, using a special small grater.*

Seasonality Charts

Buying food when it is in season ensures that you are getting the best-quality, best-value fresh produce. Although many products are available all year round, it is worth checking where they are grown and what condition they are in, and considering using a home-grown seasonal alternative instead. These charts provide a basic outline of when the food is in season in the country in which it is grown, and some of its culinary or nutritional properties and uses.

SPRING	
Apricots	Apricots appear in the shops in late spring. They are delicious poached with honey and lemon or made into tarts or sorbets.
Asparagus	Buy asparagus when it is on special offer. The stalks should snap easily and not be woody.
Aubergines (eggplants)	The first aubergines appear in mid-spring. The spongy flesh is very absorbent and carries the flavour of spices well – perfect for adding to curries and other robust dishes.
Broccoli	Dark green, vitamin-packed broccoli is a mainstay of the winter and early spring, and makes a cheap and very healthy accompaniment to most main dishes.
Broad (fava) beans	Pale green broad beans are available from the end of spring. Select firm pods.
Brussels sprouts	Small, round Brussels sprouts are available until early spring. Add to stir-fries or lightly steam or boil and serve with butter as an accompaniment.
Button (white) mushrooms	Although cultivated mushrooms are available all year, delicate button mushrooms are at their best in spring and are delicious served raw in salads or lightly sautéed.
Cabbage	Spring cabbage has tender young leaves and a mild flavour.
Carrots	Young carrots are at their best in spring and are delicious raw or lightly steamed.
Cauliflower	These are available in abundance from early spring. Pull back the leaves to check that the florets are creamy white with no discolouration.
Curly kale	Robust, dark green curly kale is available from early spring, and is packed with goodness and flavour.
Duck	Roast duck is traditionally eaten in mid-spring. The creamy flesh can be prepared in any number of ways, although since it is expensive, it is best eaten in a casserole to make it stretch further.
Greens	Spring greens are at their best towards the end of spring.
Guava	Exotic guava can be used raw in fruit salads or to make a delicate, fragrant jelly.
Halibut	These large, meaty fish are available in late spring/early summer.
Horseradish	Peel horseradish root before making into fiery horseradish sauce.
Lamb	New season lamb is the highlight of spring.
New potatoes	Many varieties are available in spring. Try to buy locally produced varieties to ensure that they are fresh.
Papaya	This tropical fruit is available most of the year round, but is particularly good in mid-spring.
Peas	Fresh peas are vibrant, sweet and tender in late spring. Select bright, firm pods.
Plaice	Buy this versatile white-fleshed fish when it is very fresh and cook it very gently.
Purple sprouting broccoli	This attractive leafy vegetable is at its best in spring and makes a change from standard green broccoli. It requires only minimal cooking.
Radishes	Crisp, fresh radishes are available from mid-spring right into the summer.
Rhubarb	The last of the forced and the first of the outdoor rhubarb is available in spring.
Rocket (arugula)	Peppery young leaves are in their prime and add a tang to salads.
Spinach	Spring heralds the arrival of baby spinach leaves, which are rich in vitamins and taste delicious.
Spring onions (scallions)	These pungent, tender onions are particularly flavoursome in late spring. Add them raw to salads, or lightly cook them by adding them to stir-fries.
Turnips	Spring turnips are small and very tender, requiring minimal cooking.

SUMMER

Apricots	These downy soft fruits do not ripen once they have been picked, so make sure they are ripe when you buy them.
Avocados	Meltingly soft, creamy and delicious, avocados are the perfect addition to any salad. Make sure that they are ripe before using, or the flavour and texture may be disappointing.
Basil	The flavour and aroma of basil is most intense during the summer months, when it is abundant.
Beef	Beef is available all year round, but make the most of tender steaks in the summer by marinading and cooking on a barbecue.
Blackcurrants	Tangy blackcurrants need to be cooked with a little sugar or mixed with other sweeter fruits.
Blueberries	Vitamin C-packed blueberries are at their best in late summer. They are very versatile, and can be added to fresh and cooked dishes.
Broad (fava) beans	Tender little broad beans are irresistible in soups, dips or steamed with a squeeze of lemon.
Cherries	Deep red, juicy cherries are divine eaten on their own, or mixed into summer fruit salads.
Corn	Freshly picked, local corn on the cob tastes fabulous when lightly steamed or baked on a barbecue and served just with some butter and ground black pepper.
Courgettes (zucchini)	Plump courgettes taste delicious and are very versatile – they can be baked, fried, cut into very thin slices and served raw or added to any number of summer soups and pasta sauces.
Crab	Make the most of the delicate flesh to make a really luxurious summer salad.
Cucumber	Although this salad vegetable is normally available all year, it is at its best during the summer.
Damsons	The intensely flavoured fruits are at their best in late summer, and can be used to make exquisite syrup, jelly, gin or cheese.
Fennel	Refreshing fennel has an aniseed flavour, and can be added raw to salads, blanched and chargrilled on a barbecue or tossed in stir-fries.
Garlic	Mild and aromatic, the first of the new season's garlic can be eaten raw in dips or marinades, or blanched and roasted for a creamy accompaniment to roast chicken.
Globe artichokes	Ideal for a lazy lunch, artichoke leaves taste delicious dipped in butter.
Gooseberries	The sharp taste and furry texture of gooseberries is unique, and since they are only around for a few weeks in mid-summer, make sure that you make the most of them.
Lettuce	Almost all varieties of lettuce are at their best in the summer. There are many different varieties, so try them out singly or in combination with other types to create a light, crisp salad.
Lovage	Leafy lovage tastes a bit like celery and can be added to salads, soups or as a flavouring for chicken or white fish.
Melons	Sweet, juicy and fragrant, melons are very versatile and can be served with cold meat and cheese as an appetizer, or simply eaten on their own as a refreshing dessert.
Mint	Most fresh herbs are at their best in the summer, and mint is no exception.
Nectarines	Allow nectarines to ripen fully before eating, so that their aromatic flavour is at its very best.
Peaches	Succulent peaches are best eaten raw, or sliced on top of natural (plain) yogurt.
Peas	Sweet new peas, straight from the pod are one of the highlights of the summer.
Peppers	Crisp and crunchy red, yellow and green (bell) peppers add flavour, texture and colour to pasta dishes and salads, or can be stuffed and baked in the oven or chargrilled on the barbecue.
Radishes	The potent, fiery flavour of radishes increases throughout the summer.
Raspberries	These soft, fragrant berries taste wonderful on their own, or mix them with peaches, nectarines and other soft summer fruits for a mouth-watering fruit salad.
Redcurrants	Jewel-like redcurrants can be served as an attractive topping to sponge cakes, as part of a mixed fruit salad or in a range of cooked summer desserts.
Strawberries	Juicy, sweet strawberries are the essence of summer, so enjoy them while they are in season.
Stringless beans	These plump beans can be cooked and eaten immediately as a side dish, or cooled and used as the basis of a substantial summer salad.
Tomatoes	All types of tomatoes are at their best in the summer. Enjoy them raw in salads or stuffed and baked. If you have a glut of tomatoes, or some that are over-ripe, convert them into sauces and soups to be enjoyed in the winter months.

AUTUMN

Apples	There are many varieties of apple available in supermarkets, but for the best locally grown varieties, buy them in greengrocers or your local food markets.
Bananas	Packed with potassium, bananas make the ideal economical snack or dessert.
Beetroot (beet)	Deep red beetroot can be boiled or baked to make a nutritious main dish or accompaniment.
Brussels sprouts	These small green brassicas are packed with vitamins. Take care not to overcook them.
Blackberries	Early autumn is the best time to go foraging in the hedgerows for wild blackberries.
Carrots	Infinitely versatile, carrots can be eaten on their own, or added to any number of soups, stews, casseroles or accompaniments.
Cauliflower	This staple autumn and winter vegetable is extremely versatile, and can be used to make creamy soups, appetizing cheese dishes or served simply boiled or steamed as an accompaniment.
Cavolo nero	Available throughout autumn and winter, cavolo nero tastes fabulous with bacon, cheese or meat.
Celery	Crisp young celery is incredibly versatile and has a subtle, sweet flavour.
Chanterelle mushrooms	Rich, earthy chanterelles require minimal preparation and are delicious added to risottos, soups and pasta. Store in a paper bag in the salad drawer of your refrigerator.
Crab apples	Tart and crisp, crab apples are ideal for converting into jams, jellies, sorbets and mousses.
Cranberries	Ruby red cranberries should be initially cooked without sugar – to prevent the waxy skin from toughening – before making into fruit tarts, or poaching and making into a piquant sauce.
Damsons	Early autumn is peak damson season, so make sure you make the most of them.
Dates	Sweet and succulent, dates are harvested in the autumn months. There are many varieties available, and their texture and sweetness ranges from toffee-like to plump and succulent.
Elderberries	Pick elderberries in early autumn and transform into cordials and jellies.
Figs	Always eat plump figs at room temperature as their flavour will be dulled if they are served chilled.
Game birds	Although usually quite expensive, the meat of game birds is rich and a little goes a long way.
Herring	Available most of the year, herring taste delicious fried or baked with a piquant citrus sauce.
Kale	Both plain and curly kale are available throughout autumn, and are packed with valuable nutrients and phytochemicals.
Leeks	Choose slender leeks whenever possible, as they will be less tough than thicker ones.
Mackerel	Omega 3-rich mackerel are at their best now. They are cheap, and easy to prepare and cook.
Marrow	Plump marrows are the ideal vessels for spicy fillings and taste wonderful baked with cheese.
Pears	Fragrant pears are the essence of autumn. Enjoy them raw, or poach them for a divine dessert.
Parsnips	These are another autumn and winter staple, and they can be used in many savoury dishes.
Passion fruit	Scrape out the flesh and seeds from these fragrant fruits and add to fruit salads for a special treat.
Pomegranates	Jewel-like pomegranates are grown in warmer climes, and are at their best now.
Pork	Pork is at its best in autumn, which coincides nicely with its traditional partner, apples.
Potatoes	Old potatoes are harvested before the cold weather really sets in, so there is an abundance of different varieties available in the autumn months.
Pumpkins	The sweet flesh can be used to create velvety soups, or can be added to stews and casseroles.
Quince	Golden yellow quinces have an aromatic flavour and are ideal for making into delicate jellies.
Rosemary	Woody-stemmed rosemary makes a great addition to many meat dishes.
Ruby chard	Red-stemmed ruby chard makes the perfect accompaniment to lamb, beef or fish dishes.
Sage	Strongly-flavoured sage is a great addition to meat dishes, and can be used to make stuffing.
Savoy cabbage	Dark green, crinkly-leaved savoy cabbage marks the start of the colder months. It can be steamed and served as an accompaniment, added to soups, or stuffed and baked.
Shallots	The first shallots come into season in early autumn.
Sloes	These grow wild in hedgerows and woodland. Use to make wonderful jellies, cordials, and sloe gin.
Squash	The many varieties of squash can be used to make a range of economical, tasty and filling dishes.
Swede (rutabaga)	Sustaining swede can be boiled and mashed, on its own or with carrots.
Swiss chard	Use the leaves of Swiss chard as you would spinach leaves, and lightly boil the white stems.

WINTER

Avocados	Creamy avocados come into season at the start of winter and last right through to the summer.
Beef	Cheaper cuts of beef, such as brisket, chuck or blade are perfectly suited to slow cooking and make warming, hearty, and economical casseroles and stews.
Brussels sprouts	Available from late autumn through to the early spring, Brussels sprouts are nutritious and cheap.
Carrots	Packed with vitamins and very economical, carrots are a key ingredient for the clever cook.
Cauliflower	The distinctive white florets of cauliflower are a mainstay on the winter menu.
Celeriac	Reminiscent of celery, celeriac has a mild flavour and can be mashed with potatoes or lightly fried.
Chicory (Belgian endive)	Red and white varieties of chicory are available during the winter months. The slightly bitter leaves can be used raw in salads, or baked with other leafy vegetables as a delicious accompaniment.
Clementines	These small, juicy fruits are delicious eaten raw and make a very handy snack food.
Cranberries	Poached cranberries can make a thick sauce that tastes wonderful with roasted game and turkey.
Goose	Some people like to eat goose during the festive period. It is reasonably expensive, so serve it with plenty of roast vegetables to make it stretch further.
Halibut	Halibut steaks or fillets are usually relatively inexpensive, and require very few additional ingredients to make them into a meal. Be careful not to overcook the flesh or it will become dry.
Leeks	These mild alliums have a delicate flavour that makes a great addition to winter soups and stews.
Mussels	These flavoursome morsels are cheap and abundant in winter.
Parsnips	Sweet white parsnips are cheap and can help to pad out a meat casserole or stew.
Physalis	Also known as Cape gooseberries, these small orange fruits make an unusual and delicious addition to fruit salads, pavlovas, sorbets and pies, and they are also very decorative.
Pomegranate	A flash of colour in the winter months, pomegranates are packed with iron and other beneficial compounds. To juice, simply press the flesh through a sieve (strainer) using the back of a ladle.
Field (portabello) mushrooms	Meaty and satisfying, field mushrooms can be grilled, stuffed and baked for a hearty vegetarian main meal, or added to any number of meat dishes.
Purple sprouting broccoli	Dramatic-looking purple sprouting broccoli makes a welcome change to green broccoli, which is available all year round.
Radicchio	The bitter white and magenta leaves of this brassica can be eaten raw or lightly cooked in a little butter. Store in a dark, dry place until required, and rinse thoroughly before use.
Red cabbage	Vibrant red cabbage can be shredded and eaten raw in salads, pickled in vinegar, or braised.
Seville oranges	These intensely-flavoured oranges are only around for a short period of time. Use for making marmalade, or adding flavour to vinaigrettes, marinades or puddings.
Squid	Unlike many other types of fish, squid prices are unaffected by bad weather since it can be caught and frozen during fair weather, so it usually good value for money.
Swede (rutabaga)	Usually white or yellow in colour, swedes can be served mashed or in stews and casseroles. They are normally very good value for money.
Sweet potatoes	Although they are available all year, sweet potatoes are particularly good in the winter months as they are both filling and warming, as well as being extremely versatile.
Turkey	Available for most of the year, but at its best during the festive months, turkey is very good value for money, and many different cuts are available, making it versatile and easy to use.
Turnips	The root of turnips can be mashed or added to slowly cooked meat dishes such as braises or casseroles, and the leaves can be steamed and eaten as an accompaniment.
Venison	Wild venison is available for most of the year as its availability varies according to the breed, sex and location of the animals. Go to your local market or butcher to get the best quality and price.
White cabbage	Extremely versatile and usually very cheap, white cabbage can be eaten raw in healthy salads, made into coleslaw, or lightly stir-fried for a warming and nutrient-packed Oriental meal.
White celery	Although green celery is available all year, frost-hardy white celery comes into its own in the winter months. Use in salads or for flavouring stocks, soups, casseroles and stuffings.
Yam	Similar in texture and flavour to sweet potatoes, yams are extremely filling and make an excellent addition to slowly cooked meat dishes, or can be served baked with butter.

Sample Menus

Whether you are planning a quick and easy mid-week family supper, a children's birthday party or a special meal for two, you can provide a dazzling array of delicious and varied dishes without blowing your budget. The key to success is to plan ahead – make sure that you know how many people are coming, if any of the guests have dietary requirements, and do as much preparation as you can ahead of time. These sample menus show what is possible, but you can easily adapt them.

Weekend Brunch

Nothing beats a hearty brunch at the weekend, and whether you want to satisfy your sweet tooth or tuck into something more substantial, there are plenty of mouthwatering options that fit the bill.

Apple and Cinnamon Muffins ✳

Served warm from the oven, muffins are the ultimate treat, and these lightly spiced ones will fill the house with an irresistible aroma.

Soufflé Omelette with Mushrooms ✳✳

Quick, cheap and very easy to make, omelettes are packed with goodness and, combined with creamy mushrooms, are truly delicious.

Focaccia with Sardines and Tomatoes ✳✳

Packed with flavour and essential Omega 3 oils, these open sandwiches are a great way to start the day.

Lazy Lunch

Sitting down to a leisurely lunch is the ultimate treat, and it is well worth taking the time to indulge yourself and your friends or family every so often. These dishes are easy to prepare, leaving you free to enjoy yourself out of the kitchen.

Warm Penne with Fresh Tomatoes and Basil ✳

Colourful, simple and satisfying, this pasta dish can be easily adapted depending on what is in season, or in your fridge.

Baby Spinach and Roast Garlic Salad ✳

Sweet, roasted garlic imparts a distinctive taste to fresh young spinach leaves, and it is the ideal partner to the simple pasta dish.

Rhubarb and Ginger Cups ✳

You can whip this dessert together in no time at all from just a few storecupboard ingredients, and it is as tasty as it is pretty.

Time for Tea

Making a selection of delectable cakes, cookies, breads and bakes for afternoon tea is extremely rewarding, and your efforts in the kitchen are sure to be appreciated by all the family.

Scones with Jam and Cream ✳

A long-standing favourite, scones served warm from the oven with a generous dollop of home-made jam and some thick cream are an essential part of a teatime spread.

Old-fashioned Treacle Cake ✳

Easy to make and extremely economical, this moist, flavoursome cake can be made with any combination of dried fruits, ensuring it will meet with everyone's approval.

Ginger Cookies ✳

Crumbly, sweet and studded with jewels of preserved stem ginger, these cookies taste as good as they look. If there are any left over, store them in an airtight container and include in packed lunches for a mid-morning snack.

Currant Cakes ✳

These tempting morsels are at their very best served warm from the pan, so try not to make more than you will need. Serve on their own or spread with butter and sprinkled with cinnamon.

  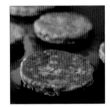

Speedy Supper

After a busy day, the last thing you feel like doing is spending hours in the kitchen, so here is an example of a nutritious and easy meal that you can rustle up in next to no time at all.

Tortellini with Ham ✳

Pasta dishes are incredibly versatile, as well as being cheap and quick to prepare. This one is an ideal way to use up any left-over ham you may have in your refrigerator.

Braised Lettuce and Peas with Spring Onions and Mint ✳

Light and colourful, this flavoursome vegetable dish is an ideal accompaniment to the tortellini, as the fresh flavour of the mint and spring onions will cut through the richness of the cream and cheese in the pasta dish.

Baked Bananas with Toffee Sauce ✳

This simple dessert is warming, nutritious, and requires just 20 minutes cooking time. Make plenty of the rich chocolate sauce so there is plenty to go round, and store any that is left over in the refrigerator for up to 3 days.

Winter Warmer

During cold, damp weather, there is nothing better than eating a really warming and sustaining meal to help drive out the chill, boost your system and raise the spirits.

Kale, Chorizo and Potato soup ✳

This sustaining and unusual soup is packed with essential nutrients and combines winter vegetables with storecupboard staples, making it an economical yet delicious option.

Chilli Con Carne ✳

This spicy meat dish makes a little meat go a long way by combining it with black beans and storecupboard ingredients. It improves with keeping, so is ideal as a make-ahead dinner.

Spiced Roasted Pumpkin✳

Chunks of pumkin are roasted with spices and topped with cheese in this easy-to-prepare side dish. The sweetness of the soft flesh complements the spiciness of the chilli con carne and it can be roasted in the oven towards the end of the chilli's cooking time.

Lemon Surprise Pudding ✳

Tangy, rich and warming, this popular pudding consists of a light lemon sponge over a zesty sauce. Serve generous portions with a scoop of vanilla ice cream or a liberal amount of cream.

Simply Slow Cooked

A way of cooking that is enjoying a resurgence in popularity, slow cooking is the ideal way to prepare many cuts of meat. Although they take time to cook, your patience will be rewarded with deep flavours and meltingly tender meat.

Braised Lamb Shanks with Cannellini Beans ✳ ✳

Warming, sustaining and extremely flavoursome, this hearty one-pot dish is ideal for a chilly evening. Although the meat may be quite expensive, it is padded out with storecupboard ingredients, making it a more economical option.

Cabbage Salad with Lemon Dressing ✳

Light, crisp and zesty, this simple salad balances the richness of the the lamb shanks perfectly.It does not keep that well, so only make as much as you need, and store any left-overs in the refrigerator for just one day.

Hot Chocolate Pudding with Rum Custard ✳

This light and intensely chocolatey steamed pudding is the perfect end to a slow-cooked meal. The rum custard provides a sophisticated note, but you could omit the rum, or serve it with cream, if you are making it for children.

Vegetarian Feast

With such a wealth of fresh, flavoursome vegetables to choose from in every season, creating a delicious vegetarian meal with the correct balance of nutrients is easy.

Spicy Red Lentil Soup ✳

Cheap and nutritious, lentils are the ideal food for vegetarians. Here they are used to make a delicious Turkish soup, which is lightly spiced with cumin, fenugreek and coriander and topped with a red onion garnish.

Vegetarian Sausages ✳

Easy to make and extremely tasty, these vegetarian sausages are made from leeks and cheese and flavoured with mustard and herbs. They will be popular with everyone, so make sure you make plenty!

Potatoes and Parsnips Baked with Garlic and Cream ✳

Rich, creamy and with a subtle hint of garlic, this baked accompaniment is the perfect partner to both meat and vegetarian sausages, as well as grilled or roasted meat.

Spiced Greens ✳

Vibrant and appetizing, this stir-fried dish makes a change from steamed greens. The spicy hit from the chillies will cut through the creaminess of the baked potato dish.

Maximum Vitality

Sometimes you really feel like you need a good boost of vitamins and minerals, and what better way to achieve this than by creating and eating lots of delicious, nutritious food!

Cannellini Bean, Tomato and Parsley Soup ✳

Tomatoes are packed with antioxidants as well as flavour, making this colourful soup a star in every regard. Make plenty, as you can freeze any you don't eat immediately, ready for when you are in a hurry or tired after a long day.

Bean Salad with Tuna and Red Onion ✳

This delicious salad contains high levels of fibre, protein and beneficial Omega 3 essential oils, and it also has a low GI, which means that it will keep you going for longer.

Fresh Fig Compote ✳ ✳

High in fibre and delicious to eat, fresh figs make an ideal light dessert when they are in season. Serve on their own or with spoonfuls of low-fat natural (plain) bio-yogurt.

Summer Supper

Salads and chilled desserts come into their own during the summer months, and they provide the perfect opportunity to really make the most of all of the fresh produce on offer.

Salad Niçoise ✳ ✳

This luxurious salad is packed with flavour. Look out for special offers on fresh tuna steaks, as they can be expensive. You could use good-quality canned tuna as a cheaper alternative, if you prefer.

Pitta Bread ✳

Fresh, home-made pitta bread served warm from the oven makes the perfect accompaniment to a substantial salad. You could also serve with any Italian bread, such as foccacia or ciabatta, depending on your personal preference.

Lemon Sorbet ✳

This tangy chilled dessert will cleanse the palate and makes the ideal end to a light summer supper. The simple ingredients are very cheap, and you can make it well in advance.

Finger Buffet

The beauty of finger food is that you can do most of the preparation in advance, leaving you free to enjoy yourself. It is a good idea to serve a wide range of dishes so that there is something for everyone.

Smoked Salmon Roulade ✳

Smoked salmon is the ultimate luxury and, combined with a herby crème fraîche and rolled in pancake, it is not as expensive as you may think. Slice the roulade into bitesize morsels so people can help themselves.

Hummus ✳

Creamy hummus is an ideal dip to accompany finger food, and it is sure to be popular so make sure that you make a lot! Serve with raw vegetable crudités, such as celery, carrot and cucumber.

Courgette Fritters with Chilli Jam ✳

Fiery chilli jam complements the light and subtle flavour of the courgette (zucchini) fritters in this unusual dish. Make plenty and keep ones that are not being served in the oven until they are needed, so you can serve them warm.

Carrot Cake ✳

Slices of moist, tangy carrot cake spread with zesty mascarpone icing are the perfect way to end a finger buffet. Just remember to have plenty of napkins to hand.

Family Barbecue

Simplicity and preparation are the key ingredients for a successful barbecue, so make sure that you have planned everything well in advance – and hope for good weather.

Potato Skewers with Mustard Dip ✳

Sticky, sweet shallots are alternated with soft new potatoes on a skewer and cooked on a barbecue, imbuing them with a slightly smokey flavour. Served with a tangy mustard dip, this delicious appetizer should satisfy everyone while you cook the chicken.

Barbecued Chicken ✳

Chicken pieces are marinated in a spicy lemon sauce before being cooked over the coals of a barbecue in this simple dish. Serve with warm pitta bread, lemon wedges and a mixed salad.

Chocolate and Banana Fool ✳

A classic combination, chocolate and bananas are combined with a sweet custard and then chilled in glasses in this simple recipe. Make in advance and keep in the refrigerator until needed.

Picnic Hamper

The key to a glorious picnic is to make plenty of food that is both portable and easy to eat. It is a good idea to take paper plates and plenty of napkins, and to include an ice pack in the basket to keep everything cool.

Fritatta with Sun-dried Tomatoes ✳

Quick and easy to make, this colourful fritatta tastes as delicious cold as it does warm. Cut it into wedges before packing into plastic containers so that it is ready to eat when you are at the picnic.

Spicy Chickpea Samosas ✳

These light-as-air vegetarian samosas contain a simple yet delicious mixture of chickpeas, coriander (cilantro) and chilli oil. They are sure to be popular, so make plenty.

Potato and Olive Salad ✳

A favourite for al fresco dining, this simple salad is less messy than the more traditional version, since it doesn't use any mayonnaise. Instead, new potatoes and olives are drizzled with garlic-flavoured olive oil and mixed with fresh herbs.

Chewy Flapjacks ✳

Subtly flavoured with orange, these moreish, chewy flapjacks are universally popular and make the perfect end to a family picnic. If there are any left over, eat them as a mid-morning snack the next day.

Sunday Lunch

Sunday lunch is a great opportunity to gather friends and family together around the table to enjoy a delicious meal together. For a vegetarian alternative, why not try Lentil and Nut Loaf in place of roasted meat?

Traditional Roast Chicken with Herb Stuffing ✳

Succulent, tender roast chicken is always a hit, especially when it is served with a herb stuffing and lashings of home-made gravy. To make the meat stretch further, serve with sausages and plenty of vegetables.

Potatoes, Peppers and Shallots ✳

Soft, floury potatoes absorb the flavour and aroma of fresh rosemary and sweet roasted shallots and peppers in this delicious accompaniment, which makes a change from standard roast potatoes.

Apple and Blackberry Wholemeal Crumble ✳

Fruit crumbles are very cheap and easy to make. When blackberries are out of season, simply use more apples, and add a handful of dried fruit and a pinch of cinammon.

  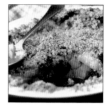

Children's Party

It is worth finding out about any food intolerances before you plan a menu for children. Keep the food simple and cut it into small, bitesize pieces to avoid any unnecessary waste.

Potato, Onion and Broad Bean Tortilla ✳

Slice this simple broad (fava) bean and potato tortilla into child-friendly chunks. If the children are older than five, thread on to cocktail sticks (toothpicks).

Turkey Patties ✳

Prepare these tasty patties in advance, so that you simply have to shallow fry them on the day of the party. Make them smaller than you would normally, and serve in a soft roll.

Oat Chocolate Chip Cookies ✳

These tasty little bites are sure to be popular, so make lots of little ones rather than several large ones. It may be a good idea to omit the pecan nuts if you are concerned about intolerances.

Victoria Sandwich Cake ✳

This simple classic makes an ideal birthday cake, as it is not too rich for young palates. You can use any flavour jam you like, and/or omit the cream, according to personal preference.

Casual Entertaining

Entertaining on a budget needn't be a strain on your time or your wallet. Simply plan your menu in advance and choose simple yet stunning dishes that can easily be adapted according to the number of guests and the season.

Pimiento Tartlets ✳

Simple to make and stunning to look at, these bitesize tartlets are a perfect way to start an informal meal. Make them in advance and serve with drinks before you sit down for dinner.

Golden Beef and Potato Puffs ✳ ✳

These light-as-air puffs are filled with an aromatic combination of spiced meat and soft mashed potato. Serve them hot, with home-made tomato sauce for dipping.

Mackerel Stuffed with Nuts and Spices ✳ ✳

Although it takes a little time to make this unusual Turkish dish, the end result is well worth the effort. Mackerel are extremely good value for money, so you will be able to feed quite a few people without breaking the bank.

Mango and Chocolate Crème Brulée ✳

Universally popular, crème brulées are a fabulous way to finish a special meal. These ones combine the soft, sweet flesh of mango with a bittersweet dark chocolate custard, topped with a crisp layer of caramel.

 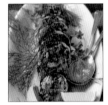 

Romantic Dinner

There is no better way of expressing your emotions than creating a special meal for two, and the ideas below show that you don't have to spend a fortune in order to impress.

Salmon Baked with Potatoes and Thyme ✳ ✳ ✳

Succulent salmon fillets are served on a bed of braised, thinly sliced potatoes and onions and garnished with thyme in this simple yet stunning all-in-one dish.

Mixed Green Leaf and Fresh Herb Salad ✳

Fresh, light and crisp, this simple salad, dressed with a light vinaigrette, makes the ideal accompaniment to the delicate flavour of the salmon and the flavoursome potatoes and onions.

Lemon Posset ✳

Effortlessly elegant, this creamy, tangy dessert simply combines lemon rind and juice with sugar and double (heavy) cream, making it a pleasure for both your senses and your pocket.

Sensational Soups

A STEAMING BOWL OF HEARTY SOUP IS THE ULTIMATE COMFORT FOOD ON A COLD DAY, AND IT MAKES AN ECONOMICAL ALL-IN-ONE LIGHT MEAL AT OTHER TIMES OF THE YEAR TOO. SOUPS ARE AN EXCELLENT WAY TO TRANSFORM A GLUT OF SEASONAL INGREDIENTS INTO A DELICIOUS MEAL, AND THEY ARE INCREDIBLY VERSATILE. CHOOSE FROM ELEGANT CHILLED SOUPS, SUCH AS AVGOLEMONO OR CUCUMBER AND YOGURT SOUP, OR EVERYDAY WARMERS, SUCH AS SPICED PARSNIP SOUP OR CORN, POTATO AND FLAGEOLET BEAN CHOWDER.

Leek and Potato Soup ✳

This classic, chilled summer soup is made from the simplest of ingredients and is very economical. Serve it garnished with fresh chives as an elegant appetizer to a special meal, or as a light lunch.

SERVES SIX

1 Melt the butter in a large, heavy pan. Add the leeks and shallots and cook gently, covered, for 15–20 minutes, until they are soft but not browned.

2 Add the potatoes and cook, uncovered, for a few minutes. Stir in the stock or water, 5ml/1 tsp salt and pepper to taste.

3 Bring to the boil, then reduce the heat and partly cover the pan. Simmer for 15 minutes, or until the potatoes are soft.

4 Cool, then process the soup until smooth in a blender or food processor. Strain the soup into a bowl and stir in the cream. Taste and adjust the seasoning, if necessary, and add a little iced water if the consistency of the soup seems too thick.

5 Chill the soup for at least 4 hours or until very cold. Taste the chilled soup for seasoning and add a squeeze of lemon juice, if required. Pour the soup into bowls and sprinkle with chopped chives. Serve immediately.

50g/2oz/^{1}/$_4$ cup unsalted (sweet) butter

450g/1lb leeks, white parts only, thinly sliced

3 large shallots, sliced

250g/9oz floury potatoes (such as King Edward or Idaho), peeled and cut into chunks

300ml/^{1}/$_2$ pint/1^1/$_4$ cups double (heavy) cream

iced water (optional)

a little lemon juice (optional)

chopped fresh chives, to garnish

FROM THE STORECUPBOARD

1 litre/1^3/$_4$ pints/4 cups light chicken stock

salt and ground black pepper, to taste

VARIATIONS

• *For hot leek and potato soup, use 1 chopped onion instead of the shallots and 450g/1lb potatoes. Halve the quantity of double (heavy) cream and reheat the soup, adding milk if it seems too thick.*

• *To make chilled leek and sorrel soup, add about 50g/2oz/1 cup shredded sorrel at the end of cooking. Finish and chill as in the main recipe, then serve garnished with a little shredded sorrel.*

Energy 547kcal/2260kJ; Protein 4.6g; Carbohydrate 17.7g, of which sugars 6.8g; Fat 51.4g, of which saturates 31.7g; Cholesterol 129mg; Calcium 79mg; Fibre 3.6g; Sodium 103mg

Avgolemono ✳

This is a great example of how a few ingredients can make a marvellous dish if carefully chosen and cooked. It is essential to use a well-flavoured stock. Add as little or as much rice as you like.

SERVES FOUR

1 Pour the chicken stock into a large pan, bring to simmering point, then add the drained rice.

2 Half cover the pan and cook for about 12 minutes until the rice is just tender. Season with salt and pepper to taste.

3 Whisk the egg yolks in a bowl, then add about 30ml/2 tbsp of the lemon juice, whisking constantly until the mixture is smooth and bubbly. Add a ladleful of soup and whisk again.

4 Remove the pan from the heat and slowly add the egg mixture to the soup, whisking all the time. The soup will turn a pretty lemon colour and will thicken slightly.

5 Taste the soup and add more lemon juice if necessary. Stir in the chopped parsley.

6 Serve at once, without reheating, garnished with lemon slices and parsley sprigs.

3 egg yolks

30–60ml/2–4 tbsp lemon juice

30ml/2 tbsp finely chopped fresh parsley

lemon slices and parsley sprigs, to garnish

FROM THE STORECUPBOARD

900ml/1^1/$_2$ pints/3^3/$_4$ cups chicken stock, preferably home-made

50g/2oz/generous ^{1}/$_3$ cup long grain rice

salt and ground black pepper, to taste

Energy 96kcal/404kJ; Protein 3.3g; Carbohydrate 10.9g, of which sugars 0.2g; Fat 4.7g, of which saturates 1.2g; Cholesterol 151mg; Calcium 39mg; Fibre 0.4g; Sodium 10mg

1 cucumber

4 garlic cloves

**75g/3oz/³/₄ cup
walnut pieces**

**40g/1¹/₂oz day-old bread,
torn into pieces**

**400ml/14fl oz/1²/₃ cups
natural (plain) yogurt**

**120ml/4fl oz/¹/₂ cup
cold water**

**5–10ml/1–2 tsp
lemon juice**

FOR THE GARNISH

**40g/1¹/₂oz/scant ¹/₂ cup
walnuts, coarsely chopped**

sprigs of fresh dill

FROM THE STORECUPBOARD

2.5ml/¹/₂ tsp salt

30ml/2 tbsp sunflower oil

25ml/1¹/₂ tbsp olive oil

Cucumber and Yogurt Soup ✳

This classic combination of cucumber and yogurt makes a particularly refreshing cold soup, perfect for lunch on a hot day.

SERVES SIX

1 Cut the cucumber in half and peel one half of it. Dice the cucumber flesh and set aside.

2 Using a large mortar and pestle, crush together the garlic and salt well, then add the walnuts and bread.

3 When the mixture is smooth, slowly add the sunflower oil and combine well.

4 Transfer the mixture to a large bowl and beat in the yogurt. Fold in the diced cucumber, then add the cold water and lemon juice to taste.

5 Pour the soup into chilled soup bowls. Garnish with the chopped walnuts and drizzle with the olive oil. Finally, arrange the sprigs of dill on top and serve immediately.

VARIATIONS

• *If you prefer your soup smooth, purée it in a food processor or blender before serving.*

• *For a creamier version, you could subsitute Greek yogurt for the natural (plain) yogurt.*

• *If you are making this dish for children, you may want to halve the amount of garlic included, or even omit it altogether.*

Energy 77kcal/322kJ; Protein 6.9g; Carbohydrate 10.3g, of which sugars 10.1g; Fat 1.3g, of which saturates 0.6g; Cholesterol 2mg; Calcium 255mg; Fibre 0.3g; Sodium 106mg.

Summer Minestrone *

This brightly coloured, fresh-tasting soup makes the most of delicious summer vegetables and fresh basil and is a meal in itself.

SERVES FOUR

1 large onion, finely chopped

450g/1lb ripe Italian plum tomatoes, peeled and finely chopped

225g/8oz green courgettes (zucchini), trimmed and roughly chopped

225g/8oz yellow courgettes, trimmed and roughly chopped

3 waxy new potatoes, washed and diced

2 garlic cloves, crushed

60ml/4 tbsp shredded fresh basil

50g/2oz/²⁄₃ cup grated grano padano cheese

FROM THE STORECUPBOARD

45ml/3 tbsp olive oil

15ml/1 tbsp sun-dried tomato purée (paste)

about 1.2 litres/2 pints/ 5 cups vegetable stock or water

salt and ground black pepper, to taste

1 Heat the oil in a large, heavy pan, add the onion and cook gently for about 5 minutes, stirring constantly, until softened but not browned.

2 Stir in the sun-dried tomato purée, chopped tomatoes, courgettes, diced potatoes and garlic. Mix well and cook gently for 10 minutes, uncovered, shaking the pan frequently to stop the vegetables sticking to the base.

3 Pour in the stock or water. Bring to the boil, lower the heat, half-cover the pan and simmer gently for 15 minutes or until the vegetables are just tender. Add more stock if necessary.

4 Remove the pan from the heat and stir in the basil and half the cheese. Taste and adjust the seasoning. Serve hot, sprinkled with the remaining cheese.

COOK'S TIP *Grano padano cheese is similar in taste and texture to Parmesan cheese, although it has a slightly milder taste. It is usually considerably cheaper than Parmesan, and makes an economical alternative.*

Energy 254kcal/1059kJ; Protein 10.2g; Carbohydrate 24.3g, of which sugars 11.1g; Fat 13.5g, of which saturates 4.1g; Cholesterol 13mg; Calcium 211mg; Fibre 4.1g; Sodium 167mg

Carrot and Orange Soup ✳

This traditional light and summery soup is always popular for its wonderfully creamy consistency and vibrantly fresh citrus flavour. Use a good, home-made chicken or vegetable stock if you can.

SERVES FOUR

1 Melt the butter in a large pan. Add the leeks and carrots and stir well, coating the vegetables with the butter.

2 Cover and cook for about 10 minutes, until the vegetables are beginning to soften but not colour.

3 Pour in the stock and the orange rind and juice. Add the nutmeg and season to taste with salt and pepper.

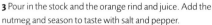

4 Bring to the boil, lower the heat, cover and simmer for about 40 minutes, or until the vegetables are tender.

5 Leave to cool slightly, then purée the soup in a food processor or blender until smooth.

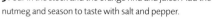

6 Return the soup to the pan and add 30ml/2 tbsp of the yogurt, then taste the soup and adjust the seasoning, if necessary. Reheat gently.

7 Ladle the soup into warm individual bowls and put a swirl of yogurt in the centre of each. Sprinkle the fresh sprigs of coriander over each bowl to garnish, and serve immediately.

50g/2oz/¹/₄ cup butter

3 leeks, sliced

450g/1lb carrots, sliced

rind and juice of 2 oranges

150ml/¹/₄ pint/²/₃ cup Greek (US strained plain) yogurt

fresh sprigs of coriander (cilantro), to garnish

FROM THE STORECUPBOARD

1.2 litres/2 pints/5 cups chicken or vegetable stock

2.5ml/¹/₂ tsp freshly grated nutmeg

salt and ground black pepper, to taste

Energy 206kcal/856kJ; Protein 5g; Carbohydrate 15.8g, of which sugars 14.2g; Fat 14.4g, of which saturates 8.3g; Cholesterol 27mg; Calcium 111mg; Fibre 5.8g; Sodium 131mg

Cream of Onion Soup ✳

This wonderfully satisfying soup has a deep, buttery flavour that is complemented perfectly by the addition of crisp croûtons or chopped chives, sprinkled over just before serving.

SERVES FOUR

115g/4oz/¹/₂ cup unsalted (sweet) butter

1kg/2¹/₄ lb yellow onions, sliced

1 fresh bay leaf

105ml/7 tbsp dry white vermouth

150ml/¹/₄ pint/²/₃ cup double (heavy) cream

a little lemon juice (optional)

croûtons (see Cook's Tip) or chopped fresh chives, to garnish

FROM THE STORECUPBOARD

1 litre/1³/₄ pints/4 cups chicken or vegetable stock

salt and ground black pepper, to taste

1 Melt 75g/3oz/6 tbsp butter in a large pan. Set about 200g/7oz of the onions aside and add the rest to the pan with the bay leaf. Stir the onions to coat in the butter, then cover and cook very gently for about 30 minutes. The onions should be soft and tender, but not browned.

2 Add the vermouth, increase the heat and boil rapidly until the liquid has evaporated. Add the stock, 5ml/1 tsp salt and pepper to taste. Bring to the boil, lower the heat and simmer gently for 5 minutes, then remove from the heat.

3 Leave the mixture to cool, then discard the bay leaf and process the soup in a blender or food processor. Return the soup to the rinsed pan.

4 Melt the remaining butter in another pan. Add the remaining onions, cover, and cook gently until soft but not browned. Uncover and continue to cook until golden yellow.

5 Add the cream to the soup and reheat gently until hot. Season to taste, adding lemon juice if liked. Add the onions and warm through for 1 minute. Serve with croûtons or chopped chives.

> **COOK'S TIP**
> To make the croûtons, preheat the oven to 200°C/400°F/Gas 6. Slice some French bread at an angle, brush with oil, and bake for 15 minutes.

Energy 522kcal/2151kJ; Protein 4g; Carbohydrate 21.5g, of which sugars 15.6g; Fat 44.5g, of which saturates 27.5g; Cholesterol 113mg; Calcium 90mg; Fibre 3.5g; Sodium 397mg

Spiced Parsnip Soup ✳

This lightly spiced, creamy soup is perfect for a cold winter day. It is very easy and cheap to make, and is packed with flavour.

SERVES SIX

1 Peel and thinly slice the parsnips. Heat the butter in a large heavy pan and add the peeled parsnips and chopped onion with the crushed garlic.

2 Cook over a gently heat until the vegetables are softened but not coloured, stirring occasionally.

3 Add the ground cumin and ground coriander to the vegetable mixture and cook, stirring, for 1–2 minutes, and then gradually blend in the hot chicken stock and mix well.

4 Cover and simmer for about 20 minutes, or until the parsnip is soft. Remove from the heat and leave to cool slightly.

5 Purée the soup in a food processor or blender. Check the texture, and adjust with extra stock or water if it seems too thick.

6 Check the seasoning and adjust as required. Add the cream and reheat without boiling.

7 Serve immediately, sprinkled with chopped chives or parsley and/or croûtons, to garnish.

900g/2lb parsnips

50g/2oz/^{1}/$_4$ cup butter

1 onion, chopped

2 garlic cloves, crushed

150ml/^{1}/$_4$ pint/^{2}/$_3$ cup single (light) cream

chopped fresh chives and/or croûtons, to garnish

FROM THE STORECUPBOARD

10ml/2 tsp ground cumin

5ml/1 tsp ground coriander

about 1.2 litres/2 pints/ 5 cups hot chicken stock

salt and ground black pepper, to taste

Energy 215kcal/899kJ; Protein 3.9g; Carbohydrate 21.3g, of which sugars 10.6g; Fat 13.3g, of which saturates 7.7g; Cholesterol 32mg; Calcium 92mg; Fibre 7.3g; Sodium 74mg

Curried Cauliflower Soup ✳

This simple yet delicious soup is perfect for lunch or as a light meal, served with warm, crusty bread and garnished with fresh coriander.

SERVES FOUR

1 Pour the milk into a large pan and place over a medium heat. Break or cut the cauliflower into florets and add to the milk with the garam masala and season to taste with salt and pepper.

2 Bring the milk to the boil, then reduce the heat, partially cover the pan with a lid and simmer for about 20 minutes, or until the cauliflower is tender.

3 Let the mixture cool for a few minutes, then transfer to a food processor and process until smooth (you may have to do this in two separate batches).

4 Return the purée to the pan and heat through gently without boiling, checking and adjusting the seasoning to taste. Serve immediately, garnished with fresh coriander, if you like.

750ml/1¼ pints/3 cups full-fat (whole) milk

1 large cauliflower

fresh coriander (cilantro) leaves, to garnish (optional)

FROM THE STORECUPBOARD

15ml/1 tbsp garam masala

salt and ground black pepper, to taste

Energy 143kcal/601kJ; Protein 12g; Carbohydrate 13.9g, of which sugars 12.6g; Fat 4.8g, of which saturates 2.3g; Cholesterol 11mg; Calcium 271mg; Fibre 3.2g; Sodium 104mg

Fresh Mushroom Soup with Tarragon

The rich, earthy flavour of brown cap mushrooms is subtly enhanced with fresh tarragon to create a hearty and satisfying appetizer or lunch. Serve with bread and cold meats for a tasty light meal.

SERVES SIX

1 Finely chop the shallots. Melt the butter in a large pan, add the shallots and cook for 5 minutes, stirring occasionally.

2 Add the mushrooms and cook gently for 3 minutes, stirring, then the stock and milk. Bring to the boil, then cover the pan and simmer for about 20 minutes until the vegetables are soft.

3 Stir in the chopped tarragon and season to taste with salt and ground black pepper.

4 Allow the soup to cool slightly, then purée in a blender or food processor, in batches if necessary, until smooth. Return to the rinsed-out pan and reheat gently.

5 Ladle the soup into warmed soup bowls and serve garnished with sprigs of tarragon.

4 shallots

15g/¹/₂oz/1 tbsp butter

450g/1lb/6 cups brown cap (cremini) mushrooms, finely chopped

300ml/¹/₂ pint/1¹/₄ cups semi-skimmed (low-fat) milk

15–30ml/1–2 tbsp chopped fresh tarragon

sprigs of fresh tarragon, to garnish

FROM THE STORECUPBOARD

300ml/¹/₂ pint/1¹/₄ cups vegetable stock

salt and ground black pepper, to taste

VARIATION *Depending on what is available, you can use a mixture of wild and button (white) mushrooms rather than just brown cap (cremini) mushrooms.*

COOK'S TIP *Brown cap (cremini) mushrooms have a more robust flavour than cultivated mushrooms, such as button (white), cap and flat mushrooms. Field (portabello) mushrooms are similar in appearance to cultivated flat mushrooms, but they are simply large brown cap mushrooms.*

Energy 58kcal/242kJ; Protein 3.4g; Carbohydrate 3.7g, of which sugars 3.3g; Fat 3.4g, of which saturates 1.9g; Cholesterol 8mg; Calcium 84mg; Fibre 1.4g; Sodium 44mg

Potato Soup ✳

This incredibly economical soup is not only excellent as it is, but it is very versatile too, as it can be used as a base for numerous other soups. Use a floury potato, such as Golden Wonder or russet.

SERVES EIGHT

1 Melt the butter in a large heavy pan and add the onions, turning them in the butter until well coated. Cover and leave to cook over a very low heat for about 10 mintues.

2 Add the potatoes to the pan, and mix well with the butter and onions. Season with salt and pepper to taste, cover and cook without colouring over a gentle heat for about 10 minutes.

3 Add most of the stock, bring to the boil and simmer for 25 minutes, or until the vegetables are tender.

4 Remove from the heat and allow to cool slightly. Purée the soup in batches in a blender or food processor.

5 Reheat over a low heat and adjust the seasoning. If it seems too thick, add extra stock to achieve the right consistency.

6 Serve the soup very hot with warm rustic bread, such as soda bread, sprinkled with chopped chives.

50g/2oz/¹⁄₄ cup butter

2 large onions, peeled and finely chopped

675g/1¹⁄₄lb potatoes, peeled and diced

a little milk, if necessary

chopped fresh chives, to garnish and rustic bread, to serve

FROM THE STORECUPBOARD

about 1.75 litres/3 pints/ 7¹⁄₂ cups hot chicken stock

salt and ground black pepper, to taste

Energy 167kcal/699kJ; Protein 2.9g; Carbohydrate 23.5g, of which sugars 5.3g; Fat 7.5g, of which saturates 4.5g; Cholesterol 18mg; Calcium 26mg; Fibre 2.1g; Sodium 201mg

Cabbage and Potato Soup with Caraway Seeds ✳

Cheap and easy to make, this soup is ideal at any time of the year. Caraway seeds come from a plant in the parsley family. They are aromatic and nutty, with a delicate anise flavour, adding a subtle accent to this soup.

SERVES FOUR

1 Pour the olive oil into a large pan, add the onion and cook gently for 5 minutes to soften. Add the garlic and the cabbage and cook over a low heat for 10 minutes, stirring occasionally to prevent the cabbage from sticking to the pan.

2 Add the potatoes, caraway seeds, salt and water. Bring to the boil, then simmer until all the vegetables are cooked through, about 20–30 minutes.

3 Remove from the heat and allow to cool slightly before mashing into a purée or passing through a seive (strainer).

2 small onions, sliced

6 garlic cloves, halved

350g/12oz/3 cups shredded green cabbage

4 potatoes, unpeeled

1.2 litres/2 pints/5 cups water

FROM THE STORECUPBOARD

30ml/2 tbsp olive oil

5ml/1 tsp caraway seeds

5ml/1 tsp salt

COOK'S TIP *Use floury potatoes to achieve the right texture. King Edward or Maris Piper (US russet or Idaho) are good choices.*

Energy 144kcal/601kJ; Protein 3.1g; Carbohydrate 20.4g, of which sugars 8.1g; Fat 6g, of which saturates 0.9g; Cholesterol 0mg; Calcium 60mg; Fibre 3.3g; Sodium 507mg.

25g/1oz/2 tbsp butter

1 onion, chopped

1 garlic clove, crushed

1 medium baking potato, chopped

2 celery sticks, sliced

1 small green (bell) pepper, seeded, halved and sliced

300ml/1/2 pint/11/4 cups milk

grated Cheddar cheese and crusty bread, to serve

FROM THE STORECUPBOARD

30ml/2 tbsp sunflower or vegetable oil

600ml/1 pint/21/2 cups stock or water

200g/7oz can flageolet (small) cannellini beans

300g/11oz can corn kernels

good pinch dried sage

salt and ground black pepper, to taste

VARIATION *You can use other types of canned bean instead of flageolet beans, including cannellini beans, butter (lima) beans or broad (fava) beans. Alternatively, add a can of mixed beans.*

Corn, Potato and Flageolet Bean Chowder ✳

This chunky soup combines creamy potatoes and flageolet beans with the sweet taste of corn. It's excellent served with thick crusty bread and topped with some melted Cheddar cheese.

SERVES FOUR

1 Heat the oil and butter in large heavy pan, then add the onion, garlic, potato, celery and green pepper. Cook gently for about 10 minutes, shaking the pan occasionally.

2 Pour in the stock or water, season with salt and pepper to taste and bring to the boil. Reduce the heat, cover again and simmer gently for about 15 minutes until the vegetables are tender.

3 Add the milk, beans and corn (including their liquids) and the sage. Simmer, uncovered, for 5 minutes.

4 Taste and adjust the seasoning if necessary. Sprinkle with grated Cheddar cheese and serve immediately in warm soup bowls, with some bread.

Energy 346kcal/1454kJ; Protein 10.3g; Carbohydrate 48.4g, of which sugars 19.6g; Fat 13.7g, of which saturates 5.1g; Cholesterol 18mg; Calcium 150mg; Fibre 6.5g; Sodium 487mg.

Pumpkin Soup with Yogurt ✳

This simple puréed soup is a great winter treat and makes a comforting lunch served with bread, or a flavoursome appetizer. It tastes especially good with some melted butter and yogurt drizzled over the top.

SERVES THREE–FOUR

1 Put the pumpkin cubes into a pan with the stock, and bring the liquid to the boil. Reduce the heat, cover the pan, and simmer for about 20 minutes, or until the pumpkin is tender.

2 Liquidize (blend) the soup in a blender, or use a potato masher to mash the flesh. Return the soup to the pan and bring it to the boil again.

3 Add the sugar to the pan and season to taste with salt and pepper. Keep the pan over a low heat while you gently melt the butter in a small pan over a low heat.

4 Ladle the hot soup into individual serving bowls. Swirl a little yogurt on to the surface of the soup and drizzle the melted butter over the top.

5 Serve immediately, offering extra yogurt so that you can enjoy the contrasting burst of sweet and tart in each mouthful.

1kg/2¹⁄₄lb pumpkin flesh, cut into cubes

25g/1oz/2 tbsp butter

60–75ml/4–5 tbsp thick and creamy natural (plain) yogurt

FROM THE STORECUPBOARD

1 litre/1³⁄₄ pints/4 cups chicken stock

10ml/2 tsp sugar

salt and ground black pepper, to taste

Energy 97kcal/406kJ; Protein 2.6g; Carbohydrate 9.3g, of which sugars 8g; Fat 5.8g, of which saturates 3.6g; Cholesterol 14mg; Calcium 104mg; Fibre 2.5g; Sodium 51mg

Pumpkin Soup with Rice ✳

This fragrant, creamy pumpkin soup is subtly spiced with cinammon and is made more substantial with the addition of a small amount of rice.

SERVES FOUR

1 Remove any seeds or strands of fibre from the pumpkin, cut off the peel and chop the flesh. Put the prepared pumpkin in a pan and add the stock, milk, sugar and seasoning.

2 Bring to the boil, then reduce the heat and simmer for about 20 minutes, until the pumpkin is tender. Drain the pumpkin, reserving the liquid, and purée it in a blender or food processor, then return it to the pan.

3 Bring the soup back to the boil again, throw in the rice and simmer for a few minutes, until the grains are reheated. Check the seasoning, pour into bowls and dust with cinnamon. Serve piping hot, with chunks of fresh, crusty bread.

about 1.1kg/2lb 7oz pumpkin

750ml/1¹/₄ pints/3 cups full-fat (whole) milk

FROM THE STORECUPBOARD

750ml/1¹/₄ pints/3 cups chicken stock

10–15ml/2–3 tsp sugar

75g/3oz/¹/₂ cup cooked white rice

salt and ground black pepper, to taste

5ml/1 tsp ground cinnamon, to garnish

Energy 148kcal/627kJ; Protein 8.8g; Carbohydrate 20.7g, of which sugars 13.5g; Fat 4g, of which saturates 2.3g; Cholesterol 11mg; Calcium 308mg; Fibre 2.8g; Sodium 81mg

Cappelletti in Broth *

This simple broth contains cappelletti, which are little stuffed pasta shapes that resemble hats. If you are unable to find capelletti, you could use stuffed tortellini or any dried pasta shapes, such as fusilli, penne, conchiglione or orechiette, depending on your personal preference.

SERVES FOUR

1 Pour the chicken stock into a large pan and bring to the boil. Add a little seasoning to taste, then drop in the pasta.

2 Stir well and bring back to the boil. Lower the heat to a simmer and cook according to the instructions on the packet, until the pasta is *al dente*, that is, tender but still firm to the bite.

3 Swirl in the finely chopped fresh flat leaf parsley, if using, then taste and adjust the seasoning, if necessary.

4 Ladle the broth into four warmed soup plates, then sprinkle with the freshly grated grano padano cheese and serve immediately with crusty bread.

45ml/3 tbsp chopped fresh flat leaf parsley (optional)

30ml/2 tbsp grated grano padano cheese

crusty bread, to serve

FROM THE STORECUPBOARD

1.2 litres/2 pints/ 5 cups chicken stock

salt and ground black pepper, to taste

90–115g/3^1/$_2$–4oz/1 cup fresh or dried cappelletti

Tiny Pasta in Broth *

This Italian soup is ideal for a light supper served with ciabatta bread and also makes a delicious first course for an *al fresco* supper. A wide variety of different types of *pastina* or soup pasta are available including stellette (stars), anellini (tiny thin rounds), risoni (rice-shaped) and farfalline (little butterflies). Choose just one shape or a combination of different varieties for an interesting result.

SERVES FOUR

1 Bring the beef stock to the boil in a large pan. Add seasoning to taste, then drop in the dried soup pasta. Stir well and bring the stock back to the boil.

2 Reduce the heat so that the soup simmers and cook for 7–8 minutes, or according to the packet instructions, until the pasta is tender but still firm to the bite.

3 Drain the pieces of roasted pepper and dice them finely. Place them in the base of four warmed soup plates.

4 Taste the soup for seasoning and adjust if necessary, then ladle it into the soup plates. Serve immediately, topped with shavings of Parmesan.

2 pieces bottled roasted red (bell) pepper

shaved Parmesan cheese

FROM THE STORECUPBOARD

1.2 litres/2 pints/ 5 cups beef stock

75g/3oz/^{3}/$_4$ cup dried tiny soup pasta

salt and ground black pepper, to taste

Top: Energy 111kcal/469kJ; Protein 5.9g; Carbohydrate 16.7g, of which sugars 0.8g; Fat 3g, of which saturates 1.6g; Cholesterol 8mg; Calcium 96mg; Fibre 0.7g; Sodium 265mg

Above: Energy 135kcal/567kJ; Protein 7.8g; Carbohydrate 16.7g, of which sugars 3.3g; Fat 4.7g, of which saturates 2.7g; Cholesterol 13mg; Calcium 159mg; Fibre 1.3g; Sodium 321mg

2 onions, chopped

1 butternut squash, peeled, seeded and cut into small chunks

4 celery stalks, chopped

2 carrots, peeled and chopped

8 large, ripe tomatoes, skinned and chopped

5–10ml/1–2 tsp store-bought *ras el hanout*

a big bunch of fresh coriander (cilantro), chopped (reserve a few sprigs for garnish)

60–75ml/4–5 tbsp creamy yogurt and fresh bread, to serve

FROM THE STORECUPBOARD

45–60ml/3–4 tbsp olive oil

3–4 cloves

5–10ml/1–2 tsp sugar

15ml/1 tbsp tomato purée (paste)

2.5ml/^{1}/$_2$ tsp ground turmeric

1.75 litres/3 pints/ 7^1/$_2$ cups vegetable stock

a handful dried egg noodles or capellini, broken into pieces

salt and ground black pepper, to taste

Chunky Tomato Soup with Noodles ✳✳

This full-flavoured Moroccan soup is given a warming kick by the *ras el hanout*, a spicy paste that you can buy in most supermarkets.

SERVES FOUR

1 In a deep, heavy pan, heat the oil and add the cloves, onions, squash, celery and carrots. Fry until they begin to colour, then stir in the tomatoes and sugar. Cook the tomatoes until the water reduces and they begin to pulp.

2 Stir in the tomato purée, *ras el hanout*, turmeric and chopped coriander. Pour in the stock and bring to the boil. Reduce the heat and simmer for 30–40 minutes, until the vegetables are tender and the liquid has reduced a little.

3 To make a puréed soup, leave the liquid to cool slightly before processing in a food processor or blender, then pour back into the pan and add the pasta. Alternatively, to make a chunky soup, simply add the pasta to the unblended soup and cook for a further 8–10 minutes, or until the pasta is soft.

4 Season the soup to taste and ladle it into bowls. Spoon a swirl of yogurt into each one, garnish with the extra coriander and serve with freshly baked bread.

Energy 258kcal/1086kJ; Protein 7.6g; Carbohydrate 36.3g, of which sugars 18.3g; Fat 10.2g, of which saturates 1.7g; Cholesterol 0mg; Calcium 175mg; Fibre 6.9g; Sodium 72mg

Carrot and Cabbage Soup with Omelette ✳

A very satisfying soup that is quick and easy to prepare. It is versatile, too, in that you can vary the vegetables according to what is available.

SERVES FOUR

1 egg

2 large carrots, finely diced

4 outer leaves Savoy cabbage, shredded

fresh coriander (cilantro) leaves, to garnish

FROM THE STORECUPBOARD

15ml/1 tbsp groundnut (peanut) oil

900ml/1^1/$_2$ pints/ 3^3/$_4$ cups vegetable stock

30ml/2 tbsp soy sauce

2.5ml/^{1}/$_2$ tsp sugar

2.5ml/^{1}/$_2$ tsp ground black pepper

1 Beat the egg in a bowl. Heat the oil in a small frying pan until it is hot, but not smoking. Pour in the egg and swirl the pan so that it coats the base evenly. Cook over a medium heat until the omelette has set and the underside is golden.

2 Slide the omelette out of the pan and roll it up like a pancake. Slice into 5mm/^{1}/$_4$in rounds and set aside for the garnish.

3 Put the stock into a large pan. Add the carrots and cabbage and bring to the boil. Reduce the heat and simmer for 5 minutes, then add the soy sauce, sugar and pepper.

4 Stir well, then pour into warmed bowls. Lay a few omelette rounds on the surface of each portion and complete the garnish with the coriander leaves.

Energy 87kcal/360kJ; Protein 3.2g; Carbohydrate 9g, of which sugars 8.6g; Fat 4.4g, of which saturates 0.8g; Cholesterol 48mg; Calcium 58mg; Fibre 2.8g; Sodium 569mg

VARIATION

If you do not want to soak dried cannelini beans, you can use ready-to-use canned ones instead. Omit stage 1 as they don't need to be cooked for as long.

COOK'S TIP

For a more substantial meal you could serve this stunning soup with fried squid, marinated anchovies or other pickled fish. Moist cubes of feta cheese also make an excellent accompaniment.

1 large onion, thinly sliced

1 celery stick, sliced

2 or 3 carrots, sliced

30ml/2 tbsp finely chopped fresh flat leaf parsley

FROM THE STORECUPBOARD

275g/10oz/1¹/₂ cups dried cannellini beans, soaked overnight in cold water

400g/14oz can tomatoes

15ml/1 tbsp tomato purée (paste)

150ml/¹/₄ pint/²/₃ cup olive oil

5ml/1 tsp dried oregano

salt and ground black pepper, to taste

Cannellini Bean, Tomato and Parsley Soup ✳

Healthy, hearty and deeply satisfying, this stunning soup is especially delicious when served with bread and olives as a light supper.

SERVES FOUR

1 Drain the beans, rinse them under cold water and drain them again. Tip them into a large pan, pour in enough water to cover the beans and bring to the boil over a medium heat. Cook for about 3 minutes, then drain.

2 Return the beans to the pan, pour in fresh water to cover them by about 3cm/1¹/₄in, then add the sliced onion, celery and carrots, and the tomatoes, and stir in.

3 Add and stir in the tomato purée, extra virgin olive oil and dried oregano. Season to taste with a little freshly ground black pepper, but don't add salt at this stage, as it would toughen the skins of the beans.

4 Bring to the boil, lower the heat and cook for about 1 hour, or until the beans are just tender. Season with salt, stir in the parsley and serve.

Energy 490kcal/2,051kJ; Protein 17.9g; Carbohydrate 47.8g, of which sugars 11.3g; Fat 26.6g, of which saturates 4.1g; Cholesterol 0mg; Calcium 89mg; Fibre 8.4g; Sodium 45mg.

Tuscan Cannellini Bean Soup with Cavolo Nero *

Cavolo nero is a very dark green cabbage with a nutty flavour that is available during the winter months. It is ideal for this Italian recipe, which is packed with flavour as well as being healthy and sustaining.

SERVES FOUR

1 Pour the tomatoes into a large pan and add a can of cold water. Season with salt and pepper to taste and bring to the boil, then reduce the heat to a simmer.

2 Roughly shred the cabbage leaves and add them to the pan. Partially cover the pan and simmer gently for about 15 minutes, or until the cabbage is tender.

3 Add the cannellini beans to the pan and warm through over a gentle heat for a few minutes.

4 Check and adjust the seasoning, then ladle the soup into bowls, drizzle each one with a little olive oil and serve.

250g/9oz cavolo nero leaves, or Savoy cabbage

FROM THE STORECUPBOARD

2 x 400g/14oz cans chopped tomatoes with herbs

400g/14oz can cannellini beans, drained and rinsed

60ml/4 tbsp extra virgin olive oil

salt and ground black pepper, to taste

Energy 227kcal/950kJ; Protein 8.2g; Carbohydrate 22.3g, of which sugars 10.4g; Fat 12.2g, of which saturates 1.9g; Cholesterol 0mg; Calcium 60mg; Fibre 7.9g; Sodium 443mg

Broad Bean and Potato Soup **

This elegant soup tastes best if you use fresh broad beans, when they are in season in the summer months, rather than dried ones. Fresh coriander adds a distinctive, fragrant note to the creamy mixture, without overpowering the subtle and delicious taste of the beans.

SERVES FOUR

1 Heat the oil in a large pan, add the onions and cook gently for 5 minutes until soft.

2 Add the potatoes, most of the beans (reserving a few for the garnish) and the stock to the pan, and bring to the boil. Simmer for 5 minutes, then add the coriander and simmer for a further 10 minutes.

3 Blend the soup in batches in a food processor or blender, then return to the rinsed pan.

4 Stir in the cream, season with salt and pepper to taste, and bring to a simmer. Serve imediately, garnished with coriander, the reserved beans and a drizzle of cream.

2 onions, chopped

3 large floury potatoes, peeled and diced

450g/1lb fresh shelled broad (US fava) beans

1 bunch fresh coriander (cilantro), roughly chopped

150ml/^{1}/$_4$ pint/^{2}/$_3$ cup single (light) cream, plus a little extra, to garnish

FROM THE STORECUPBOARD

30ml/2 tbsp olive oil

1.75 litres/3 pints/7^1/$_2$ cups vegetable stock

salt and ground black pepper, to taste

Energy 187kcal/784kJ; Protein 8.1g; Carbohydrate 19.2g, of which sugars 3.5g; Fat 9.2g, of which saturates 3.7g; Cholesterol 14mg; Calcium 89mg; Fibre 6.1g; Sodium 22mg

Chickpea Soup ✳

This nutritious soup is enjoyable in any season, even during the hot summer months. Compared to other soups based on beans, peas and lentils, which are often very hearty, this has a unique lightness in terms of both flavour and texture. It can be enjoyed as an appetizer, or can be a delicious healthy main meal when served with fresh bread and feta cheese.

SERVES FOUR

1 Heat the olive oil in a heavy pan, add the onion and cook gently until it starts to colour.

2 Meanwhile, drain the chickpeas, rinse them and drain again. Add to the pan, coat in the oil, then pour in enough hot water to cover them by about 4cm/1^1/$_2$in. Slowly bring to the boil.

3 Skim off and discard any white froth that rises to the surface. Lower the heat, add some freshly ground black pepper, cover and cook for 1–1^1/$_4$ hours, or until the chickpeas are soft.

4 Combine the flour and lemon juice. When the chickpeas are soft, add this mixture to them. Mix, then add seasoning to taste. Cover and cook for 5–10 minutes more, stirring occasionally.

5 To thicken the soup, take out about two cupfuls of the chickpeas and process them in a food processor or blender, until the chickpeas are broken up, then stir into the soup. Add the parsley, then taste and add more lemon juice if bland. Serve in heated bowls with a drizzle of olive oil on top.

1 large onion, chopped

juice of 1 lemon, or to taste

45ml/3 tbsp chopped fresh flat leaf parsley

FROM THE STORECUPBOARD

150ml/^{1}/$_4$ pint/^{2}/$_3$ cup olive oil, plus extra for drizzling and serving

350g/12oz/1^3/$_4$ cups dried chickpeas, soaked in cold water overnight

15ml/1 tbsp plain (all-purpose) flour

salt and ground black pepper, to taste

Energy 544kcal/2,274kJ; Protein 20.1g; Carbohydrate 51.6g, of which sugars 6.1g; Fat 30g, of which saturates 4g; Cholesterol 0mg; Calcium 184mg; Fibre 10.9g; Sodium 40mg

Spicy Red Lentil Soup *

This stunning, light lentil soup is subtly spiced with cumin, fenugreek and coriander. Served with a pretty and flavoursome garnish of chopped red onion and flat leaf parsley and a squeeze of lemon juice, it makes a refreshing appetizer or snack at any time of the year.

SERVES SIX

1 Heat the oil in a heavy pan and stir in the onion, garlic, chilli, cumin and coriander seeds. When the onion begins to colour, toss in the carrot and cook for 2–3 minutes. Add the fenugreek, sugar and tomato purée and stir in the lentils.

2 Pour in the stock, stir well and bring to the boil. Lower the heat, partially cover the pan and simmer for 30–40 minutes, until the lentils have broken up.

3 If the soup is too thick, thin it down with a little water. Season with salt and pepper to taste.

4 Serve the soup straight from the pan or, if you prefer a smooth texture, whiz it in a blender, then reheat if necessary.

5 Ladle the soup into bowls and sprinkle liberally with the chopped onion and parsley. Serve with a wedge of lemon to squeeze over the soup.

1 large onion,
finely chopped

2 garlic cloves,
finely chopped

1 fresh red chilli, seeded
and finely chopped

1 carrot, finely chopped

scant 5ml/1 tsp
ground fenugreek

TO SERVE

1 small red onion,
finely chopped

1 large bunch of fresh flat
leaf parsley, finely chopped

4–6 lemon wedges

FROM THE STORECUPBOARD

30–45ml/2–3 tbsp olive
or sunflower oil

5–10ml/1–2 tsp cumin
seeds

5–10ml/1–2 tsp coriander
seeds

5ml/1 tsp sugar

15ml/1 tbsp tomato
purée (paste)

250g/9oz/generous 1 cup
split red lentils

1.75 litres/3 pints/
7¹/₂ cups chicken stock

salt and ground black
pepper, to taste

Energy 203kcal/856kJ; Protein 11.1g; Carbohydrate 31.8g, of which sugars 7.3g; Fat 4.4g, of which saturates 0.6g; Cholesterol 0mg; Calcium 45mg; Fibre 3.5g; Sodium 26mg

Brown Lentil Soup ✳

Lentils do not need soaking, so they make an easy option for a quick meal. The secret of good lentil soup is to be generous with the olive oil. The soup can be served as a substantial appetizer, or as a warming lunch dish when accompanied by plenty of fresh bread.

SERVES EIGHT

1 Rinse the brown-green lentils thoroughly, drain them and put them in a large pan with cold water to cover. Bring the water to the boil and boil for 3–4 minutes. Strain, discarding the liquid, and set the lentils aside.

2 Wipe the pan clean and add the olive oil. Place it over a medium heat until hot and then add the thinly sliced onion and sauté until translucent.

3 Stir in the sliced garlic, then, as soon as it becomes aromatic, return the lentils to the pan. Add the carrot, tomatoes, tomato purée and oregano. Stir in the hot water and pepper to taste.

4 Bring the soup to the boil, then lower the heat, cover the pan and cook gently for 20–30 minutes, until the lentils feel soft but have not begun to disintegrate. Add salt, if required, and the chopped herbs before serving.

1 onion, thinly sliced

2 garlic cloves, sliced into thin matchsticks

1 carrot, sliced into discs

1 litre/1³/₄ pints/4 cups hot water

30ml/2 tbsp chopped fresh herbs, to garnish

FROM THE STORECUPBOARD

275g/10oz/1¹/₄ cups brown-green lentils, preferably the small variety

150ml/¹/₄ pint/²/₃ cup olive oil

400g/14oz can chopped tomatoes

15ml/1 tbsp tomato purée (paste)

2.5ml/¹/₂ tsp dried oregano

salt and ground black pepper, to taste

Energy 462kcal/1,935kJ; Protein 18.4g; Carbohydrate 40g, of which sugars 6.6g; Fat 26.6g, of which saturates 3.7g; Cholesterol 0mg; Calcium 86mg; Fibre 8g; Sodium 64mg

200g/7oz smoked
mackerel fillets

4 tomatoes

1 lemon grass stalk,
finely chopped

5cm/2in piece fresh
galangal, finely diced

4 shallots, finely chopped

2 garlic cloves,
finely chopped

45ml/3 tbsp thick
tamarind juice,
made by mixing
tamarind paste with
warm water

small bunch of fresh
chives or spring onions
(scallions), to garnish

FROM THE STORECUPBOARD

1 litre/1³/₄ pints/4 cups
vegetable stock

2.5ml/¹/₂ tsp dried
chilli flakes

15ml/1 tbsp Thai
fish sauce

5ml/1 tsp light muscovado
(brown) sugar

Smoked Mackerel and Tomato Soup ✳

All the ingredients for this unusual soup are cooked in a single pan, so it is
not only quick and easy to prepare, but requires minimal washing up.

SERVES FOUR

1 Prepare the smoked mackerel fillets. Remove and discard the
skin, if necessary, then chop the flesh into large pieces. Remove
any stray bones with your fingers or a pair of tweezers.

2 Cut the tomatoes in half, squeeze out most of the seeds with
your fingers, then finely dice the flesh with a sharp knife. Set
aside until required.

3 Pour the stock into a large pan and add the lemon grass,
galangal, shallots and garlic. Bring to the boil, reduce the heat
and simmer for 15 minutes.

4 Add the fish, tomatoes, chilli flakes, fish sauce, muscovado
sugar and tamarind juice. Simmer for 4–5 minutes, until the fish
and tomatoes are heated through.

5 Serve immediately, garnished with chives or spring onions,
with some plain boiled noodles for a more substantial meal.

VARIATION

*For a spicier soup, you
could use smoked
peppered mackerel
fillets. These are usually
available in many large
supermarkets, and add a
delicious peppery flavour.*

Energy 203kcal/845kJ; Protein 10.3g; Carbohydrate 5.3g, of which sugars 5g; Fat 15.8g, of which saturates 3.3g; Cholesterol 53mg; Calcium 21mg; Fibre 1.2g; Sodium 385mg

Crab, Coconut, Chilli and Coriander Soup **

Although fresh crab meat has a better flavour, you can use canned crab meat in this sensational soup to keep the cost down.

SERVES FOUR

1 Heat the olive oil in a pan over a low heat. Stir in the chopped onion and celery, and sauté gently for 5 minutes, until the onion is soft and translucent.

2 Add the garlic and chilli, mix to combine well, and cook for a further 2 minutes.

3 Add the tomato and half the coriander and increase the heat. Cook, stirring, for 3 minutes, then add the stock. Bring to the boil, then simmer for 5 minutes.

4 Stir the crab, coconut milk and palm oil into the pan and simmer over a very low heat for a further 5 minutes. The consistency should be thick, but not stew-like, so add some water if needed.

5 Stir in the lime juice and remaining coriander, then season with salt to taste. Serve in heated bowls with the chilli oil and lime wedges on the side.

1 onion, finely chopped

1 celery stick, chopped

2 garlic cloves, crushed

1 fresh red chilli, seeded and chopped

1 large tomato, peeled and chopped

45ml/3 tbsp chopped fresh coriander (cilantro)

500g/1¼lb crab meat

250ml/8fl oz/1 cup coconut milk

30ml/2 tbsp palm oil

juice of 1 lime

hot chilli oil and lime wedges, to serve

FROM THE STORECUPBOARD

30ml/2 tbsp olive oil

1 litre/1¾ pints/4 cups fresh crab or fish stock

salt, to taste

Energy 228kcal/951kJ; Protein 23.6g; Carbohydrate 5.4g, of which sugars 5g; Fat 12.6g, of which saturates 3.7g; Cholesterol 90mg; Calcium 199mg; Fibre 1.1g; Sodium 767mg

Chicken, Leek and Celery Soup *

This makes a substantial main course soup in winter, served with fresh crusty bread. You will need nothing more than a mixed green salad or fresh winter fruit to follow, such as satsumas or tangerines.

SERVES FOUR–SIX

1 Cut the breasts off the chicken and set aside. Chop the rest of the chicken carcass into 8–10 pieces and place them in a large pan or stockpot.

2 Chop 4–5 of the outer sticks of the head of celery and add them to the pan with the coarsely chopped onion. Tie the bay leaf, parsley stalks and tarragon sprigs together to make a bouquet garni and add to the pan. Pour in the cold water to cover the ingredients and bring to the boil. Reduce the heat and cover the pan with a lid, then simmer for 1¹/₂ hours.

3 Remove the chicken from the pan using a slotted spoon and cut off and reserve the meat.

4 Strain the stock through a sieve (strainer), then return it to the cleaned pan and boil rapidly until it has reduced in volume to about 1.5 litres/2¹/₂ pints/6¹/₄ cups.

5 Meanwhile, set about 150g/5oz of the leeks aside. Slice the remaining leeks and the remaining celery, reserving any celery leaves. Chop the celery leaves and set them aside to garnish the soup, or reserve a few of the leek pieces.

6 Heat half the oil in a large, heavy pan. Add the sliced leeks and celery, cover and cook over a low heat for about 10 minutes, or until the vegetables are softened but not browned. Add the potatoes, wine and 1.2 litres/2 pints/5 cups of the stock.

7 Season with a little salt and plenty of black pepper, bring to the boil and reduce the heat. Part-cover the pan and simmer the soup for 15–20 minutes, or until the potatoes are cooked.

8 Check and adjust the seasoning as required, bring to the boil and reduce the heat. Part-cover the pan and simmer the soup for 15–20 minutes, or until the potatoes are cooked.

9 Thickly slice the reserved leeks, add to the frying pan and cook, stirring occasionally, for a further 3–4 minutes until they are just cooked.

10 Stir in the cream, if using, and the chicken and leek mixture. Reheat the soup gently.

11 Serve in warmed bowls. Crumble the pancetta over the soup and sprinkle with the celery leaves or reserved leek slices.

1.3kg/3lb chicken

1 small head of celery, trimmed

1 onion, coarsely chopped

1 fresh bay leaf

a few fresh parsley stalks

a few fresh tarragon sprigs

2.5 litres/4 pints/10 cups cold water

3 large leeks

2 potatoes, cut into chunks

150ml/¹/₄ pint/²/₃ cup dry white wine

30–45ml/2–3 tbsp single (light) cream

90g/3¹/₂oz pancetta, grilled until crisp, to garnish

FROM THE STORECUPBOARD

75ml/5 tbsp olive oil

salt and ground black pepper, to taste

VARIATIONS

• If you prefer, you can use ready-cut chicken portions instead of jointing a whole chicken, although this may bump the cost up.

• Streaky (fatty) bacon can be used instead of pancetta to add a delicious flavour to the soup.

Energy 253kcal/1056kJ; Protein 16.5g; Carbohydrate 10.3g, of which sugars 2.4g; Fat 14.7g, of which saturates 3.4g; Cholesterol 48mg; Calcium 31mg; Fibre 2g; Sodium 231mg

Pumpkin, Rice and Chicken Soup ✳

This comforting soup is a complete meal in itself, served with warm, crusty bread for scooping up the delicious liquid. For an even more substantial meal, add a little more rice.

SERVES FOUR

1 Skin the pumpkin and remove all the seeds and pith, so that you have about 350g/12oz flesh. Cut the flesh into small cubes.

2 Heat the oil and butter in a pan and fry the cardamom pods for 2–3 minutes, until slightly swollen. Add the leeks and pumpkin. Cook, stirring, for 3–4 minutes over a medium heat, then lower the heat, cover and sweat for 5 minutes, until the pumpkin is soft.

3 Pour 600ml/1 pint/2¹/₂ cups of the stock into the pan. Bring to the boil, then lower the heat, cover and simmer gently for 10–15 minutes, until the pumpkin is soft.

4 Pour the remaining stock into a measuring jug and make up with water to 300ml/¹/₂ pint/1¹/₄ cups. Drain the rice and put it into a pan. Pour in the stock, bring to the boil, then simmer for about 10 minutes until the rice is tender. Add seasoning to taste.

5 Remove the cardamom pods, then process the soup in a blender or food processor until smooth. Pour back into a clean pan and stir in the milk, chicken and rice (with any stock that has not been absorbed). Heat until simmering. Garnish with the orange rind and black pepper, and serve with bread.

COOK'S TIP *Once made, chicken stock will keep in an airtight container in the refrigerator for 3–4 days. Alternatively, use stock (bouillon) cubes.*

1 wedge of pumpkin, about 450g/1lb

25g/1oz/2 tbsp butter

2 leeks, chopped

350ml/12fl oz/1¹/₂ cups milk

strips of pared orange rind, to garnish

granary or wholemeal (wholewheat) bread, to serve

FROM THE STORECUPBOARD

15ml/1 tbsp sunflower or vegetable oil

6 green cardamom pods

750ml/1¹/₄ pints/3 cups chicken stock

115g/4oz/generous ¹/₂ cup basmati rice, soaked

salt and ground black pepper, to taste

Energy 315kcal/1320kJ; Protein 24.6g; Carbohydrate 29.9g, of which sugars 6.3g; Fat 10.8g, of which saturates 4.9g; Cholesterol 71mg; Calcium 140mg; Fibre 2.1g; Sodium 122mg

25g/1oz/2 tbsp butter

225g/8oz lamb, cut into 1cm/¹/₂in pieces

1 onion, chopped

450g/1lb tomatoes

60ml/4 tbsp chopped fresh coriander (cilantro)

30ml/2 tbsp chopped fresh parsley

600ml/1 pint/2¹/₂ cups cold water

4 baby onions or small shallots, peeled

FOR THE GARNISH

chopped fresh coriander (cilantro)

lemon slices

ground cinnamon

FROM THE STORECUPBOARD

2.5ml/1/2 tsp ground turmeric

2.5ml/¹/₂ tsp ground cinnamon

50g/2oz/¹/₄ cup red lentils

75g/3oz/¹/₂ cup dried chickpeas, soaked overnight

25g/1oz/¹/₄ cup soup noodles

salt and ground black pepper, to taste

Moroccan Harira ✶✶

A cheaper cut of lamb, such as scrag end, middle neck or knuckle, would be ideal for this substantial meat and vegetable soup, which is a meal in itself.

SERVES FOUR

1 Heat the butter in a large pan or flameproof casserole and fry the lamb and onion for 5 minutes, stirring frequently.

2 Peel the tomatoes, if you wish, by plunging them into boiling water to loosen the skins. Wait for them to cool a little before peeling off the skins. Cut them into quarters and add to the lamb with the herbs and spices.

3 Place the lentils in a sieve (strainer) and rinse under cold running water, then drain the chickpeas. Add both to the pan with the water. Season with salt and pepper to taste. Bring to the boil, cover and simmer gently for 1¹/₂ hours.

4 Add the baby onions or small shallots and cook for a further 30 minutes. Add the noodles 5 minutes before the end of the cooking time.

5 Serve the soup when the noodles are tender, garnished with the coriander, lemon slices and cinnamon.

Energy 303kcal/1271kJ; Protein 19.8g; Carbohydrate 27.6g, of which sugars 6.2g; Fat 13.2g, of which saturates 6.4g; Cholesterol 56mg; Calcium 78mg; Fibre 4.7g; Sodium 113mg

Beef and Barley Soup ✳

This traditional Irish farmhouse soup makes a wonderfully restorative dish on a cold day. The flavours develop particularly well if the soup is made in advance and then reheated before serving.

SERVES SIX–EIGHT

1 Bone the meat and put the bones and half an onion, roughly sliced, into a large pan. Cover with cold water, season and bring to the boil. Skim if necessary, then simmer until needed.

2 Meanwhile, trim any fat or gristle from the meat and cut into small pieces. Chop the remaining onions finely. Drain the stock from the bones, make it up with water to 2 litres/3$^{1}/_{2}$ pints/ 8 cups, and return to the rinsed pan with the meat, onions, barley and split peas.

3 Season, bring to the boil, and skim if necessary. Reduce the heat, cover and simmer for about 30 minutes.

4 Add the rest of the vegetables and simmer for 1 hour, or until the meat is tender. Check the seasoning and adjust if necessary. Serve in large warmed bowls, generously sprinkled with parsley.

450–675g/1–1$^{1}/_{2}$lb rib steak, or other stewing beef on the bone

2 large onions

50g/2oz/$^{1}/_{4}$ cup pearl barley

3 large carrots, chopped

2 white turnips, peeled and chopped into dice

3 celery stalks, chopped

1 large or 2 medium leeks, thinly sliced

chopped fresh parsley, to serve

FROM THE STORECUPBOARD

50g/2oz/$^{1}/_{4}$ cup green split peas

salt and ground black pepper, to taste

Energy 167kcal/705kJ; Protein 16g; Carbohydrate 21.4g, of which sugars 7.8g; Fat 2.6g, of which saturates 0.8g; Cholesterol 34mg; Calcium 54mg; Fibre 3.6g; Sodium 58mg

1 large onion,
finely chopped

2 garlic cloves,
finely chopped

25g/1oz fresh root ginger,
finely chopped

350g/12oz pork rump or
tenderloin, cut widthways
into bitesize slices

TO SERVE

2 garlic cloves,
finely chopped

2 spring onions
(scallions), white parts
only, finely sliced

2–3 green or red chillies,
seeded and quartered
lengthways (optional)

FROM THE STORECUPBOARD

15–30ml/1–2 tbsp palm or
groundnut (peanut) oil

5–6 black peppercorns

115g/4oz/1 cup plus
15ml/1 tbsp short
grain rice

2 litres/3¹⁄₂ pints/8 cups
pork or chicken stock

30ml/2 tbsp *patis*
(fish sauce)

salt, to taste

Pork and Rice Soup ✳

Made with tender chunks of pork, this aromatic and sustaining rice soup from the Philippines is ideal for a special lunch. A complete meal in itself, it tastes particularly good served with spring onions, garlic and raw chilli.

SERVES FOUR–SIX

1 Heat the oil in a wok or deep, heavy pan that has a lid. Stir in the onion, garlic and ginger and fry until fragrant and beginning to colour. Add the pork and fry, stirring frequently, for 5–6 minutes, until lightly browned. Stir in the peppercorns.

2 Meanwhile, put the rice in a sieve (strainer), rinse under cold running water until the water runs clear, then drain. Toss the rice into the pan, making sure that it is coated in the mixture.

3 Pour in the stock, add the *patis* and bring to the boil. Reduce the heat and partially cover with a lid. Simmer for 40 minutes, stirring ocassionally to make sure that the rice doesn't stick to the bottom of the pan. Season with salt to taste.

4 Just before serving, dry-fry the garlic in a small, heavy pan, until golden brown, then stir it into the soup. Ladle the soup into individual warmed bowls and sprinkle the spring onions over the top. Serve the chillies separately, to chew on, if you like.

Energy 195kcal/813kJ; Protein 14.8g; Carbohydrate 19.9g, of which sugars 3.4g; Fat 6.2g, of which saturates 1.3g; Cholesterol 37mg; Calcium 24mg; Fibre 0.8g; Sodium 399mg

Leek and Bacon Soup ✳

This simple yet attractive soup makes good use of winter vegetables, combining them with tender chunks of flavoursome bacon to create a refreshing broth that makes an ideal light lunch.

COOK'S TIP

For a quicker version, fry 4 finely chopped bacon rashers in butter. Omit step 1 and add the bacon to a pan with 1.5l/2¹⁄₂ pints vegetable or chicken stock and the vegetables. Continue as in the recipe.

SERVES SIX

1 Trim the bacon of any excess fat, put into a large pan and pour over enough cold water to cover it. Bring to the boil, then discard the water. Add 1.5 litres/2¹⁄₂ pints cold water, bring to the boil again, then cover and simmer gently for 30 minutes.

2 Meanwhile, thickly slice the white and pale green parts of the leeks, reserving the dark green leaves. Add to the pan together with the carrot, potato and oatmeal, then bring back to the boil. Cover and simmer gently for a further 30–40 minutes until the vegetables and bacon are tender.

3 Slice the reserved dark green leek leaves very thinly and finely chop the parsley.

4 Lift the bacon out of the pan and either slice it and serve separately or cut it into bitesize chunks and return it to the pan.

5 Taste and adjust the seasoning as required. Bring the soup just to the boil once more. Finally, add the sliced dark green leeks with the parsley and simmer gently for 5 minutes before serving.

1 unsmoked bacon joint, such as corner or collar, weighing about 1kg/2¹⁄₄ lb

500g/1¹⁄₄ lb/4¹⁄₂ cups leeks, thoroughly washed

1 large carrot, peeled and finely chopped

1 large main-crop potato, peeled and sliced

15ml/1 tbsp fine or medium oatmeal

handful of fresh parsley

FROM THE STORECUPBOARD

salt and ground black pepper, to taste

Energy 273kcal/1135kJ; Protein 18.8g; Carbohydrate 10.9g, of which sugars 3.5g; Fat 17.3g, of which saturates 6.3g; Cholesterol 53mg; Calcium 33mg; Fibre 2.7g; Sodium 1550mg

115g/4oz/¹/₂ cup butter

150g/5oz streaky (fatty) bacon, roughly chopped

2 onions, finely chopped

1 carrot, chopped

1 celery stick, chopped

15ml/1 tbsp chopped fresh rosemary

2 fresh bay leaves

2 garlic cloves, halved

FOR THE TORTILLA CHIPS

75g/3oz/6 tbsp butter

175g/6oz plain tortilla chips

FROM THE STORECUPBOARD

400g/14oz/2 cups dried chickpeas, soaked overnight in cold water

2.5ml/¹/₂ tsp sweet paprika

1.5ml/¹/₄ tsp ground cumin

salt and ground black pepper, to taste

VARIATION *For a smoky flavour, use smoked bacon or pancetta instead of the non-smoked version. You could also use smoked sweet paprika for the tortilla chips.*

Bacon and Chickpea Soup ✳

This silky-smooth nutty soup is absolutely delicious and so easy to make. Served with a bowl of warm and spicy tortilla chips and dip, it makes an ideal midweek supper dish and will be enjoyed by all the family.

SERVES SIX

1 Drain the chickpeas, put them in a pan and cover with water. Bring to the boil and simmer for 20 minutes. Strain and set aside.

2 Melt the butter in a large pan and add the pancetta or bacon. Fry over a medium heat until just beginning to turn golden. Add the chopped vegetables and cook for 5–10 minutes until soft.

3 Add the chickpeas to the pan with the rosemary, bay leaves, garlic cloves and enough water to cover completely. Bring to the boil, half cover with a lid, turn down the heat and simmer for 45–60 minutes, stirring occasionally. Leave to cool slightly.

4 Process the soup until smooth in a blender or food processor. Return to the rinsed-out pan, taste and season. Reheat gently.

5 To make the chips, preheat the oven to 180°C/350°F/Gas 4. Melt the butter with the paprika and cumin in a pan, then brush over the tortilla chips. Reserve any leftover butter. Spread the chips out on a baking sheet and warm in the oven for 5 minutes.

6 Ladle the soup into bowls, pour some of the reserved butter over each and sprinkle with paprika. Serve with warm tortilla chips.

Energy 996kcal/4154kJ; Protein 31.4g; Carbohydrate 80.1g, of which sugars 6.6g; Fat 63.3g, of which saturates 30.1g; Cholesterol 126mg; Calcium 252mg; Fibre 14.3g; Sodium 1186mg

Mediterranean Sausage and Pesto Soup ✳

This delicious soup makes a satisfying one-pot meal that brings the summery flavour of basil to midwinter meals. The lentils enhance the flavour of the smoked sausage.

SERVES FOUR

1 Heat the oil in a large pan and cook the onion until softened. Coarsely chop all but one of the sausages and add them to the pan. Cook for 5 minutes, stirring, or until they are cooked.

2 Stir in the lentils, tomatoes and water, and bring to the boil. Reduce the heat, cover and simmer for about 20 minutes. Cool the soup slightly before puréeing it in a blender. Return the soup to the rinsed pan.

3 Cook the remaining sausage in a little oil in a small frying pan, turning it often, for 10 minutes, until browned. Transfer to a chopping board or plate and leave to cool, then slice thinly.

4 Heat the oil for deep-frying to 180°C/350°F or until a cube of day-old bread browns in about 15 seconds. Deep-fry the sausage slices and basil until the sausages are brown and the basil leaves are crisp. Lift them out using a slotted spoon and drain on kitchen paper.

5 Reheat the soup, add seasoning to taste, then ladle into warmed soup bowls. Sprinkle with the sausage slices and basil and swirl a little pesto through each portion. Serve with bread.

1 red onion, chopped

450g/1lb smoked pork sausages

1 litre/1³/₄ pints/4 cups water

60ml/4 tbsp pesto and fresh basil sprigs, to garnish

FROM THE STORECUPBOARD

15ml/1 tbsp olive oil, plus extra for frying

225g/8oz/1 cup red lentils

400g/14oz can chopped tomatoes

oil, for deep-frying

salt and ground black pepper, to taste

Energy 656kcal/2741kJ; Protein 30.9g; Carbohydrate 46.7g, of which sugars 8.2g; Fat 39.7g, of which saturates 13.1g; Cholesterol 75mg; Calcium 250mg; Fibre 4.8g; Sodium 1109mg

Kale, Chorizo and Potato Soup *

This hearty, warming winter soup has a spicy kick to it, which comes from the chorizo sausage, and it is a meal in itself. The spicy flavour becomes more potent if the soup is chilled overnight.

SERVES EIGHT

1 Place the kale in a food processor and process for a few seconds to chop it finely.

2 Prick the sausages and place in a pan with enough water to cover. Simmer for 15 minutes. Drain and cut into thin slices.

3 Cook the potatoes in a pan of boiling water for about 15 minutes or until tender. Drain and place in a bowl, then mash, adding a little of the cooking liquid to form a thick paste.

4 Bring the vegetable stock to the boil and add the kale. Add the chorizo and simmer for 5 minutes. Add the mashed potato gradually, and simmer for 20 minutes. Season to taste with black and cayenne pepper.

5 Place bread slices in each bowl, and pour over the soup. Serve, generously sprinkled with pepper.

225g/8oz kale, stems removed

225g/8oz chorizo sausage

675g/1¹/₂lb red potatoes

12 slices baguette, lightly grilled

FROM THE STORECUPBOARD

1.75 litres/3 pints/ 7¹/₂ cups vegetable stock

pinch cayenne pepper (optional)

salt and ground black pepper, to taste

Energy 290kcal/1228kJ; Protein 11.6g; Carbohydrate 49.3g, of which sugars 3.4g; Fat 6.5g, of which saturates 1.8g; Cholesterol 32mg; Calcium 120mg; Fibre 3.4g; Sodium 619mg

First Courses and Finger Food

IT IS ALWAYS A TREAT TO HAVE A FIRST COURSE TO
WHET THE APPETITE, AND THERE IS A WIDE RANGE
OF DELICIOUS, ECONOMICAL RECIPES SUITABLE FOR
EVERY OCCASION, WHETHER YOU ARE PLANNING
A SUSTAINING FAMILY MEAL, AN INFORMAL GATHERING
OR AN ELEGANT DINNER PARTY. CHOOSE FROM
EASY-TO-MAKE DIPS, SUCH AS HUMMUS, OR
FOR SOMETHING MORE SUBSTANTIAL, TRY FOCACCIA
WITH SARDINES AND TOMATOES, SPICY CHICKPEA
SAMOSAS OR POACHED EGGS FLORENTINE.

Salmon Mousse ✳

This deliciously creamy mousse makes a little salmon go a long way. If you can find it, it is equally good made with sea trout.

SERVES SIX

1 Put the salmon in a shallow pan. Pour in the fish stock and heat to simmering point. Poach the fish for about 3–4 minutes, until it is lightly cooked. Strain the stock into a jug (pitcher) and leave the fish to cool. Add the gelatine to the hot stock and stir until it has dissolved completely. Set the stock aside until required.

2 Remove the skin from the fish and flake the flesh. Pour the stock into a food processor or blender. Process briefly, then add the salmon, lemon juice, sherry or vermouth and grano padano, and process until smooth. Scrape into a bowl and leave to cool.

3 Lightly whip the cream, then fold it into the salmon mixture. Season, then cover with clear film (plastic wrap) and chill until just beginning to set; it should have the consistency of mayonnaise.

4 In a grease-free bowl, beat the egg whites with a pinch of salt until they form soft peaks. Using a metal spoon, stir one-third into the mixture to slacken it, then fold in the rest.

5 Grease six ramekins with oil, then divide the mousse among them and level the surface. Chill for 2–3 hours, until set. Just before serving, arrange a few slices of cucumber and a herb sprig on each mousse and add a little chopped dill or chervil.

250g/9oz salmon fillet

2 sheets leaf gelatine, or 15ml/1 tbsp powdered gelatine

juice of 1/2 lemon

30ml/2 tbsp dry sherry or dry vermouth

30ml/2 tbsp freshly grated grano padano cheese

300ml/1/2 pint/11/4 cups whipping cream

2 egg whites

FOR THE GARNISH

5cm/2in piece cucumber, with peel, halved and thinly sliced

fresh dill or chervil

FROM THE STORECUPBOARD

120ml/4fl oz/1/2 cup fish stock

15ml/1 tbsp sunflower oil

salt and ground white pepper, to taste

VARIATION *You could serve the mousse with Melba toast. Toast thin slices of bread on both sides under the grill (broiler). Cut off the crusts and slice each piece of toast in half horizontally. Return to the grill pan, untoasted sides up, and toast again, taking care not to let it burn.*

Energy 285kcal/1183kJ; Protein 12.6g; Carbohydrate 5.8g, of which sugars 3.2g; Fat 22.7g, of which saturates 8.7g; Cholesterol 57mg; Calcium 73mg; Fibre 0.2g; Sodium 103mg

Smoked Salmon Roulade ✳

Make the most of a small amount of smoked salmon by using it in the filling for this delicately flavoured roulade.

SERVES SIX–EIGHT

1 Melt the butter in a heavy pan, stir in the flour and cook over a low heat to a thick paste. Gradually add the milk, whisking constantly until it boils, then cook for 1–2 minutes more. Stir in the egg yolks, two-thirds of the grano padano cheese, the parsley and half the dill. Add salt and black pepper to taste.

2 Prepare a 33 x 28cm/13 x 11in Swiss roll tin (jelly roll pan) and preheat the oven to 180°C/350°F/Gas 4. Whisk the egg whites and fold into the yolk mixture, then pour into the tin and bake for 12–15 minutes.

3 Cover with baking parchment and set aside for 10–15 minutes, then tip out on to another sheet of parchment, sprinkled with a little grano padano. Leave to cool.

4 Mix the smoked salmon with the crème fraîche or sour cream and remaining chopped dill. Season to taste.

5 Peel off the lining paper from the roulade, spread the filling evenly over the surface and roll up, then leave to firm up in a cold place. Sprinkle with the rest of the Parmesan and garnish with the lamb's lettuce.

25g/1oz/2 tbsp butter

175ml/6fl oz/³/₄ cup milk, warmed

3 large eggs, separated

50g/2oz/²/₃ cup freshly grated grano padano cheese

30ml/2 tbsp chopped fresh parsley

60ml/4 tbsp chopped fresh dill

115g/4oz smoked salmon trimmings, chopped

150ml/¹/₄ pint/²/₃ cup full fat crème fraîche or sour cream

lamb's lettuce, to garnish

FROM THE STORECUPBOARD

25g/1oz/¹/₄ cup plain (all-purpose) flour

salt and ground black pepper, to taste

Energy 196kcal/814kJ; Protein 10.4g; Carbohydrate 4.1g, of which sugars 1.6g; Fat 15.5g, of which saturates 9g; Cholesterol 119mg; Calcium 144mg; Fibre 0.4g; Sodium 402mg

Chicken Liver and Brandy Pâté ✳

This pâté really could not be simpler to make, and tastes so much better than anything you can buy ready-made in the supermarkets. Serve with crispy toast for an elegant appetizer.

SERVES FOUR

1 Heat the butter in a large frying pan until it is foamy. Add the chopped chicken livers and cook them over a medium heat for 3–4 minutes, or until they are browned and cooked through.

2 Add the brandy and allow it to bubble for a few minutes. Remove the pan from the heat, allow the mixture to cool slightly, then tip it into a food processor with the cream and some salt and pepper to taste.

3 Process the mixture until smooth and spoon into ramekin dishes. Level the surface and chill overnight to set.

4 Serve garnished with sprigs of parsley to add a little colour, and some lightly toasted bread.

50g/2oz/¹/₄ cup butter

350g/12oz chicken livers, trimmed and roughly chopped

30ml/2 tbsp brandy

30ml/2 tbsp double (heavy) cream

FROM THE STORECUPBOARD

salt and ground black pepper, to taste

Energy 227kcal/942kJ; Protein 15.7g; Carbohydrate 0.2g, of which sugars 0.2g; Fat 16.3g, of which saturates 9.6g; Cholesterol 369mg; Calcium 13mg; Fibre 0g; Sodium 144mg

Mushroom Caviar ✳

The name caviar refers to the dark colour and texture of this dish of chopped mushrooms. Serve with toasted rye bread, and garnish with chopped hard-boiled egg, spring onion and parsley, if you like.

SERVES FOUR

1 Heat the oil in a large pan, add the chopped mushrooms, shallots and garlic, and cook gently for about 5 minutes, stirring occasionally, until browned.

2 Season the mixture with salt and pepper to taste, then continue cooking until the mushrooms give up their liquor.

3 Continue cooking, stirring frequently, until the liquor has evaporated and the mushrooms are brown and dry.

4 Leave the mixture to cool slightly, then scrape it in to a food processor or blender and process briefly until a chunky paste is formed.

5 Spoon the mushroom caviar into dishes and serve with plenty of toasted bread.

450g/1lb mushrooms, coarsely chopped

5–10 shallots, chopped

4 garlic cloves, chopped

FROM THE STORECUPBOARD

45ml/3 tbsp olive or vegetable oil

salt and ground black pepper, to taste

COOK'S TIP

For a rich wild mushroom caviar, soak 10–15g/ ¼–½oz dried porcini in about 120ml/4fl oz/ ½ cup water for about 30 minutes. Add the porcini and their soaking liquid to the browned mushrooms in step 2. Continue as in the recipe.

Energy 116kcal/479kJ; Protein 2.9g; Carbohydrate 6.4g, of which sugars 4.4g; Fat 9g, of which saturates 1.3g; Cholesterol 0mg; Calcium 26mg; Fibre 2.3g; Sodium 8mg

Baba Ganoush with Flatbread

Baba Ganoush is a delectable aubergine dip from the Middle East. It makes a very good appetizer served with raw vegetable crudités or bread for a party, or serve it at a barbecue as a side dish.

SERVES SIX

1 Start by making the Lebanese flatbread. Split the pitta breads through the middle and carefully open them out. Mix the sesame seeds, chopped thyme and poppy seeds in a mortar. Work them lightly with a pestle to release the flavour.

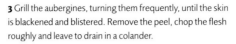

2 Stir in 150ml/¼ pint/⅔ cup olive oil. Spread the mixture over the cut sides of the pitta bread. Grill (broil) until golden brown and crisp. When cool, break into pieces and set aside.

3 Grill the aubergines, turning them frequently, until the skin is blackened and blistered. Remove the peel, chop the flesh roughly and leave to drain in a colander.

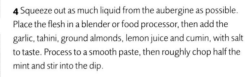

4 Squeeze out as much liquid from the aubergine as possible. Place the flesh in a blender or food processor, then add the garlic, tahini, ground almonds, lemon juice and cumin, with salt to taste. Process to a smooth paste, then roughly chop half the mint and stir into the dip.

5 Spoon the paste into a bowl, scatter the remaining mint leaves on top and drizzle with the remaining olive oil. Serve with the Lebanese flatbread.

2 small aubergines (eggplants)

1 garlic clove, crushed

60ml/4 tbsp tahini

25g/1oz/¼ cup ground almonds

juice of ½ lemon

30ml/2 tbsp fresh mint leaves

FOR THE FLATBREAD

4 pitta breads

45ml/3 tbsp sesame seeds

45ml/3 tbsp fresh thyme leaves

45ml/3 tbsp poppy seeds

FROM THE STORECUPBOARD

175ml/6fl oz/¾ cup olive oil

2.5ml/½ tsp ground cumin

salt, to taste

COOK'S TIPS

• Tahini is a paste that is made from sesame seeds, cumin and sesame oil. It is used in many Middle Eastern recipes, including hummus and tahini yogurt dip, so it is a useful ingredient to have to hand.

• Run the prongs of a fork down the woody stem to remove the leaves from fresh thyme.

Energy 129kcal/535kJ; Protein 3.3g; Carbohydrate 1.9g, of which sugars 1.6g; Fat 12.2g, of which saturates 1.6g; Cholesterol 0mg; Calcium 85mg; Fibre 2.5g; Sodium 4mg

Hummus ✳

Blending chickpeas with garlic and oil creates a surprisingly creamy purée that is delicious as part of a Turkish-style mezze, or as a dip with bread and cherry tomatoes. Leftovers make a good sandwich filler.

SERVES FOUR–SIX

1 Put the chickpeas in a large bowl with plenty of cold water and leave them to soak overnight.

2 Thoroughly rinse and drain the chickpeas, then place them in a large pan and cover with fresh water. Bring to the boil and boil rapidly for 10 minutes. Reduce the heat and simmer gently for 1¹/₄–2 hours until soft.

3 Drain the chickpeas in a colander, then purée in a food processor until they form a smooth paste.

4 Add the lemon juice, garlic, olive oil, cayenne pepper and tahini paste and blend until creamy, scraping the mixture down from the sides of the bowl.

5 Season the purée with plenty of salt and ground black pepper and transfer to a serving dish.

6 Sprinkle with a little olive oil and cayenne pepper, and garnish with a few parsley sprigs. Serve with toasted pitta bread and olives, if you like.

juice of 2 lemons

2 garlic cloves, sliced

150ml/¹/₄ pint/²/₃ cup tahini paste

flat leaf parsley sprigs, to garnish

FROM THE STORECUPBOARD

150g/5oz/³/₄ cup dried chickpeas

30ml/2 tbsp olive oil

pinch of cayenne pepper

salt and ground black pepper, to taste

extra olive oil and cayenne pepper, for sprinkling

Energy 453kcal/1887kJ; Protein 15.7g; Carbohydrate 32.1g, of which sugars 13.8g; Fat 30g, of which saturates 4.2g; Cholesterol 0mg; Calcium 345mg; Fibre 10.5g; Sodium 49mg

2 garlic cloves, crushed

1 fresh red chilli, seeded and finely sliced

15ml/1 tbsp chopped fresh mint

15ml/1 tbsp chopped fresh parsley

2 spring onions (scallions), finely chopped

1 large egg, beaten

sesame seeds, for coating

FOR THE TAHINI YOGURT DIP

30ml/2 tbsp light tahini

200g/7oz/scant 1 cup natural (plain) yogurt

15ml/1 tbsp chopped fresh mint

1 spring onion (scallion), finely sliced

fresh herbs, to garnish

FROM THE STORECUPBOARD

250g/9oz/1¹/₃ cups dried chickpeas

5ml/1 tsp cayenne pepper, plus extra for sprinkling

5ml/1 tsp ground coriander

5ml/1 tsp ground cumin

sunflower oil, for frying

salt and ground black pepper, to taste

Falafel with Tahini Dip ✳

Sesame seeds are used to give a delightfully crunchy coating to these spicy chickpea patties. Serve them with the tahini yogurt dip, and some warmed pitta bread for a delicious appetizer or warming snack.

SERVES SIX

1 Place the chickpeas in a large bowl, cover with cold water and leave to soak overnight.

2 Drain and rinse the chickpeas, then place them in a large pan and cover with cold water. Bring to the boil and boil rapidly for 10 minutes. Reduce the heat and simmer for 1¹/₄–2 hours until the chickpeas are tender.

3 Meanwhile, make the tahini yogurt dip. Mix together the tahini, yogurt, cayenne pepper and mint in a small bowl. Sprinkle the spring onion and extra cayenne pepper on top and chill in the refrigerator until required.

4 Combine the chickpeas with the garlic, chilli, ground spices, herbs, spring onions and seasoning, then mix in the egg. Place in a food processor and blend until the mixture forms a coarse paste. If the paste seems too soft, chill it for 30 minutes.

5 Form the chilled chick-pea paste into 12 patties with your hands, then roll each one in the sesame seeds to coat evenly.

6 Heat enough oil to cover the base of a large frying pan. Fry the falafel, in batches if necessary, for 6 minutes, turning once. Serve with the tahini yogurt dip garnished with fresh herbs.

Energy 372kcal/1557kJ; Protein 19.3g; Carbohydrate 35.3g, of which sugars 5.8g; Fat 18.1g, of which saturates 2.6g; Cholesterol 48mg; Calcium 280mg; Fibre 8g; Sodium 89mg

Potato Skewers with Mustard Dip ✳

Tender new potatoes cooked on the barbecue have a great flavour and crisp skin, but you could also cook these simple skewers under a hot grill (broiler). Serve with a creamy mustard and garlic dip at a family barbecue or as an appetizer at a summer dinner party.

SERVES FOUR

FOR THE DIP

4 garlic cloves, crushed

2 egg yolks

30ml/2 tbsp freshly squeezed lemon juice

FOR THE SKEWERS

200g/7oz shallots

1kg/2¼lb small new potatoes

FROM THE STORECUPBOARD

350ml/12fl oz/1½ cups extra virgin olive oil

10ml/2 tsp wholegrain mustard

salt and ground black pepper, to taste, plus 15ml/1 tbsp salt

1 Prepare and light the barbecue or preheat the grill (broiler) to high.

2 To make the dip, place the garlic, egg yolks and lemon juice in a blender or a food processor and process for a few seconds until the mixture is smooth.

3 Keep the blender motor running and add 300ml/½ pint/ 1¼ cups of the olive oil very gradually, pouring it in a thin stream, until the mixture forms a thick, glossy cream.

4 Add the mustard and stir the ingredients together, then season with salt and pepper. Chill until ready to use.

5 Skin the shallots and then cut them in half. Par-boil the potatoes in their skins in a pan of boiling water for 5 minutes.

6 Drain well and then thread the potatoes on to metal skewers, alternating with the shallots.

7 Brush the skewers with the remaining olive oil and sprinkle with 15ml/1 tbsp salt. Cook over a barbecue or under a hot grill for 10–12 minutes, turning occasionally. Serve the skewers immediately with the dip.

COOK'S TIPS

• Early or "new" potatoes, and salad potatoes have the firmness and waxy texture that is necessary for the potatoes to stay on the skewer. Don't be tempted to use other types of small potato, since they will probably split or fall off the skewers during cooking.

• If you do not like mustard, you can omit it from this creamy home-made mayonnaise dip. You could add a dash of paprika instead.

Energy 2731kcal/11338kJ; Protein 28g; Carbohydrate 181.3g, of which sugars 25g; Fat 215.4g, of which saturates 32.8g; Cholesterol 403mg; Calcium 174mg; Fibre 14.3g; Sodium 297mg

Pea and Potato Pakoras with Coconut and Mint Chutney ✳

These delicious golden bites are sold as street food throughout India. Fragrant and flavoursome, they combine potato, onions and peas with a range of spices, including cumin, turmeric and coriander seeds. They make a wonderful snack drizzled with the fragrant chutney, or you could sandwich them in a crusty roll for a light lunch.

MAKES TWENTY FIVE

1 Add the diced potatoes to a large pan of lightly salted boiling water and cook for 10 minutes, until tender.

2 Heat a wok or large frying pan over a medium heat and add the sunflower oil. When hot, add the cumin and mustard seeds and stir-fry for 1–2 minutes.

3 Add the onion, ginger and chillies to the wok or large pan and cook for 3–4 minutes, stirring constantly to prevent the onion from burning.

4 Add the cooked potatoes and peas, stir well to combine and stir-fry for 3–4 minutes. Season to taste, then stir in the lemon juice and coriander leaves.

5 Leave the mixture to cool slightly, then divide into 25 portions. Using damp hands, shape each portion into a small ball and chill in the refrigerator.

6 To make the batter, put the besan, self-raising flour and rice flour in a large bowl. Season with salt and pepper and add the turmeric and coriander seeds. Gradually whisk in the water to make a smooth, thick batter.

7 To make the coconut and mint chutney place all the ingredients in a blender or food processor and process until smooth. Season to taste with salt and ground black pepper, then chill in the refrigerator until required.

8 To cook the pakoras, fill a wok or large, heavy pan one-third full of vegetable oil and heat to 180°C/350°F. (A cube of bread, dropped into the oil, should brown in 15 seconds.)

9 Working in batches, dip the chilled pea and potato balls in the batter, then carefully slip each into the hot oil, using a slotted spoon. Deep-fry for 1–2 minutes, or until golden.

10 Drain on kitchen paper and keep warm while you cook the rest of the balls. Serve hot, with the chutney.

600g/1lb 6oz potatoes, peeled and diced

1 small onion, chopped

10ml/2 tsp grated fresh root ginger

2 green chillies, seeded and chopped

200g/7oz peas

juice of 1 lemon

90ml/6 tbsp chopped fresh coriander (cilantro) leaves

115g/4oz/1 cup besan (chickpea flour)

350ml/12fl oz/1¹/₂ cups water

FOR THE CHUTNEY

105ml/7 tbsp coconut cream

200ml/7fl oz/scant 1 cup natural (plain) yogurt

50g/2oz mint leaves, finely chopped

juice of 1 lime

FROM THE STORECUPBOARD

15ml/1 tbsp sunflower oil

20ml/4 tsp cumin seeds

5ml/1 tsp black mustard seeds

25g/1oz/¹/₄ cup self-raising (self-rising) flour

40g/1¹/₂oz/¹/₃ cup rice flour

large pinch of turmeric

10ml/2 tsp crushed coriander seeds

5ml/1 tsp sugar

vegetable oil, for frying

salt and ground black pepper, to taste

Energy 126kcal/525kJ; Protein 4.1g; Carbohydrate 8.3g, of which sugars 2.6g; Fat 8.8g, of which saturates 5.2g; Cholesterol 0mg; Calcium 35mg; Fibre 1.3g; Sodium 16mg.

Courgette Fritters with Chilli Jam ✳

Chilli jam is hot, sweet and sticky – rather like a thick chutney. It adds a delicious piquancy to these light fritters, which are always popular with adults and children alike.

SERVES SIX

1 First make the chilli jam. Heat the olive oil in a frying pan until hot, then add the onions and the garlic. Reduce the heat to low, then cook for 20 minutes, stirring frequently, until the onions are very soft.

2 Leave the onion mixture to cool, then transfer to a food processor or blender. Add the chillies and sugar and blend until smooth, then return the mixture to the pan. Cook for a further 10 minutes, stirring frequently, until the liquid evaporates and the mixture has the consistency of jam. Cool slightly.

3 To make the fritters, squeeze the courgettes in a dish towel to remove any excess liquid, then combine with the grano padano, eggs, flour and salt and pepper.

4 Heat enough oil to cover the base of a large frying pan. Add 30ml/2 tbsp of the mixture for each fritter and cook three fritters at a time. Cook for 2–3 minutes on each side until golden, then keep warm while you cook the rest of the fritters.

5 Drain on kitchen paper and serve warm with a spoonful of the chilli jam.

COOK'S TIP *Stored in an airtight jar in the refrigerator, the chilli jam will keep for up to 1 week.*

450g/1lb/3¹/₂ cups coarsely grated courgettes (zucchini)

50g/2oz/²/₃ cup freshly grated grano padano cheese

2 eggs, beaten

FOR THE CHILLI JAM

4 large onions, diced

4 garlic cloves, chopped

1–2 green chillies, seeded and sliced

FROM THE STORECUPBOARD

75ml/5 tbsp olive oil

30ml/2 tbsp soft dark brown sugar

60ml/4 tbsp plain flour

vegetable oil, for frying

salt and ground black pepper, to taste

Energy 326kcal/1355kJ; Protein 10g; Carbohydrate 22.3g, of which sugars 13.2g; Fat 22.6g, of which saturates 4.7g; Cholesterol 103mg; Calcium 177mg; Fibre 2.6g; Sodium 131mg

Crab Cakes *

Definitely one for younger members of the family who like flavourful fish cakes. They may even help you make some fish-shaped cakes.

SERVES FOUR

1 Put the crab meat in a large bowl and stir in the mayonnaise with the mustard and egg. Season to taste with Tabasco, salt, pepper and cayenne.

2 Stir in the chopped parsley, spring onions, if using, and 50g/2oz/¹/₂ cup of the breadcrumbs. The mixture should be just firm enough to hold together; you may need to add some more breadcrumbs.

3 Divide the mixture into eight portions, roll each into a ball and flatten slightly to make a thick flat disc. Spread out the crab cakes on a platter and put in the refrigerator for 30 minutes before frying.

4 Pour the oil into a heavy pan to a depth of about 5mm/¹/₄in. Cook the crab cakes, in two batches, until golden brown.

5 Drain on kitchen paper and keep hot. Serve with a spring onion garnish and red onion marmalade.

30ml/2 tbsp mayonnaise

2.5–5ml/¹/₂–1 tsp mustard powder

1 egg, lightly beaten

45ml/3 tbsp chopped fresh parsley

4 spring onions (scallions), finely chopped (optional)

50–75g/2–3oz/¹/₂–³/₄ cup dried breadcrumbs

chopped spring onions (scallions), to garnish

red onion marmalade, to serve

FROM THE STORECUPBOARD

450g/1lb canned crab meat

Tabasco sauce

salt, ground black pepper and cayenne pepper

sunflower oil, for frying

Energy 285kcal/1187kJ; Protein 23.9g; Carbohydrate 10.3g, of which sugars 0.9g; Fat 16.7g, of which saturates 2.4g; Cholesterol 134mg; Calcium 178mg; Fibre 0.8g; Sodium 768mg

600g/1lb 6oz courgettes (zucchini)

90g/3¹/₂oz/³/₄ cup besan (chickpea flour)

250ml/8fl oz/1 cup beer

steamed basmati rice, natural (plain) yogurt and pickles, to serve

FROM THE STORECUPBOARD

5ml/1 tsp baking powder

2.5ml/¹/₂ tsp turmeric

10ml/2 tsp ground coriander

5ml/1 tsp ground cumin

5ml/1 tsp chilli powder

sunflower oil, for frying

salt, to taste

Courgette Tempura ✳

This quick-and-easy dish is a twist on the classic Japanese tempura, using besan in the batter. Also known as gram flour, golden besan is more commonly used in Indian cooking and gives a wonderfully crisp texture while the courgette inside becomes meltingly tender.

SERVES FOUR

1 Using a large. sharp knife, slice the courgettes into thick, finger-sized batons and set aside.

2 Sift the besan, baking powder, turmeric, ground coriander, cumin and chilli powder into a large bowl.

3 Season the mixture with salt and gradually add the beer, mixing to make a thick batter – do not overmix.

4 Fill a wok or large, heavy pan one-third full of sunflower oil and heat to 180°C/350°F (or until a cube of bread, dropped into the oil, browns in 15 seconds).

5 Working in batches, dip the courgette batons in the spiced batter and then deep-fry for 1–2 minutes, or until crisp and golden. Carefully lift out of the wok or pan using a slotted spoon and drain on kitchen paper.

6 Serve the courgettes immediately with steamed basmati rice, yogurt, pickles and chutney.

VARIATIONS

• You can cook all kinds of vegetables in this way. Try using onion rings, aubergine (eggplant) slices, cauliflower or broccoli florets, or even whole mild chillies.

• For a spicer version, try adding 15ml/1 tbsp Chinese five-spice powder to the batter before you coat the courgettes (zucchini).

Energy 241kcal/999kJ; Protein 7.3g; Carbohydrate 15.3g, of which sugars 4.6g; Fat 15.6g, of which saturates 1.9g; Cholesterol 0mg; Calcium 83mg; Fibre 3.8g; Sodium 15mg

Seven-spice Aubergines ✳

Crisp, fragrant and very moreish, these tasty bites make a delicious snack or appetizer. The Chinese seven-spice powder gives the aubergines a warm flavour that goes well with the light, curry batter. If you are unable to find it, you can use Chinese five-spice powder instead.

SERVES FOUR

500g/1¹⁄₄ lb aubergines (eggplant)

2 egg whites

fresh mint leaves, to garnish

steamed rice or noodles and hot chilli sauce, to serve

FROM THE STORECUPBOARD

90ml/6 tbsp cornflour (cornstarch) or plain (all-purpose) flour

5ml/1 tsp salt

15ml/1 tbsp Chinese seven-spice powder

15ml/1 tbsp mild chilli powder

sunflower oil, for frying

COOK'S TIPS

• Choose small, firm aubergines that feel heavy. Select ones with shiny, unblemished skins, and avoid any that feel soft or that are beginning to wrinkle.

• Thai seven-spice powder is a blend of spices, including cumin, ground cinnamon, star anise, chilli, cloves and lemon peel.

1 Using a large, sharp knife, slice the aubergines into thin discs. Pat dry with kitchen paper.

2 Whisk the egg whites in a large bowl until they are light and foamy, but not dry.

3 Combine the cornflour or flour, salt, seven-spice powder and chilli powder and spread evenly on to a large plate.

4 Fill a wok or large, heavy pan one-third full of sunflower oil and heat to 180°C/350°F (or until a cube of bread, dropped into the oil, browns in 15 seconds).

5 Working in batches, dip the aubergine slices in the egg white and then into the spiced flour mixture to coat. Deep-fry for 3–4 minutes, or until crisp and golden.

6 Remove the aubergines with a wire skimmer or slotted spoon and drain well on kitchen paper.

7 Serve immediately, garnished with mint leaves and accompany with steamed rice or noodles, and hot chilli sauce for dipping.

Energy 203kcal/850kJ; Protein 2.7g; Carbohydrate 23.5g, of which sugars 2.5g; Fat 11.7g, of which saturates 1.4g; Cholesterol 0mg; Calcium 17mg; Fibre 2.5g; Sodium 45mg

Crispy Fried Whitebait with Sherry Salsa ✳

Whitebait are the small fry of herring and sprats, and are especially delicious when fried and eaten whole. Here, they are served with an intensely flavoured tomato, garlic and sherry salsa and wedges of zesty lemon to squeeze over the hot, crispy fish.

SERVES FOUR

1 Preheat the oven to 150°C/300°F/Gas 2. Wash the fresh or thawed whitebait thoroughly, drain well and dry on kitchen paper, then dust in the seasoned flour.

2 To make the salsa, place the chopped shallot, garlic, tomatoes, chilli and 30ml/2 tbsp olive oil in a pan. Cover with a lid and cook gently for about 10 minutes.

3 Pour the sherry into the pan and season with salt and pepper to taste. Stir in the herbs and breadcrumbs, then cover and keep the salsa hot until the whitebait are ready.

4 Heat the oils together in a heavy frying pan and cook the fish in batches until crisp and golden. Drain on kitchen paper and keep warm until all the fish are cooked. Serve immediately with the salsa and crusty bread.

225g/8oz whitebait, thawed if frozen

FOR THE SALSA

1 shallot, finely chopped

2 garlic cloves, finely chopped

4 ripe tomatoes, chopped

1 small red chilli, seeded and finely chopped

60ml/4 tbsp sweet sherry

30–45ml/2–3 tbsp chopped mixed fresh herbs, such as parsley or basil

25g/1oz/¹/₂ cup stale white breadcrumbs

FROM THE STORECUPBOARD

30ml/2 tbsp seasoned plain (all-purpose) flour

90ml/6 tbsp olive oil

60ml/4 tbsp sunflower oil

salt and ground black pepper, to taste

COOK'S TIP *Frozen whitebait are good value for money and are especially useful if you are unable to buy fresh ones from your supermarket or local fishmonger.*

Energy 360kcal/1498kJ; Protein 12.6g; Carbohydrate 13.2g, of which sugars 5.2g; Fat 27.2g, of which saturates 0.1g; Cholesterol 0mg; Calcium 504mg; Fibre 1.5g; Sodium 188mg

Crispy Salt and Pepper Squid with Dipping Sauce **＊＊**

These delicious morsels of squid look stunning skewered on small or large wooden sticks and are perfect served with drinks, or as an appetizer. The crisp, golden coating contrasts with the succulent squid inside, and they taste divine dipped into sweet-and-sour or chilli sauce.

SERVES FOUR

750g/1lb 10oz fresh or frozen squid, cleaned (see Cook's Tip) and thawed, if frozen

juice of 4–5 lemons

3 egg whites, lightly beaten

skewers, to serve

FROM THE STORECUPBOARD

15ml/1 tbsp ground black pepper

15ml/1 tbsp salt

10ml/2 tsp caster (superfine) sugar

115g/4oz/1 cup cornflour (cornstarch)

sunflower oil, for frying

sweet-and-sour or chilli sauce, for dipping

1 Cut the squid into large bitesize pieces and score a diamond pattern on each piece.

2 Trim the tentacles. Place in a large mixing bowl and pour over the lemon juice. Cover and marinate for 10–15 minutes. Drain well and pat dry.

3 In a separate bowl mix together the pepper, salt, sugar and cornflour. Dip the squid pieces in the egg white and then toss lightly in the seasoned flour, shaking off any excess.

4 Fill a wok or large, heavy pan one-third full of sunflower oil and heat to 180°C/350°F. (A cube of bread, dropped into the oil, should brown in 15 seconds.)

5 Working in batches, deep-fry the squid for 1 minute, until crispy. Drain on kitchen paper and serve threaded on to skewers with sweet-and-sour or chilli sauce.

COOK'S TIP To clean the squid, pull the head and tentacles away from the body; the intestines and quill should pull away at the same time. Reserve the tentacles but discard the head and innards. Gripping firmly with your fingers, pull off the purplish membrane from the body, then slit the body open and wash under cold water.

Energy 346kcal/1462kJ; Protein 31.2g; Carbohydrate 31.3g, of which sugars 2.6g; Fat 11.6g, of which saturates 1.8g; Cholesterol 422mg; Calcium 32mg; Fibre 0g; Sodium 1741mg

Chargrilled Spicy Chicken Wings **

Chicken wings, thighs and drumsticks have a very good flavour and are often excellent value for money. Here, the wings are marinated in a spicy paste and then grilled over charcoal or fried. They can be served on their own with a few sprigs of coriander as an appetizer at a barbecue, or include them as part of a selection of dishes at a buffet or informal lunch.

SERVES FOUR

1 First make the spice paste. Using a mortar and pestle or food processor, grind the shallots, garlic, ginger, chillies and lemon grass to a paste. Bind with the oil and stir in the tomato purée, sugar and lime juice. Season with salt and pepper.

2 Rub the spice paste into the chicken wings and leave to marinate for 2 hours.

3 Prepare and light the barbecue or preheat a grill (broiler). Lift the wings out of the marinade and place them on the rack.

4 Cook them for about 5 minutes each side until cooked through, brushing with marinade while they cook. Serve immediately, garnished with coriander and chillies.

12 chicken wings

fresh coriander (cilantro) leaves, roughly chopped, and 2–3 green chillies, seeded and quartered lengthways, to garnish

FOR THE SPICE PASTE

4 shallots, chopped

4 garlic cloves, chopped

25g/1oz fresh root ginger, chopped

8 red chillies, seeded and chopped

1 lemon grass stalk, trimmed and chopped

juice of 2 limes

FROM THE STORECUPBOARD

30ml/2 tbsp sesame or groundnut (peanut) oil

15ml/1 tbsp tomato purée (paste)

10ml/2 tsp sugar

salt and ground black pepper, to taste

Energy 350kcal/1455kJ; Protein 30.7g; Carbohydrate 2.6g, of which sugars 2.6g; Fat 24.1g, of which saturates 5.9g; Cholesterol 134mg; Calcium 11mg; Fibre 0.1g; Sodium 99mg

2 onions, finely chopped

2 garlic cloves,
finely chopped

1 green chilli, seeded
and finely chopped

25g/1oz fresh root ginger,
finely chopped

250g/9oz lean minced
(ground) lamb

4 eggs

fresh coriander (cilantro)
leaves, roughly chopped,
to garnish

1 lemon, quartered,
to serve

FROM THE STORECUPBOARD

150g/5oz/generous 1/2 cup
red, brown, yellow or
green lentils, rinsed

30ml/2 tbsp vegetable oil

10ml/2 tsp Indian
curry powder

5ml/1 tsp turmeric powder

vegetable oil, for frying

salt and ground black
pepper, to taste

Lentil and Meat Patties ✳✳

Otherwise known as shami kebabs, these lentil and lamb patties are
originally from Malaysia. They make a delicious appetizer served with a
piqant sambal or some lemon wedges, or they can be eaten as a snack
between chunks of bread with tomato ketchup, like a burger.

SERVES FOUR

1 Put the lentils in a pan and cover with plenty of water. Bring to
a gentle boil and cook until they have softened but still have a
bite to them – this can take 20–40 minutes depending on the
type of lentil. Drain well.

2 Heat the oil in a heavy pan and stir in the onions, garlic, chilli
and ginger. Fry until they begin to colour, then add the lentils and
minced lamb. Cook for a few minutes, then add the curry powder
and turmeric. Season and cook over a high heat until the moisture
has evaporated. Remove from the heat and leave until the
mixture is cool enough to handle.

3 Beat one of the eggs in a bowl and mix it into the meat. Using
damp hands, take small portions of the mixture and roll them
into balls about the size of a plum or apricot. Press each ball in
the palm of your hand to form thick, flat patties.

4 Beat the remaining eggs in a bowl. Heat enough oil in a heavy
pan for shallow frying. Dip each patty in the egg and place them
all into the oil. Fry for 3–4 minutes each side, until golden. Garnish
with coriander and serve with lemon wedges to squeeze over.

VARIATION The patties are delicious served in a baguette, halved lengthways, layered with lettuce leaves, coriander, mint, yogurt and a hot chutney or a chilli sauce.

Energy 488kcal/2033kJ; Protein 28g; Carbohydrate 25.7g, of which sugars 3.7g; Fat 31.2g, of which saturates 7.4g; Cholesterol 238mg; Calcium 87mg; Fibre 3.1g; Sodium 140mg

675g/1¹/₂ lb spinach, washed and drained

30ml/2 tbsp butter

60ml/4 tbsp double (heavy) cream

FOR THE TOPPING

30ml/2 tbsp butter

300ml/¹/₂ pint/1¹/₄ cups hot milk

115g/4oz/1 cup Gruyère cheese, grated

4 eggs

30ml/2 tbsp freshly grated grano padano cheese, plus shavings to serve

FROM THE STORECUPBOARD

pinch of freshly grated nutmeg

salt and ground black pepper, to taste

25g/1oz/¹/₄ cup plain (all-purpose) flour

pinch of ground mace

Poached Eggs Florentine ✳✳

In this elegant appetizer, soft poached eggs are served on a bed of wilted spinach and baked in the oven with a creamy, cheesy sauce.

SERVES FOUR

1 Place the spinach in a large pan with very little water. Cook for 3–4 minutes or until tender, then drain and chop finely. Return the spinach to the pan, add the butter, cream, nutmeg and seasoning and heat through. Place on the bottom of one large or four small gratin dishes.

2 To make the topping, heat the butter in a small pan, add the flour and cook for 1 minute into a paste. Gradually blend in the hot milk, beating well as it thickens to break up any lumps.

3 Cook for 1–2 minutes, stirring. Remove from the heat and stir in the mace and three-quarters of the Gruyère cheese.

4 Preheat the oven to 200°C/400°F/Gas 6. Bring a pan of water to the simmer, then carefully drop in the eggs. Poach gently for 3–4 minutes, then lift out of the water with a slotted spoon.

5 Make hollows in the spinach with the back of a spoon, and place a poached egg in each one. Cover with the cheese sauce and sprinkle with the remaining Gruyère and grano padanao. Bake for 10 minutes, until golden. Serve with grano padano shavings.

Energy 459kcal/1901kJ; Protein 21.7g; Carbohydrate 11.5g, of which sugars 6.5g; Fat 36g, of which saturates 20.3g; Cholesterol 270mg; Calcium 636mg; Fibre 3.7g; Sodium 626mg

Baked Eggs with Creamy Leeks ✳

This simple but elegant appetizer is perfect for last-minute entertaining or quick dining. It is extremely economical, as well as being nourishing, sustaining and delicious.

SERVES FOUR

1 Preheat the oven to 190°C/375°F/Gas 5. Butter the base and sides of four small ramekins or individual soufflé dishes.

2 Melt the butter in a frying pan and cook the leeks over a medium heat, stirring frequently, for 3–5 minutes, until softened and translucent, but not browned.

3 Add 45ml/3 tbsp of the cream and cook over a low heat for 5 minutes, until the leeks are very soft and the cream has thickened a little. Season to taste.

4 Place the ramekins in a small roasting pan and divide the cooked leek mixture among them. Break an egg into each, spoon over the remaining cream and season to taste with salt and pepper.

5 Pour boiling water into the roasting pan to come about halfway up the sides of the ramekins. Transfer the pan to the preheated oven and bake for about 10 minutes, until just set. Garnish with fried sage leaves and serve immediately.

15g/¹/₂oz/1 tbsp butter, plus extra for greasing

225g/8oz small leeks, thinly sliced

75–90ml/5–6 tbsp whipping cream

4 small-medium (US medium-large) eggs

crisp, fried sage leaves, to garnish

FROM THE STORECUPBOARD

salt and ground black pepper, to taste

Energy 149kcal/614kJ; Protein 4.4g; Carbohydrate 2.2g, of which sugars 1.8g; Fat 13.7g, of which saturates 7.5g; Cholesterol 123mg; Calcium 39mg; Fibre 1.3g; Sodium 64mg

Deep-fried Eggs with Tamarind Dressing ✳✳

This tasty salad combines crispy fried eggs with crunchy, refreshing beansprouts and salad leaves, and a deliciously sweet and tangy tamarind dresssing. Serve as an appetizer or light meal.

SERVES FOUR

1 Place the eggs in a pan and cover with cold water. Bring to the boil and cook for 4 minutes. Remove with a slotted spoon, then drain and rinse in cold water. Shell and set aside.

2 Fill a wok one-third full of oil and heat to 180°C/350°F (or until a cube of bread, dropped into the oil, browns in 15 seconds).

3 Using a slotted spoon, lower the eggs, one at a time, into the hot oil. Deep-fry for 2–3 minutes, or until lightly golden. Remove and drain on kitchen paper. Keep warm.

4 Place the palm sugar, tamarind juice and fish sauce in a clean wok with 30ml/2 tbsp of water and bring to the boil, stirring until the sugar dissolves. Reduce the heat, then simmer gently for 3–4 minutes. Transfer the mixture to a bowl and set aside.

5 Wipe out the wok and add 30ml/2 tbsp oil. When hot, fry the shallots, garlic and chillies until they are all lightly browned.

6 In a large bowl, toss together the salad leaves, coriander leaves and beansprouts with the tamarind mixture. Divide this among four plates.

7 Cut the fried eggs in half and and divide among the prepared plates. Sprinkle over the shallot mixture and serve immediately.

6 large (US extra large) eggs

75g/3oz/scant ¹/₂ cup palm sugar

90ml/6 tbsp tamarind juice

6 shallots, finely sliced

4 garlic cloves, thinly sliced

2 red chillies, seeded and thinly sliced

115g/4oz salad leaves

a small handful of coriander (cilantro) leaves

25g/1oz beansprouts

FROM THE STORECUPBOARD

sunflower oil, for frying

75ml/5 tbsp Thai fish sauce

COOK'S TIP *For a lower-fat version of this dish, you could omit step 3 and serve the salad with plain hard-boiled eggs. You could also omit the fried shallots, garlic and chillies.*

Energy 351kcal/1462kJ; Protein 13g; Carbohydrate 23.3g, of which sugars 21.5g; Fat 23.8g, of which saturates 4.4g; Cholesterol 333mg; Calcium 117mg; Fibre 1.3g; Sodium 165mg

Potato, Onion and Broad Bean Tortilla *

The classic tortilla is simple to make and tastes fabulous. Serve it as a light summer lunch dish with a green leafy salad, or cut it into pieces, thread on to cocktail sticks (toothpicks) and serve as an appetizer.

SERVES SIX

1 Heat 30ml/2 tbsp of the oil in a deep 23cm/9in non-stick frying pan. Add the onions and potatoes and season with salt and pepper to taste. Stir to mix, then cover and cook gently, stirring, for 20–25 minutes.

2 Meanwhile, cook the beans in lightly salted, boiling water for 5 minutes. Drain well and set aside to cool. When the beans are cool enough to handle, peel off the grey outer skins. Add to the frying pan, together with the thyme or summer savory. Stir and cook for a further 2–3 minutes.

3 Beat the eggs with salt and pepper to taste and the mixed fresh herbs, then pour over the potatoes and onions and increase the heat slightly. Cook gently until the egg on the base sets and browns, gently pulling the omelette away from the sides of the pan and tilting it to allow the uncooked egg to run underneath.

4 Invert the tortilla on to a plate. Add the remaining oil to the pan and heat. Slip the tortilla back into the pan, uncooked side down, and cook for another 3–5 minutes. Slide the tortilla out on to a plate. Divide as you like, and serve warm rather than piping hot.

2 Spanish (Bermuda) onions, thinly sliced

300g/11oz waxy potatoes, cut into 1cm/^{1}/$_2$ in dice

250g/9oz/1^3/$_4$ cups shelled broad (fava) beans

5ml/1 tsp chopped fresh thyme or summer savory

6 large (US extra large) eggs

45ml/3 tbsp chopped mixed fresh chives and flat leaf parsley

FROM THE STORECUPBOARD

45ml/3 tbsp olive oil

salt and ground black pepper, to taste

Energy 673kcal/2812kJ; Protein 34.9g; Carbohydrate 59.2g, of which sugars 18.1g; Fat 35.2g, of which saturates 7.3g; Cholesterol 571mg; Calcium 272mg; Fibre 14.3g; Sodium 252mg

Mini Baked Potatoes with Sour Cream and Blue Cheese ✳

These attractive miniature baked potatoes are packed with flavour and can be eaten with the fingers. They provide an economical and unusual way of starting off an informal supper party.

MAKES TWENTY

1 Preheat the oven to 180°C/350°F/Gas 4. Wash and dry the potatoes. Toss with the oil in a bowl to coat.

2 Dip the potatoes in the salt to coat lightly, then spread them out on a large baking sheet. Bake for 45–50 minutes until they are tender.

3 In a small bowl, combine the sour cream and blue cheese, mixing together well to combine thoroughly.

4 Cut a cross in the top of each potato. Press gently with your fingers to open the potatoes. Top each one with a dollop of the blue cheese mixture.

5 Place on a serving dish and garnish with the chives.

20 small new or salad potatoes

120ml/4fl oz/¹/₂ cup sour cream

25g/1oz blue cheese, crumbled

30ml/2 tbsp snipped fresh chives, to garnish

FROM THE STORECUPBOARD

60ml/4 tbsp vegetable oil

salt

Energy 71kcal/299kJ; Protein 1.3g; Carbohydrate 8.3g, of which sugars 0.9g; Fat 3.9g, of which saturates 1.3g; Cholesterol 5mg; Calcium 15mg; Fibre 0.5g; Sodium 23mg

Mushrooms with Garlic and Chilli Sauce ✳

These spicy, garlic-flavoured mushrooms make an ideal vegetarian alternative for a dinner party or summer barbecue.

SERVES FOUR

1 If using wooden skewers, soak eight of them in cold water for at least 30 minutes before making the kebabs. This will prevent them from burning over the barbecue or under the grill (broiler).

2 Make the dipping sauce by heating 15ml/1 tbsp of the sugar, rice vinegar and salt in a small pan, stirring occasionally until the sugar and salt have dissolved. Add the garlic and chilli, pour into a serving dish and keep warm.

3 Thread three mushroom halves on to each skewer. Lay the skewers side by side in a shallow dish.

4 In a mortar or spice grinder, pound or blend the garlic and coriander roots. Scrape into a bowl and mix with the remaining sugar, soy sauce and a little pepper.

5 Brush the soy sauce mixture over the mushrooms and leave to marinate for 15 minutes. Prepare the barbecue or preheat the grill, and cook the mushrooms for 2–3 minutes on each side. Serve with the dipping sauce.

COOK'S TIP *If you like really spicy foods, do not remove the seeds from the red chilli.*

12 large field (portabello), brown cap (cremini) or oyster mushrooms, or a mixture of the three, halved

4 garlic cloves, coarsely chopped

6 coriander (cilantro) roots, coarsely chopped

FOR THE DIPPING SAUCE

1 garlic clove, crushed

1 small fresh red chilli, seeded and finely chopped

FROM THE STORECUPBOARD

30ml/2 tbsp sugar

90ml/6 tbsp rice vinegar

5ml/1 tsp salt

30ml/2 tbsp light soy sauce

ground black pepper, to taste

Energy 78kcal/329kJ; Protein 5.8g; Carbohydrate 11.5g, of which sugars 9.1g; Fat 1.3g, of which saturates 0.3g; Cholesterol 0mg; Calcium 23mg; Fibre 3.3g; Sodium 1039mg

Mushrooms on Spicy Toast ✳

This recipe uses a technique called dry-panning, which is a quick way of cooking mushrooms that makes the most of their flavour. The juices run when the mushrooms are heated, so they become really moist and tender.

SERVES FOUR

1 Preheat the oven to 200°C/400°F/Gas 6. Peel the mushrooms, if necessary, and remove the stalks. Heat a dry frying pan until very hot.

2 Place the mushrooms in the hot frying pan, with the gills on top. Using half the butter, add a piece the size of a hazelnut to each one, then sprinkle all the mushrooms lightly with salt.

3 Cook over a medium heat until the butter begins to bubble and the mushrooms are juicy and tender.

4 Meanwhile, mix the remaining butter with the curry powder. Spread on the bread. Bake in the oven for 10 minutes, pile the mushrooms on top and serve.

8–12 large flat field (portabello) mushrooms

50g/2oz/¼ cup butter

4 slices thickly-sliced white or brown bread, toasted, to serve

FROM THE STORECUPBOARD

5ml/1 tsp curry powder

salt, to taste

VARIATIONS

• Using a flavoured butter makes these mushrooms even more special. Try one of the following:

• Herb butter – mix softened butter with chopped fresh herbs, such as parsley and thyme, or marjoram and chopped chives.

• Olive butter – mix softened butter with diced green olives and spring onions (scallions).

• Tomato butter – mix softened butter with sun-dried tomato purée (paste).

• Garlic butter – mix softened butter with finely chopped garlic.

• Pepper and paprika butter – mix softened butter with 2.5ml/½ tsp paprika and 2.5ml/½ tsp black pepper.

Energy 230kcal/966kJ; Protein 6.1g; Carbohydrate 25.1g, of which sugars 1.6g; Fat 12.5g, of which saturates 6.7g; Cholesterol 27mg; Calcium 63mg; Fibre 1.9g; Sodium 341mg

Focaccia with Sardines and Tomatoes ✳✳

Fresh sardines not only have a lovely flavour and texture, but are also cheap to buy so make an economical yet utterly delicious lunch in next to no time. Use plump, ripe vine tomatoes when they are in season, or you can use drained canned tomatoes during the winter months.

SERVES FOUR

1 Preheat the oven to 190°C/375°F/Gas 5. Put the cherry tomatoes in a small roasting pan and drizzle 30ml/2 tbsp of the olive oil over the top.

2 Season the tomatoes with salt and pepper and roast for 10–15 minutes, shaking the pan gently once or twice so that the tomatoes cook evenly on all sides. When they are tender and slightly charred, remove from the oven and set aside.

3 While the tomatoes are cooking, preheat the grill (broiler) to high. Brush the sardine fillets with the remaining oil and lay them on a baking sheet. Grill (broil) for 4–5 minutes on each side, until cooked through.

4 Split the focaccia in half horizontally and cut each piece in half to give four equal pieces. Toast the cut side under the grill. Top with the sardines and tomatoes and an extra drizzle of oil. Season with black pepper and serve.

20 cherry tomatoes

12 fresh sardine fillets

1 focaccia loaf

FROM THE STORECUPBOARD

45ml/3 tbsp olive oil

salt and ground black pepper, to taste

VARIATION *If you have some left-over boiled potatoes in the refrigerator, slice them and fry them in oil, then pile the sardines and tomatoes on top.*

Energy 301kcal/1262kJ; Protein 15.8g; Carbohydrate 27.6g, of which sugars 3.1g; Fat 15g, of which saturates 2.9g; Cholesterol 0mg; Calcium 106mg; Fibre 1.7g; Sodium 334mg

Creamy Chicken Livers with Toasted Baguette ✳

Cheap, versatile, nutritious and packed with flavour, chicken livers are a much under-rated ingredient. Here, they are combined with onion, garlic, sherry and cream and served with lightly toasted sliced baguette to make a quick-and-easy appetizer, light lunch or snack.

SERVES FOUR

1 Trim any green spots and sinews from the chicken livers. Heat the oil in a frying pan, then add the onion, garlic, chicken livers and thyme and fry for 3 minutes.

2 Stir the sherry into the pan, then add the cream and cook briefly to warm through.

3 Preheat the grill (broiler) and lightly toast the slices of baguette on both sides.

4 Season the liver mixture to taste with salt and pepper and add paprika. Garnish with fresh thyme and serve immediately with the toasted baguette.

225g/8oz chicken livers,
thawed if frozen, trimmed

1 small onion,
finely chopped

2 small garlic cloves,
finely chopped

5ml/1 tsp fresh
thyme leaves

30ml/2 tbsp sweet
oloroso sherry

30ml/2 tbsp crème fraîche
or double (heavy) cream

fresh thyme, to garnish

1 thin baguette, sliced
into 12, to serve

FROM THE STORECUPBOARD

15ml/1 tbsp olive oil

2.5ml/¹/₂ tsp paprika

salt and ground black
pepper, to taste

Energy 436kcal/1846kJ; Protein 21.1g; Carbohydrate 69.2g, of which sugars 4.9g; Fat 9.4g, of which saturates 3.2g; Cholesterol 222mg; Calcium 158mg; Fibre 3.1g; Sodium 785mg

Fried Black Pudding with Onions on Toast ✳

Black pudding is flavoured with spices and herbs, usually including garlic and oregano, and has a wonderfully rich, spicy taste. Often eaten as part of an English breakfast, it can also be used to make delectable savoury snacks that are perfect for serving as nibbles at a party.

SERVES FOUR

1 Heat the olive oil in a large frying pan, add the sliced onion, garlic, oregano and paprika and fry for 7–8 minutes until the onion is softened and has turned golden brown.

2 Add the slices of black pudding to the pan, then increase the heat and cook them for 3 minutes, without stirring. Turn them over carefully with a spatula and cook for a further 3 minutes, until crisp.

3 Arrange the rounds of bread on a large serving plate and top each with a slice of black pudding. Stir the sherry into the onions and add a little sugar to taste. Heat, swirling the mixture around the pan until bubbling, then season with salt and black pepper.

4 Spoon a little of the onion mixture on top of each slice of black pudding. Scatter the oregano over and serve.

1 onion, thinly sliced
into rings

2 garlic cloves, thinly sliced

225g/8oz black pudding
(blood sausage), cut into
12 thick slices

1 thin baguette,
sliced into 12

30ml/2 tbsp fino sherry

chopped fresh oregano,
to garnish

FROM THE STORECUPBOARD

15ml/1 tbsp olive oil

5ml/1 tsp dried oregano

5ml/1 tsp paprika

sugar, to taste

salt and ground black
pepper, to taste

Energy 506kcal/2137kJ; Protein 18.4g; Carbohydrate 77.8g, of which sugars 4.7g; Fat 14.8g, of which saturates 5.2g; Cholesterol 38mg; Calcium 171mg; Fibre 3.1g; Sodium 1422mg

Spicy Chickpea Samosas ✳

A blend of crushed chickpeas and coriander sauce makes an interesting alternative to the more familiar meat or vegetable fillings in these crisp little pastries. The samosas look pretty garnished with fresh coriander leaves and finely sliced onion and are delicious served with a simple dip such as Fresh Tomato Sauce, Hummus or a mixture of Greek (US strained plain) yogurt and chopped fresh mint leaves.

MAKES EIGHTEEN

1 Preheat the oven to 220°C/425°F/Gas 7. Process half the chickpeas to a paste in a food processor. Tip into a bowl and add the whole chickpeas, the hara masala or coriander sauce, and a little salt. Mix until well combined.

2 Cut a sheet of filo pastry into three strips. Brush with a little of the oil. Place 10ml/2 tsp of the filling at one end of a strip. Turn one corner diagonally over the filling to meet the long edge. Continue folding the filling and the pastry along the length of the strip, keeping the triangular shape.

3 Transfer to a baking sheet and repeat with the remaining filling and pastry. Brush with any remaining oil and bake for 15 minutes. Serve garnished with coriander and sliced red onion.

120ml/4fl oz/¹⁄₂ cup hara masala or coriander (cilantro) sauce

275g/10oz filo pastry

FROM THE STORECUPBOARD

2 x 400g/14oz cans chickpeas, drained and rinsed

**60ml/4 tbsp chilli and garlic oil
(*see* page 31)**

Energy 119kcal/499kJ; Protein 4.1g; Carbohydrate 13.7g, of which sugars 0.4g; Fat 5.7g, of which saturates 0.8g; Cholesterol 0mg; Calcium 36mg; Fibre 2.2g; Sodium 99mg

Red Onion and Goat's Cheese Pastries ✳

These attractive little tartlets couldn't be easier to make. Garnish them with fresh thyme sprigs and serve with a selection of salad leaves and a tomato and basil salad for a light lunch or quick supper. A wide variety of different types of goat's cheeses are available – the creamy log-shaped types without a rind are most suitable for these pastries. Ordinary onions can be used instead of red, if you prefer.

SERVES FOUR

1 Heat the oil in a large, heavy frying pan, add the onions and cook over a gentle heat for 10 minutes, or until softened, stirring occasionally to prevent them from browning.

2 Add seasoning to taste and cook for a further 2 minutes. Remove the pan from the heat and leave to cool.

3 Preheat the oven to 220°C/425°F/Gas 7. Roll out the puff pastry on a lightly floured board and cut out four rounds, using a 15cm/6in plate as a guide.

4 Place the pastry rounds on a dampened baking sheet and, using the point of a sharp knife, score a border, 2cm/³⁄₄in inside the edge of each pastry round.

5 Divide the cooked onions among the pastry rounds and top with the cubed goat's cheese.

6 Bake the pastries for 25–30 minutes, until the pastry is golden brown and the goat's cheese has melted. Serve immediately, garnished with thyme sprigs, if you like.

450g/1lb red onions, peeled and sliced

425g/15oz packet puff pastry

115g/4oz/1 cup goat's cheese, cubed

thyme sprigs, to garnish (optional)

FROM THE STORECUPBOARD

15ml/1 tbsp olive oil

salt and ground black pepper, to taste

Energy 554kcal/2308kJ; Protein 13.5g; Carbohydrate 48.5g, of which sugars 8g; Fat 36.4g, of which saturates 5.6g; Cholesterol 27mg; Calcium 128mg; Fibre 1.6g; Sodium 506mg

1 red (bell) pepper

1 yellow (bell) pepper

75g/3oz/6 tbsp chilled butter, diced

30–45ml/2–3 tbsp cold water

60ml/4 tbsp double (heavy) cream

1 egg

15ml/1 tbsp freshly grated grano padano cheese

FROM THE STORECUPBOARD

175g/6oz/1¹/₂ cups plain (all-purpose) flour

salt and ground black pepper, to taste

Pimiento Tartlets ✳

Originally from Spain, these pretty little tartlets are filled with strips of roasted sweet peppers and a deliciously creamy, cheesy custard. They make the perfect snack to serve with drinks.

SERVES FOUR

1 Preheat the oven to 200°C/400°F/Gas 6, and heat the grill (broiler). Place the peppers on a baking sheet and grill for 10 minutes, turning occasionally, until blackened. Cover with a dish towel and leave for 5 minutes. Peel away the skin, then discard the seeds and cut the flesh into very thin strips.

2 Sift the flour and a pinch of salt into a bowl. Add the butter and rub it in until the mixture resembles fine breadcrumbs. Stir in enough of the water to make a firm, not sticky, dough.

3 Roll the dough out on a floured surface and line 12 individual moulds or a 12-hole tartlet tin (muffin pan). Prick the bases and fill the pastry cases with crumpled foil. Bake for 10 minutes. Remove the foil from the pastry cases and divide the pepper strips among the pastry cases.

4 Whisk the cream and egg in a bowl. Season and pour over the peppers. Sprinkle with grano padano and bake for 20 minutes. Cool for 2 minutes, then transfer to a wire rack. Serve warm or cold.

VARIATIONS

• To ring the changes, you could use strips of grilled aubergine (eggplant) mixed with chopped sun-dried tomatoes, or drained and chopped marinated artichoke hearts, in place of the strips of roasted (bell) peppers.

• For an even cheesier flavour, add 30ml/2 tbsp finely grated grano padano cheese to the pastry mixture in step 2.

Energy 427kcal/1778kJ; Protein 8.4g; Carbohydrate 40g, of which sugars 6.4g; Fat 27g, of which saturates 16.1g; Cholesterol 112mg; Calcium 131mg; Fibre 2.8g; Sodium 180mg

Egg and Salmon Puff Parcels ✳

These elegant parcels hide a mouthwatering mixture of flavours, and make a delicious appetizer or lunch dish. Serve with curry-flavoured mayonnaise or hollandaise sauce and a green salad.

SERVES SIX

350g/12oz tail pieces of salmon

juice of 1/2 lemon

15ml/1 tbsp chopped fresh dill

15ml/1 tbsp chopped fresh parsley

6 small (US medium) eggs, soft-boiled and cooled

425g/15oz flaky or puff pastry, thawed if frozen

1 egg, beaten

FROM THE STORECUPBOARD

75g/3oz/scant 1/2 cup long grain rice, cooked according to pack instructions, cooled

300ml/1/2 pint/11/4 cups good-quality fish stock

10ml/2 tsp mild curry powder

salt and ground black pepper, to taste

VARIATIONS

• You could replace the hen's eggs with quail's eggs for a luxury touch.

• You could substitute trout for the salmon if you like.

• For a slightly nutty flavour, use brown rice in place of the long grain rice.

1 Preheat the oven to 220°C/425°F/Gas 7. Place the salmon in a large pan and cover with cold water. Gently heat until almost simmering and cook the fish for 8–10 minutes until it flakes easily.

2 Lift the salmon out of the pan and remove the bones and skin. Flake the fish into the cooled rice, add the lemon juice, herbs, curry powder and seasoning, and mix well. Shell the eggs.

3 Roll out the pastry and cut into six 15cm/6in squares. Brush the edges with the beaten egg. Place a spoonful of the rice mixture in the middle of each square, push an egg into the centre and top with a little more of the rice mixture.

4 Pull over the pastry corners to the middle to form a neat, square parcel, pressing the joins together with your fingers firmly to seal.

5 Brush the parcels with more beaten egg, place on a baking sheet and bake for 20 minutes, then reduce the oven temperature to 190°C/375°F/Gas 5. Cook for 10 minutes more, until golden and crisp. Cool slightly before serving.

Energy 494kcal/2063kJ; Protein 23.4g; Carbohydrate 36.9g, of which sugars 1.1g; Fat 29.7g, of which saturates 2.7g; Cholesterol 219mg; Calcium 112mg; Fibre 0.8g; Sodium 326mg

Flatbreads with Spicy Lamb and Tomato *

These flavoursome flatbreads make an ideal snack or appetizer. The thin crispy base is smeared with a layer of lightly spiced lamb and rolled into a cone with fresh parsley, sumac and a squeeze of lemon.

SERVES TWO–FOUR

1 Make the dough. Put the yeast and 2.5ml/^{1}/$_2$ tsp sugar into a small bowl with half the lukewarm water. Set aside for about 15 minutes until frothy.

2 Sift the flour and 2.5ml/^{1}/$_2$ tsp salt into a large bowl, make a well in the middle and add the creamed yeast and the rest of the lukewarm water. Using your hand, draw in the flour and work the mixture to a dough, adding more water if necessary.

3 Turn the dough on to a lightly floured surface and knead until it is smooth and elastic. Drip a few drops of sunflower oil into the base of the bowl and roll the dough in it. Cover the bowl with a damp dish towel and leave in a warm place for about 1 hour or until the dough has doubled in size.

4 Meanwhile, prepare the topping. Heat the oil and butter in a heavy pan and gently fry the onion and garlic until they soften. Leave to cool in the pan.

5 Put the lamb in a bowl, add the tomato purée, the remaining sugar, red pepper or chilli and mint, then the softened onion and garlic. Season with salt and pepper, and mix and knead with your hands. Cover with clear film (plastic wrap) and keep in the refrigerator until you are ready to use.

6 Place two baking sheets in the oven. Preheat the oven to 220°C/425°F/Gas 7.

7 Punch down the risen dough, knead it on a lightly floured surface, then divide into 2 or 4 equal pieces. Roll each piece into a thin flat round, stretching the dough with your hands as you roll.

8 Oil the hot baking sheets and place the rounds on them, then cover with a thin layer of meat mixture, spreading it right to the edges. Bake for 15–20 minutes, until the meat is nicely cooked.

9 As soon as the flatbreads are ready, sprinkle them with the sumac or paprika and parsley. Squeeze a little lemon juice over the top and roll them up while the dough is still pliable. Eat like a pizza, with your hands, or on plates with a knife and fork.

5ml/1 tsp active dried yeast

150ml/^{1}/$_4$ pint/^{2}/$_3$ cup lukewarm water

FOR THE TOPPING

15ml/1 tbsp butter

1 onion, finely chopped

2 garlic cloves, chopped

225g/8oz/1 cup finely minced (ground) lean lamb

5–10ml/1–2 tsp Turkish red pepper, or 1 fresh red chilli, finely chopped

5–10ml/1–2 tsp sumac or paprika

1 bunch of fresh flat leaf parsley, roughly chopped

1 lemon, halved

FROM THE STORECUPBOARD

17.5ml/3^1/$_2$ tsp sugar

350g/12oz/3 cups strong white bread flour

a few drops of sunflower oil

15ml/1 tbsp olive oil

30ml/2 tbsp tomato purée (paste)

5ml/1 tsp dried mint

salt and ground black pepper, to taste

Energy 496kcal/2092kJ; Protein 20g; Carbohydrate 75.2g, of which sugars 8.1g; Fat 14.9g, of which saturates 6.1g; Cholesterol 51mg; Calcium 167mg; Fibre 3.8g; Sodium 333mg

Golden Beef and Potato Puffs

These crisp, golden pillows of pastry filled with fragrant spiced beef and creamy mashed potato are delicious served piping hot, straight from the wok. The light, flaky pastry puffs up wonderfully in the hot oil and contrasts enticingly with the fragrant spiced beef within. Serve with tomato ketchup as a snack with drinks, or as an appealing appetizer for an informal dinner.

SERVES FOUR

1 Heat the oil in a wok or large, heavy pan, then add the onion, garlic, ginger and chilli. Stir-fry over a medium heat for 2–3 minutes. Add the curry powder and beef and stir-fry over a high heat for a further 4–5 minutes, or until the beef is browned and just cooked through, then remove from the heat.

2 Transfer the beef mixture to a large bowl and add the mashed potato and coriander. Stir well, then season and set aside.

3 Lay the pastry sheets on a clean, dry surface and cut out 8 rounds, using a 7.5cm/3in pastry (cookie) cutter. Place a large spoonful of the beef mixture in the centre of each pastry round. Brush the edges of the pastry with the beaten egg and fold each round in half to enclose the filling. Press and crimp the edges with the tines of a fork to seal.

4 Fill a wok one-third full of oil and heat to 180°C/350°F (or until a cube of bread, dropped into the oil, browns in 15 seconds). Deep-fry the puffs, in batches, for 2–3 minutes until puffed up and golden brown. Drain on kitchen paper, garnish with fresh coriander leaves and serve with tomato ketchup, for dipping.

¹/₂ small onion, finely chopped

3 garlic cloves, crushed

5ml/1 tsp finely grated fresh root ginger

1 red chilli, seeded and finely chopped

75g/3oz minced (ground) beef

115g/4oz mashed potato

60ml/4 tbsp chopped fresh coriander (cilantro)

2 sheets ready-rolled, puff pastry

1 egg, lightly beaten

fresh coriander leaves, to garnish

FROM THE STORECUPBOARD

15ml/1 tbsp sunflower oil

30ml/2 tbsp curry powder

vegetable oil, for frying

salt and ground black pepper, to taste

tomato ketchup, to serve

VARIATION *You can use ready-made shortcrust pastry in place of the puff pastry. The puffs will be transformed into little golden crescents with a firmer, crisper shell and the same beef filling.*

Energy 408kcal/1695kJ; Protein 9g; Carbohydrate 24.2g, of which sugars 1.8g; Fat 31.8g, of which saturates 4.2g; Cholesterol 67mg; Calcium 46mg; Fibre 0.5g; Sodium 202mg

Spiced Lamb Poppadums ✳

Crisp, melt-in-the-mouth mini poppadums make a great base for these divine little bites. Top them with a drizzle of yogurt and a spoonful of mango chutney, then serve immediately. To make an equally tasty variation, you can use chicken or pork in place of the lamb.

MAKES TWENTY FIVE

1 Heat the oil in a wok or large, heavy pan over a medium heat and add the shallots. Stir-fry for 4–5 minutes, until softened.

2 Add the curry paste, stir-fry for 1–2 minutes, then add the lamb. Stir-fry over a high heat for a further 4–5 minutes, then stir in the tomato purée, sugar and coconut cream.

3 Cook the lamb over a gentle heat for 25–30 minutes, or until the meat is tender and all the liquid has been absorbed.

4 Season to taste and stir in the lime juice and mint leaves. Remove from the heat and keep warm.

5 Fill a separate wok one-third full of oil and deep-fry the mini poppadums for 30–40 seconds, until puffed up and crisp. Drain on kitchen paper.

6 Place the poppadums on a serving platter. Put a spoonful of spiced lamb on each one, then top with a little yogurt and mango chutney. Serve immediately, garnished with slivers of red chilli and mint leaves.

4 shallots, finely chopped

300g/11oz minced (ground) lamb

200ml/7fl oz/scant 1 cup coconut cream

juice of 1 lime

60ml/4 tbsp chopped fresh mint leaves

25 mini poppadums

natural (plain) yogurt and mango chutney, to drizzle

red chilli slivers and mint leaves, to garnish

FROM THE STORECUPBOARD

30ml/2 tbsp sunflower oil

30ml/2 tbsp medium curry paste

90ml/6 tbsp tomato purée (paste)

5ml/1 tsp sugar

vegetable oil, for frying

salt and ground black pepper, to taste

Energy 63kcal/260kJ; Protein 2.7g; Carbohydrate 2.7g, of which sugars 1.3g; Fat 4.7g, of which saturates 1.4g; Cholesterol 9mg; Calcium 7mg; Fibre 0.3g; Sodium 45mg

Substantial Salads

WHETHER YOU WANT A LIGHT SALAD FOR A SUMMER LUNCH OR QUICK MEAL, OR A TASTY DISH FOR A HEALTHY SUPPER, THERE IS A SALAD HERE TO SUIT YOU. CHOOSE FROM SIMPLE SUMMER DISHES SUCH AS SALAD NIÇOISE, WATERMELON SALAD WITH FETA CHEESE OR MIXED VEGETABLE SALAD WITH AIOLI DRESSING, OR WHY NOT TRY SOMETHING MORE UNUSUAL, SUCH AS LENTIL AND SPINACH SALAD WITH ONIONS, CUMIN AND GARLIC, GADO GADO SALAD OR TANGY FISH SALAD?

Orange and Red Onion Salad ✳

Thinly sliced oranges can be used to make unusual and refreshing salads. In this Spanish version, the oranges are partnered with thinly sliced red onions and black olives, and flavoured with cumin seeds and mint.

SERVES SIX

1 Using a sharp knife, slice the oranges thinly, working over a bowl to catch any juice. Then, holding each orange slice in turn over the bowl, cut round the middle fleshy section with scissors to remove the peel and pith. Reserve the juice.

2 Slice the two red onions as thinly as possible and separate into individual rings.

3 Arrange the orange and onion slices in layers in a shallow dish, sprinkling each layer with cumin seeds, pepper, mint, olive oil and salt. Pour in the reserved orange juice.

4 Leave to marinate in a cool place for about 2 hours. Just before serving, scatter with the mint sprigs and black olives.

6 oranges

2 red onions

15ml/1 tbsp chopped fresh mint

fresh mint sprigs and black olives, to garnish

FROM THE STORECUPBOARD

15ml/1 tbsp cumin seeds

5ml/1 tsp coarsely ground black pepper

90ml/6 tbsp olive oil

salt, to taste

COOK'S TIP It is important to let the salad stand before serving. This allows the flavours to develop and the pungent taste of the onion to soften slightly.

Mixed Salad with Capers ✳✳

Colourful salads are a great start to a summer meal, and can be a communal affair, with everyone helping themselves with a fork from a large bowl placed in the middle of the table.

SERVES FOUR

1 To peel the tomatoes, place them in a heatproof bowl, cover with boiling water and leave to stand for 1 minute. Plunge into a bowl of cold water. Leave for 1 minute, then drain. Slip off the skins and dice the flesh finely. Put in a salad bowl.

2 Peel the cucumber, dice finely and add to the tomatoes. Trim and chop half the spring onions, and add to the bowl.

3 Toss the vegetables together, then break the watercress or rocket into sprigs. Add to the tomato mixture, with the olives and capers.

4 Make the dressing. Put the garlic in a bowl and mix in the vinegar and spices. Whisk in the oil and taste for seasoning.

5 Dress the salad, then garnish with the remaining spring onions.

4 large tomatoes

1/2 cucumber

1 bunch spring onions (scallions)

1 bunch watercress or rocket (arugula), washed

8 pimiento-stuffed olives

30ml/2 tbsp drained pickled capers

FROM THE STORECUPBOARD

1 garlic clove, crushed

30ml/2 tbsp red wine vinegar

5ml/1 tsp paprika

2.5ml/1/2 tsp ground cumin

75ml/5 tbsp virgin olive oil

salt and ground black pepper, to taste

Top: Energy 157kcal/652kJ; Protein 1.9g; Carbohydrate 12.8g, of which sugars 11.3g; Fat 11.3g, of which saturates 1.6g; Cholesterol 0mg; Calcium 70mg; Fibre 2.6g; Sodium 11mg

Above: Energy 162Kcal/670kJ; Protein 1.9g; Carbohydrate 4.3g, of which sugars 4.2g; Fat 15.4g, of which saturates 2.3g; Cholesterol 0mg; Calcium 49mg; Fibre 2g; Sodium 243mg

Watermelon Salad with Feta Cheese ✳✳

This delicious dish combines the contrasting flavours and textures of sweet and juicy watermelon with salty feta cheese, resulting in a stunning salad that is perfect for the hot summer months.

SERVES FOUR

1 Pour the extra virgin olive oil, lemon juice and vinegar into a bowl or jug (pitcher). Add the fresh thyme and ground cumin, and whisk until well combined. Set the dressing aside until you are ready to serve the salad.

2 Cut the rind off the watermelon and remove as many seeds as possible. Cut the flesh into triangular-shaped chunks.

3 Put the lettuce leaves in a bowl, pour over the dressing and toss together to combine thoroughly.

4 Arrange the leaves on a serving dish or individual plates and add the watermelon, feta cheese, pumpkin and sunflower seeds and black olives. Serve the salad immediately.

juice of 1/2 lemon

sprinkling of fresh thyme

4 large slices of watermelon, chilled

1 frisée lettuce, core removed

130g/4 1/2 oz feta cheese, preferably sheep's milk feta, cut into bitesize pieces

handful of lightly toasted pumpkin seeds

handful of sunflower seeds

10–15 black olives

FROM THE STORECUPBOARD

30–45ml/2–3 tbsp extra virgin olive oil

5ml/1 tsp vinegar of choice, or to taste

pinch of ground cumin

Energy 256kcal/1066kJ; Protein 7.7g; Carbohydrate 12.9g, of which sugars 11.6g; Fat 19.7g, of which saturates 6.2g; Cholesterol 23mg; Calcium 165mg; Fibre 1.4g; Sodium 616mg

This delicious and colourful salad can be made using any combination of chopped, cooked vegetables, such as broad (fava) beans, courgette (zucchini), marrow (large zucchini), aubergine (eggplant) turnip, parsnip, sweet potato or pumpkin. Use whatever is in season or is readily available.

8 new potatoes, scrubbed and quartered

1 large carrot, diced

115g/4oz fine green beans, cut into 2cm/³/₄ in lengths

75g/3oz/³/₄ cup peas

¹/₂ Spanish (Bermuda) onion, chopped

4 cornichons or small gherkins, sliced

1 small red (bell) pepper, seeded and diced

50g/2oz/¹/₂ cup pitted black olives

15ml/1 tbsp drained pickled capers

15ml/1 tbsp freshly squeezed lemon juice

30ml/2 tbsp chopped fresh fennel or parsley, to garnish

FOR THE AIOLI

2 garlic cloves, finely chopped

150ml/¹/₄ pint/²/₃ cup mayonnaise

FROM THE STORECUPBOARD

salt and ground black pepper, to taste

Mixed Vegetable Salad with Aioli Dressing ✳

This colourful salad, often called Russian salad, contains a range of diced summer vegetables, including new potatoes, green beans, peas and red pepper, which are tossed in a pungent aioli dressing.

SERVES FOUR

1 Make the aioli. Crush the garlic with a pinch of salt in a mortar and whisk or stir into the mayonnaise.

2 Cook the potatoes and diced carrot in a pan of boiling lightly salted water for 5–8 minutes, until almost tender. Add the beans and peas to the pan and cook for 2 minutes, or until all the vegetables are tender. Drain well.

3 Tip the vegetables into a large bowl. Add the onion, cornichons or gherkins, red pepper, olives and capers. Stir in the aioli and season to taste with pepper and lemon juice.

4 Toss the vegetables and aioli together until well combined, check the seasoning and chill well. Serve garnished with fennel or parsley.

Energy 395kcal/1636kJ; Protein 5.2g; Carbohydrate 25.6g, of which sugars 8.1g; Fat 30.9g, of which saturates 4.8g; Cholesterol 28mg; Calcium 68mg; Fibre 4.9g; Sodium 472mg

Beetroot Salad with Oranges and Cinnamon ✳

The combination of sweet beetroot, zesty orange and warm cinnamon is both unusual and delicious, and this dish makes a healthy light meal served with some warm, crusty bread to mop up the vibrant juices.

SERVES SIX

1 Quarter the cooked beetroot, then slice the quarters. Arrange the beetroot on a plate with the orange slices or toss them together in a bowl.

2 Gently heat the orange flower water with the sugar, stir in the cinnamon and season to taste. Pour over the beetroot and orange salad and chill for at least 1 hour before serving.

675g/1¹⁄₂ lb beetroot (beet), steamed or boiled, then peeled

1 orange, peeled and sliced

30ml/2 tbsp orange flower water

FROM THE STORECUPBOARD

15ml/1 tbsp sugar

5ml/1 tsp ground cinnamon

salt and ground black pepper, to taste

Energy 58kcal/247kJ; Protein 2.2g; Carbohydrate 12.9g, of which sugars 12.2g; Fat 0.1g, of which saturates 0g; Cholesterol 0mg; Calcium 33mg; Fibre 2.5g; Sodium 75mg

Grated Beetroot Salad with Yogurt and Garlic *

The earthy flavour of beetroot is perfectly balanced by creamy yogurt and a hint of garlic in this stunning and simple salad. It is delicious served on its own with pitta bread, or as an accompaniment to grilled meat or chicken.

SERVES FOUR

1 Add the beetroot to a large pan of boiling water and cook for 35–40 minutes until tender, but the flesh is not soft or mushy.

2 Drain in a sieve (strainer) and refresh immediately under cold running water to prevent it from cooking further.

3 Peel off the skins and grate the beetroot on to a plate. Squeeze it with your fingers to drain off excess water.

4 In a bowl, beat the yogurt with the garlic and season to taste with salt and pepper.

5 Add the beetroot, reserving a little to garnish the top, and mix well. Garnish with mint leaves.

4 raw beetroot (beets), washed and trimmed

500g/1¹/₄lb/2¹/₄ cups thick and creamy natural (plain) yogurt

2 garlic cloves, crushed

a few fresh mint leaves, shredded, to garnish

FROM THE STORECUPBOARD

salt and ground black pepper, to taste

Energy 95kcal/403kJ; Protein 7.8g; Carbohydrate 14.4g, of which sugars 13g; Fat 1.4g, of which saturates 0.6g; Cholesterol 2mg; Calcium 249mg; Fibre 1.3g; Sodium 137mg

Warm Salad with Poached Eggs ✳✳

Soft poached eggs, chilli oil, hot croûtons and cool, crisp salad leaves make a lively and unusual combination. This delicious salad will provide a sustaining lunch or supper, served with bread.

SERVES TWO

1 Heat the chilli oil in a large, heavy frying pan. Add the cubes of bread and cook for 5 minutes, tossing the cubes occasionally, until they are crisp and golden. Remove from the pan and drain on a sheet of kitchen paper.

2 Bring a large pan of water to a gentle boil. Break each egg into a jug (pitcher) and slide it carefully into the water. Poach for 3–4 minutes.

3 Meanwhile, divide the salad leaves equally between two small serving plates. Scatter the croûtons over the mixed salad leaves.

4 Wipe the frying pan clean, then add the olive oil and heat gently. Add the crushed garlic and balsamic or sherry vinegar and cook over a high heat for about 1 minute, stirring occasionally. Pour the warm dressing over the salad leaves.

5 Remove the poached eggs from the pan with a slotted spoon, and pat them dry on kitchen paper. Place one egg on top of each plate of salad, then top with shavings of fresh grano padano cheese and season with black pepper. Serve immediately.

1 slice wholegrain bread, crusts removed and cubed

2 eggs

115g/4oz mixed salad leaves

2 garlic cloves, crushed

50g/2oz grano padano cheese, shaved

FROM THE STORECUPBOARD

25ml/1¹/₂ tbsp chilli oil

45ml/3 tbsp extra virgin olive oil

15ml/1 tbsp balsamic or sherry vinegar

ground black pepper

Energy 697kcal/2907kJ; Protein 25.9g; Carbohydrate 41.3g, of which sugars 2.8g; Fat 49g, of which saturates 11.5g; Cholesterol 215mg; Calcium 408mg; Fibre 6.3g; Sodium 914mg

225g/8oz new potatoes, scrubbed and halved

2 carrots, cut into sticks

115g/4oz green beans

$^1/_2$ small cauliflower, broken into florets

$^1/_4$ firm white cabbage, shredded

200g/7oz bean or lentil sprouts

4 eggs, hard-boiled and quartered

small bunch of watercress (optional)

FOR THE SAUCE

90ml/6 tbsp crunchy peanut butter

300ml/$^1/_2$ pint/1$^1/_4$ cups cold water

1 garlic clove, crushed

15ml/1 tbsp dry sherry

15ml/1 tbsp fresh lemon juice

5ml/1 tsp anchovy essence (extract)

FROM THE STORECUPBOARD

30ml/2 tbsp dark soy sauce

10ml/2 tsp caster (superfine) sugar

COOK'S TIP
There is a range of nut butters available in health-food stores and supermarkets. Alternatively, you can make your own peanut butter by blending 225g/8oz/2 cups peanuts with 120ml/4fl oz/$^1/_2$ cup oil in a food processor.

Gado Gado Salad ✳

This Indonesian salad combines steamed vegetables and hard-boiled eggs with a richly flavoured peanut and soy sauce dressing.

SERVES SIX

1 Place the halved potatoes in a metal colander or steamer and set over a pan of gently boiling water. Cover the pan or steamer with a lid and cook the potatoes for 10 minutes.

2 Add the rest of the vegetables to the steamer and steam for a further 10 minutes, until tender.

3 Cool and arrange on a platter with the egg quarters and the watercress, if using.

4 Beat together the peanut butter, water, garlic, sherry, lemon juice, anchovy essence, soy sauce and sugar in a large mixing bowl until smooth. Drizzle a little sauce over each portion then pour the rest into a small bowl and serve separately.

Energy 235kcal/979kJ; Protein 12.7g; Carbohydrate 18.3g, of which sugars 10.6g; Fat 12.5g, of which saturates 3.2g; Cholesterol 127mg; Calcium 91mg; Fibre 4.8g; Sodium 494mg

Fried Egg Salad ✳✳

Chillies and eggs may seem unlikely partners, but they actually work very well together. The peppery flavour of the watercress complements the spicy eggs perfectly in this tasty and unusual salad.

SERVES TWO

1 Heat the oil in a frying pan. Add the garlic and cook over a low heat until it starts to turn golden. Crack in the eggs. Break the yolks with a wooden spatula, then fry until the eggs are almost firm. Remove from the pan and set aside.

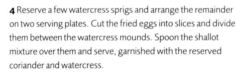

2 Mix the shallots, chillies, cucumber and ginger in a bowl. In a separate bowl, whisk the lime juice with the soy sauce and sugar. Pour this dressing over the vegetables and toss lightly.

3 Set aside a few coriander sprigs for the garnish. Chop the rest and add them to the salad. Toss it again.

4 Reserve a few watercress sprigs and arrange the remainder on two serving plates. Cut the fried eggs into slices and divide them between the watercress mounds. Spoon the shallot mixture over them and serve, garnished with the reserved coriander and watercress.

1 garlic clove, thinly sliced

4 eggs

2 shallots, thinly sliced

2 small fresh red chillies, seeded and thinly sliced

$^1/_2$ small cucumber, finely diced

1cm/$^1/_2$ in piece fresh root ginger, peeled and grated

juice of 2 limes

small bunch coriander (cilantro)

bunch watercress, coarsely chopped

FROM THE STORECUPBOARD

15ml/1 tbsp groundnut (peanut) oil

30ml/2 tbsp soy sauce

5ml/1 tsp caster (superfine) sugar

Energy 235kcal/977kJ; Protein 14.8g; Carbohydrate 6.4g, of which sugars 5.6g; Fat 17.2g, of which saturates 3.9g; Cholesterol 381mg; Calcium 154mg; Fibre 1.2g; Sodium 1234mg

2 aubergines (eggplant)

30ml/2 tbsp dried shrimp, soaked in warm water for 10 minutes

15ml/1 tbsp coarsely chopped garlic

1 hard-boiled egg, chopped

4 shallots, thinly sliced into rings

fresh coriander (cilantro) leaves and 2 fresh red chillies, seeded and sliced, to garnish

FOR THE DRESSING

30ml/2 tbsp fresh lime juice

FROM THE STORECUPBOARD

5ml/1 tsp light muscovado (brown) sugar

30ml/2 tbsp Thai fish sauce

15ml/1 tbsp vegetable oil

Aubergine Salad with Egg *

This appetizing and unusual salad combines grilled aubergines, salty shrimp, hard-boiled eggs and sweet shallots with a zesty lime dressing and slivers of spicy red chilli. It makes an ideal appetizer or light lunch.

SERVES FOUR–SIX

VARIATIONS
- For a special occasion, use salted duck's or quail's eggs, cut in half, instead of hen's eggs.

- If you don't like spicy food, omit the chilli.

1 Preheat the grill (broiler) to medium. Prick the aubergines several times with a skewer, then arrange on a baking sheet. Cook them under the grill for 30–40 minutes, or until they are charred and tender. Remove the aubergines and set aside until they are cool enough to handle.

2 Meanwhile, make the dressing. Put the lime juice, muscovado sugar and fish sauce into a small bowl. Whisk, then cover with clear film (plastic wrap) and set aside until required.

3 When the aubergines are cool enough to handle, peel off the skin and cut the flesh into medium slices.

4 Heat the oil in a small frying pan. Drain the dried shrimp thoroughly and add them to the pan with the garlic. Cook over a medium heat for about 3 minutes, until golden. Remove from the pan and set aside.

5 Arrange the aubergine slices on a serving dish. Top with the hard-boiled egg, shallots and dried shrimp mixture. Drizzle over the dressing and garnish with the coriander and red chillies.

Energy 58kcal/242kJ; Protein 4.6g; Carbohydrate 3.1g, of which sugars 2.8g; Fat 3.2g, of which saturates 0.6g; Cholesterol 57mg; Calcium 74mg; Fibre 1.5g; Sodium 230mg

Spiced Aubergine Salad with Yogurt and Parsley ✳

The delicate flavours of aubergine, tomatoes and cucumber are lightly spiced with cumin and coriander in this fresh-tasting salad. Make it in the summer, when the vegetables are at their best, and serve with bread.

SERVES FOUR

1 Preheat the grill (broiler). Lightly brush the aubergine slices with olive oil and cook them under a high heat, turning once, until they are golden and tender. Alternatively, cook them on a griddle pan.

2 When they are done, remove the aubergine slices to a chopping board and cut them into quarters.

3 Mix together the remaining oil, the vinegar, garlic, lemon juice, cumin and coriander. Season with salt and pepper to taste and mix thoroughly.

4 Add the warm aubergines to the bowl, stir well and chill for at least 2 hours. Add the cucumber and tomatoes.

5 Transfer to a serving dish and spoon the yogurt on top. Sprinkle with parsley and serve with warm crusty bread.

2 small aubergines (eggplants), sliced

2 garlic cloves, crushed

15ml/1 tbsp lemon juice

$^1/_2$ cucumber, thinly sliced

2 well-flavoured tomatoes, thinly sliced

30ml/2 tbsp natural (plain) yogurt

chopped fresh flat leaf parsley, to garnish

FROM THE STORECUPBOARD

75ml/5 tbsp extra virgin olive oil

50ml/2fl oz/$^1/_4$ cup red wine vinegar

2.5ml/$^1/_2$ tsp ground cumin

2.5ml/$^1/_2$ tsp ground coriander

salt and ground black pepper, to taste

Energy 155kcal/642kJ; Protein 1.9g; Carbohydrate 4.9g, of which sugars 4.7g; Fat 14.4g, of which saturates 2.2g; Cholesterol 0mg; Calcium 35mg; Fibre 2.7g; Sodium 14mg

Roasted Shallot and Squash Salad with Feta ✳

This sustaining salad combines sweet chunks of squash and roasted shallots with salty feta cheese and spicy red chillies. It is especially good for lunch, served with plenty of crusty bread to mop up the juices.

SERVES FOUR–SIX

1 Preheat the oven to 200°C/400°F/Gas 6. Beat the olive oil, balsamic vinegar and soy sauce together in a large bowl, then season to taste with a little salt and plenty of freshly ground black pepper.

2 Toss the shallots and two of the chillies in the oil mixture and tip into a large roasting pan or ovenproof dish. Roast in the oven for 15 minutes, stirring once or twice.

3 Add the squash and roast for a further 30–35 minutes, stirring once, until the squash is tender and browned. Remove from the oven, stir in the thyme and leave to cool.

4 Chop the parsley and garlic together and mix with the walnuts. Seed and finely chop the remaining chilli.

5 Stir the parsley, garlic and walnut mixture into the vegetables. Add chopped chilli to taste and adjust the seasoning, adding a little extra balsamic vinegar, if you like. Crumble the feta and add to the salad. Transfer to a serving dish and serve immediately.

350g/12oz shallots, peeled but left whole

3 fresh red chillies

1 butternut squash, peeled, seeded and cut into chunks

5ml/1 tsp finely chopped fresh thyme

15g/1/2oz flat leaf parsley

1 small garlic clove, finely chopped

75g/3oz/3/4 cup walnuts, roughly chopped

150g/5oz feta cheese

FROM THE STORECUPBOARD

75ml/5 tbsp olive oil

15ml/1 tbsp balsamic vinegar, plus a little extra, if you like

15ml/1 tbsp sweet soy sauce

salt and ground black pepper, to taste

Energy 275kcal/1136kJ; Protein 7.7g; Carbohydrate 9.3g, of which sugars 7g; Fat 23.2g, of which saturates 5.6g; Cholesterol 18mg; Calcium 165mg; Fibre 2.9g; Sodium 541mg

Hot and Sour Noodle Salad ✳✳

Noodles make the perfect basis for a salad, absorbing the dressing and providing a contrast in texture to the crisp vegetables. Here, they are served with a piquant sauce made from chillies, lime juice and soy sauce.

SERVES TWO

1 Bring a large pan of lightly salted water to the boil. Snap the rice noodles into short lengths, add to the pan and cook for 3–4 minutes. Drain, then rinse under cold water and drain again.

2 Set aside a few coriander leaves for the garnish. Chop the remaining leaves and place them in a large serving bowl.

3 Add the noodles to the bowl, with the tomato slices, corn cobs, spring onions, red pepper, lime juice, chillies, sugar and toasted peanuts. Season with the soy sauce, then taste and add a little salt if you think the mixture needs it.

4 Toss the salad lightly but thoroughly, then garnish with the reserved coriander leaves and serve immediately.

small bunch fresh coriander (cilantro)

2 tomatoes, seeded and sliced

130g/4¹/₂oz baby corn cobs, sliced

4 spring onions (scallions), thinly sliced

1 red (bell) pepper, seeded and finely chopped

juice of 2 limes

2 small fresh green chillies, seeded and finely chopped

115g/4oz/1 cup peanuts, toasted and chopped

FROM THE STORECUPBOARD

200g/7oz thin rice noodles

10ml/2 tsp sugar

30ml/2 tbsp soy sauce

salt, to taste

Energy 783kcal/3269kJ; Protein 24.7g; Carbohydrate 106.4g, of which sugars 20.4g; Fat 27.9g, of which saturates 5.2g; Cholesterol 0mg; Calcium 129mg; Fibre 8.5g; Sodium 1845mg

450g/1lb firm rectangular tofu, rinsed, patted dry and cut into blocks

1 small cucumber, partially peeled in strips, seeded and shredded

2 spring onions (scallions), trimmed, halved and shredded

2 handfuls of fresh beansprouts rinsed and drained

fresh coriander (cilantro) leaves, to garnish

FOR THE SAUCE

30ml/2 tbsp tamarind pulp, soaked in water until soft

4 shallots, finely chopped

4 garlic cloves, chopped

2 red chillies, seeded

2.5ml/¹/₂ tsp shrimp paste

115g/4oz/1 cup roasted peanuts, crushed

30–45ml/2–3 tbsp kecap manis

FROM THE STORECUPBOARD

vegetable oil, for deep-frying

15ml/1 tbsp sesame or groundnut (peanut) oil

15ml/1 tbsp tomato ketchup

Fried Tofu Salad ✳

Tofu is extremely nutritious and is ideal for use in salads made with strong flavours, such as spring onions, coriander, garlic and chilli. This delicious Asian version can be served on its own or with stir-fried noodles.

SERVES FOUR

1 First make the sauce. Squeeze the tamarind pulp to soften it in the water, and then strain through a sieve (strainer). Measure out 120ml/4fl oz/¹/₂ cup tamarind pulp.

2 Heat the oil in a wok or heavy pan, add the shallots, garlic and chillies, and cook until fragrant. Stir in the shrimp paste and the peanuts, and cook until they emit a nutty aroma. Add the kecap manis, tomato ketchup and tamarind pulp and blend to form a thick sauce. Set aside and leave to cool.

3 Heat enough oil for deep-frying to 180°C/350°F in a wok or heavy pan. Slip in the blocks of tofu and fry until golden brown all over. Pat dry on kitchen paper and cut each block into slices.

4 Arrange on a plate with the cucumber, spring onions and beansprouts. Drizzle over the sauce and garnish with coriander.

Energy 423kcal/1749kJ; Protein 17.9g; Carbohydrate 7.8g, of which sugars 4.5g; Fat 35.8g, of which saturates 5.3g; Cholesterol 0mg; Calcium 607mg; Fibre 2.8g; Sodium 296mg

Grilled Aubergine, Mint and Couscous Salad ✳

Packets of flavoured couscous are available in most supermarkets – you can use whichever you like, but garlic and coriander is particularly good for this recipe. Serve with a crisp green salad.

SERVES TWO

1 Preheat the grill (broiler) to high. Cut the aubergine into large chunky pieces and toss them with the olive oil.

2 Season with salt and pepper to taste and spread the aubergine pieces on a non-stick baking sheet.

3 Grill the aubergine pieces for 5–6 minutes, turning occasionally, until they are golden brown.

4 Meanwhile, prepare the couscous according to the instructions on the packet.

5 Stir the grilled aubergine and chopped mint into the couscous, toss thoroughly and serve immediately with a crisp green salad.

1 large aubergine (eggplant)

110g/4oz packet flavoured couscous

30ml/2 tbsp chopped fresh mint

FROM THE STORECUPBOARD

30ml/2 tbsp olive oil

salt and ground black pepper, to taste

Energy 251kcal/1044kJ; Protein 4.8g; Carbohydrate 32.5g, of which sugars 2g; Fat 12.1g, of which saturates 1.7g; Cholesterol 0mg; Calcium 53mg; Fibre 2g; Sodium 5mg

Quinoa Salad with Zesty Citrus Dressing ✳

Quinoa is quick to prepare and reasonably priced. It is packed with protein and is also gluten free, making it ideal for those with intolerances. Here it is combined with strong flavours, including chilli and citrus juice.

SERVES SIX

1 Put the quinoa in a sieve (strainer), rinse thoroughly under cold water, then tip into a large pan. Pour in enough cold water to cover and bring to the boil. Lower the heat and simmer for 10–12 minutes, until tender. Drain and leave to cool.

2 Make a dressing by whisking the oil with the citrus juices. Stir in the chillies and garlic and season with salt to taste.

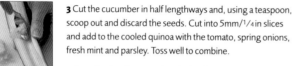

3 Cut the cucumber in half lengthways and, using a teaspoon, scoop out and discard the seeds. Cut into 5mm/¹⁄₄ in slices and add to the cooled quinoa with the tomato, spring onions, fresh mint and parsley. Toss well to combine.

4 Pour the dressing over the salad and toss again until well mixed. Check the seasoning and serve.

175g/6oz/1 cup quinoa

juice of 2 limes

juice of 1 large orange

2 fresh green chillies, seeded and finely chopped

2 garlic cloves, crushed

¹⁄₂ cucumber, peeled

1 large tomato, seeded and cubed

4 spring onions (scallions), sliced

30ml/2 tbsp chopped fresh mint

15ml/1 tbsp chopped fresh flat leaf parsley

FROM THE STORECUPBOARD

90ml/6 tbsp olive oil

salt, to taste

Energy 213kcal/885kJ; Protein 3.4g; Carbohydrate 24.3g, of which sugars 2g; Fat 11.6g, of which saturates 1.6g; Cholesterol 0mg; Calcium 26mg; Fibre 0.5g; Sodium 5mg

1 bunch spring onions
(scallions), finely sliced

1 green (bell) pepper,
seeded and finely diced

1 yellow (bell) pepper,
seeded and finely diced

225g/8oz tomatoes, peeled,
seeded and chopped

30ml/2 tbsp chopped
fresh flat leaf parsley or
coriander (cilantro)

FROM THE STORECUPBOARD

275g/10oz/1¹/₂ cups long
grain rice

75ml/5 tbsp mixed olive oil
and extra virgin olive oil

15ml/1 tbsp sherry vinegar

5ml/1 tsp strong
Dijon mustard

salt and ground black
pepper, to taste

Simple Rice Salad ✳

Sometimes called confetti salad, this stunning dish features brightly
coloured chopped vegetables served in a well-flavoured dressing.
It makes an ideal light lunch at home or at a picnic.

SERVES SIX

1 Cook the rice in a large pan of lightly salted boiling water for
10–12 minutes, until tender but still al dente. Be careful not to
overcook it.

2 Drain the rice well in a sieve (strainer), rinse thoroughly under
cold running water and drain again. Leave the rice to cool.

3 Make the dressing by whisking together the olive oil, sherry
vinegar and mustard in a small bowl. Transfer the rice to a large
bowl, add half the dressing, stir to moisten the rice, then leave
to cool further.

4 Add the spring onions, peppers, tomatoes and parsley or
coriander with the remaining dressing, and toss well to mix.
Season with salt and pepper to taste.

COOK'S TIP To peel the tomatoes,
place them in a heatproof
bowl, cover with boiling
water and leave to stand
for 1 minute. Plunge into a
bowl of cold water. Leave
for 1 minute, then drain.
Slip off the skins, then
slice them in half, scoop
out the seeds and dice.

Energy 276kcal/1150kJ; Protein 4.6g; Carbohydrate 41.9g, of which sugars 5.2g; Fat 9.9g, of which saturates 1.4g; Cholesterol 0mg; Calcium 29mg; Fibre 1.7g; Sodium 8mg

Thai Rice Salad ✳

The sky's the limit with this recipe. Use whatever fruit, vegetables and even left-over meat that you might have, mix with cooked rice and pour over the fragrant dressing.

SERVES FOUR–SIX

1 Asian pear, cored
and diced

50g/2oz dried
shrimp, chopped

1 avocado, peeled, stoned
(pitted) and diced

1/2 medium cucumber,
finely diced

2 lemon grass stalks,
finely chopped

1 fresh green or red chilli,
seeded and finely sliced

115g/4oz/1 cup flaked
(sliced) almonds, toasted

small bunch fresh coriander
(cilantro), chopped

fresh Thai sweet basil
leaves, to garnish

FOR THE DRESSING

300ml/1/2 pint/1 1/4 cups
water

10ml/2 tsp shrimp paste

2 kaffir lime leaves,
torn into small pieces

1/2 lemon grass
stalk, sliced

FROM THE STORECUPBOARD

15ml/1 tbsp light
muscovado (brown) sugar

350g/12oz/3 cups
cooked rice

30ml/2 tbsp sweet
chilli sauce

1 Make the dressing. Put the measured water in a small pan with the shrimp paste, sugar, kaffir lime leaves and lemon grass. Heat gently, stirring, until the sugar dissolves, then bring to boiling point and simmer for 5 minutes. Strain into a bowl and set aside until cold.

2 Put the cooked rice in a large salad bowl and fluff up the grains with a fork. Add the Asian pear, dried shrimp, avocado, cucumber, lemon grass and sweet chilli sauce. Mix well.

3 Add the diced chilli, almonds and coriander to the bowl and toss well. Garnish with Thai basil leaves and serve with the bowl of dressing to spoon over the top of individual portions.

Energy 125kcal/523kJ; Protein 2.6g; Carbohydrate 20.9g, of which sugars 1.4g; Fat 4.1g, of which saturates 0.6g; Cholesterol 0mg; Calcium 38mg; Fibre 1.3g; Sodium 7mg

Bulgur Salad ✳

This Turkish *meze* dish of bulgur and tomato is easy to make and very tasty. Packed with fresh mint and parsley, it is both filling and refreshing. It is good served at room temperature as part of a buffet or barbecue spread, with lemon wedges for squeezing over it.

SERVES FOUR–SIX

1 Put the bulgur into a wide bowl, pour over enough boiling water to cover it by about 2.5cm/1in, and give it a quick stir.

2 Cover the bowl with a plate or pan lid and leave the bulgur to steam for about 25 minutes, until it has soaked up the water and doubled in quantity.

3 Pour the oil and lemon juice over the bulgur and toss to mix, then add the tomato purée and toss the mixture again until the bulgur is well coated.

4 Add the sugar, onion, Turkish red pepper or chillies, and the herbs. Season with salt and pepper. Serve at room temperature, garnished with a little mint and parsley.

juice of 1–2 lemons

1 large or 2 small red onions, cut in half lengthways, in half again crossways, and sliced along the grain

10ml/2 tsp Turkish red pepper, or 1–2 fresh red chillies, seeded and finely chopped

1 bunch each of fresh mint and flat leaf parsley, finely chopped

a few fresh mint and parsley leaves, to garnish

FROM THE STORECUPBOARD

175g/6oz/1 cup bulgur wheat, rinsed and drained

45–60ml/3–4 tbsp olive oil

30ml/2 tbsp tomato purée (paste)

10ml/2 tsp sugar

salt and ground black pepper, to taste

COOK'S TIP *This salad should be light and lemony, packed full of the refreshing flavours of parsley and mint, with a slight tang of chilli, so be liberal with these ingredients. The sugar intensifies the tomato flavour of the purée.*

VARIATION *Substitute the juice of sour pomegranates in place of lemon juice and add extra hot red pepper to the mixture. To offset the added spice, mould the mixture into small balls and serve wrapped in individual lettuce leaves.*

Energy 149kcal/620kJ; Protein 3g; Carbohydrate 21.6g, of which sugars 5.4g; Fat 6.1g, of which saturates 0.8g; Cholesterol 0mg; Calcium 54mg; Fibre 1.7g; Sodium 19mg

1 large bunch spring
onions (scallions),
thinly sliced

1 cucumber, finely
chopped or diced

3 tomatoes, chopped

1 large bunch fresh
parsley, chopped

1 large bunch fresh
mint, chopped

juice of 2 lemons,
or to taste

cos or romaine lettuce
and natural (plain) yogurt,
to serve (optional)

6 olives, lemon wedges,
tomato wedges, cucumber
slices and mint sprigs,
to garnish (optional)

FROM THE STORECUPBOARD

**250g/9oz/1¹/₂ cups
bulgur wheat**

**1.5–2.5ml/¹/₄–¹/₂ tsp
ground cumin**

**30ml/2 tbsp extra virgin
olive oil**

salt, to taste

VARIATION *You can use couscous
soaked in boiling water in
place of the bulgur wheat
and use chopped fresh
coriander (cilantro)
instead of the parsley.*

Tabbouleh ✳

This is a wonderfully refreshing, tangy salad of soaked bulgur wheat and
masses of fresh mint, parsley and spring onions. Feel free to increase the
amount of herbs for a greener salad. It can be served as an appetizer or as
an accompaniment to a main course of grilled meat or fish.

SERVES FOUR–SIX

1 Pick over the bulgur wheat to remove any dirt. Place it in
a bowl, cover with cold water and leave to soak for about
30 minutes. Tip the bulgur wheat into a sieve (strainer) and drain,
shaking to remove any excess water, then return it to the bowl.

2 Add the spring onions to the bulgur wheat, then mix and
squeeze together with your hands to combine.

3 Add the cucumber, tomatoes, cumin, parsley, mint, lemon
juice, oil and salt to the bulgur wheat and toss to combine.

4 Heap the tabbouleh on to a bed of lettuce and garnish with
olives, lemon wedges, tomato, cucumber and mint sprigs.
Serve with a bowl of natural yogurt, if you like.

Energy 232kcal/965kJ; Protein 5.2g; Carbohydrate 34.6g, of which sugars 2.7g; Fat 8.4g, of which saturates 1.1g; Cholesterol 0mg; Calcium 51mg; Fibre 1.4g; Sodium 12mg

White Beans with Green Peppers in Spicy Dressing ✳

Tender white beans are delicious served in a spicy sauce with the bite of fresh, crunchy green pepper. Using canned beans means that the salad is very quick and easy to make. Satisfying and flavoursome, it is perfect for eating with some wedges of pitta bread for lunch or at a picnic.

SERVES FOUR

1 Finely chop the tomatoes, onion, mild chilli, green pepper and garlic cloves, then place in a large bowl. Add the sugar, drained cannellini beans, salt and plenty of ground black pepper and toss together until everything is well combined.

2 Add the olive oil, grated lemon rind, lemon juice and vinegar to the salad and toss lightly to combine.

3 For the best flavour, cover the bowl with clear film (plastic wrap) and chill in the refrigerator for at least an hour, to allow the flavours to mingle and intensify. Cut the pitta bread into wedges.

4 Serve garnished with chopped fresh parsley and wedges of pitta bread.

750g/1lb 10oz tomatoes

1 onion

1/2–1 mild fresh chilli

1 green (bell) pepper

4 garlic cloves

grated rind and juice of 1 lemon

chopped fresh parsley, to garnish

pitta bread, to serve

FROM THE STORECUPBOARD

pinch of sugar

400g/14oz can cannellini beans, drained

45–60ml/3–4 tbsp olive oil

15ml/1 tbsp cider vinegar or wine vinegar

salt and ground black pepper, to taste

Energy 226kcal/947kJ; Protein 8.8g; Carbohydrate 27.6g, of which sugars 12.9g; Fat 9.6g, of which saturates 1.5g; Cholesterol 0mg; Calcium 92mg; Fibre 9g; Sodium 409mg

Bean Salad with Red Onion, Eggs, Olives and Anchovies ✳

Colourful, good value for money and packed with flavour, this versatile salad can be made with a wide range of beans, including haricot, soya, borlotti or black-eyed beans – whatever you have in your storecupboard. It makes a nutritious snack or light meal when served with crusty bread, or it can be used as an accompaniment to grilled, broiled or barbecued meat or fish.

SERVES FOUR

1 red onion, cut in half lengthways, in half again crossways, and sliced along the grain

45–60ml/3–4 tbsp black olives, drained

1 bunch of fresh flat leaf parsley, roughly chopped

juice of 1 lemon

3–4 eggs, boiled until just firm, shelled and quartered

12 canned or bottled anchovy fillets, rinsed and drained

lemon wedges, to serve

FROM THE STORECUPBOARD

225g/8oz/1¼ cups dried haricot (navy), soya or black-eyed beans (peas), soaked in cold water for at least 6 hours or overnight

60ml/4 tbsp olive oil

salt and ground black pepper, to taste

1 Drain the beans, tip them into a pan and fill the pan with plenty of cold water. Bring to the boil and boil for 1 minute, then lower the heat and partially cover the pan. Simmer the beans for about 45 minutes, until they are cooked but still firm – they should have a bite to them, and not be soft and mushy.

2 Drain the beans, rinse well under cold running water and remove any loose skins.

3 Mix the beans in a wide shallow bowl with the onion, olives and most of the parsley. Toss in the oil and lemon juice, and season with salt and pepper.

4 Place the eggs and anchovy fillets on top of the salad and sprinkle with the remaining parsley. Serve with lemon wedges for squeezing.

Energy 402kcal/1674kJ; Protein 28g; Carbohydrate 10.4g, of which sugars 4.2g; Fat 28g, of which saturates 4.4g; Cholesterol 149mg; Calcium 221mg; Fibre 10g; Sodium 696mg

Warm Black-eyed Bean Salad with Rocket and Black Olives ✳

This is an easy dish, as black-eyed beans do not need to be soaked overnight. By adding spring onions and dill, it is transformed into a refreshing and healthy meal. It can be served hot or cold.

SERVES FOUR

1 Thoroughly rinse the beans and drain them well. Tip into a pan and pour in cold water to just about cover them. Slowly bring to the boil over a low heat. As soon as the water is boiling, remove from the heat and drain the water off immediately.

2 Put the beans back in the pan with fresh cold water to cover and add a pinch of salt – this will make their skins harder and stop them from disintegrating when they are cooked.

3 Bring the beans to the boil over a medium heat, then lower the heat and cook them until they are soft but not mushy. They will take 20–30 minutes only, so keep an eye on them.

4 Drain the beans, reserving 75–90ml/5–6 tbsp of the cooking liquid. Tip the beans into a large salad bowl. Immediately add the remaining ingredients, including the reserved liquid, and mix well. Serve immediately, piled on the lettuce leaves, or leave to cool slightly and serve later.

5 spring onions (scallions), sliced into rounds

a large handful of fresh rocket (arugula) leaves, chopped if large

45–60ml/3–4 tbsp chopped fresh dill

juice of 1 lemon, or to taste

10–12 black olives

small cos or romaine lettuce leaves, to serve

FROM THE STORECUPBOARD

275g/10oz/1$^{1}/_{2}$ cups black-eyed beans (peas)

150ml/$^{1}/_{4}$ pint/$^{2}/_{3}$ cup extra virgin olive oil

salt and ground black pepper, to taste

Energy 434kcal/1,811kJ; Protein 16.6g; Carbohydrate 31.4g, of which sugars 2.7g; Fat 27.8g, of which saturates 4g; Cholesterol 0mg; Calcium 149mg; Fibre 12.5g; Sodium 334mg

1 celery stick

fresh thyme sprig

1 onion or 3–4 shallots,
finely chopped

400g/14oz young spinach

30–45ml/2–3 tbsp
chopped fresh parsley

toasted baguette,
to serve

FOR THE DRESSING

1 small garlic clove,
finely chopped

2.5ml/¹/₂ tsp finely
grated lemon rind

FROM THE STORECUPBOARD

225g/8oz/1 cup Puy lentils

1 fresh bay leaf

105ml/7 tbsp olive oil

5ml/1 tsp Dijon mustard

15–25ml/1–1¹/₂ tbsp red
wine vinegar

salt and ground black
pepper, to taste

10ml/2 tsp crushed
toasted cumin seeds

Lentil and Spinach Salad with Onion, Cumin and Garlic ✳✳

This earthy and sustaining salad combines Puy lentils with onions, bay, thyme, parsley and cumin in a mustard, garlic and lemon dressing.

SERVES SIX

1 Rinse the lentils and place them in a large pan. Add enough water to cover. Tie the bay leaf, celery and thyme into a bundle and add to the pan, then bring to the boil. Reduce the heat and cook the lentils for 30–45 minutes, or until just tender.

2 Meanwhile, to make the dressing, mix 75ml/5 tbsp of the olive oil, the mustard and 15ml/1 tbsp red wine vinegar with the garlic and lemon rind, and season well with salt and pepper.

3 Thoroughly drain the lentils and turn them into a bowl. Add most of the dressing and toss well, then set the lentils aside.

4 Heat the remaining olive oil in a deep frying pan and sauté the chopped onion or shallots over a low heat for 4–5 minutes, then add the cumin and cook for a further 1 minute.

5 Add the spinach and season to taste with salt and pepper, then cover and cook until wilted. Stir the spinach into the lentils and leave to cool.

6 Stir in the remaining dressing and chopped parsley. Adjust the seasoning, and add extra red wine vinegar, if necessary. Turn on to a serving dish and serve with toasted baguette.

Energy 248kcal/1037kJ; Protein 11.2g; Carbohydrate 20.3g, of which sugars 2.1g; Fat 14.1g, of which saturates 2g; Cholesterol 0mg; Calcium 150mg; Fibre 5.1g; Sodium 102mg

Summer Salad ✳

Ripe tomatoes, creamy mozzarella and juicy olives make a good base for a fresh pasta salad that is perfect for a light summer lunch.

SERVES FOUR

1 Cook the pasta for 10–12 minutes, or according to the instructions on the packet. Tip it into a colander and rinse briefly under cold running water, then shake the colander to remove as much water as possible and leave to drain.

2 Make the dressing. Whisk the olive oil and balsamic vinegar or lemon juice in a jug (pitcher) with a little salt and pepper to taste.

3 Place the pasta, mozzarella, tomatoes, olives and spring onion in a large bowl, pour the dressing over and toss together well. Taste for seasoning before serving, sprinkled with basil leaves.

150g/5oz packet buffalo
mozzarella, drained and diced

3 ripe tomatoes, diced

10 pitted black olives, sliced

10 pitted green olives, sliced

1 spring onion (scallion), thinly
sliced on the diagonal

1 handful fresh basil leaves

FOR THE DRESSING

15ml/1 tbsp balsamic vinegar
or lemon juice

FROM THE STORECUPBOARD

350g/12oz/3 cups dried penne

90ml/6 tbsp olive oil

salt and ground black pepper,
to taste

Country Pasta Salad ✳

Colourful, tasty and nutritious, this is the ideal pasta salad for a summer picnic or an *al fresco* lunch. Serve with plenty of bread and butter.

SERVES SIX

1 Cook the pasta according to the instructions on the packet. Drain it into a colander, rinse under cold running water until cold, then shake the colander to remove as much water as possible. Leave to drain and dry.

2 Trim the beans and cut them into 5cm/2in lengths, and dice the potato. Put the beans and the potato in a pan of boiling water for 5–6 minutes or steam for 8–10 minutes. Drain and leave to cool.

3 To make the dressing, put the olive oil, balsamic vinegar and parsley in a large bowl with a little salt and ground black pepper to taste and whisk well to mix.

4 Halve the tomatoes, finely chop the spring onions, and add to the dressing with the grano padano, olive rings and capers. Stir in the cold pasta, beans and potato. Toss well to mix. Cover and leave to stand for about 30 minutes. Taste for seasoning before serving.

150g/5oz fine green beans

1 potato

200g/7oz cherry tomatoes

2 spring onions (scallions)

90g/3^1/$_2$oz/scant 1^1/$_4$ cups
grano padano cheese, shaved

6–8 pitted black olives,
cut into rings

15–30ml/1–2 tbsp capers

FOR THE DRESSING

15ml/1 tbsp chopped fresh
flat leaf parsley

FROM THE STORECUPBOARD

300g/11oz/2^3/$_4$ cups
dried fusilli

90ml/6 tbsp extra virgin
olive oil

15ml/1 tbsp balsamic vinegar

salt and ground black pepper,
to taste

Top: Energy 577kcal/2420kJ; Protein 18.2g; Carbohydrate 67.2g, of which sugars 5.3g; Fat 28g, of which saturates 8.1g; Cholesterol 22mg; Calcium 175mg; Fibre 3.9g; Sodium 580mg

Above: Energy 381kcal/1600kJ; Protein 13.3g; Carbohydrate 44.4g, of which sugars 3.8g; Fat 18g, of which saturates 5g; Cholesterol 15mg; Calcium 212mg; Fibre 2.9g; Sodium 341mg

Bean Salad with Tuna and Red Onion ✳

This makes a great main meal dish if served with a green salad, some garlic mayonnaise and plenty of warm, crusty bread. Using good-quality canned tuna brings the overall cost of the dish right down, making it affordable as well as healthy and absolutely delicious.

SERVES FOUR

1 Drain the dried beans and bring them to the boil in fresh water with the bay leaf added. Boil rapidly for 10 minutes, then reduce the heat and boil steadily for 1–1½ hours, until tender. Drain well. Discard the bay leaf.

2 Meanwhile, place the olive oil, tarragon vinegar and mustard, and garlic in a jug (pitcher) and whisk until mixed. Season to taste with salt, pepper, lemon juice and a pinch of caster sugar, if you like. Leave to stand.

3 Blanch the green beans in boiling water for 3–4 minutes. Drain, refresh under cold water and drain thoroughly again.

4 Place both types of beans in a bowl. Add half the dressing and toss to mix. Stir in the onion and half the chopped parsley, then season to taste with salt and pepper.

5 Flake the tuna into large chunks with a knife and toss it into the beans with the tomato halves.

6 Arrange the salad on four individual plates. Drizzle the remaining dressing over the salad and sprinkle the remaining chopped parsley on top. Garnish with a few onion rings and serve immediately, at room temperature.

200–250g/7–9oz fine green beans, trimmed

1 large red onion, sliced

45ml/3 tbsp chopped fresh flat leaf parsley

200–250g/7–9oz good-quality canned tuna in olive oil, drained

200g/7oz cherry tomatoes, halved

a few onion rings, to garnish

FOR THE DRESSING

1 garlic clove, finely chopped

5ml/1 tsp finely grated lemon rind

a little lemon juice

FROM THE STORECUPBOARD

250g/9oz/1⅓ cups dried haricot (navy) or cannellini beans, soaked overnight in cold water

1 bay leaf

90ml/6 tbsp olive oil

15ml/1 tbsp tarragon vinegar

5ml/1 tsp tarragon mustard

pinch of caster (superfine) sugar (optional)

salt and ground black pepper, to taste

Energy 461kcal/1929kJ; Protein 29.9g; Carbohydrate 37g, of which sugars 8.7g; Fat 22.6g, of which saturates 3.3g; Cholesterol 25mg; Calcium 131mg; Fibre 13g; Sodium 167mg

115g/4oz green beans,
trimmed and cut in half

115g/4oz mixed
salad leaves

¹/₂ small cucumber,
thinly sliced

4 ripe tomatoes, quartered

50g/2oz can
anchovies, drained

4 eggs, hard-boiled

1 tuna steak, about
175g/6oz

¹/₂ bunch of small
radishes, trimmed

50g/2oz/¹/₂ cup small
black olives

FOR THE DRESSING

2 garlic cloves, crushed

FROM THE STORECUPBOARD

90ml/6 tbsp extra virgin
olive oil, plus extra
for brushing

15ml/1 tbsp white
wine vinegar

salt and ground black
pepper, to taste

VARIATIONS

• Opinions vary on
whether Salad Niçoise
should include potatoes
or not, but, if you like,
include a handful of small
cooked new potatoes for
a more substantial salad.

• Fresh tuna can be
expensive, so buy it when
it is on special offer.
Alternatively, you could
use a 250g/9oz can of
tuna instead. Simply drain
the canned fish in a sieve
(strainer) and flake the
flesh with a fork.

Salad Niçoise ✷✷

Made with the freshest of seasonal ingredients, this classic Provençal
salad makes a simple yet unbeatable summer dish. Serve with warm
country-style bread for a nutritious and sustaining main meal.

SERVES FOUR

1 To make the dressing, whisk together 90ml/6 tbsp of the
olive oil, the garlic and the vinegar in a bowl and season to
taste with salt and pepper. Alternatively, shake together in a
screw-top jar. Set aside.

2 Cook the green beans in a pan of boiling water for 2 minutes,
until just tender, then drain.

3 Mix together the salad leaves, sliced cucumber, tomatoes
and green beans in a large, shallow bowl. Halve the anchovies
lengthways and shell and quarter the eggs.

4 Preheat the grill (broiler). Brush the tuna with olive oil and
sprinkle with salt and black pepper. Grill (broil) for 3–4 minutes
on each side until cooked through. Cool, then flake with a fork.

5 Sprinkle the flaked tuna, sliced anchovies, quartered eggs,
radishes and olives over the salad. Pour over the dressing and
toss together lightly to combine. Serve immediately.

Energy 351kcal/1457kJ; Protein 21.7g; Carbohydrate 5.3g, of which sugars 5g; Fat 27.3g, of which saturates 5g; Cholesterol 210mg; Calcium 114mg; Fibre 2.6g; Sodium 876mg

2.5cm/1in piece fresh
root ginger, peeled and
finely grated

1 garlic clove, crushed

grated rind and juice of
2 lemons

450g/1lb trout
fillet, skinned

900g/2lb new potatoes

15ml/1 tbsp whole or
chopped fresh chives,
to garnish

FROM THE STORECUPBOARD

5ml/1 tsp hot chilli powder

15ml/1 tbsp coriander
seeds, lightly crushed

60ml/4 tbsp olive oil

5–10ml/1–2 tsp salt

ground black pepper,
to taste

Spiced Trout Salad ✳

Most of the preparation for this delicious salad is done in advance, so it
makes an ideal mid-week supper. The trout is marinated in a mixture of
coriander, ginger and chilli and served with cold baby roast potatoes.

SERVES FOUR

1 Mix the ginger, garlic, chilli powder, coriander seeds and
lemon rind in a bowl. Whisk in the lemon juice with 15ml/1 tbsp
of the olive oil to make a marinade.

2 Place the trout in a shallow, non-metallic dish and cover with
the marinade. Turn the fish to make sure they are well coated,
cover with clear film (plastic wrap) and chill for at least 2 hours
or overnight.

3 Preheat the oven to 200°C/400°F/Gas 6. Place the potatoes
in a roasting pan, toss them in 30ml/2 tbsp olive oil and season
with salt and pepper. Roast for 45 minutes or until tender.
Remove from the oven and set aside to cool.

4 Reduce the oven temperature to 190°C/375°F/Gas 5. Remove
the trout from the marinade and place in a roasting pan. Bake for
20 minutes or until cooked through. Remove from the oven and
leave to cool.

5 Cut the potatoes into chunks, flake the trout into bitesize
pieces and toss them together in a serving dish with the
remaining olive oil. Sprinkle with the chives and serve.

VARIATION *If you don't
like spicy
food, omit the
hot chilli
powder from
the marinade.*

COOK'S TIP *Look for firm pieces of
fresh root ginger, with
smooth skin. If bought
really fresh, root ginger
will keep for up to 2
weeks in a cool, dry place,
away from strong light.
Root ginger freezes
successfully and can be
shaved or grated straight
from the freezer.*

Energy 365kcal/1535kJ; Protein 26g; Carbohydrate 37.1g, of which sugars 2.9g; Fat 13.5g, of which saturates 1.5g; Cholesterol 0mg; Calcium 28mg; Fibre 2.3g; Sodium 580mg

Tangy Fish Salad ✳✳

Flakes of halibut are deep-fried until crispy and make a wonderful topping for this refreshing main course salad. The combination of crispy, crunchy textures and fragrant, spicy flavours is unbeatable.

SERVES FOUR

1 Place the fish in a wok or heavy pan and cover with cold water. Place over a medium heat and bring to the boil. Reduce the heat and cook gently for 6–8 minutes, or until the fish is cooked.

2 Remove the fish from the wok or pan and pat dry on kitchen paper. Break up into large flakes. Place in a food processor and pulse until the mixture resembles coarse breadcrumbs.

3 Fill a wok or pan one-third full with oil and heat to 180°C/350°F (or until a cube of bread, dropped into the oil, browns in about 15 seconds). Working in batches, deep-fry the fish mixture for 1–2 minutes until browned and crispy. Drain and set aside.

4 Combine the cucumber, tomatoes, red onion and herbs in a bowl.

5 Mix together the sweet chilli sauce, fish sauce, lime juice and sugar and pour this over the salad. Sprinkle over the deep-fried fish and chopped peanuts. Serve immediately.

250g/9oz halibut fillet, skinned

1 cucumber, seeded and thinly sliced

2 plum tomatoes, seeded and diced

1 red onion, halved and thinly sliced

1 bunch fresh coriander (cilantro) leaves

1 bunch fresh mint leaves

juice of 2 limes

45ml/3 tbsp roasted peanuts, chopped

FROM THE STORECUPBOARD

sunflower oil, for frying

30ml/2 tbsp sweet chilli sauce

30ml/2 tbsp Thai fish sauce

15ml/1 tbsp soft light brown sugar

Energy 252kcal/1050kJ; Protein 17.9g; Carbohydrate 11.9g, of which sugars 10.6g; Fat 15g, of which saturates 2.2g; Cholesterol 22mg; Calcium 70mg; Fibre 2.4g; Sodium 705mg

Pasta Salad with Salami ✳✳

This pasta dish is easy to make and would be perfect for a picnic or packed lunch. Take the dressing and salad leaves separately and mix everything at the last moment to prevent the salad leaves from wilting.

SERVES FOUR

1 Cook the pasta in a large pan of lightly salted boiling water for 12 minutes, or according to the instructions on the packet, until tender but not soft. Drain thoroughly and rinse with cold water, then drain again.

2 Drain the peppers and reserve 60ml/4 tbsp of the oil for the dressing. Cut the peppers into long, fine strips and mix them with the olives, sun-dried tomatoes and Roquefort in a large bowl. Stir in the pasta and peppered salami.

3 Divide the salad leaves among four individual bowls and spoon the pasta salad on top. Whisk the reserved oil with the vinegar, oregano, garlic and seasoning to taste. Spoon this dressing over the salad and serve at once.

275g/10oz jar charcoal-roasted peppers in oil

115g/4oz/1 cup pitted black olives

4 drained sun-dried tomatoes in oil, quartered

115g/4oz Roquefort cheese, crumbled

10 slices peppered salami, cut into strips

115g/4oz packet mixed leaf salad

30ml/2 tbsp chopped fresh oregano

2 garlic cloves, crushed

FROM THE STORECUPBOARD

225g/8oz pasta twists

30ml/2 tbsp white wine vinegar

salt and ground black pepper, to taste

Energy 429kcal/1797kJ; Protein 17.8g; Carbohydrate 46.7g, of which sugars 6.6g; Fat 20.3g, of which saturates 8.9g; Cholesterol 37mg; Calcium 188mg; Fibre 3.9g; Sodium 1341mg

225g/8oz new potatoes, halved if large

50g/2oz green beans

115g/4oz young spinach leaves

2 spring onions (scallions), sliced

4 eggs, hard-boiled and quartered

50g/2oz cooked ham, cut into strips

juice of ¹/₂ lemon

FOR THE DRESSING

50g/2oz/¹/₃ cup shelled hazelnuts

FROM THE STORECUPBOARD

salt and ground black pepper, to taste

60ml/4 tbsp olive oil

5ml/1 tsp ground turmeric

5ml/1 tsp ground cumin

VARIATION An even quicker salad can be made by using a 400g/14oz can of mixed beans and pulses instead of the potatoes. Drain and rinse the beans and pulses, then drain again.

Ham and New Potato Salad ✴

Combining warm new potatoes, young spinach leaves, cooked ham and hard-boiled eggs with a lightly spiced, nutty dressing, this delicious warm salad is an excellent choice for a casual summer supper with friends.

SERVES FOUR

1 Cook the potatoes in boiling salted water for 10–15 minutes, or until tender. Meanwhile, cook the beans in boiling salted water for 2 minutes.

2 Drain the potatoes and beans. Toss with the spinach and spring onions.

3 Arrange the hard-boiled egg quarters on the salad and sprinkle the strips of ham over the top. Drizzle with the lemon juice and season with plenty of salt and pepper.

4 To make the dressing, put the oil, turmeric, cumin and hazelnuts in a large, heavy frying pan and cook, stirring frequently, until the nuts turn golden. Pour the hot, nutty dressing over the salad and serve immediately.

Energy 318kcal/1319kJ; Protein 12.4g; Carbohydrate 11g, of which sugars 2.2g; Fat 25.4g, of which saturates 4g; Cholesterol 198mg; Calcium 106mg; Fibre 2.3g; Sodium 268mg

Chicken and Tomato Salad with Hazelnut Dressing ✳✳

This simple, warm salad combines pan-fried chicken and spinach with a light, nutty dressing. Serve it with bread for a sustaining main meal.

SERVES FOUR

1 First make the dressing: place 30ml/ 2 tbsp of the olive oil, the hazelnut oil, vinegar, garlic and chopped herbs in a small bowl or jug (pitcher) and whisk together until mixed. Set aside.

2 Trim any long stalks from the spinach leaves, then place in a large serving bowl with the tomatoes and spring onions, and toss together to mix.

3 Heat the remaining olive oil in a frying pan, and stir-fry the chicken over a high heat for 7–10 minutes, until it is cooked, tender and lightly browned.

4 Arrange the cooked chicken pieces over the salad. Give the dressing a quick whisk to blend, then drizzle it over the salad. Add salt and pepper to taste, toss lightly and serve immediately.

225g/8oz baby spinach leaves

250g/9oz cherry tomatoes, halved

1 bunch of spring onions (scallions), chopped

2 skinless, chicken breast fillets, cut into thin strips

FOR THE DRESSING

30ml/2 tbsp hazelnut oil

1 garlic clove, crushed

15ml/1 tbsp chopped fresh mixed herbs

FROM THE STORECUPBOARD

45ml/3 tbsp olive oil

15ml/1 tbsp white wine vinegar

salt and ground black pepper, to taste

Energy 247kcal/1029kJ; Protein 23.5g; Carbohydrate 3.6g, of which sugars 3.5g; Fat 15.5g, of which saturates 2.1g; Cholesterol 61mg; Calcium 114mg; Fibre 2.2g; Sodium 139mg

Rice Salad with Chicken, Orange and Cashew Nuts ✳✳

With their tangy flavour, orange segments are the perfect partner for tender chicken in this tasty and wholesome rice salad.

SERVES FOUR

3 large seedless oranges

450g/1lb cooked chicken, diced

45ml/3 tbsp chopped fresh chives

75g/3oz/³/₄ cup almonds or cashew nuts, toasted

mixed salad leaves, to serve

FROM THE STORECUPBOARD

175g/6oz/scant 1 cup long grain rice

175ml/6fl oz/³/₄ cup home-made vinaigrette (*see* Cook's Tip)

10ml/2 tsp strong Dijon mustard

2.5ml/¹/₂ tsp caster (superfine) sugar

salt and ground black pepper, to taste

COOK'S TIPS

• To make a simple vinaigrette, whisk 45ml/3 tbsp wine vinegar with 90ml/ 6 tbsp olive oil. Add 60ml/4 tbsp extra virgin olive oil and season well.

• This healthy salad is a great way to use up left-over roast chicken and cold rice, and is a meal in itself.

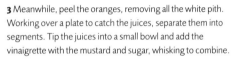

1 Pare one of the oranges thinly, removing only the rind, not the white pith. Put the pieces of rind in a pan and add the rice.

2 Pour in 475ml/16fl oz/2 cups water and bring to the boil. Cover and cook over a very low heat for about 15 minutes, or until the rice is tender and all the water has been absorbed.

3 Meanwhile, peel the oranges, removing all the white pith. Working over a plate to catch the juices, separate them into segments. Tip the juices into a small bowl and add the vinaigrette with the mustard and sugar, whisking to combine.

4 When the rice is cooked, remove it from the heat and discard the pieces of orange rind. Spoon into a bowl, let it cool slightly, then add half the dressing. Toss well, then set aside to cool.

5 Add the chicken, chives, toasted nuts and orange segments to the cooled rice. Pour over the remaining dressing and toss gently to combine. Serve on a bed of mixed salad leaves.

Energy 668kcal/2785kJ; Protein 35.9g; Carbohydrate 47.8g, of which sugars 12.3g; Fat 37.2g, of which saturates 4.8g; Cholesterol 79mg; Calcium 141mg; Fibre 4.1g; Sodium 80mg

Tangy Chicken Salad ✳✳

This fresh and lively dish typifies the character of Thai cuisine. It is ideal for a light lunch on a hot and lazy summer's day.

SERVES FOUR–SIX

1 Place the chicken in a large dish. Rub with the garlic, soy sauce and 15ml/1 tbsp of the oil. Cover with clear film (plastic wrap) and leave to marinate for 1–2 hours.

2 Heat the remaining oil in a wok or frying pan and stir-fry the chicken for 3–4 minutes on each side, or until cooked. Remove and set aside to cool.

3 In a pan, heat the coconut cream, fish sauce, lime juice and sugar. Stir until the sugar has dissolved; set aside.

4 Tear the cooked chicken into strips and put it in a bowl. Add the water chestnuts, cashew nuts, shallots, kaffir lime leaves, lemon grass, galangal, red chilli, spring onions and mint leaves.

5 Pour the coconut dressing over the mixture and toss well. Serve the chicken on a bed of lettuce leaves and garnish with sliced red chillies.

4 skinless, boneless chicken breast portions

2 garlic cloves, crushed

120ml/4fl oz/¹/₂ cup coconut cream

juice of 1 lime

115g/4oz/¹/₂ cup water chestnuts, sliced

50g/2oz/¹/₂ cup cashew nuts, roasted and coarsely chopped

4 shallots, thinly sliced

4 kaffir lime leaves, thinly sliced

1 lemon grass stalk, thinly sliced

5ml/1 tsp chopped fresh galangal

1 large fresh red chilli, seeded and finely chopped

2 spring onions (scallions), thinly sliced

10–12 fresh mint leaves, torn

1 lettuce, separated into leaves, to serve

2 fresh red chillies, seeded and sliced, to garnish

FROM THE STORECUPBOARD

30ml/2 tbsp soy sauce

30ml/2 tbsp vegetable oil

30ml/2 tbsp Thai fish sauce

30ml/2 tbsp light muscovado (brown) sugar

Energy 349kcal/1453kJ; Protein 24.3g; Carbohydrate 11.5g, of which sugars 9.8g; Fat 23.2g, of which saturates 12.3g; Cholesterol 43mg; Calcium 49mg; Fibre 1.7g; Sodium 200mg

675g/1¹/₂lb fillet (tenderloin) or rump (round) steak

2 small mild red chillies, seeded and sliced

225g/8oz/3¹/₄ cups fresh shiitake mushrooms, stems removed and caps sliced

FOR THE DRESSING

3 spring onions (scallions), finely chopped

2 garlic cloves, finely chopped

juice of 1 lime

30ml/2 tbsp chopped fresh coriander (cilantro)

TO SERVE

1 cos or romaine lettuce, torn into strips

175g/6oz cherry tomatoes, halved

5cm/2in piece cucumber, peeled, halved and thinly sliced

45ml/3 tbsp toasted sesame seeds

FROM THE STORECUPBOARD

30ml/2 tbsp olive oil

15–30ml/1–2 tbsp Thai fish sauce

5ml/1 tsp soft light brown sugar

Beef and Mushroom Salad ✳✳✳

This flavoursome and sustaining salad combines tender strips of beef and earthy mushrooms with fresh salad vegetables and a zesty sauce.

SERVES FOUR

1 Preheat the grill (broiler) to medium, then cook the steak for 2–4 minutes on each side, depending on how well done you like it. Leave to cool for at least 15 minutes. Slice the meat as thinly as possible and place the slices in a bowl.

2 Heat the olive oil in a small frying pan. Add the seeded and sliced red chillies and the sliced shiitake mushroom caps. Cook for 5 minutes, stirring occasionally.

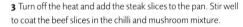

3 Turn off the heat and add the steak slices to the pan. Stir well to coat the beef slices in the chilli and mushroom mixture.

4 Make the dressing by mixing all the ingredients in a bowl, then pour it over the meat mixture and toss gently.

5 Arrange the lettuce, tomatoes and cucumber on a serving plate. Spoon the steak mixture in the centre and sprinkle the sesame seeds over. Serve at once.

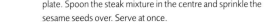

Energy 441kcal/1834kJ; Protein 42.3g; Carbohydrate 3.9g, of which sugars 3.8g; Fat 28.5g, of which saturates 8.3g; Cholesterol 98mg; Calcium 110mg; Fibre 2.6g; Sodium 119mg

Versatile
Vegetable Dishes

VEGETABLE DISHES ARE HEALTHY, ECONOMICAL
AND EXTREMELY ADAPTABLE. TRY USING DIFFERENT
COMBINATIONS OF VEGETABLES, DEPENDING ON
YOUR PERSONAL PREFERENCES AND THE
SEASON. FROM QUICK-AND-EASY DISHES SUCH
AS FRITTATA WITH SUN-DRIED TOMATOES OR TOFU,
ROASTED PEANUT AND PEPPER KEBABS TO LEEK,
SQUASH AND TOMATO GRATIN OR HOT AND SPICY
PARSNIPS WITH CHICKPEAS, THERE IS A DELICIOUS DISH
FOR EVERYONE.

Baked Potatoes with a Choice of Three Fillings ✳

Potatoes baked in their skins until they are crisp on the outside and fluffy in the middle make an excellent and nourishing meal on their own. But for an even better treat, add one of these delicious and easy toppings.

SERVES FOUR

1 Preheat the oven to 200°C/400°F/Gas 6. Score the potatoes with a cross and rub all over with the olive oil.

2 Place on a baking sheet and cook for 45 minutes to 1 hour, until a knife inserted into the centres indicates they are cooked. Alternatively, cook in the microwave according to your manufacturer's instructions.

3 Cut the potatoes open along the score lines and push up the flesh. Season to taste and fill with your chosen filling.

STIR-FRY VEG

1 Heat the sunflower oil in a wok or large frying pan, then add the leeks, carrots, courgette and baby corn and stir-fry together for about 2 minutes. Add the mushrooms and stir-fry for a further minute.

2 Mix together the soy sauce, sherry and sesame oil and pour over the vegetables. Heat through until just bubbling and scatter the sesame seeds over the top.

RED BEAN CHILLIES

1 Heat the beans in a pan and stir in the cottage or cream cheese, chilli sauce and cumin.

2 Serve topped with more chilli sauce.

CHEESE AND CREAMY CORN

1 Heat the corn gently with the cheese and mixed herbs until well blended.

2 Use to fill the potatoes and garnish with fresh parsley sprigs.

> **COOK'S TIP**
> Choose floury potatoes, such as Maris Piper or King Edward, which are evenly sized and have undamaged skins. Scrub them thoroughly under hot running water. If they are cooked before you are ready to serve them, take them out of the oven and wrap them up in a warmed cloth until they are needed.

---

4 medium baking potatoes

filling of your choice
(*see* below)

STIR-FRIED VEG

2 leeks, thinly sliced

2 carrots, cut into sticks

1 courgette, thinly sliced

115g/4oz baby corn, halved

115g/4oz/1^1/2 cup button mushrooms, sliced

30ml/2 tbsp dry sherry

sesame seeds, to garnish

RED BEAN CHILLIES

200g/7oz/scant 1 cup low-fat cottage or cream cheese

CHEESE AND CREAMY CORN

425g/15oz can creamed corn

115g/4oz/1 cup hard cheese, grated

fresh parsley sprigs, to garnish

FROM THE STORECUPBOARD

olive oil

salt and ground black pepper, to taste

45ml/3 tbsp sunflower oil

45ml/3 tbsp soy sauce

15ml/1 tbsp sesame oil

425g/15oz can red kidney beans, drained

30ml/2 tbsp mild chilli sauce

5ml/1 tsp ground cumin

5ml/1 tsp mixed dried herbs

Energy 223kcal/941kJ; Protein 7.3g; Carbohydrate 38.6g, of which sugars 8.3g; Fat 4.5g, of which saturates 0.8g; Cholesterol 0mg; Calcium 55mg; Fibre 5.4g; Sodium 1150mg

Layered Vegetable Terrine ✳

Serve this delicious combination of vegetables and herbs layered and baked in a spinach-lined loaf tin hot or warm with a simple salad garnish.

SERVES SIX

1 Preheat the oven to 180°C/350°F/Gas 4. Place the peppers in a roasting tin and roast, cores in place, for 30–45 minutes until charred. Remove from the oven. Place in a plastic bag to cool. Peel the skins and remove the cores. Halve the potatoes and boil in lightly salted water for 10–15 minutes.

2 Blanch the spinach for a few seconds in boiling water. Drain and pat dry on kitchen paper. Line the base and sides of a 900g/2lb loaf tin, making sure the leaves overlap slightly.

3 Slice the potatoes thinly and lay one-third of the potatoes over the base, dot with a little of the butter and season with salt, pepper and nutmeg. Sprinkle a little cheese over.

4 Arrange 3 of the peeled pepper halves on top. Sprinkle a little cheese over and then a layer of courgettes. Lay another one-third of the potatoes on top with the remaining peppers and some more cheese, seasoning as you go. Lay the final layer of potato on top and scatter over any remaining cheese. Fold the spinach leaves over. Cover with foil.

5 Place the loaf tin in a roasting tin and pour boiling water around the outside, so the water comes halfway up the sides of the tin. Bake for 45 minutes–1 hour. Remove from the oven and turn the loaf out. Serve sliced with lettuce and tomatoes.

3 red (bell) peppers, halved

450g/1lb waxy potatoes

115g/4oz spinach leaves, trimmed

25g/1oz/2 tbsp butter

115g/4oz/1 cup Cheddar cheese, grated

1 medium courgette, sliced lengthways and blanched

FROM THE STORECUPBOARD

salt and ground black pepper, to taste

pinch grated nutmeg

VARIATIONS

• Depending on what is available, you could use orange, yellow and green peppers along with or in place of the red ones.

• You can add a range of fresh, seasonal vegetables to this versatile terrine. Good additions include lightly steamed French beans, peas and corn.

• For a stronger cheese flavour, use mature (sharp) Cheddar cheese, or add some Parmesan or grano padano cheese.

Energy 205kcal/854kJ; Protein 8.3g; Carbohydrate 19.2g, of which sugars 7.7g; Fat 10.6g, of which saturates 6.6g; Cholesterol 27mg; Calcium 196mg; Fibre 3g; Sodium 203mg

2.5ml/¹/₂ tsp easy-blend (rapid-rise) dried yeast

350g/12oz small new or salad potatoes

2 garlic cloves, crushed

1 red onion, thinly sliced

150g/5oz/1¹/₄ cups smoked mozzarella cheese, grated

10ml/2 tsp chopped fresh rosemary or sage

30ml/2 tbsp freshly grated grano padano cheese, to garnish

FROM THE STORECUPBOARD

225g/8oz/2 cups strong white bread flour, sifted, plus extra for dusting

5ml/1 tsp salt

75ml/5 tbsp olive oil, plus extra for greasing

salt and ground black pepper, to taste

VARIATION

For a non-vegetarian alternative, add sliced smoked pork sausage, salami or pastrami, or some chunks of cooked ham or chicken to this delicious pizza.

Potato and Garlic Pizza ✳

This simple pizza uses a flavoursome and unusual combination of sliced new potatoes, smoked mozzarella and garlic.

SERVES TWO–THREE

1 To make the pizza base, place the flour, salt and easy-blend dried yeast in a large bowl. Make a well in the centre and add 45ml/3 tbsp oil and 150ml/¹/₄ pint/²/₃ cup warm water. Mix with a round-bladed knife to form a soft dough. Turn out on to a lightly floured work surface and knead for 5 minutes.

2 Cover the dough with a dish towel and leave to rest for about 5 minutes, then knead for a further 5 minutes, until smooth and elastic. Place in a lightly oiled bowl and cover with clear film (plastic wrap). Leave for 45 minutes, or until doubled in size.

3 Preheat the oven to 220°C/425°F/Gas 7. Cook the potatoes in boiling salted water for 5 minutes. Drain well and leave to cool. Peel and slice thinly. Heat 30ml/2 tbsp of the oil in a frying pan. Add the potatoes and garlic and fry for 5–8 minutes, until tender.

4 Knead the risen dough lightly, then roll out to form a rough 30cm/12in round. Place on a lightly oiled baking sheet and push up the edges of the dough to form a shallow, even rim.

5 Brush the pizza base with the remaining oil. Scatter the onion over, then arrange the potatoes on top. Sprinkle over the mozzarella and rosemary or sage and plenty of black pepper. Bake for 15–20 minutes until golden. Remove from the oven, sprinkle with grano padano and more black pepper.

Energy 690kcal/2899kJ; Protein 24.8g; Carbohydrate 85.2g, of which sugars 6.4g; Fat 30.1g, of which saturates 10.6g; Cholesterol 39mg; Calcium 410mg; Fibre 4.2g; Sodium 620mg

Rocket and Tomato Pizza ✳

Simple, colourful and irresistible, this stunning pizza will be loved by all the family. Rocket, with its pronounced flavour, adds the final touch.

SERVES TWO

1 To make the pizza base, place the flour, salt and easy-blend dried yeast in a large bowl. Make a well in the centre and add 45ml/3 tbsp oil and 150ml/¼ pint/²/₃ cup warm water. Mix with a round-bladed knife to form a soft dough. Turn out on to a lightly floured work surface and knead for 5 minutes.

2 Cover the dough with a dish towel and leave to rest for about 5 minutes, then knead for a further 5 minutes, until smooth and elastic. Place in a lightly oiled bowl and cover with clear film (plastic wrap). Leave for 45 minutes, or until doubled in size.

3 Preheat the oven to 220°C/425°F/Gas 7. To make the topping, heat 15ml/1 tbsp oil in a frying pan and fry the garlic for 1 minute. Add the canned tomatoes and sugar, and cook for 5–7 minutes, or until reduced and thickened. Stir in the basil and seasoning to taste, then set aside.

4 Knead the risen dough lightly, then roll out to form a rough 30cm/12in round. Place on a lightly oiled baking sheet and push up the edges of the dough to form a shallow, even rim.

5 Spoon the tomato mixture over the pizza base, then top with the chopped fresh tomatoes, and the mozzarella. Season to taste, then drizzle with olive oil.

6 Bake in the top of the oven for 10–12 minutes, or until crisp and golden. Scatter with rocket and serve.

2.5ml/¹/₂ tsp easy-blend (rapid-rise) dried yeast

1 garlic clove, crushed

30ml/2 tbsp torn fresh basil leaves

2 tomatoes, seeded and chopped

150g/5oz mozzarella cheese, sliced

20g/³/₄oz rocket (arugula) leaves

FROM THE STORECUPBOARD

225g/8oz/2 cups strong white bread flour, sifted, plus extra for dusting

5ml/1 tsp salt

90ml/6 tbsp olive oil, plus extra for greasing

150g/5oz canned chopped tomatoes

2.5ml/¹/₂ tsp sugar

salt and ground black pepper, to taste

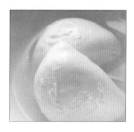

VARIATION To make a Roquefort cheese and walnut pizza, replace half the strong white flour with wholemeal flour. Use 75g/3oz/³/₄ cup crumbled Roquefort cheese instead of the mozzarella. Omit the rocket and use 30ml/2 tbsp chopped walnuts.

Energy 683kcal/2874kJ; Protein 26.1g; Carbohydrate 92.3g, of which sugars 6.5g; Fat 25.8g, of which saturates 11.9g; Cholesterol 44mg; Calcium 494mg; Fibre 5.7g; Sodium 1312mg

Fiorentina Pizza ✳

An egg adds the finishing touch to this classic Italian spinach pizza; try not to overcook it though, as it's best when the yolk is slightly soft in the middle.

SERVES TWO–THREE

2.5ml/¹/₂ tsp easy-blend (rapid-rise) dried yeast

1 garlic clove, crushed

30ml/2 tbsp torn fresh basil leaves

1 small red onion, thinly sliced

175g/6oz fresh spinach, stalks removed

150g/5oz mozzarella cheese, thinly sliced

1 egg

25g/1oz/¹/₄ cup Gruyère cheese, grated

FROM THE STORECUPBOARD

225g/8oz/2 cups strong white bread flour, sifted, plus extra for dusting

5ml/1 tsp salt

90ml/6 tbsp olive oil, plus extra for greasing

150g/5oz canned chopped tomatoes

2.5ml/¹/₂ tsp sugar

salt and ground black pepper, to taste

freshly grated nutmeg

1 To make the pizza base, place the flour, salt and dried yeast in a large bowl. Make a well in the centre and add 45ml/3 tbsp oil and 150ml/¹/₄ pint/²/₃ cup warm water. Mix to form a soft dough. Turn out on to a floured surface and knead for 5 minutes.

2 Cover the dough with a dish towel and leave to rest for about 5 minutes, then knead for a further 5 minutes, until smooth and elastic. Place in a lightly oiled bowl and cover with clear film (plastic wrap). Leave for 45 minutes, or until doubled in size.

3 To make the topping, heat 15ml/1 tbsp oil in a frying pan and fry the garlic for 1 minute. Add the canned tomatoes and sugar, and cook for 5–7 minutes, until thickened. Season to taste.

4 Heat 15ml/1 tbsp of the oil and fry the onion until soft. Add the spinach and fry until wilted. Drain any excess liquid.

5 Knead the risen dough lightly, then roll out to form a rough 30cm/12in round. Place on a lightly oiled baking sheet and push up the edges of the dough to form a shallow, even rim.

6 Preheat the oven to 220°C/425°F/Gas 7. Brush the base with half the remaining olive oil. Spread the tomato sauce over the base, then top with the spinach mixture. Sprinkle over a little nutmeg and arrange the mozzarella on top. Drizzle over the remaining oil. Bake for 10 minutes, then remove from the oven.

7 Make a small well in the centre of the topping and break the egg into the hole. Sprinkle over the Gruyère cheese and return to the oven for a further 5–10 minutes until crisp and golden.

VARIATION *A calzone is like a pizza but is folded in half. To make, add the egg with the rest of the pizza topping, fold over the dough, seal the edges and bake for 20 minutes.*

Energy 503kcal/2100kJ; Protein 20.8g; Carbohydrate 40.3g, of which sugars 5.9g; Fat 29.7g, of which saturates 10.9g; Cholesterol 101mg; Calcium 417mg; Fibre 2.8g; Sodium 668mg

Potato Gnocchi with Parmesan Cheese and Basil ✳

Gnocchi make a substantial and tasty alternative to pasta. Serve with a green side salad for a simple yet delicious light meal.

SERVES SIX

1 Cook the potatoes in their skins in a large pan of boiling water until tender but not falling apart. Drain and peel while warm.

2 Spread a layer of flour on a work surface. Pass the hot potatoes through a food mill, dropping them directly on to the flour. Sprinkle with half of the remaining flour and mix in very lightly. Break the egg into the mixture. Add the nutmeg and knead, adding more flour if the mixture is too loose. When the dough is no longer moist, it is ready to be rolled.

3 Divide the dough into four pieces. On a lightly floured surface, form each into a roll about 2cm/³⁄₄ in in diameter. Cut the rolls crossways into pieces about 2cm/³⁄₄ in long. One by one, press and roll the gnocchi lightly along the prongs of a fork towards the points, making ridges on one side, and a depression from your thumb on the other.

4 Bring a large pan of lightly salted water to a fast boil, then drop in half the gnocchi. When they rise to the surface, they are done. Drain well, and place in a warmed serving bowl. Dot with butter. Cover to keep warm while cooking the remainder. As soon as they are cooked, toss the gnocchi with the butter, garnish with grano padano shavings and basil leaves, and serve immediately.

1kg/2¹⁄₄lb waxy potatoes

1 egg

25g/1oz/2 tbsp butter

grano padano cheese cut in shavings, to garnish

fresh basil leaves, to garnish

FROM THE STORECUPBOARD

250–300g/9–11oz/ 2¹⁄₄–2³⁄₄ cups plain (all-purpose) flour, plus more if necessary

pinch of freshly grated nutmeg

a pinch of salt

Energy 302kcal/1279kJ; Protein 7.8g; Carbohydrate 59.2g, of which sugars 2.8g; Fat 5.4g, of which saturates 2.7g; Cholesterol 41mg; Calcium 74mg; Fibre 3g; Sodium 57mg

Baked Cheese Polenta with Tomato Sauce ✳

Polenta, or cornmeal, is very cheap. It is prepared like a sort of oatmeal, and eaten soft, or left to set, cut into shapes, then cooked.

SERVES FOUR

1 Preheat the oven to 200°C/400°F/ Gas 6. Line a 28 x 18cm/11 x 7in tin (pan) with clear film (plastic wrap). Boil 1 litre/1³/₄ pints/4 cups water in a large pan.

2 Add the salt and pour in the polenta in a steady stream and cook, stirring constantly, for 5 minutes. Beat in the paprika and nutmeg. Pour into the tin and smooth the surface. Leave to cool.

3 Heat the oil in a pan and cook the onion and garlic until soft. Add the tomatoes, tomato purée and sugar. Season. Simmer for 20 minutes.

4 Cut the polenta into 5cm/2in squares. Layer the polenta and tomato sauce in an ovenproof dish. Sprinkle with the cheese and bake for 25 minutes, until golden. Serve immediately.

1 large onion, finely chopped

2 garlic cloves, crushed

75g/3oz Gruyère cheese or other mild cheese, grated

FROM THE STORECUPBOARD

5ml/1 tsp salt

250g/9oz/1¹/₂ cups quick-cook polenta

5ml/1 tsp paprika

2.5ml/¹/₂ tsp ground nutmeg

30ml/2 tbsp extra virgin olive oil

2 x 400g/14oz cans chopped tomatoes, or 450g/1lb fresh tomatoes

15ml/1 tbsp tomato purée (paste)

5ml/1 tsp sugar

salt and ground black pepper, to taste

Energy 425kcal/1777kJ; Protein 13.1g; Carbohydrate 59.4g, of which sugars 12g; Fat 14.5g, of which saturates 5.1g; Cholesterol 18mg; Calcium 175mg; Fibre 4.5g; Sodium 165mg

Vegetable Hot-pot ✳✳

Make this healthy one-dish meal in the summer, when the vegetables are in season, and serve with Italian bread, such as foccacia.

SERVES FOUR

1 Preheat the oven to 190°C/375°F/ Gas 5. Heat 45ml/3 tbsp of the oil in a heavy pan, and cook the onion until golden.

2 Add the aubergines, sauté for 3 minutes, then add the courgettes, peppers, peas, beans and potatoes, and stir in the spices and seasoning. Cook for 3 minutes, stirring constantly.

3 Cut the tomatoes in half and scoop out the seeds. Chop the tomatoes finely and place them in a bowl.

4 Stir in the canned tomatoes with the chopped fresh parsley, crushed garlic and the remaining olive oil.

5 Spoon the aubergine mixture into a shallow ovenproof dish and level the surface.

6 Pour the stock over the aubergine mixture and then spoon over the prepared tomato mixture.

7 Cover the dish with foil and bake for 30–45 minutes, until the vegetables are tender. Serve hot, garnished with black olives and parsley.

1 large onion,
finely chopped

2 small or medium
aubergines (eggplants),
cut into small cubes

4 courgettes (zucchini),
cut into small chunks

2 red, yellow or green
(bell) peppers, seeded
and chopped

115g/4oz/1 cup
frozen peas

115g/4oz green beans

450g/1lb new or salad
potatoes, peeled
and cubed

4–5 tomatoes, peeled

30ml/2 tbsp chopped
fresh parsley

3–4 garlic cloves, crushed

black olives and fresh
parsley, to garnish

FROM THE STORECUPBOARD

60ml/4 tbsp extra virgin
olive oil

200g/7oz can flageolet
(small cannellini) beans,
rinsed and drained

2.5ml/^{1}/$_2$ tsp
ground cinnamon

2.5ml/^{1}/$_2$ tsp
ground cumin

5ml/1 tsp paprika

400g/14oz can
chopped tomatoes

350ml/12fl oz/1^1/$_2$ cups
vegetable stock

salt and ground black
pepper, to taste

Energy 386kcal/1618kJ; Protein 15.4g; Carbohydrate 51.7g, of which sugars 22.6g; Fat 14.5g, of which saturates 2.5g; Cholesterol 0mg; Calcium 142mg; Fibre 14.3g; Sodium 234mg

Hot and Spicy Parsnips and Chickpeas ✳

The sweet flavour of parsnips goes very well with the aromatic spices in this hearty and healthy Indian-style vegetable stew. Offer Indian breads such as naan to mop up the delicious sauce.

SERVES FOUR

7 garlic cloves, chopped

1 small onion, chopped

5cm/2in piece fresh root ginger, chopped

2 green chillies, seeded and finely chopped

450ml/³/₄ pint/scant 2 cups plus 75ml/5 tbsp water

50g/2oz cashew nuts, toasted and ground

250g/9oz tomatoes, peeled and chopped

900g/2lb parsnips, cut into chunks

juice of 1 lime, to taste

fresh coriander (cilantro) leaves, to garnish

cashew nuts, toasted, to garnish

FROM THE STORECUPBOARD

200g/7oz dried chickpeas, soaked overnight in cold water, then drained

60ml/4 tbsp vegetable oil

5ml/1 tsp cumin seeds

10ml/2 tsp ground coriander seeds

5ml/1 tsp ground turmeric

2.5–5ml/¹/₂–1 tsp chilli powder or mild paprika

5ml/1 tsp ground roasted cumin seeds

salt and ground black pepper, to taste

1 Put the chickpeas in a pan, cover with cold water and bring to the boil. Boil for 10 minutes, then reduce the heat and cook for 1–1¹/₂ hours until the chickpeas are tender. Drain well.

2 Set 10ml/2 tsp of the garlic aside, then place the remainder in a food processor or blender with the onion, ginger and half the chillies. Add 75ml/5 tbsp water and process to make a paste.

3 Heat the oil in a large, deep, frying pan and cook the cumin seeds for 30 seconds. Stir in the coriander seeds, turmeric, chilli powder or paprika and the ground cashew nuts. Add the ginger and chilli paste and cook, stirring frequently, until the water begins to evaporate. Add the tomatoes and stir-fry until the mixture begins to turn red-brown in colour.

4 Mix in the chickpeas and parsnips with the rest of the water, the lime juice, 5ml/1 tsp salt and black pepper. Bring to the boil, stir, then simmer, uncovered, for 15–20 minutes, until tender.

5 Reduce the liquid until the sauce is thick. Add the ground cumin and reserved garlic and chilli, and cook for 1–2 minutes. Sprinkle over the coriander and cashew nuts and serve.

Energy 506kcal/2124kJ; Protein 18.4g; Carbohydrate 60.1g, of which sugars 18.2g; Fat 23.1g, of which saturates 3.4g; Cholesterol 0mg; Calcium 192mg; Fibre 17.1g; Sodium 86mg

Leek, Squash and Tomato Gratin

You can use virtually any kind of squash for this colourful and succulent gratin, from patty pans and acorn squash to pumpkins, depending on what is in season and your personal preference.

SERVES SIX

1 Steam the prepared squash in a steamer set over boiling salted water for 10 minutes.

2 Heat half the oil in a frying pan and cook the leeks gently for 5–6 minutes, until lightly coloured. Try to keep the slices intact. Preheat the oven to 190°C/375°F/Gas 5.

3 Layer all the squash, leeks and tomatoes in a 2 litre/3^1/$_2$ pint/8 cup gratin dish, arranging them in rows. Season with salt, pepper and cumin.

4 Pour the cream into a small pan and add the chilli and garlic. Bring to the boil over a low heat, then stir in the mint. Pour the mixture evenly over the layered vegetables, using a rubber spatula to scrape all the sauce out of the pan.

5 Cook for 50–55 minutes, or until the gratin is bubbling and tinged brown. Sprinkle the parsley and breadcrumbs on top and drizzle over the remaining oil.

6 Bake for another 15–20 minutes until the breadcrumbs are browned and crisp. Serve immediately.

450g/1lb peeled and seeded squash, cut into 1cm/^{1}/$_2$in slices

450g/1lb leeks, cut into thick, diagonal slices

675g/1^1/$_2$lb tomatoes, peeled and thickly sliced

300ml/^{1}/$_2$ pint/1^1/$_4$ cups single (light) cream

1 fresh red chilli, seeded and sliced

1 garlic clove, finely chopped

15ml/1 tbsp chopped fresh mint

30ml/2 tbsp chopped fresh parsley

60ml/4 tbsp fine white breadcrumbs

FROM THE STORECUPBOARD

60ml/4 tbsp olive oil

2.5ml/^{1}/$_2$ tsp ground toasted cumin seeds

salt and ground black pepper, to taste

VARIATIONS

• For a curried version of this dish, use ground coriander as well as cumin seeds, and coconut milk instead of cream. Use fresh coriander (cilantro) instead of mint and parsley.

• You can remove or add more fresh chilli, with or without the seeds, depending on how spicy you like it.

Energy 248kcal/1032kJ; Protein 5.7g; Carbohydrate 16.7g, of which sugars 7.8g; Fat 18g, of which saturates 7.4g; Cholesterol 28mg; Calcium 126mg; Fibre 3.8g; Sodium 104mg

Courgette and Potato Bake ✳

Cook this delicious dish in early autumn, and the aromas spilling from the kitchen will recall the rich summer tastes and colours just past.

SERVES FOUR

1 Preheat the oven to 190°C/375°F/Gas 5. Scrape the courgettes lightly under running water to dislodge any grit and then slice them into thin rounds.

2 Put the courgettes in a large baking dish and add the chopped potatoes, onion, garlic, red pepper and tomatoes. Mix well, then stir in the olive oil, hot water and dried oregano.

3 Spread the mixture evenly, then season with salt and ground black pepper. Bake for 30 minutes in the centre of the preheated oven, then stir in the parsley and a little more water.

4 Return the baking dish to the oven and cook for 1 hour, increasing the temperature to 200°C/400°F/Gas 6 for the final 10–15 minutes, so that the potatoes brown.

5 Serve immediately, garnished with the remaining parsley. You could also serve this as an accompaniment to grilled (broiled) meats, such as sausages, pork chops or steak.

675g/1¹/₂lb courgettes (zucchini)

450g/1lb potatoes, peeled and cut into chunks

1 onion, finely sliced

3 garlic cloves, chopped

1 large red (bell) pepper, seeded and cubed

150ml/¹/₄ pint/²/₃ cup hot water

45ml/3 tbsp chopped fresh flat leaf parsley, plus a few extra sprigs, to garnish

FROM THE STORECUPBOARD

400g/14oz can chopped tomatoes

150ml/¹/₄ pint/²/₃ cup extra virgin olive oil

5ml/1 tsp dried oregano

salt and ground black pepper, to taste

Energy 374kcal/1,554kJ; Protein 6.6g; Carbohydrate 28.6g, of which sugars 11.2g; Fat 26.7g, of which saturates 4g; Cholesterol 0mg; Calcium 86mg; Fibre 5.1g; Sodium 29mg

Mediterranean Bake ✳

Peppers, tomatoes and onions are baked together to make a colourful, soft vegetable dish that is studded with olives. In the summer the vegetables can be cooked on the barbecue. Serve with warm bread.

SERVES EIGHT

1 Cut the peppers in half lengthways with a large knife and remove the seeds. Cut each pepper lengthways into 12 strips. Preheat the oven to 200°C/400°F/Gas 6.

2 Place the peppers, onion, garlic, olives and tomatoes in a large roasting pan.

3 Sprinkle the vegetables with the sugar, then pour in the sherry. Season well with salt and pepper, cover with foil and bake for 45 minutes.

4 Remove the foil from the pan and stir the mixture well. Add the rosemary sprigs and drizzle with the olive oil. Return the pan to the oven and cook for a further 30 minutes, uncovered, until the vegetables are very tender. Serve hot or cold with plenty of chunks of fresh crusty bread.

2 red (bell) peppers

2 yellow (bell) peppers

1 red onion, sliced

2 garlic cloves, halved

50g/2oz/¼ cup black olives

6 large ripe tomatoes, quartered

45ml/3 tbsp amontillado sherry

3–4 fresh rosemary sprigs

fresh bread, to serve

FROM THE STORECUPBOARD

5ml/1 tsp soft light brown sugar

30ml/2 tbsp olive oil

salt and ground black pepper, to taste

COOK'S TIPS

• Good quality Spanish olives are best for this dish, although you can use other ones if you prefer. Choose unpitted ones as they have a better flavour.

• Amontillado sherry has a dry to medium, slightly nutty flavour that perfectly complements the saltiness of the olives.

Energy 151kcal/635kJ; Protein 6.3g; Carbohydrate 23g, of which sugars 7.9g; Fat 4.4g, of which saturates 1.2g; Cholesterol 35mg; Calcium 113mg; Fibre 2.5g; Sodium 37mg

4 garlic cloves, crushed

4 shallots, finely chopped

30ml/2 tbsp yellow
curry paste

400ml/14fl oz/1²/₃ cups
near-boiling vegetable stock

300ml/¹/₂ pint/1¹/₄ cups
coconut milk

2 kaffir lime leaves, torn

15ml/1 tbsp chopped
fresh galangal

450g/1lb pumpkin, peeled,
seeded and diced

225g/8oz sweet
potatoes, diced

90g/3¹/₂ oz/1¹/₂ cups
chestnut mushrooms,
sliced

90g/3¹/₂ oz/scant 1 cup
peanuts, roasted and
chopped

50g/2oz/¹/₃ cup pumpkin
seeds, toasted, and fresh
green or red chilli flowers,
to garnish

FROM THE STORECUPBOARD

30ml/2 tbsp vegetable oil

15ml/1 tbsp soy sauce

30ml/2 tbsp Thai
fish sauce

COOK'S TIP

To make chilli flowers,
hold each chilli by the
stem and slit the chilli in
half lengthways, keeping
the stem end intact.
Continue slitting the chilli
in the same way to make
thin strips. Put the chillies
in a bowl of iced water
and leave for several
hours to curl up like
flower petals.

Pumpkin and Peanut Curry ✳

Rich, sweet, spicy and fragrant, the flavours of this delicious Thai-style
curry really come together with long, slow cooking. Serve with rice or
noodles for a substantial supper dish.

SERVES FOUR

1 Heat the oil in a frying pan. Add the garlic and shallots and
cook over a medium heat, stirring occasionally, for 10 minutes,
until softened and beginning to turn golden.

2 Add the yellow curry paste to the pan and stir-fry over a
medium heat for 30 seconds, until fragrant. Tip the mixture into
a ceramic cooking pot.

3 Add the lime leaves, galangal, pumpkin and sweet potatoes
to the cooking pot. Pour the stock and 150ml/¹/₄ pint/²/₃ cup
of the coconut milk over the vegetables, and stir to combine.
Cover with the lid and cook on high for 1¹/₂ hours.

4 Stir the mushrooms, soy sauce and Thai fish sauce into the
curry, then add the chopped peanuts and pour in the remaining
coconut milk. Cover and cook on high for a further 3 hours, or
until the vegetables are very tender.

5 Spoon the curry into warmed serving bowls, garnish with the
pumpkin seeds and chillies, and serve immediately.

Energy 337kcal/1404kJ; Protein 10.3g; Carbohydrate 21.7g, of which sugars 10.8g; Fat 23.8g, of which saturates 4g; Cholesterol 0mg; Calcium 168mg; Fibre 5.1g; Sodium 554mg

Potato Curry with Yogurt ✳

Combining an aromatic mixture of herbs and spices with creamy yogurt and potatoes, this simple Indian curry is a feast for all the senses. It is delicious on its own, served with yogurt and a spicy pickle or chutney, or with some flatbread and wedges of lemon for a more substantial meal.

SERVES FOUR

1 Using a mortar and pestle or a food processor, grind the garlic and ginger to a coarse paste.

2 Heat the ghee in a heavy pan, add the shallots and chillies and cook until fragrant. Add the garlic and ginger paste with the sugar, and stir until the mixture begins to colour.

3 Stir in the curry leaves, cinnamon sticks, turmeric and garam masala, and toss in the potatoes, making sure they are coated in the spice mixture.

4 Pour in just enough cold water to cover the potatoes. Bring to the boil, then reduce the heat and simmer until the potatoes are just cooked – they should still have a bite to them.

5 Season with salt and pepper to taste. Add the tomatoes and heat them through. Fold in the yogurt, then sprinkle with the chilli powder, coriander and mint. Serve immediately with lemon to squeeze over it and flatbread for scooping it up.

6 garlic cloves, chopped

25g/1oz fresh root ginger, peeled and chopped

30ml/2 tbsp ghee, or 15ml/1 tbsp oil and 15g/¹⁄₂oz/1 tbsp butter

6 shallots, halved lengthways and sliced along the grain

2 green chillies, seeded and finely sliced

a handful of fresh or dried curry leaves

500g/1¹⁄₄lb waxy potatoes, cut into bitesize pieces

2 tomatoes, peeled, seeded and quartered

250ml/8fl oz/1 cup Greek (US strained plain) yogurt

fresh coriander (cilantro) and mint leaves, finely chopped, to garnish

1 lemon, quartered, to serve

FROM THE STORECUPBOARD

10ml/2 tsp sugar

2 cinnamon sticks

5–10ml/1–2 tsp ground turmeric

15ml/1 tbsp garam masala

salt and ground black pepper, to taste

5ml/1 tsp red chilli powder, to garnish

VARIATION *This recipe also works well with sweet potatoes, butternut squash or pumpkin, all of which absorb the aromatic spices well.*

Energy 231kcal/967kJ; Protein 6.7g; Carbohydrate 26.2g, of which sugars 7.4g; Fat 12.4g, of which saturates 4.1g; Cholesterol 0mg; Calcium 110mg; Fibre 2g; Sodium 63mg

200ml/7fl oz/scant 1 cup coconut cream

300ml/½ pint/1¼ cups coconut milk

200g/7oz snake beans, cut into 2cm/¾in lengths

200g/7oz baby corn

4 baby courgettes (zucchini), sliced

1 small aubergine (eggplant), cubed or sliced

fresh coriander (cilantro) leaves, to garnish

FOR THE CURRY PASTE

15ml/1 tbsp chopped fresh galangal

10ml/2 tsp finely grated garlic

30ml/2 tbsp finely chopped lemon grass

4 red Asian shallots, finely chopped

5ml/1 tsp shrimp paste

5ml/1 tsp finely chopped lime rind

FROM THE STORECUPBOARD

10ml/2 tsp hot chilli powder

10ml/2 tsp ground coriander

10ml/2 tsp ground cumin

5ml/1 tsp turmeric

30ml/2 tbsp sunflower oil

150ml/¼ pint/⅔ cup vegetable stock

30ml/2 tbsp Thai fish sauce

10ml/2 tsp light muscovado (brown) sugar

noodles or rice, to serve

Thai Yellow Vegetable Curry ✳✳

This hot and spicy curry has a creamy richness that contrasts well with the heat of chilli. Yellow curry paste is available in supermarkets and is useful if you're in a hurry, but you will really taste the difference when you make this one using fresh herbs, spices and aromatics.

SERVES FOUR

1 Make the curry paste. Place the chilli powder, coriander, cumin, turmeric, galangal, garlic, lemon grass, shallots, shrimp paste and lime rind in a small food processor and blend with 30–45ml/2–3 tbsp of cold water to make a smooth paste. Add a little more water if the paste seems too dry.

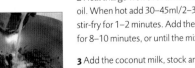

2 Heat a large wok over a medium heat and add the sunflower oil. When hot add 30–45ml/2–3 tbsp of the curry paste and stir-fry for 1–2 minutes. Add the coconut cream and cook gently for 8–10 minutes, or until the mixture starts to separate.

3 Add the coconut milk, stock and vegetables and cook gently for 8–10 minutes, until the vegetables are just tender. Stir in the fish sauce and sugar, garnish with coriander leaves and serve with noodles or rice.

Energy 279kcal/1161kJ; Protein 9.8g; Carbohydrate 17.4g, of which sugars 13.3g; Fat 19.4g, of which saturates 3.6g; Cholesterol 5mg; Calcium 99mg; Fibre 3.3g; Sodium 824mg

Peppers Filled with Spiced Vegetables ✳

Indian spices season the potato and aubergine stuffing in these colourful baked peppers. They are good with plain rice and a lentil dhal. Alternatively, serve them with a crisp green salad, Indian breads and a cucumber or mint and yogurt raita.

SERVES SIX

1 Cut the tops off the red or yellow peppers then remove and discard the seeds. Cut a thin slice off the base of the peppers, if necessary, to make them stand upright.

2 Bring a large pan of lightly salted water to the boil. Add the peppers and cook for 5–6 minutes. Drain well and leave the peppers upside down in a colander to drain completely.

3 Cook the potatoes in large pan of lightly salted, boiling water for 10–12 minutes, until just tender. Drain, cool and peel, then cut into 1cm/^{1}/$_2$in dice.

4 Put the onion, garlic, ginger and green chillies in a food processor or blender with 60ml/4 tbsp of the water and process to a purée.

5 Heat 45ml/3 tbsp of the oil in a large, deep frying pan and cook the aubergine, stirring occasionally, until browned on all sides. Remove from the pan and set aside. Add another 30ml/2 tbsp of the oil to the pan and cook the potatoes until lightly browned. Remove from the pan and set aside.

6 If necessary, add another 15ml/1 tbsp oil to the pan, then add the cumin and *kalonji* seeds. Cook briefly until they darken, then add the turmeric, coriander and ground cumin. Cook for 15 seconds. Stir in the onion and garlic purée and cook, scraping the pan, until it begins to brown.

7 Return the potatoes and aubergines to the pan, season with salt, pepper and 1–2 pinches of cayenne. Add the remaining water and 15ml/1 tbsp lemon juice and then cook, stirring, until the liquid evaporates. Preheat the oven to 190°C/375°F/Gas 5.

8 Fill the peppers with the potato mixture and place on a lightly greased baking sheet. Brush the peppers with a little oil and bake for 30–35 minutes, until the peppers are cooked. Leave to cool a little, then sprinkle with a little more lemon juice, garnish with the coriander and serve.

---

6 large red or yellow (bell) peppers

500g/1^1/$_4$lb waxy potatoes

1 small onion, chopped

4–5 garlic cloves, chopped

5cm/2in piece fresh root ginger, chopped

1–2 fresh green chillies, seeded and chopped

105ml/7 tbsp water

1 aubergine (eggplant), cut into 1cm/^{1}/$_2$in dice

5ml/1 tsp *kalonji* seeds

about 30ml/2 tbsp lemon juice

30ml/2 tbsp chopped fresh coriander (cilantro), to garnish

FROM THE STORECUPBOARD

90–105ml/6–7 tbsp groundnut (peanut) oil

10ml/2 tsp cumin seeds

2.5ml/^{1}/$_2$ tsp ground turmeric

5ml/1 tsp ground coriander

5ml/1 tsp ground toasted cumin seeds

pinch of cayenne pepper

salt and ground black pepper, to taste

COOK'S TIP

Kalonji, or nigella as it is sometimes known, is a tiny black seed. It is widely used in Indian cookery, especially sprinkled over breads or in potato dishes, and is available from large supermarkets. It has a mild, slightly nutty flavour and is best toasted for a few seconds in a dry frying pan over a medium heat. This helps to bring out its flavour.

Energy 234kcal/976kJ; Protein 4.2g; Carbohydrate 28.1g, of which sugars 14.8g; Fat 12.4g, of which saturates 2.4g; Cholesterol 0mg; Calcium 45mg; Fibre 5.5g; Sodium 21mg

Roasted Aubergines Stuffed with Feta Cheese and Fresh Coriander ✳✳

Aubergines take on a lovely smoky flavour when grilled on a barbecue. Choose a good-quality Greek feta cheese for the best flavour.

SERVES SIX

1 Prepare a barbecue. Cook the aubergines for 20 minutes on the barbecue, turning occasionally, until they are slightly charred and soft. Remove and cut in half lengthways.

2 Carefully scoop the aubergine flesh into a bowl, reserving the skins. Mash the flesh roughly with a fork.

3 Crumble the feta cheese, and then stir it into the mashed aubergine with the chopped coriander and olive oil. Season with salt and ground black pepper to taste.

4 Spoon the feta mixture back into the skins and return to the barbecue for 5 minutes to warm through.

5 Serve immediately with a fresh green salad coated with fruity extra virgin olive oil, garnished with sprigs of fresh coriander.

3 medium to large aubergines (eggplant)

400g/14oz feta cheese

a small bunch of fresh coriander (cilantro), roughly chopped, plus extra sprigs to garnish

FROM THE STORECUPBOARD

60ml/4 tbsp extra virgin olive oil

salt and freshly ground black pepper

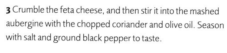

Energy 257kcal/1,066kJ; Protein 12g; Carbohydrate 4.2g, of which sugars 3.9g; Fat 21.5g, of which saturates 10.3g; Cholesterol 47mg; Calcium 286mg; Fibre 3.3g; Sodium 968mg

4 large onions

150g/5oz goat's cheese, crumbled or cubed

50g/2oz/1 cup fresh breadcrumbs

8 sun-dried tomatoes in oil, drained and chopped

1–2 garlic cloves, chopped

2.5ml/½ tsp chopped fresh thyme

30ml/2 tbsp chopped fresh parsley

1 small (US medium) egg, beaten

45ml/3 tbsp pine nuts, toasted

30ml/2 tbsp oil from the sun-dried tomatoes

FROM THE STORECUPBOARD

salt and ground black pepper, to taste

VARIATIONS

• *Use feta cheese in place of the goat's cheese and substitute mint, currants and pitted black olives for the other flavourings.*

• *Stuff the onions with wilted spinach and cooked long grain rice mixed with smoked mozzarella cheese and toasted flaked almonds.*

• *Substitute 175g/6oz Roquefort or Gorgonzola for the goat's cheese, omit the sun-dried tomatoes and pine nuts, and add 75g/3oz chopped walnuts and 115g/4oz chopped celery, cooked until soft with the chopped onion in 25ml/1½ tbsp olive oil.*

Onions Stuffed with Goat's Cheese and Sun-dried Tomatoes **✳✳**

Roasted onions and tangy cheese are a winning combination. They make an excellent main course when served with rice.

SERVES FOUR

1 Bring a large pan of lightly salted water to the boil. Add the whole onions in their skins and boil for 10 minutes. Drain and cool, then cut each onion in half horizontally and peel.

2 Using a teaspoon, remove the centre of each onion, leaving a thick shell around the outside. Reserve the flesh and place the shells in an oiled ovenproof dish. Preheat the oven to 190°C/375°F/Gas 5.

3 Chop the scooped-out onion flesh and place in a bowl. Add the goat's cheese, breadcrumbs, sun-dried tomatoes, garlic, thyme, parsley and egg. Mix well, then season with salt and pepper and add the toasted pine nuts.

4 Divide the stuffing among the onions and cover with foil. Bake for about 25 minutes.

5 Uncover the onions, drizzle with the oil and cook for another 30–40 minutes, until bubbling and well cooked. Baste occasionally during cooking.

Energy 402kcal/1669kJ; Protein 14.8g; Carbohydrate 25.1g, of which sugars 11.7g; Fat 27.7g, of which saturates 8.8g; Cholesterol 82mg; Calcium 120mg; Fibre 3.2g; Sodium 346mg

Bubble and Squeak ✳

Whether you have leftovers or cook this old-fashioned classic from fresh, be sure to give it a really good "squeak" in the pan so it turns a rich honey brown. Serve with warm bread for a quick vegetarian supper, or as an accompaniment to grilled pork chops or fried eggs.

SERVES FOUR

1 Heat 30ml/2 tbsp of the oil in a heavy frying pan. Add the onion and cook over a medium heat, stirring frequently, until softened but not browned.

2 In a large bowl, mix together the potatoes and cooked cabbage or Brussels sprouts and season with salt and plenty of ground black pepper to taste.

3 Add the vegetables to the pan with the cooked onions, stir well, then press the vegetable mixture into a large, even cake.

4 Cook over a medium heat for about 15 minutes, until the cake has browned underneath.

5 Invert a large plate over the pan and, holding it tightly against the pan, turn them both over together.

6 Lift off the frying pan, return it to the heat and add the remaining oil. When hot, slide the cake back into the pan, browned side uppermost.

7 Cook over a medium heat for 10 minutes, or until the underside is golden brown. Serve hot, in wedges.

1 medium onion, chopped

450g/1lb floury potatoes, cooked and mashed

225g/8oz cooked cabbage or Brussels sprouts, finely chopped

FROM THE STORECUPBOARD

60ml/4 tbsp vegetable oil

salt and ground black pepper, to taste

VARIATIONS

• Add any left-over gravy from a roast dinner for a really delicious flavour.

• Use bacon fat in place of the vegetable oil for a non-vegetarian version.

Energy 205kcal/857kJ; Protein 3.5g; Carbohydrate 23.3g, of which sugars 4.2g; Fat 11.5g, of which saturates 1.2g; Cholesterol 0mg; Calcium 34mg; Fibre 3g; Sodium 15mg

Peanut and Tofu Cutlets ✳✳

These delicious, high-protein patties make a filling and satisfying vegetarian mid-week meal served with lightly steamed green vegetables or a crisp salad, and a tangy salsa or ketchup. They make an ideal alternative to beef or turkey patties when served in bread rolls.

SERVES FOUR

1 Cook the rice according to the instructions on the packet until tender, then drain. Heat the vegetable oil in a large, heavy frying pan and cook the onion and garlic over a low heat, stirring occasionally, for about 5 minutes, until softened and golden.

2 Meanwhile, spread out the peanuts on a baking sheet and toast under the grill (broiler) for a few minutes, until browned. Place the peanuts, onion, garlic, rice, tofu, coriander or parsley, if using, and soy sauce in a blender or food processor and process until the mixture comes together in a thick paste.

3 Divide the paste into eight equal-size mounds and form each mound into a cutlet shape or square.

4 Heat the olive oil for shallow frying in a large, heavy frying pan. Add the cutlets, in two batches if necessary, and cook for 5–10 minutes on each side, until golden and heated through.

5 Remove from the pan with a fish slice or metal spatula and drain on kitchen paper. Keep warm while you cook the remaining batch, then serve immediately.

1 onion, finely chopped

1 garlic clove, crushed

200g/7oz/1³/₄ cups unsalted peanuts

small bunch of fresh coriander (cilantro) or parsley, chopped (optional)

250g/9oz firm tofu, drained and crumbled

FROM THE STORECUPBOARD

90g/3¹/₂oz/¹/₂ cup brown rice

15ml/1 tbsp vegetable oil

30ml/2 tbsp soy sauce

30ml/2 tbsp olive oil, for shallow frying

Energy 495kcal/2059kJ; Protein 20.2g; Carbohydrate 27.1g, of which sugars 5.3g; Fat 34.7g, of which saturates 5.9g; Cholesterol 0mg; Calcium 381mg; Fibre 4.4g; Sodium 543mg

Tofu and Green Bean Thai Red Curry ✳✳

This is one of those versatile recipes that should be in every cook's repertoire. This version uses green beans, but other types of vegetable work equally well, depending on what is available. The tofu takes on the flavour of the spice paste and also boosts the nutritional value.

SERVES FOUR

1 Pour about one-third of the coconut milk into a wok or large frying pan. Cook gently until it starts to separate and an oily sheen appears on the surface.

2 Add the red curry paste, fish sauce and sugar to the coconut milk. Mix thoroughly, then add the mushrooms. Stir and cook for 1 minute.

3 Stir in the remaining coconut milk. Bring back to the boil, then add the green beans and tofu cubes. Simmer gently for 4–5 minutes more.

4 Stir in the kaffir lime leaves and sliced red chillies. Spoon the curry into a serving dish, garnish with the coriander leaves and serve immediately.

600ml/1 pint/2¹/₂ cups canned coconut milk

15ml/1 tbsp Thai red curry paste

225g/8oz/3¹/₄ cups button (white) mushrooms

115g/4oz/scant 1 cup green beans, trimmed

175g/6oz firm tofu, rinsed, drained and cut in 2cm/³/₄in cubes

4 kaffir lime leaves, torn

2 fresh red chillies, seeded and sliced

fresh coriander (cilantro) leaves, to garnish

FROM THE STORECUPBOARD

45ml/3 tbsp Thai fish sauce

10ml/2 tsp light muscovado (brown) sugar

Energy 59kcal/250kJ; Protein 3.8g; Carbohydrate 7.5g, of which sugars 7.1g; Fat 1.8g, of which saturates 0.4g; Cholesterol 0mg; Calcium 188mg; Fibre 0.8g; Sodium 291mg

Tofu, Roasted Peanut and Pepper Kebabs ✳✳

A coating of ground, dry-roasted peanuts pressed on to cubed tofu provides plenty of flavour along with the peppers. Use metal or bamboo skewers for the kebabs – if you use bamboo, then soak them in cold water for 30 minutes before using, to prevent scorching.

SERVES FOUR

1 Pat the tofu dry on kitchen paper, then cut it into small cubes. Finely grind the peanuts in a blender or food processor and transfer to a plate. Coat the tofu in the ground nuts.

2 Preheat the grill (broiler) to moderate. Cut the halved and seeded peppers into large chunks. Thread the chunks of pepper on to four large skewers with the tofu cubes and place on a foil-lined grill rack.

3 Grill (broil) the kebabs, turning them often, for 10–12 minutes, or until the peppers and peanuts are beginning to brown. Transfer the kebabs to plates and serve with the dipping sauce.

250g/9oz firm tofu, drained

50g/2oz/¹/₂ cup dry-roasted peanuts

2 red and 2 green (bell) peppers, halved and seeded

60ml/4 tbsp sweet chilli dipping sauce

Energy 175kcal/730kJ; Protein 10g; Carbohydrate 12.9g, of which sugars 11.4g; Fat 9.6g, of which saturates 1.6g; Cholesterol 0mg; Calcium 339mg; Fibre 3.6g; Sodium 108mg

Vegetable Pancakes with Tomato Salsa ✳

Spinach and egg pancakes are tasty, inexpensive and nutritious. Serve with flavoursome sun-dried tomato salsa and bread for a light snack, or with boiled new potatoes for a more sustaining main meal.

MAKES TEN

1 Prepare the tomato salsa: place the tomatoes, chilli, sun-dried tomatoes, onion, garlic, olive oil, sherry and brown sugar in a bowl and toss together to combine. Cover and leave to stand in a cool place for 2–3 hours.

2 To make the pancakes, finely chop the spinach, leek and coriander or parsley, then place in a bowl and beat in the eggs and seasoning. Blend in the flour and 30–45ml/2–3 tbsp water and leave to stand for 20 minutes.

3 Drop spoonfuls of the batter into a lightly oiled frying pan and cook until golden underneath. Using a fish slice (metal spatula), turn the pancakes over and cook on the other side.

4 Lift the pancakes out of the pan, drain on kitchen paper and keep warm while you cook the remaining mixture. Sprinkle with Parmesan cheese and serve with the salsa.

225g/8oz spinach

1 small leek

a few sprigs of fresh coriander (cilantro) or parsley

3 large (US extra large) eggs

25g/1oz/¹⁄₃ cup freshly grated Parmesan cheese

FOR THE SALSA

2 tomatoes, peeled and chopped

¹⁄₄ fresh red chilli, chopped

2 pieces sun-dried tomato in oil, drained and chopped

1 small red onion, chopped

1 garlic clove, crushed

30ml/2 tbsp sherry

FROM THE STORECUPBOARD

60ml/4 tbsp olive oil

2.5ml/¹⁄₂ tsp soft light brown sugar

50g/2oz/¹⁄₂ cup plain (all-purpose) flour, sifted

vegetable oil, for frying

salt, ground black pepper and freshly grated nutmeg

COOK'S TIP Try to find sun-ripened tomatoes for the salsa, as these have the best flavour and are superior to those ripened under glass.

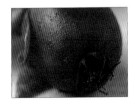

Energy 153kcal/634kJ; Protein 4.6g; Carbohydrate 6.2g, of which sugars 2.1g; Fat 11.8g, of which saturates 2.2g; Cholesterol 63mg; Calcium 92mg; Fibre 1.3g; Sodium 84mg

25g/1oz/1 cup chopped
fresh herbs

120ml/4fl oz/¹⁄₂ cup milk

3 eggs

FOR THE SAUCE

1 small onion, chopped

2 garlic cloves, crushed

FOR THE FILLING

450g/1lb fresh spinach,
cooked and drained

175g/6oz/³⁄₄ cup
ricotta cheese

25g/1oz/¹⁄₄ cup
pine nuts, toasted

5 sun-dried tomato
halves in olive oil,
drained and chopped

30ml/2 tbsp shredded
fresh basil

4 egg whites

FROM THE STORECUPBOARD

15ml/1 tbsp sunflower
oil, plus extra for frying
and greasing

25g/1oz/¹⁄₄ cup plain
(all-purpose) flour

pinch of salt

30ml/2 tbsp olive oil

400g/14oz can
chopped tomatoes

pinch of soft light
brown sugar

grated nutmeg and
ground black pepper

Baked Herb Crêpes with Spinach and Ricotta ✳✳

Turn light herb crêpes into something special. Fill with a spinach, cheese and pine nut filling, then bake and serve with a delicious tomato sauce.

SERVES FOUR

1 To make the crêpes, place the herbs and sunflower oil in a food processor and process until smooth. Add the milk, eggs, flour and salt and process again. Leave to rest for 30 minutes.

2 Heat a small non-stick frying pan and add a small amount of sunflower oil. Pour in a ladleful of the batter. Swirl around until the batter covers the base evenly. Cook for 2 minutes, turn over and cook for a further 1–2 minutes. Make seven more crêpes.

3 To make the sauce, heat the olive oil in a pan, add the onion and garlic, and cook for 5 minutes. Stir in the tomatoes and sugar, and cook for 10 minutes until thickened. Process in a blender, then sieve (strain). Preheat the oven to 190°C/375°F/ Gas 5.

4 To make the filling, mix together the spinach and the ricotta, pine nuts, tomatoes, basil, nutmeg and pepper. Whisk the egg whites until they are stiff. Stir one-third into the spinach mixture, then gently fold in the rest.

5 Place one crêpe at a time on a lightly oiled baking sheet, add a spoonful of filling and fold into quarters. Bake for 12 minutes. Meanwhile, pour the tomato sauce into a small pan and reheat it gently, stirring occasionally. Serve the sauce with the hot crêpes.

Energy 434kcal/1800kJ; Protein 14.9g; Carbohydrate 15.1g, of which sugars 9.8g; Fat 35.4g, of which saturates 8.3g; Cholesterol 161mg; Calcium 251mg; Fibre 5g; Sodium 229mg

Carrot and Apricot Rolls ✳

Served with a dollop of yogurt flavoured with mint and garlic, these sweet, herby carrot rolls make a delicious light lunch or supper with a green salad and warm crusty bread. Alternatively, you can mould the mixture into miniature balls and serve them on sticks as a nibble to go with drinks.

SERVES FOUR

1 Steam the carrot slices for about 25 minutes, or until they are very soft.

2 Meanwhile, make the mint yogurt. Beat the yogurt in a bowl with the lemon juice and garlic, season to taste with salt and pepper and stir in the mint. Set aside, or chill in the refrigerator.

3 Mash the carrots to a paste while they are warm. Add the breadcrumbs, spring onions, apricots and pine nuts and mix well with a fork. Beat in the egg and stir in the red pepper or chilli and herbs. Season to taste with salt and pepper.

4 Tip a small heap of flour on to a flat surface. Take a plum-sized portion of the carrot mixture in your fingers and mould it into an oblong roll. Coat the carrot roll in the flour and put it on a plate. Repeat with rest of the mixture, to make 12–16 rolls altogether.

5 Heat enough sunflower oil for shallow frying in a heavy frying pan. Place the carrot rolls in the oil and fry over a medium heat for 8–10 minutes, turning them from time to time, until they are golden brown. Remove with a slotted spoon and drain on kitchen paper. Serve hot, with lemon wedges and the mint yogurt.

8–10 carrots, sliced

2–3 slices of day-old bread, ground into crumbs

4 spring onions (scallions), finely sliced

150g/5oz/generous 1/2 cup dried apricots, chopped

45ml/3 tbsp pine nuts

1 egg

5ml/1 tsp Turkish red pepper, or 1 fresh red chilli, seeded and chopped

1 bunch of fresh dill, chopped

1 bunch of fresh basil, finely shredded

lemon wedges, to serve

FOR THE MINT YOGURT

about 225g/8oz/1 cup natural (plain) yogurt

juice of 1/2 lemon

1–2 garlic cloves, crushed

1 bunch of fresh mint, finely chopped

FROM THE STORECUPBOARD

salt and ground black pepper, to taste

plain (all-purpose) flour

sunflower oil, for shallow frying

Energy 401kcal/1673kJ; Protein 8.7g; Carbohydrate 46g, of which sugars 29.1g; Fat 21.5g, of which saturates 2.5g; Cholesterol 48mg; Calcium 144mg; Fibre 8.5g; Sodium 145mg

Vegetarian Sausages ✳

These flavoursome cheese and leek sausages are a delicious meat-free alternative for all the family. Quick and easy to cook, they make a fabulous lunch or light meal served with a crisp salad and a fruit-based sauce or chutney. For a more substantial meal, serve in a bread roll.

MAKES EIGHT

1 In a large mixing bowl, stir together the breadcrumbs, cheese, leek, herbs, mustard and seasoning to taste.

2 Separate 1 egg and lightly beat the yolk with the whole egg (reserving the white). Stir the beaten eggs into the breadcrumb mixture. You need to add sufficient milk to make a mixture that can then be gathered together into a sticky (but not wet) ball.

3 Using your hands, divide the mixture into eight and shape into sausages of equal size. Cover and refrigerate for about 1 hour, or until needed.

4 Lightly whisk the reserved egg white. Coat each sausage in flour, egg white and then in fresh breadcrumbs.

5 Heat enough oil for deep-frying in a large pan to 180°C/350°F. Lower the sausages into the oil and cook for 5 minutes until crisp and brown. Lift out, drain on kitchen paper and serve immediately.

150g/5oz/3 cups fresh breadcrumbs, plus extra for coating

100g/3³/₄oz/1 cup mature (sharp) Caerphilly or Cheddar cheese, grated

1 small leek, washed and thinly sliced

15–30ml/1–2 tbsp chopped fresh herbs, such as parsley, thyme and a very little sage

2 eggs

milk to mix, if necessary

FROM THE STORECUPBOARD

5ml/1 tsp mustard powder

plain (all-purpose) flour, for coating

oil, for deep-frying

salt and ground black pepper, to taste

Energy 202kcal/844kJ; Protein 7.6g; Carbohydrate 17.6g, of which sugars 1g; Fat 11.5g, of which saturates 3.8g; Cholesterol 60mg; Calcium 134mg; Fibre 1g; Sodium 251mg

Cheesy Aubergines ✳

This warming and nourishing dish is sure to be a hit with all the family, and especially with children. Serve it as a main dish for lunch or supper with chunks of fresh, crusty bread and a juicy green salad.

SERVES FOUR

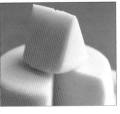

1 Preheat the oven to 200°C/400°F/ Gas 6. Put the aubergines on the gas flame on top of the stove, or under a grill (broiler), and turn them until the skin is charred on all sides and the flesh feels soft. Place in a plastic bag and leave for a few minutes.

2 Hold each aubergine under cold running water and peel off the charred skin. Squeeze the flesh to get rid of any excess water, remove the stalks and chop the flesh to a pulp.

3 To make the sauce, melt the butter in a heavy pan, remove from the heat and stir in the flour. Slowly beat in the milk, then return the pan to a medium heat and cook, stirring constantly, until the sauce is smooth and thick. Beat in the grated Cheddar cheese a little at a time, then beat in the aubergine pulp and season to taste with salt and pepper.

4 Tip the mixture into a baking dish and sprinkle a generous layer of grano padano over the top. Bake in the oven for about 25 minutes, until the top is nicely browned.

2 large aubergines (eggplants)

50g/2oz/¹⁄₄ cup butter

600ml/1 pint/2¹⁄₂ cups milk

115g/4oz Cheddar cheese, grated

finely grated grano padano cheese, for the topping

FROM THE STORECUPBOARD

30ml/2 tbsp plain (all-purpose) flour

salt and ground black pepper, to taste

Energy 322kcal/1344kJ; Protein 14.1g; Carbohydrate 15.2g, of which sugars 9.3g; Fat 22.7g, of which saturates 14.5g; Cholesterol 63mg; Calcium 415mg; Fibre 2.2g; Sodium 350mg

Cheese Pudding ✳

This light, soufflé-like pudding is simply made with cheese, breadcrumbs, milk and eggs. Serve it with green vegetables, such as beans or broccoli, or with a crisp salad tossed in an oil and vinegar dressing.

SERVES FOUR

1 Preheat the oven to 200°C/400°F/Gas 6. Butter the insides of a 1.2 litre/2 pint/5 cup ovenproof soufflé dish.

2 Mix together three-quarters of the grated Cheddar cheese with the breadcrumbs.

3 Put the remaining ingredients into a pan and stir well. Heat gently, stirring, until the butter has just melted (if the mixture gets too hot then the eggs will start to set).

4 Stir into the cheese mixture and tip into the prepared dish. Scatter the remaining cheese evenly over the top.

5 Put into the hot oven and cook for about 30 minutes or until golden brown and just set (a knife inserted in the centre should come out clean).

225g/8oz/2 cups grated mature (sharp) Cheddar-style cheese

115g/4oz/2 cups fresh breadcrumbs

600ml/1 pint/2¹⁄₂ cups milk

40g/1¹⁄₂oz/3 tbsp butter

3 eggs, beaten

FROM THE STORECUPBOARD

5ml/1 tsp mustard (such as wholegrain or English) or 2.5ml/¹⁄₂ tsp mustard powder

salt and ground black pepper, to taste

Energy 534kcal/2232kJ; Protein 27.5g; Carbohydrate 29.5g, of which sugars 7.9g; Fat 33.9g, of which saturates 20.2g; Cholesterol 227mg; Calcium 656mg; Fibre 0.6g; Sodium 803mg

Cheese and Tomato Soufflés ✳

Guests are always impressed by a home-made soufflé and this recipe for little individual ones is the ultimate in effortless entertaining. Serve with a green salad and some warm bread.

SERVES SIX

1 Melt the butter in a pan, then stir in the flour to form a paste and cook for 1 minute. Pour in the milk and stir until smooth, then bring to the boil, stirring continuously. Stir in the Cheddar and mix until the cheese has melted and the sauce is smooth.

2 Preheat the oven to 200°C/400°F/Gas 6. Tip the cheese sauce into a bowl. Thinly slice the sun-dried tomatoes and add them to the sauce with 90g/3¹/₂oz/generous 1 cup of the grano padano and the egg yolks. Season well and stir.

3 Brush the base and sides of six 200ml/7fl oz/scant 1 cup ramekins or individual soufflé dishes with the oil, then coat the insides with half of the remaining cheese, tilting them until evenly covered. Tip out any excess cheese and set aside.

4 Whisk the egg whites in a clean, grease-free bowl until stiff. Use a large metal spoon to stir one-quarter of the egg whites into the sauce, then fold in the remaining egg whites.

5 Spoon the mixture into the ramekins or soufflé dishes and sprinkle with the reserved cheese. Place on a baking sheet and bake for about 15–18 minutes, or until the soufflé is well risen and golden. Serve immediately with a mixed green salad.

25g/1oz/2 tbsp butter

350ml/¹/₂ pint/1¹/₄ cups full-fat (whole) milk

115g/4oz/1 cup grated Cheddar cheese

50g/2oz sun-dried tomatoes in olive oil, drained, plus 10ml/ 2 tsp of the oil

130g/4¹/₂ oz/1¹/₂ cups grated grano padano cheese

4 large (US extra large) eggs, separated

FROM THE STORECUPBOARD

25g/1oz/2 tbsp plain (all-purpose) flour

salt and ground black pepper, to taste

Energy 328kcal/1364kJ; Protein 20g; Carbohydrate 6.2g, of which sugars 3g; Fat 24.7g, of which saturates 13.6g; Cholesterol 184mg; Calcium 497mg; Fibre 0.2g, Sodium 473mg

Frittata with Sun-dried Tomatoes ✳

This Italian omelette, made with tangy Parmesan cheese, can be eaten warm or cold. It is perfect as a light vegetarian meal when served with a large mixed salad.

SERVES FOUR

1 Place the tomatoes in a bowl and pour over hot water to cover. Leave to soak for 15 minutes, then pat dry on kitchen paper. Reserve the soaking water. Cut the tomatoes into strips.

2 Heat the olive oil in a large non-stick frying pan. Cook the onion for 5–6 minutes. Add the thyme and tomatoes and cook for a further 2–3 minutes.

3 Break the eggs into a bowl and beat lightly. Stir in 45ml/3 tbsp of the tomato soaking water and the Parmesan and season to taste. Raise the heat under the pan. When the oil is sizzling, add the eggs. Mix quickly into the other ingredients, then stop stirring. Lower the heat to medium and cook for 4–5 minutes, or until the base is golden and the top puffed.

4 Take a large plate, invert it over the pan and, holding it firmly with oven gloves, turn the pan and the frittata over on to it. Slide the frittata back into the pan, and continue cooking for 3–4 minutes until golden brown on the second side. Remove the pan from the heat. Cut the frittata into wedges, garnish with thyme sprigs and Parmesan, and serve immediately.

6 sun-dried tomatoes

1 small onion, finely chopped

pinch of fresh thyme leaves

6 eggs

25g/1oz/¹⁄₃ cup freshly grated Parmesan cheese, plus shavings to serve

thyme sprigs, to garnish

FROM THE STORECUPBOARD

60ml/4 tbsp olive oil

salt and ground black pepper, to taste

Energy 170kcal/705kJ; Protein 5.7g; Carbohydrate 3g, of which sugars 2.6g; Fat 15.2g, of which saturates 4.1g; Cholesterol 13mg; Calcium 158mg; Fibre 0.6g; Sodium 167mg

Soufflé Omelette with Mushrooms ✳✳

Nourishing and flavoursome, a soufflé omelette makes an ideal meal. It is very quick and easy to make, ideal for when you are in a hurry or are too tired to spend a long time in the kitchen.

SERVES ONE

1 To make the mushroom sauce, melt the butter in a pan or frying pan and add the sliced mushrooms. Fry gently for 4–5 minutes, stirring occasionally. The mushrooms will exude quite a lot of liquid, but this will rapidly be reabsorbed.

2 Stir in the flour, then gradually add the milk, stirring all the time. Cook until the sauce boils and thickens. Add the parsley and season to taste with salt and pepper. Keep warm.

3 Make the omelette. Beat the egg yolks with 15ml/1 tbsp water and season with a little salt and pepper. Whisk the egg whites until stiff, then fold into the egg yolks. Preheat the grill (broiler).

4 Melt the butter in a large frying pan and pour in the egg mixture. Cook over a gentle heat for 2–4 minutes. Place the frying pan under the grill and cook for a further 3–4 minutes until the top is golden brown.

5 Slide the omelette on to a warmed serving plate, pour the mushroom sauce over the top and fold the omelette in half. Serve, garnished with parsley.

2 eggs, separated

15g/¹⁄₂oz/1 tbsp butter

flat leaf parsley or coriander (cilantro) leaves, to garnish

FOR THE MUSHROOM SAUCE

15g/¹⁄₂oz/1 tbsp butter

75g/3oz/generous 1 cup button (white) mushrooms, thinly sliced

85–120ml/3–4fl oz/ ¹⁄₃–¹⁄₂ cup milk

5ml/1 tsp chopped fresh parsley

FROM THE STORECUPBOARD

15ml/1 tbsp plain (all-purpose) flour

salt and ground black pepper, to taste

COOK'S TIP *For extra flavour, stir in a few drops of soy sauce and some additional chopped parsley to the mushroom sauce at the end of step 2.*

Energy 838kcal/3514kJ; Protein 45.5g; Carbohydrate 53.7g, of which sugars 42.1g; Fat 51.4g, of which saturates 28.3g; Cholesterol 497mg; Calcium 1150mg; Fibre 1.3g; Sodium 707mg

1 onion, finely chopped

1 garlic clove, crushed

1 or 2 fresh green chillies, finely chopped

a few coriander (cilantro) sprigs, chopped, plus extra, to garnish

1 firm tomato, chopped

1 small potato, cubed and boiled

25g/1oz/¹/₄ cup cooked peas

25g/1oz/¹/₄ cup cooked corn, or drained canned corn

2 eggs

25g/1oz/¹/₄ cup grated Cheddar cheese

FROM THE STORECUPBOARD

30ml/2 tbsp vegetable oil

2.5ml/¹/₂ tsp ground cumin

salt and ground black pepper, to taste

VARIATION You can use any type of vegetable with the potatoes. Try adding thickly sliced mushrooms instead of the corn.

Spicy Omelette ✳

Packed with vegetables and flavoured with chilli and coriander, this delectable omelette is a treat for all the senses – and the wallet!

SERVES FOUR–SIX

1 Heat the vegetable oil in a large pan, add the onion, garlic, chillies, coriander, cumin, tomato, potato, peas and corn and fry for 2–3 minutes until they are well blended but the potato and tomato are still firm. Season to taste with salt and black pepper.

2 Increase the heat, beat the eggs and pour in to the pan. Reduce the heat, cover the pan and cook until the bottom of the omelette is golden brown.

3 Sprinkle the omelette with the grated cheese. Place under a hot grill (broiler) and cook until the egg sets and the cheese has melted.

4 Garnish the omelette with sprigs of coriander and serve with salad for a light lunch or supper.

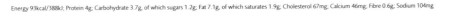

Energy 93kcal/388kJ; Protein 4g; Carbohydrate 3.7g, of which sugars 1.2g; Fat 7.1g, of which saturates 1.9g; Cholesterol 67mg; Calcium 46mg; Fibre 0.6g; Sodium 104mg

Cheesy Baked Eggs ✳

This delicious dish of potatoes, leeks, eggs and cheese sauce is perfect for a cold day. Serve with boiled potatoes and green vegetables, if you like.

SERVES FOUR

1 Cook the peeled potatoes in boiling, lightly salted water for about 15 minutes or until soft. Meanwhile, cook the leeks in a little water for about 10 minutes until soft. Hard-boil the eggs, drain and put under cold running water to cool.

2 Preheat the oven to 200°C/400°F/Gas 6. Drain and mash the potatoes. Drain the leeks and stir into the potatoes with a little black pepper to taste. Remove the shells from the eggs and cut in half or into quarters lengthways.

3 Pour the milk into a pan and add the butter and flour. Stirring continuously with a whisk, bring slowly to the boil and bubble gently for 2 minutes, until thickened and smooth. Remove from the heat, stir in half the cheese and season to taste.

4 Arrange the eggs in four shallow ovenproof dishes (or use one large one). Spoon the potato and leek mixture around the edge of the dishes. Pour the cheese sauce over and top with the remaining cheese.

5 Bake in the hot oven for about 15–20 minutes, until bubbling and golden brown.

500g/1¹⁄₄lb potatoes, peeled

3 leeks, sliced

6 eggs

600ml/1 pint/2¹⁄₂ cups milk

50g/2oz/3 tbsp butter, cut into small pieces

100g/3³⁄₄oz/1 cup Caerphilly or Cheddar cheese, grated

FROM THE STORECUPBOARD

50g/2oz/¹⁄₂ cup plain (all-purpose) flour

salt and ground black pepper, to taste

COOK'S TIPS

• *You can brown the dish by putting it under a medium-hot grill (broiler).*

• *Grate a little fresh nutmeg over the top of the dish, to add flavour.*

Energy 540kcal/2259kJ; Protein 26.6g; Carbohydrate 41.3g, of which sugars 12.3g; Fat 30.6g, of which saturates 16.2g; Cholesterol 345mg; Calcium 471mg; Fibre 5g; Sodium 443mg

Flamenco Eggs ✶✶

This adaptable dish is a swirl of red, green, yellow and white. You can use different vegetables, but should always include chorizo.

SERVES FOUR

115g/4oz diced smoked bacon or pancetta

2 frying chorizos, cubed

1 onion, chopped

2 garlic cloves, finely chopped

1 red and 1 green (bell) pepper, seeded and chopped

500g/1¼lb tomatoes, chopped

15–30ml/1–2 tbsp fino sherry

45ml/3 tbsp finely chopped parsley

8 large (US extra large) eggs

FOR THE GARLIC CRUMBS

4 thick slices stale bread

2 garlic cloves, bruised

FROM THE STORECUPBOARD

30ml/2 tbsp olive oil

salt, paprika and cayenne pepper, to taste

vegetable oil, for frying

COOK'S TIPS
• The vegetable mixture should not be too dry, so add more sherry if necessary to moisten.

• Do not leave the dish in the oven for too long, or you'll overcook the eggs.

1 Preheat the oven to 180°C/350°F/Gas 4. Warm four individual baking dishes.

2 Heat the oil in a large pan and fry the diced bacon and chorizo until they yield their fat. Add the onion and garlic and cook gently until softened, stirring. Add the peppers and tomatoes and cook to reduce, stirring occasionally. Add some paprika and stir in the sherry.

3 Divide the vegetable mixture evenly among the baking dishes. Sprinkle with parsley. Swirl the eggs together with a fork and season with salt and cayenne pepper. Pour over the vegetable mixture and bake for 8 minutes, until the eggs are just set.

4 Make the garlic crumbs. Cut the crusts off the bread and reduce to crumbs in a food processor or with a hand grater.

5 Heat plenty of vegetable oil in a large frying pan over a high heat, add the garlic cloves for a few moments to flavour it, then remove and discard them.

6 Add the breadcrumbs and brown, scooping them out on to kitchen paper with a slotted spoon. Season the breadcrumbs with salt and paprika, then sprinkle around the edge of the eggs.

Energy 597kcal/2485kJ; Protein 27.3g; Carbohydrate 28g, of which sugars 11.1g; Fat 42.4g, of which saturates 11.7g; Cholesterol 429mg; Calcium 163mg; Fibre 3.2g; Sodium 1116mg

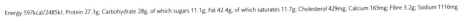

Perfect Pasta, Beans and Grains

PASTA, BEANS, LENTILS, RICE AND COUSCOUS ARE
LOW IN FAT, SUSTAINING AND EXTREMELY GOOD VALUE
FOR MONEY, AS WELL AS BEING INCREDIBLY VERSATILE.
USE THEM TO CREATE WHOLESOME VEGETARIAN
DISHES, SUCH AS WARM PENNE WITH GREEN
VEGETABLE SAUCE, PORCINI RISOTTO OR AUBERGINE
PILAFF WITH CINNAMON AND MINT, OR TO BULK
OUT MORE EXPENSIVE INGREDIENTS SUCH AS MEAT
AND FISH, AS IN TURKEY LASAGNE, FARFALLE WITH
TUNA, OR TORTELLINI WITH HAM.

Spaghetti with Lemon ✳

This very quick and easy dish combines simple yet flavoursome ingredients. It is ideal for when you rush home for a quick bite to eat.

SERVES FOUR

1 Cook the pasta in a large pan of lightly salted boiling water for 10–12 minutes, or according to the instructions on the packet, until it is just tender.

2 Drain the cooked pasta thoroughly in a colander, then return it to the pan.

3 Pour the olive oil and lemon juice over the pasta, sprinkle in the slivers of garlic and add seasoning to taste.

4 Toss the pasta over a medium to high heat for 1–2 minutes. Serve immediately in four warmed bowls.

juice of 1 large lemon

2 garlic cloves, cut into very thin slivers

FROM THE STORECUPBOARD

350g/12oz dried spaghetti

90ml/6 tbsp olive oil

salt and ground black pepper, to taste

Energy 448kcal/1886kJ; Protein 10.5g; Carbohydrate 64.9g, of which sugars 3g; Fat 18.1g, of which saturates 2.5g; Cholesterol 0mg; Calcium 22mg; Fibre 2.6g; Sodium 3mg

Spaghetti with Fresh Tomato Sauce ✳

This is an ideal dish to make in the summer when you have a glut of soft, ripe, juicy tomatoes. Do not be tempted to use under-ripe tomatoes, as they will have an inferior flavour and be too firm.

SERVES FOUR

1 Cut a cross in the base end of each tomato, then plunge into a bowl of boiling water. Leave for around 30 seconds, then lift them out with a slotted spoon and drop them into a bowl of cold water. Drain well, then remove the skins from the tomatoes. Place on a chopping board and cut them into quarters, then eighths, and chop as finely as possible.

2 Heat the oil in a large pan, add the onion and cook gently for 5 minutes, until softened and lightly coloured.

3 Add the tomatoes, season with salt and pepper, bring to a simmer, then turn the heat down to low and cover. Cook, stirring occasionally, for 30–40 minutes, until the mixture is thick.

4 Meanwhile, cook the pasta according to the instructions on the packet. Shred the basil leaves or tear them into small pieces.

5 Remove the sauce from the heat, stir in the basil and check the seasoning. Drain the pasta, then tip into a warmed bowl. Pour the sauce over and toss the mixture well. Serve immediately, with shaved Parmesan handed round in a separate bowl.

675g/1¹/₂lb ripe Italian plum tomatoes or sweet cherry tomatoes

1 onion, finely chopped

a small handful of fresh basil leaves

coarsely shaved Parmesan cheese, to serve

FROM THE STORECUPBOARD

60ml/4 tbsp extra virgin olive oil or sunflower oil

350g/12oz dried spaghetti

salt and ground black pepper, to taste

Energy 436kcal/1840kJ; Protein 12.2g; Carbohydrate 71.5g, of which sugars 9.2g; Fat 13.2g, of which saturates 1.9g; Cholesterol 0mg; Calcium 58mg; Fibre 4.9g; Sodium 22mg

Warm Penne with Fresh Tomatoes and Basil ✳

Basil and tomatoes are a match made in heaven, and in this dish they are combined with just pasta and olive oil, allowing their flavours to shine.

SERVES FOUR

1 Cook the pasta in a large pan of lightly salted boiling water for 12–14 minutes, or according to packet instructions, until tender.

2 Meanwhile, roughly chop the plum tomatoes and tear up the basil leaves.

3 Drain the pasta thoroughly in a colander and return it to the clean pan. Toss with the tomatoes, basil and olive oil.

4 Season to taste with salt and freshly ground black pepper and serve immediately.

5 very ripe plum tomatoes

1 small bunch fresh basil

FROM THE STORECUPBOARD

500g/1¹/₄lb dried penne

60ml/4 tbsp extra virgin olive oil

salt and ground black pepper, to taste

COOK'S TIP *If you are unable to find ripe tomatoes, roast those you have to bring out their full flavour. Simply put the tomatoes in a roasting pan, drizzle with a little olive oil and roast at 190°C/375°F/Gas 5 for 20 minutes. Allow to cool slightly, then mash roughly with a fork.*

Energy 552kcal/2336kJ; Protein 16.3g; Carbohydrate 96.9g, of which sugars 8.3g; Fat 13.8g, of which saturates 2g; Cholesterol 0mg; Calcium 65mg; Fibre 5.5g; Sodium 19mg

Warm Penne with Green Vegetable Sauce ✳

Lightly cooked fresh green vegetables are tossed with pasta to create this low-fat Italian dish, ideal for a light lunch or supper.

SERVES FOUR

1 Heat the oil in a medium frying pan or saucepan. Add the carrots and leek. Sprinkle the sugar over and cook, stirring frequently, for about 5 minutes.

2 Stir in the courgette, French beans, peas and plenty of salt and pepper. Cover and cook over a low to medium heat for 5–8 minutes until the vegetables are tender, stirring occasionally.

3 Meanwhile, cook the pasta in a large saucepan of boiling salted water, according to the packet instructions, until it is tender or al dente. Drain the pasta well and keep it hot until it is ready to serve.

4 Stir the parsley and chopped plum tomatoes into the vegetable mixture and adjust the seasoning to taste. Toss with the cooked pasta and serve at once.

2 carrots, finely diced

1 small leek, washed and thinly sliced

1 courgette (zucchini), finely diced

75g/3oz French beans, topped and tailed and cut into 2cm/³/₄in lengths

115g/4oz/1 cup frozen peas

1 handful flat leaf parsley, finely chopped

2 ripe plum tomatoes, skinned and diced

FROM THE STORECUPBOARD

15ml/1 tbsp olive oil

2.5ml/¹/₂ tsp sugar

350g/12oz/3 cups dried penne

salt and ground black pepper, to taste

Energy 401Kcal/1698kJ; Protein 15.5g; Carbohydrate 76.7g, of which sugars 11.3g; Fat 5.7g, of which saturates 0.9g; Cholesterol 0mg; Calcium 99mg; Fibre 8.1g; Sodium 26mg

2 carrots, peeled and cut
into matchsticks

1 leek, cut into matchsticks

2 celery sticks, cut
into matchsticks

225g/8oz smoked trout
fillets, skinned and cut
into strips

200g/7oz cream cheese

15ml/1 tbsp chopped
fresh dill or fennel

fresh dill sprigs, to garnish

FROM THE STORECUPBOARD

150ml/¼ pint/⅔ cup
vegetable stock

150ml/¼ pint/⅔ cup
fish stock

225g/8oz/2 cups long
curly fusilli or other dried
pasta shapes

salt and ground black
pepper, to taste

Fusilli with Smoked Trout ✳

Smoked trout has a strong flavour, so a little goes a long way. Here, it is
combined with a rich, creamy sauce and colourful vegetables to make a
flavoursome and satisfying pasta dish; perfect for a quick supper.

SERVES FOUR–SIX

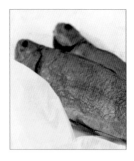

1 Put the carrot, leek and celery matchsticks into a pan and
add the vegetable stock. Bring to the boil and cook quickly for
4–5 minutes, until most of the stock has evaporated. Remove
from the heat and add the smoked trout.

2 Put the cream cheese and fish stock into a pan over a medium
heat, and whisk until smooth. Add the dill or fennel and salt and
pepper to taste.

3 Cook the fusilli in a pan of salted boiling water according to the
instructions on the packet. When the pasta is tender, but still
firm to the bite, drain it thoroughly, and return it to the pan.

4 Add the sauce, toss lightly and transfer to a serving bowl.
Top with the cooked vegetables and trout. Serve immediately,
garnished with the dill sprigs.

COOK'S TIP

*Once regarded as poor
man's smoked salmon,
smoked trout is now
regarded as a delicious
treat in its own right. It is
often sold in supermarkets
or fishmongers as skinned
fillets, but you can also
occasionally find them
sold whole.*

Energy 348kcal/1455kJ; Protein 15.9g; Carbohydrate 31.4g, of which sugars 4.5g; Fat 18.5g, of which saturates 10.3g; Cholesterol 45mg; Calcium 74mg; Fibre 2.8g; Sodium 822mg

Farfalle with Tuna ✳

Passata and canned tuna are very good value for money and endlessly versatile for making weekday suppers. A variety of herbs can be added – choose from basil, marjoram or oregano – and use fresh herbs, as the short cooking time does not allow the flavour of dried herbs to develop fully.

SERVES FOUR

1 Cook the pasta in a large pan of lightly salted boiling water according to the instructions on the packet.

2 Meanwhile, gently heat the passata in a separate pan and add the olive rings.

3 Drain the canned tuna and flake it with a fork. Add the tuna to the sauce with about 60ml/4 tbsp of the hot water used for cooking the pasta. Mix well to combine. Taste and adjust the seasoning, as necessary.

4 Drain the pasta thoroughly and tip it into a large, warmed serving bowl. Pour the tuna sauce over the top and toss lightly to mix. Serve immediately.

8–10 pitted black olives, cut into rings

175g/6oz can tuna in olive oil

FROM THE STORECUPBOARD

400g/14oz/3¹/₂ cups dried farfalle

600ml/1 pint/2¹/₂ cups passata (bottled strained tomatoes)

Energy 459kcal/1949kJ; Protein 25.2g; Carbohydrate 78.6g, of which sugars 7.8g; Fat 7.1g, of which saturates 1.1g; Cholesterol 22mg; Calcium 53mg; Fibre 4.2g; Sodium 756mg

Mixed Mushroom and Courgette Lasagne **

This is the perfect main-course lasagne for vegetarians. Adding dried porcini to fresh chestnut mushrooms intensifies the flavour. The dish can be made in advance and then simply reheated in the oven when you want to eat it. Serve with warm bread to mop up the delicious juices.

SERVES SIX

1 Put the dried porcini mushrooms in a bowl. Pour over the hot water and leave to soak for 15 minutes.

2 Tip the porcini and liquid into a sieve (strainer) set over a bowl and squeeze the mushrooms with your hands to release as much liquid as possible. Chop the mushrooms finely and set aside. Strain the soaking liquid through a fine sieve and reserve.

3 To make the tomato sauce, heat 30ml/2 tbsp olive oil in a pan, add the vegetables and fry until softened. Place in a food processor with the tomatoes, tomato purée, sugar, dried basil, porcini and soaking liquid, and blend to a purée. Preheat the oven to 190°C/375°F/Gas 5.

4 For the lasagne, heat the remaining olive oil and half the butter in a large pan. Add half the courgette slices and season to taste. Cook over a medium heat for 5–8 minutes, until lightly coloured on both sides. Remove from the pan with a slotted spoon and transfer to a bowl. Repeat with the remaining courgettes.

5 Melt the remaining butter in the pan, and cook the onion for 3 minutes, stirring. Add the chestnut mushrooms, chopped porcini and garlic and cook for 5 minutes. Add to the courgettes.

6 For the white sauce, melt the butter in a large pan, then add the flour and cook, stirring, for 1 minute. Gradually whisk in the milk, then bring to the boil and cook, stirring, until the sauce is smooth and thick. Season to taste with salt and pepper.

7 Ladle half of the tomato sauce into a shallow ovenproof dish and spread out to cover the base. Add half the vegetable mixture, spreading it evenly. Top with about one-third of the white sauce, then about half the lasagne sheets, breaking them to fit the dish. Repeat these layers, then top with the remaining white sauce and sprinkle with grated grano padano cheese.

8 Bake in the oven for 30–45 minutes, until the top is bubbling and golden and the lasagne is tender. Garnish with a sprinkling of fresh oregano leaves.

FOR THE TOMATO SAUCE

15g/¹/₂oz dried porcini mushrooms

120ml/4fl oz/¹/₂ cup hot water

1 onion, chopped

1 carrot, chopped

1 celery stick, chopped

FOR THE LASAGNE

50g/2oz/¹/₄ cup butter

450g/1lb courgettes (zucchini), thinly sliced

1 onion, finely chopped

450g/1lb/6 cups chestnut mushrooms, thinly sliced

2 garlic cloves, crushed

50g/2oz/¹/₂ cup freshly grated grano padano cheese

oregano leaves, to garnish

FOR THE WHITE SAUCE

40g/1¹/₂oz/3 tbsp butter

900ml/1¹/₂ pints/3³/₄ cups milk

FROM THE STORECUPBOARD

60ml/4 tbsp olive oil

salt and ground black pepper, to taste

2 x 400g/14oz cans chopped tomatoes

15ml/1 tbsp tomato purée (paste)

5ml/1 tsp sugar

5ml/1 tsp dried basil

40g/1¹/₂oz/¹/₃ cup plain (all-purpose) flour

6–8 non-pre-cook lasagne sheets

Energy 421kcal/1757kJ; Protein 15.5g; Carbohydrate 32.9g, of which sugars 15g; Fat 26.2g, of which saturates 12.4g; Cholesterol 49mg; Calcium 346mg; Fibre 3.8g; Sodium 310mg

Macaroni Cheese ✳

Rich and creamy, this is a deluxe macaroni cheese. It goes well with either a tomato and basil salad or a leafy green salad.

SERVES FOUR

1 Preheat the oven to 180°C/350°F/Gas 4. Cook the macaroni according to the instructions on the packet.

2 Meanwhile, gently melt the butter in a pan, add the flour and cook, stirring, for 1–2 minutes.

3 Add the milk a little at a time, whisking vigorously after each addition. Stir in the cream, then the dry white wine. Bring to the boil. Cook, stirring constantly, until the sauce thickens. Remove from the heat.

4 Add the Gruyère or Emmenthal, Gorgonzola and about a third of the grated grano padano cheese to the sauce. Stir well to mix in the cheeses, then taste for seasoning and add salt and pepper if necessary.

5 Thoroughly drain the macaroni and tip it into a baking dish. Pour the sauce over the pasta and mix well, then sprinkle the remaining grano padano over the top.

6 Place in the preheated oven and bake for 25–30 minutes or until golden brown. Serve immediately.

50g/2oz/$^{1}/_{4}$ cup butter

600ml/1 pint/2$^{1}/_{2}$ cups milk

100ml/3$^{1}/_{2}$ fl oz/ scant $^{1}/_{2}$ cup double (heavy) cream

100ml/3$^{1}/_{2}$ fl oz/ scant $^{1}/_{2}$ cup dry white wine

100g/4oz/1 cup grated Gruyère or Emmenthal cheese

50g/2oz Gorgonzola cheese, crumbled

75g/3oz/1 cup freshly grated grano padano cheese

FROM THE STORECUPBOARD

250g/9oz/2$^{1}/_{4}$ cups short-cut macaroni

50g/2oz/$^{1}/_{2}$ cup plain (all-purpose) flour

salt and ground black pepper, to taste

Energy 743kcal/3104kJ; Protein 30.3g; Carbohydrate 52.1g, of which sugars 8.9g; Fat 45.4g, of which saturates 27.8g. Cholesterol 123mg; Calcium 673mg; Fibre 0.4g; Sodium 593mg

Turkey Lasagne ✳✳

This easy-to-make baked pasta dish is delicious made with cooked turkey left over from a roast dinner and broccoli florets in a creamy cheese sauce.

SERVES FOUR

1 onion, chopped

2 garlic cloves,
finely chopped

450g/1lb cooked turkey
meat, finely diced

225g/8oz/1 cup
mascarpone

30ml/2 tbsp chopped
fresh tarragon

300g/11oz broccoli,
broken into florets

FOR THE SAUCE

50g/2oz/¹/₄ cup butter

600ml/1 pint/2¹/₂ cups
milk

75g/3oz/1 cup
freshly grated grano
padano cheese

FROM THE STORECUPBOARD

30ml/2 tbsp light olive oil

salt and ground black
pepper, to taste

30ml/2 tbsp plain
(all-purpose) flour

115g/4oz no pre-cook
lasagne verdi

VARIATION Boost your daily
vegetable intake by
adding some thawed,
frozen peas, chopped
green beans, or broad
(fava) beans to the
mixture with the broccoli.

1 Preheat the oven to 180°C/350°F/Gas 4. Heat the oil in a pan and cook the onion and garlic until softened but not coloured. Remove from the heat and stir in the diced turkey, mascarpone and tarragon and season with salt and pepper to taste.

2 Blanch the broccoli for 1 minute, then drain and rinse under cold water. Drain well and set aside.

3 To make the sauce, melt the butter in a pan, stir in the flour and cook for 1 minute, still stirring. Remove from the heat and gradually stir in the milk.

4 Return to the heat and bring the sauce to the boil, stirring constantly. Simmer for 1 minute, then add 50g/2oz/²/₃ cup of the grano padano and seasoning to taste.

5 Spoon a layer of the turkey mixture into a large, shallow ovenproof dish. Add a layer of broccoli and cover with sheets of lasagne. Coat with cheese sauce.

6 Repeat these layers, finishing with a layer of sauce on top. Sprinkle with the remaining cheese and bake for 35–40 minutes.

Energy 673kcal/2819kJ; Protein 49.4g; Carbohydrate 44.3g, of which sugars 11g; Fat 34.4g, of which saturates 18.4g; Cholesterol 142mg; Calcium 471mg; Fibre 2.5g; Sodium 409mg

Tortellini with Ham ✳

This is a very easy recipe that can be made quickly from storecupboard ingredients. It is therefore ideal for an after-work supper.

SERVES FOUR

1 Cook the pasta according to the instructions on the packet. Meanwhile, heat the oil in a large pan, add the onion and cook over a low heat, stirring frequently, for about 5 minutes until softened. Add the ham and cook, stirring occasionally, until it darkens.

2 Add the passata to the pan. Stir well, then add salt and pepper to taste. Bring to the boil, lower the heat and simmer the sauce for a few minutes, stirring occasionally, until it has reduced slightly. Stir in the cream. Drain the pasta well and add it to the sauce.

3 Add a handful of grated grano padano to the pan. Stir to combine well and taste for seasoning. Serve in warmed bowls, topped with the remaining grano padano.

COOK'S TIP Passata (bottled strained tomatoes) is handy for making quick sauces.

250g/9oz meat-filled tortellini

$^1/_4$ large onion, finely chopped

115g/4oz cooked ham, diced

100ml/3$^1/_2$fl oz/scant $^1/_2$ cup double (heavy) cream

about 90g/3$^1/_2$oz/generous 1 cup freshly grated grano padano cheese

FROM THE STORECUPBOARD

30ml/2 tbsp olive oil

150ml/$^1/_4$ pint/$^2/_3$ cup passata (bottled strained tomatoes)

salt and ground black pepper, to taste

Bolognese Sauce ✳

This is a versatile meat sauce. You can toss it with freshly cooked pasta or, alternatively, you can layer it in a baked dish like lasagne.

SERVES FOUR

1 Heat the oil in a large pan, then add the chopped onion, carrot, celery and garlic and cook over a low heat, stirring frequently, for 5–7 minutes until softened.

2 Add the minced beef and cook for 5 minutes, stirring frequently and breaking up any lumps in the meat with a wooden spoon. Stir in the red wine and mix well.

3 Cook for 1–2 minutes, then add the passata, tomato purée, fresh parsley, dried oregano and 60ml/4 tbsp of the stock. Season with salt and pepper to taste. Stir well and bring the mixture to the boil.

4 Cover the pan, and cook gently for 30 minutes, stirring from time to time and adding more stock as necessary.

5 Taste for seasoning and toss with hot, freshly cooked pasta, or use in baked pasta dishes.

1 onion, finely chopped

1 small carrot, finely chopped

1 celery stick, finely chopped

2 garlic cloves, finely chopped

400g/14oz minced (ground) beef

120ml/4fl oz/$^1/_2$ cup red wine

15ml/1 tbsp chopped fresh flat leaf parsley

FROM THE STORECUPBOARD

45ml/3 tbsp olive oil

200ml/7fl oz/scant 1 cup passata (strained bottled tomatoes)

15ml/1 tbsp tomato purée (paste)

5ml/1 tsp dried oregano

about 350ml/12fl oz/1$^1/_2$ cups beef stock

salt and ground black pepper

Top: Energy 373kcal/1549kJ; Protein 17.4g; Carbohydrate 10.9g, of which sugars 3.5g; Fat 29.2g, of which saturates 14.8g; Cholesterol 79mg; Calcium 302mg; Fibre 1g; Sodium 1025mg

Above: Energy 340kcal/1410kJ; Protein 20.6g; Carbohydrate 4.3g, of which sugars 3.9g; Fat 24.5g, of which saturates 8.1g; Cholesterol 60mg; Calcium 27mg; Fibre 1g; Sodium 214mg

Indian Mee Goreng ✳

This is a truly international dish combining Indian, Chinese and Western ingredients. It is a delicious and nutritious treat for lunch or supper.

SERVES SIX

1 Bring a large pan of water to the boil, add the fresh or dried egg noodles and cook according to the packet instructions. Drain the noodles and immediately rinse them under cold water to halt cooking. Drain again and set aside.

2 Heat 30ml/2 tbsp of the oil in a large frying pan. Cut the tofu into cubes and cook until brown, then lift it out with a slotted spoon and set aside.

3 Beat the eggs with the water and seasoning. Add to the oil in the frying pan and cook without stirring until set. Flip over, cook the other side, then slide out of the pan, roll up and slice thinly.

4 Heat the remaining oil in a wok or large frying pan and cook the onion and garlic for 2–3 minutes. Add the drained noodles, soy sauce, ketchup and chilli sauce. Toss well over medium heat for 2 minutes, then add the diced potato.

5 Reserve a few spring onions to garnish, and stir the rest into the noodles with the chilli, if using, and the tofu.

6 Stir in the sliced omelette. Serve immediately on a hot plate, garnished with the remaining spring onion.

150g/5oz firm tofu

2 eggs

30ml/2 tbsp water

1 onion, sliced

1 garlic clove, crushed

1 large cooked
potato, diced

4 spring onions
(scallions), shredded

1–2 fresh green chillies,
seeded and thinly
sliced (optional)

FROM THE STORECUPBOARD

450g/1lb fresh or 225g/8oz
dried egg noodles

60–90ml/4–6 tbsp
vegetable oil

15ml/1 tbsp light
soy sauce

30–45ml/2–3 tbsp
tomato ketchup

15ml/1 tbsp chilli sauce
(or to taste)

Energy 421kcal/1772kJ; Protein 13.7g; Carbohydrate 59g, of which sugars 4.2g; Fat 16.2g, of which saturates 3.2g; Cholesterol 85mg; Calcium 165mg; Fibre 2.7g; Sodium 416mg

1/2 cucumber, sliced
lengthways, seeded and diced

4–6 spring onions (scallions)

a bunch of radishes,
about 115g/4oz

225g/8oz mooli
(daikon), peeled

115g/4oz/2 cups beansprouts,
rinsed then left in iced water
and drained

2 garlic cloves, crushed

45ml/3 tbsp toasted
sesame paste

roasted peanuts or cashew
nuts, to garnish

FROM THE STORECUPBOARD

225g/8oz dried egg noodles

60ml/4 tbsp groundnut
(peanut) oil or sunflower oil

15ml/1 tbsp sesame oil

15ml/1 tbsp light soy sauce

5–10ml/1–2 tsp chilli sauce,
to taste

15ml/1 tbsp rice vinegar

120ml/4fl oz/1/2 cup chicken
stock or water

5ml/1 tsp sugar, or to taste

salt and ground black pepper,
to taste

Sichuan Noodles ✳

This tasty vegetarian dish combines egg noodles with plenty of fresh
vegetables in a rich, nutty sauce, with just a hint of chilli.

SERVES FOUR

1 Bring a large pan of water to the boil, add the noodles and
cook according to the packet instruction. Drain and rinse
them under cold water. Drain again and set aside.

2 Sprinkle the cucumber with salt, leave for 15 minutes,
rinse well, then drain and pat dry on kitchen paper. Place
in a large salad bowl.

3 Cut the spring onions into fine shreds. Cut the radishes
in half and slice finely. Coarsely grate the mooli, using a
mandolin or a food processor. Add all the vegetables to the
cucumber and toss gently.

4 Heat half the oil in a wok or large frying pan and stir-fry the
noodles for about 1 minute. Using a slotted spoon, transfer
the noodles to a large serving bowl and keep warm.

5 Heat the remaining oil in the wok or frying pan and add the
garlic to flavour the oil. Stir in the sesame paste, sesame oil,
soy and chilli sauces, vinegar and chicken stock or water.
Add a little sugar and season. Warm over a gentle heat.

6 Pour the sauce over the noodles and toss well. Garnish
with peanuts or cashew nuts and serve with the vegetables.

Energy 499kcal/2088kJ; Protein 11.8g; Carbohydrate 60.3g, of which sugars 7.1g; Fat 25g, of which saturates 5.3g; Cholesterol 23mg; Calcium 85mg; Fibre 4.5g; Sodium 510mg

200g/7oz baby leeks, sliced lengthways

200g/7oz baby courgettes (zucchini), halved lengthways

200g/7oz sugarsnap peas, trimmed

200g/7oz peas

5 garlic cloves, sliced

45ml/3 tbsp yellow bean sauce

cashew nuts, to garnish

FROM THE STORECUPBOARD

150g/5oz thin egg noodles

15ml/1 tbsp sunflower oil

45ml/3 tbsp sweet chilli sauce

30ml/2 tbsp sweet soy sauce

Vegetable Noodles with Yellow Bean Sauce ✳✳

Yellow bean sauce adds a distinctive Chinese flavour to this wonderfully simple dish of spicy vegetables and noodles.

SERVES FOUR

1 Cook the noodles according to the packet instructions, drain and set aside.

2 Line a large bamboo steamer with perforated baking parchment and place the leeks, courgettes and both types of peas in it. Cover and suspend over a pan of simmering water. Steam the vegetables for 5 minutes, then remove and set aside.

3 Pour the water from the pan and wipe dry with kitchen paper. Pour the sunflower oil into the pan and place over a medium heat. Add the sliced garlic and stir-fry for 1–2 minutes.

4 In a separate bowl, mix together the yellow bean, sweet chilli and soy sauces, then pour into the wok. Stir to mix with the garlic, then add the steamed vegetables and the noodles and toss together to combine.

5 Cook the vegetables and noodles for 2–3 minutes, stirring frequently, until heated through. To serve, divide the vegetable noodles among four warmed serving bowls and and scatter over the cashew nuts to garnish.

COOK'S TIP *Yellow bean sauce is made from fermented yellow beans and has a marvellous texture and spicy, aromatic flavour. However, be very careful not too add too much, because it is very salty – and if you overdo it, the final flavour of the dish will be spoiled.*

Energy 354kcal/1487kJ; Protein 14.6g; Carbohydrate 46.4g, of which sugars 13g; Fat 13.5g, of which saturates 2.7g; Cholesterol 11mg; Calcium 76mg; Fibre 6.8g; Sodium 1008mg

250ml/8fl oz/1 cup coconut cream

15ml/1 tbsp magic paste (*see* Cook's Tip)

5ml/1 tsp Thai red curry paste

450g/1lb chicken thigh meat, chopped into small pieces

2 red (bell) peppers, seeded and finely diced

FOR THE GARNISHES

2 pickled garlic cloves, chopped

small bunch fresh coriander (cilantro), chopped

2 limes, cut into wedges

FROM THE STORECUPBOARD

30ml/2 tbsp dark soy sauce

600ml/1 pint/2½ cups chicken or vegetable stock

vegetable oil, for deep-frying

90g/3½oz fine dried rice noodles

90g/3½oz fresh or dried rice noodles

COOK'S TIPS

• *Magic paste is made from garlic, coriander (cilantro) and white pepper and is available from Asian stores.*

• *To make the noodle garnish a few hours in advance, deep-fry the noodles and drain on kitchen paper. Transfer to a wire rack lined with fresh sheets of kitchen paper and set aside until ready to use.*

Thai Noodles with Chicken ✳✳

This noodle dish combines soft, boiled noodles with crisp deep-fried ones and adds a range of Thai sweet, hot and sour flavours.

SERVES FOUR

1 Pour the coconut cream into a large frying pan, bring to the boil and boil, stirring frequently, for 8–10 minutes, until the milk separates and an oily sheen appears on the surface. Add the magic paste and red curry paste and cook, stirring constantly, for 3–5 seconds, until fragrant.

2 Add the chicken and toss over the heat until sealed on all sides. Stir in the soy sauce and peppers and stir-fry for 3–4 minutes. Pour in the stock. Bring to the boil, then lower the heat and simmer for 10–15 minutes, until the chicken is fully cooked.

3 Meanwhile, make the garnish. Heat the oil in a pan to 180°C/350°F, or until a cube of bread, added to the oil, browns in 15 seconds. Break all the fine dried noodles in half, then divide them into four portions. Add one portion at a time to the hot oil. They will puff up on contact. As soon as they are crisp, lift the noodles out with a slotted spoon and drain on kitchen paper.

4 Bring a large pan of water to the boil and cook the fresh or dried noodles until tender, following the instructions on the packet. Drain well, divide among four warmed individual dishes, then spoon the curry sauce over them.

5 Top each portion with fried noodles. Sprinkle with the pickled garlic and coriander and serve with lime wedges for squeezing.

Energy 433kcal/1830kJ; Protein 17.7g; Carbohydrate 62.7g, of which sugars 8.8g; Fat 14.2g, of which saturates 3g; Cholesterol 43mg; Calcium 115mg; Fibre 2.9g; Sodium 965mg

1 onion, chopped

2 garlic cloves, crushed

175ml/6fl oz/³/₄ cup dry white wine

60ml/4 tbsp mascarpone

65g/2¹/₂oz/scant 1 cup freshly grated grano padano cheese, plus extra, to serve (optional)

5ml/1 tsp chopped fresh rosemary

FROM THE STORECUPBOARD

400g/14oz can borlotti beans

30ml/2 tbsp olive oil

275g/10oz/1¹/₂ cups risotto rice

900ml–1 litre/ 1¹/₂–1³/₄ pints/ 3³/₄–4 cups simmering vegetable or chicken stock

salt and ground black pepper, to taste

Rosemary Risotto ✳

This is a classic risotto with a subtle and complex taste. It is very filling and quite rich, so it only requires a simple side salad as an accompaniment.

SERVES FOUR

1 Drain the beans, rinse under cold water and drain again. Purée about two-thirds of the beans fairly coarsely in a food processor or blender. Set the remaining beans aside.

2 Heat the oil in a large pan and gently fry the onion and garlic for 6–8 minutes until very soft. Add the rice and cook over a medium heat for a few minutes, stirring constantly, until the grains are thoroughly coated in oil and are slightly translucent.

3 Pour in the wine. Cook over a medium heat for 2–3 minutes, stirring all the time, until the wine has been absorbed. Add the stock a ladleful at a time, waiting for each quantity to be absorbed before adding more, and continuing to stir.

4 When the rice is three-quarters cooked, stir in the bean purée. Continue to cook, adding the remaining stock, until it is creamy and the rice is tender but still has a bit of "bite". Add the reserved beans, with the mascarpone, grano padano and rosemary, then season to taste. Stir, then cover and leave to stand for about 5 minutes. Serve with extra grano padano.

COOK'S TIPS

• Arborio rice is the best type of rice to use for making a risotto because it has shorter, fatter grains than other short grain rices, and a high starch content, which makes for a creamier risotto. By being coated in olive oil, the grains of rice absorb the liquid slowly and release their starch gradually, which helps to produce a creamy end result.

• You should use a large pan for making risotto, as it makes it easier to stir and allows the grains of rice to cook evenly and more quickly.

Energy 531kcal/2220kJ; Protein 20g; Carbohydrate 74.6g, of which sugars 5.2g; Fat 14g, of which saturates 5.6g; Cholesterol 23mg; Calcium 287mg; Fibre 6.4g; Sodium 569mg

Porcini Risotto ✳

This risotto is easy to make because you don't have to stand over it stirring constantly as it cooks, as you do with a traditional risotto. Serve with steamed green vegetables for a sustaining main meal.

SERVES FOUR

1 Soak the mushrooms for 30 minutes in 750ml/1¼ pints/ 3 cups boiling water. Drain through a sieve (strainer) lined with kitchen paper, reserving the soaking liquor. Rinse and pat dry.

2 Preheat the oven to 180°C/350°F/Gas 4. Heat the oil in a roasting pan on the hob (stovetop) and add the onion. Cook for 2–3 minutes, or until softened but not coloured.

3 Add the rice and stir for 2 minutes, then add the mushrooms. Mix in the mushroom liquor, then season, and cover with foil.

4 Bake in the oven for 30 minutes, stirring occasionally, until all the stock has been absorbed and the rice is tender. Divide between warm serving bowls and serve immediately.

25g/1oz/¹⁄₂ cup dried porcini mushrooms

1 onion, finely chopped

FROM THE STORECUPBOARD

225g/8oz/generous 1 cup risotto rice

30ml/2 tbsp garlic-infused olive oil

salt and ground black pepper, to taste

Energy 258kcal/1074kJ; Protein 4.5g; Carbohydrate 46.1g, of which sugars 0.9g; Fat 5.8g, of which saturates 0.8g; Cholesterol 0mg; Calcium 15mg; Fibre 0.3g; Sodium 1mg

Barley Risotto with Roasted Squash and Leeks ✳✳

This healthy risotto is made with slightly chewy, nutty-flavoured pearl barley, which is perfectly complemented by leeks and roasted squash.

SERVES FOUR

1 Rinse the barley, then cook it in simmering water, keeping the pan part-covered, for 35–45 minutes, or until tender. Drain. Preheat the oven to 200°C/400°F/Gas 6.

2 Place the squash in a roasting pan with half of the thyme. Season with pepper and toss with half the oil. Roast, stirring once, for 30–35 minutes, until the squash is tender and beginning to brown.

3 Heat half the butter with the remaining olive oil in a large frying pan. Cook the leeks and garlic gently for 5 minutes. Add the mushrooms and remaining thyme, then cook until the liquid from the mushrooms evaporates and they begin to fry.

4 Stir in the carrots and cook for about 2 minutes, then add the barley and most of the vegetable stock. Season well and part-cover the pan. Cook for a further 5 minutes. Pour in the remaining stock if the mixture seems dry.

5 Stir in the parsley, the remaining butter and half the cheese, then stir in the squash. Add seasoning to taste and serve immediately, sprinkled with the toasted pumpkin seeds or walnuts and the remaining cheese.

200g/7oz/1 cup
pearl barley

1 butternut squash,
peeled, seeded and cut
into chunks

10ml/2 tsp chopped
fresh thyme

25g/1oz/2 tbsp butter

4 leeks, cut into fairly
thick diagonal slices

2 garlic cloves, chopped

175g/6oz/2^{1}/$_{2}$ cups
brown cap (cremini)
mushrooms, sliced

2 carrots, coarsely grated

30ml/2 tbsp chopped
fresh flat leaf parsley

50g/2oz/^{2}/$_{3}$ cup grano
padano cheese, grated

45ml/3 tbsp pumpkin
seeds, toasted, or
chopped walnuts

FROM THE STORECUPBOARD

60ml/4 tbsp olive oil

about 120ml/4fl oz/^{1}/$_{2}$ cup
vegetable stock

salt and ground black
pepper, to taste

VARIATIONS

• You could make the risotto with brown rice instead of barley – cook following the packet instructions and continue from step 2.

• Any type of fresh mushrooms can be used in this recipe – try sliced field (portabello) mushrooms, or rehydrated dried shiitake mushrooms for a rich, hearty flavour.

Energy 398kcal/1670kJ; Protein 9.1g; Carbohydrate 52.8g, of which sugars 7.7g; Fat 18.1g, of which saturates 2.4g; Cholesterol 0mg; Calcium 121mg; Fibre 5g; Sodium 21mg

1 small onion,
finely chopped

2 fresh green
chillies, seeded
and finely chopped

25g/1oz garlic chives,
roughly chopped

15g/$\frac{1}{2}$oz fresh coriander
(cilantro) sprigs

250g/9oz mixed
mushrooms, wiped
clean and thickly sliced

50g/2oz cashew nuts,
fried in 15ml/1 tbsp
olive oil until
golden brown

FROM THE STORECUPBOARD

350g/12oz/generous
1$\frac{3}{4}$ cups long grain rice

60ml/4 tbsp groundnut
(peanut) oil

600ml/1 pint/2$\frac{1}{2}$ cups
good-quality vegetable
or mushroom stock, hot

salt and ground black
pepper, to taste

COOK'S TIPS

• Garlic chives have flat
leaves, unlike standard
chives, and a mild garlic
flavour. They make an
excellent addition to
salads, soups, stir-fries,
risottos and Asian dishes.

• Ensure that you use
good home-made stock
for making risotto.

• The stock that is added
to the risotto must always
be hot. Add it slowly,
ladleful by ladleful,
making sure that all of
the liquid has been
absorbed before adding
the next ladleful.

Garlic Chive Rice with Mixed Mushrooms ✳

A mixture of fresh mushrooms combines well with rice and garlic chives
to make a tasty accompaniment to vegetarian dishes, fish or chicken.

SERVES FOUR

1 Wash and drain the rice in a sieve (strainer). Heat half the oil in
a pan and cook the onion and chillies over a gentle heat, stirring
occasionally, for 10–12 minutes until soft.

2 Set half the garlic chives aside. Cut the stalks off the coriander
and set the leaves aside. Purée the remaining chives and the
coriander stalks with the stock in a food processor or blender.

3 Add the rice to the onions and fry gently for 4–5 minutes.
Pour in the stock mixture, then season to taste. Bring to the boil,
then stir and reduce the heat to very low. Cover and cook for
15–20 minutes, or until the rice has absorbed all the liquid.

4 Remove from the heat and lay a clean dish towel over the pan,
under the lid, and press on the lid to wedge it firmly in place.
Leave to stand for a further 10 minutes.

5 Meanwhile, heat the remaining oil and cook the mushrooms
for 5–6 minutes, then add the remaining garlic chives and cook
for another 1–2 minutes. Stir the mushroom mixture and
coriander leaves into the rice. Adjust the seasoning to taste,
then transfer to a warmed serving dish. Serve immediately,
scattered with the fried cashew nuts.

Energy 535kcal/2227kJ; Protein 11g; Carbohydrate 74.7g, of which sugars 1.9g; Fat 21g, of which saturates 3g; Cholesterol 0mg; Calcium 37mg; Fibre 1.8g; Sodium 41mg

2 limes

1 lemon grass stalk

1 onion, chopped

2.5cm/1in piece of fresh root ginger, peeled and finely chopped

60ml/4 tbsp chopped fresh coriander (cilantro)

spring onion (scallion) green, toasted coconut strips and lime wedges, to serve

FROM THE STORECUPBOARD

225g/8oz/generous 1 cup brown long grain rice

15ml/1 tbsp olive oil

7.5ml/1½ tsp coriander seeds

7.5ml/1½ tsp cumin seeds

750ml/1¼ pints/3 cups vegetable stock

VARIATION *Spicy stir-fried prawns (shrimp) would make an excellent addition to this dish. To make, simply thaw, peel and devein 150g/5oz frozen prawns, then fry in 30ml/ 2 tbsp hot oil for 4 minutes. Sprinkle with 5ml/1 tsp dried chilli flakes and serve with the Thai Rice.*

Thai Rice ✳

This is soft, fluffy rice dish is perfumed with fresh lemon grass and limes, and is ideal as a light vegetarian supper dish.

SERVES FOUR

1 Pare the limes using a canelle knife (zester) or grate them using a fine grater, taking care to avoid cutting the bitter pith. Set aside the rind. Finely chop the lower portion of the lemon grass stalk and set aside.

2 Rinse the rice in plenty of cold water until the water runs clear. Tip into a sieve (strainer) and drain thoroughly.

3 Heat the olive oil in a large pan. Add the onion, ginger, spices, lemon grass and lime rind and fry gently over a low heat for 2–3 minutes.

4 Add the drained rice and cook for 1 minute, then pour in the stock and bring to the boil. Reduce the heat to very low and cover the pan. Cook gently for 30 minutes, then check the rice. If it is still crunchy, cover the pan and leave for 3–5 minutes more. Remove the pan from the heat.

5 Stir in the fresh coriander, fluff up the grains of rice, cover and leave for about 10 minutes. Garnish the rice with spring onion green and toasted coconut strips, and serve with lime wedges, if you like.

Energy 234kcal/992kJ; Protein 4.3g; Carbohydrate 47.2g, of which sugars 1.8g; Fat 4.5g, of which saturates 0.8g; Cholesterol 0mg; Calcium 30mg; Fibre 1.8g; Sodium 6mg

75g/3oz/6 tbsp butter

1 small onion,
finely chopped

150ml/¹/₄ pint/²/₃ cup dry
white wine

225g/8oz/2 cups frozen
peas, thawed

115g/4oz cooked
ham, diced

50g/2oz/²/₃ cup freshly
grated grano padano
cheese, to serve

FROM THE STORECUPBOARD

about 1 litre/1³/₄ pints/
4 cups simmering
chicken stock

275g/10oz/1¹/₂ cups
risotto rice

salt and ground black
pepper, to taste

COOK'S TIPS

• *Always use fresh grano padano cheese, grated off a block. It has a far superior flavour to ready-grated grano padano and is usually better value for money.*

• *Frozen peas are much cheaper than fresh peas, and have the added bonus of being available all year round. They also often have a better flavour than fresh ones, since they are frozen at source immediately after being picked, which helps to preserve their sweet taste and their freshness.*

• *Serve this tasty risotto with generous hunks of warm crusty bread and some butter for a delicious, warming supper dish.*

Risi e Bisi ✳

Use good quality ham in this classic Italian risotto; you only need a small amount, and the overall flavour of the dish will be greatly improved.

SERVES FOUR

1 Melt 50g/2oz/4 tbsp of the butter in a large heavy pan until foaming. Add the onion and cook gently for about 3 minutes, stirring frequently, until softened. Have the hot stock ready in an adjacent pan.

2 Add the rice to the onion mixture. Stir until the grains start to swell, then pour in the wine. Stir until the wine stops sizzling and most of it has been absorbed, then pour in a little hot stock, with salt and pepper to taste. Stir continuously, over a low heat, until all the stock has been absorbed.

3 Add the remaining stock, a little at a time, allowing the rice to absorb all the liquid before adding more, and stirring constantly. Add the peas after about 20 minutes. After 25–30 minutes, the the risotto should be moist and creamy.

4 Gently stir in the diced cooked ham and the remaining butter. Heat through until the butter has melted, then taste for seasoning and adjust as necessary. Transfer the risotto to a warmed serving bowl. Grate or shave a little grano padano over the top and serve the rest separately.

Energy 545kcal/2268kJ; Protein 19.3g; Carbohydrate 61.9g, of which sugars 1.9g; Fat 21.6g, of which saturates 12.8g; Cholesterol 69mg; Calcium 184mg; Fibre 2.7g; Sodium 597mg

Indian Pilaff with Peas ✳

This fragrant, versatile rice dish can be served on its own or with a range of other Indian dishes, including several meat and vegetable curries, a yogurt dish, and chutneys. Garnish the pilaff with chopped fresh mint and coriander (cilantro), if you like, or with roasted chilli and coconut.

SERVES FOUR

1 Rinse the rice and put it in a bowl. Cover with plenty of water and leave to soak for 30 minutes. Drain thoroughly.

2 Heat the ghee, or oil and butter, in a heavy pan. Stir in the cinnamon stick, cardamom and cloves. Add the onion, ginger and sugar, and fry until golden. Add the peas, followed by the rice, and stir for 1 minute to coat the rice in ghee.

3 Pour in 600ml/1 pint/2¹/₂ cups water with the salt, stir once and bring the liquid to the boil. Reduce the heat and allow the mixture to simmer for 15–20 minutes, until all the liquid has been absorbed.

4 Turn off the heat, cover the pan with a clean dishtowel and the lid, and leave the rice to steam for a further 10 minutes. Spoon the rice on to a serving dish.

1 onion, halved lengthways and sliced

25g/1oz fresh root ginger, peeled and grated

130g/4¹/₂oz fresh peas, shelled, or frozen peas

FROM THE STORECUPBOARD

350g/12oz/1³/₄ cups basmati rice

45ml/3 tbsp ghee or 30ml/2 tbsp vegetable oil and a little butter

1 cinnamon stick

6–8 cardamom pods, crushed

4 cloves

5ml/1 tsp sugar

5ml/1 tsp salt

Energy 451kcal/1880kJ; Protein 8.9g; Carbohydrate 75.7g, of which sugars 2.6g; Fat 12.2g, of which saturates 5.4g; Cholesterol 0mg; Calcium 28mg; Fibre 1.8g; Sodium 328mg

Rice Tortitas ✳

Like miniature tortillas, these flavoursome little rice pancakes are delicious served hot, either plain or with tomato sauce for dipping. They also make an excellent scoop for any soft vegetable mixture or dip, such as hummus, guacamole, baba ganoush, tahini or mustard dip.

SERVES FOUR

1 Heat half the olive oil in a large frying pan and stir-fry the rice, with the potato, spring onions and garlic, over a high heat for 3 minutes, until golden.

2 Tip the rice and vegetable mixture into a bowl and stir in the parsley and eggs, with the paprika and salt and pepper to taste. Mix well to combine thoroughly.

3 Heat the remaining oil in the frying pan and drop in large spoonfuls of the rice mixture, leaving room for spreading. Cook the tortitas for 1–2 minutes on each side.

4 Drain the tortitas on kitchen paper and keep hot while cooking the remaining mixture. Serve hot.

1 potato, grated

4 spring onions (scallions), thinly sliced

1 garlic clove, finely chopped

15ml/1 tbsp chopped fresh parsley

3 large (US extra large) eggs, beaten

FROM THE STORECUPBOARD

30ml/2 tbsp olive oil

115g/4oz/1 cup cooked long grain white rice

2.5ml/^{1}/$_2$ tsp paprika

salt and ground black pepper, to taste

Energy 185kcal/776kJ; Protein 6.8g; Carbohydrate 17.6g, of which sugars 1.2g; Fat 10.4g, of which saturates 2.1g; Cholesterol 143mg; Calcium 56mg; Fibre 1.3g; Sodium 63mg

Aubergine Pilaff with Cinnamon and Mint ✳

This wonderful rice dish combines a range of spices and herbs with juicy tomatoes and meaty aubergines. Eat it on its own accompanied by a green salad, or serve it with grilled, broiled or barbecued meat.

SERVES FOUR–SIX

1 Place the aubergine chunks in a bowl of salted water. Cover with a plate to keep them submerged, and soak for 30 minutes.

2 Meanwhile, heat the olive oil in a heavy pan, stir in the pine nuts and cook until they turn golden. Add the onion and soften it, then stir in the coriander seeds and currants. Add the sugar, cinnamon, mint and dill and stir in the tomatoes.

3 Stir in the rice, then pour in the water, season and bring to the boil. Lower the heat and partially cover the pan, then simmer for 10–12 minutes, until most of the water has been absorbed. Turn off the heat, cover with a dish towel and press the lid on top. Leave to steam for about 15 minutes.

4 Heat enough sunflower oil for deep-frying in a deep-sided pan. Drain the aubergines and squeeze them dry, then toss them in batches in the oil, for a few minutes at a time. When they are brown, lift them out and drain on kitchen paper.

5 Tip the rice into a bowl and toss the aubergine chunks through it with the lemon juice. Garnish with mint and serve warm or cold, with lemon wedges for squeezing.

2 large aubergines (eggplants), peeled lengthways in stripes, then cut into bitesize chunks

30–45ml/2–3 tbsp pine nuts

1 large onion, chopped

30ml/2 tbsp currants, soaked in warm water for 5–10 minutes and drained

1 small bunch of fresh dill, finely chopped

3 tomatoes, skinned, seeded and finely chopped

900ml/1½ pints/3¾ cups water

juice of ½ lemon

fresh mint sprigs and lemon wedges, to serve

FROM THE STORECUPBOARD

30–45ml/2–3 tbsp olive oil

5ml/1 tsp coriander seeds

10–15ml/2–3 tsp sugar

15–30ml/1–2 tbsp ground cinnamon

15–30ml/1–2 tbsp dried mint

350g/12oz/generous 1¾ cups long or short grain rice, well rinsed and drained

sunflower oil, for deep-frying

salt and ground black pepper, to taste

VARIATIONS

• You could use bulgur wheat , or tiny pasta "tears" in place of the rice.

• For a spicy version, add 5ml/1 tsp paprika to the rice mixture in step 2.

Energy 369kcal/1539kJ; Protein 6.1g; Carbohydrate 52.2g, of which sugars 11g; Fat 15.2g, of which saturates 1.8g; Cholesterol 0mg; Calcium 38mg; Fibre 2.7g; Sodium 8mg

Anatolian Bulgur with Nuts and Dates ✳

This hearty dish can be made with rice or bulgur wheat, and includes a combination of vegetables, dried fruit and nuts. Serve it with a dollop of thick, creamy yogurt and some melted butter as a substantial lunch dish.

SERVES FOUR–SIX

25g/1oz butter

2 medium carrots, cut into matchsticks

75g/3oz/³⁄₄ cup blanched almonds

30–45ml/2–3 tbsp pine nuts

30–45ml/2–3 tbsp shelled pistachio nuts, chopped

175g/6oz/1 cup soft dried dates, roughly chopped

a handful of fresh coriander (cilantro), chopped, to serve

thick and creamy natural (plain) yogurt, to serve

FROM THE STORECUPBOARD

350g/12oz/2 cups coarse-grain bulgur wheat, rinsed and drained

salt, to taste

about 25g/1oz/2 tbsp ghee or butter, melted (optional)

> **COOK'S TIP**
> Look for soft and succulent whole dates (which usually come from Iran or Iraq) rather than blocks of hard ones, or use soft dried figs or apricots instead.

1 Put the bulgur into a bowl, pour over enough boiling water to cover it by 2.5cm/1in, and give it a quick stir. Cover the bowl and leave the bulgur to steam for about 25 minutes, until it has soaked up the water and doubled in volume.

2 Meanwhile, melt the butter in a wide, heavy pan, add the carrots and fry for about 10 minutes, until tender and golden. Toss in the nuts and cook for a further minute, or until they give off a nutty aroma and begin to colour.

3 Add the dates and, if they look dry, pour in 15–30ml/1–2 tbsp water. Tip the bulgur into the pan and toss until everything is mixed well together. Turn off the heat, cover the pan with a dish towel and lid, and leave to steam for 5–10 minutes.

4 To serve, stir the coriander through the bulgur, and pour over the ghee or butter, if you like. Hand round yogurt in a small bowl.

Energy 412kcal/1719kJ; Protein 9g; Carbohydrate 54g, of which sugars 23.4g; Fat 19.1g, of which saturates 3.9g; Cholesterol 11mg; Calcium 71mg; Fibre 3.4g; Sodium 74mg

Spiced Vegetable Stew with Chickpeas and Couscous *

This tasty, satisfying vegetarian main course is cheap and easy to make and can be prepared with any number of seasonal vegetables such as spinach, peas, broad (fava) beans or baby corn.

SERVES SIX

1 Heat 30ml/2 tbsp olive oil in a large pan, add the onion and garlic and cook until soft. Stir in the tomato purée, turmeric, cayenne, ground coriander and cumin. Cook for 2 minutes.

2 Add the cauliflower, carrots and pepper, with enough water to come halfway up the vegetables. Bring to the boil, then lower the heat, cover and simmer for 10 minutes. Add the courgettes, chickpeas and tomatoes and cook for 10 minutes. Stir in the fresh coriander and season. Keep hot.

3 To cook the couscous, bring about 475ml/16fl oz/2 cups water to the boil in a large pan. Add the remaining olive oil and a pinch of salt. Remove from the heat and add the couscous. Allow to swell for 2 minutes, then add the sunflower oil and heat through, stirring to separate the grains.

4 Turn the couscous out on to a warm serving dish, and spoon the cooked vegetables on top, pouring over any liquid. Garnish with coriander and serve immediately.

1 large onion, finely chopped

2 garlic cloves, crushed

225g/8oz/1¹⁄₂ cups cauliflower florets

225g/8oz baby carrots, washed and trimmed

1 red (bell) pepper, seeded and diced

225g/8oz courgettes (zucchini), sliced

4 beefsteak tomatoes, skinned and sliced

45ml/3 tbsp chopped fresh coriander (cilantro)

coriander sprigs, to garnish

FROM THE STORECUPBOARD

45ml/3 tbsp olive oil

15ml/1 tbsp tomato purée (paste)

2.5ml/¹⁄₂ tsp ground turmeric

2.5ml/¹⁄₂ tsp cayenne pepper

5ml/1 tsp ground coriander

5ml/1 tsp ground cumin

400g/14oz can chickpeas, drained and rinsed

salt and ground black pepper, to taste

450g/1lb/2²⁄₃ cups couscous

50ml/3¹⁄₂ tbsp sunflower oil

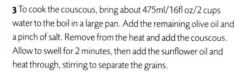

Energy 419kcal/1749kJ; Protein 12.9g; Carbohydrate 61.8g, of which sugars 11.8g; Fat 14.8g, of which saturates 1.9g; Cholesterol 0mg; Calcium 87mg; Fibre 6.7g; Sodium 178mg

4 (bell) peppers

50g/2oz dried apricots, finely chopped

75g/3oz feta cheese, cut into tiny cubes

3 ripe tomatoes, skinned, seeded and chopped

45ml/3 tbsp toasted pine nuts

30ml/2 tbsp chopped fresh parsley

fresh flat leaf parsley, to garnish

FROM THE STORECUPBOARD

75g/3oz/^{1}/$_2$ cup couscous

75ml/2^1/$_2$ fl oz/^{1}/$_3$ cup boiling vegetable stock

15ml/1 tbsp olive oil

10ml/2 tsp white wine vinegar

salt and ground black pepper, to taste

Couscous-stuffed Baked Sweet Peppers ✳

Colourful red, yellow or orange peppers are softened in boiling water before being filled with a delicious mixture of couscous, apricots and pine nuts, to ensure really tender results in this simple vegetarian dish.

SERVES FOUR

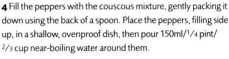

1 Preheat the oven to 190°C/375°F/Gas 5. Halve the peppers lengthways, then remove the core and seeds. Place the peppers in a large heatproof bowl and pour over boiling water to cover. Leave to stand for 3 minutes, then drain and set aside.

2 Meanwhile, put the couscous in a small bowl and pour over the stock. Leave to stand for about 5 minutes until all the liquid has been absorbed.

3 Using a fork, fluff up the couscous, then stir in the oil, vinegar, apricots, feta cheese, tomatoes, pine nuts and parsley, and season to taste with salt and ground black pepper.

4 Fill the peppers with the couscous mixture, gently packing it down using the back of a spoon. Place the peppers, filling side up, in a shallow, ovenproof dish, then pour 150ml/^{1}/$_4$ pint/^{2}/$_3$ cup near-boiling water around them.

5 Put the dish in the preheated oven and bake for 20 minutes, until the peppers are tender and the topping is browned. Serve immediately, garnished with parsley.

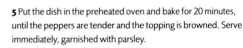

Energy 303kcal/1266kJ; Protein 33.7g; Carbohydrate 33.6g, of which sugars 17g; Fat 15.8g, of which saturates 3.9g; Cholesterol 13mg; Calcium 105mg; Fibre 4.3g; Sodium 285mg

Couscous with Dried Fruit, Nuts and Cinnamon ✳

This simple yet delicious dish of couscous with dates, raisins and nuts can be served as a course on its own, or as an accompaniment to a spicy tagine or roasted or grilled meat or poultry.

SERVES SIX

1 Preheat the oven to 180°C/350°F/Gas 4. Put the couscous in a bowl. Mix together the water, salt and saffron and pour it over the couscous, stirring. Leave to stand for 10 minutes. Add the sunflower oil and, using your fingers, rub it through the grains. Set aside.

2 Chop the dates and slice the apricots into slivers. In a heavy pan, heat the olive oil and butter and stir in the dates, apricots, raisins, most of the almonds and pistachio nuts.

3 Cook until the raisins plump up, then tip the nuts and fruit into the couscous and toss together to mix. Tip the couscous into an ovenproof dish and cover with foil. Place in the oven for about 20 minutes, until heated through.

4 Toast the reserved slivered almonds. Pile the hot couscous in a mound on a large serving dish and sprinkle with the cinnamon and sugar – these look attractive sprinkled in stripes down the mound. Scatter the toasted almonds over the top and serve hot.

600ml/1 pint/2¹/₂ cups warm water

pinch of saffron threads

75g/3oz/¹/₂ cup dried dates

115g/4oz/¹/₂ cup dried apricots

a little butter

75g/3oz/generous ¹/₂ cup seedless raisins

115g/4oz/²/₃ cup blanched almonds, cut into slivers

75g/3oz/¹/₂ cup pistachio nuts

FROM THE STORECUPBOARD

500g/1¹/₄lb/3 cups couscous

5ml/1 tsp salt

45ml/3 tbsp sunflower oil

30ml/2 tbsp olive oil

10ml/2 tsp ground cinnamon

45ml/3 tbsp caster (superfine) sugar

COOK'S TIP
Although saffron is expensive, a little goes a long way, and it is useful for adding both flavour and colour to dishes.

Energy 567kcal/2367kJ; Protein 11.9g; Carbohydrate 71.5g, of which sugars 27.9g; Fat 27.7g, of which saturates 3g; Cholesterol 0mg; Calcium 94mg; Fibre 3.3g; Sodium 79mg

3 red onions, peeled and quartered

2–3 courgettes (zucchini), halved lengthways and cut across into 2–3 pieces

2–3 red, green or yellow (bell) peppers, seeded and quartered

2 aubergines (eggplants), cut into 6–8 long segments

2–3 leeks, trimmed and cut into long strips

2–3 sweet potatoes, peeled, halved lengthways and cut into long strips

4–6 tomatoes, quartered

6 garlic cloves, crushed

25g/1oz fresh root ginger, sliced

a few large fresh rosemary sprigs

natural (plain) yogurt or harissa and bread, to serve

FOR THE COUSCOUS

600ml/1 pint/2^{1}/$_{2}$ cups warm water

about 25g/1oz/2 tbsp butter, diced

FROM THE STORECUPBOARD

about 150ml/^{1}/$_{4}$ pint/ ^{2}/$_{3}$ cup olive oil

10ml/2 tsp sugar or clear honey

salt and ground black pepper, to taste, plus a pinch of salt

500g/1^{1}/$_{4}$lb/3 cups medium couscous

45ml/3 tbsp sunflower oil

Casablancan Couscous with Roasted Vegetables **

This delicious summer dish is packed with seasonal vegetables. Serve with yogurt and bread for a stunning vegetarian dinner-party dish and follow with a simple lemon sorbet for dessert.

SERVES SIX

1 Preheat the oven to 200°C/400°F/Gas 6. Arrange all the vegetables in a roasting pan. Tuck the garlic, ginger and rosemary around the vegetables. Pour the olive oil over the vegetables, sprinkle with the sugar or honey, and salt and pepper to taste, and roast, turning occasionally, for about 1^{1}/$_{2}$ hours until they are tender and slightly caramelized.

2 When the vegetables are nearly ready, put the couscous in a bowl. Stir a pinch of salt into the water, then pour it over the couscous, stirring to make sure it is absorbed evenly. Leave to stand for 10 minutes, then, using your fingers, rub the sunflower oil into the grains and break up any lumps. Tip into an ovenproof dish, arrange the butter over the top, cover with foil and heat in the oven for about 20 minutes.

3 To serve, use your fingers to work the melted butter into the couscous and fluff it up, then pile it on a large dish and shape into a mound with a pit at the top. Spoon some vegetables into the pit and arrange the rest around the dish. Pour the oil from the pan over the couscous. Serve immediately with yogurt, or harissa if you prefer, and bread for mopping up the juices.

Energy 607kcal/2531kJ; Protein 11.3g; Carbohydrate 81.3g, of which sugars 22.2g; Fat 28.3g, of which saturates 5.7g; Cholesterol 9mg; Calcium 115mg; Fibre 9.2g; Sodium 76mg

Mixed Bean and Aubergine Tagine with Mint Yogurt ✳

Beans are not only cheap, but they are also a very good source of protein. Here they are combined with aubergine (eggplant), fresh herbs, garlic and chillies to make a very healthy dish that is perfect for a cold winter's day.

SERVES FOUR

1 Place the soaked and drained kidney beans in a large pan of unsalted boiling water. Bring back to the boil and boil rapidly for 10 minutes, then drain.

2 Place the soaked and drained black-eyed or cannellini beans in a separate large pan of boiling unsalted water and boil rapidly for 10 minutes, then drain.

3 Place 600ml/1 pint/2^1/$_2$ cups of water in a large tagine or casserole, and add the bay leaves, celery and beans. Cover and place in an unheated oven.

4 Set the oven to 190°C/375°F/Gas 5. Cook for 1–1^1/$_2$ hours or until the beans are tender, then drain.

5 Heat 60ml/4 tbsp of the oil in a large frying pan or cast-iron tagine base. Pat the aubergine chunks dry, then add to the pan and cook, stirring, for 4–5 minutes. Remove and set aside.

6 Add the remaining oil to the tagine base or frying pan, then add the sliced onion and cook, stirring, for about 4–5 minutes, until softened. Add the crushed garlic and chopped red chillies and cook for a further 5 minutes, stirring frequently, until the onion is golden and has softened.

7 Reset the oven temperature to 160°C/325°F/Gas 3. Add the tomato purée and paprika to the onion mixture and cook for 1–2 minutes. Add the tomatoes, aubergine, beans and stock, then season to taste.

8 Cover the tagine base with the lid or, if using a frying pan, transfer the contents to a clay tagine or casserole. Place in the oven and cook for 1 hour.

9 Meanwhile, mix together the yogurt, mint and spring onions. Just before serving, add the fresh mint, parsley and coriander to the tagine and lightly mix through the vegetables.

10 Garnish with fresh herb sprigs and serve immediately with the mint yogurt and some couscous or brown rice.

2 bay leaves

2 celery sticks, each cut into 4 matchsticks

1 aubergine (eggplant), about 350g/12oz, cut into chunks

1 onion, thinly sliced

3 garlic cloves, crushed

1–2 fresh red chillies, seeded and chopped

2 large tomatoes, roughly chopped

15ml/1 tbsp each chopped fresh mint, parsley and coriander (cilantro)

fresh herb sprigs, to garnish

FOR THE MINT YOGURT

150ml/^{1}/$_4$ pint/^{2}/$_3$ cup natural (plain) yogurt

30ml/2 tbsp chopped fresh mint

2 spring onions (scallions), chopped

FROM THE STORECUPBOARD

115g/4oz/generous ^{1}/$_2$ cup dried red kidney beans, soaked overnight in cold water and drained

115g/4oz/generous ^{1}/$_2$ cup dried black-eyed beans (peas) or cannellini beans, soaked overnight in cold water and drained

75ml/5 tbsp olive oil

30ml/2 tbsp tomato purée (paste)

5ml/1 tsp paprika

300ml/^{1}/$_2$ pint/1^1/$_4$ cups vegetable stock

salt and ground black pepper, to taste

Energy 209kcal/890kJ; Protein 16.6g; Carbohydrate 33.9g, of which sugars 9.4g; Fat 1.9g, of which saturates 0.5g; Cholesterol 1mg; Calcium 173mg; Fibre 12.3g; Sodium 62mg

Mixed Bean and Tomato Chilli ✳

This warming dish is based on store-cupboard ingredients, making it an ideal end-of-the week supper dish when you have eaten everything in the refrigerator. Serve with warm bread.

SERVES FOUR

1 Seed and thinly slice the chilli, then put it into a pan. Add the tomatoes and mixed beans and simmer gently on a medium heat for 5 minutes.

2 Finely chop the fresh coriander. Set some aside for the garnish and add the remainder to the tomato and bean mixture. Stir to mix all the ingredients together.

3 Bring the mixture to the boil, then reduce the heat, cover and simmer gently for 10 minutes. Stir the mixture occasionally and add a dash of water if the sauce starts to dry out.

4 Ladle the chilli into warmed individual bowls and top with sour cream. Sprinkle with coriander and serve immediately.

1 fresh red chilli

a large handful of fresh coriander (cilantro)

120ml/4fl oz/¹/₂ cup sour cream

FROM THE STORECUPBOARD

1 x 400g/14oz can chopped tomatoes

2 x 400g/14oz cans mixed beans, drained and rinsed

Energy 309kcal/1302kJ; Protein 16.7g; Carbohydrate 43.7g, of which sugars 14.1g; Fat 8.7g, of which saturates 4.2g; Cholesterol 18mg; Calcium 193mg; Fibre 12.4g; Sodium 1202mg

Braised Beans and Lentils ✳

Easy to make and very healthy, this dish requires little effort. It is important, however, to soak the pulses for at least 12 hours.

SERVES FOUR

1 Drain the pulse mixture, rinse it thoroughly under cold water and drain again. Put the mixture in a large pan. Cover with cold water, bring to the boil, and cook for about 1¹/₂ hours, by which time the beans and lentils will be quite soft and tender.

2 Strain, reserving 475ml/16fl oz/2 cups of the cooking liquid. Return the bean mixture to the clean pan.

3 Heat the oil in a frying pan and fry the onion until light golden. Add the garlic and sage. As soon as the garlic becomes aromatic, add the mixture to the beans.

4 Stir in the reserved liquid, add plenty of seasoning and simmer for about 15 minutes, or until the pulses are piping hot.

5 Stir in the lemon juice, then spoon into serving bowls, top with a sprinkling of spring onions and dill, and serve.

**1 large onion,
finely chopped**

2 garlic cloves, crushed

**5 or 6 fresh sage
leaves, chopped**

juice of 1 lemon

**3 spring onions (scallions),
thinly sliced**

**60–75ml/4–5 tbsp
chopped fresh dill**

FROM THE STORECUPBOARD

**200g/7oz/generous 1 cup
mixed beans and lentils,
soaked overnight in water**

**150ml/¹/₄ pint/²/₃ cup
extra virgin olive oil**

**salt and ground black
pepper, to taste**

Energy 428kcal/1,788kJ; Protein 13.4g; Carbohydrate 37.7g, of which sugars 4.3g; Fat 26g, of which saturates 3.7g; Cholesterol 0mg; Calcium 62mg; Fibre 3.7g; Sodium 24mg

Lentil Casserole with Mushrooms and Anis ✳

Lentils are very good value and make a good partner for stronger flavours, such as the powerful anis used in this recipe. Serve this dish on its own, or partnered with grilled pork or chicken.

SERVES FOUR

1 Heat the oil in a large, flameproof casserole. Add the onion and fry gently, with the garlic, for 5 minutes, until softened but not browned.

2 Add the sliced mushrooms and stir to combine with the onion and garlic. Continue cooking, stirring gently, for a couple of minutes, until the mushrooms soften.

3 Add the lentils, tomatoes and bay leaf with 175ml/6fl oz/³/₄ cup water. Simmer gently, covered, for 30–40 minutes until the lentils are soft, and the liquid has almost disappeared.

4 Stir in the chopped parsley and anis. Season to taste with salt, paprika and black pepper.

1 large onion, sliced

2 garlic cloves, finely chopped

250g/9oz/3 cups brown cap (cremini) mushrooms, sliced

4 tomatoes, cut in eighths

25g/1oz/¹/₂ cup chopped fresh parsley

30ml/2 tbsp anis spirit or anisette

FROM THE STORECUPBOARD

30ml/2 tbsp olive oil

150g/5oz/generous ¹/₂ cup brown or green lentils, soaked overnight

1 bay leaf

salt, paprika and black pepper, to taste

Energy 212kcal/892kJ; Protein 11.5g; Carbohydrate 23.2g, of which sugars 4.8g; Fat 7g, of which saturates 1g; Cholesterol 0mg; Calcium 64mg; Fibre 5.8g; Sodium 21mg

Braised Lentils with Carrots and Sage *

Serve this simple dish of lentils flavoured with sage with grilled, broiled or barbecued meats, or on their own with a dollop of yogurt seasoned with crushed garlic, salt and pepper, and lemon wedges. for squeezing.

SERVES FOUR–SIX

1 onion, cut in half lengthways, in half again crossways, and sliced along the grain

3–4 plump garlic cloves, roughly chopped and bruised with the flat side of a knife

4 carrots, sliced

1 bunch of fresh sage or flat leaf parsley, to garnish

FROM THE STORECUPBOARD

175g/6oz/³/₄ cup green lentils, rinsed and picked over to remove grit

45–60ml/3–4 tbsp olive oil

5ml/1 tsp coriander seeds

a handful of dried sage leaves

5–10ml/1–2 tsp sugar

15–30ml/1–2 tbsp tomato purée (paste)

salt and ground black pepper, to taste

1 Bring a pan of water to the boil and tip in the lentils. Lower the heat, partially cover the pan and simmer for 10 minutes. Drain and rinse well under cold running water.

2 Heat the oil in a heavy pan, stir in the onion, garlic, coriander, sage and sugar, and cook until the onion begins to colour. Toss in the carrots and cook for 2–3 minutes.

3 Add the lentils and pour in 250ml/8fl oz/1 cup water, making sure the lentils and carrots are covered. Stir in the tomato purée and cover the pan, then cook the lentils and carrots gently for about 20 minutes, until most of the liquid has been absorbed. The lentils and carrots should both be tender, but still have some bite. Season with salt and pepper to taste.

4 Garnish with the fresh sage or flat leaf parsley, and serve hot or at room temperature.

Energy 166kcal/696kJ; Protein 7.6g; Carbohydrate 21.1g, of which sugars 6.7g; Fat 6.2g, of which saturates 0.9g; Cholesterol 0mg; Calcium 38mg; Fibre 4g; Sodium 22mg

Creamy Puy Lentils ✳

Wholesome lentils are filling, nutritious, and very good value for money. A poached egg is the perfect companion to the creamy lentils, making this a very healthy and tasty supper dish.

SERVES SIX

1 Put the Puy lentils and bay leaf in a large pan, cover with cold water, and slowly bring to the boil. Reduce the heat and simmer, partially covered, for about 25 minutes, or until the lentils are tender. Stir the lentils occasionally and add more water, if necessary. Drain.

2 Heat the oil in a frying pan and cook the spring onions and garlic for 1 minute. Add the mustard, lemon rind and juice, tomatoes and seasoning, then mix together and cook gently for 1–2 minutes until the tomatoes are heated through. Add a little water if the mixture becomes too dry.

3 Meanwhile, poach the eggs in a pan of lightly salted barely simmering water for 4 minutes, adding them one at a time.

4 Stir the lentils and crème fraîche into the tomato mixture, remove and discard the bay leaf, then heat through for 1 minute. Divide among six serving plates. Top each portion with a poached egg, and sprinkle with parsley.

4 spring onions (scallions), sliced

2 large garlic cloves, chopped

finely grated rind and juice of 1 large lemon

4 plum tomatoes, seeded and diced

6 eggs

60ml/4 tbsp crème fraîche

30ml/2 tbsp chopped fresh flat leaf parsley, to garnish

FROM THE STORECUPBOARD

250g/9oz/generous 1 cup Puy lentils

1 bay leaf

30ml/2 tbsp olive oil

15ml/1 tbsp Dijon mustard

salt and ground black pepper, to taste

Energy 281kcal/1179kJ; Protein 17.2g; Carbohydrate 22.8g, of which sugars 3g; Fat 14.2g, of which saturates 4.9g; Cholesterol 202mg; Calcium 71mg; Fibre 4.5g; Sodium 84mg

Lentil and Nut Loaf ✳

For a vegetarian alternative at a special celebration, serve this with all the trimmings, including a vegetarian gravy. Garnish with fresh cranberries and flat leaf parsley for a really festive effect.

SERVES SIX

115g/4oz/1 cup
hazelnuts, skinned

115g/4oz/1 cup walnuts

1 large carrot,
coarsely chopped

2 celery sticks,
coarsely chopped

1 large onion,
coarsely chopped

115g/4oz/1¹/₂ cups
fresh mushrooms,
coarsely chopped

50g/2oz/¹/₄ cup butter,
plus extra for greasing

1 egg, beaten

60ml/4 tbsp chopped
fresh parsley

150ml/¹/₄ pint/²/₃ cup
water

fresh flat leaf parsley
and cranberries, to
garnish (optional)

FROM THE STORECUPBOARD

115g/4oz/¹/₂ cup
red lentils

10ml/2 tsp mild
curry powder

30ml/2 tbsp
tomato ketchup

30ml/2 tbsp vegetarian
Worcestershire sauce

10ml/2 tsp salt

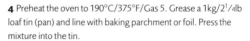

1 Cover the lentils with cold water and soak for 1 hour. Grind the nuts in a food processor, then place them in a large bowl. Put the carrot, celery, onion and mushrooms in the food processor and process until finely chopped.

2 Heat the butter in a pan. Add the vegetables and fry gently, stirring occasionally, for 5 minutes. Stir in the curry powder and cook for 1 minute more. Remove from the heat and set aside.

3 Drain the lentils and stir them into the ground nuts. Add the vegetables, ketchup, vegetarian Worcestershire sauce, egg, salt, chopped parsley and water.

4 Preheat the oven to 190°C/375°F/Gas 5. Grease a 1kg/2¹/₄lb loaf tin (pan) and line with baking parchment or foil. Press the mixture into the tin.

5 Bake for 1–1¹/₄ hours, until just firm, covering the top with foil if it starts to burn. Leave to stand for 15 minutes, turn out, and peel off the paper. Serve immediately, garnished with parsley and cranberries, if you like.

Energy 410kcal/1703kJ; Protein 11.9g; Carbohydrate 16.5g, of which sugars 5.2g; Fat 33.5g, of which saturates 6.6g; Cholesterol 49mg; Calcium 81mg; Fibre 3.6g; Sodium 222mg

Fabulous Fish and Shellfish

THE COST OF FISH AND SHELLFISH CAN VARY
TREMENDOUSLY, DEPENDING ON WHERE YOU LIVE,
THE TYPE OF FISH, AND WHAT SEASON IT IS. OILY FISH,
SUCH AS SARDINES AND MACKEREL, FIRM-FLESHED
WHITE FISH SUCH AS HALIBUT AND HADDOCK,
AND SQUID ARE ALL USUALLY GOOD VALUE FOR
MONEY. SO WHY NOT INDULGE YOURSELF WITHOUT
BREAKING THE BANK WITH DELICATE SALMON QUICHE,
SUPER-HEALTHY PAN-FRIED MACKEREL WITH
RATATOUILLE AND LEMON, OR SPICY SQUID STEW?

500g/1¼lb fresh spinach, trimmed of thick stalks

4 x 200g/7oz fresh hake steaks

175ml/6fl oz/¾ cup white wine

3–4 strips of pared lemon rind

FOR THE EGG AND LEMON SAUCE

2 large (US extra large) eggs, at room temperature

juice of ½ lemon

FROM THE STORECUPBOARD

30ml/2 tbsp plain (all-purpose flour)

75ml/5 tbsp olive oil

salt and ground black pepper, to taste

2.5ml/½ tsp cornflour (cornstarch)

Hake with Lemon Sauce ✱✱✱

This healthy dish is perfect on its own as a light lunch, or can be served with steamed new potatoes for a more substantial main course.

SERVES FOUR

1 Place the spinach leaves in a large pan with just the water that clings to the leaves after washing. Cover and cook over a medium heat for 5–7 minutes, then drain and set aside.

2 Dust the fish with the flour. Heat the oil in a large frying pan, add the fish and sauté gently for 2–3 minutes on each side. Pour in the wine, and add the lemon rind and some seasoning. Lower the heat and simmer gently for a few minutes, then add the spinach, and let it simmer for 3–4 minutes more. Remove from the heat.

3 To make the sauce, mix the cornflour to a paste with a little water. Beat the eggs in a bowl, then add the lemon juice and the cornflour mixture and beat until smooth. Gradually beat in a ladleful of the liquid from the fish pan, then beat for 1 minute. Add a second ladleful in the same way, and continue until all of the liquid is incorporated.

4 Pour the sauce over the fish and spinach, and return the pan to the hob. Allow to cook gently for 2–3 minutes, then serve immediately.

COOK'S TIP

Spinach can have a gritty texture if it is not washed properly. The best way to wash it is to swirl the leaves gently with your hand in a large bowl of cold water, then lift them out by hand into a colander positioned over a sink. Repeat the process until the water that drains from the colander runs clear.

Energy 441kcal/1,839kJ; Protein 43.6g; Carbohydrate 10.6g, of which sugars 2.3g; Fat 22.1g, of which saturates 3.5g; Cholesterol 141mg; Calcium 273mg; Fibre 2.9g; Sodium 413mg

1 large red (bell) pepper

4 rashers (strips)
streaky (fatty) bacon,
roughly chopped

4 garlic cloves,
finely chopped

1 onion, sliced

5ml/1 tsp hot pimentón
(smoked Spanish paprika)

large pinch of saffron
threads or 1 sachet
powdered saffron, soaked
in 45ml/3 tbsp hot water

6 large plum
tomatoes, quartered

350g/12oz fresh
skinned cod fillet, cut
into large chunks

45ml/3 tbsp chopped fresh
coriander (cilantro), plus
a few sprigs to garnish

crusty bread, to serve

FROM THE STORECUPBOARD

45ml/3 tbsp olive oil

10ml/2 tsp paprika

400g/14oz can haricot
(navy) beans, drained
and rinsed

about 600ml/1 pint/
2¹/₂ cups fish stock

salt and ground black
pepper, to taste

COOK'S TIP

Cod is a popular white fish despite having been over-fished. Ensure that you buy fish that comes from a carefully controlled source, or else use an alternative white fish, such as hoki, hake, haddock, whiting, coley or pollack.

Cod and Bean Stew ✷✷

Everything is cooked in one pot in this divine dish, which combines fresh cod with luxurious saffron and smoked paprika-spiced beans.

SERVES EIGHT

1 Preheat the grill (broiler) and line the pan with foil. Halve the red pepper and scoop out the seeds. Place the halves, cut side down, in the pan and cook under a hot grill for about 10–15 minutes, until the skin is charred.

2 Put the pepper into a plastic bag, seal and leave for 10 minutes to steam. Remove from the bag, peel off the skin and discard. Chop the pepper into large pieces.

3 Heat the oil in a pan, then add the bacon and garlic. Fry for 2 minutes, then add the onion. Cover and cook for 5 minutes until the onion is soft. Stir in the paprika and pimentón, the saffron and its soaking water, and salt and pepper to taste.

4 Stir in the beans and add just enough stock to cover. Bring to the boil and simmer, uncovered, for about 15 minutes, stirring to prevent sticking. Stir in the chopped pepper and tomato quarters. Drop in the chunks of cod and bury them in the sauce.

5 Cover and simmer for 5 minutes. Stir in the chopped coriander. Serve in warmed soup plates or bowls, garnished with the coriander sprigs. Eat with lots of crusty bread.

Energy 181kcal/757kJ; Protein 14.4g; Carbohydrate 13.4g, of which sugars 6g; Fat 8.1g, of which saturates 1.8g; Cholesterol 28mg; Calcium 59mg; Fibre 4.6g; Sodium 388mg

60ml/4 tbsp lemon juice

750g/1lb 11oz thick halibut fillets, skinned and cubed

1 onion, finely chopped

3 garlic cloves, finely grated

30ml/2 tbsp finely grated fresh root ginger

10ml/2 tsp black mustard seeds

chopped coriander (cilantro) and sliced green chilli, to garnish

natural (plain) yogurt, to drizzle (optional)

basmati rice, pickles and poppadums, to serve

FROM THE STORECUPBOARD

60ml/4 tbsp rice wine vinegar

30ml/2 tbsp cumin seeds

5ml/1 tsp turmeric

5ml/1 tsp chilli powder

5ml/1 tsp salt

60ml/4 tbsp sunflower oil

2 x 400g/14oz cans chopped tomatoes

5ml/1 tsp sugar

Halibut and Tomato Curry ✳✳✳

The chunky cubes of white fish contrast beautifully with the rich red spicy tomato sauce and taste just as good as they look.

SERVES FOUR

1 Mix together the lemon juice, vinegar, cumin, turmeric, chilli powder and salt in a shallow glass bowl. Add the cubed fish and turn to coat evenly. Cover and put in the refrigerator to marinate for 25–30 minutes.

2 Meanwhile, heat a large pan over a high heat and add the oil. When hot, add the onion, garlic, ginger and mustard seeds. Reduce the heat to low and cook very gently for 10 minutes, stirring occasionally.

3 Add the tomatoes and sugar to the wok, bring to a boil, reduce the heat, cover and cook gently for 15–20 minutes, stirring occasionally.

4 Add the fish and its marinade to the wok, stir gently to mix, then cover and simmer gently for 15–20 minutes, or until the fish is cooked through and flakes easily with a fork.

5 Serve the curry ladled into shallow bowls with basmati rice, pickles and poppadums. Garnish with fresh coriander and green chillies, and drizzle over some natural yogurt if liked.

VARIATIONS

• Halibut is used here, but you can use any type of firm white fish, such as hake, coley or gurnard, for this recipe.

• For a spicier version of this curry, add more chilli powder, but be careful not to add too much or you will mask the lovely flavour of the halibut.

Energy 335kcal/1409kJ; Protein 41.9g; Carbohydrate 8.4g, of which sugars 8.1g; Fat 15.2g, of which saturates 2.1g; Cholesterol 66mg; Calcium 73mg; Fibre 2.2g; Sodium 622mg

Halibut with Leek and Ginger ✳✳

Generally fish needs to be absolutely fresh, but halibut needs to mature for a day or two to bring out the flavour. In this simple recipe the delicate flavour is subtly complemented by leeks and fresh root ginger.

SERVES FOUR

1 Trim the leeks, discarding the coarse outer leaves, the very dark green tops and the root end. Cut them into 5cm/2in lengths then slice into thin matchsticks. Wash thoroughly.

2 Peel the fresh ginger as best you can then slice it very thinly and cut the slices into thin matchsticks.

3 Pat the halibut steaks dry on kitchen paper. Heat a large pan with the olive oil and add 50g/2oz/¹⁄₄ cup of the butter. As it begins to bubble place the fish steaks carefully in the pan, skin side down. Allow the halibut to colour – this will take 3–4 minutes. Then turn the steaks over, reduce the heat and cook for about a further 10 minutes.

4 Remove the fish from the pan, set aside and keep warm. Add the leek and ginger to the pan, stir to mix then allow the leek to soften (they may colour slightly but this is fine). Once softened, season with a little salt and ground black pepper. Cut the remaining butter into small pieces then, off the heat, gradually stir into the pan. Serve immediately.

2 leeks

50g/2oz piece fresh root ginger

4 halibut steaks, approximately 175g/6oz each (see Cook's Tip)

75g/3oz/6 tbsp butter

FROM THE STORECUPBOARD

15ml/1 tbsp olive oil

COOK'S TIP *Look out for flattish, reasonably thin halibut steaks, as you want to cook them quite quickly in a pan on the stove rather than in the oven.*

Energy 364kcal/1520kJ; Protein 39.1g; Carbohydrate 2.7g, of which sugars 2.1g; Fat 21.9g, of which saturates 10.8g; Cholesterol 101mg; Calcium 75mg; Fibre 1.9g; Sodium 221mg

Smoked Haddock Flan ✳

The classic combination of potatoes and smoked fish is reworked in pastry. Always ask your fishmonger for "pale" smoked rather than "yellow" haddock as the latter tends to have been dyed to look bright and often has not been smoked properly at all. It is worth paying the extra for the real thing.

SERVES FOUR

1 Preheat the oven to 200°C/400°F/Gas 6. Use a food processor to make the pastry. Put the flour, salt and butter into the food processor bowl and process until the mixture resembles fine breadcrumbs.

2 Pour in a little cold water (you will need about 40ml/8 tsp but *see* Cook's Tip) and continue to process until the mixture forms a ball. If this takes longer than 30 seconds add a dash or two more water.

3 Take the pastry ball out of the food processor, wrap it in clear film (plastic wrap) and leave it to rest in a cool place for about 30 minutes.

4 Roll out the pastry and use it to line a 20cm/8in flan tin (quiche pan). Prick the base of the pastry all over with a fork then bake blind in the preheated oven for 20 minutes.

5 Put the haddock fillets in a pan with the milk, peppercorns and thyme. Poach for 10 minutes. Remove the fish from the pan using a slotted spoon and flake the flesh into small chunks. Allow the poaching liquor to cool.

6 Whisk the cream and eggs together in a large bowl, then whisk in the cooled poaching liquid.

7 Arrange the flaked fish and diced potato in the base of the pastry case, and season to taste with black pepper. Pour the cream mixture over the top.

8 Put the flan in the oven and bake for 40 minutes, until lightly browned on top and set.

VARIATION

This recipe is also delicious if you add roughly chopped hard-boiled eggs when you arrange the fish and potatoes in the base of the pastry case.

FOR THE PASTRY

115g/4oz/1¹/₂ cup cold butter, cut into chunks

cold water, to mix

FOR THE FILLING

2 pale smoked haddock fillets (approximately 200g/7oz)

600ml/1 pint/2¹/₂ cups full-fat (whole) milk

150ml/¹/₄ pint/²/₃ cup double (heavy) cream

2 eggs

200g/7oz potatoes, peeled and diced

FROM THE STORECUPBOARD

225g/8oz/2 cups plain (all-purpose) flour

pinch of salt

3–4 black peppercorns

sprig of fresh thyme

ground black pepper, to taste

COOK'S TIPS

• *Different flours absorb water at different rates. A traditional rule of thumb is to use the same number of teaspoons of water as the number of ounces of flour, but some flours will require less water and others more, so add the water gradually. If you add too much water, the pastry will become unworkable and you will need to add more flour.*

• *The key to making light pastry is to ensure that the butter and water are cold, and that your hands are as cool as possible. Try not to handle the pastry too much.*

Energy 734kcal/3064kJ; Protein 23.8g; Carbohydrate 58.4g, of which sugars 8.2g; Fat 46.8g, of which saturates 27.9g; Cholesterol 225mg; Calcium 280mg; Fibre 2.3g; Sodium 636mg

Smoked Haddock with Cabbage ✳✳✳

This simple and colourful dish of poached smoked haddock served with grilled tomatoes and sautéed shredded cabbage makes a healthy and delicious family meal.

SERVES FOUR

1 Cut the cabbage in half, remove the central core and thick ribs, then shred the cabbage. Cook in a pan of lightly salted boiling water, or steam over boiling water for about 10 minutes, until just tender. Leave in the pan or steamer until required.

2 Meanwhile put the haddock in a large, shallow pan with the milk, onion and bay leaves. Add the lemon and peppercorns. Bring to simmering point, cover and poach until the fish flakes easily when tested with the tip of a sharp knife. This will take 8–10 minutes, depending on the thickness of the fillets. Take the pan off the heat and set aside until needed. Preheat the grill.

3 Cut the tomatoes in half horizontally, season them to taste with salt and pepper and grill until lightly browned. Drain the cabbage, refresh under cold water and drain again.

4 Melt the butter in a shallow pan, add the cabbage and toss over the heat for 2 minutes. Mix in the mustard and season to taste, then tip the cabbage into a warmed serving dish.

5 Drain the haddock. Skin and cut the fish into four pieces. Place on top of the cabbage with some onion rings and tomato halves. Pour on the lemon juice, then sprinkle with parsley and serve.

1 Savoy or
pointu cabbage

675g/1¹⁄₂ lb undyed
smoked haddock fillet

300ml/¹⁄₂ pint/1¹⁄₄ cups
milk

¹⁄₂ onion, peeled and
sliced into rings

¹⁄₂ lemon, sliced

4 ripe tomatoes

50g/2oz/¹⁄₄ cup butter

juice of 1 lemon

30ml/2 tbsp chopped fresh
parsley, to garnish

FROM THE STORECUPBOARD

2 bay leaves

4 white peppercorns

30ml/2 tbsp wholegrain
mustard

salt and ground black
pepper, to taste

Energy 319kcal/1340kJ; Protein 36.1g; Carbohydrate 14.2g, of which sugars 13.7g; Fat 13.1g, of which saturates 7.3g; Cholesterol 90mg; Calcium 146mg; Fibre 4.2g; Sodium 1512mg

Haddock with Fennel Butter ✳✳✳

Fresh fish tastes fabulous cooked in a simple herb butter. Here the liquorice flavour of fennel complements the haddock beautifully to make a simple dish that is ideal for a dinner party.

SERVES FOUR

1 Preheat the oven to 220°C/425°F/Gas 7. Season the fish on both sides with salt and pepper. Melt one-quarter of the butter in a non-stick frying pan and cook the fish over a medium heat briefly on both sides.

2 Transfer the fish to a shallow ovenproof dish. Cut four wafer-thin slices from the lemon and squeeze the juice from the remainder over the fish. Place the lemon slices on top and then bake for 15–20 minutes, or until the fish is cooked.

3 Meanwhile, melt the remaining butter in the frying pan and add the fennel and a little seasoning.

4 Transfer the cooked fish to plates and pour the cooking juices into the herb butter. Heat the butter gently for a few seconds, then pour over the fish. Serve immediately.

675g/1¹/₂ lb haddock fillet, skinned and cut into 4 portions

50g/2oz/¹/₄ cup butter

1 lemon

45ml/3 tbsp chopped fennel

Energy 269kcal/1125kJ; Protein 36.5g; Carbohydrate 0.4g, of which sugars 0.3g; Fat 13.5g, of which saturates 7g; Cholesterol 86mg; Calcium 54mg; Fibre 0.3g; Sodium 178mg

450g/1lb haddock or
cod fillet

225g/8oz smoked
haddock or cod

150ml/¹/₄ pint/²/₃ cup
milk

150ml/¹/₄ pint/²/₃ cup
water

1 slice of lemon

a few fresh
parsley stalks

FOR THE SAUCE

25g/1oz/2 tbsp butter

5ml/1 tbsp lemon juice,
or to taste

45ml/3 tbsp chopped
fresh parsley

FOR THE TOPPING

450g/1lb potatoes,
boiled and mashed

25g/1oz/2 tbsp butter

FROM THE STORECUPBOARD

1 small bay leaf

25g/1oz/¹/₄ cup plain
(all-purpose) flour

ground black pepper,
to taste

Seafood Pie ✶✶

A well-made fish pie is perfect comfort food, and is particularly good
made with a mixture of fresh and smoked fish.

SERVES FOUR–FIVE

1 Preheat the oven to 190°C/375°F/Gas 5. Rinse the fish, cut
it into bitesize pieces and put into a pan with the milk, water,
lemon, bay leaf and parsley stalks. Bring slowly to the boil,
then simmer gently for 15 minutes until tender.

2 Strain and reserve 300ml/¹/₂ pint/1¹/₄ cups of the cooking
liquor. Leave the fish until cool, then flake the flesh and discard
the skin and bones. Set aside.

3 To make the sauce, melt the butter in a heavy pan, add the
flour and cook for 1–2 minutes over low heat stirring constantly.
Then gradually add the reserved cooking liquor, stirring well to
make a smooth sauce.

4 Simmer the sauce gently for 1–2 minutes, then remove from
the heat and stir in the flaked fish, chopped parsley and lemon
juice. Season to taste with ground black pepper.

5 Turn into a buttered 1.75 litre/3 pint/7¹/₂ cup pie dish or
shallow casserole, cover with the mashed potato for the topping
and dot with the butter.

6 Cook in the oven for about 20 minutes, or until thoroughly
heated through. The top should be golden brown and crunchy.
Divide the pie among 4–5 warmed plates and serve with a
lightly cooked green vegetable, such as fresh broccoli spears.

Energy 336kcal/1413kJ; Protein 35.1g; Carbohydrate 24.3g, of which sugars 0.9g; Fat 11.6g, of which saturates 6.7g; Cholesterol 87mg; Calcium 45mg; Fibre 1.7g, Sodium 587mg

Salmon Quiche ✳✳

There are so many wonderful ways of making smoked salmon stretch a bit further. Here it forms the filling for a light quiche made with potato pastry.

SERVES SIX

115g/4oz floury
potatoes, diced

115g/4oz/¹/₂ cup
butter, diced

¹/₂ egg, beaten

10ml/2 tsp chilled water

salad leaves and chopped
fresh dill, to serve

FOR THE FILLING

6 eggs, beaten

150ml/¹/₄ pint/²/₃ cup
full cream (whole) milk

300ml/¹/₂ pint/1¹/₄ cups
double (heavy) cream

30–45ml/2–3 tbsp
chopped fresh dill

30ml/2 tbsp drained
bottled capers, chopped

275g/10oz smoked salmon,
cut into bitesize pieces

FROM THE STORECUPBOARD

225g/8oz/2 cups plain
(all-purpose) flour, sifted

salt and ground black
pepper, to taste

VARIATION
These quantities can also be used to make six individual quiches, which make an ideal first course or light summer lunch. Prepare them as above, but reduce the cooking time by about 15 minutes.

1 Cook the potatoes in a large pan of lightly salted boiling water for 15 minutes or until tender. Drain and return to the pan. Mash the potatoes until smooth and set aside to cool completely.

2 Place the flour in a bowl and rub or cut in the butter to form fine crumbs. Beat in the potatoes and egg. Bring the mixture together, adding chilled water if needed.

3 Roll the pastry out on a floured surface to a 28cm/11in round. Use the pastry to line a deep, 23cm/9in round, loose-based, fluted quiche pan. Trim the edges. Chill for 1 hour.

4 Preheat the oven to 200°C/400°F/Gas 6. Place a baking sheet in the oven to heat it.

5 Make the filling. In a bowl, beat the eggs with the milk and cream. Stir in the dill and capers and season with pepper. Add in the salmon and stir to combine.

6 Remove the pastry case (pie shell) from the refrigerator, prick the base well and pour the mixture into it. Bake on a baking sheet for 35–45 minutes. Serve warm with mixed salad leaves and some more dill.

Energy 679kcal/2825kJ; Protein 23.3g; Carbohydrate 34.1g, of which sugars 2.7g; Fat 51.1g, of which saturates 28.9g; Cholesterol 317mg; Calcium 142mg; Fibre 1.4g; Sodium 1070mg

Lemony Salmon Loaf with Cucumber Sauce ✳

This stunning fish loaf is made using canned salmon, making it an economical option for the savvy cook. Served with the lemony cucumber sauce it is perfect as a light and elegant summer lunch or supper dish, or you can slice the loaf and eat it at picnics on its own.

SERVES FOUR–SIX

1 Put the breadcrumbs in a large bowl, pour in the milk and add the beaten eggs. Mix well to combine, then leave to stand for 10 minutes.

2 Preheat the oven to 180°C/350°F/Gas 4. Grease a 450g/1lb loaf tin (pan) with butter.

3 Drain the salmon, the put in a bowl and flake with a fork. Add to the breadcrumb mixture with the chopped celery, grated lemon rind and juice. Season to taste with salt and pepper.

4 Stir the mixture until evenly blended. Pour into the prepared loaf tin and bake for 1 hour or until a skewer inserted into the centre of the loaf comes out clean. Leave the loaf in the tin to cool slightly.

5 Make the sauce. Place the cucumber pieces in a small pan, cover with cold water and simmer until just tender. Using a slotted spoon, remove the cucumber and set it aside. Pour the cooking liquid into a measuring jug (cup). Add enough water to make up the liquid to 300ml/¹/₂ pint/1¹/₄ cups.

6 Melt the butter in the small pan. Stir in the flour using a wooden spoon. Cook, stirring constantly, for 1 minute, then gradually add the reserved cooking liquid, stirring until it boils and thickens.

7 Add the lemon rind and juice to the pan, then stir in the cooked cucumber.

8 Beat the egg yolk in a separate container and stir in a little of the hot sauce. Pour into the pan and heat gently, without boiling, until the sauce thickens a little more. Season to taste with salt and ground black pepper.

9 Using a spatula, loosen the salmon loaf from the sides of the tin and invert it on a serving dish. Garnish the loaf with lemon slices. Serve warm or cold, in slices, with the warm cucumber sauce on the side.

115g/4oz/2 cups fresh white breadcrumbs

150ml/¹/₄ pint/²/₃ cup milk

2 eggs, beaten

butter, for greasing

75g/3oz celery, chopped

400g/14oz can salmon

grated rind and juice of 1 lemon

lemon slices, to garnish

FOR THE SAUCE

1 cucumber, peeled, seeded and chopped

25g/1oz/2 tbsp butter

rind and juice of ¹/₂ lemon

1 egg yolk

FROM THE STORECUPBOARD

salt and ground black pepper, to taste

15ml/1 tbsp plain (all-purpose) flour

VARIATION *Fennel could be used instead of the celery. Quarter and core a fennel bulb, then chop finely and toss it with the lemon juice so that it doesn't discolour.*

Energy 265kcal/1109kJ; Protein 20g; Carbohydrate 19.1g, of which sugars 2.8g; Fat 12.3g, of which saturates 4.2g; Cholesterol 130mg; Calcium 152mg; Fibre 1g; Sodium 596mg

Salmon Baked with Potatoes and Thyme ✳✳✳

In this simple, elegant dish, pepper-crusted salmon fillets are baked on a bed of potatoes and onions braised in thyme-flavoured vegetable or fish stock. It makes an impressive main course for a dinner party.

SERVES FOUR

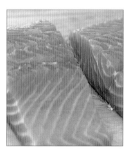

1 Preheat the oven to 190°C/375°F/Gas 5. Layer the potato and onion slices in a shallow baking dish, such as a lasagne dish, seasoning each layer and sprinkling with thyme. Pour over the stock, dot with butter, cover with foil and place in the oven.

2 Bake the potatoes for 40 minutes then remove the foil and bake for a further 20 minutes, or until they are almost cooked.

3 Meanwhile brush the salmon fillets with olive oil and coat with crushed black peppercorns, pressing them in to the flesh, if necessary, with the back of a spoon.

4 Place the salmon on top of the potatoes, cover with foil and bake for 15 minutes, or until the salmon is opaque, removing the foil for the last 5 minutes.

5 Garnish with fresh thyme sprigs and serve with mangetouts or sugar snap peas.

675g/1¹/₂ lb waxy potatoes, thinly sliced

1 onion, thinly sliced

10ml/2 tsp fresh thyme leaves, plus extra to garnish

450ml/³/₄ pint/scant 2 cups vegetable or fish stock

40g/1¹/₂ oz/3 tbsp butter, finely diced

4 salmon fillets, each about 150g/5oz, skinned

mangetouts (snow peas) or sugar snap peas, to serve

FROM THE STORECUPBOARD

30ml/2 tbsp olive oil

15ml/1 tbsp black peppercorns, crushed

salt and ground black pepper, to taste

COOK'S TIP *If you have a fish clay pot, use it for cooking this dish and the results will be even more spectacular. Soak the clay pot for 20 minutes in cold water, drain and add the layered potatoes. Cover with foil and place in a cold oven. Bake for 40 minutes, then for 20 minutes more without a lid. Proceed as in the recipe.*

Energy 517kcal/2160kJ; Protein 33.4g; Carbohydrate 28.4g, of which sugars 3.1g; Fat 30.8g, of which saturates 9g; Cholesterol 96mg; Calcium 47mg; Fibre 1.9g; Sodium 147mg

150g/5oz salmon fillet, skinned and any bones removed

50g/2oz fresh shiitake mushrooms, stalks removed

1 small carrot, peeled

¹/₂ mooli (daikon), peeled

5g/¹/₈oz *dashi-konbu* (dried kelp seaweed), about 10cm/4in square

60ml/4 tbsp water

15ml/1 tbsp *shoyu* (Japanese soy sauce)

7.5ml/1¹/₂ tsp *mirin* or dry sherry

2.5cm/1in fresh root ginger, peeled, to garnish

FROM THE STORECUPBOARD

salt

400g/14oz canned black-eyed beans (peas) in brine

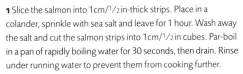

> **COOK'S TIP** Dashi-konbu *is usually covered with a fine white powder, which is a natural by-product of the drying process. It simply needs to be wiped off with a damp dish towel or piece of kitchen paper, rather than rinsed off with running water.*

Japanese Salmon and Black-eyed Bean Stew ✳✳

The addition of fresh salmon to this Asian stew helps to make it an extremely nourishing dish, as well as a delicious winter warmer. The canned beans are an added energy boost.

SERVES TWO

1 Slice the salmon into 1cm/¹/₂in-thick strips. Place in a colander, sprinkle with sea salt and leave for 1 hour. Wash away the salt and cut the salmon strips into 1cm/¹/₂in cubes. Par-boil in a pan of rapidly boiling water for 30 seconds, then drain. Rinse under running water to prevent them from cooking further.

2 Slice the ginger for the garnish thinly lengthways, then stack the slices and cut them into thin threads. Soak in cold water for about 30 minutes, then drain well.

3 Drain the can of black-eyed beans into a medium pan. Reserve the liquid. Chop all the fresh vegetables into 1cm/¹/₂in cubes. Wipe the *dashi-konbu* with a damp dish towel, then snip with scissors. Cut everything as close to the same size as possible.

4 Put the salmon, *dashi-konbu* and vegetables into the pan containing the liquid from the beans. Add the beans, 60ml/4 tbsp water and 1.5ml/¹/₄ tsp salt. Bring to the boil. Reduce the heat and cook for 6 minutes or until the carrot is cooked.

5 Add the *shoyu* and cook for a further 4 minutes. Add the *mirin* or sherry and remove the pan from the heat. Mix well. Leave to rest for 1 hour. Serve warm or cold, with the ginger threads.

Energy 387kcal/1633kJ; Protein 33.7g; Carbohydrate 43.5g, of which sugars 5.6g; Fat 9.9g, of which saturates 1.9g; Cholesterol 38mg; Calcium 70mg; Fibre 8.2g; Sodium 589mg

Smoked Trout Risotto ✳✳✳

Risottos are a great way of making more expensive ingredients, in this case smoked trout, stretch further. The strong flavour of the smoked fish permeates all the way through the dish, and, in combination with the cream and white wine, produces a rich and delicious all-in-one-dish supper, perfect for the cold months of winter.

SERVES FOUR

1 Heat the oil in a large, heavy pan. Add the chopped onion and fry it gently over a low heat for about 5 minutes until softened. Do not allow the onion to brown.

2 Add the rice to the pan and stir well with a wooden spoon to coat each grain thoroughly in oil. Cook over a low heat for 2–3 minutes until the rice grains have turned translucent.

3 Pour the white wine over the rice in the pan, stirring constantly. Continue to stir for 1–2 minutes until all of the wine has been absorbed.

4 Keeping the pan over a medium heat, add the hot stock, a ladleful at a time, stirring all the time.

5 Add another ladleful of stock to the rice only when the previous quantity has been absorbed, and continue in this way until all the stock has been used up.

6 During cooking, adjust the heat so that the risotto bubbles merrily. Do not let it boil or the stock will evaporate before it can be absorbed by the rice. This will take around 20 minutes. As the rice cooks the mixture will thicken – the risotto is cooked when the rice has a velvety texture. When you taste them, the grains of rice should still have a bit of bite in the centre.

7 Remove the pan from the heat and stir in the crème fraîche or sour cream and the grated grano padano cheese.

8 Add three-quarters of the chopped smoked trout and the chopped chervil.

9 Season to taste with plenty of salt and freshly ground black pepper and stir well to mix. Cover the pan and leave to stand for about 2 minutes.

10 Divide the risotto among four warmed serving plates, top with the remaining smoked trout and garnish with the fresh chervil sprigs. Serve immediately. Extra grated grano padano cheese can be offered separately.

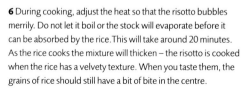

**1 medium onion,
finely chopped**

**150ml/¹/₄ pint/²/₃ cup
dry white wine**

**45ml/3 tbsp crème fraîche
or sour cream**

**45ml/3 tbsp grated grano
padano cheese, plus extra,
to serve**

**350g/12oz smoked trout,
roughly chopped**

**60ml/4 tbsp chopped
fresh chervil**

**fresh chervil sprigs,
to garnish**

FROM THE STORECUPBOARD

30ml/2 tbsp olive oil

**1.2 litres/2 pints/5 cups
hot fish stock**

**400g/14oz/2 cups risotto
rice, preferably arborio**

**salt and ground black
pepper, to taste**

COOK'S TIPS

• For the creamiest risotto the stock needs to be hot when it is added to the rice, so keep it simmering in a pan on top of the stove, next to the risotto pan.

• For best results, use a well-flavoured fish stock.

Energy 656kcal/2741kJ; Protein 34.5g; Carbohydrate 81.5g, of which sugars 1.3g; Fat 18.2g, of which saturates 6.9g; Cholesterol 55mg; Calcium 184mg; Fibre 0.2g; Sodium 1772mg

350g/12oz trout
fillet, skinned

150ml/¹/₄ pint/²/₃ cup
milk

4 spring onions (scallions),
thinly sliced

350g/12oz cooked
potatoes, peeled

1 egg, beaten

50g/2oz/1 cup fresh
white breadcrumbs

TO SERVE

120ml/4fl oz/¹/₂ cup
mayonnaise

45ml/3 tbsp drained
canned corn

1 red (bell) pepper, seeded
and finely diced

8 burger buns

salad leaves

4 ripe tomatoes, sliced

FROM THE STORECUPBOARD

150ml/¹/₄ pint/²/₃ cup
hot fish stock

5ml/1 tsp tartare sauce

60ml/4 tbsp semolina

salt and ground white
pepper, to taste

vegetable oil, for
shallow frying

Trout Burgers with Corn and Pepper Mayonnaise ✳

These home-made fish burgers really are a treat for all the family. They provide the ideal way of persuading children who claim they don't like fish to try it, and also include salad, corn and peppers. Cook chilled burgers on the barbecue, if you prefer, on a lightly oiled grill (broiler) rack.

MAKES SIX

1 Place the trout in a frying pan with the milk, stock and spring onions. Simmer for 5 minutes, or until the fish is cooked. Lift it out of the pan and set it aside. Strain the stock into a bowl, reserving the spring onions.

2 Mash the potatoes and stir in the tartare sauce, egg and breadcrumbs. Flake the trout and add the reserved spring onions. Fold into the potato mixture and season to taste.

3 Divide the potato mixture into eight and shape into burgers, using your hands. Coat thoroughly in the semolina and pat them into shape. Chill in the refrigerator for 1 hour.

4 Meanwhile, in a bowl, mix the mayonnaise with the corn kernels and diced red pepper.

5 Heat the oil in a frying pan and fry the burgers for 10 minutes, turning once. To serve, split open the buns and spread a little of the mayonnaise over each half. Fill with a few salad leaves, a couple of tomato slices and a fish burger. Serve immediately.

VARIATIONS

• Not all children like tartare sauce. If you have any doubts about adding it to the burger mixture, you could substitute tomato ketchup instead.

• Substitute the trout for salmon, mackerel or any other oily fish.

Energy 497kcal/2080kJ; Protein 19.5g; Carbohydrate 45.7g, of which sugars 6.9g; Fat 27.5g, of which saturates 3.8g; Cholesterol 47mg; Calcium 93mg; Fibre 2.9g; Sodium 400mg

Pan-fried Mackerel with Ratatouille and Lemon ✳✳

Make this colourful dish during the summer when peppers and tomatoes have the sweetest flavour and are better value for money. Ratatouille is rather like a chunky vegetable stew. This version is particularly lemony, to offset the richness of the mackerel.

SERVES FOUR

2 large mackerel, filleted, or 4 fillets

lemon wedges, to serve

FOR THE RATATOUILLE

1 large aubergine (eggplant), sliced

1 large onion, chopped

2 garlic cloves, finely chopped

1 large courgette (zucchini), sliced

1 red and 1 green (bell) pepper, seeded and chopped

800g/1³⁄₄lb ripe tomatoes, roughly chopped

FROM THE STORECUPBOARD

90ml/6 tbsp olive oil

1 bay leaf

plain (all-purpose) flour, for dusting

salt and ground black pepper, to taste

> **COOK'S TIP** Sprinkling the slices of aubergine (eggplant) with salt helps to draw out the bitter juices and allows the aubergine to absorb more flavour.

1 Sprinkle the aubergine slices with salt and leave to stand in a colander for 30 minutes.

2 Heat 15ml/3 tsp of the olive oil in a large flameproof casserole. Gently fry the onion until it colours slightly. Add the garlic, then the courgette and peppers and stir-fry. Add the tomatoes and bay leaf, partially cover and simmer until the tomatoes just soften.

3 Rinse off the salt from the aubergine. Using kitchen paper, squeeze the slices dry, then cut into cubes. Heat 15ml/3 tsp of the olive oil in a frying pan until smoking. Add the aubergine cubes a handful at a time and cook, stirring over a high heat until the cubes are brown on all sides. Stir into the tomato sauce.

4 Cut each mackerel fillet into three, then dust the filleted side with flour. Heat 60ml/4 tbsp of the oil in a frying pan and fry the fish, floured side down, for 3 minutes. Turn and cook for a further minute, then slip into the sauce and simmer, covered, for 5 minutes. Check the seasoning before serving hot or cold.

Energy 544kcal/2260kJ; Protein 28.4g; Carbohydrate 22.9g, of which sugars 17.9g; Fat 38.2g, of which saturates 6.9g; Cholesterol 68mg; Calcium 78mg; Fibre 6.3g; Sodium 104mg

Mackerel Stuffed with Nuts and Spices ✳✳

This dish of whole mackerel stuffed with nuts and spices is a classic dish from Turkey. The fish is skilfully massaged to empty it of flesh while keeping the skin intact, so that it can then be stuffed to resemble the whole fish once more. Although it can be quite time-consuming and fiddly to prepare, it is a satisfying and impressive dish to make for a buffet spread or a special meal for friends and family.

SERVES FOUR

1 Take a sharp knife and cut an opening just below the gills of the mackerel, making sure the head and backbone remain intact. Push your finger into the opening and remove the guts, then rinse the fish inside and out.

2 Using a rolling pin or mallet, gently bash the fish on both sides, making sure you smash the backbone. Now, with your hands, gently massage the skin to loosen it away from the flesh – don't pummel it too hard or the skin will tear.

3 Working from the tail end towards the head, squeeze the loosened flesh out of the opening below the gills – use a similar motion to squeezing a half-empty tube of toothpaste. Remove any bits of bone from the loosened flesh, then rinse out the mackerel sack and set aside.

4 Heat the oil in a frying pan, stir in the shallots and cook until soft. Add the nuts and stir until they begin to colour. Add the currants, apricots, spices, Turkish red pepper or chilli and sugar. Mix in the fish flesh and cook through for 2–3 minutes, then toss in the herbs and lemon juice and season with salt and pepper.

5 Lift up the empty mackerel skin and push the filling through the opening, shaking the sack a little to jiggle the filling down towards the tail.

6 As the skin begins to fill, gently squeeze the mixture downwards to make it compact, until it looks like a plump, fresh mackerel once more.

7 To cook the mackerel, toss it in flour and fry in sunflower oil, or brush with a little oil and grill (broil) until the skin begins to turn brown and buckle.

8 To serve, cut the fish crossways into thick slices and arrange on a dish in the shape of the fish. Surround with dill and parsley and serve with lemon wedges.

1 large, fresh mackerel, scaled and thoroughly washed, but not gutted

4–5 shallots, finely chopped

30ml/2 tbsp pine nuts

30ml/2 tbsp blanched almonds, finely slivered

45ml/3 tbsp walnuts, finely chopped

15–30ml/1–2 tbsp currants, soaked in warm water for 5–10 minutes and drained

6–8 dried apricots, finely chopped

1 small bunch each of fresh flat leaf parsley and dill, finely chopped

juice of 1 lemon

1 bunch of fresh dill, to serve

a few fresh flat leaf parsley sprigs, to serve

1 lemon, cut into wedges, to serve

FROM THE STORECUPBOARD

30–45ml/2–3 tbsp olive oil

5–10ml/1–2 tsp ground cinnamon

5ml/1 tsp ground allspice

2.5ml/1/2 tsp ground cloves

2.5ml/1/2 tsp chilli powder

5ml/1 tsp sugar

plain (all-purpose) flour

sunflower oil, for shallow frying

salt and ground black pepper, to taste

Energy 520kcal/2154kJ; Protein 20.2g; Carbohydrate 13.7g, of which sugars 10.1g; Fat 43.1g, of which saturates 5.5g; Cholesterol 40mg; Calcium 86mg; Fibre 3.1g; Sodium 53mg

Grilled Mackerel with Spicy Dhal ✳✳

Oily fish like mackerel are essential as part of a balanced diet and are good value for money. Here they are complemented by tamarind-flavoured dhal, chopped fresh tomatoes, onion salad and flat bread.

SERVES FOUR

1 Rinse the lentils, drain them well and put them in a pan. Pour in 1 litre/1³/₄ pints/4 cups water and bring to the boil. Lower the heat, partially cover the pan and simmer the lentils for about 30–40 minutes, stirring occasionally, until they are tender and soft.

2 Heat the oil in a wok or shallow pan. Add the mustard seeds, then cover and cook for a few seconds, until they pop. Remove the lid, add the rest of the seeds, with the turmeric and chillies and cook for a few more seconds.

3 Stir in the lentils, with salt to taste. Mix well, then stir in the tamarind paste and sugar. Bring to the boil, then simmer for 10 minutes, until thick. Stir in the chopped fresh coriander.

4 Meanwhile, clean the fish then heat a ridged griddle pan or the grill (broiler) until very hot. Make six diagonal slashes on either side of each fish and remove the head if you like. Season inside and out, then cook for 5–7 minutes on each side, until the skin is crisp. Serve with the dhal, flat bread and tomatoes, garnished with chilli and coriander.

3–4 dried red chillies, crumbled

30ml/2 tbsp tamarind paste

30ml/2 tbsp chopped fresh coriander (cilantro)

4 mackerel or 8 large sardines

fresh red chilli slices and finely chopped coriander (cilantro), to garnish

flat bread and tomatoes, to serve

FROM THE STORECUPBOARD

250g/9oz/1 cup red lentils

30ml/2 tbsp sunflower oil

2.5ml/¹/₂ tsp each mustard seeds, cumin seeds, fennel seeds, and fenugreek or cardamom seeds

5ml/1 tsp ground turmeric

5ml/1 tsp soft brown sugar

salt and ground black pepper, to taste

Energy 586kcal/2453kJ; Protein 43.3g; Carbohydrate 36.5g, of which sugars 2.8g; Fat 30.6g, of which saturates 5.7g; Cholesterol 81mg; Calcium 72mg; Fibre 3.6g; Sodium 121mg

Grilled Sardines with Chilli and Onion Marinade ✳

This unusual dish is packed with flavour and is an ideal make-ahead dish for a summer dinner party or *al fresco* meal. Serve with roasted summer vegetables and flatbread to mop up the marinade.

SERVES FOUR

1 Cut the heads off the sardines and split each of them along the belly. Turn the fish over so that the backbone is uppermost. Press down along the backbone to loosen it, then carefully lift out the backbone and as many of the remaining little bones as possible. Close the sardines up again and dust them with seasoned flour.

2 Heat 30ml/2 tbsp of the olive oil in a frying pan and fry the sardines for 2–3 minutes on each side. With a metal spatula, remove the fish from the pan to a plate and allow to cool, then pack them in a single layer in a large shallow dish.

3 To make the marinade, add the remaining olive oil to the oil in the frying pan. Fry the onion and garlic for 5–10 minutes until translucent. Add the bay leaves, cloves, chilli and paprika, with pepper to taste. Fry for another 1–2 minutes.

4 Stir in the vinegar, wine and a little salt. Allow to bubble up, then pour over the sardines to cover the fish completely. When cool, cover and chill overnight or for up to three days. Serve garnished with the onion, pepper and tomatoes.

12–16 sardines, cleaned

roasted red onion, green (bell) pepper and tomatoes, to garnish

FOR THE MARINADE

1 onion, sliced

1 garlic clove, crushed

1 dried red chilli, seeded and chopped

120ml/4fl oz/^{1}/$_2$ cup white wine

FROM THE STORECUPBOARD

seasoned plain (all-purpose) flour, for dusting

90 ml/6 tbsp olive oil

3–4 bay leaves

2 cloves

5ml/1 tsp paprika

120ml/4fl oz/^{1}/$_2$ cup wine or sherry vinegar

salt and ground black pepper, to taste

Energy 353kcal/1467kJ; Protein 23.7g; Carbohydrate 4.2g, of which sugars 1g; Fat 26g, of which saturates 5.1g; Cholesterol 0mg; Calcium 124mg; Fibre 0.3g; Sodium 129mg

Baked Sardines with Tomatoes and Thyme *

Served with chunks of crusty bread to mop up the sauce, and a green salad, this simple dish is all you need for a tasty, satisfying meal. Whole mackerel and anchovies can also be prepared and cooked this way.

SERVES FOUR

1 Preheat the oven to 180°C/350°F/ Gas 4. Lay the prepared sardines side by side in a shallow, ovenproof dish, place a sprig of fresh thyme between each one and squeeze the lemon juice over them.

2 In a large bowl, mix the drained tomatoes, olive oil, smashed garlic and sugar. Season to taste with salt and pepper and stir in most of the fresh purple or green basil leaves, then tip the mixture over the sardines.

3 Put the dish in the preheated oven and bake, uncovered, for 25 minutes. Sprinkle the remaining basil leaves over the top and serve hot, with lemon wedges for squeezing.

8 large sardines, scaled, gutted and thoroughly washed

6–8 fresh thyme sprigs

juice of $^{1}/_{2}$ lemon

4 garlic cloves, smashed flat

1 bunch of fresh purple or green basil

lemon wedges, to serve

FROM THE STORECUPBOARD

2 x 400g/14oz cans chopped tomatoes, drained of juice

60–75ml/4–5 tbsp olive oil

5ml/1 tsp sugar

salt and ground black pepper, to taste

Energy 219kcal/915kJ; Protein 11.7g; Carbohydrate 7.3g, of which sugars 7.3g; Fat 16.2g, of which saturates 3.1g; Cholesterol 0mg; Calcium 57mg; Fibre 2g; Sodium 78mg

12 sardines, scaled, gutted and thoroughly washed

juice of 1/2 lemon

12 fresh or preserved vine leaves (see Cook's Tip)

4–6 vine tomatoes, halved or quartered

lemon wedges, to serve

FOR THE DRESSING

juice of 1 lemon

5–10ml/1–2 tsp clear honey

5ml/1 tsp Turkish red pepper, or 1 fresh red chilli, finely chopped

a few fresh dill fronds and flat leaf parsley sprigs, finely chopped

FROM THE STORECUPBOARD

90ml/6 tbsp olive oil, plus extra for brushing

15ml/1 tbsp balsamic or white wine vinegar

salt and ground black pepper, to taste

COOK'S TIP *Fresh vine leaves are sold in Middle Eastern and Mediterranean stores when they are in season in the autumn. Plunged into boiling water for a minute, the bright green leaves soften and turn a deep olive colour, ready for use. If you can't get fresh vine leaves, use the ones preserved in brine. Before using, place them in a bowl, pour boiling water over them and leave to soak for about an hour. Drain and rinse under cold running water, then pat dry.*

Chargrilled Sardines Wrapped in Vine Leaves ✳

Although this dish can be cooked under a grill (broiler), there is nothing to beat the taste when it is cooked over a charcoal barbecue. The charred vine leaves and tomatoes make perfect partners for the oily fish.

SERVES THREE–FOUR

1 Put 60ml/4 tbsp oil and the rest of the dressing ingredients in a bowl, season with salt and pepper and mix well.

2 Pat the sardines dry and lay them in a flat dish. Mix 30ml/2 tbsp oil with the lemon juice and brush over the sardines.

3 Get the barbecue ready for cooking. Meanwhile, spread the vine leaves out on a flat surface and place a sardine on each leaf. Sprinkle with a little salt and wrap loosely in the leaf like a cigar, with the tail and head poking out.

4 Brush each leaf with a little oil and place seam side down. Thread the tomatoes on skewers and sprinkle with a little salt.

5 Cook the sardines and tomatoes on the barbecue for 2–3 minutes on each side, until the vine leaves are charred and the tomatoes are soft. Transfer to a serving dish and drizzle with the dressing. Serve immediately, with lemon wedges for squeezing.

Energy 300kcal/1245kJ; Protein 16.5g; Carbohydrate 5.3g, of which sugars 5.3g; Fat 23.7g, of which saturates 4.5g; Cholesterol 0mg; Calcium 82mg; Fibre 1.5g; Sodium 101mg

Barbecued Sardines with Orange and Parsley ✳

Sardines are ideal for the barbecue – the meaty flesh holds together and the skin crisps nicely – but they are equally delicious cooked under a grill (broiler). Serve them with boiled potatoes and a green salad.

SERVES SIX

1 Arrange the sardines and orange slices in a single layer in a shallow, non-metallic dish. Sprinkle over the chopped parsley and season with salt and pepper, to taste.

2 Drizzle the oil over the sardines and orange slices and stir to coat. Cover with clear film (plastic wrap) and chill for 2 hours.

3 Meanwhile, prepare the barbecue or preheat the grill (broiler) to high. Remove the sardines and orange slices from the marinade and place them directly on to a grill rack.

4 Cook the fish over the barbecue or under the hot grill for 7–8 minutes on each side, until the fish are cooked through. Serve immediately.

6 whole sardines, gutted

1 orange, sliced

a small bunch of fresh flat leaf parsley, chopped

FROM THE STORECUPBOARD

60ml/4 tbsp extra virgin olive oil

salt and ground black pepper, to taste

Energy 156kcal/649kJ; Protein 13.1g; Carbohydrate 1.7g, of which sugars 1.7g; Fat 10.8g, of which saturates 2.3g; Cholesterol 0mg; Calcium 73mg; Fibre 0.3g; Sodium 72mg

Fish Curry with Shallots and Lemon Grass ✳✳

This is a thin fish curry made with salmon fillets. It has wonderfully strong, aromatic flavours, and should ideally be served in small bowls with plenty of crusty bread or plain boiled rice.

SERVES FOUR

1 Place the salmon fillets in the freezer for about 30–40 minutes to firm up the flesh slightly. Remove and discard the skin, then use a sharp knife to cut the fish into 2.5cm/1in cubes, removing any stray bones as you do so.

2 Pour the vegetable stock into a pan and bring it slowly to the boil. Add the chopped shallots, garlic, ginger, lemon grass, dried chilli flakes, fish sauce and sugar. Bring back to the boil, stir well to ensure the ingredients are thoroughly mixed, then reduce the heat and simmer gently for about 15 minutes.

3 Add the fish pieces, bring back to the boil, then turn off the heat. Leave the curry to stand for 10–15 minutes, then serve in small bowls.

450g/1lb salmon fillets

4 shallots, finely chopped

**2 garlic cloves,
finely chopped**

**2.5cm/1in piece fresh root
ginger, finely chopped**

**1 lemon grass stalk,
finely chopped**

**2.5ml/¹/₂ tsp dried
chilli flakes**

FROM THE STORECUPBOARD

**500ml/17fl oz/2¹/₄ cups
vegetable stock**

**15ml/1 tbsp Thai
fish sauce**

**5ml/1 tsp light muscovado
(brown) sugar**

Energy 218kcal/910kJ; Protein 23.4g; Carbohydrate 3.1g, of which sugars 2.7g; Fat 12.6g, of which saturates 2.2g; Cholesterol 56mg; Calcium 51mg; Fibre 0.8g; Sodium 322mg

Prawn and New Potato Stew ✳

New potatoes with plenty of flavour, such as Jersey Royals, Maris Piper or Nicola, are essential for this effortless seasonal stew. Use fresh prawns if they are on special offer, otherwise use good-quality frozen ones as they will usually be much more economical and taste almost as good.

SERVES FOUR

1 Cook the new potatoes in lightly salted, boiling water for 15 minutes, until tender. Drain and return to the pan.

2 Meanwhile, finely chop the coriander and crumble the dried chilli. Heat the oil in a large pan and fry the garlic for 1 minute. Pour in the chopped tomatoes, and add the chilli, coriander and 90ml/6 tbsp water. Bring to the boil, reduce the heat, cover and simmer gently for 5 minutes.

3 Stir in the prawns and the cooked new potatoes and heat briefly until they are warmed through. Be careful not to overcook the prawns or they will quickly shrivel, becoming tough and tasteless.

4 Spoon the stew into shallow bowls and serve sprinkled with the remaining coriander, torn into pieces. Serve with bread and salad, or steamed seasonal vegetables.

675g/1¹/₂lb small new potatoes, scrubbed

15g/¹/₂ oz/¹/₂ cup fresh coriander (cilantro)

1 garlic clove

300g/11oz cooked peeled prawns (shrimp), thawed and drained if frozen

FROM THE STORECUPBOARD

15ml/1 tbsp olive oil

400g/14oz can chopped tomatoes

1 dried red chilli, crumbled

Energy 218kcal/924kJ; Protein 16.9g; Carbohydrate 30.4g, of which sugars 5.4g; Fat 4.1g, of which saturates 0.7g; Cholesterol 146mg; Calcium 84mg; Fibre 2.9g; Sodium 171mg

Prawn, Tomato and Potato Omelette ✳

This simple dish makes a delicious lunch when served with a fresh leafy green salad, or a healthy light meal when served with steamed seasonal vegetables. The sweet prawns are cooked gently inside the omelette, which helps them to stay tender and succulent.

SERVES FOUR

1 Cook the potatoes in a pan of salted boiling water for about 10 minutes or until tender.

2 Meanwhile, pour the oil into a 23cm/9in frying pan which can safely be used under the grill (broiler). Place over a medium heat. Add the onion slices and stir well to coat evenly in the oil. Cook for 5 minutes until the onions begin to soften. Sprinkle over the paprika and cook for 1 minute more.

3 Stir in the tomatoes. Drain the cooked potatoes thoroughly and add to the pan. Stir gently to mix. Increase the heat and cook for 10 minutes, or until the mixture has thickened and the potatoes have absorbed the flavour of the tomatoes. Remove from the heat and stir in the prawns.

4 Preheat the grill. Beat the eggs, stir in the baking powder and salt. Pour into the pan and mix thoroughly. Cover and cook for 8–10 minutes until the omelette has almost set, then finish under the grill.

200g/7oz potatoes, peeled and diced

1 onion, finely sliced

2 large tomatoes, peeled, seeded and chopped

200g/7oz frozen peeled raw prawns (shrimp), thawed

6 eggs

FROM THE STORECUPBOARD

30ml/2 tbsp olive oil

2.5ml/¹/₂ tsp paprika

2.5ml/¹/₂ tsp baking powder

pinch of salt

Energy 247kcal/1031kJ; Protein 19.6g; Carbohydrate 10.8g, of which sugars 3.1g; Fat 14.5g, of which saturates 3.3g; Cholesterol 383mg; Calcium 93mg; Fibre 1.2g; Sodium 211mg

Baked Prawns with Tomatoes, Pepper and Garlic ✳✳✳

This easy-to-make dish can be cooked in one large earthenware dish, or several small ones. It is delicious simply served with a green salad.

SERVES FOUR

1 Heat the oil in a heavy pan, stir in the onion, green pepper, garlic, coriander seeds and red pepper or chilli and cook until they begin to colour.

2 Stir in the sugar, vinegar, tomatoes and parsley, then cook gently for about 25 minutes, until you have a chunky sauce. While the sauce is cooking, preheat the oven to 200°C/400°F/Gas 6.

3 Season the sauce with salt and pepper and toss in the prawns, making sure they are mixed in well.

4 Spoon the mixture into one large or four individual earthenware pots and sprinkle the top with the grated cheese. Bake for 25 minutes, or until the cheese is browned on top.

1 onion, cut in half lengthways and finely sliced along the grain

1 green (bell) pepper, seeded and finely sliced

2–3 garlic cloves, chopped

5–10ml/1–2 tsp Turkish red pepper, or 1 fresh red chilli, seeded and chopped

1 small bunch of fresh flat leaf parsley, chopped

500g/1¼lb raw prawns (shrimp), thawed if frozen and peeled (with the tail shells intact)

about 120g/4oz grano padano or mature (sharp) Cheddar cheese, grated

FROM THE STORECUPBOARD

30–45ml/2–3 tbsp olive oil

5–10ml/1–2 tsp coriander seeds

5–10ml/1–2 tsp sugar

splash of white wine vinegar

2 x 400g/14oz cans chopped tomatoes

salt and ground black pepper, to taste

Energy 338kcal/1413kJ; Protein 35.9g; Carbohydrate 11.2g, of which sugars 10.8g; Fat 16.9g, of which saturates 7.3g; Cholesterol 274mg; Calcium 481mg; Fibre 2.9g; Sodium 585mg

1 onion, chopped

$^1/_2$ red (bell) pepper, seeded and cubed

675g/1$^1/_2$lb ripe tomatoes, peeled and roughly chopped

450g/1lb raw tiger prawns (jumbo shrimp), thawed if frozen and peeled (with the tail shells intact)

30ml/2 tbsp finely chopped fresh flat leaf parsley

75g/3oz feta cheese, cubed

FROM THE STORECUPBOARD

75ml/5 tbsp olive oil

generous pinch of sugar

2.5ml/$^1/_2$ tsp dried oregano

salt and ground black pepper, to taste

COOK'S TIPS

• When tomatoes are not in season, substitute fresh ones with 2 x 400g/14oz cans chopped tomatoes, drained of their juices.

• Tiger prawns are absolutely delicious but they can be expensive, so either buy them when they are on offer, or use frozen ones.

Baked Prawns with Tomatoes and Feta ✳✳

Tangy, salty feta cheese provides the perfect contrast to the sweet, succulent prawns in this simple baked dish. Serve with a green salad.

SERVES FOUR

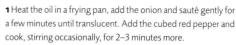
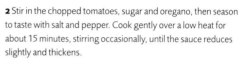

1 Heat the oil in a frying pan, add the onion and sauté gently for a few minutes until translucent. Add the cubed red pepper and cook, stirring occasionally, for 2–3 minutes more.

2 Stir in the chopped tomatoes, sugar and oregano, then season to taste with salt and pepper. Cook gently over a low heat for about 15 minutes, stirring occasionally, until the sauce reduces slightly and thickens.

3 Preheat the oven to 180°C/350°F/Gas 4. Stir the prawns and chopped parsley into the tomato sauce, tip into a baking dish and spread evenly. Sprinkle the cheese cubes on top, then bake for 30 minutes. Serve hot with a fresh green salad.

Energy 308kcal/1,282kJ; Protein 24.8g; Carbohydrate 10g, of which sugars 9.1g; Fat 19g, of which saturates 4.8g; Cholesterol 233mg; Calcium 194mg; Fibre 2.9g; Sodium 504mg

2 frozen octopuses, total weight about 675–800g/1¹/₂–1³/₄lb, thawed and cleaned well

2 large onions, sliced

3 garlic cloves, chopped

1 fresh red or green chilli, seeded and thinly sliced

175ml/6fl oz/³/₄ cup red wine

300ml/¹/₂ pint/1¹/₄ cups warm water

300ml/¹/₂ pint/1¹/₄ cups boiling water

45ml/3 tbsp finely chopped fresh flat leaf parsley, to garnish (optional)

FROM THE STORECUPBOARD

150ml/¹/₄ pint/²/₃ cup olive oil

1 or 2 bay leaves

5ml/1 tsp dried oregano

1 piece of cinnamon stick

2 or 3 grains allspice (optional)

30ml/2 tbsp tomato purée (paste) diluted in 300ml/¹/₂ pint/1¹/₄ cups water

225g/8oz/2 cups dried penne or small macaroni-type pasta

ground black pepper

Octopus and Pasta Bake ✳

A mouthwatering dish, this slow-cooked combination of octopus and pasta in a spicy tomato sauce makes a tasty supper dish.

SERVES FOUR

1 Cut the octopuses into large pieces and place in a heavy pan over a low heat. Cook gently; they will produce some liquid, the colour of the flesh will change and they will become scarlet. Keep turning the pieces until all the liquid has evaporated.

2 Add the olive oil to the pan and sauté the octopus pieces for 4–5 minutes. Add the onions and cook for a further 4–5 minutes, stirring them constantly until they start to turn golden.

3 Stir in the garlic, chilli, bay leaf or leaves, oregano, cinnamon stick and allspice, if using. As soon as the garlic becomes aromatic, pour in the wine and let it bubble for a few minutes.

4 Pour in the tomato purée, add some black pepper, cover and cook gently for 1¹/₂ hours, or until the octopus is perfectly soft. Stir occasionally and add a little hot water if needed.

5 Preheat the oven to 160°C/325°F/Gas 3. Bring the octopus mixture to the boil, and then add the boiling water.

6 Stir in the dried pasta, coating it in the mixture. Tip into a large roasting dish and level the surface.

7 Transfer to the oven and bake for 30–35 minutes, stirring occasionally and adding a little hot water if the mixture starts to look dry. Sprinkle the parsley on top, if using, and serve.

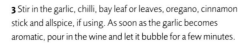

COOK'S TIP

• Do not add salt to octopus as it makes it tough and indigestible.

• The octopus mixture can be cooked more quickly in a pressure cooker, if you prefer. It will take about 20 minutes under full pressure.

Energy 637kcal/2,669kJ; Protein 38.9g; Carbohydrate 52.9g, of which sugars 10.2g; Fat 28.5g, of which saturates 4.2g; Cholesterol 81mg; Calcium 108mg; Fibre 3.6g; Sodium 25mg

Fried Squid with Split Pea Purée ✳

Medium-sized squid work well for this tasty fried squid recipe, although the tender baby squid are also popular and add a lovely crispness to the texture, which contrasts well with the smooth purée.

SERVES FOUR

**1.5 litres/2¹/₂ pints/
6¹/₄ cups cold water**

1 onion, finely chopped

**4 medium frozen squid,
thawed, total weight
about 900g/2lb**

**2 or 3 shallots,
finely chopped**

juice of ¹/₂ lemon

**15ml/1 tbsp finely
chopped fresh parsley,
to garnish**

FROM THE STORECUPBOARD

**225g/8oz/1 cup fava or
yellow split peas**

**50g/2oz/¹/₂ cup plain
(all-purpose) flour**

75ml/5 tbsp sunflower oil

**60–75ml/4–5 tbsp extra
virgin olive oil**

**salt and ground black
pepper, to taste**

COOK'S TIPS

- Squid require either very fast or very slow cooking. Anything in between renders them very rubbery and almost inedible.

- Towards the end of the cooking time, watch the pea mixture closely and stir it frequently as it may start to stick to the bottom of the pan. Once cooked, the peas should be perfectly soft and moist.

1 Soak the fava or split peas in cold water to cover for 1 hour. Drain, rinse several times, then drain again. Pour the measured water in to a large, heavy pan. Add the fava or split peas, bring to the boil and skim away any scum using a slotted spoon.

2 Add the onion and simmer, uncovered, for 1 hour or more, depending on the age of the peas, stirring occasionally, until soft.

3 Season the flour with salt and freshly ground black pepper and then toss the squid in it until each is evenly coated.

4 Purée the pea mixture in a food processor or blender while it is still hot, as it will solidify if you allow it to cool. The purée should be smooth, with the consistency of thick cream. Add salt to taste.

5 Heat the sunflower oil in a large frying pan. When it is hot enough to sizzle but is not smoking, add the squid bodies, without letting them touch each other. Cook until pale golden all over. Add the tentacles and cook until they are crisp and golden all over.

6 Spread the pea mixture on individual plates in a thin layer and let it cool a little. Sprinkle the chopped shallots over the top, then drizzle with the olive oil and lemon juice. Place the fried squid on top. Grind a little pepper over the top and add the chopped parsley. Serve warm or at room temperature.

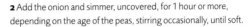
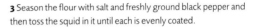
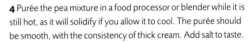
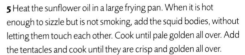
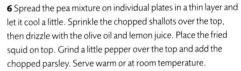

Energy 637kcal/2,677kJ; Protein 49.6g; Carbohydrate 46.5g, of which sugars 3.3g; Fat 29.5g, of which saturates 4.6g; Cholesterol 506mg; Calcium 83mg; Fibre 3.6g; Sodium 269mg

Spicy Squid Stew ✳✳

This hearty stew is ideal on a cold evening, served with plenty of fresh crusty bread or steamed rice. The potatoes disintegrate to thicken and enrich the sauce, making a warming, comforting main course.

SERVES SIX

1 Clean the squid under cold water. Pull the tentacles away from the body. The squid's entrails will come out easily.

2 Remove the cartilage from inside the body cavity and discard it. Wash the body thoroughly.

3 Pull away the membrane that covers the body. Cut between the tentacles and head, discarding the head and entrails. Leave the tentacles whole but discard the hard beak in the middle. Cut the body into thin rounds.

4 Heat the oil, add the garlic, chillies and celery and cook gently over a low heat for 5 minutes.

5 Stir in the potatoes, then add the wine and stock. Bring to the boil, then simmer, covered, for 25 minutes.

6 Remove from the heat and stir in the squid, tomatoes and parsley. Cover the pan and leave to stand until the squid is cooked. Serve immediately.

600g/1lb 6oz frozen squid, thawed

5 garlic cloves, crushed

4 fresh jalapeño chillies, seeded and finely chopped

2 celery sticks, diced

500g/1¹/₄lb small new potatoes scrubbed, scraped or peeled and quartered

400ml/14fl oz/1²/₃ cups dry white wine

4 tomatoes, diced

30ml/2 tbsp chopped fresh flat leaf parsley

white rice or *arepas* (corn breads), to serve

FROM THE STORECUPBOARD

45ml/3 tbsp olive oil

400ml/14fl oz/1²/₃ cups fish stock

salt

Energy 247kcal/1041kJ; Protein 17.6g; Carbohydrate 17.4g, of which sugars 3.8g; Fat 7.8g, of which saturates 1.3g; Cholesterol 225mg; Calcium 48mg; Fibre 2g; Sodium 136mg

Squid Stuffed with Rice and Ham *

Squid are often just stuffed with their own tentacles but, in this recipe, ham and raisins, which contrast wonderfully with the subtle flavour of the squid, are also included. The stuffed squid are cooked in a richly flavoured tomato sauce and make a perfect main course served with plain boiled rice.

SERVES FOUR

2 frozen squid, about 275g/10oz each, thawed

1 small onion, chopped

2 garlic cloves, chopped

50g/2oz Serrano ham or gammon steak, diced small

30ml/2 tbsp raisins, chopped

30ml/2 tbsp finely chopped fresh parsley

¹/₂ small (US medium) egg, beaten

250ml/8fl oz/1 cup white wine

30ml/2 tbsp chopped fresh parsley, plus extra, to garnish

FOR THE TOMATO SAUCE

1 onion, finely chopped

2 garlic cloves, chopped

FROM THE STORECUPBOARD

90ml/6 tbsp olive oil

200g/7oz can tomatoes

salt and cayenne pepper

75g/3oz/scant ¹/₂ cup long grain rice

plain (all-purpose) flour, for dusting

1 bay leaf

salt, paprika and black pepper, to taste

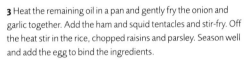
1 Make the tomato sauce. Heat 30ml/2 tbsp oil in a large, flameproof casserole. Add the onion and garlic and cook over a gentle heat. Add the tomatoes and cook for 10 minutes. Season with salt and cayenne pepper.

2 To prepare the squid, use the tentacles to pull out the body. Cut off the tentacles, discarding the eyes and everything below. Pop out the spinal structure. Chop the fin flaps and rinse the bodies.

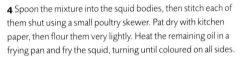
3 Heat the remaining oil in a pan and gently fry the onion and garlic together. Add the ham and squid tentacles and stir-fry. Off the heat stir in the rice, chopped raisins and parsley. Season well and add the egg to bind the ingredients.

4 Spoon the mixture into the squid bodies, then stitch each of them shut using a small poultry skewer. Pat dry with kitchen paper, then flour them very lightly. Heat the remaining oil in a frying pan and fry the squid, turning until coloured on all sides.

5 Arrange the squid in the tomato sauce. Add the wine and bay leaf. Cover and simmer for 30 minutes, turning the squid over if the sauce does not cover them completely. Serve sliced into rings, surrounded by the sauce and garnished with parsley.

Energy 344kcal/1449kJ; Protein 28.9g; Carbohydrate 25.5g, of which sugars 4.2g; Fat 9.6g, of which saturates 1.5g; Cholesterol 298mg; Calcium 104mg; Fibre 1.8g; Sodium 701mg

Crab and Tofu Stir-fry ✳✳

For a year-round light meal, this stir-fry is a delicious choice. Use canned crab meat, as it is much more economical than fresh. Serve with fine egg noodles, if you like, as a special supper for two.

SERVES TWO

1 Drain the silken tofu, if necessary. Using a sharp knife, cut the tofu into 1cm/¹/₂in cubes.

2 Heat the oil in a wok or large, heavy frying pan. Add the tofu cubes and stir-fry until golden. Remove the tofu with a slotted spoon and set aside.

3 Add the garlic to the wok or pan and stir-fry for about 1 minute, or until golden. Add the tofu, crab meat, corn, spring onions, chilli, soy sauce, fish sauce and sugar. Cook, stirring constantly, until the vegetables are just tender.

4 Stir in the lime juice, sprinkle with coriander and serve in dishes with lime wedges, and fine egg noodles, if you like.

200g/7oz silken tofu

2 garlic cloves, finely chopped

115g/4oz canned crab meat

100g/3³/₄oz baby corn, halved lengthways

2 spring onions (scallions), chopped

1 fresh red chilli, seeded and finely chopped

juice of 1 lime

small bunch fresh coriander (cilantro), chopped, to garnish

lime wedges, to serve

FROM THE STORECUPBOARD

60ml/4 tbsp vegetable oil

30ml/2 tbsp soy sauce

15ml/1 tbsp Thai fish sauce

5ml/1 tsp light muscovado (brown) sugar

COOK'S TIPS

• *Store fresh tofu in plenty of water in the refrigerator and use within three days. Change the water daily. Follow the use-by dates on cartoned or vacuum-packed tofu.*

• *Silken tofu is delicate, so handle it with care.*

Energy 357kcal/1478kJ; Protein 21.5g; Carbohydrate 6.6g, of which sugars 5.6g; Fat 27.3g, of which saturates 3.2g; Cholesterol 41mg; Calcium 637mg; Fibre 2g; Sodium 2501mg

225g/8oz cooked white crab meat

juice of ¹/₂ lemon

15ml/1 tbsp chopped fresh herbs, such as parsley, chives and fennel

20ml/4 tsp gin

60ml/4 tbsp grated hard cheese, such as Cheddar

FOR THE BÉCHAMEL SAUCE

1 small onion

300ml/¹/₂ pint/1¹/₄ cups milk

25g/1oz/2 tbsp butter

FROM THE STORECUPBOARD

3 cloves

¹/₂ bay leaf

5ml/1 tsp smooth Dijon mustard

5ml/1 tsp wholegrain Dijon mustard

ground black pepper

25g/1oz/¹/₄ cup plain (all-purpose) flour

Crab Bake ✳

The addition of a splash of dry gin brings an extra dimension to this creamy, cheesy baked crab dish. Serve hot with plain boiled rice or fresh crusty bread and a fresh green side salad.

SERVES TWO

COOK'S TIP *Fresh crab meat gives the best flavour to this dish, but for a more economical option you could use canned crab, drained, instead.*

1 First make an infusion for the béchamel sauce: stud the onion with the cloves, and then put it into a small pan with the milk and bay leaf. Bring slowly to the boil, then allow to infuse (steep) for 15 minutes, and strain.

2 Preheat the oven to 180°C/350°F/Gas 4 and butter two medium gratin dishes. Toss the crab meat in the lemon juice. Divide it between the dishes and add a pinch of herbs to each. Sprinkle each dish with 5ml/1 tsp gin and pepper.

3 Melt the butter for the sauce in a pan, stir in the flour and cook over a low heat for 1–2 minutes. Gradually add the infused milk, stirring constantly to make a smooth sauce. Simmer over a low heat for 1–2 minutes.

4 Blend the béchamel sauce with the two mustards and use to cover the crab. Sprinkle the cheese on top, and bake in the oven for 20–25 minutes, or until bubbling. Serve immediately.

Energy 224kcal/936kJ; Protein 17.4g; Carbohydrate 9.6g, of which sugars 4.5g; Fat 11.9g, of which saturates 7.4g; Cholesterol 73mg; Calcium 282mg; Fibre 0.4g; Sodium 489mg

Perfect Poultry

CHICKEN, TURKEY AND DUCK ARE VERY POPULAR AND INFINITELY VERSATILE. THE SUCCULENT FLESH IS THE PERFECT PARTNER FOR A WIDE RANGE OF DIVERSE INGREDIENTS, AND CAN BE COOKED IN MANY DIFFERENT WAYS. FROM QUICK-AND-EASY STIR-FRIED DUCK WITH NOODLES AND PINEAPPLE OR CHARGRILLED CHICKEN WITH GARLIC AND PEPPERS TO CHICKEN AND LEEK PIES OR TURKEY MEATBALLS WITH A TOMATO SAUCE, THERE IS A RECIPE TO SUIT EVERY BUDGET, TASTE AND OCCASION.

Stir-fried Chicken with Thai Basil ✳✳

Thai basil, sometimes called holy basil, has purple-tinged leaves and a more pronounced, slightly aniseedy flavour than other varieties. It is available in most Asian food stores but if you can't find any, use a handful of ordinary basil instead. Serve this fragrant stir-fry with plain steamed rice or boiled noodles and soy sauce on the side as a quick and easy supper dish.

SERVES SIX

1 Using a sharp knife, slice the chicken breast portions into strips. Halve the peppers, remove the seeds, then cut each piece of pepper into strips.

2 Heat the oil in a wok or large frying pan. Add the chicken and red peppers and stir-fry over a high heat for about 3 minutes, until the chicken is golden and cooked through. Season with salt and ground black pepper to taste.

3 Roughly tear up the basil leaves, add to the chicken and peppers and toss briefly to combine. Serve immediately with rice or noodles.

4 skinless chicken breast fillets

2 red (bell) peppers

1 small bunch of fresh Thai basil

FROM THE STORECUPBOARD

30ml/2 tbsp garlic-infused olive oil

salt and ground black pepper, to taste

Crème Fraîche and Coriander Chicken ✳

Boneless chicken thighs are usually better value for money than chicken breast fillets, and the meat has a stronger taste. There is no need to buy ready-skinned thighs, since it takes seconds to skin them yourself. Be generous with the coriander leaves, as they have a wonderful fragrant flavour, or use chopped parsley instead. Serve with creamy mashed potatoes or steamed rice, and steamed vegetables.

SERVES FOUR

1 Remove the skin from the chicken thighs, then cut each into three or four pieces.

2 Heat the oil in a wok or large frying pan, add the chicken and cook for about 6 minutes, turning occasionally, until cooked through.

3 Add the crème fraîche to the pan and stir until melted, then allow to bubble for 1–2 minutes.

4 Add the chopped coriander to the chicken and stir to combine. Season with salt and ground black pepper to taste, and serve immediately with mashed potatoes or rice, and steamed seasonal green vegetables.

6 boneless chicken thighs

60ml/4 tbsp crème fraîche

1 small bunch of fresh coriander (cilantro), roughly chopped

FROM THE STORECUPBOARD

15ml/1 tbsp sunflower oil

salt and ground black pepper, to taste

Top: Energy 161kcal/675kJ; Protein 24.8g; Carbohydrate 4g, of which sugars 3.8g; Fat 5.1g, of which saturates 0.9g; Cholesterol 70mg; Calcium 26mg; Fibre 1.4g; Sodium 65mg

Above: Energy 222kcal/927kJ; Protein 26.8g; Carbohydrate 0.7g, of which sugars 0.6g; Fat 12.4g, of which saturates 5.4g; Cholesterol 148mg; Calcium 43mg; Fibre 0.6g; Sodium 120mg

Barbecued Chicken ✳

In this simple recipe, chicken pieces are marinated in a strongly-scented marinade made with garlic, lemon juice, cumin, cinnamon and paprika, and then cooked on a barbecue or under a hot grill.

SERVES FOUR

1 In a bowl, combine the garlic, cumin, cinnamon, paprika, lemon juice, oil, and salt and pepper to taste. Add the chicken and turn to coat thoroughly in the marinade.

2 Leave to marinate for at least 1 hour or cover with clear film (plastic wrap) and leave in the refrigerator overnight.

3 Prepare and light the barbecue or preheat a grill (broiler). Place the dark meat on the grill pan and cook for 10 minutes, turning once.

4 Place the remaining chicken on the grill pan and cook for 7–10 minutes, turning occasionally, until golden brown and the juices run clear when pricked with a skewer. Serve immediately, with pitta bread, lemon wedges and salad.

5 garlic cloves, chopped

juice of 1 lemon

1.3kg/3lb chicken, cut into 8 portions

fresh coriander (cilantro) leaves, to garnish

warmed pitta bread, salad and lemon wedges, to serve

FROM THE STORECUPBOARD

30ml/2 tbsp ground cumin

7.5ml/1¹/₂ tsp ground cinnamon

5ml/1 tsp paprika

30ml/2 tbsp olive oil

salt and ground black pepper, to taste

Energy 313kcal/1315kJ; Protein 52.7g; Carbohydrate 0.9g, of which sugars 0g; Fat 11g, of which saturates 2.3g; Cholesterol 219mg; Calcium 20mg; Fibre 0g; Sodium 188mg

Devilled Chicken ✳

Grilling is a very healthy, low-fat way of cooking meat, and these spicy chicken skewers are a good source of protein. Serve them with a crisp leaf salad and pitta bread for a nutritious main meal.

SERVES FOUR

1 In a shallow dish, combine the oil, lemon rind and juice, garlic, dried chillies and seasoning. Add the chicken pieces and turn to coat thoroughly in the marinade. Cover and place in the refrigerator for at least 4 hours, or overnight.

2 When ready to cook, thread the marinated chicken on to eight oiled skewers and cook under a pre-heated grill (broiler) for 6–8 minutes, turning frequently. Garnish with parsley and serve with lemon wedges.

finely grated rind and juice of 1 lemon

2 garlic cloves, finely chopped

10ml/2 tsp crumbled dried red chillies

8 boneless chicken thighs, skinned and each cut into 3 or 4 pieces

flat leaf parsley leaves, to garnish

lemon wedges, to serve

FROM THE STORECUPBOARD

60ml/4 tbsp olive oil

salt and ground black pepper, to taste

Energy 320kcal/1339kJ; Protein 42.1g; Carbohydrate 0.3g, of which sugars 0.2g; Fat 16.7g, of which saturates 3.2g; Cholesterol 210mg; Calcium 34mg; Fibre 0.5g; Sodium 183mg

Chargrilled Chicken with Garlic and Peppers **✳✳**

An imaginative marinade can make all the difference to the sometimes bland flavour of chicken. This garlicky marinade, with mustard and chilli, gives tender chicken a real punch. Make sure the chicken has plenty of time to absorb the flavours before cooking.

SERVES SIX

1½ chickens, total weight about 2.25kg/5lb, jointed, or 12 chicken pieces

2 red or green (bell) peppers, quartered and seeded

5 ripe tomatoes, halved horizontally

lemon wedges, to serve

FOR THE MARINADE

juice of 1 large lemon

4 garlic cloves, crushed

2 fresh red or green chillies, seeded and chopped

FROM THE STORECUPBOARD

90ml/6 tbsp extra virgin olive oil

5ml/1 tsp French mustard

5ml/1 tsp dried oregano

salt and ground black pepper, to taste

1 Beat together the oil, lemon juice, garlic, chilli, mustard, oregano and seasoning in a large bowl. Add the chicken pieces and turn to coat thoroughly in the marinade. Cover with clear film (plastic wrap) and place in the refrigerator for 4–8 hours.

2 Prepare the barbecue or preheat a grill (broiler). When the barbecue or grill is hot, lift the chicken pieces out of the marinade and place them on the grill rack. Add the pepper pieces and the tomatoes to the marinade and set aside for 15 minutes. Grill the chicken pieces for 20–25 minutes.

3 Turn the chicken pieces over and cook for 20–25 minutes more. Meanwhile, thread the peppers on two metal skewers. Add them to the grill rack, with the tomatoes, for the last 15 minutes of cooking. Serve with the lemon wedges.

COOK'S TIP *If you are jointing the chicken yourself, divide the legs into two and make slits in the deepest part of the flesh. This will help the marinade to be absorbed more and let the chicken cook thoroughly.*

Energy 760kcal/3,156kJ; Protein 61.7g; Carbohydrate 11.1g, of which sugars 10.8g; Fat 52.2g, of which saturates 13.3g; Cholesterol 313mg; Calcium 40mg; Fibre 3.1g; Sodium 235mg

Chicken and Preserved Lemon Tagine ✳✳

This fragrant Moroccan dish is perfect for a casual dinner party. Slowly cooked chicken pieces are served in an aromatic sauce, which melds the mellow flavour of the preserved lemons with the earthiness of the olives.

SERVES FOUR

1 onion, chopped

3 garlic cloves, crushed

1cm/¹/₂in fresh root ginger, peeled and grated

pinch of saffron threads

4 chicken quarters, halved if liked

30ml/2 tbsp chopped fresh coriander (cilantro)

30ml/2 tbsp chopped fresh parsley

1 preserved lemon

115g/4oz/²/₃ cup Moroccan tan olives

lemon wedges and fresh coriander (cilantro) sprigs, to garnish

FROM THE STORECUPBOARD

30ml/2 tbsp olive oil

2.5–5ml/¹/₂–1 tsp ground cinnamon

750ml/1¹/₄ pints/3 cups chicken stock

salt and ground black pepper, to taste

1 Heat the oil in a large flameproof casserole and fry the onion for 6–8 minutes over a moderate heat until lightly golden.

2 Meanwhile, blend the garlic with the ginger, cinnamon, saffron and a little salt and pepper. Stir into the pan and fry for 1 minute. Add the chicken in batches and fry over a medium heat for 2–3 minutes, until browned.

3 Add the stock, coriander and parsley, bring to the boil, then cover and simmer for 45 minutes, until the chicken is tender.

4 Rinse the preserved lemon, discard the flesh and cut the peel into small pieces. Stir into the pan with the olives and simmer for a further 15 minutes, until the chicken is very tender.

5 Transfer the chicken to a plate and keep warm. Bring the sauce to the boil and bubble for 3–4 minutes, until reduced and fairly thick. Pour the sauce over the chicken and serve, garnished with lemon wedges and coriander sprigs.

COOK'S TIP The salty juice that is used to preserve the lemons can also be used to flavour salad dressings or added to hot sauces.

Energy 474kcal/1967kJ; Protein 36.3g; Carbohydrate 5.3g, of which sugars 3.8g; Fat 34.3g, of which saturates 8.1g; Cholesterol 209mg; Calcium 83mg; Fibre 2.6g; Sodium 807mg.

Chicken Fricassée ✱✱

Traditionally made with chicken, rabbit or veal, this fricassée dish has a wonderfully rich and flavoursome sauce that is further enhanced with cream and fresh herbs. The meat is first seared in fat, then braised in stock with vegetables until tender. It is a perfect dish for entertaining because you can prepare it in advance and then simply leave it to simmer while you enjoy the company of your guests.

SERVES FOUR

1 Preheat the oven to 180°C/350°F/Gas 4. Put the onions or shallots in a bowl, add just enough boiling water to cover them, and leave to soak.

2 Meanwhile, rinse the chicken pieces well in cold water, and pat dry with kitchen paper.

3 Melt half the butter with the oil in a large frying pan. Add the chicken pieces and cook on a high heat, turning occasionally, until lightly browned all over. Using a slotted spoon or tongs, transfer the chicken pieces to a large casserole, leaving the juices behind.

4 Stir the flour into the pan juices, then blend in the wine. Stir in the stock and add the bouquet garni and the lemon juice.

5 Bring the mixture to the boil, stirring all the time, until the sauce has thickened. Season well and pour over the chicken. Cover the pot with the lid and put in the oven. Cook for 1 hour.

6 Drain and peel the onions or shallots. (Soaking them in boiling water loosens the skins, making them easy to peel.) Trim the stalks from the mushrooms.

7 Clean the frying pan, then add the remaining butter and heat gently until melted. Add the mushrooms and onions or shallots and cook for 5 minutes, turning frequently until they are lightly browned. Tip into the casserole with the chicken.

8 Cook for a further hour, until the chicken is cooked and tender. (To test that the chicken is cooked through, pierce the thickest part of one of the portions with a skewer or thin knife; the juices should run clear.)

9 Using a slotted spoon, remove the chicken and vegetables to a warmed serving dish. Add the cream and 30ml/2 tbsp of the parsley to the sauce and whisk to combine. Check the seasoning and adjust if necessary, then pour the sauce over the chicken and vegetables.

10 Sprinkle the fricassée with the remaining parsley and serve with mashed potatoes and seasonal vegetables.

20 small even-size button (pearl) onions or shallots

1.2–1.3kg/2¹/₂–3lb chicken, cut into pieces

25g/1oz/2 tbsp butter

250ml/8fl oz/1 cup dry white wine

600ml/1 pint/2¹/₂ cups boiling chicken stock

1 bouquet garni

5ml/1 tsp lemon juice

225g/8oz/3 cups button (white) mushrooms

75ml/2¹/₂fl oz/¹/₃ cup double (heavy) cream

45ml/3 tbsp chopped fresh parsley

mashed potatoes and steamed seasonal vegetables, to serve

FROM THE STORECUPBOARD

30ml/2 tbsp sunflower oil

45ml/3 tbsp plain (all-purpose) flour

salt and ground black pepper, to taste

COOK'S TIP

A bouquet garni is made up of parsley stalks, a sprig of thyme and a bay leaf. Tie together with a piece of string, or enclose in muslin (cheesecloth).

Energy 613kcal/2563kJ; Protein 53.1g; Carbohydrate 36.4g, of which sugars 17.9g; Fat 25g, of which saturates 11.1g; Cholesterol 196mg; Calcium 128mg; Fibre 5.3g; Sodium 396mg

Baked Mediterranean Chicken ✳✳

This colourful and versatile chicken dish can have an infinite number of variations. Cubed ham can replace the bacon, but the fat the latter gives off adds flavour and character.

SERVES FOUR

1 Rub paprika and salt into the chicken portions. Heat 30ml/ 2 tbsp oil in a large frying pan. Put in the chicken portions, skin side down, and fry gently.

2 Heat 15ml/1 tbsp oil in a flameproof casserole and add the bacon or pancetta.

3 When the bacon or pancetta starts to give off fat, add the chopped onion and garlic, frying very gently until soft.

4 Remove and discard the stalks and seeds from the peppers and roughly chop the flesh. Spoon off a little fat from the chicken pan, then add the peppers, fitting them into the spaces between the chicken portions, and cook gently.

5 When the onions are soft, stir in the tomatoes and season to taste with salt and pepper. Arrange the chicken pieces in the sauce, and stir in the cooked peppers.

6 Cover the casserole tightly and simmer over a low heat for 15 minutes. Check the seasoning, stir in the chopped parsley and serve with rice, if you like.

4 chicken portions

150g/5oz smoked bacon lardons, or diced pancetta

1 large onion, chopped

2 garlic cloves, finely chopped

1 green (bell) pepper

1 red (bell) pepper

450g/1lb tomatoes or 400g/14oz canned tomatoes

30ml/2 tbsp chopped fresh parsley

FROM THE STORECUPBOARD

5ml/1 tsp paprika

45ml/3 tbsp olive oil

salt and ground black pepper, to taste

boiled rice, to serve (optional)

Energy 462kcal/1947kJ; Protein 46.9g; Carbohydrate 41.3g, of which sugars 24.5g; Fat 13.4g, of which saturates 4.5g; Cholesterol 118mg; Calcium 156mg; Fibre 9.2g; Sodium 133mg

Spiced Coconut Chicken ✳✳

You need to plan ahead in order to make this luxurious chicken curry. The chicken legs are marinated in yogurt and spices before being simmered with chillies in coconut milk. Serve with rice or Indian breads.

SERVES FOUR

1.6kg/3¹/₂lb large chicken drumsticks

400ml/14fl oz/1²/₃ cups coconut milk

4–6 large green chillies, halved

45ml/3 tbsp finely chopped coriander (cilantro)

natural (plain) yogurt, to drizzle

FOR THE MARINADE

15ml/1 tbsp grated fresh root ginger

10ml/2 tsp finely grated garlic

105ml/7 tbsp natural (plain) yogurt

2 green chillies, seeded and chopped

finely grated zest and juice of 1 lime

FROM THE STORECUPBOARD

15ml/1 tbsp crushed cardamom pods

5ml/1 tsp ground cumin

5ml/1 tsp ground coriander

5ml/1 tsp turmeric

salt and ground black pepper, to taste

30ml/2 tbsp sunflower oil

1 Make the marinade. Place the cardamom, ginger, garlic, half the yogurt, green chillies, cumin, coriander, turmeric and lime zest and juice in a blender. Process until smooth, season and pour into a large glass bowl.

2 Add the chicken to the marinade and toss to coat evenly. Cover the bowl and marinate in the refrigerator for 6–8 hours, or overnight if time permits.

3 Heat the oil in a large, non-stick pan over a low heat. Remove the chicken from the marinade, reserving the marinade. Add the chicken to the pan and brown all over, then add the coconut milk, remaining yogurt, reserved marinade and green chillies and bring to a boil.

4 Reduce the heat and simmer, uncovered for 30–35 minutes. Check and adjust the seasoning, if needed. Stir in the coriander, ladle into warmed bowls and serve immediately. Drizzle with yogurt if liked.

Energy 706kcal/2935kJ; Protein 48.1g; Carbohydrate 15.8g, of which sugars 15.6g; Fat 50.4g, of which saturates 12.8g; Cholesterol 240mg; Calcium 91mg; Fibre 1.5g; Sodium 305mg

1 chicken, about
2.25kg/5lb

1 parsley sprig

300g/11oz baby
carrots

175g/6oz baby leeks

25g/1oz/2 tbsp butter

300g/11oz shallots,
halved if large

200ml/7fl oz/scant 1 cup
dry white wine

800g/1³/₄lb baby
new potatoes

120ml/4fl oz/¹/₂ cup
double (heavy) cream

small bunch parsley or
tarragon, chopped,
to garnish

FROM THE STORECUPBOARD

15ml/1 tbsp black
peppercorns

1 bay leaf

15ml/1 tbsp olive oil

salt and ground black
pepper, to taste

Chicken Pot-au-feu ✳✳✳

This rustic recipe combines a lovely white wine and herb-scented stock with tender morsels of chicken and spring vegetables. It is cooked slowly, which allows the flavours to mingle and tenderizes the meat.

SERVES FOUR

1 Joint the chicken into eight pieces and place the carcass in a large stockpot. Add the parsley sprig, peppercorns, bay leaf and the trimmings from the carrots and leeks. Cover with cold water and bring to the boil. Simmer for 45 minutes, then strain.

2 Meanwhile, melt the butter with the olive oil in a frying pan, then add the chicken pieces, season, and brown all over. Lift out the chicken pieces on to a plate and add the shallots to the pan. Cook over a low heat for 20 minutes, stirring occasionally, until softened, but not browned.

3 Return the chicken to the pan and add the wine. Scrape up any juices from the bottom of the pan, then add the carrots, leeks and potatoes with enough of the stock to cover. Bring to the boil, then cover and simmer for 20 minutes. Stir in the cream.

4 Serve immediately on warmed serving plates, garnished with fresh herbs, with plain boiled rice or mashed potatoes, if you like.

COOK'S TIPS

• Any left-over stock can be kept in the refrigerator and used in other recipes. Alternatively, pour into an ice cube tray and freeze. Then, when you need some stock, simply pop out the cubes.

• You could use large potatoes when new ones are not in season. They will need to be cut into small chunks or par-boiled first so that they will cook in the same amount of time as the other vegetables in the pot.

Energy 309kcal/1304kJ; Protein 33.2g; Carbohydrate 30.7g, of which sugars 9.2g; Fat 6.7g, of which saturates 1.7g; Cholesterol 98mg; Calcium 79mg; Fibre 7.7g; Sodium 143mg

Ethiopian Chicken ✳✳

This long-simmered Ethiopian stew contains hard-boiled eggs, which soak up the flavour of the aromatic spices. Nourishing and warming, it makes an unusual family meal, perfect for the dark winter months. Serve with boiled rice or flatbreads, and thinly sliced red onion rings.

SERVES FOUR

2 large onions, chopped

3 garlic cloves, chopped

2.5cm/1in piece peeled and finely chopped fresh root ginger

1.3kg/3lb chicken, cut into 8–12 portions

4 hard-boiled eggs

cayenne pepper or hot paprika, to taste

roughly chopped fresh coriander (cilantro) and onion rings, to garnish

flatbread or rice, to serve

FROM THE STORECUPBOARD

30ml/2 tbsp vegetable oil

175ml/6fl oz/³/₄ cup chicken or vegetable stock

250ml/8fl oz/1 cup passata (bottled strained tomatoes) or 400g/14oz can chopped tomatoes

seeds from 5 cardamom pods

2.5ml/¹/₂ tsp ground turmeric

large pinch of ground cinnamon

large pinch of ground cloves

large pinch of grated nutmeg

salt and ground black pepper, to taste

1 Preheat the oven to 180°C/350°F/Gas 4. Heat the oil in a large, heavy pan, add the onions and cook for 10 minutes until softened. Add the garlic and ginger and cook for 1–2 minutes.

2 Add the stock and the passata or chopped tomatoes to the pan. Bring to the boil and cook, stirring frequently, for about 10 minutes, until it has thickened, then season to taste.

3 Transfer the mixture to a ceramic cooking pot and stir in the cardamom pods, turmeric, cinnamon, cloves and nutmeg.

4 Add the chicken in a single layer, pushing the pieces down into the sauce so they are completely coated. Cover the dish with the lid, place in the oven and cook for 1 hour.

5 Remove the shells from the eggs, then prick them a few times with a fork or very fine skewer. Add to the sauce and cook for 30–45 minutes, or until the chicken is cooked through and tender. Season to taste with cayenne pepper or paprika.

6 Garnish with coriander and onion rings and serve with flatbread or rice.

Energy 388kcal/1629kJ; Protein 54.6g; Carbohydrate 13g, of which sugars 9.6g; Fat 13.4g, of which saturates 2.8g; Cholesterol 13mg; Calcium 81mg; Fibre 2.5g; Sodium 311mg

Chicken Casserole ✳✳

This is a very simple and economical dish to prepare and cook, and with its strong Mediterranean undertones it is also packed with colour and flavour. It is delicious served with French fries or plain boiled rice, but it goes equally well with steamed new potatoes.

SERVES FOUR

1 Preheat the oven to 180°C/350°F/Gas 4. Heat the olive oil in a wide flameproof casserole and brown the chicken pieces on both sides. Lift them out and set them aside.

2 Add the shallots, carrots and celery to the oil remaining in the casserole and sauté them for a few minutes. Stir in the garlic. As soon as it becomes aromatic, return the chicken to the pan and pour the lemon juice over the mixture. Let it bubble for a few minutes, then add the water and season with salt and pepper.

3 Cover the casserole and bake for 1 hour, turning the chicken pieces over occasionally.

4 Remove the casserole from the oven and stir in the parsley and olives. Re-cover the casserole and return it to the oven for about 30 minutes more. Check that it is cooked by piercing with a sharp knife. The juices should run clear. Serve immediately.

**1 chicken, about
1.6kg/3¹/₂lb, jointed**

**3 or 4 shallots,
finely chopped**

2 carrots, sliced

**1 celery stick,
roughly chopped**

2 garlic cloves, chopped

juice of 1 lemon

**300ml/¹/₂ pint/1¹/₄ cups
hot water**

**30ml/2 tbsp chopped
flat leaf parsley**

12 black or green olives

FROM THE STORECUPBOARD

**75ml/5 tbsp extra virgin
olive oil**

**salt and ground black
pepper, to taste**

Energy 726kcal/3,008kJ; Protein 54.9g; Carbohydrate 3.8g, of which sugars 3.5g; Fat 54.5g, of which saturates 13.1g; Cholesterol 289mg; Calcium 55mg; Fibre 1.9g; Sodium 435mg

Spicy Chicken Casserole ✳✳

This spicy take on classic chicken casserole combines a rich red wine sauce with warming cinnamon and allspice, to create an aromatic dish that will be a treat for all the senses. Serve with orzo, plain boiled rice, or thick-cut fried potatoes for a satisfying supper.

SERVES FOUR

1 Heat the oil in a large pan and brown the chicken pieces on all sides, ensuring that the skin is cooked and lifts away from the flesh slightly. Lift the chicken pieces out, set them aside on a plate, and keep them warm.

2 Add the chopped onion to the hot oil in the same pan and stir it over a medium heat until it becomes translucent.

3 Return the chicken pieces to the pan, pour over the wine and cook for 2–3 minutes, until it has reduced. Add the tomato purée mixture, cinnamon, allspice and bay leaves. Season well with salt and pepper.

4 Cover the pan and cook gently for 1 hour or until the chicken is tender. Serve with rice, orzo or fried potatoes.

1.6kg/3¹/₂lb chicken, jointed

1 large onion, peeled and roughly chopped

250ml/8fl oz/1 cup red wine

boiled rice, orzo or fried potatoes, to serve

FROM THE STORECUPBOARD

75ml/5 tbsp extra virgin olive oil

30ml/2 tbsp tomato purée (paste) diluted in 450ml/³/₄ pint/ scant 2 cups hot water

1 cinnamon stick

3 or 4 whole allspice

2 bay leaves

salt and ground black pepper, to taste

Energy 767kcal/3,195kJ; Protein 53.3g; Carbohydrate 32.5g, of which sugars 2.9g; Fat 47.7g, of which saturates 11.8g; Cholesterol 264mg; Calcium 51mg; Fibre 2.6g; Sodium 206mg

Curried Chicken and Rice ✳

This simple one-pot meal is perfect for casual entertaining. It can be made using virtually any meat or vegetables that you have to hand.

SERVES FOUR

1 Heat the oil in a wok or flameproof casserole, which has a lid. Add the garlic and cook over a low to medium heat until golden brown. Add the chicken in batches, increase the heat and brown the pieces on all sides.

2 Add the garam masala to the wok or casserole, stir well to coat the chicken all over in the spice, then tip in the drained rice. Add the salt and stir to mix.

3 Pour in the stock, stir well, then cover the wok or casserole and bring to the boil. Reduce the heat to low and simmer gently for 10 minutes, until the rice is cooked and tender.

4 Lift off the heat, leaving the lid on, and leave to stand for about 10 minutes. Fluff up the rice with a fork and transfer to a platter. Sprinkle with the coriander and serve immediately.

4 garlic cloves, finely chopped

1 chicken (about 1.5kg/ 3–3 1/2 lb) or chicken pieces, skin and bones removed and meat cut into bitesize pieces

small bunch fresh coriander (cilantro), chopped, to garnish

FROM THE STORECUPBOARD

60ml/4 tbsp vegetable oil

5ml/1 tsp garam masala

450g/1lb/2 2/3 cups jasmine rice, rinsed and drained

10ml/2 tsp salt

1 litre/1 3/4 pints/4 cups chicken stock

Energy 719kcal/3012kJ; Protein 56.7g; Carbohydrate 90.1g, of which sugars 0.3g; Fat 13.9g, of which saturates 1.9g; Cholesterol 140mg; Calcium 57mg; Fibre 0.6g; Sodium 1107mg

225g/8oz skinless, boneless chicken breast portions

175g/6oz piece raw smoked gammon or bacon

1 large onion, peeled and chopped

2 garlic cloves, crushed

2 sticks celery, diced

5ml/1 tsp chopped fresh thyme or 2.5ml/¹/₂ tsp dried thyme

115g/4oz chorizo sausage (cooked), sliced

30ml/2 tbsp chopped fresh flat leaf parsley, plus extra, to garnish

FROM THE STORECUPBOARD

salt and ground black pepper, to taste

30ml/2 tbsp olive oil

5ml/1 tsp mild chilli powder

2.5ml/¹/₂ tsp ground ginger

10ml/2 tsp tomato purée (paste)

2 dashes of Tabasco sauce

750ml/1¹/₄ pints/3 cups boiling chicken stock

300g/11oz/1¹/₂ cups easy-cook (converted) rice

Spicy Chicken Jambalaya ✳

This classic Creole dish is great for a family supper, served with a simple salad. Spicy red Spanish chorizo sausage gives the stew a real boost.

SERVES SIX

1 Preheat the oven to 180°C/350°F/Gas 4. Cut the chicken into 2.5cm/1in cubes and season. Trim any fat off the gammon or bacon, then cut the meat into 1cm/¹/₂in cubes.

2 Heat 15ml/1 tbsp of the olive oil in a pan, add the onion and fry gently for about 5 minutes, until beginning to colour. Stir in the garlic, celery, thyme, chilli powder and ginger and cook for about 1 minute. Transfer the mixture to a large ovenproof dish.

3 Heat the remaining 15ml/1 tbsp olive oil in the pan, add the chicken pieces and fry until lightly browned. Add the chicken to the ovenproof dish with the gammon or bacon cubes.

4 Add the tomato purée and Tabasco sauce to the stock and whisk together. Pour into the dish, cover with the lid and cook in the oven for 45 minutes.

5 Add the rice to the dish. Cover and cook for 20–30 minutes, or until the rice is almost tender and most of the stock has been absorbed. Stir in the chorizo and cook for a further 15 minutes, or until heated through. Stir in the chopped parsley, then taste and adjust the seasoning.

6 Remove from the oven and leave to stand for 10 minutes. Stir with a fork to fluff up the rice, then serve garnished with parsley.

Energy 384kcal/1617kJ; Protein 21.2g; Carbohydrate 48.6g, of which sugars 2.9g; Fat 13g, of which saturates 3.6g; Cholesterol 43mg; Calcium 57mg; Fibre 1.1g; Sodium 630mg

Chicken, Split Pea and Aubergine Koresh ✳✳

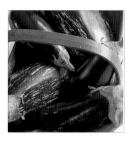

Koresh is traditionally a hearty meat dish, but here it has been transformed to a lighter chicken and vegetable stew.

SERVES FOUR

1 Put the split peas in a bowl, pour over cold water to cover, then leave to soak for about 4 hours. Drain well.

2 Heat a little of the oil in a pan, add two-thirds of the onions and cook for about 5 minutes. Add the chicken and cook until golden brown on all sides.

3 Add the soaked split peas to the chicken mixture, then the stock, turmeric, cinnamon and nutmeg. Cook over a medium-low heat for about 40 minutes, until the split peas are tender.

4 Heat the remaining oil in a pan, add the aubergines and remaining onions and cook until lightly browned. Add the tomatoes, garlic and mint. Season.

5 Just before serving, stir the aubergine mixture into the chicken and split pea stew. Garnish with fresh mint leaves and serve with boiled rice.

1 large or 2 small onions, finely chopped

500g/1¼lb boneless chicken thighs

2 aubergines (eggplants), roughly diced

8–10 ripe tomatoes, diced

2 garlic cloves, crushed

fresh mint, to garnish

FROM THE STORECUPBOARD

50g/2oz/¼ cup green split peas

45–60ml/3–4 tbsp olive oil

500ml/17fl oz/2¼ cups chicken stock

5ml/1 tsp ground turmeric

2.5ml/½ tsp ground cinnamon

1.5ml/¼ tsp grated nutmeg

30ml/2 tbsp dried mint

salt and ground black pepper, to taste

boiled rice, to serve

VARIATION To make a traditional lamb koresh, use 675g/1½lb stewing lamb in place of chicken. Add to the onions, pour over water to cover and cook for 1½ hours, then proceed as above.

Energy 324kcal/1359kJ; Protein 32.4g; Carbohydrate 20.4g, of which sugars 12.6g; Fat 13.1g, of which saturates 2.5g; Cholesterol 131mg; Calcium 61mg; Fibre 6.2g; Sodium 136mg

3 onions, sliced

4 boneless chicken thighs

3 garlic cloves, chopped

5ml/1 tsp chopped fresh
root ginger

juice of 1 lemon

4 tomatoes, sliced

30ml/2 tbsp chopped
fresh coriander (cilantro)

150ml/^{1}/$_4$ pint/^{2}/$_3$ cup
natural (plain) yogurt,
plus extra to serve

4–5 saffron threads,
soaked in 10ml/2 tsp
hot milk

150ml/^{1}/$_4$ pint/^{2}/$_3$ cup
cold water

toasted flaked (sliced)
almonds and fresh
coriander (cilantro)
sprigs, to garnish

FROM THE STORECUPBOARD

10 whole green
cardamom pods

275g/10oz/1^1/$_2$ cups
basmati rice, soaked
and drained

2.5ml/^{1}/$_2$ tsp salt

2–3 whole cloves

5cm/2in cinnamon stick

45ml/3 tbsp vegetable oil

1.5ml/^{1}/$_4$ tsp
ground cloves

1.5ml/^{1}/$_4$ tsp hot
chilli powder

5ml/1 tsp ground cumin

5ml/1 tsp ground
coriander

2.5ml/^{1}/$_2$ tsp ground
black pepper

Chicken Biryani with Saffron Milk and Coriander ✳✳

Easy to make and very tasty, this delicious, fairly mild curry is bursting with flavours and is ideal for a family supper or relaxed dinner party.

SERVES FOUR

1 Preheat the oven to 190°C/375°F/ Gas 5. Remove the seeds from half the cardamom pods and grind them finely, using a mortar and pestle. Set them aside. Bring a pan of water to the boil and add the rice, salt, whole cardamom pods, cloves and cinnamon stick. Boil for 2 minutes, then drain, leaving the whole spices in the rice.

2 Heat the oil in a frying pan and cook the onions for 8 minutes, until softened and browned. Add the chicken and the ground spices, including the ground cardamom seeds. Mix well, then add the garlic, ginger and lemon juice. Stir-fry for 5 minutes.

3 Transfer the chicken mixture to a casserole and arrange the tomatoes on top. Sprinkle on the chopped fresh coriander, spoon the yogurt evenly on top and cover with the drained rice.

4 Drizzle the saffron milk over the rice and pour over the water. Cover tightly and bake for 1 hour.

5 Transfer to a warmed serving platter and remove the whole spices from the rice. Garnish with toasted almonds and fresh coriander sprigs and serve with extra yogurt.

Energy 536kcal/2243kJ; Protein 31.3g; Carbohydrate 74.2g, of which sugars 14.6g; Fat 13g, of which saturates 2.1g; Cholesterol 105mg; Calcium 163mg; Fibre 3.6g; Sodium 139mg

1 onion, chopped

120ml/4fl oz/¹/₂ cup
white wine

4 large chicken breasts

300ml/¹/₂ pint/1¹/₄ cups
double (heavy) cream

15ml/1 tbsp chopped
fresh tarragon

FOR THE DUMPLINGS

225g/8oz main crop
potatoes, boiled
and mashed

175g/6oz/1¹/₄ cups suet

30ml/2 tbsp chopped
mixed fresh herbs

50ml/2fl oz/¹/₄ cup water

FROM THE STORECUPBOARD

300ml/¹/₂ pint/1¹/₄ cups
vegetable stock

salt and ground black
pepper, to taste

115g/4oz/1 cup self-
raising (self-rising) flour

Creamy Chicken Stew with Potato Dumplings ✳✳

Poached chicken breast in a creamy sauce topped with light herb and potato dumplings makes a delicate yet hearty and warming meal.

SERVES SIX

1 Place the onion, stock and wine in a deep-sided frying pan. Add the chicken and simmer for 20 minutes, covered. Remove the chicken, cut into chunks and reserve the stock.

2 Strain the stock and discard the onion. Reduce the stock by about one-third. Remove from the heat, then stir in the cream and tarragon and reheat gently, stirring, until just thickened. Stir in the chicken and season to taste.

3 Preheat the oven to 190°C/375°F/Gas 5. Spoon the mixture into a 900ml/1¹/₂ pint/3³/₄ cup ovenproof dish.

4 Mix together the potatoes, flour, suet and herbs and stir in the water. Knead to make a soft dough. Divide into six and shape into balls with floured hands. Place on top of the chicken mixture and bake uncovered for 30 minutes. Serve immediately.

COOK'S TIP
Make sure that you do not reduce the sauce too much before it is cooked in the oven as the dumplings absorb quite a lot of the liquid.

Energy 552kcal/2299kJ; Protein 28.2g; Carbohydrate 26.5g, of which sugars 2.6g; Fat 37.4g, of which saturates 21g; Cholesterol 121mg; Calcium 83mg; Fibre 1.3g; Sodium 80mg

Chicken and Mushroom
Potato Bake ✳✳

A delicious and moist combination of chicken, vegetables and gravy in a simple, one-dish meal topped with crunchy slices of potato.

SERVES FOUR–SIX

1 Preheat the oven to 180°C/350°F/Gas 4. Heat the oil in a large saucepan. Fry the chicken for 5 minutes until browned. Add the leek and fry for a further 5 minutes.

2 Add half the butter to the pan and allow it to melt. Sprinkle the flour over and stir in the milk. Cook over a low heat until thickened, then stir in the mustard. Add the carrot with the mushrooms. Season to taste with salt and black pepper.

3 Lay enough potato slices to line the base of a 1.75 litre/3 pint/ 7¹⁄₂ cup ovenproof dish. Spoon one-third of the chicken mixture over. Cover with another layer of potatoes. Repeat layering, finishing with a layer of potatoes. Top with the remaining butter in knobs.

4 Bake for 1¹⁄₂ hours in the oven, covering the dish with foil after 30 minutes. Serve immediately.

4 large chicken breasts, cut into chunks

1 leek, finely sliced into rings

50g/2oz/¹⁄₄ cup butter

475ml/16fl oz/2 cups milk

1 carrot, very finely diced

225g/8oz/3 cups button (white) mushrooms, finely sliced

900g/2lb potatoes, finely sliced

FROM THE STORECUPBOARD

15ml/1 tbsp olive oil

25g/1oz/¹⁄₄ cup plain (all-purpose) flour

5ml/1 tsp wholegrain mustard

salt and ground black pepper, to taste

Energy 358kcal/1510kJ; Protein 31g; Carbohydrate 33.6g, of which sugars 7.8g; Fat 12.1g, of which saturates 6g; Cholesterol 92mg; Calcium 130mg; Fibre 3.1g; Sodium 192mg

Chicken and Mushroom Pie ✳

Versatile and delicous, chicken pie is a classic family favourite that will be enjoyed time after time. It is an ideal way to use up left-over roast chicken, but if you don't have any then use chicken wings and thighs, which have a good flavour and tend to be much better value than chicken breast portions.

SERVES SIX

1 To make the pastry, sift 225g/8oz/2 cups of the flour and the salt into a bowl. Rub in the butter and white vegetable fat until the mixture resembles breadcrumbs. Sprinkle with 90ml/6 tbsp chilled water and mix until the dough holds together. If it is too crumbly, add a little more water, 15ml/1 tbsp at a time.

2 Gather the dough into a ball and flatten it into a round. Wrap in clear film (plastic wrap) so that it is airtight and chill in the refrigerator for at least 30 minutes.

3 Preheat the oven to 190°C/375°F/Gas 5. To make the filling, melt half the butter in a heavy pan over a low heat. Whisk in the remaining flour and cook until bubbling, whisking constantly. Add the stock and whisk over a medium heat until the mixture boils. Cook for 2–3 minutes, then whisk in the cream. Season to taste with salt and ground black pepper, and set aside.

4 Heat the remaining butter in a frying pan, add the onion and carrots and cook over a low heat for about 5 minutes. Add the celery and mushrooms and cook for a further 5 minutes, until they have softened. Add the cooked chicken and peas and stir.

5 Add the chicken mixture to the hot cream sauce and stir to mix. Taste and adjust the seasoning if necessary. Spoon the mixture into a 2.5 litre/4 pint/2½ quart oval baking dish.

6 Roll out the pastry on a floured surface to a thickness of about 3mm/⅛in. Cut out an oval 2.5cm/1in larger all around than the dish. Lay the pastry over the filling. Gently press around the edge of the dish to seal, then trim off the excess pastry. Crimp the edge of the pastry by pushing the forefinger of one hand into the edge and, using the thumb and forefinger of the other hand, pinch the pastry. Continue all round the pastry edge.

7 Press together the pastry trimmings and roll out again. Cut out mushroom shapes with a sharp knife and stick them on to the pastry lid with a little of the beaten egg. Glaze the entire lid with beaten egg, then cut several slits in the pastry to allow the steam to escape.

8 Bake the pie in the preheated oven for about 30 minutes, until the pastry has browned. Serve hot.

50g/2oz/¼ cup butter

60ml/4 tbsp single (light) cream

1 onion, coarsely chopped

2 carrots, sliced

2 celery sticks, coarsely chopped

50g/2oz fresh (preferably wild) mushrooms, quartered

450g/1lb cooked chicken meat, cubed

50g/2oz/½ cup fresh or frozen peas

beaten egg, to glaze

FOR THE PASTRY

115g/4oz/½ cup cold butter, diced

65g/2½oz/⅓ cup white vegetable fat (shortening), diced

90–120ml/6–8 tbsp chilled water

FROM THE STORECUPBOARD

250g/9oz/2¼ cups plain (all-purpose) flour

1.5ml/¼ tsp salt

250ml/8fl oz/1 cup hot chicken stock

salt and ground black pepper, to taste

Energy 600kcal/2501kJ; Protein 23.7g; Carbohydrate 38.8g, of which sugars 3.7g; Fat 40g, of which saturates 21.8g; Cholesterol 132mg; Calcium 92mg; Fibre 2.7g; Sodium 226mg

Chicken and Leek Pies ✳

Make these individual chicken and leek pies in small tart tins or in a four-hole Yorkshire pudding tin. Alternatively, as in the main picture, make one large pie using a 20cm/8in tart tin or pie plate. Comforting and sustaining, they are excellent served hot, warm or cold and are ideal for picnics.

SERVES FOUR

1 To make the pastry, sift the flour and the salt into a bowl. Rub in the butter and fat until the mixture resembles breadcrumbs. Sprinkle with 90ml/6 tbsp chilled water and mix until the dough holds together. If it is too crumbly, add a little more water.

2 Gather the dough into a ball and flatten it into a round. Wrap in clear film (plastic wrap) and chill in the refrigerator for 30 minutes.

3 Preheat the oven to 200°C/400°F/Gas 6. Roll out the pastry on a lightly floured surface to a thickness of about 3mm/$\frac{1}{8}$in. Cut out four circles, each large enough to line an individual tart tin (pan) and line the four pans. Cut the remaining pastry into four slightly smaller circles ready to make lids for the pies.

4 Melt the butter in a small pan, add the leek and cook gently for about 5 minutes, stirring occasionally, until soft but not brown.

5 Beat the eggs in a bowl and stir in the chicken, herbs and seasoning. Add the leek and its juices, mix and spoon into the pastry cases. Brush the edges of the pastry with egg and place the lids on top, pressing the edges together to seal them. Brush the tops with egg and make a small slit in the centre of each.

6 Put into the hot oven and cook for about 30 minutes, until golden brown and cooked through.

15g/$\frac{1}{2}$oz/1 tbsp butter

1 leek, thinly sliced

2 eggs

225g/8oz skinless chicken breast fillets, finely chopped

small handful of fresh parsley or mint, finely chopped

beaten egg, to glaze

FOR THE PASTRY

115g/4oz/$\frac{1}{2}$ cup cold butter, diced

65g/2$\frac{1}{2}$oz/$\frac{1}{3}$ cup white vegetable fat (shortening), diced

90–120ml/6–8 tbsp chilled water

FROM THE STORECUPBOARD

225g/8oz/2 cups plain (all-purpose) flour

1.5ml/$\frac{1}{4}$ tsp salt

salt and ground black pepper, to taste

Energy 588kcal/2459kJ; Protein 23.4g; Carbohydrate 48.4g, of which sugars 2.1g; Fat 34.9g, of which saturates 11.7g; Cholesterol 157mg; Calcium 133mg; Fibre 3.4g; Sodium 496mg

Bacon, Chicken and Leek Pudding ✳✳

Old-fashioned suet puddings are still a family favourite, and this one, made with chunks of chicken, leek and bacon is bursting with flavour. The pastry is quite thin, but to make it thicker, simply increase the flour to 225g/8oz/2 cups and the suet to 100g/3^{1}/$_{2}$oz/^{2}/$_{3}$ cup. Serve it with seasonal vegetables.

SERVES FOUR

200g/7oz unsmoked lean, rindless bacon

400g/14oz skinless boneless chicken, preferably thigh meat

2 small or medium leeks, finely chopped

30ml/2 tbsp finely chopped fresh parsley

butter for greasing

FOR THE PASTRY

75g/3oz/^{1}/$_{2}$ cup shredded suet

FROM THE STORECUPBOARD

175g/6oz/1^{1}/$_{2}$ cups self-raising (self-rising) flour

120ml/4fl oz/1^{1}/$_{2}$ cups chicken or vegetable stock

ground black pepper

COOK'S TIP Check the water level in the pan during the cooking time to ensure it does not get too low. Top up with boiling water as and when necessary.

1 Cut the bacon and chicken into bitesize pieces into a bowl. Mix with the leeks and half the parsley. Season with black pepper.

2 Sift the flour into another large bowl and stir in the suet and the remaining parsley. Stir in sufficient cold water to make a soft dough. On a lightly floured surface, roll out the dough to a circle measuring about 33cm/13in across. Cut out one quarter of the circle (starting from the centre), roll up and reserve.

3 Butter a 1.2 litre/2 pint/5 cup pudding bowl. Use the dough to line the bowl, pressing the cut edges together to seal them and allowing the pastry to overlap the top of the bowl slightly.

4 Spoon the bacon and chicken mixture into the lined bowl. Pour the chicken or vegetable stock over the bacon mixture making sure it does not overfill the bowl.

5 Roll out the reserved pastry into a circle and lay it over the filling, pinching the edges together to seal them well. Cover with baking parchment (pleated in the centre to allow the pudding to rise) and then a large sheet of foil (again pleated at the centre). Tuck the edges under until well sealed.

6 Steam over boiling water for 3^{1}/$_{2}$ hours. Uncover the pudding, slide a knife around the sides and turn out on to a warmed plate.

Energy 535kcal/2236kJ; Protein 28.2g; Carbohydrate 39.4g, of which sugars 2.9g; Fat 31.3g, of which saturates 14.8g; Cholesterol 86mg; Calcium 111mg; Fibre 4g; Sodium 999mg

Traditional Roast Chicken with Herb Stuffing ✳

Nothing beats a tender roast chicken for Sunday lunch. Traditional accompaniments include roast potatoes, sausages, bacon rolls, bread sauce and a fruit sauce or jelly, such as cranberry sauce or elderberry jelly.

SERVES SIX

1 Remove the giblets from the chicken. Wipe out the inside of the bird thoroughly. Separate the liver from the rest of the giblets and set it aside to use in the gravy.

2 Put the remaining giblets and the neck into a pan with the onion, carrot, parsley, thyme and some salt and pepper. Add cold water to cover, bring to the boil and simmer for 1 hour. Strain the stock and discard the giblets. Preheat the oven to 200°C/400°F/Gas 6.

3 Meanwhile, make the herb stuffing: cook the chopped onion in the butter in a large pan over a low heat for a few minutes. Remove from the heat, and add the breadcrumbs, herbs and lemon rind. Mix thoroughly. Mix in the lemon juice, beaten egg and a generous amount of salt and pepper.

4 Spoon the stuffing into the neck cavity of the chicken, without packing it in too tightly, and secure the opening with a small skewer. Spread the breast with the butter, then put the oil into a roasting pan and lay the bird in it. Season and lay the bacon rashers over the top of the bird to protect it in the oven.

5 Weigh the stuffed chicken and work out the cooking time (see Cook's Tip), then put into the oven. After 20 minutes, reduce the temperature to 180°C/350°F/Gas 4 and cook for another 45–60 minutes, or until cooked. Test by inserting a knife between the body and thigh: if the juices run clear, it is cooked. Transfer to a serving dish and allow it to rest for 10 minutes.

6 To make the gravy, pour off the excess fat from the roasting pan. Finely chop the liver, add to the pan and stir over a low heat for 1 minute. Sprinkle in just enough flour to absorb the remaining chicken fat and cook, stirring to blend, for 2 minutes. Gradually add some of the stock, scraping the pan to dissolve the residues and stirring to make a smooth gravy. Bring to the boil, stirring, adding more stock until the consistency is as you like it. Adjust the seasoning, then pour into a sauceboat to hand round separately.

7 Carve the chicken. Serve on heated plates with the herb stuffing and gravy, and any other accompaniments you like.

1 large chicken, about 1.8kg/4lb, with giblets and neck if possible

1 small onion, sliced

1 small carrot, sliced

small bunch of fresh parsley and thyme

15g/¹⁄₂oz/1 tbsp butter

6 rashers (strips) of streaky (fatty) bacon

FOR THE STUFFING

1 onion, finely chopped

50g/2oz/¹⁄₄ cup butter

150g/5oz/2¹⁄₂ cups fresh white breadcrumbs

15ml/1 tbsp fresh chopped parsley

15ml/1 tbsp fresh chopped mixed herbs, such as thyme, marjoram and chives

finely grated rind and juice of ¹⁄₂ lemon

1 small egg, lightly beaten

FROM THE STORECUPBOARD

salt and ground black pepper, to taste

30ml/2 tbsp vegetable oil

15ml/1 tbsp plain (all-purpose) flour

COOK'S TIPS

• To work out the amount of time required to roast a chicken, allow 20 minutes per 450g/1lb plus an additional 20 minutes.

• Allow the chicken to rest in a warm place for at least 10 minutes, and ensure that you use a really sharp knife to carve.

Energy 562kcal/2342kJ; Protein 40.9g; Carbohydrate 23.2g, of which sugars 2.7g; Fat 34.5g, of which saturates 11.9g; Cholesterol 216mg; Calcium 72mg; Fibre 1.5g; Sodium 381mg

Baked Chicken with Fennel ✳✳

This simple dish is perfect as a make-ahead meal. It combines succulent chicken pieces with garlic, shallots and the aniseed flavour of fennel, and is served in a delicious creamy herb sauce.

SERVES FOUR

1 Place the chicken pieces, shallots and all but one of the garlic cloves in a flameproof dish or roasting pan. Add the oil, vinegar, wine or vermouth, if using, and fennel seeds. Season with pepper, then marinate for at least 2–3 hours.

2 Preheat the oven to 190°C/375°F/Gas 5. Add the fennel to the chicken, season with salt and stir to mix. Cook the chicken in the oven for 50–60 minutes, stirring once or twice. The chicken juices should run clear, not pink, when the thick thigh meat is pierced with a skewer.

3 Transfer the chicken and vegetables to a serving dish and keep them warm. Skim off some of the fat and bring the cooking juices to the boil, then pour in the cream. Stir, then whisk in the redcurrant jelly followed by the mustard. Check the seasoning.

4 Chop the remaining garlic clove with the feathery fennel tops and mix with the chopped parsley. Pour the sauce over the chicken and sprinkle the chopped garlic and herb mixture over the top. Serve immediately.

1.6–1.8kg/3¹/₂–4lb chicken, cut into 8 pieces or 8 chicken portions

250g/9oz shallots, peeled

1 garlic bulb, separated into cloves and peeled

45ml/3 tbsp white wine or vermouth (optional)

2 bulbs fennel, cut into wedges, feathery tops reserved

150ml/¹/₄ pint/²/₃ cup double (heavy) cream

5ml/1 tsp redcurrant jelly

30ml/2 tbsp chopped fresh parsley

FROM THE STORECUPBOARD

60ml/4 tbsp olive oil

45ml/3 tbsp tarragon vinegar

5ml/1 tsp fennel seeds, crushed

15ml/1 tbsp tarragon mustard

salt and ground black pepper, to taste

COOK'S TIPS

• *The cut surfaces of fennel quickly discolour, so make sure that you cook it soon after you have prepared it.*

• *Use new season garlic if possible, as the cloves will be more tender.*

Energy 568kcal/2349kJ; Protein 24.3g; Carbohydrate 6.5g, of which sugars 5.3g; Fat 49.6g, of which saturates 19.4g; Cholesterol 163mg; Calcium 76mg; Fibre 2.9g; Sodium 112mg

Roasted Duckling with Potatoes ✳✳

The rich flavour of duck combined with these sweetened potatoes glazed with honey makes an excellent treat for a dinner party or special occasion. Serve with steamed seasonal green vegetables.

SERVES FOUR

1 Preheat the oven to 200°C/400°F/ Gas 6. Place the duckling in a roasting pan. Prick the skin well. Combine the soy sauce and orange juice and pour over the duck. Cook for 20 minutes.

2 Place the potato chunks in a bowl, stir in the honey and toss to mix well. Remove the duckling from the oven and spoon the potatoes all around and under the duckling.

3 Roast for 35 minutes, then remove from the oven. Toss the potatoes in the juices and turn the duck over. Put the pan back in the oven and cook for a further 30 minutes.

4 Remove the duckling from the oven and carefully scoop off the excess fat, leaving the juices behind. Sprinkle the sesame seeds over the potatoes, season and turn the duckling back over, breast side up, and cook for a further 10 minutes. Remove from the oven and keep warm.

5 Pour off the excess fat and simmer the juices on the hob (stovetop). Serve the juices with the duckling and potatoes.

**1 duckling,
giblets removed**

**150ml/¹/₄ pint/²/₃ cup
fresh orange juice**

**3 large floury potatoes,
cut into chunks**

30ml/2 tbsp clear honey

15ml/1 tbsp sesame seeds

FROM THE STORECUPBOARD

**60ml/4 tbsp light
soy sauce**

**salt and ground black
pepper, to taste**

Energy 363kcal/1523kJ; Protein 23.3g; Carbohydrate 30.4g, of which sugars 11.8g; Fat 18.7g, of which saturates 4.9g; Cholesterol 108mg; Calcium 50mg; Fibre 1.6g; Sodium 198mg

250g/9oz fresh
sesame noodles

2 duck breasts,
thinly sliced

3 spring onions (scallions),
cut into strips

2 celery sticks, cut into
matchstick strips

1 fresh pineapple,
peeled, cored and cut
into strips

300g/11oz mixed
vegetables, such as
carrots, (bell) peppers,
beansprouts and green
cabbage, shredded or
cut into strips

90ml/6 tbsp plum sauce

Stir-fried Duck with Noodles and Pineapple ✳✳

The fatty skin on duck makes it ideal for stir-frying: as soon as the duck is added to the hot pan the fat is released, creating delicious crisp skin and tender flesh when cooked. Stir-fried vegetables and noodles make this a meal in itself, perfect for entertaining friends or a special supper.

SERVES FOUR

COOK'S TIPS

• Fresh sesame noodles can be bought from large supermarkets or Asian stores – you'll find them in the chiller cabinets alongside fresh pasta. If they aren't available, then use fresh egg noodles instead. Cook according to the instructions on the packet. For extra flavour, add a little sesame oil to the cooking water.

• Ensure you cut the vegetables into similar-sized strips.

1 Cook the noodles in a saucepan of boiling water for 3 minutes. Drain in a colander.

2 Meanwhile, heat a wok. Add the duck to the hot wok and stir-fry for about 2 minutes, until crisp. If the duck yields a lot of fat, drain off all but 30ml/2 tbsp.

3 Add the spring onions and celery to the wok and stir-fry for 2 minutes more. Use a draining spoon to remove the ingredients from the wok and set aside. Add the pineapple strips and mixed vegetables, and stir-fry for 2 minutes.

4 Add the cooked noodles and plum sauce to the wok, then replace the duck, spring onion and celery mixture.

5 Stir-fry the duck mixture for about 2 minutes more, or until the noodles and vegetables are hot and the duck is cooked through. Serve at once.

Energy 455Kcal/1927kJ; Protein 28.3g; Carbohydrate 69g, of which sugars 22.6g; Fat 11g, of which saturates 1.4g; Cholesterol 110mg; Calcium 81mg; Fibre 5.7g; Sodium 143mg

Slow-cooked Duck Legs in a Spicy Orange Sauce ✳✳

This unusual dish combines the traditional partnership of duck and orange with exotic spices, fragrant lemongrass, fiery chilli and chunks of sweet, juicy pineapple to create a taste sensation. Serve simply with steamed rice and wedges of lime for squeezing over.

SERVES FOUR

4 duck legs

4 garlic cloves, crushed

50g/2oz fresh root ginger, peeled and finely sliced

2 lemon grass stalks, trimmed, cut into 3 pieces and crushed

2 dried whole red Thai chillies

30ml/2 tbsp *nuoc cham* or *tuk trey* (*see* Cook's Tip)

900ml/1¹/₂ pints/3³/₄ cups fresh orange juice

1 lime, cut into quarters

FROM THE STORECUPBOARD

15ml/1 tbsp palm sugar

5ml/1 tsp five-spice powder

salt and ground black pepper, to taste

1 Place the duck legs, skin side down, in a large heavy pan or flameproof clay pot. Cook them on both sides over a medium heat for about 10 minutes, until browned and crispy. Transfer them to a plate and set aside.

2 Stir the garlic, ginger, lemon grass and chillies into the fat left in the pan, and cook until golden. Add the sugar, five-spice powder and *nuoc cham* or *tuk trey*.

3 Stir in the orange juice and place the duck legs back in the pan. Cover the pan and gently cook the duck for 1–2 hours, until the meat is tender and the sauce has reduced.

4 Season to taste and serve immediately, with lime wedges to squeeze over it.

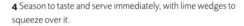

Energy 280kcal/1181kJ; Protein 31g; Carbohydrate 23.8g, of which sugars 23.8g; Fat 10g, of which saturates 2g; Cholesterol 165mg; Calcium 48mg; Fibre 0.4g; Sodium 250mg

Turkey Meatballs with a Tomato Sauce ✳

In this delicious dish, turkey is shaped into small balls and simmered with rice in a richly flavoured tomato sauce, creating a one-pot meal in itself.

SERVES FOUR

1 Using a serrated knife, remove the crusts from the bread and cut into cubes. Place the bread in a mixing bowl and sprinkle with the milk, then leave to soak for about 5 minutes.

2 Add the garlic clove, caraway seeds, turkey, and salt and pepper to the bread and mix together well.

3 Whisk the egg white until stiff, then fold, half at a time, into the turkey mixture. Chill in the refrigerator for half an hour.

4 Preheat the oven to 190°C/375°F/Gas 5. Pour the stock into a large ovenproof dish. Add the tomatoes and tomato purée, cover with a lid and cook for 1/2 hour.

5 Meanwhile, shape the turkey mixture into 16 small balls. Stir the rice into the tomato mixture, then add the turkey balls.

6 Cook for a further 1/2 hour, or until the turkey balls and rice are cooked. Serve immediately.

white bread loaf, unsliced

30ml/2 tbsp milk

1 garlic clove, crushed

225g/8oz minced (ground) turkey

1 egg white

15ml/1 tbsp chopped fresh basil, to garnish (optional)

FROM THE STORECUPBOARD

2.5ml/1/2 tsp caraway seeds

350ml/12fl oz/11/2 cups near-boiling chicken stock

400g/14oz can chopped tomatoes

15ml/1 tbsp tomato purée (paste)

90g/31/2 oz/1/2 cup easy-cook (converted) rice

salt and ground black pepper, to taste

VARIATIONS

• *You could make these meatballs using any type of minced (ground) meat, including chicken, pork, beef and lamb.*

• *For a richer tomato sauce, add 75ml/5 tbsp red wine to the mixture in step 4.*

Energy 187kcal/797kJ; Protein 18.2g; Carbohydrate 26.6g, of which sugars 3.9g; Fat 1.7g, of which saturates 0.5g; Cholesterol 32mg; Calcium 44mg; Fibre 1g; Sodium 212mg

15g/¹/₂oz/1 tbsp butter

1 small onion,
finely chopped

50g/2oz/¹/₂ cup
small chestnut
mushrooms, quartered

75g/3oz/³/₄ cup
cranberries, fresh
or frozen

60–75ml/4–5 tbsp water

about 275g/10oz cooked
turkey breast, cut into
2cm/³/₄in cubes

150ml/¹/₄ pint/²/₃ cup
sour cream

30ml/2 tbsp freshly grated
grano padano cheese

FOR THE PANCAKES

1 egg

350ml/12fl oz/
1¹/₂ cups semi-skimmed
(low-fat) milk

FROM THE STORECUPBOARD

175g/6oz/1¹/₂ cups plain
(all-purpose) flour

oil, for frying

50g/2oz/generous ¹/₄ cup
wild rice, cooked according
to packet instructions

2.5ml/¹/₂ tsp sunflower oil

25ml/1¹/₂ tbsp sugar

salt and ground black
pepper, to taste

COOK'S TIP

These healthy pancakes make a change from the rich fare eaten at Christmas, and are a good way of using up leftovers. If you have cranberry jelly you can use that in place of the fresh berries.

Stuffed Pancakes with Turkey and Cranberries ✳

This is a wonderful way of using left-over roast turkey. Cranberries add their bitter-sweet flavour, while the wild rice contributes a nutty flavour.

MAKES SIX–EIGHT

1 Preheat the oven to 190°C/375°F/Gas 5. Make the pancakes. Sift the flour and a pinch of salt into a bowl. Beat in the egg and milk to make a smooth batter. Heat a little oil in a frying pan, pour in about 30ml/2 tbsp of the batter and tilt to cover the bottom of the pan. Cook until the underside is a pale brown colour, then flip the pancake over and cook the other side briefly. Slide it out of the pan and cook 5–7 more pancakes in the same way.

2 Heat the butter and sunflower oil in a separate frying pan and fry the onion for 3–4 minutes, until soft. Add the mushrooms and fry for 2–3 minutes, until they are a pale golden colour. Put the cooked rice in a bowl and add the onions and mushrooms.

3 Put the cranberries in a saucepan and add the sugar and water. Cover and simmer for 10 minutes, or until the cranberries burst.

4 Transfer the cranberries to a bowl with a slotted spoon, and pour in 45ml/3 tbsp of the cooking liquid. Add the rice mixture and 60ml/4 tbsp of the sour cream. Season to taste and stir to mix.

5 Fold the pancakes in four and spoon the stuffing into one of the pockets. Arrange in a lightly greased baking dish. Mix the remaining sour cream with the grano padano and spoon over the top. Bake for 10 minutes to heat through, then serve.

Energy 305kcal/1279kJ; Protein 19.1g; Carbohydrate 29.4g, of which sugars 7.6g; Fat 13g, of which saturates 5.5g; Cholesterol 71mg; Calcium 157mg; Fibre 1g; Sodium 120mg

PERFECT POULTRY   **309**

VARIATIONS

These crisp, tasty little parcels can be made with a variety of fillings and they are a great way of using up a range of left-over cooked meats and the sauces that accompany them.

• To make ham and Cheddar bundles, replace the turkey with cubed cooked ham and use Cheddar cheese in place of the brie. A fruit-flavoured chutney would make a good alternative to the cranberry sauce, if you like.

• To make chicken and Stilton bundles, use diced cooked chicken in place of the cooked turkey and white Stilton instead of brie. Replace the cranberry sauce with mango chutney.

Turkey Filo Pastry Bundles ✳

After the traditional Christmas or Thanksgiving meal, it is easy to end up with lots of turkey leftovers. These delicious filo pastry parcels are a marvellous way of using up the small pieces of cooked turkey.

SERVES SIX

1 Preheat the oven to 200°C/400°F/Gas 6. Mix the turkey, diced brie, cranberry sauce and chopped parsley. Season with salt and pepper.

2 Cut the filo sheets in half widthways and trim to make 18 squares. Layer three pieces of pastry together, brushing them with a little melted butter so that they stick together. Repeat with the remaining filo squares to give six pieces.

3 Divide the turkey mixture among the pastry, making neat piles on each piece. Gather up the pastry to enclose the filling in bundles. Place on a baking sheet, brush with a little melted butter and bake for 20 minutes, or until the pastry is crisp and golden. Serve hot or warm with a green salad.

450g/1lb cooked turkey, cut into chunks

115g/4oz/1 cup diced brie cheese

30ml/2 tbsp cranberry sauce

30ml/2 tbsp chopped fresh parsley

9 sheets filo pastry, 45 x 28cm/18 x 11in each, thawed if frozen

50g/2oz/¼ cup butter, melted

green salad, to serve

FROM THE STORECUPBOARD

salt and ground black pepper, to taste

Energy 307kcal/1286kJ; Protein 24.8g; Carbohydrate 23.1g, of which sugars 4g; Fat 13g, of which saturates 8.1g; Cholesterol 78mg; Calcium 99mg; Fibre 1g; Sodium 199mg

Turkey Patties ✳

Minced turkey is very good value for money and makes deliciously light patties, which are ideal for summer meals and are especially popular with children. The recipe is a flavourful variation on a classic burger.

SERVES SIX

1 Mix together the minced turkey, chopped onion, lime rind and juice, thyme and seasoning in a large bowl.

2 Cover the bowl with clear film (plastic wrap) and chill for up to 4 hours to allow the flavours to infuse, then divide the mixture into six equal portions and shape into round patties.

3 Preheat a griddle pan. Brush the patties with oil, then place them on the pan and cook for 10–12 minutes.

4 Turn the patties over, brush with more olive oil and cook for 10–12 minutes on the second side, or until cooked through.

5 Serve the patties immediately with bread rolls, salad and chips (French fries), if you like.

VARIATIONS
- During the summer, when fresh herbs are at their best, try using fresh oregano, parsley or basil in place of thyme.
- Use minced chicken in place of the turkey.

675g/1¹/₂lb minced (ground) turkey

1 small red onion, finely chopped

grated rind and juice of 1 lime

small handful of fresh thyme leaves

FROM THE STORECUPBOARD

15–30ml/1–2 tbsp olive oil

salt and ground black pepper, to taste

Energy 141kcal/592kJ; Protein 27.7g; Carbohydrate 1.2g, of which sugars 0.6g; Fat 2.8g, of which saturates 0.6g; Cholesterol 64mg; Calcium 23mg; Fibre 0.1g; Sodium 57mg

Marvellous Meat

THERE IS A HUGE RANGE OF DIFFERENT TYPES
AND CUTS OF MEAT, ALL OF WHICH VARY IN PRICE AND
IN THEIR COOKING REQUIREMENTS. BY CHOOSING
GOOD-VALUE CUTS, COMBINING THEM WITH CHEAPER
INGREDIENTS AND COOKING IN AN APPROPRIATE
MANNER, MOST TYPES OF MEAT BECOME AFFORDABLE.
SO ADD A LITTLE SPICE TO YOUR LIFE WITH MEXICAN
SPICY BEEF TORTILLA, TUCK INTO A SUCCULENT LAMB
POT-ROAST OR FOR A SUPER-HEALTHY AND CHEAP
MEAL ENJOY LAMB'S LIVER AND BACON CASSEROLE.

Beef Patties with Onions and Peppers ✳

This is a firm family favourite. It is easy to make, delicious and good value for money. Try adding other vegetables, such as sliced red peppers, broccoli or mushrooms, and serve with salad and bread.

SERVES FOUR

1 Place the minced beef, chopped onion and 15ml/1 tbsp of the garlic-flavoured oil in a bowl and combine. Season well and form into four large or eight small patties.

2 Heat the remaining oil in a large non-stick pan, then add the patties and cook on both sides until browned. Sprinkle over 15ml/1 tbsp water and add a little seasoning.

3 Cover the patties with the sliced onions and peppers. Sprinkle in another 15ml/1 tbsp water and a little seasoning, then cover the pan. Reduce the heat to low and braise for 20–30 minutes.

4 When the onions are turning golden brown, remove the pan from the heat. Serve the patties with the onions and peppers, and a side salad and some bread or potatoes, if you like.

500g/1¹/₂lb lean minced (ground) beef

4 onions, 1 finely chopped and 3 sliced

2–3 green (bell) peppers, seeded and sliced lengthways into strips

FROM THE STORECUPBOARD

30ml/2 tbsp garlic-flavoured olive oil

salt and ground black pepper, to taste

Energy 431kcal/1789kJ; Protein 27.9g; Carbohydrate 21.1g, of which sugars 17.2g; Fat 26.6g, of which saturates 9.6g; Cholesterol 75mg; Calcium 60mg; Fibre 4.4g; Sodium 110mg

Spaghetti with Meatballs ✳

For a great introduction to the charm of chillies, this simple pasta dish is hard to beat. Children love the gentle heat of the sweet and spicy tomato sauce.

SERVES FOUR

1 Put the beef in a bowl. Add the egg, with half the parsley and half the crushed chillies. Season with plenty of salt and pepper.

2 Tear the bread into pieces and place in a bowl. Moisten with the milk. Leave to soak for a few minutes, then squeeze out the excess milk and crumble the bread over the meat mixture. Mix everything together with a wooden spoon, then use your hands to knead the mixture so that it becomes smooth and quite sticky.

3 Wash your hands, rinse them under the cold tap, then pick up small pieces of the mixture and roll them to make about 20–30 small balls. Place on a tray and chill for 30 minutes.

4 Heat the oil in a large non-stick frying pan. Cook the meatballs in batches until browned on all sides.

5 Meanwhile, pour the passata and stock into a pan. Heat gently, then add the remaining chillies and the sugar, and season. Add the meatballs and simmer for 20 minutes.

6 Cook the pasta until it is just tender, following the instructions on the packet. Drain and tip it into a large heated bowl. Pour over the sauce and toss gently. Sprinkle with the remaining parsley and shavings of grano padano. Serve immediately.

COOK'S TIP
This is an ideal dish to make ahead and freeze. Leave to cool at the end of step 5, then freeze.

350g/12oz minced (ground) beef

1 egg

60ml/4 tbsp roughly chopped fresh flat leaf parsley

2.5ml/$^{1}/_{2}$ tsp crushed dried red chillies

1 thick slice white bread, crusts removed

30ml/2 tbsp milk

shavings of grano padano cheese, to serve

FROM THE STORECUPBOARD

salt and ground black pepper, to taste

about 30ml/2 tbsp olive oil

300ml/$^{1}/_{2}$ pint/1$^{1}/_{4}$ cups passata (bottled strained tomatoes)

400ml/14fl oz/1$^{2}/_{3}$ cups vegetable stock

5ml/1 tsp sugar

350–450g/12oz–1lb dried spaghetti

Energy 598kcal/2517kJ; Protein 30.7g; Carbohydrate 71.8g, of which sugars 6.7g; Fat 22.9g, of which saturates 7.5g; Cholesterol 101mg; Calcium 61mg; Fibre 3.1g; Sodium 301mg

500g/1¼lb braising steak

2 onions, chopped

1 garlic clove, crushed

1 fresh green chilli, seeded and finely chopped

1 dried red chilli, crumbled

5ml/1 tsp hot pepper sauce

1 fresh red (bell) pepper, seeded and chopped

fresh coriander (cilantro), to garnish

FROM THE STORECUPBOARD

225g/8oz/1¼ cups dried black beans

30ml/2 tbsp vegetable oil

15ml/1 tbsp paprika

10ml/2 tsp ground cumin

10ml/2 tsp ground coriander

400g/14oz can chopped tomatoes

300ml/½ pint/1¼ cups beef stock

salt and ground black pepper, to taste

boiled rice, to serve

Chilli Con Carne ✳

Fresh green and dried red chillies add plenty of fire to this classic Tex-Mex dish of tender beef cooked in a spicy tomato sauce.

SERVES SIX

1 Put the beans in a large pan. Add enough cold water to cover, bring to the boil and boil vigorously for 10 minutes. Drain, tip into a bowl, cover with cold water and soak for 8 hours.

2 Preheat the oven to 150°C/300°F/Gas 2. Cut the braising steak into small dice. Heat the vegetable oil in a large, flameproof casserole. Add the onion, garlic and green chilli and cook gently for 5 minutes, then transfer the mixture to a plate.

3 Increase the heat to high, add the diced meat to the casserole and brown on all sides. Stir in the paprika, ground cumin and ground coriander.

4 Add the tomatoes, beef stock, dried chilli and hot pepper sauce. Drain the beans and add them to the casserole, with enough water to cover. Bring to simmering point, cover and cook in the oven for 2 hours. Stir occasionally and add extra water, if necessary.

5 Season the casserole to taste and add the chopped red pepper. Replace the lid, return the casserole to the oven and cook for 30 minutes more, or until the meat and beans are tender. Sprinkle over the fresh coriander and serve with rice.

VARIATION
You could use minced (ground) beef in place of the diced braising steak, if you want to.

Energy 331kcal/1387kJ; Protein 29.1g; Carbohydrate 26.6g, of which sugars 8.5g; Fat 12.7g, of which saturates 3.9g; Cholesterol 48mg; Calcium 70mg, Fibre 8g, Sodium 70mg

1 onion, chopped

2 garlic cloves, crushed

1 fresh red chilli, seeded
and sliced

350g/12oz braising steak,
cut into small cubes

3 large wheat tortillas

FOR THE SALSA PICANTE

2 garlic cloves, halved

1 onion, quartered

1–2 fresh red
chillies, seeded and
roughly chopped

5ml/1 tsp chopped
fresh oregano

water, if required

FOR THE CHEESE SAUCE

50g/2oz/¼ cup butter

600ml/1 pint/
2½ cups milk

115g/4oz/1 cup grated
Cheddar cheese

FROM THE STORECUPBOARD

2 x 400g/14oz cans
chopped tomatoes

5ml/1 tsp ground cumin

2.5–5ml/½–1 tsp
cayenne pepper

50g/2oz/½ cup plain
(all-purpose) flour

15ml/1 tbsp oil

225g/8oz/2 cups cooked
long grain rice

beef stock, to moisten

salt and ground black
pepper, to taste

Mexican Spicy Beef Tortilla ✳✳

This dish is not unlike a lasagne, except that the spicy meat is mixed with
rice and is layered between Mexican tortillas with a hot salsa sauce.

SERVES FOUR

1 Make the salsa picante. Place the tomatoes, garlic, onion and chillies in a blender or food processor and process until smooth. Pour into a pan, add the spices and oregano, and season with salt. Bring to the boil, stirring occasionally.

2 Boil for 1–2 minutes, then lower the heat, cover and simmer for 15 minutes. The sauce should be thick, but of a pouring consistency. If it is too thick, dilute it with a little water. Preheat the oven to 180°C/350°F/Gas 4.

3 Make the cheese sauce. Melt the butter in a pan and stir in the flour. Cook for 1 minute. Add the milk, stirring all the time until the sauce boils and thickens. Stir in all but 30ml/2 tbsp of the cheese and season. Set aside.

4 Put the onion, garlic and chilli in a large bowl. Mix in the meat. Heat the oil in a pan and fry the meat until it has browned. Stir in the rice and stock to moisten. Season to taste.

5 Pour about one-quarter of the cheese sauce into the base of a round ovenproof dish. Add a tortilla and then spread over half the salsa followed by half the meat mixture. Repeat these layers, then add half the remaining cheese sauce and the final tortilla. Pour over the remaining cheese sauce and sprinkle the reserved cheese. Bake in the oven for 15–20 minutes until golden on top.

Energy 907kcal/3802kJ; Protein 43.8g; Carbohydrate 106.5g, of which sugars 15.1g; Fat 34.8g, of which saturates 18.3g; Cholesterol 114mg; Calcium 514mg; Fibre 4.1g; Sodium 598mg

Madras Beef Curry with Spicy Rice **

Chillies are an indispensable ingredient of a hot and spicy Madras curry. After long, gentle simmering, they merge with the other flavourings to give a delectable result that goes perfectly with the spicy rice.

SERVES FOUR

1 Heat half the vegetable oil with half the butter in a large, shallow pan. When it is hot, fry the meat, in batches if necessary, until it is browned on all sides. Transfer to a plate and set aside.

2 Heat the remaining vegetable oil and butter and fry the onion for about 3–4 minutes until it is softened and lightly browned.

3 Add 3 of the cardamom pods and fry for 1 minute, then stir in the chillies, ginger and garlic, and fry for 2 minutes more.

4 Stir in the curry paste, 5ml/1 tsp each of ground cumin and coriander, then return the meat to the pan.

5 Stir in the stock. Season with salt, bring to the boil, then reduce the heat and simmer very gently for 1–1^1/$_2$ hours, until the meat is tender.

6 When the curry is almost ready, prepare the spicy rice. Put the basmati in a bowl and pour over enough boiling water to cover.

7 Set aside for 10 minutes, then drain, rinse under cold water and drain again. The rice will still be uncooked but should have lost its brittle texture.

8 Heat the sunflower oil and butter in a flameproof casserole and fry the onion and garlic gently for 3–4 minutes until softened and lightly browned.

9 Stir in the remaining ground cumin, coriander and green cardamom pods and the cinnamon stick. Fry for 1 minute, then add the diced peppers.

10 Add the rice, stirring well to coat the grains thoroughly in the spice mixture, and pour in the chicken stock.

11 Bring to the boil, then reduce the heat, cover the pan tightly and simmer for about 8–10 minutes, or until the rice is tender and the stock has been absorbed.

12 Spoon the spicy rice into a bowl and serve immediately with the curry. You can also serve this with a generous dollop of natural (plain) yogurt and some naan bread.

25g/1oz/2 tbsp butter

675g/1^1/$_2$lb stewing beef, cut into bitesize cubes

1 onion, chopped

2 fresh green chillies, seeded and finely chopped

2.5cm/1in piece of fresh root ginger, grated

2 garlic cloves, crushed

FOR THE RICE

25g/1oz/2 tbsp butter

1 onion, finely chopped

1 garlic clove, crushed

1 small red (bell) pepper, seeded and diced

1 small green (bell) pepper, seeded and diced

FROM THE STORECUPBOARD

30ml/2 tbsp vegetable oil

7 green cardamom pods

15ml/1 tbsp Madras curry paste

10ml/2 tsp ground cumin

7.5ml/1^1/$_2$ tsp ground coriander

150ml/^{1}/$_4$ pint/^{2}/$_3$ cup beef stock

salt

225g/8oz/generous 1 cup basmati rice

15ml/1 tbsp sunflower oil

1 cinnamon stick

300ml/^{1}/$_2$ pint/1^1/$_4$ cups beef stock

Energy 717kcal/2984kJ; Protein 44.2g; Carbohydrate 53.8g, of which sugars 7.1g; Fat 36g, of which saturates 14.2g; Cholesterol 125mg; Calcium 41mg; Fibre 1.8g; Sodium 189mg

Beef and Aubergine Casserole ✳✳

Easy to make but with an exotic taste, this slow-cooked combination of beef and aubergines in a rich tomato sauce would make an excellent main course for a dinner party. Use good-quality stewing steak and cook it slowly, so that it is meltingly tender and full of flavour, and a reasonably dry white wine. Serve with toasted pitta bread and a fresh green salad.

SERVES FOUR

1 Heat the olive oil in a large pan and brown the pieces of meat on both sides. As each piece browns, take it out and set it aside.

2 Add the onion to the pan and sauté until translucent. Add the oregano and the garlic, then, as soon as the garlic becomes aromatic, return the meat to the pan and pour in the wine. Cook for a few minutes, then add the tomatoes, with enough hot water to just cover the meat. Bring to the boil, lower the heat, cover and cook for about 1 hour, until the meat is tender.

3 Meanwhile, slice the aubergines into 2cm/³/₄ in thick rounds, then slice each round in half. Heat the sunflower oil and fry the aubergines in batches over a high heat, turning them as they become golden. Drain on kitchen paper and season to taste.

4 Season the meat, then add the aubergine pieces and shake the pan to distribute them evenly. From this point, do not stir the mixture as the aubergines will be quite fragile. Add a little hot water so that the aubergines are submerged, cover and simmer for 30 minutes more, or until the meat is very tender.

5 Sprinkle the parsley over the top and simmer for a few more minutes before transferring to a serving dish. Serve with hot toasted pitta bread and a fresh green or mixed salad.

1kg/2¹/₄lb good-quality stewing steak or feather steak, sliced in 4 thick pieces

1 onion, chopped

2 garlic cloves, chopped

175ml/6fl oz/³/₄ cup white wine

2 or 3 aubergines (eggplants), total weight about 675g/1¹/₂lb

45ml/3 tbsp finely chopped fresh parsley

toasted pitta bread and green or mixed salad, to serve

FROM THE STORECUPBOARD

60ml/4 tbsp olive oil

2.5ml/¹/₂ tsp dried oregano

400g/14oz can chopped tomatoes

150ml/¹/₄ pint/²/₃ cup sunflower oil

salt and ground black pepper, to taste

COOK'S TIP

When browning meat in a hot pan don't put too much in at once as this lowers the temperature in the pan too quickly and the meat will poach instead of fry.

Energy 838kcal/3,479kJ; Protein 59.2g; Carbohydrate 8.3g, of which sugars 7.6g; Fat 60.2g, of which saturates 14.4g; Cholesterol 145mg; Calcium 44mg; Fibre 4.6g; Sodium 175mg

COOK'S TIP

Stewing steak is very good value for money, and a little goes a long way. It requires slow cooking over a low heat to achieve a meltingly tender consistency and for its full flavour to be properly realised, and it is best paired with strong flavours, such as red wine and garlic.

900g/2lb stewing beef

225g/8oz onions, peeled and chopped

50g/2oz/¹/₄ cup butter

100g/4oz button (white) mushrooms, quartered

2 garlic cloves, crushed with a little salt

15ml/1 tbsp bitter marmalade

300ml/¹/₂ pint/1¹/₄ cups red wine

FROM THE STORECUPBOARD

50g/2oz/¹/₂ cup plain (all-purpose) flour

2.5ml/¹/₂ tsp paprika

30ml/2 tbsp vegetable oil

150ml/¹/₄ pint/²/₃ cup beef stock

salt and ground black pepper, to taste

Rich Beef Stew ✳✳✳

Marmalade adds a zesty and sweet note to this hearty beef stew, made with tender chunks of slow-cooked stewing beef, red wine and mushrooms. It makes an excellent family meal served with warming creamy mashed potatoes and steamed winter greens.

SERVES FOUR

1 Preheat the oven to 180°C/350°F/Gas 4. Cut the meat into 2.5cm/1in cubes. Season the flour with salt, black pepper and the paprika, spread it on a tray and coat the meat in it.

2 Heat a large pan, add the vegetable oil and brown the meat. Do this in batches if your pan is small.

3 Transfer the meat to a casserole. Brown the onions in the original pan, adding a little butter if they seem too dry. Add to the casserole.

4 Keeping the pan hot, add the rest of the butter and brown the mushrooms then transfer to the casserole.

5 Add the rest of the ingredients to the casserole and bring to the boil, stirring to combine the marmalade and evenly distribute the meat and mushrooms. Cover the casserole and place in the preheated oven for about 3 hours, until the meat is tender. Serve with creamy mashed potatoes.

Energy 544kcal/2276kJ; Protein 53.3g; Carbohydrate 17.1g, of which sugars 6.2g; Fat 24.1g, of which saturates 10.4g; Cholesterol 177mg; Calcium 53mg; Fibre 1.5g; Sodium 242mg

All-in-the-pot Beef Stew **✳✳**

This one-pot stew makes a superb alternative to a standard Sunday roast and is less hassle as the beef, being boiled, can sit and wait until you are ready to eat and you don't have to worry about cooking accompaniments.

SERVES EIGHT

1 Make a beurre manié by combining the butter and flour thoroughly. This will be used to thicken the sauce.

2 Put the beef in a large pan, pour in cold water to cover and put on the lid. Bring to the boil and simmer for 2 hours, topping up with boiling water.

3 After 2 hours add the prepared vegetables to the pan and simmer for a further 30 minutes, until the vegetables are just cooked. Test by inserting the point of a knife into them.

4 Remove the beef and vegetables from the pan, arrange on a serving dish and keep warm. Ladle about 350ml/12fl oz/ 1¹/₂ cups of the cooking liquor into a clean pan and bring to the boil. Whisk in the beurre manié to thicken it and add the chopped fresh parsley.

5 When you are ready to eat, pour the thickened sauce over the beef and vegetables, retaining some to pass round the table in a separate jug (pitcher). Serve the meat in thick slices, accompanied by a generous serving of the vegetables.

25g/1oz/2 tbsp butter, softened

1.6kg/3¹/₂lb silverside (pot roast), boned and rolled

450g/1lb small whole onions, peeled

450g/1lb small carrots, peeled and halved

8 celery sticks, peeled and quartered

12 small potatoes

30ml/2 tbsp chopped fresh parsley

FROM THE STORECUPBOARD

25g/1oz/¹/₄ cup plain (all-purpose) flour

Energy 875kcal/3656kJ; Protein 89.8g; Carbohydrate 38.5g, of which sugars 16.7g; Fat 41.1g, of which saturates 17.7g; Cholesterol 231mg; Calcium 121mg; Fibre 6.3g; Sodium 358mg

Beef and Chickpea Stew ✳✳

This aromatic stew combines aubergines, chickpeas and left-over meat with a subtly spiced tomato sauce to create a taste sensation. It is often made with cold roast beef, but you can use any meat and even stuffing.

SERVES FOUR

2 small aubergines (eggplant)

1 large onion, chopped

3 garlic cloves, finely chopped

1 fresh, or baked, red (bell) pepper, seeded and sliced (optional)

400g/14oz cooked beef, cubed (or mixed turkey, ham, or any other left-over meat)

chopped fresh mint, to garnish

FROM THE STORECUPBOARD

90ml/6 tbsp olive oil

400g/14oz can plum tomatoes

250ml/8fl oz/1 cup meat stock

2.5ml/¹/₂ tsp ground cumin

2.5ml/¹/₂ tsp ground allspice

pinch of ground cloves

2.5ml/¹/₂ tsp cayenne pepper

400g/14oz can chickpeas, drained

salt and ground black pepper, to taste

1 Cut the aubergines into cubes and put them into a colander. Sprinkle with 10ml/2 tsp salt, turning the cubes over with your hands. Leave to drain for about 1 hour. Rinse, then squeeze them dry using kitchen paper.

2 Meanwhile put 30ml/2 tbsp oil in a wide flameproof casserole and fry the onion and garlic until soft. If using the fresh pepper, add it to the casserole and stir-fry until softened.

3 Add the tomatoes and the baked pepper, if using, the meat stock, cumin, allspice, ground cloves and cayenne pepper. Season to taste. Add the cubed meat and simmer gently.

4 Heat 45ml/3 tbsp oil over a high heat in a large frying pan. Fry the aubergine, in batches if necessary, until they are brown on all sides. (If you need to add more oil, add it to an empty pan, and reheat to a high heat, before adding more cubes.)

5 Add the aubergine and chickpeas and bring to a simmer, adding more stock to cover, if necessary – the dish should be almost solid. Check the seasonings, garnish with mint and serve.

Energy 483kcal/2018kJ; Protein 32.1g; Carbohydrate 23.7g, of which sugars 7.4g; Fat 29.6g, of which saturates 6.7g; Cholesterol 58mg; Calcium 74mg; Fibre 8.3g; Sodium 297mg

Slow Baked Beef with Potato Crust ✳✳

This recipe makes the very most of the delicious taste and tender texture of braising beef by marinating it in red wine and topping it with a cheesy grated potato crust that bakes to a golden, crunchy consistency. For a change, instead of grating the potatoes, slice them thinly and layer over the top of the beef with onion rings and crushed garlic.

SERVES FOUR

1 Place the diced beef in a non-metallic bowl. Add the red wine and orange peel and season with black pepper. Mix the ingredients together and then cover and marinate in the refrigerator for at least 4 hours or overnight if possible.

2 Preheat the oven to 160°C/325°F/Gas 3. Drain the beef, reserving the marinade.

3 Heat 30ml/2 tbsp of the oil in a large flameproof casserole and cook the meat, in batches, for 5 minutes to seal. Add the onions, carrots and garlic and cook for 5 minutes. Stir in the mushrooms, red wine marinade and beef stock. Simmer.

4 Mix the cornflour with water to make a smooth paste. Stir into the pan. Season, cover and cook in the oven for 1¹/₂ hours.

5 Make the crust 30 minutes before the end of the cooking time for the beef. Start by blanching the grated potatoes in boiling water for 5 minutes. Drain well and then squeeze out all the extra liquid.

6 Stir in the remaining oil, the horseradish and the cheese, then sprinkle evenly over the surface of the beef.

7 Increase the oven temperature to 200°C/400°F/Gas 6 and cook the dish for a further 30 minutes so that the top is crispy and slightly browned.

COOK'S TIPS

• Use a large grater on the food processor for the potatoes. They will hold their shape better than if you use a finer blade.

• It is worth remembering that the better the quality of the wine you use when cooking, the better the dish will taste. It is a mistake to use a nasty-tasting wine that you wouldn't be prepared to drink on the grounds that it will do for cooking. There are plenty of inexpensive good-quality wines available. In fact, a good rule of thumb is to use the same wine for cooking that you plan to serve with the dish.

675g/1¹/₂lb stewing beef, diced

300ml/¹/₂ pint/1¹/₄ cups red wine

slice of orange peel

2 onions, cut into chunks

2 carrots, cut into chunks

1 garlic clove, crushed

225g/8oz/3 cups button (white) mushrooms

FOR THE CRUST

450g/1lb potatoes, grated

30ml/2 tbsp creamed horseradish

50g/2oz/¹/₂ cup grated mature (sharp) Cheddar cheese

FROM THE STORECUPBOARD

30ml/2 tbsp olive oil

150ml/¹/₄ pint/²/₃ cup beef stock

45ml/3 tbsp cornflour (cornstarch)

salt and ground black pepper, to taste

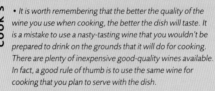

Energy 630kcal/2632kJ; Protein 45.9g; Carbohydrate 40.1g, of which sugars 10.8g; Fat 26.9g, of which saturates 10.2g; Cholesterol 111mg; Calcium 152mg; Fibre 4.2g; Sodium 308mg

Lamb Meatballs ✳

These flavoursome meatballs contain an exciting mixture of flavours and textures – sweet currants, creamy pine nuts and a harmonious blend of spices. Serve with lemon, a salad and some creamy yogurt.

SERVES SIX

1 In a bowl, pound the lamb with the onion, garlic and cinnamon. Knead with your hands and knock out the air, then add the pine nuts with the currants, red pepper or paprika, breadcrumbs, egg and ketchup. Season with salt and pepper.

2 Finely chop the herbs, reserving 1–2 sprigs of parsley for the garnish, and knead into the mixture, making sure all the ingredients are mixed well together.

3 Take apricot-size portions of the mixture in your hands and roll into balls. Flatten each ball so that it resembles a thick disc, then coat lightly in the flour.

4 Heat a thin layer of oil in a heavy pan. Add the meatballs and cook for 8–10 minutes, until browned on all sides.

5 Remove with a slotted spoon and drain on kitchen paper. Serve hot with lemon wedges and garnish with parsley.

250g/9oz/generous 1 cup lean minced (ground) lamb

1 onion, finely chopped

2 garlic cloves, crushed

30ml/2 tbsp pine nuts

30ml/2 tbsp currants, soaked in warm water for 5–10 minutes and drained

2 slices of day-old white or brown bread, ground into crumbs

1 egg, lightly beaten

1 bunch each of fresh flat leaf parsley and dill

lemon wedges, to serve

FROM THE STORECUPBOARD

10–15ml/2–3 tsp ground cinnamon

5ml/1 tsp Turkish red pepper or paprika

15ml/1 tbsp tomato ketchup

salt and ground black pepper, to taste

60ml/4 tbsp plain (all-purpose) flour

sunflower oil, for shallow frying

VARIATION *For a delicious spicy meatball sandwich, omit the currants and pine nuts and add 5ml/1 tsp ground cumin and 1 chopped fresh hot chilli in step 1. Shape the mixture into small balls, cook as above for 5–6 minutes, then tuck the browned meatballs into toasted pitta bread pockets with sliced red onion, finely chopped flat leaf parsley and garlic-flavoured yogurt.*

Energy 261kcal/1088kJ; Protein 11.4g; Carbohydrate 15.4g, of which sugars 5.2g; Fat 17.5g, of which saturates 4g; Cholesterol 64mg; Calcium 40mg; Fibre 0.7g; Sodium 129mg

2 onions

2 garlic cloves, crushed

900g/2lb boneless shoulder of lamb, trimmed and cut into bitesize pieces

TO SERVE

1 large red onion, cut in half lengthways, in half again crossways, and sliced along the grain

1 large bunch of fresh flat leaf parsley, chopped

2–3 lemons, cut into wedges

FROM THE STORECUPBOARD

7.5ml/1¹/₂ tsp salt

10ml/2 tsp cumin seeds, crushed

225g/8oz/2 cups strong white bread flour

50g/2oz/¹/₂ cup wholemeal (whole-wheat) flour

5ml/1 tsp salt

COOK'S TIP The bread is cooked at the same time as the meat, so it will help if you have someone to flip it over while you do the kebabs, or vice versa.

Grilled Lamb with Flatbread ✳

In this popular kebab recipe small pieces of cooked meat are wrapped in freshly griddled home-made flatbread with red onion, flat leaf parsley and a squeeze of lemon. You can use store-bought pitta bread, if you like.

SERVES SIX

1 Grate the onions on to a plate, sprinkle with the salt and leave to weep for 15 minutes. Place a sieve (strainer) over a bowl, tip in the onions and press down to extract the juice. Discard the onions, then mix the garlic and cumin seeds into the onion juice and toss in the lamb. Cover and leave to marinate for 3–4 hours.

2 Meanwhile, prepare the dough for the breads. Sift the flours and salt into a bowl. Make a well in the middle and gradually add 200ml/7fl oz/scant 1 cup lukewarm water, drawing in the flour from the sides. Using your hands, knead the dough until firm and springy – if the dough is at all sticky, add more flour.

3 Divide the dough into 24 pieces and knead each one into a ball. Place on a floured surface and cover with a damp cloth. Leave to rest for 45 minutes while you get the barbecue ready.

4 Just before cooking, roll each ball of dough into a wide, thin circle. Dust with flour and cover with a damp dish towel.

5 Thread the meat on to metal skewers and cook on the barbecue for 2–3 minutes on each side. At the same time, cook the flat breads on a hot griddle or other flat pan, flipping them over as they begin to go brown and buckle. Pile up on a plate.

6 Slide the meat off the skewers on to the flat breads. Sprinkle onion and parsley over each pile and squeeze lemon juice over the top. Wrap the breads into parcels and eat with your hands.

Energy 433kcal/1821kJ; Protein 34.3g; Carbohydrate 37.1g, of which sugars 4.4g; Fat 17.5g, of which saturates 7.9g; Cholesterol 114mg; Calcium 83mg; Fibre 2.5g; Sodium 460mg

Lamb Şiş Kebab ✳✳

This is the ultimate kebab for an outdoor barbecue – chargrilled meat served with chunks of spiced flat bread with yogurt and tomatoes. Designed to use up day-old pitta bread or a plain Indian naan, the dish is succulent and tasty, and should be devoured on its own.

SERVES FOUR

1 Make the kebabs. Put the lamb into a bowl with the Turkish red pepper or paprika, 5ml/1 tsp sumac, the onions, chilli, garlic and chopped parsley. Knead well to form a smooth paste that is quite sticky. Cover with plastic wrap (clear film) and chill in the refrigerator for about 15 minutes.

2 Meanwhile, make the sauce. Heat the oil and butter in a heavy pan, stir in the onion, garlic and chilli and cook until they just begin to colour.

3 Add the sugar and tomatoes and cook, uncovered, for about 30 minutes until quite thick and saucy. Season to taste with salt and pepper, remove from the heat and keep warm.

4 Get the barbecue ready for cooking and shape the kebabs by moulding them around metal skewers using damp hands. As soon as the kebabs are shaped, put them on the barbecue and cook for 6–8 minutes, turning once.

5 Meanwhile, thread the whole plum tomatoes on to four skewers, place them on the barbecue and cook until the tomatoes are charred.

6 While the kebabs are cooking, melt the butter in a heavy pan and toss in the bread. Cook until it is golden-brown all over.

7 Sprinkle the bread with a little sumac and the oregano, then arrange on a large serving dish, spreading the pieces out so they form a flat base.

8 Splash a little of the tomato sauce over the bread – not too much or it will go soggy – and spoon half the yogurt on top.

9 When the kebabs are cooked on both sides, slip the meat off the skewers and cut it into bitesize pieces.

10 Arrange the meat on the bread with the chargrilled tomatoes, sprinkle with salt and the rest of the sumac and oregano, and garnish with the chopped parsley.

11 Serve hot, topped with dollops of the remaining tomato sauce and yogurt.

---

12 plum tomatoes

30ml/2 tbsp butter

1 large pide, or 4 pitta or small naan, cut into bitesize chunks

225g/8oz/1 cup creamy natural (plain) yogurt

1 bunch of fresh flat leaf parsley, chopped, to garnish

FOR THE KEBABS

500g/1¼lb/2¼ cups lean minced (ground) lamb

2 onions, finely chopped

1 fresh green chilli, seeded and finely chopped

4 garlic cloves, crushed

1 bunch of fresh flat leaf parsley, finely chopped

FOR THE SAUCE

15ml/1 tbsp butter

1 onion, finely chopped

2 garlic cloves, finely chopped

1 fresh green chilli, seeded and finely chopped

FROM THE STORECUPBOARD

5ml/1 tsp Turkish red pepper or paprika

10ml/2 tsp ground sumac

30ml/2 tbsp olive oil

5–10ml/1–2 tsp sugar

400g/14oz can chopped tomatoes

salt and ground black pepper, to taste

5ml/1 tsp dried oregano

Energy 642kcal/2688kJ; Protein 35.2g; Carbohydrate 52.8g, of which sugars 24.1g; Fat 33.9g, of which saturates 15.1g; Cholesterol 121mg; Calcium 253mg; Fibre 6.3g; Sodium 456mg

Shepherd's Pie ✳✳

Economical, comforting and absolutely delicious, this classic pie is sure to be a hit. You could add finely chopped celery and a sprinkling of frozen peas if you want to sneak in some extra vegetables.

SERVES FOUR

1 Heat the oil in a large pan, add the onion, carrot and mushrooms and cook, stirring occasionally, until browned. Stir the beef into the pan and cook, stirring to break up the lumps, until lightly browned.

2 Blend a few spoonfuls of the stock or water with the flour, then stir this mixture into the pan. Stir in the remaining stock or water and bring to a simmer, stirring.

3 Add the bay leaf, Worcestershire sauce and tomato purée, then cover and cook very gently for 1 hour, stirring occasionally. Uncover the pan towards the end of cooking to allow any excess water to evaporate, if necessary.

4 Preheat the oven to 190°C/375°F/ Gas 5. Gently heat the potatoes for a couple of minutes, then mash with the butter, milk and seasoning, to taste.

5 Add the tarragon and seasoning to the mince, then pour into a pie dish. Cover the mince with an even layer of potato and mark the top with the prongs of a fork. Bake for about 25 minutes, until golden brown.

1 onion, finely chopped

1 carrot, finely chopped

115g/4oz mushrooms, wiped and chopped

500g/1¼lb/2¼ cups lean minced (ground) lamb

675g/1½lb potatoes, boiled

25g/1oz/2 tbsp butter

45ml/3 tbsp hot milk

15ml/1 tbsp chopped fresh tarragon

FROM THE STORECUPBOARD

30ml/2 tbsp oil

300ml/½ pint/1¼ cups brown veal stock or water

15ml/1 tbsp plain (all-purpose) flour

bay leaf

10–15ml/2–3 tsp Worcestershire sauce

15ml/1 tbsp tomato purée (paste)

salt and ground black pepper, to taste

VARIATIONS

• To make Cottage Pie, replace the minced (ground) lamb with lean minced beef.

• Add some cooked, mashed parsnip to the potato mixture.

Energy 426kcal/1788kJ; Protein 33.9g; Carbohydrate 39.2g, of which sugars 6.3g; Fat 15.9g, of which saturates 5.9g; Cholesterol 0mg; Calcium 66mg; Fibre 3.7g; Sodium 240mg

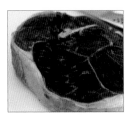

Lamb and Potato Pies ✳✳

These tasty pies are made using mutton, which is packed with flavour and normally much better value for money than lamb. Serve the pies hot with steamed vegetables, or cold as a delicious packed lunch.

SERVES FOUR

450g/1lb boneless mutton

1 large onion, diced

2 carrots, diced

1 potato, diced

2 celery sticks, diced

1 egg, beaten

FOR THE
SHORTCRUST PASTRY

250g/9oz/generous 1 cup butter

120ml/4fl oz/¹/₂ cup chilled water

FROM THE STORECUPBOARD

500g/1¹/₄lb/5 cups plain (all-purpose) flour

salt and ground black pepper, to taste

1 To make the pastry, sieve the flour into a large bowl and add the butter. Rub the butter into the flour with the fingertips until it resembles coarse breadcrumbs. Add the chilled water. Mix with a knife until the mixture clings together. Turn on to a floured worktop and knead once or twice until smooth. Wrap in baking parchment and chill for 20 minutes before using.

2 Trim any fat or gristle from the meat and cut it up into very small pieces. Place in a large bowl and add the diced onion, carrots, potato and celery. Mix well and season to taste.

3 Preheat the oven to 180°C/350°F/Gas 4. Cut a third off the ball of pastry and reserve to make the lids of the pies. Roll out the rest and cut out six circles. Divide the meat mixture between the circles, piling it in the middle of each.

4 Roll out the remaining pastry and cut out six smaller circles, about 10cm/4in across. Lay these on top. Dampen the edges of the pastry bases, bring the pastry up around the meat, pleat it to fit the lid and pinch the edges together.

5 Make a small hole in the top of each pie, brush with beaten egg and slide the pies on to baking sheets. Bake for an hour, then serve hot or cold.

Energy 784kcal/3275kJ; Protein 25.1g; Carbohydrate 74.6g, of which sugars 5.2g; Fat 44.9g, of which saturates 26.1g; Cholesterol 178mg; Calcium 155mg; Fibre 4g; Sodium 345mg

Mutton Hotpot ✳

Mutton is hard to come by today but it really is worth looking out for. Try your local farmers' market or ask your butcher if he could get it for you. It often has a superior flavour to lamb, although it does require longer, slower cooking. Serve with steamed seasonal vegetables.

SERVES SIX

1 Preheat the oven to 180°C/350°F/Gas 4. Trim the mutton chops, leaving a little fat but no bone. Slice the kidneys in two horizontally and remove the fat and core with sharp scissors.

2 Place three of the chops in a deep casserole and season well with salt and ground black pepper.

3 Add a layer of half the kidneys, then half the onion and finally half the potatoes. Season lightly.

4 Repeat the process, seasoning as you go and making sure that you finish with an even layer of potatoes.

5 Heat the stock and pour it into the casserole, almost covering everything but leaving the potatoes just showing at the top. Cover and cook in the preheated oven for 2 hours, removing the lid for the last 30 minutes to allow the potatoes to brown.

6 mutton chops

6 lamb's kidneys

1 large onion, sliced

450g/1lb potatoes, sliced

FROM THE STORECUPBOARD

600ml/1 pint/2¹/₂ cups dark stock

salt and ground black pepper, to taste

Energy 626kcal/2629kJ; Protein 76.9g; Carbohydrate 23.1g, of which sugars 5g; Fat 25.8g, of which saturates 11.6g; Cholesterol 374mg; Calcium 76mg; Fibre 2g; Sodium 269mg

Lamb Pot-roast ✳

This slow-braised dish of lamb and tomatoes, spiced with cinnamon and stewed with green beans, has a Greek influence. It is good served with warm crusty bread to mop up the delicious juices.

SERVES EIGHT

1kg/2¹/₄lb lamb on the bone

8 garlic cloves, chopped

juice of 1 lemon

2 onions, thinly sliced

400g/14oz/scant 3 cups runner (green) beans, cut into 2.5cm/1in lengths

chopped fresh parsley, to garnish

FROM THE STORECUPBOARD

2.5–5ml/¹/₂–1 tsp ground cumin

45ml/3 tbsp olive oil

salt and ground black pepper, to taste

about 500ml/17fl oz/ 2¹/₄ cups lamb, beef or vegetable stock

75–90ml/5–6 tbsp tomato purée (paste)

1 cinnamon stick

2–3 large pinches of ground allspice or ground cloves

15–30ml/1–2 tbsp sugar

VARIATION You could substitute sliced courgettes for the green beans if you prefer. They will take less time to cook than the beans, so check them often during the cooking time.

1 Preheat the oven to 160°C/325°F/Gas 3. Coat the joint of lamb with the garlic, cumin, olive oil, lemon juice, salt and pepper.

2 Heat a flameproof casserole. Sear the lamb on all sides. Add the onions and pour the stock over the meat to cover. Stir in the tomato purée, spices and sugar. Cover and cook in the oven for 2–3 hours.

3 Remove the casserole from the oven and pour the stock into a pan. Move the onions to the side of the dish and return to the oven, uncovered, for 20 minutes.

4 Meanwhile, add the beans to the stock and cook until tender. Slice the meat and serve with the pan juices, onions and beans. Garnish with parsley and serve immediately.

Energy 307kcal/1279kJ; Protein 28.4g; Carbohydrate 9.8g, of which sugars 8.5g; Fat 17.4g, of which saturates 6.8g; Cholesterol 103mg; Calcium 39mg; Fibre 1.9g; Sodium 83mg

North African Lamb **

This dish is full of contrasting flavours that create a rich, spicy and fruity main course. For best results, use lamb that still retains some fat, as this will help keep the meat moist and succulent during roasting. Serve the lamb with couscous and steamed seasonal green vegetables.

SERVES FOUR

1 Preheat the oven to 200°C/400°F/Gas 6. Season the lamb with salt and pepper. Heat a frying pan, preferably non-stick, and cook the lamb on all sides until beginning to brown. Transfer to a roasting pan, reserving any fat in the frying pan.

2 Peel the onions and cut each into six wedges. Toss with the lamb and roast for about 30–40 minutes, until the lamb is cooked through and the onions are deep golden brown.

3 Tip the cooked lamb and onions back into the frying pan. Mix the harissa with 250ml/8fl oz/1 cup boiling water and add to the roasting pan. Scrape up any residue left in the pan and pour the mixture over the lamb and onions.

4 Stir in the prunes and heat until just simmering. Cover and simmer for 5 minutes, then serve.

675g/1¹/₂lb lamb fillet or shoulder steaks, cut into chunky pieces

5 small onions

7.5ml/1¹/₂ tsp harissa

115g/4oz ready-to-eat pitted prunes, halved

FROM THE STORECUPBOARD

salt and ground black pepper, to taste

Energy 379kcal/1585kJ; Protein 35g; Carbohydrate 17.7g, of which sugars 15.4g; Fat 19.2g, of which saturates 8.8g; Cholesterol 128mg; Calcium 48mg; Fibre 3.1g; Sodium 151mg

Lamb and Carrot Casserole with Barley ✳

Barley and carrots make natural partners for lamb and mutton. In this delicious casserole the barley bulks out the meat and adds to the flavour and texture as well as thickening the sauce. The dish is comfort food at its best. Serve with boiled or baked potatoes and steamed green vegetables.

SERVES SIX

1 Trim the lamb of any fat or gristle and cut it into bitesize pieces. Heat the oil in a flameproof casserole, add the lamb and toss until the lamb is browned all over.

2 Add the vegetables to the casserole and fry them briefly with the meat. Add the barley and enough stock or water to cover, and season to taste.

3 Cover the casserole and simmer gently or cook in a slow oven, 150°C/300°F/Gas 2 for 1–1¹⁄₂ hours until the meat is tender. Add extra stock or water during cooking if necessary. Serve immediately with potatoes and vegetables.

4 Alternatively, allow the casserole to cool, then refrigerate or freeze until needed. This will allow the flavours to mature. Thaw, if necessary, and reheat until piping hot before serving.

675g/1¹⁄₂lb stewing lamb

2 onions, sliced

675g/1¹⁄₂lb carrots, sliced

4–6 celery sticks, sliced

45ml/3 tbsp pearl barley, rinsed

FROM THE STORECUPBOARD

15ml/1 tbsp oil

stock or water

salt and ground black pepper, to taste

Energy 304kcal/1263kJ; Protein 23.2g; Carbohydrate 13g, of which sugars 11.3g; Fat 18g, of which saturates 7.5g; Cholesterol 84mg; Calcium 53mg; Fibre 3.6g; Sodium 110mg

Braised Lamb Shanks with Cannellini Beans ✳✳

Earthy and substantial, this is the ideal dish for chilly autumn evenings. The beans acquire layers of taste when slow-cooked in the rich sauce provided by the meat. A lemon-dressed salad is all it needs on the side.

SERVES FOUR–SIX

1 Preheat the oven to 160°C/325°F/Gas 3. Season the lamb shanks and coat them lightly in flour. Heat the oil in a large flameproof casserole over a high heat and brown the meat on all sides. Lift them out and set them aside.

2 Add the onion to the oil remaining in the casserole and sauté until golden, stir in the garlic, celery, carrot, rosemary and bay leaves.

3 Put the meat back in the pan and pour the wine slowly over it. Let it bubble and reduce, then stir in the tomato purée diluted in 450ml/^{3}/$_4$ pint/scant 2 cups hot water.

4 Drain the beans and add them to the pan with pepper to taste. Mix well. Cover the casserole, transfer it to the oven and bake for 1 hour. Stir in salt to taste and add 150ml/^{1}/$_4$ pint/^{2}/$_3$ cup hot water. Cover and cook for 1 hour more, or until tender.

4 lamb shanks

1 large onion, chopped

2 garlic cloves, sliced

1 celery stick, sliced

1 carrot, sliced

leaves from 2 fresh rosemary sprigs

175ml/6fl oz/^{3}/$_4$ cup white wine

FROM THE STORECUPBOARD

45ml/3 tbsp plain (all-purpose) flour

45ml/3 tbsp olive oil

2 bay leaves

30ml/2 tbsp tomato purée (paste)

225g/8oz/1^1/$_4$ cups dried cannellini beans, soaked overnight in water to cover

salt and ground black pepper, to taste

COOK'S TIPS

• You could use drained, canned cannellini beans in place of the dried ones, if you prefer.

• This dish will improve with time, so you could make it a day in advance, store in the refrigerator and then reheat.

Energy 588kcal/2,465kJ; Protein 43.9g; Carbohydrate 39.9g, of which sugars 6.7g; Fat 26.2g, of which saturates 9.1g; Cholesterol 114mg; Calcium 110mg; Fibre 10.5g; Sodium 161mg

1.5kg/3¼lb lean boneless lamb, cubed

250ml/8fl oz/1 cup natural (plain) yogurt

3 onions

2 red (bell) peppers, seeded and cut into chunks

3 garlic cloves, finely chopped

1 fresh red chilli, seeded and chopped

2.5cm/1in piece fresh root ginger, peeled and chopped

large pinch of saffron strands

800g/1¾lb plum tomatoes, halved, seeded and cut into chunks

chopped fresh coriander, to garnish

FROM THE STORECUPBOARD

30ml/2 tbsp sunflower oil

30ml/2 tbsp mild curry paste

2 x 400g/14oz cans chopped tomatoes

salt and ground black pepper, to taste

Spiced Lamb with Tomatoes and Peppers ✳✳✳

Select lean tender lamb from the leg for this lightly spiced curry with succulent peppers and wedges of onion. Serve warm naan or pitta bread to mop up the tomato-rich juices, or some boiled rice.

SERVES SIX

1 Mix the lamb with the yogurt in a bowl. Cover and chill for about 1 hour.

2 Heat the oil in a large pan. Drain the lamb and reserve the yogurt, then cook the lamb in batches until it is golden on all sides. Remove from the pan and set aside.

3 Cut two of the onions into wedges and add to the oil remaining in the pan. Fry for about 10 minutes, until they begin to colour. Add the peppers and cook for a further 5 minutes. Remove the vegetables from the pan and set aside.

4 Chop the remaining onion. Add it to the pan with the garlic, chilli and ginger, and cook, stirring, until softened. Stir in the curry paste and tomatoes with the reserved marinade. Replace the lamb, add seasoning to taste and stir. Bring to the boil, reduce the heat and simmer for 30 minutes.

5 Pound the saffron to a powder in a mortar, then stir in a little boiling water to dissolve it. Add to the curry. Replace the onion and pepper mixture. Stir in the fresh tomatoes and bring back to simmering point, then cook for 15 minutes. Garnish with chopped coriander to serve.

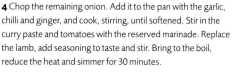

Energy 559kcal/2343kJ; Protein 54.4g; Carbohydrate 20.5g, of which sugars 18.8g; Fat 29.6g, of which saturates 13.5g; Cholesterol 191mg; Calcium 139mg; Fibre 4.6g; Sodium 278mg.

Spiced Pork Roast with Apple and Thyme Cream Sauce **

Belly of pork (sometimes called "lap" of pork) makes a tasty and tender roasting joint. In this unusual dish, the pork is boned and skinned, then stuffed with a simple herb stuffing, rolled, and roasted. The rich, creamy apple and thyme sauce complements the flavour of the pork perfectly and makes a good alternative to standard gravy. Serve with mashed or roasted potatoes, steamed carrots and broccoli for a delectable Sunday lunch.

SERVES SIX

1 Gently melt the butter in a medium pan, then add the finely chopped onion and garlic and cook for 5 minutes, until soft. Add the chopped herbs and breadcrumbs to the pan and mix well to combine.

2 Cool the stuffing mixture a little before mixing in the egg, and season well with salt and ground pepper. Preheat the oven to 150°C/300°F/Gas 2.

3 Meanwhile, trim off any fat from the meat and prick the centre with a fork.

4 In a small bowl, combine the butter, chutney, lemon juice, garlic and mustard.

5 Spread the stuffing over the meat, then roll it up and tie it with cotton string. Liberally brush the outside of the joint with the spicy paste.

6 Brown the meat in the oil in a hot roasting pan on the stove, then put in the oven and cook for 3 hours. Halfway through cooking remove the joint from the oven and liberally brush the joint with the spicy paste; turn over, return to the oven, and continue cooking.

7 To make the thyme cream sauce, put the cooking apples, onion and garlic in a large pan and add the thyme sprigs, cider and stock. Bring to the boil and simmer gently for 15 minutes, then discard the thyme. Add the cream.

8 Process the sauce mixture in a blender or food processor, strain through a sieve (strainer) and season to taste with salt and black pepper. If the sauce seems too thick, adjust the texture with extra stock. Keep the sauce warm until it is required.

9 To serve, cut the meat into generous slices and serve immediately, with the hot sauce.

75g/3oz/6 tbsp butter

1 medium onion, finely chopped

3 garlic cloves, crushed

bunch of mixed fresh herbs, leaves finely chopped

225g/8oz/4 cups fine fresh breadcrumbs

1 egg, beaten

1 piece of pork belly, about 1.3kg/3lb

FOR THE SPICY PASTE

25g/1oz/2 tbsp butter, melted

30ml/2 tbsp chutney

15ml/1 tbsp lemon juice

2 garlic cloves, crushed

FOR THE SAUCE

2 large cooking apples, peeled, cored and chopped

1 medium onion, chopped

2 garlic cloves, crushed

1 or 2 thyme sprigs

150ml/¼ pint/²/₃ cup medium cider

300ml/½ pint/1¼ cups single (light) cream

FROM THE STORECUPBOARD

15ml/1 tbsp oil

salt and ground black pepper, to taste

30ml/2 tbsp mild mustard

about 150ml/¼ pint/ ²/₃ cup chicken stock

Energy 814kcal/3409kJ; Protein 73.2g; Carbohydrate 41.9g, of which sugars 12.6g; Fat 39.8g, of which saturates 20.2g; Cholesterol 264mg; Calcium 145mg; Fibre 2.4g; Sodium 581mg

Stir-fried Pork with Chilli and Scrambled Egg ✳

This tasty combination of rice, pork and Asian flavours is a meal in itself, perfect when you are in a hurry or for a mid-week supper. You could add sliced pepper, green beans or baby corn to the mixture, if you like.

SERVES FOUR

1 Cook the rice according to the instructions on the packet. Spread out and leave to cool.

2 Heat the oil in a wok or large frying pan. Add the onion and garlic and cook for about 2 minutes, until softened.

3 Add the pork to the softened onion and garlic. Stir-fry until the pork changes colour and is cooked.

4 Add the eggs and cook until scrambled into small lumps. Add the rice and continue to stir and toss, to coat it with the oil and prevent it from sticking.

5 Stir in the fish sauce, soy sauce and sugar and mix well. Continue to fry until the rice is thoroughly heated.

6 Spoon into warmed individual bowls and serve, garnished with sliced spring onions, chillies and lime wedges.

1 onion, chopped

15ml/1 tbsp finely chopped garlic

115g/4oz pork, cut into small cubes

2 eggs, beaten

4 spring onions (scallions), finely sliced, to garnish

2 fresh red chillies, sliced, to garnish

1 lime, cut into wedges, to garnish

FROM THE STORECUPBOARD

500g/1¼lb/2½ cups long grain rice

45ml/3 tbsp vegetable oil

30ml/2 tbsp Thai fish sauce

15ml/1 tbsp dark soy sauce

2.5ml/½ tsp caster (superfine) sugar

Energy 602kcal/2512kJ; Protein 18.8g; Carbohydrate 101.3g, of which sugars 1.1g; Fat 12.8g, of which saturates 2.2g; Cholesterol 113mg; Calcium 45mg; Fibre 0.2g; Sodium 323mg

Sweet and Sour Thai-style Pork with Vegetables **

The fresh flavours, attractive colours and crisp textures of the fruit and vegetables combined with tender pork in this dish are a treat for the eyes and the stomach. Serve on its own or with some plain egg noodles.

SERVES FOUR

350g/12oz lean pork

4 garlic cloves, thinly sliced

1 small red onion, sliced

1 red (bell) pepper, seeded and diced

1/2 cucumber, seeded and very thinly sliced

2 plum tomatoes, cut into wedges

115g/4oz piece fresh pineapple, cut into small chunks

2 spring onions (scallions), cut into short lengths

TO GARNISH

coriander (cilantro) leaves

spring onions (scallions), shredded

FROM THE STORECUPBOARD

30ml/2 tbsp vegetable oil

30ml/2 tbsp Thai fish sauce

15ml/1 tbsp sugar

ground black pepper, to taste

1 Cut the pork into very thin strips. This is easier to do if you freeze it for 30 minutes first.

2 Heat the oil in a wok or large frying pan. Add the garlic. Cook over a medium heat until golden, then add the pork and stir-fry for 4–5 minutes. Add the onion slices and toss to mix.

3 Add the fish sauce, sugar and ground black pepper to taste. Toss the mixture over the heat for 3–4 minutes more.

4 Stir in the red pepper, cucumber, tomatoes, pineapple and spring onions. Stir-fry for 3–4 minutes more, then spoon into individual serving bowls. Garnish with the coriander and spring onions and serve immediately.

Energy 211kcal/885kJ; Protein 20g; Carbohydrate 12.4g, of which sugars 11.8g; Fat 9.4g, of which saturates 2g; Cholesterol 55mg; Calcium 29mg; Fibre 1.8g; Sodium 68mg

Pork Casserole with Onions, Chilli and Dried Fruit ✳✳

Inspired by South American cooking, a mole – paste – of chilli, shallots and nuts is added to this casserole of pork and onions. Part of the mole is added at the end of cooking to retain its fresh flavour. Serve with rice and a green salad for an unusual and sustaining family meal.

SERVES SIX

1 Make the mole paste. Toast the chillies in a dry pan over a low heat for 1–2 minutes, until they are aromatic, then soak them in warm water for 30 minutes. Drain, reserving the soaking water, and discard the stalks and seeds.

2 Preheat the oven to 160°C/325°F/Gas 3. Heat 30ml/2 tbsp oil in a small frying pan and fry the shallots, garlic, fresh green chilli and ground coriander over a very low heat for 5 minutes.

3 Transfer the shallot mixture to a food processor or blender and add the drained chillies, paprika, almonds and oregano. Process the mixture, adding 45–60ml/3–4 tbsp of the chilli soaking liquid to make a workable paste.

4 Season the flour with salt and black pepper, then use to coat the pork. Heat 45ml/3 tbsp of the olive oil in a large, heavy frying pan and fry the pork, stirring frequently, until sealed on all sides. Transfer the pork cubes to a flameproof casserole.

5 If necessary, add an extra 15ml/1 tbsp oil to the pan and cook the onions and garlic for 8–10 minutes, stirring occasionally.

6 Add the wine and 105ml/7 tbsp water to the frying pan. Cook for 2 minutes. Stir in half the mole paste, bring back to the boil and bubble for a few seconds before pouring over the pork.

7 Season lightly with salt and pepper and stir to mix, then cover and cook in the oven for 1½ hours.

8 Increase the oven temperature to 180°C/350°F/Gas 4. Stir in the prunes, apricots and orange juice to the casserole. Taste to check the seasoning, adding the muscovado sugar if necessary, and more salt and pepper. Then cover and cook for another 30–45 minutes until the meat is succulent and delicious.

9 Place the casserole over a direct heat and stir in the remaining mole paste. Simmer, stirring once or twice, for 5 minutes. Serve immediately, sprinkled with the orange rind, chopped parsley and fresh chilli, if using.

1kg/2¼lb shoulder or leg of pork, cut into 5cm/2in cubes

2 large onions, chopped

2 garlic cloves, chopped

600ml/1 pint/2½ cups fruity white wine

115g/4oz ready-to-eat prunes

115g/4oz ready-to-eat dried apricots

grated rind and juice of 1 orange

30ml/2 tbsp chopped fresh parsley

½–1 fresh green chilli, seeded and finely chopped (optional)

FOR THE MOLE

3 large, medium-hot dried red chillies

2 shallots, chopped

2 garlic cloves, chopped

1 fresh green chilli, seeded and chopped

50g/2oz/½ cup blanched almonds, toasted

FROM THE STORECUPBOARD

75–90ml/5–6 tbsp olive oil

10ml/2 tsp ground coriander

5ml/1 tsp mild paprika

2.5ml/½ tsp dried oregano

25ml/1½ tbsp plain (all-purpose) flour

salt and ground black pepper, to taste

pinch of muscovado (molasses) sugar (optional)

Energy 468kcal/1956kJ; Protein 38.8g; Carbohydrate 17.1g, of which sugars 16.9g; Fat 20.7g, of which saturates 4g; Cholesterol 105mg; Calcium 64mg; Fibre 2.9g; Sodium 134mg

Stewed Pork with Chickpeas and Orange ✳

This healthy and colourful dish is perfect comfort food on a cold winter day. Serve with fresh bread and green salad.

SERVES FOUR

1 Drain the chickpeas, rinse them under cold water and drain them again. Place them in a large pan. Pour in cold water to cover, cover and bring to the boil. Skim the surface, replace the lid and cook gently for 1–1¹/₂ hours, until the chickpeas are soft. Drain, reserving the cooking liquid, and set them aside.

2 Heat the olive oil in the clean pan and brown the meat cubes in batches. As each cube browns, lift it out with a slotted spoon and put it on a plate. When all the meat cubes have been browned, add the onion to the oil remaining in the pan and sauté until light golden. Stir in the garlic, then as soon as it becomes aromatic, add the tomatoes and orange rind.

3 Crumble in the chilli. Return the chickpeas and meat to the pan, and pour in enough of the reserved cooking liquid to cover. Add the black pepper, but not salt at this stage.

4 Mix well, cover and simmer for about 1 hour, or until the meat is tender. Stir occasionally and add more of the reserved liquid if needed. The result should be a moist casserole; not soupy, but not dry either. Season with salt before serving.

675g/1¹/₂lb boneless leg of pork, cut into large cubes

1 large onion, sliced

2 garlic cloves, chopped

grated rind of 1 orange

1 small dried red chilli

FROM THE STORECUPBOARD

350g/12oz/1³/₄ cups dried chickpeas, soaked overnight in water to cover

75–90ml/5–6 tbsp olive oil

400g/14oz can chopped tomatoes

salt and ground black pepper, to taste

Energy 663kcal/2,781kJ; Protein 56.7g; Carbohydrate 54.4g, of which sugars 11g; Fat 25.7g, of which saturates 4.9g; Cholesterol 106mg; Calcium 184mg; Fibre 11.8g; Sodium 164mg

Bacon Chops with Apple and Cider Sauce **✳✳**

Either thick bacon or pork chops could be used in this recipe. Serve with lots of creamy mashed potatoes and steamed buttered cabbage.

SERVES FOUR

1 Heat the oil in a large, heavy frying pan, over a medium heat, add the bacon chops and fry for 10–15 minutes, browning well on both sides.

2 Peel, core and slice the apples. Remove the chops from the pan and keep warm. Add the butter and apples to the pan and cook until the juices begin to brown.

3 Add the finely chopped garlic and sugar to the pan, and cook for 1 minute, then stir in the cider, cider vinegar, mustard and chopped thyme. Boil for a few minutes until the liquid has reduced to a saucy consistency.

4 Season to taste and place the chops on warmed serving plates. Garnish with the thyme sprigs and serve.

4 bacon chops

1 or 2 cooking apples

knob (pat) of butter

1 or 2 garlic cloves, finely chopped

150ml/¹/₄ pint/²/₃ cup dry (hard) cider

10ml/2 tsp chopped fresh thyme

sprigs of thyme, to garnish

FROM THE STORECUPBOARD

15ml/1 tbsp oil

5ml/1 tsp sugar

5ml/1 tsp cider vinegar

15ml/1 tbsp wholegrain mustard

salt and ground black pepper, to taste

Energy 285kcal/1190kJ; Protein 26.4g; Carbohydrate 6.5g, of which sugars 6.5g; Fat 16.1g, of which saturates 5.4g; Cholesterol 40mg; Calcium 17mg; Fibre 0.8g; Sodium 1.34g

Sausage and Pepper Stew ✳✳

Bursting with flavour, this stunning yet simple recipe makes a fabulous brunch or lazy lunch dish. Serve with warm, crusty bread.

SERVES FOUR

1 Halve and seed the peppers and cut them into quarters. Heat the olive oil in a large, heavy pan, add the prepared peppers and sauté them over a medium heat for 10–15 minutes until they start to brown.

2 Meanwhile, slice the sausages into bitesize chunks. Then carefully tip the hot olive oil into a frying pan.

3 Add the sausages and fry them briefly, turning them frequently, to get rid of the excess fat but not to cook them. As soon as they are brown, remove from the pan with a slotted spoon and drain on kitchen paper.

4 Add the tomatoes, sausages and oregano to the peppers. Stir in the water and season with salt and pepper, then cover the pan and cook gently for about 30 minutes. Mix in the chopped parsley, garnish with thyme and serve piping hot.

675g/1¹/₂lb red and green (bell) peppers

500g/1¹/₄lb spicy sausages (such as Italian garlic sausages, Merguez or Toulouse sausages)

400g/14oz tomatoes, skinned and roughly sliced

150ml/¹/₄ pint/²/₃ cup hot water

45ml/3 tbsp chopped fresh flat leaf parsley

chopped fresh thyme, to garnish

FROM THE STORECUPBOARD

75ml/5 tbsp olive oil

5ml/1 tsp dried oregano

salt and ground black pepper, to taste

Energy 573kcal/2,378kJ; Protein 14.8g; Carbohydrate 28.9g, of which sugars 15.9g; Fat 45g, of which saturates 14.7g; Cholesterol 50mg; Calcium 106mg; Fibre 5g; Sodium 1,033mg

Dublin Coddle ✳

This simple dish combines bacon and sausages, and is best accompanied by a crisp green vegetable, such as Brussels sprouts, broccoli or cabbage.

SERVES SIX

1 Cut the ham or bacon into chunks and cook with the sausages in a large pan containing 1.2 litres/2 pints/5 cups boiling water for 5 minutes. Drain, but reserve the cooking liquor.

2 Put the meat into a large pan with the sliced onions, potatoes and the parsley. Season, and add just enough of the reserved cooking liquor to cover completely.

3 Lay a piece of buttered foil or baking parchment on top of the mixture in the pan, then cover with a tight-fitting lid.

4 Simmer gently over a low heat for about 1 hour, or until the liquid is reduced by half and all the ingredients are cooked but not mushy.

5 Serve the coddle immediately with the Brussels sprouts or broccoli, or any other vegetable of your choice.

6 x 8mm/^{1}/₃in thick ham or dry-cured bacon slices

6 best-quality lean pork sausages

4 large onions, sliced

900g/2lb potatoes, peeled and sliced

90ml/6 tbsp chopped fresh parsley

FROM THE STORECUPBOARD

salt and ground black pepper, to taste

Energy 336kcal/1409kJ; Protein 12.7g; Carbohydrate 39.3g, of which sugars 9g; Fat 15.4g, of which saturates 6.2g; Cholesterol 33mg; Calcium 80mg; Fibre 3.6g; Sodium 695mg

Potato and Sausage Bake ✳✳

This easy-to-make bake combines top-quality sausages, bacon, onions, garlic and potatoes to create a warming and sustaining dish that is perfect for a cold winter's day. Serve with seasonal cabbage or broccoli.

SERVES SIX

1 Preheat the oven to 180°C/350°F/Gas 4. Grease a large ovenproof dish and set aside.

2 Heat the oil in a frying pan. Add the bacon to the pan and cook for 2 minutes, then add the onions and cook for 5–6 minutes, until golden. Add the garlic and cook for 1 minute, then remove the mixture from the pan and set aside. Add the sausages to the pan and cook for 5–6 minutes, until golden.

3 Arrange the potatoes in the base of the prepared dish. Spoon the bacon and onion mixture on top. Season with the salt and pepper and sprinkle with the fresh sage.

4 Pour on the stock and top with the sausages. Cover and bake for 1 hour. Serve hot with soda bread if you like.

4 bacon rashers (strips), cut into 2.5cm/1in pieces

2 large onions, chopped

2 garlic cloves, crushed

8 large pork sausages

4 large baking potatoes, thinly sliced

1.5ml/¼ tsp fresh sage

FROM THE STORECUPBOARD

15ml/1 tbsp vegetable oil

300ml/½ pint/1¼ cups vegetable stock

salt and ground black pepper, to taste

Energy 451kcal/1879kJ; Protein 14g; Carbohydrate 35.2g, of which sugars 7.5g; Fat 29.2g, of which saturates 10.5g; Cholesterol 44mg; Calcium 61mg; Fibre 2.9g; Sodium 844mg

Toad in the Hole ✳

This is one of those dishes that is classic comfort food – perfect for lifting the spirits on cold days. Use only the best sausages for this grown-up version, which includes chives in the satisfying batter.

SERVES FOUR–SIX

1 Preheat the oven to 220°C/425°F/Gas 7. Sift the flour into a large bowl with a pinch of salt and pepper. Make a well in the centre of the flour.

2 Whisk the chives, if using, with the eggs and milk, then gradually pour into the well in the flour in the bowl. Whisk the flour into the liquid to make a smooth batter. Cover with clear film (plastic wrap) and leave to rest for at least 30 minutes.

3 Put the vegetable fat or lard into a small roasting pan and place in the oven for 3–5 minutes until very hot. Add the sausages and cook for 15 minutes. Turn the sausages twice during cooking.

4 Pour the batter over the sausages and cook for about 20 minutes, or until the batter is risen and golden. Serve immediately with vegetables.

30ml/2 tbsp chopped fresh chives (optional)

2 eggs

300ml/¹/₂ pint/1¹/₄ cups milk

50g/2oz/¹/₃ cup white vegetable fat (shortening)

450g/1lb good-quality pork sausages

FROM THE STORECUPBOARD

175g/6oz/1¹/₂ cups plain (all-purpose) flour

salt and ground black pepper, to taste

VARIATION *To make individual dishes, cook cocktail sausages in patty tins (muffin pans) until golden. Add the batter and cook for 15 minutes, or until puffed and brown.*

Energy 497kcal/2070kJ; Protein 14.5g; Carbohydrate 32.1g, of which sugars 3.8g; Fat 35.4g, of which saturates 13.6g; Cholesterol 109mg; Calcium 141mg; Fibre 1.3g; Sodium 616mg

Lamb's Liver and Bacon Casserole ✳

Boiled new potatoes tossed in butter go well with this simple casserole. The trick when cooking liver is to seal it quickly, then simmer it gently and briefly. Prolonged and/or fierce cooking makes liver hard and grainy.

SERVES FOUR

1 Heat the oil in a frying pan and cook the bacon until crisp. Add the onions to the pan and cook for about 10 minutes, stirring frequently, or until softened. Add the mushrooms to the pan and cook for a further 1 minute.

2 Use a slotted spoon to remove the bacon and vegetables from the pan and set aside. Add the liver to the pan and cook over a high heat for 3–4 minutes, turning once to seal the slices on both sides. Remove the liver from the pan and keep warm.

3 Melt the butter in the pan, add the soy sauce and flour and blend together. Stir in the stock and bring to the boil, stirring until thickened. Return the liver and vegetables to the pan and heat through for 1 minute. Season with salt and pepper to taste, and serve with new potatoes and lightly cooked green beans.

225g/8oz rindless unsmoked back (lean) bacon rashers (strips), cut into pieces

2 onions, halved and sliced

175g/6oz/2^1/₃ cups chestnut mushrooms, wiped clean and halved

450g/1lb lamb's liver, trimmed and sliced

25g/1oz/2 tbsp butter

FROM THE STORECUPBOARD

30ml/2 tbsp sunflower oil

15ml/1 tbsp soy sauce

30ml/2 tbsp plain (all-purpose) flour

150ml/^{1}/₄ pint/^{2}/₃ cup chicken stock

salt and ground black pepper, to taste

Energy 440kcal/1832kJ; Protein 35g; Carbohydrate 14.3g, of which sugars 6.1g; Fat 27.4g, of which saturates 9.4g; Cholesterol 527mg; Calcium 50mg; Fibre 2.1g; Sodium 1259mg

Pan-fried Calf's Liver with Crisp Onions ✳✳

Sautéed or creamy mashed potatoes go well with fried calf's liver. Serve a salad of mixed leaves with plenty of delicate fresh herbs, such as fennel, dill and parsley, to complement the simple flavours of this main course.

SERVES FOUR

1 Melt the butter in a large, heavy pan with a lid. Add the onions and mix well to coat with butter. Cover the pan with a lid and cook gently for 10 minutes, stirring occasionally.

2 Stir in the sugar and cover the pan. Cook the onions for a further 10 minutes, or until they are soft and golden. Increase the heat, remove the lid and stir the onions over a high heat, until they are deep gold and crisp. Use a draining spoon to remove the onions from the pan, draining off the fat.

3 Meanwhile, rinse the calf's liver in cold water and pat it dry on kitchen paper. Season the flour, put it on a plate and turn the slices of liver in it until they are lightly coated in flour.

4 Heat the oil in a large frying pan, add the liver and cook for about 2 minutes on each side, or until lightly browned and just firm. Arrange the liver on warmed plates, with the crisp onions. Garnish with parsley and serve with sautéed or mashed potatoes.

50g/2oz/¼ cup butter

4 onions, finely sliced

4 slices calf's liver, each weighing about 115g/4oz

parsley, to garnish

FROM THE STORECUPBOARD

5ml/1 tsp sugar

30ml/2 tbsp plain (all-purpose) flour

30ml/2 tbsp olive oil

salt and ground black pepper, to taste

Energy 315kcal/1310kJ; Protein 22.7g; Carbohydrate 11.8g, of which sugars 4.4g; Fat 19.9g, of which saturates 8.5g; Cholesterol 452mg; Calcium 39mg; Fibre 1.3g; Sodium 160mg

Lamb's Kidneys and Bacon with Sherry ✳

Kidneys cooked in sherry make an excellent family supper. As a first course, partner the dish with fried toast triangles or crusty bread. As a main course, serve with some boiled new potatoes.

SERVES FOUR

1 Halve and skin the kidneys, then remove the cores. Cut the kidneys into cubes. Heat half the oil in a large frying pan and fry the bacon or pancetta until the fat starts to run. Add the onion and garlic and fry until softened. Remove to a plate.

2 Add the remaining oil to the pan and divide the kidneys into four batches. Put in one handful, and stir-fry over a high heat until sealed. (They should not give off any juice.) Remove to a plate and repeat with a second handful and remove to the plate. Continue until they are all cooked.

3 Return the onion and bacon mixture to the pan. Sprinkle with flour and cook, stirring gently. Add the sherry and stir until thickened. Add the tomato purée and parsley. Return the kidneys to the pan, and heat through. Season well and serve hot with buttered new potatoes, if you like.

12 plump lamb's kidneys

115g/4oz smoked bacon lardons

1 large onion, finely chopped

2 garlic cloves, finely chopped

150ml/¼ pint/⅔ cup fino sherry

30ml/2 tbsp chopped fresh parsley

new potatoes, boiled and buttered, to serve (optional)

FROM THE STORECUPBOARD

60ml/4 tbsp olive oil

30ml/2 tbsp plain (all-purpose) flour

15ml/1 tbsp tomato purée (paste)

salt and ground black pepper, to taste

COOK'S TIP

Kidneys are packed with goodness as well as flavour, and are extremely good value for money. Look for ones that are firm, with a rich, even colour. Avoid those with dry spots or a dull surface. Always remove the fatty core before cooking.

Energy 542kcal/2246kJ; Protein 26g; Carbohydrate 1.1g, of which sugars 1g; Fat 48.3g, of which saturates 25.1g; Cholesterol 566mg; Calcium 29mg; Fibre 0g; Sodium 609mg

Lamb's Kidneys with Creamy Mustard Sauce ✳

This piquant recipe is simple and flexible, so the exact amounts of any one ingredient are unimportant. It would be suitable as a supper dish for two or four, in which case rice and green salad make a good accompaniment.

SERVES FOUR

1 Skin the kidneys and slice them horizontally. Remove the cores with scissors, and then wash them thoroughly in plenty of cold water. Drain and dry off with kitchen paper.

2 Heat a little butter in a heavy frying pan and gently cook the kidneys in it for a few minute, until cooked as you like them. Remove the kidneys from the pan and keep warm.

3 Add a spoonful of mustard to the pan with the wine, herbs and garlic. Simmer to reduce by about half, then add enough cream to make a smooth sauce.

4 Return the kidneys to their sauce and reheat gently, without cooking any further, or the kidneys will be tough. Serve garnished with parsley, and with rice or a green salad.

4–6 lamb's kidneys

butter, for frying

250ml/8fl oz/1 cup white wine

5ml/1 tsp chopped fresh mixed herbs, such as rosemary, thyme, parsley and chives

1 small garlic clove, crushed

about 30ml/2 tbsp single (light) cream

fresh parsley, to garnish

FROM THE STORECUPBOARD

Dijon mustard or other mild mustard, to taste

salt and ground black pepper, to taste

Energy 138kcal/578kJ; Protein 15.6g; Carbohydrate 0.6g, of which sugars 0.6g; Fat 3.8g, of which saturates 1.7g; Cholesterol 288mg; Calcium 20mg; Fibre 0g; Sodium 140mg

Scrumptious Side Dishes

Side dishes not only add nutritional value to main courses, but they also help more expensive dishes to stretch further, and provide extra flavours, colours and textures. This section contains some simple ideas for using seasonal vegetables, such as Braised Red Cabbage, Radicchio and Chicory Gratin or Baked Winter Squash with Tomatoes, as well as year-round family favourites such as Root Vegetable Mash, Creamed Leeks or Potato and Olive Salad.

Steamed Cauliflower and Broccoli with Breadcrumbs and Eggs ✳

Steamed vegetables are a delicious and extremely healthy accompaniment for any main meal.
Here they are given a tasty twist with the addition of an egg and breadcrumb topping.

SERVES SIX

1 Trim the cauliflower and broccoli and break into medium-sized florets, then place in a steamer over a pan of boiling water and steam for about 12 minutes, or until tender. Alternatively, if you prefer, you can boil the vegetables in a large pan of salted water for 5–7 minutes, until just tender.

2 Drain the vegetables well in a colander (strainer) and transfer to a warmed serving dish.

3 While the vegetables are cooking, make the topping. In a bowl, combine the lemon rind, garlic and breadcrumbs.

4 Finely chop the eggs, add to the bowl and mix into the breadcrumb mixture.

5 Season the mixture with salt and black pepper to taste, then sprinkle the chopped egg mixture over the cooked vegetables and serve immediately.

500g/1¼lb cauliflower and broccoli

finely grated rind of ½ lemon

1 garlic clove, crushed

25g/1oz/½ cup wholegrain breadcrumbs, lightly baked or grilled (broiled) until crisp

2 eggs, hard-boiled and shelled

FROM THE STORECUPBOARD

salt and ground black pepper, to taste

Energy 67kcal/280kJ; Protein 6.2g; Carbohydrate 4.7g, of which sugars 1.4g; Fat 2.7g, of which saturates 0.7g; Cholesterol 63mg; Calcium 62mg; Fibre 2.3g; Sodium 62mg

50g/2oz/^{1}/$_4$ cup butter

4 Little Gem (Bibb) lettuces, halved lengthways

2 bunches spring onions (scallions), trimmed and cut into 5cm/2in lengths

400g/14oz shelled peas (about 1kg/2^1/$_2$lb in pods), or frozen peas, thawed

4 fresh mint sprigs

120ml/4fl oz/^{1}/$_2$ cup chicken or vegetable stock

15ml/1 tbsp chopped fresh mint, to garnish

FROM THE STORECUPBOARD

5ml/1 tsp caster (superfine) sugar

salt and ground black pepper, to taste

Braised Lettuce and Peas with Spring Onions and Mint ✳

This simple recipe is delicious served with steamed or baked fish, or roast duck. You can use fresh or frozen peas, depending on your preference.

SERVES FOUR

VARIATION Fry 115g/4oz chopped pancetta or dry cured streaky (fatty) bacon with 1 small chopped onion in the butter.

COOK'S TIP Frozen peas tend to be much cheaper than fresh peas, and since the peas are frozen very shortly after being picked, they are often fresher too.

1 Gently melt half the butter in a large pan over a low heat. Add the lettuces and spring onions.

2 Turn the vegetables in the butter, then sprinkle in the caster sugar, 2.5ml/^{1}/$_2$ tsp salt and plenty of black pepper. Cover and cook very gently for about 5 minutes, stirring once.

3 Add the peas and mint sprigs. Turn them in the buttery juices and pour in the stock, then cover and cook over a gentle heat for a further 5 minutes. Uncover and increase the heat to reduce the liquid to a few tablespoons.

4 Stir in the remaining butter and adjust the seasoning. Transfer to a warmed serving dish and sprinkle with the chopped mint. Serve immediately.

Energy 191kcal/790kJ; Protein 8g; Carbohydrate 13.3g, of which sugars 4.2g; Fat 12.3g, of which saturates 6.9g; Cholesterol 27mg; Calcium 52mg; Fibre 5.7g; Sodium 81mg

Stir-fried Brussels Sprouts with Bacon ✳

This is a great way of cooking Brussels sprouts, helping to retain their sweet flavour and crunchy texture. Stir-frying guarantees that there will not be a single soggy sprout.

SERVES FOUR

1 Using a sharp knife, carefully cut all the Brussels sprouts into fine shreds.

2 Heat the oil in a wok or large frying pan. Add the shredded sprouts and turn quickly over the heat, season to taste with salt and ground black pepper, then remove and set aside.

3 Use the the same wok or pan to cook the chopped bacon. Stir-fry for 1–2 minutes until golden.

4 Return the seasoned sprouts to the pan containing the bacon and stir in the caraway seeds. Cook for a further 1–2 minutes, then serve immediately.

450g/1lb Brussels sprouts, trimmed and washed

2 streaky (fatty) bacon rashers (strips), finely chopped

FROM THE STORECUPBOARD

30ml/2 tbsp sunflower oil

10ml/2 tsp caraway seeds, lightly crushed

salt and ground black pepper, to taste

Energy 131kcal/545kJ; Protein 5.9g; Carbohydrate 4.6g, of which sugars 3.5g; Fat 10g, of which saturates 2g; Cholesterol 8mg; Calcium 30mg; Fibre 4.6g; Sodium 164mg

Braised Cabbage with Chorizo ✳

Salty, flavoursome chorizo really complements the subtle flavour of the cabbage in this simple braised cabbage dish. Serve as an accompaniment to simply grilled meat, chicken or fish.

SERVES FOUR

50g/2oz/¹/₄ cup butter

225g/8oz green cabbage, shredded

2 garlic cloves, finely chopped

50g/2oz cured chorizo sausage, roughly chopped

60ml/4 tbsp dry sherry or white wine

FROM THE STORECUPBOARD

5ml/1 tsp coriander seeds

salt and ground black pepper, to taste

1 Gently melt the butter in a frying pan over a low heat, add the coriander seeds and cook for 1 minute, until they start to give off an aroma.

2 Add the shredded cabbage to the frying pan with the chopped garlic and chorizo. Stir-fry over a high heat for about 5 minutes, until the cabbage is tender.

3 Add the sherry or wine and plenty of salt and pepper to the frying pan. Cover the pan and cook for 15–20 minutes, until the cabbage is tender.

4 Taste to check the seasoning. Adjust if necessary, then transfer to a serving dish and serve immediately.

VARIATION *Smoked bacon makes a good substitute for chorizo sausage in this recipe, but it should only be cooked briefly.*

COOK'S TIP *There two main categories of chorizo: red chorizo, which require cooking; and cured chorizo, which can be eaten raw or cooked.*

Energy 163kcal/673kJ; Protein 2.1g; Carbohydrate 4.6g, of which sugars 3.3g; Fat 13.4g, of which saturates 7.8g; Cholesterol 32mg; Calcium 37mg; Fibre 1.3g; Sodium 183mg

Wilted Spinach with Rice ✳

Spinach and rice make a very successful combination, and the dill adds its distinctive aniseed flavour to this delicious, easy-to-make dish. Serve it as an accompaniment to fried or grilled fish or chicken.

SERVES FOUR

1 Thoroughly wash the spinach in several changes of water until clean, then drain it in a colander. Shake off the excess water and put the spinach leaves on a board. Shred them coarsely.

2 Heat the olive oil in a large pan and sauté the onion until translucent. Add the spinach and stir for a few minutes to coat it with the oil.

3 As soon as the spinach looks wilted, add the lemon juice and the measured water and bring to the boil.

4 Add the rice and half of the dill, then cover and cook gently for about 10 minutes or until the rice is cooked to your taste. Spoon into a serving dish and sprinkle the sprigs of dill over the top.

675g/1¹/₂ lb fresh spinach, trimmed of any hard stalks

1 large onion, chopped

juice of ¹/₂ lemon

150ml/¹/₄ pint/²/₃ cup water

45ml/3 tbsp chopped fresh dill, plus extra sprigs to garnish

FROM THE STORECUPBOARD

105ml/7 tbsp olive oil

115g/4oz/generous ¹/₂ cup long grain rice

salt and ground black pepper, to taste

Energy 337kcal/1392kJ; Protein 7.5g; Carbohydrate 29.6g, of which sugars 5.3g; Fat 20.8g, of which saturates 2.9g; Cholesterol 0mg; Calcium 305mg; Fibre 4.3g; Sodium 238mg

Spiced Greens ✳

Here is a really good way to enliven your greens, excellent for crunchy cabbages but also good for kale or even Brussels sprout tops. It's a very good way of persuading children to try leafy green vegetables.

SERVES FOUR

1 Remove any tough outer leaves from the cabbage then quarter it and remove the core. Shred the leaves.

2 Pour the groundnut oil into a large pan and as it heats stir in the ginger and garlic. Add the shallots and as the pan becomes hotter add the chillies.

3 Add the greens and toss to mix thoroughly. Cover the pan and reduce the heat to create some steam. Cook, shaking the pan occasionally, for about 3 minutes.

4 Remove the lid and increase the heat in order to dry off the steam, season to taste with salt and ground black pepper and serve immediately.

1 medium cabbage, or the equivalent in quantity of your chosen green vegetable

5ml/1 tsp grated fresh root ginger

2 garlic cloves, grated

2 shallots, finely chopped

2 red chillies, seeded and finely sliced

FROM THE STORECUPBOARD

15ml/1 tbsp groundnut (peanut) oil

salt and ground black pepper, to taste

Energy 77kcal/322kJ; Protein 2.6g; Carbohydrate 9.9g, of which sugars 9.4g; Fat 3.1g, of which saturates 0.5g; Cholesterol 0mg; Calcium 90mg; Fibre 3.9g; Sodium 13mg

Fresh Green Beans with Tomato Sauce ✳

This colourful dish can be served as an appetizer, side dish or light lunch, accompanied by feta cheese and fresh bread. When the beans are tender and the tomatoes sweet, the dish, although simple, has an excellent flavour.

SERVES FOUR

1 If the green beans are very long, cut them in half. Drop them into a bowl of cold water so that they are completely submerged. Leave them to absorb the water for a few minutes.

2 Heat the olive oil in a large pan, add the onion and sauté until translucent. Add the garlic, then, when it becomes aromatic, stir in the potatoes and sauté the mixture for a few minutes.

3 Add the tomatoes and the hot water and cook for 5 minutes. Drain the beans, rinse them and drain again, then add them to the pan with a little salt and pepper to season. Cover and simmer for 30 minutes.

4 Stir in the chopped parsley, with a little more hot water if the mixture looks dry. Cook for 10 minutes more, until the beans are very tender. Serve hot with slices of feta cheese, if you like.

800g/1³⁄₄lb green beans, trimmed

1 large onion, thinly sliced

2 garlic cloves, chopped

2 small potatoes, peeled and chopped into cubes

150ml/¹⁄₄ pint/²⁄₃ cup hot water

45–60ml/3–4 tbsp chopped fresh parsley

slices of feta cheese, to serve (optional)

FROM THE STORECUPBOARD

150ml/¹⁄₄ pint/²⁄₃ cup olive oil

400g/14oz can plum tomatoes, chopped

salt and ground black pepper, to taste

Energy 350kcal/1,448kJ; Protein 6.6g; Carbohydrate 21.9g, of which sugars 13.4g; Fat 26.9g, of which saturates 4g; Cholesterol 0mg; Calcium 121mg; Fibre 7.7g; Sodium 25mg

Slow-cooked Okra with Tomato Sauce ✳

Okra makes a deliciously sweet casserole and, combined with fresh tomatoes, at the height of the summer, it makes a delicious accompaniment to poultry or meat. Serve it hot or at room temperature.

SERVES SIX

1 Cut off the conical head from each okra pod, without cutting into the body of the okra. Remove the black tip at the other end and rinse the pod.

2 Heat the oil in a large, deep pan or sauté pan and fry the onion slices until light golden. Stir in the fresh or canned tomatoes, with the sugar, and salt and pepper to taste. Cook for 5 minutes.

3 Add the okra and shake the pan to distribute them evenly and coat them in the sauce. The okra should be immersed in the sauce, so add a little hot water if necessary.

4 Cook gently for 30–40 minutes, depending on the size of the okra. Shake the pan occasionally, but do not stir. Add the parsley just before serving.

675g/1¹/₂ lb fresh okra

1 large onion, sliced

675g/1¹/₂ lb fresh tomatoes, sliced

30ml/2 tbsp finely chopped flat leaf parsley

FROM THE STORECUPBOARD

150ml/¹/₄ pint/²/₃ cup olive oil

2.5ml/¹/₂ tsp sugar

salt and ground black pepper, to taste

Energy 326kcal/1,350kJ; Protein 6.5g; Carbohydrate 14.8g, of which sugars 12.8g; Fat 27.3g, of which saturates 4.3g; Cholesterol 0mg; Calcium 295mg; Fibre 9.1g; Sodium 30mg

Creamed Leeks ✳

This dish is delicious with a full roast dinner, or even served on its own with some bread as a light lunch or snack. It is very important to use fresh, firm leeks or they may become flaccid with cooking.

SERVES FOUR

1 Split the leeks down the middle then cut across so you make pieces approximately 2cm/³⁄₄in square. Wash thoroughly and drain in a colander.

2 Melt the butter in a large pan, then add the leeks, stirring to coat them in the butter, and heat through. They will wilt but should not exude water. Keep the heat high but don't allow them to colour. You need to create a balance between keeping the temperature high so the water steams out of the vegetable, keeping the leeks bright green, whilst not burning them.

3 Pour in the cream, mix in and allow to bubble and reduce. Season to taste with salt and ground black pepper. When the texture is smooth, thick and creamy the leeks are ready to serve.

2 leeks, tops trimmed and roots removed

50g/2oz/¹⁄₄ cup butter

200ml/7fl oz/scant 1 cup double (heavy) cream

FROM THE STORECUPBOARD

salt and ground black pepper, to taste

Energy 363kcal/1496kJ; Protein 2.5g; Carbohydrate 3.8g, of which sugars 3.1g; Fat 37.6g, of which saturates 23.3g; Cholesterol 95mg; Calcium 51mg; Fibre 2.2g; Sodium 89mg

Baked Tomatoes with Mint ✳

This is a dish for the height of the summer when the tomatoes are falling off the vines and are very ripe, juicy and full of flavour. Mint makes an ideal partner to the tomatoes, and the fresh flavour cuts through the rich, creamy sauce. This tomato dish goes especially well with lamb.

SERVES FOUR

1 Preheat the oven to 220°C/425°F/Gas 7. Bring a pan of water to the boil and have a bowl of iced water ready. Cut the cores out of the tomatoes and make a cross at the base. Plunge the tomatoes into the boiling water for 10 seconds and then straight into the iced water. Leave to cool completely.

2 Put the cream and mint in a pan and bring to the boil. Reduce the heat and allow to simmer until it has reduced by about half.

3 Peel the cooled tomatoes and slice them thinly. Brush a shallow gratin dish lightly with a little olive oil. Layer the sliced tomatoes in the dish, overlapping slightly, and season to taste with salt and pepper. Sprinkle a little sugar over the top.

4 Strain the reduced cream evenly over the top of the tomatoes. Sprinkle on the cheese and bake in the preheated oven for 15 minutes, or until the top is browned and bubbling. Serve immediately in the gratin dish.

6 large ripe tomatoes

300ml/¹/₂ pint/1¹/₄ cups double (heavy) cream

2 sprigs of fresh mint

30ml/2 tbsp grated hard goat's cheese

FROM THE STORECUPBOARD

olive oil, for brushing

a few pinches of caster (superfine) sugar

salt and ground black pepper, to taste

Energy 443kcal/1831kJ; Protein 5g; Carbohydrate 6.7g, of which sugars 6.7g; Fat 44.1g, of which saturates 27.4g; Cholesterol 113mg; Calcium 123mg; Fibre 1.8g; Sodium 105mg

Onion Cake ✳

Serve this simple but delicious dish with sausages, lamb chops or any roasted meat. The cooking time will depend on the potatoes and how thinly they are sliced: use a food processor or mandolin (if you have one) to make paper-thin slices. The mound of potatoes will cook down to make a buttery cake.

SERVES SIX

1 Preheat the oven to 190°C/375°F/Gas 5. Lightly butter a 20cm/8in round cake tin (pan) and line the base with a circle of baking parchment.

2 Arrange some of the potato slices evenly in the bottom of the tin and then sprinkle some of the onions over them. Season to taste with salt and pepper. Reserve 25g/1oz/2 tbsp of the butter and dot the mixture with tiny pieces of the remaining butter.

3 Repeat these layers, using up all the ingredients and finishing with a layer of potatoes. Melt the reserved butter and brush it over the top.

4 Cover the potatoes with foil, put in the hot oven and cook for 1–1¹/₂ hours, until tender and golden. Remove from the oven and leave to stand, still covered, for 10–15 minutes.

5 Carefully turn out the onion cake on to a warmed serving plate and serve immediately.

900g/2lb new potatoes, peeled and thinly sliced

2 medium onions, very finely chopped

115g/4oz/¹/₂ cup butter

FROM THE STORECUPBOARD

salt and ground black pepper, to taste

COOK'S TIP *If using old potatoes, cook in an earthenware or ovenproof dish. Remove the cover for the final 10–15 minutes to lightly brown the top.*

Energy 272kcal/1133kJ; Protein 3.5g; Carbohydrate 29.5g, of which sugars 5.8g; Fat 16.3g, of which saturates 10.1g; Cholesterol 41mg; Calcium 29mg; Fibre 2.4g; Sodium 135mg

Braised Red Cabbage ✳

Cook this very economical, vibrantly coloured dish in the oven at the same time as a pork casserole or joint of meat for a simple, easy-to-prepare meal that is perfect for a cold winter day.

SERVES EIGHT

1 Cut the red cabbage into fine shreds, discarding any tough outer leaves and the core, and place in an ovenproof dish.

2 Thinly slice the onion, then fry in the olive oil in a frying pan until the onion is soft and golden.

3 Preheat the oven to 190°C/375°F/Gas 5. Peel, core and slice the apples, and peel and coarsely grate the beetroot.

4 Stir the apple slices, vegetable stock and red wine vinegar into the onions, then transfer to the ovenproof dish.

5 Season with salt and pepper to taste, and cover. Put the dish in the preheated oven and cook for 1 hour. Stir in the beetroot, re-cover the dish and cook for a further 20–30 minutes, or until the cabbage and beetroot are tender.

6 Serve immediately with a roasted joint of meat or a casserole, or on its own with plenty of creamy mashed potatoes.

675g/1¹/₂lb red cabbage

1 onion

2 tart eating apples

375g/13oz raw beetroot (beet)

FROM THE STORECUPBOARD

30ml/2 tbsp olive oil

300ml/¹/₂ pint/1¹/₄ cups vegetable stock

60ml/4 tbsp red wine vinegar

salt and ground black pepper, to taste

Energy 74kcal/309kJ; Protein 2.1g; Carbohydrate 10g, of which sugars 9.5g; Fat 3g, of which saturates 0.4g; Cholesterol 0mg; Calcium 53mg; Fibre 3.1g; Sodium 38mg

Radicchio and Chicory Gratin ✳

Baking seasonal salad vegetables in a creamy sauce creates a dish that is wholesome, warming and sustaining. It is delicious served with grilled meat or fish, or with a bean or lentil casserole.

SERVES FOUR

1 Preheat the oven to 180°C/350°F/Gas 4. Grease a 1.2 litre/2 pint/5 cup ovenproof dish and arrange the radicchio and chicory in it.

2 Sprinkle over the sun-dried tomatoes and brush the vegetables with oil from the jar.

3 Season to taste and cover with foil. Bake for 15 minutes, then uncover and bake for a further 10 minutes.

4 To make the sauce, place the butter in a small pan and melt over a medium heat. When it is foaming, add the flour and cook for 1 minute, stirring.

5 Remove from the heat and gradually add the milk, whisking all the time until smooth.

6 Return to the heat and bring to the boil, then simmer for 3 minutes to thicken. Season to taste and add the nutmeg.

7 Pour the sauce over the vegetables and sprinkle with the cheese. Bake for about 20 minutes. Serve immediately.

2 heads radicchio, quartered lengthways

2 heads chicory (Belgian endive), quartered lengthways

25g/1oz/1/2 cup drained sun-dried tomatoes in oil, coarsely chopped

25g/1oz/2 tbsp butter

250ml/8fl oz/1 cup milk

50g/2oz/1/2 cup grated Emmenthal cheese

FROM THE STORECUPBOARD

15g/1/2oz/2 tbsp plain (all-purpose) flour

pinch of freshly grated nutmeg

salt and ground black pepper, to taste

VARIATION
You could use fennel in place of the radicchio and chicory. Par-boil the fennel before putting it in the ovenproof dish, then continue as in the recipe.

Energy 159kcal/662kJ; Protein 6.3g; Carbohydrate 8g, of which sugars 4.4g; Fat 11.6g, of which saturates 6.9g; Cholesterol 29mg; Calcium 196mg; Fibre 1g; Sodium 158mg

Baked Winter Squash with Tomatoes ✳

Acorn, butternut or Hubbard squash can all be used in this simple recipe. Serve the squash as a light main course, with warm crusty bread, or as a side dish for grilled meat or poultry.

SERVES SIX

1 Preheat the oven to 160°C/325°F/Gas 3. Heat the oil in a large frying pan and cook the pumpkin or squash slices, in batches, until they are golden brown. Remove them from the pan and set them aside as they are cooked.

2 Add the tomatoes to the pan and cook over a medium-high heat for 10 minutes, or until the mixture is of a thick sauce consistency. Stir in the rosemary and season to taste with salt and ground black pepper.

3 Layer the pumpkin slices and tomatoes in an ovenproof dish, ending with a layer of tomatoes.

4 Bake for 35 minutes, or until the top is lightly glazed and beginning to turn golden brown, and the pumpkin is tender. Serve immediately.

1kg/2¹⁄₄lb pumpkin or orange winter squash, peeled and sliced

2–3 fresh rosemary sprigs, stems removed and leaves chopped

FROM THE STORECUPBOARD

45ml/3 tbsp garlic-flavoured olive oil

2 x 400g/14oz cans chopped tomatoes

salt and ground black pepper, to taste

Energy 94kcal/392kJ; Protein 2.1g; Carbohydrate 7.8g, of which sugars 7g; Fat 6.2g, of which saturates 1.1g; Cholesterol 0mg; Calcium 58mg; Fibre 3g; Sodium 12mg

Spiced Roasted Pumpkin ✳

In this delicious dish, chunks of pumpkin are roasted with spices and herbs and topped with cheese. It makes a good accompaniment to roast meats, sausages or lamb chops, or serve with watercress for a light lunch.

SERVES THREE–FOUR

1 Preheat the oven to 200°C/400°F/Gas 6. Lightly crush or bruise the fennel seeds with a mortar and pestle.

2 Put the oil into a large bowl and stir in the fennel, garlic, ginger, thyme and chilli, if using. Season and mix well.

3 Cut the skin off the pumpkin, scrape out and discard the seeds. Cut the flesh into rough chunks of about 2.5cm/1in.

4 Toss the chunks in the oil until evenly coated, then spread them in a single layer on a large baking tray. Cook for 40 minutes, or until tender and golden brown on the edges.

5 Sprinkle the cheese over the top and return to the oven for 5 more minutes. Serve straight from the baking tray, making sure all the bits of cheese are scraped up with the pumpkin.

1 garlic clove, crushed

piece of pumpkin weighing about 1.5kg/3lb 6oz

75g/3oz/³/₄ cup cheese, such as Caerphilly or mature (sharp) Cheddar cheese, grated

FROM THE STORECUPBOARD

5ml/1 tsp fennel seeds

30ml/2 tbsp olive oil

5ml/1 tsp ground ginger

5ml/1 tsp dried thyme

pinch of chilli powder (optional)

salt and ground black pepper, to taste

Energy 171kcal/712kJ; Protein 7.1g; Carbohydrate 8.3g, of which sugars 6.4g; Fat 12g, of which saturates 5g; Cholesterol 17mg; Calcium 238mg; Fibre 3.8g; Sodium 127mg

Carrot and Parsnip Purée ✳

Carrots and parsnips are good value, flavoursome and popular winter vegetables. The combination of the two works well together in this simple side dish, which is an ideal accompaniment to grilled (broiled) meats.

SERVES FOUR

1 Peel the carrots and slice them fairly thinly. Peel the parsnips and cut into bitesize chunks (they are softer and will cook more quickly than the carrots). Boil the two vegetables, separately, in lightly salted water, until tender.

2 Drain them well and put them through a mouli-légumes (food mill) or food processor with the grated nutmeg, a good seasoning of salt and ground black pepper, and the butter. Purée together and taste for seasoning.

3 If you like, blend in some single cream to taste, and add chopped parsley for extra flavour. Transfer the purée to a warmed serving bowl, sprinkle with freshly chopped parsley to garnish and serve immediately.

350g/12oz carrots

450g/1lb parsnips

15g/¹/₂oz/1 tbsp butter

about 15ml/1 tbsp single (light) cream (optional)

1 small bunch parsley leaves, chopped (optional), plus extra to garnish

FROM THE STORECUPBOARD

pinch of grated nutmeg

salt and ground black pepper, to taste

COOK'S TIP *Any leftover purée can be thinned to taste with good-quality chicken stock and heated to make a quick home-made soup.*

Energy 92kcal/385kJ; Protein 1.8g; Carbohydrate 14.1g, of which sugars 8.7g; Fat 3.5g, of which saturates 1.8g; Cholesterol 7mg; Calcium 48mg; Fibre 4.9g; Sodium 38mg

Root Vegetable Mash ✳

This root vegetable dish is excellent with sausages or on top of shepherd's pie in place of just potato. Turnips give an earthy flavour, and swede introduces a sweet accent. It is also slightly less heavy than mashed potato, which makes it ideal for a lighter meal or supper.

SERVES FOUR

1 Chop the potatoes and turnips or swede into chunks. Place in a pan and cover with cold water. Bring to the boil over a medium heat, then reduce the heat and simmer until both vegetables are cooked, which will take about 15–20 minutes. Test the vegetables by pushing the point of a sharp knife into one of the cubes; if it goes in easily and the cube begins to break apart, then it is cooked.

2 Drain the vegetables in a colander. Return to the pan and allow them to dry out for a few minutes over a low heat, stirring occasionally to prevent any from sticking to the base of the pan.

3 Melt the butter with the milk in a small pan over a low heat. Mash the potato mixture, then add the milk mixture.

4 Grate in the nutmeg, add the parsley, mix thoroughly and season to taste. Serve immediately with roast meat or game.

450g/1lb potatoes, peeled

450g/1lb turnips or swede (rutabaga), peeled

50g/2oz/$^1/_4$ cup butter

50ml/2fl oz/$^1/_4$ cup milk

30ml/2 tbsp chopped fresh parsley

FROM THE STORECUPBOARD

5ml/1 tsp freshly grated nutmeg

salt and ground black pepper, to taste

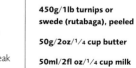

Energy 204kcal/852kJ; Protein 3.4g; Carbohydrate 24.1g, of which sugars 7.2g; Fat 11.2g, of which saturates 6.8g; Cholesterol 27mg; Calcium 78mg; Fibre 3.8g; Sodium 111mg

Mashed Potato with Cabbage ✳

This is versatile side dish makes a welcome change to standard mashed potatoes, and is a good way to encourage children to eat leafy greens. Since the cabbage is stir-fried rather than boiled or steamed, it retains more of its goodness and has a more interesting texture.

SERVES FOUR

1 Peel and chop the potatoes, then place in boiling water and boil for 15–20 minutes, until tender.

2 Return the potatoes to the pan and allow them to dry out for a few minutes over a low heat, stirring occasionally to prevent any from sticking to the base of the pan.

3 Melt the butter with the milk in a small pan over a low heat. Mash the potato mixture, then add the milk mixture.

4 Heat the olive oil in a large frying pan, add the shredded cabbage and fry for a few minutes.

5 Season to taste with salt and ground black pepper. Add the mashed potato to the cabbage, mix well then stir in the cream. Serve immediately.

450g/1lb potatoes, peeled and chopped

50g/2oz/¹/₄ cup butter

50ml/2fl oz/¹/₄ cup milk

450g/1lb cabbage, washed and finely shredded

50ml/2fl oz/¹/₄ cup double (heavy) cream

FROM THE STORECUPBOARD

30ml/2 tbsp olive oil

salt and ground black pepper, to taste

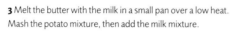
Energy 183kcal/766kJ; Protein 3.9g; Carbohydrate 24g, of which sugars 7.3g; Fat 8.5g, of which saturates 2.4g; Cholesterol 7mg; Calcium 73mg; Fibre 3.5g; Sodium 24mg

Simple Pan-fried Potatoes and Onions *

This dish uses left-over cooked potatoes that have been boiled in their skins. It makes a tasty accompaniment to grilled meat or fish or as a light meal.

SERVES FOUR–SIX

1 Slice the peeled onions in half, then cut them into crescents across the grain.

2 Put the onions in a large pan and scald them briefly in boiling water. Refresh under cold water and drain well. Peel and thinly slice the potatoes.

3 Put the butter and oil into a large, heavy frying pan and heat well. When the fat is hot, fry the onion until tender.

4 Add the potato slices and brown them together, turning the potato slices to brown as evenly as possible on both sides.

5 Transfer to a warmed serving dish and season to taste with salt and pepper. Serve very hot.

2 onions, peeled

450–675g/1–1¹/₂ lb whole cooked potatoes, boiled in their skins

15g/¹/₂oz/1 tbsp butter

FROM THE STORECUPBOARD

15ml/1 tbsp oil, for shallow frying

salt and ground black pepper, to taste

Energy 163kcal/681kJ; Protein 3.4g; Carbohydrate 26.4g, of which sugars 5g; Fat 5.5g, of which saturates 3.3g; Cholesterol 13mg; Calcium 26mg; Fibre 2.6g; Sodium 49mg

Roasted Potatoes, Peppers and Shallots ✳

These potatoes soak up both the taste and wonderful aromas of the shallots and rosemary – just wait till you open the oven door.

SERVES FOUR

1 Preheat the oven to 200°C/400°F/Gas 6. Par-boil the potatoes in their skins, then drain and leave to cool. Peel and cut in half. Peel the shallots, and cut each pepper lengthways into eight strips, discarding the seeds and pith.

2 Oil a shallow ovenproof dish. Arrange the potatoes and peppers in alternating rows and stud with the shallots.

3 Cut the rosemary sprigs into 5cm/2in lengths and tuck among the vegetables. Season, pour over the olive oil and roast, uncovered, for 30–40 minutes until all the vegetables are tender. Turn the vegetables occasionally to brown evenly. Serve hot or at room temperature, with crushed peppercorns.

500g/1¹/₄lb waxy potatoes

12 shallots

2 yellow (bell) peppers

2 rosemary sprigs

FROM THE STORECUPBOARD

olive oil, for drizzling

crushed black peppercorns, to garnish

salt and ground black pepper, to taste

Energy 192kcal/806kJ; Protein 3.9g; Carbohydrate 31.7g, of which sugars 11.2g; Fat 6.4g, of which saturates 1g; Cholesterol 0mg; Calcium 33mg; Fibre 3.7g; Sodium 20mg

Potatoes and Parsnips Baked with Garlic and Cream ✳

This creamy, flavoursome baked dish is the ideal accompaniment to any number of main course dishes and is particularly good during the winter months. As the potatoes and parsnips cook, they gradually absorb the garlic-flavoured cream, while the cheese browns to a crispy finish. You could use sweet potatoes or other root vegetables, such as carrots, swede (rutabaga) or turnips in place of the standard potatoes.

SERVES FOUR–SIX

1 Peel the potatoes and parsnips and cut them into thin slices using a sharp knife. Place them in a steamer and cook for 5 minutes. Leave to cool slightly.

2 Meanwhile, pour the cream and milk into a medium, heavy pan, add the crushed garlic and bring to the boil over a medium heat.

3 Remove the pan from the heat and leave to stand at room temperature for about 10 minutes to allow the flavour of the garlic to infuse into the cream and milk mixture.

4 Lightly grease a 25cm/10in long, shallow rectangular earthenware baking dish with butter or oil. Preheat the oven to 180°C/350°F/Gas 4.

5 Arrange the thinly sliced potatoes and parsnips in layers in the greased earthenware dish, sprinkling each layer of vegetables with a little freshly grated nutmeg, a little salt and plenty of ground black pepper.

6 Pour the infused cream and milk mixture into the dish and then press the sliced potatoes and parsnips down into the liquid. The liquid should come to just underneath the top layer of vegetables.

7 Cover the dish with a piece of lightly buttered foil or baking parchment and bake in the oven for 45 minutes.

8 Remove the dish from the oven and remove the foil or paper from the dish. Sprinkle the grated Cheddar cheese over the vegetables in an even layer.

9 Return the dish to the oven and bake uncovered for a further 20–30 minutes, or until the potatoes and parsnips are tender (see Cook's Tip) and the topping is golden brown.

3 large potatoes, total weight about 675g/1¹/₂lb

350g/12oz small– medium parsnips

200ml/7fl oz/scant 1 cup single (light) cream

105ml/7 tbsp milk

2 garlic cloves, crushed

butter or olive oil, for greasing

75g/3oz/³/₄ cup coarsely grated Cheddar cheese

FROM THE STORECUPBOARD

about 5ml/1 tsp freshly grated nutmeg

salt and ground black pepper, to taste

COOK'S TIPS

• *If you have one, use a mandolin or food processor fitted with a slicing blade to slice the potatoes and parsnips thinly and evenly.*

• *To test if the vegetables are tender, insert a knife through the middle. The knife should slide in easily, and the vegetables should feel soft. If not, give them a few more minutes.*

Energy 1443kcal/6055kJ; Protein 47g; Carbohydrate 161.8g, of which sugars 38.1g; Fat 70.4g, of which saturates 43.1g; Cholesterol 189mg; Calcium 1042mg; Fibre 22.8g; Sodium 755mg

Mixed Green Leaf and Fresh Herb Salad ✳

This flavourful salad makes an ideal side dish that goes well with meat and fish. You could turn it into a more substantial dish for a light lunch by adding some cooked asparagus tips and pitted green olives.

SERVES FOUR

1 Wash and dry the herbs and salad leaves in a salad spinner, or use two clean, dry dish towels to pat them dry.

2 To make the dressing, blend together the olive oil and cider vinegar in a small bowl and season with salt and ground black pepper to taste.

3 Place the prepared mixed herbs and salad leaves in a large salad bowl.

4 Just before serving, pour over the dressing and toss thoroughly to mix well, using your hands. Serve immediately.

15g/¹/₂oz/¹/₂ cup mixed fresh herbs, such as chervil, tarragon (use sparingly), dill, basil, marjoram (use sparingly), flat leaf parsley, mint, sorrel, fennel and coriander (cilantro)

350g/12oz mixed salad leaves, such as rocket (arugula), radicchio, chicory (Belgian endive), watercress, frisée, baby spinach, oakleaf lettuce and dandelion

FROM THE STORECUPBOARD

50ml/2fl oz/¹/₄ cup extra virgin olive oil

15ml/1 tbsp cider vinegar

salt and ground black pepper, to taste

Energy 92kcal/377kJ; Protein 0.7g; Carbohydrate 1.6g, of which sugars 1.6g; Fat 9.2g, of which saturates 1.4g; Cholesterol 0mg; Calcium 26mg; Fibre 0.8g; Sodium 3mg

Baby Spinach and Roast Garlic Salad ✳

Tender young spinach leaves are packed with flavour and goodness. Here they are combined with sweet roasted garlic, crunchy pine nuts and zesty lemon juice to create a healthy and delicious side dish.

SERVES FOUR

1 Preheat the oven to 190°C/375°F/Gas 5. Place the unpeeled garlic cloves in a small roasting pan, drizzle over 30ml/2 tbsp of the olive oil and toss to coat. Bake the garlic cloves for about 15 minutes until the skins are slightly charred.

2 Place the garlic cloves, still in their skins, in a salad bowl. Add the spinach, pine nuts, lemon juice and remaining olive oil. Toss well to mix thoroughly, and season with plenty of salt and ground black pepper to taste.

3 Serve immediately, gently squeezing the softened garlic purée out of the skins to eat.

12 garlic cloves, unpeeled

450g/1lb baby spinach leaves

50g/2oz/$^1/_2$ cup pine nuts, lightly toasted

juice of $^1/_2$ lemon

FROM THE STORECUPBOARD

60ml/4 tbsp olive oil

salt and ground black pepper, to taste

Energy 238kcal/980kJ; Protein 6.9g; Carbohydrate 6.4g, of which sugars 2.6g; Fat 20.6g, of which saturates 2.3g; Cholesterol 0mg; Calcium 198mg; Fibre 3.6g; Sodium 159mg

Cucumber and Shallot Salad ✳

This light, refreshing cucumber salad makes a good alternative to cooling, mint-flavoured raita when you eat Indian food. It is also good with spicy fish and grilled meat dishes. It can be made ahead of time and kept in the refrigerator. Serve it as a salad, or a relish.

SERVES FOUR

1 Slice the cucumber halves finely, place in a sieve (strainer) and sprinkle with salt. Set aside for about 15 minutes. Rinse well under cold running water, then drain off any excess water.

2 Put the cucumber, shallots and chillies in a bowl. Pour in the coconut milk and toss well. Sprinkle most of the roasted cumin over the top.

3 Just before serving, toss the salad again, season with salt and sprinkle the rest of the cumin over the top. Serve immediately with juicy lime wedges to squeeze over the salad.

1 cucumber, peeled, halved lengthways and seeded

4 shallots, halved lengthways and sliced finely along the grain

1–2 green chillies, seeded and sliced finely lengthways

60ml/4 tbsp coconut milk

1 lime, quartered, to serve

FROM THE STORECUPBOARD

5–10ml/1–2 tsp cumin seeds, dry-roasted and ground to a powder

salt, to taste

Energy 17kcal/68kJ; Protein 0.7g; Carbohydrate 3.3g, of which sugars 2.7g; Fat 0.1g, of which saturates 0g; Cholesterol 0mg; Calcium 19mg; Fibre 0.7g; Sodium 15mg

Celery and Coconut Salad ✳

Juicy and refreshing, this unusual salad is perfect on a hot sunny day as part of a buffet spread outdoors, or as an accompaniment to grilled, broiled or barbecued meats and spicy dishes. It looks especially appealing served in coconut shell halves, so take care when splitting the shell.

SERVES THREE–FOUR

1 Mix the yogurt and garlic in a small bowl, add the lime rind and juice and season to taste with salt and pepper.

2 Fold in the grated celery and coconut, then set aside and leave for 15–20 minutes to let the celery juices weep. Don't leave it for too long or it will become watery.

3 To serve, spoon the salad into a bowl and garnish with celery and parsley. Serve immediately.

45–60ml/3–4 tbsp thick and creamy natural (plain) yogurt

2 garlic cloves, crushed

5ml/1 tsp grated lime rind

juice of 1 lime

8 long celery sticks, grated (leaves reserved for the garnish)

flesh of 1/2 fresh coconut, grated

a few sprigs of fresh flat leaf parsley, to garnish

FROM THE STORECUPBOARD

salt and ground black pepper, to taste

Energy 126kcal/521kJ; Protein 2.1g; Carbohydrate 2.9g, of which sugars 2.9g; Fat 11.9g, of which saturates 10.1g; Cholesterol 0mg; Calcium 63mg; Fibre 3.6g; Sodium 69mg

Turnip Salad in Sour Cream ✳

Usually served cooked, raw young tender turnips have a tangy, slightly peppery flavour and a crunchy texture. Serve this as an accompaniment for grilled poultry or meat. It is also delicious as an appetizer, garnished with parsley and paprika, and served with warmed flat breads such as pitta or naan. Garnish the salad with fresh flat leaf parsley and paprika, if you like.

SERVES FOUR

1 Thinly slice or coarsely grate the turnips. Alternatively, slice half the turnips and grate the remaining half. Put in a bowl.

2 Add the onion and vinegar and season to taste with salt and plenty of freshly ground black pepper. Toss together, then stir in the sour cream. Chill well before serving.

VARIATIONS
• You can use large white radishes instead of turnips for a more peppery flavour. Simply peel, then thinly slice or coarsely grate the radishes.

• Crème fraîche or natural (plain) yogurt can be substituted for the sour cream, if you prefer.

2–4 young, tender turnips, peeled

¹/₄–¹/₂ onion, finely chopped

60–90ml/4–6 tbsp sour cream

FROM THE STORECUPBOARD

2–3 drops white wine vinegar, or to taste

Energy 48kcal/198kJ; Protein 1.1g; Carbohydrate 4.1g, of which sugars 3.7g; Fat 3.2g, of which saturates 1.9g; Cholesterol 9mg; Calcium 42mg; Fibre 1.4g; Sodium 14mg

Potato and Olive Salad ✳

This delicious salad is simple and zesty – the perfect choice for lunch, as an accompaniment, or as an appetizer. Similar in appearance to flat leaf parsley, fresh coriander has a distinctive pungent, almost spicy flavour. It is widely used in India, the Middle and Far East and in eastern Mediterranean countries. If new potatoes are not in season, you can substitute another waxy variety, such as Charlotte potatoes.

SERVES FOUR

1 Cut the new potatoes into chunks. Put them in a pan, pour in water to cover and add a pinch of salt.

2 Bring to the boil, then reduce the heat and cook gently for about 10 minutes, or until the potatoes are just tender.

3 Drain the potatoes well and leave in a colander to dry thoroughly and cool slightly.

4 When they are cool enough to handle, chop the potatoes and put them in a large serving bowl.

5 Drizzle the garlic oil over the potatoes. Toss well and sprinkle with the chopped fresh herbs, and black olives. Chill in the refrigerator for at least 1 hour before serving.

8 large new potatoes

60–90ml/4–6 tbsp chopped fresh herbs, such as coriander (cilantro) and chives

10–15 black olives

FROM THE STORECUPBOARD

45–60ml/3–4 tbsp garlic oil (*see* page 31)

Energy 238kcal/998kJ; Protein 4g; Carbohydrate 32.6g, of which sugars 2.9g; Fat 11.1g, of which saturates 1.7g; Cholesterol 0mg; Calcium 49mg; Fibre 3.2g; Sodium 448mg

Cabbage Salad with Lemon Dressing ✳

Fresh, colourful and appetizing, this simple salad combines very thin shreds of raw cabbage and olives with a zesty lemon and parsley dressing to produce a rather sweet-tasting, unusual salad. It makes a healthier alternative to coleslaw, and can be served with grilled or fried meat, poultry or fish.

SERVES FOUR

1 Cut the cabbage in quarters, discard the outer leaves and trim off any thick, hard stems as well as the hard base.

2 Lay each quarter in turn on its side and cut long, very thin slices until you reach the central core, which should be discarded.

3 Place the shredded cabbage in a large mixing bowl and stir in the black olives.

4 Make the dressing by whisking the extra virgin olive oil, lemon juice, garlic, chopped parsley and salt to taste together in a bowl until well blended.

5 Pour the dressing over the cabbage and olives, and toss the salad until everything is evenly coated.

1 white cabbage

12 black olives

FOR THE DRESSING

30ml/2 tbsp lemon juice

1 garlic clove, crushed

30ml/2 tbsp finely chopped flat leaf parsley

FROM THE STORECUPBOARD

75–90ml/5–6 tbsp extra virgin olive oil

salt, to taste

Energy 208kcal/861kJ; Protein 4g; Carbohydrate 12.9g, of which sugars 12.5g; Fat 15.8g, of which saturates 2.2g; Cholesterol 0mg; Calcium 155mg; Fibre 6.2g; Sodium 303mg

Curried Red Cabbage Slaw ✳

Vibrant and fresh, this stunning, crisp slaw combines red cabbage, red pepper and red onion with a creamy mayonnaise sauce. It is particularly good served with rich meat, such as game or duck.

SERVES FOUR–SIX

1 Put the sliced cabbage, pepper and red onion in a large bowl and toss to combine.

2 In a small pan, heat the vinegar and sugar until the sugar has dissolved, then pour over the vegetables. Leave to cool slightly.

3 Combine the yogurt and mayonnaise, then mix into the cabbage mixture. Season to taste with curry powder, salt and ground black pepper, then mix in the raisins.

4 Chill the salad in the refrigerator before serving, if you have time. Just before serving, drain off any excess liquid and briefly stir the slaw again.

¹/₂ red cabbage, very thinly sliced

1 red (bell) pepper, very thinly sliced

¹/₂ red onion, chopped

120ml/4fl oz/¹/₂ cup Greek (US strained plain) yogurt

120ml/4fl oz/¹/₂ cup mayonnaise

2–3 handfuls raisins

FROM THE STORECUPBOARD

60ml/4 tbsp red or white wine vinegar or cider vinegar

60ml/4 tbsp sugar

1.5ml/¹/₄ tsp curry powder

salt and ground black pepper, to taste

Energy 272kcal/1136kJ; Protein 3g; Carbohydrate 27.9g, of which sugars 27.5g; Fat 17.5g, of which saturates 3.4g; Cholesterol 15mg; Calcium 74mg; Fibre 2g; Sodium 120mg

Beetroot with Lemon ✳

With its distinctive, vibrant colour and earthy taste, fresh beetroot is packed with fibre as well as flavour. Served with a simple lemon and oil dressing, it makes a simple accompaniment to meat dishes.

SERVES FOUR

1 Twist off the tops from the beetroot using your fingers, rather than slicing them off with a knife.

2 Put the beetroot in a large pan of salted boiling water and cook for about 30 minutes, or until the beetroot is tender. Pinch the skin between two fingers: when cooked, the skin will come away easily. Drain the beetroot and allow it to cool.

3 When the beetroot are cool enough to handle, peel them and slice into wedges.

4 Put in a large bowl. Add the lemon rind and juice, and the oil, then season to taste with salt and ground black pepper. Mix gently in the dressing and serve immediately.

450g/1lb evenly-sized raw beetroot (beets)

grated rind and juice of 1/2 lemon

chopped fresh chives, to garnish (optional)

FROM THE STORECUPBOARD

about 150ml/1/4 pint/ 2/3 cup extra virgin olive oil

salt and ground black pepper, to taste

Energy 265kcal/1097kJ; Protein 1.9g; Carbohydrate 8.6g, of which sugars 7.9g; Fat 25.1g, of which saturates 3.6g; Cholesterol 0mg; Calcium 23mg; Fibre 2.2g; Sodium 74mg

Grated Beetroot and Yogurt Salad ✳

Spiked with garlic and a pretty shade of pink, this colourful and unusual salad makes a simple yet delicious appetizer scooped on to flatbread or chunks of a warm, crusty loaf. It can also be served as an accompaniment to roasted, grilled or fried meat, poultry and fish.

SERVES FOUR

4 raw beetroot (beets), washed and trimmed

500g/1¹/₄ lb/2¹/₄ cups thick and creamy natural (plain) yogurt

2 garlic cloves, crushed

a few fresh mint leaves, shredded, to garnish

FROM THE STORECUPBOARD

salt and ground black pepper, to taste

1 Put the beetroot in a large pan of salted boiling water and cook for about 30 minutes, or until the beetroot is tender, but not mushy or soft.

2 Drain and refresh under cold running water, then peel off the skins and grate the beetroot on to a plate. Squeeze it lightly with your fingers to drain off excess water.

3 In a bowl, beat the yogurt with the garlic and season to taste with salt and pepper.

4 Add the beetroot to the yogurt mixture, reserving a little to garnish the top, and mix well to combine. Garnish with mint leaves and serve immediately.

VARIATIONS

• To make a carrot version of this dish, cut four carrots into bitesize chunks and steam for about 15 minutes, until they are tender but still with some bite. Leave to cool slightly, then grate and mix with the yogurt and garlic. Season to taste with salt and pepper and garnish with fresh mint or dill.

• To make warm beetroot salad, dice the beetroot and put it in a pan with coriander seeds, sugar and a splash of apple vinegar. Stir-fry for about 5 minutes, until the beetroot is tender, then serve warm with the cooling garlic-flavoured yogurt and garnished with dill.

• For a lower-fat version, use fat-free yogurt.

Energy 95kcal/403kJ; Protein 7.8g; Carbohydrate 14.4g, of which sugars 13g; Fat 1.4g, of which saturates 0.6g; Cholesterol 2mg; Calcium 249mg; Fibre 1.3g; Sodium 137mg

Delectable Desserts

Home-made desserts make an impressive and irresistible end to a meal, and with a wealth of hot and cold ones to choose from, there is something for every taste, whatever the weather. Decadent, rich treats include Coffee and Ginger Pudding, Plum Crumble and Boston Banoffee Pie, or for something a bit lighter have a go at making Lemon Posset, Blackcurrant Fool or Classic Vanilla Ice Cream.

Moroccan Rice Pudding ✳

This comforting dessert is a simple and delicious alternative to traditional and much-loved rice pudding. In this recipe, the rice is slowly cooked in almond-flavoured milk and flavoured with warming cinnamon.

SERVES SIX

1 Put the almonds in a food processor or blender with 60ml/4 tbsp of very hot water. Process until finely chopped, then push through a sieve (strainer) into a bowl. Return to the food processor or blender, add a further 60ml/4 tbsp hot water, and process again. Push through the sieve into a pan.

2 Add 300ml/$^1/_2$ pint/$1^1/_4$ cups water and bring the mixture to the boil. Add the rice, caster sugar, cinnamon stick, half the butter, the almond essence, half the milk and half the cream, and mix to combine thoroughly.

3 Bring to the boil, then simmer, covered, for about 30 minutes, adding more milk and cream as the rice mixture thickens. Continue to cook the rice, stirring, and adding the remaining milk and cream, until the pudding becomes thick and creamy.

4 At the end of the cooking time, taste the rice pudding for sweetness, adding a little extra sugar, if necessary.

5 Pour the rice pudding into a serving bowl and sprinkle with the toasted flaked almonds. Dot with the remaining butter and dust with a little ground cinnamon. Serve the pudding hot.

25g/1oz/$^1/_4$ cup almonds

50g/2oz/$^1/_4$ cup butter

1.5ml/$^1/_4$ tsp almond essence (extract)

175ml/6fl oz/$^3/_4$ cup milk

175ml/6fl oz/$^3/_4$ cup single (light) cream

toasted flaked (sliced) almonds and ground cinnamon, to decorate

FROM THE STORECUPBOARD

450g/1lb/$2^1/_4$ cups short grain rice

25g/1oz/$^1/_4$ cup caster (superfine) sugar

1 cinnamon stick

COOK'S TIP
There are many different types of rice pudding eaten around the world – from traditional Western puddings served with jam, and Persian ones made with saffron to East Asian versions made with glutinous black rice and Latin American versions made with coconut milk.

VARIATION
To ring the changes, simply add 2 cardamom pods to the milk mixture in step 2, cook them with the rice, then remove before serving.

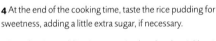

Energy 443kcal/1847kJ; Protein 8.5g; Carbohydrate 66.6g, of which sugars 6.6g; Fat 15.6g, of which saturates 8.4g; Cholesterol 36mg; Calcium 89mg; Fibre 0.3g; Sodium 72mg

Lemon Surpise Pudding ✳

This much-loved dessert is cheap and easy to make, and is perfect for all the family on a cold day. The surprise is the unexpected, rich, tangy sauce that is concealed beneath the delectable light sponge.

SERVES FOUR

1 Preheat the oven to 190°C/375°F/Gas 5. Use a little butter to grease a 1.2 litre/2 pint/5 cup baking dish.

2 Beat the lemon rind, remaining butter and caster sugar in a bowl until pale and fluffy. Add the egg yolks and flour and beat together well. Gradually whisk in the lemon juice and milk (the mixture will curdle, but this is supposed to happen).

3 Fold the egg whites lightly into the lemon mixture using a metal spoon, then pour into the prepared baking dish.

4 Place the dish in a roasting pan and pour in hot water to come halfway up the side of the dish. Bake for 45 minutes until golden. Serve immediately.

50g/2oz/¼ cup butter, plus extra for greasing

grated rind and juice of 2 lemons

2 eggs, separated

300ml/½ pint/1¼ cups milk

FROM THE STORECUPBOARD

115g/4oz/½ cup caster (superfine) sugar

50g/2oz/½ cup self-raising (self-rising) flour

COOK'S TIP *Lemons are often waxed, so you should either buy unwaxed lemons or scrub the peel thoroughly under hot water to remove the wax before grating.*

Energy 320kcal/1346kJ; Protein 7.1g; Carbohydrate 43.4g, of which sugars 33.8g; Fat 14.5g, of which saturates 8.1g; Cholesterol 126mg; Calcium 139mg; Fibre 0.4g; Sodium 145mg

Coffee and Ginger Pudding ✳

This coffee-capped feather-light sponge is made with breadcrumbs and ground almonds. Serve with creamy custard or scoops of vanilla ice cream.

SERVES FOUR

1 Preheat the oven to 180°C/350°F/Gas 4. Grease and line the base of a 750ml/1¼ pint/3 cup ovenproof bowl, then sprinkle in the muscovado sugar and chopped stem ginger.

2 Put the ground coffee in a small, heatproof bowl. Heat the ginger syrup in a small pan, until almost boiling, then pour into the coffee. Stir well and leave for 4 minutes. Pour through a fine sieve (strainer) into the ovenproof bowl.

3 Beat half the sugar with the egg yolks until light and fluffy. Sift the flour and ground ginger together and fold into the egg yolk mixture with the breadcrumbs and ground almonds.

4 Whisk the egg whites until stiff, then gradually whisk in the remaining caster sugar. Fold into the mixture, in two batches. Spoon into the pudding basin and smooth the top.

5 Cover the basin with a piece of pleated greased baking parchment and secure with string. Bake for 40 minutes, or until the sponge is firm to the touch. Turn out and serve immediately.

25g/1oz/2 tbsp preserved stem ginger, chopped, plus 75ml/5 tbsp ginger syrup

30ml/2 tbsp mild-flavoured ground coffee

3 eggs, separated

65g/2½oz/ generous 1 cup fresh white breadcrumbs

25g/1oz/¼ cup ground almonds

FROM THE STORECUPBOARD

30ml/2 tbsp light muscovado (brown) sugar

115g/4oz/generous ½ cup caster (superfine) sugar

25g/1oz/¼ cup plain (all-purpose) flour

5ml/1 tsp ground ginger

Energy 382kcal/1617kJ; Protein 9.7g; Carbohydrate 70.6g, of which sugars 53.5g; Fat 8.9g, of which saturates 1.7g; Cholesterol 171mg; Calcium 93mg; Fibre 1g; Sodium 240mg

Sticky Toffee Pudding ✷✷

Rich, sweet and utterly irresistible, this gooey pudding is sure to be a hit every time you make it. Serve with cream or vanilla ice cream.

SERVES SIX

1 Grease a 900ml/1¹/₂ pint/3³/₄ cup heatproof bowl and put half the nuts in the bottom.

2 Heat 50g/2oz/¹/₄ cup of the butter with 50g/2oz/¹/₄ cup of the sugar, the cream and 15ml/1 tbsp lemon juice in a small pan, stirring until smooth. Pour half into the heatproof bowl, then swirl to coat it a little way up the sides.

3 Beat the remaining butter and sugar until fluffy, then beat in the eggs. Fold in the flour, remaining nuts and lemon juice and spoon into the basin.

4 Cover the bowl with greaseproof (waxed) paper with a pleat folded in the centre, then tie securely with string. Steam the pudding for about 1¹/₄ hours, until a skewer inserted in the centre comes out clean.

5 Just before serving, gently warm the remaining sauce. Unmould the pudding on to a warm plate and pour over the sauce.

115g/4oz/1 cup toasted walnuts, chopped

175g/6oz/³/₄ cup butter

60ml/4 tbsp double (heavy) cream

30ml/2 tbsp lemon juice

2 eggs, beaten

FROM THE STORECUPBOARD

175g/6oz/scant 1 cup light muscovado (brown) sugar

115g/4oz/1 cup self-raising (self-rising) flour

Energy 606kcal/2523kJ; Protein 7.5g; Carbohydrate 46g, of which sugars 31.6g; Fat 44.9g, of which saturates 20.3g; Cholesterol 152mg; Calcium 122mg; Fibre 1.3g; Sodium 279mg

Hot Chocolate Pudding with Rum Custard ✳

These delicious chocolate puddings are sure to be a hit. The rum custard turns them into a more adult pudding; for a family dessert, flavour the custard with vanilla or orange rind instead, if you like.

SERVES SIX

1 Lightly grease a 1.2 litre/2 pint/5 cup heatproof bowl or six individual dariole moulds. Cream the butter and sugar until pale and creamy. Gently blend in the eggs and the vanilla essence.

2 Sift together the cocoa powder and flour, and fold gently into the egg mixture with the chopped chocolate and sufficient milk to give a soft dropping consistency.

3 Spoon the mixture into the basin or moulds, cover with buttered greaseproof paper and tie down. Fill a pan with 2.5–5cm/1–2in water, place the puddings in the pan, cover with a lid and bring to the boil. Steam the large pudding for $1^1/_2$–2 hours and the individual puddings for 45–50 minutes, topping up the pan with water if necessary. When firm, turn out on to warm plates.

4 To make the rum custard, bring the milk and sugar to the boil. Whisk together the egg yolks and cornflour in a heatproof bowl, then pour on the hot milk, whisking constantly. Return the mixture to the pan and stir continuously while it slowly comes back to the boil. Allow the sauce to simmer gently as it thickens, stirring all the time. Remove from the heat and stir in the rum.

115g/4oz/$^1/_2$ cup butter, plus extra for greasing

2 eggs, beaten

a few drops of vanilla essence (extract)

45ml/3 tbsp unsweetened cocoa powder, sifted

75g/3oz bitter (semisweet) chocolate, chopped

a little milk, warmed

FOR THE RUM CUSTARD

250ml/8fl oz/1 cup milk

2 egg yolks

30–45ml/2–3 tbsp rum

FROM THE STORECUPBOARD

115g/4oz/$^1/_2$ cup light muscovado (brown) sugar

115g/4oz/1 cup self-raising (self-rising) flour

15ml/1 tbsp caster (superfine) sugar

10ml/2 tsp cornflour (cornstarch)

Energy 458kcal/1915kJ; Protein 8.3g; Carbohydrate 49g, of which sugars 31.5g; Fat 25.6g, of which saturates 14.5g; Cholesterol 186mg; Calcium 145mg; Fibre 1.8g; Sodium 302mg

Bread and Butter Pudding with Whiskey Sauce ✳

This traditional dessert is a great way of using up stale white bread. The whiskey sauce is heavenly, but the pudding can also be served with chilled cream or vanilla ice cream, if you prefer.

SERVES SIX

8 slices of white bread, crusts removed and buttered

115–150g/4–5oz/²/₃–³/₄ cup sultanas (golden raisins), or mixed dried fruit

2 large (US extra large) eggs

300ml/¹/₂ pint/1¹/₄ cups single (light) cream

450ml/³/₄ pint/ scant 2 cups milk

5ml/1 tsp vanilla essence (extract)

FOR THE WHISKEY SAUCE

150g/5oz/10 tbsp butter

1 egg

45ml/3 tbsp Irish whiskey

FROM THE STORECUPBOARD

2.5ml/¹/₂ tsp grated nutmeg

260g/9¹/₂oz/1¹/₄ cups caster (superfine) sugar

light muscovado (brown) sugar, for sprinkling (optional)

1 Preheat the oven to 180°C/350°F/Gas 4. Put four slices of bread, buttered side down, in the base of an ovenproof dish. Sprinkle with the sultanas or mixed dried fruit, some of the nutmeg and 15ml/1 tbsp sugar.

2 Place the remaining four slices of bread on top, buttered side down, and sprinkle again with nutmeg and 15ml/1 tbsp sugar.

3 Beat the eggs, add the cream, milk, vanilla essence and 115g/4oz/generous ¹/₂ cup caster sugar, and mix to make a custard. Pour over the bread, and sprinkle light muscovado sugar over the top, if you would like to have a crispy crust. Bake for 1 hour, or until the pudding has risen and is brown.

4 Meanwhile, make the sauce: melt the butter in a heavy pan, add the remaining caster sugar and dissolve over a gentle heat. Remove from the heat and add the egg, whisking, then add the whiskey. Serve with the whiskey sauce poured over the top.

Energy 757kcal/3168kJ; Protein 11.7g; Carbohydrate 82g, of which sugars 65.2g; Fat 40.8g, of which saturates 24.3g; Cholesterol 207mg; Calcium 232mg; Fibre 0.9g; Sodium 472mg

Scone and Butter Pudding ✳

This simple yet elegant pudding is a good way to use up scones that are slightly stale. Either use home-made ones, or good quality store-bought ones. You can use any type of dried fruit, depending on what is in your cupboard and your personal preference.

SERVES FOUR

1 Place the dried fruit and whisky in a small bowl, cover and leave to soak overnight or for at least 2 hours. Preheat the oven to 200°C/400°F/Gas 6.

2 Whisk the milk, cream, egg yolks, sugar and vanilla extract. Slice the tops off the scones and then slice each into three rounds. Butter each round and then layer with the fruit and custard in buttered ramekins. Set aside for 1 hour.

3 Place the ramekins in a deep baking tin (pan) and pour in enough boiling water to come half way up the ramekins. Bake for 40 minutes until risen slightly and golden-brown in colour.

4 Remove from the oven and brush with the warmed apricot jam. Serve immediately in the ramekins.

50g/2oz/scant ¹/₂ cup
sultanas (golden raisins)

50g/2oz/¹/₄ cup dried
apricots, cut into
small pieces

50ml/2fl oz/¹/₄ cup whisky

300ml/¹/₂ pint/1¹/₄ cups
milk

300ml/¹/₂ pint/1¹/₄ cups
double (heavy) cream

5 egg yolks

6 scones

75g/3oz/6 tbsp butter

60ml/4 tbsp apricot
jam, warmed

FROM THE STORECUPBOARD

50g/2oz/1/4 cup caster
(superfine) sugar

2 drops vanilla extract

Energy 796kcal/3305kJ; Protein 8.1g; Carbohydrate 43.2g, of which sugars 43.2g; Fat 63.9g, of which saturates 37.6g; Cholesterol 399mg; Calcium 178mg; Fibre 0.5g; Sodium 187mg

Plum Crumble ✳

The crumble is an infinitely versatile and perennially popular dessert. Plums can be divided into three categories – dessert, dual and cooking. Choose whichever dual or cooking plum is available locally. Serve with hot custard, cream or scoops of vanilla ice cream.

SERVES FOUR

1 Preheat the oven to 200°C/400°F/Gas 6. Place a large pan over a medium heat. Put the plums in the pan and add the sugar, water and lemon juice. Mix thoroughly and bring to the boil, stirring continuously until the sugar dissolves.

2 Cook the plums until they are just beginning to soften, then place the fruit with the juices in a deep pie dish.

3 Place the flour, oats, sugar and butter in a bowl and mix with your fingers until the mixture resembles breadcrumbs.

4 Sprinkle the crumble topping evenly over the fruit so that it is a good thickness. Bake in the preheated oven for 20 minutes, or until the top is crunchy and brown.

450g/1lb stoned (pitted) plums

50g/2oz/¹/₄ cup light muscovado (brown) sugar

15ml/1 tbsp water

juice of 1 lemon

FOR THE CRUMBLE TOPPING

25g/1oz/generous ¹/₄ cup coarse rolled oats

50g/2oz/¹/₄ cup butter, softened

FROM THE STORECUPBOARD

50g/2oz/¹/₂ cup plain (all-purpose) flour

50g/2oz/¹/₄ cup light muscovado (brown) sugar

Energy 304kcal/1284kJ; Protein 2.9g; Carbohydrate 51.5g, of which sugars 37.4g; Fat 11.1g, of which saturates 6.5g; Cholesterol 27mg; Calcium 53mg; Fibre 2.8g; Sodium 82mg

Apple and Blackberry
Wholemeal Crumble ✳

The pinhead oatmeal in the topping makes this traditional hot dessert especially crunchy and flavoursome. Serve with crème fraîche or ice cream.

SERVES EIGHT

1 Preheat the oven to 200°C/400°F/Gas 6. To make the crumble topping, rub the butter into the flour, and then add the oatmeal and brown sugar and continue to rub in until the mixture begins to stick together, forming large crumbs. Mix in the grated lemon rind, if using.

2 Peel and core the cooking apples, then slice into wedges. Put the apples, blackberries, lemon juice (if using), 30ml/2 tbsp water and the sugar into a shallow ovenproof dish, about 2 litres/3¹/₂ pints/9 cups capacity.

3 Cover the fruit with the crumble topping and sprinkle with a little cold water. Bake for 15 minutes, then reduce the heat to 190°C/375°F/Gas 5 and cook for another 15–20 minutes until crunchy and brown on top.

4 Serve the crumble hot with lashings of custard, crème fraîche or vanilla ice cream.

900g/2lb cooking apples

450g/1lb/4 cups blackberries

juice of ¹/₂ lemon (optional)

FOR THE TOPPING

115g/4oz/¹/₂ cup butter

50g/2oz/¹/₂ cup fine or medium pinhead oatmeal

grated lemon rind (optional)

FROM THE STORECUPBOARD

115g/4oz/1 cup wholemeal (whole-wheat) flour

50g/2oz/¹/₂ cup soft light brown sugar

175g/6oz/scant 1 cup sugar

VARIATION *You can use almost any combination of fruit in a crumble, including rhubarb, blackcurrants and gooseberries.*

Energy 470kcal/1974kJ; Protein 5.1g; Carbohydrate 78.2g, of which sugars 60.3g; Fat 17.2g, of which saturates 10g; Cholesterol 41mg; Calcium 71mg; Fibre 7g; Sodium 128mg

675g/1¹/₂lb fresh forced rhubarb, cut into chunks

grated rind and juice of 1 lime

225g/8oz fresh or frozen raspberries

custard or clotted cream, to serve

FOR THE CRUMBLE

50g/2oz/¹/₂ cup ground almonds

115g/4oz/¹/₂ cup cold butter

115g/4oz/1 cup blanched almonds, chopped

FROM THE STORECUPBOARD

a pinch of ground allspice

225g/8oz/scant 1¹/₂ cups caster (superfine) sugar

115g/4oz/1 cup plain (all-purpose) flour

a pinch of salt

Rhubarb and Raspberry Almond Crumble ✳✳

The distinctive sharp flavour of rhubarb is beautifully offset by sweet raspberries and a sweet almond crumble topping in this stunning dessert.

SERVES FOUR

COOK'S TIP *The pretty, pink and slender rhubarb available at the beginning of the season is called "forced" rhubarb. It has a sweeter flavour and less tough texture than later rhubarb, although this can also be used to make this dessert.*

1 Preheat the oven to 200°C/400°F/Gas 6 and put a baking sheet inside to heat up. Cut the rhubarb into chunks and put in a pan with the allspice, lime rind and juice and 175g/6oz/ scant 1 cup caster sugar.

2 Cook over a gentle heat for 2 minutes, stirring occasionally, until the chunks of rhubarb are tender but still hold their shape when probed with a knife. Pour into a sieve (strainer), set over a bowl to catch the juices. Leave to cool. Reserve the juices.

3 To make the crumble, put the flour, pinch of salt, ground almonds and butter into a food processor and process until the mixture resembles fine breadcrumbs. Tip into a bowl and stir in the blanched almonds and remaining sugar.

4 Spoon the rhubarb into a large ovenproof dish, and stir in the raspberries. Sprinkle the almond mixture evenly over the surface, mounding it up a little towards the centre.

5 Place the dish on the baking sheet and bake for 35 minutes until crisp and golden on top. Cool for 5 minutes before serving with custard or clotted cream and the reserved rhubarb juices.

Energy 812kcal/3403kJ; Protein 14.2g; Carbohydrate 88.1g, of which sugars 65.1g; Fat 47.4g, of which saturates 16.9g; Cholesterol 61mg; Calcium 345mg; Fibre 7.7g; Sodium 191mg

2 eggs, lightly beaten

10ml/2 tsp vanilla essence (extract)

25g/1oz desiccated (dry unsweetened shredded) coconut

FROM THE STORECUPBOARD

175g/6oz cooked basmati rice

60ml/4 tbsp caster (superfine) sugar

a pinch of nutmeg

2.5ml/¹/₂ tsp ground cinnamon

a pinch of ground cloves

50g/2oz/¹/₂ cup plain (all-purpose) flour

10ml/2 tsp baking powder

a pinch of salt

sunflower oil, for frying

icing (confectioners') sugar, to dust

Sweet and Spicy Rice Fritters ✳

These delicious little golden balls of rice are scented with sweet, warm spices and will fill the kitchen with wonderful aromas while you're cooking. To enjoy them at their best, serve piping hot, as soon as you have dusted them with sugar. They are great at any time of day – as a mid-morning or late afternoon snack or a simple dessert.

SERVES FOUR

COOK'S TIP
Unlike many cakes and cookies, these little fritters are gluten-free, so they make a perfect sweet snack for anyone with a gluten intolerance.

1 Place the cooked rice, eggs, sugar, nutmeg, cinnamon, cloves and vanilla essence in a large bowl and whisk to combine. Sift in the flour, baking powder and salt and add the coconut. Mix well until thoroughly combined.

2 Fill a wok or deep frying pan one-third full of the oil and heat to 180°C/350°F (or until a cube of bread, dropped into the oil, browns in 15 seconds).

3 Very gently, drop tablespoonfuls of the mixture into the oil, one at a time, and fry for 2–3 minutes, or until golden. Carefully remove the fritters from the wok using a slotted spoon and drain well on kitchen paper.

4 Divide the fritters into four portions, or simply pile them up on a single large platter. Dust them with icing sugar and serve immediately.

Energy 316kcal/1321kJ; Protein 6.6g; Carbohydrate 45.7g, of which sugars 16.3g; Fat 12.4g, of which saturates 4.8g; Cholesterol 95mg; Calcium 46mg; Fibre 1.3g; Sodium 38mg

Sesame and Banana Fritters ✳

Deep-fried bananas are popular all over South-east Asia, and this version coated in coconut and sesame seeds is particularly good. Small apple bananas, which have a lovely sweet, luscious flavour, are used here, but if you can't find them, you can use standard bananas instead – just cut them into bitesize pieces before coating in batter and frying.

SERVES FOUR

1 Place the coconut, caster sugar, cinnamon, baking powder, rice flour, sesame seeds and coconut milk in a large mixing bowl. Whisk thoroughly to form a smooth batter. Cover with clear film (plastic wrap) and leave to rest for 30 minutes–1 hour.

2 Fill a wok or deep frying pan one-third full of the oil and heat to 180°C/350°F (or until a cube of bread, dropped into the oil, browns in 15 seconds).

3 Working in batches, dip the halved bananas into the batter, drain off any excess and gently lower into the oil. Deep-fry for 3–4 minutes, or until golden.

4 Remove the bananas using a slotted spoon and drain well on kitchen paper. Serve hot or warm, dusted with icing sugar, with scoops of vanilla ice cream.

50g/2oz desiccated
(dry unsweetened
shredded) coconut

30ml/2 tbsp sesame seeds

600ml/1 pint/2¹/₂ cups
coconut milk

6 baby or apple bananas,
peeled and cut in half
lengthways

vanilla ice cream, to serve

FROM THE STORECUPBOARD

50g/2oz/¹/₄ cup caster
(superfine) sugar

5ml/1 tsp ground
cinnamon

2.5ml/¹/₂ tsp baking
powder

115g/4oz/1 cup rice flour

sunflower oil, for frying

icing (confectioners')
sugar, to dust

Energy 407kcal/1696kJ; Protein 4.4g; Carbohydrate 44.3g, of which sugars 21.3g; Fat 23.8g, of which saturates 8.9g; Cholesterol 0mg; Calcium 110mg; Fibre 2.9g; Sodium 172mg

Baked Bananas with Toffee Sauce *

Bananas make one of the cheapest and easiest of all hot desserts, and they are just as welcome as a comforting winter treat as they are to follow a barbecue. For an extra sweet finishing touch, grate some plain (semisweet) chocolate on the bananas, over the sauce, just before serving. If you are baking them on a barbecue, turn the bananas occasionally to ensure even cooking.

SERVES FOUR

1 Preheat the oven to 180°C/350°F/Gas 4. Put the unpeeled bananas in an ovenproof dish and bake for 15–20 minutes, until the skins are very dark and the flesh feels soft when squeezed.

2 Meanwhile, heat the light muscovado sugar in a small, heavy pan with 75ml/5 tbsp water until dissolved. Bring to the boil and add the double cream. Cook for 5 minutes, until the sauce has thickened and is toffee coloured. Remove from the heat.

3 Transfer the baked bananas in their skins to serving plates and split them lengthways to reveal the flesh. Pour some of the sauce over the bananas and top with scoops of vanilla ice cream. Serve any remaining sauce separately.

4 large bananas

75ml/5 tbsp double (heavy) cream

4 scoops good-quality vanilla ice cream, to serve

FROM THE STORECUPBOARD

75g/3oz/scant $^1/_2$ cup light muscovado (brown) sugar

Energy 368kcal/1546kJ; Protein 3.8g; Carbohydrate 55g, of which sugars 52g; Fat 15.5g, of which saturates 10g; Cholesterol 40mg; Calcium 85mg; Fibre 1.1g; Sodium 42mg

Treacle Tart ✳

It is worth taking the time to make your own pastry for this old-fashioned favourite, with its sticky filling and twisted lattice topping. Smooth creamy custard is the classic accompaniment, but it is also delicious served with cream or vanilla ice cream. For a more textured filling, use wholemeal (whole-wheat) breadcrumbs or crushed cornflakes instead of the white breadcrumbs.

SERVES FOUR–SIX

1 On a lightly floured surface, roll out three-quarters of the pastry to a thickness of 3mm/¹/₈in. Transfer to a 20cm/8in fluted flan tin (pan) and trim off the overhang. Chill the pastry case (pie shell) for 20 minutes. Reserve the trimmings.

2 Put a baking sheet in the oven and preheat to 200°C/400°F/Gas 6. To make the filling, warm the syrup in a pan until it melts. Grate the lemon rind and squeeze the juice.

3 Remove the syrup from the heat and stir in the breadcrumbs and lemon rind. Leave to stand for 10 minutes, then add more crumbs if the mixture is too thin and moist. Stir in 30ml/2 tbsp of the lemon juice, then spread the mixture evenly in the pastry case.

4 Roll out the reserved pastry and cut into 10–12 thin strips. Twist the strips into spirals, then lay half of them on the filling. Arrange the remaining strips at right angles to form a lattice. Press the ends on to the rim.

5 Place the tart on the hot baking sheet and bake for 10 minutes. Lower the oven temperature to 190°C/375°F/Gas 5. Bake for 15 minutes more, until golden. Serve warm.

350g/12oz unsweetened shortcrust pastry (*see* Cook's Tip)

260g/9¹/₂oz/ generous ³/₄ cup golden (light corn) syrup

1 lemon

75g/3oz/1¹/₂ cups fresh white breadcrumbs

COOK'S TIP *To make the pastry: place 225g/8oz/2cups plain (all-purpose) flour into a bowl. Rub in 115g/4oz/¹/₂cup cold butter, until the mixture resembles breadcrumbs. Sprinkle over 45–60ml/3–4 tbsp water, and gently knead to bind. Wrap and chill for 30 minutes.*

Energy 437kcal/1837kJ; Protein 4.9g; Carbohydrate 71.2g, of which sugars 35.1g; Fat 16.6g, of which saturates 5.1g; Cholesterol 8mg; Calcium 73mg; Fibre 1.4g; Sodium 445mg

Lemon Meringue Tart ✳

In this popular dessert a crisp, light pastry shell is generously filled with a tangy lemon custard and topped with soft, sweet meringue. The tart is best served at room temperature, with or without cream.

SERVES SIX

1 To make the pastry, sift the flour and salt into a bowl and add the lard and butter. With the fingertips, lightly rub the fats into the flour until the mixture resembles fine crumbs.

2 Stir in about 30ml/2 tbsp cold water until the mixture can be gathered together into a smooth ball of dough. (Alternatively make the pastry using a food processor.)

3 Wrap the pastry and refrigerate for at least 30 minutes. Meanwhile, preheat the oven to 200°C/400°F/Gas 6.

4 Roll out the pastry on a lightly floured surface and use to line a 20cm/8in flan tin (pan). Prick the base with a fork, line with baking parchment or foil and add a layer of baking beans to prevent the pastry rising.

5 Put the pastry case (pie shell) into the hot oven and cook for 15 minutes. Remove the beans and parchment or foil, return the pastry to the oven and cook for a further 5 minutes until crisp and golden brown. Reduce the oven temperature to 150°C/300°F/Gas 2.

6 To make the lemon filling, put the cornflour into a pan and add 175g/6oz/³/₄ cup sugar, lemon rind and 300ml/¹/₂ pint/ 1¹/₄ cups water. Heat the mixture, stirring continuously, until it comes to the boil and thickens.

7 Reduce the heat and simmer very gently for 1 minute. Remove the pan from the heat and stir in the lemon juice.

8 Add the egg yolks to the lemon mixture, one at a time, beating after each addition, and then stir in the butter. Tip the mixture into the baked pastry case and level the surface.

9 To make the meringue topping, whisk the egg whites until stiff peaks form then whisk in half the remaining sugar. Fold in the rest of the sugar using a metal spoon.

10 Spread the meringue over the lemon filling, covering it completely. Cook for about 20 minutes, until the top of the meringue is lightly browned.

11 Remove from the oven and leave to cool slightly before cutting into slices and serving on its own or with cream.

FOR THE PASTRY

25g/1oz/2 tbsp lard

25g/1oz/2 tbsp butter, diced

FOR THE FILLING

finely grated rind and juice of 2 lemons

2 egg yolks

15g/¹/₂oz/1 tbsp butter, diced

FOR THE MERINGUE TOPPING

2 egg whites

FROM THE STORECUPBOARD

115g/4oz/1 cup plain (all-purpose) flour

pinch of salt

50g/2oz/¹/₂ cup cornflour (cornstarch)

250g/9oz/1¹/₄ cup caster (superfine) sugar

VARIATIONS

• To make lemon and lime meringue pie, substitute the finely grated rind and juice of 2 limes for the rind and juice of 1 lemon.

• Using lard to make the pastry ensures a light result, but you can substitute an equal quantity of additional butter, if you prefer.

Energy 357kcal/1497kJ; Protein 6.8g; Carbohydrate 42.8g, of which sugars 25.1g; Fat 18.9g, of which saturates 9g; Cholesterol 129mg; Calcium 108mg; Fibre 0.7g; Sodium 137mg

3 eggs, beaten

grated rind and juice of
1 lemon

40g/1¹/₂oz/3 tbsp
butter, melted

450g/1lb/2 cups curd
(farmer's) cheese

75g/3oz/scant ¹/₂ cup
raisins

FOR THE PASTRY

115g/4oz/¹/₂ cup
butter, diced

1 egg yolk

15–30ml/1–2 tbsp
chilled water

FROM THE STORECUPBOARD

225g/8oz/2 cups plain
(all-purpose) flour

90g/3¹/₂oz/scant ¹/₂ cup
light muscovado (brown)
sugar

pinch of ground allspice

Curd Tart ✳

Moist and succulent, this traditional tart made from curd cheese and
subtly flavoured with allspice is so good that it is difficult to resist second
helpings. Serve for dessert or for a special tea.

SERVES EIGHT

1 To make the pastry, sift the flour into a large mixing bowl and
rub or cut in the chilled butter until the mixture resembles fine
breadcrumbs. Stir the egg yolk into the flour mixture and add
just enough of the water to bind the mixture together to form a
soft dough.

2 Put the dough on a floured surface, knead lightly and briefly,
then form into a ball. Roll out the pastry thinly and use to line a
20cm/8in fluted loose-based flan tin (tart pan). Cover with clear
film (plastic wrap) and chill for about 15 minutes.

3 Preheat the oven to 190°C/375°F/Gas 5. Mix the sugar with
the ground allspice in a bowl, then stir in the eggs, lemon rind
and juice, butter, curd cheese and raisins. Mix well.

4 Pour the filling into the pastry case, then bake for 40 minutes,
or until the pastry is cooked and the filling is lightly set and
golden brown. Cut the tart into wedges while it is still slightly
warm, and serve with cream, if you like.

Energy 406kcal/1700kJ; Protein 14g; Carbohydrate 41.4g, of which sugars 20g; Fat 21.7g, of which saturates 12.4g; Cholesterol 159mg; Calcium 110mg; Fibre 1.1g; Sodium 371mg

Bakewell Tart ✳

This simple tart combines soft puff pastry with jam and a rich almond sponge. Served hot, warm or cold it is absolutely delicious with custard, cream or ice cream, and is sure to be a hit with all the family.

SERVES FOUR

225g/8oz puff pastry

30ml/2 tbsp raspberry or apricot jam

2 eggs, plus 2 egg yolks

115g/4oz/¹/₂ cup butter, melted

50g/2oz/¹/₂ cup ground almonds

grated rind of 1 lemon

FROM THE STORECUPBOARD

115g/4oz/¹/₂ cup caster (superfine) sugar

a few drops of almond essence (extract)

icing (confectioners') sugar, for dusting

1 Preheat the oven to 200°C/400°F/Gas 6. Roll out the pastry on a lightly floured surface and use to line an 18cm/7in pie plate. Trim the edge.

2 Re-roll the pastry trimmings and cut out wide strips of pastry. Use these to decorate the edge of the pastry case by gently twisting them around the rim, joining the strips together as necessary.

3 Prick the pastry case all over with a fork, then spread the jam over the base.

4 Whisk the eggs, egg yolks and sugar together in a bowl until the mixture is thick and pale.

5 Gently stir the melted butter, ground almonds, almond essence and lemon rind into the whisked egg mixture.

6 Pour the mixture into the pastry case and bake for 30 minutes, or until the filling is just set and is lightly browned. Dust with icing sugar before serving hot, warm or cold.

VARIATIONS
- You could use shortcrust pastry instead of puff pastry, if you like. Either make some (see Cook's Tip on page 403) or use good-quality ready-made pastry.

- You can use any jam.

COOK'S TIP
Since this pastry case is not baked blind before being filled, place a baking sheet in the oven while it preheats, then place the tart on the hot sheet. This will ensure that the base of the pastry case cooks right through.

Energy 417kcal/1753kJ; Protein 8.6g; Carbohydrate 56.1g, of which sugars 36g; Fat 19.9g, of which saturates 1.7g; Cholesterol 215mg; Calcium 78mg; Fibre 0g; Sodium 226mg

Apple Pie ✳

There are many variations on this classic all-time-favourite recipe, and it is a great way of enjoying seasonal apples. For a slightly different twist, you could add ground cinnamon or dried cranberries to the filling, if you like. Bake in a traditional metal pie plate so that the pastry base will be perfectly cooked. Serve warm or cold with chilled whipped cream, or vanilla ice cream.

SERVES SIX

1 Sift the flour into a large mixing bowl, add the butter and cut it into small pieces.

2 Rub the butter, or butter and fat, into the flour with the fingertips, or using a pastry (cookie) cutter, lifting the mixture as much as possible to aerate, which will make the pastry lighter.

3 Mix 25g/1oz/2 tbsp caster sugar with the chilled milk or water, add to the bowl and mix with a knife or fork until the mixture clings together.

4 Turn the pastry on to a floured worktop and knead lightly once or twice until smooth.

5 Wrap in baking parchment or foil and leave in the refrigerator to relax for 20 minutes before using. Meanwhile, preheat the oven to 200°C/400°F/Gas 6.

6 Roll out one-third of the pastry and use to line a 23cm/9in pie plate. Use any trimmings to make a rim of pastry around the top edge of the pie plate.

7 To make the filling, peel, core and slice the apples and arrange half of them on the pastry base, then sprinkle over the sultanas and lemon rind, if using. Top with the caster sugar, the remaining apples and butter or water.

8 Roll out the remainder of the pastry to make a circle about 2.5cm/1in larger than the pie plate.

9 Dampen the pastry edging on the rim and lay the top over the apples, draping it gently over any lumps to avoid straining the pastry. Press the rim well to seal. Pinch the edges with your fingers to make a fluted edge.

10 Brush the pastry lightly with milk and bake the pie in the preheated oven for about 30 minutes, or until the pastry has browned and is crisp, and the fruit is cooked.

11 To serve, dust the pastry with icing sugar and serve hot, warm or cold, but not straight from the refrigerator. The pie is delicious with vanilla ice cream or whipped cream.

130g/4¹/₂oz/generous ¹/₂ cup butter, or mixed butter and white vegetable fat (shortening)

45ml/3 tbsp very cold milk or water

FOR THE FILLING

675g/1¹/₂lb cooking apples

75g/3oz/¹/₂ cup sultanas (golden raisins) (optional)

a little grated lemon rind (optional)

a knob (pat) of butter or 15ml/1 tbsp of water

a little milk, to glaze

icing (confectioners') sugar and whipped cream, to serve

FROM THE STORECUPBOARD

225g/8oz/2 cups plain (all-purpose) flour

100g/4oz/8 tbsp caster (superfine) sugar

Energy 393kcal/1650kJ; Protein 4.1g; Carbohydrate 56.3g, of which sugars 27.7g; Fat 18.4g, of which saturates 11.4g; Cholesterol 46mg; Calcium 68mg; Fibre 2.5g; Sodium 136mg

Summer Berries in Warm Sabayon Glaze ✳

This luxurious combination consists of summer berries under a light and fluffy sauce flavoured with liqueur. The topping is lightly grilled to form a crisp, caramelized crust.

SERVES FOUR

1 Arrange the fruit in four heatproof ramekins. Preheat the grill (broiler) to high.

2 Whisk the yolks in a large bowl with the sugar and liqueur. Place over a pan of hot water and whisk constantly until thick, fluffy and pale.

3 Pour equal quantities of the sauce over the summer berries in each dish. Place under the preheated grill for 1–2 minutes until just turning brown.

4 Dust the fruit with icing sugar and sprinkle with mint leaves just before serving. You could also add an extra splash of liqueur, if you like.

450g/1lb/4 cups mixed summer berries

4 egg yolks

120ml/4fl oz/¹/₂ cup liqueur, such as Cointreau

mint leaves, to decorate

FROM THE STORECUPBOARD

50g/2oz/¹/₄ cup caster (superfine) sugar

icing (confectioners') sugar, sifted, to decorate

Energy 235kcal/984kJ; Protein 3.9g; Carbohydrate 27.1g, of which sugars 27.1g; Fat 5.6g, of which saturates 1.6g; Cholesterol 202mg; Calcium 48mg; Fibre 1.3g; Sodium 18mg

Autumn Pudding ✳

Although summer pudding is made more often, this pudding is equally easy to make, using autumnal fruit instead of the soft fruits of summer.

SERVES EIGHT

1 Use several slices of bread to line the base and sides of a 900ml–1.2 litres/1^1/$_2$–2 pints/3^3/$_4$–5 cup pudding bowl or soufflé dish, cutting them so that the pieces fit closely together.

2 Put all the fruit into a wide, heavy pan, sprinkle the sugar over and bring very gently to the boil. Cook for 2–3 minutes, or until the sugar has dissolved and the juices run.

3 Remove from the heat and set aside 30–45ml/2–3 tbsp of the juices. Spoon the fruit and the remaining juices into the bread-lined dish and cover the top with the remaining slices of bread. Put a plate on top of the pudding and weigh it down with a heavy can or jar. Leave in the refrigerator for at least 8 hours.

4 Before serving, remove the weight and plate, cover with a serving plate and turn upside down to unmould the pudding. Use the reserved fruit juice to pour over any patches of the bread that have not been completely soaked by the fruit juices. Serve cold, cut into wedges with cream or crème fraîche.

1 loaf white bread, 2 or 3 days old, crusts removed and sliced thinly

675g/1^1/$_2$lb/6 cups mixed soft fruit, such as blackberries, autumn raspberries, late strawberries, and peeled and chopped eating apples

FROM THE STORECUPBOARD

115g/4oz/generous ^{1}/$_2$ cup caster (superfine) sugar

Energy 261kcal/1112kJ; Protein 7.7g; Carbohydrate 57.5g, of which sugars 27.1g; Fat 1.7g, of which saturates 0.4g; Cholesterol 0mg; Calcium 153mg; Fibre 4.2g; Sodium 398mg

Oranges in Syrup ✳

This recipe works well with most citrus fruits – for example, try pink grapefruit or sweet, perfumed clementines, which have been peeled but left whole. Serve the oranges with 300ml/½ pint/1¼ cups whipped cream flavoured with 5ml/1 tsp ground cinnamon, or 5ml/1 tsp ground nutmeg or with Greek (US strained plain) yogurt for an elegant summer dessert.

SERVES SIX

1 Finely pare, shred and reserve the rind from one orange. Peel the remaining oranges. Cut each crossways into slices, then re-form them, with a cocktail stick (toothpick) through the centre.

2 Put the sugar in a heavy pan and add 50ml/2fl oz/¼ cup water. Heat gently until the sugar dissolves, then bring to the boil and cook until the syrup turns pale gold.

3 Remove from the heat and carefully pour 100ml/3½fl oz/ scant ½ cup freshly boiling water into the pan. Return to the heat until the syrup has dissolved in the water. Stir in the coffee.

4 Add the oranges and the rind to the coffee syrup. Simmer for 15–20 minutes, turning the oranges once during cooking. Leave to cool, then chill. Serve sprinkled with pistachio nuts, if using.

6 medium oranges

100ml/3½fl oz/ scant ½ cup fresh strong brewed coffee

50g/2oz/½ cup pistachio nuts, chopped (optional)

FROM THE STORECUPBOARD

200g/7oz/1 cup sugar

Fresh Fig Compote ✳✳

A vanilla and coffee syrup brings out the wonderful flavour of figs. Serve Greek (US strained plain) yogurt or vanilla ice cream with the poached fruit. A good selection of different honeys is available – the aroma and flavour will be subtly scented by the plants surrounding the hives. Orange blossom honey works particularly well in this recipe, although any clear variety is suitable.

SERVES SIX

1 Choose a frying pan with a lid, large enough to hold the figs in a single layer. Pour in the coffee and add the honey.

2 Split the vanilla pod lengthways and scrape the seeds into the pan. Add the vanilla pod, then bring to a rapid boil and cook until reduced to about 175ml/6fl oz/¾ cup.

3 Wash the figs and pierce the skins several times with a sharp skewer. Cut in half and add to the syrup. Reduce the heat, cover and simmer for 5 minutes. Remove the figs from the syrup with a slotted spoon and set aside to cool.

4 Strain the syrup over the figs. Allow to stand at room temperature for 1 hour before serving.

400ml/14fl oz/ 1²/₃ cups fresh brewed coffee

115g/4oz/½ cup clear honey

1 vanilla pod (bean)

12 slightly under-ripe fresh figs

Top: Energy 191kcal/815kJ; Protein 2g; Carbohydrate 48.5g, of which sugars 48.5g; Fat 0.2g, of which saturates 0g; Cholesterol 0mg; Calcium 93mg; Fibre 2.7g; Sodium 10mg

Above: Energy 147kcal/628kJ; Protein 1.7g; Carbohydrate 36g, of which sugars 35.8g; Fat 0.6g, of which saturates 0g; Cholesterol 0mg; Calcium 103mg; Fibre 3g; Sodium 27mg

VARIATIONS

• To make individual custards in ramekin dishes, coat 6–8 small ramekins with the hot caramel and divide the custard mixture among them. Place in a roasting tin and pour in just enough boiling water to come halfway up the dishes. Bake for 25–30 minutes or until set.

• Slice the strawberries and marinate them with a little sugar and a liqueur or dessert wine, such as Amaretto or Muscat wine.

Baked Caramel Custard ✳

Simple and nourishing, custards are classic nursery puddings. This more sophisticated take has a rich caramel flavour which is wonderful with fresh cream and sweet, ripe strawberries.

SERVES SIX–EIGHT

1 Put 175g/6oz/generous ³/₄ cup of the sugar in a heavy pan with just enough water to moisten the sugar. Bring to the boil, swirling the pan until the sugar is dissolved. Boil for 5 minutes, without stirring, until the syrup turns a dark caramel colour.

2 Working quickly, pour the caramel into a 1 litre/1³/₄ pint/4 cup soufflé dish. Holding the dish with oven gloves, swirl to coat the base and sides with the hot caramel mixture. Set aside to cool.

3 Preheat the oven to 160°C/325°F/Gas 3. Put the vanilla essence and cream in a pan and bring just to the boil, stirring frequently. Remove from the heat, cover and set aside to cool.

4 In a bowl, whisk the eggs and egg yolks with the remaining sugar for 2–3 minutes until smooth and creamy. Whisk in the cream and strain into the caramel-lined dish. Cover with foil.

5 Place in a roasting tin and pour in just enough boiling water to come halfway up the side of the dish. Bake for 40–45 minutes until just set. Remove from the roasting tin and leave to cool for at least 30 minutes, then place in the fridge and chill overnight.

6 To turn out, run a knife around the edge of the dish, then cover with a serving plate and, holding them together tightly, invert, allowing the custard to drop down on to the plate. Lift one edge of the dish, allowing the caramel to run down, then carefully lift off the dish. Serve with cream and strawberries.

10ml/2 tsp vanilla essence (extract)

425ml/15fl oz/1³/₄ cups double (heavy) cream

5 large eggs, plus 2 extra yolks

thick cream and fresh strawberries, to serve

FROM THE STORECUPBOARD

250g/9oz/1¹/₄ cups sugar

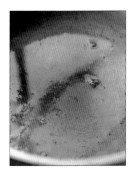

Energy 622kcal/2587kJ; Protein 9.6g; Carbohydrate 44.8g, of which sugars 44.8g; Fat 46.4g, of which saturates 26g; Cholesterol 386mg; Calcium 98mg; Fibre 0g; Sodium 103mg

Mango and Chocolate Crème Brulée ✳

A very popular dessert, crème brulée is extremely easy to make at home. This decadent version combines dark chocolate with sweet, ripe mango for a truly stunning dinner party dessert.

SERVES SIX

2 ripe mangoes, peeled and stoned (pitted)

300ml/¹/₂ pint/1¹/₄ cups double (heavy) cream

300ml/¹/₂ pint/1¹/₄ cups crème fraîche

1 vanilla pod

115g/4oz plain (semisweet) dark chocolate, chopped into small pieces

4 egg yolks

15ml/1 tbsp clear honey

FROM THE STORECUPBOARD

90ml/6 tbsp demerara (raw) sugar, for the topping

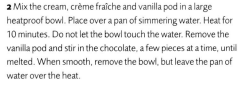

VARIATION *You can use almost any soft fruit in the bottom of the ramekins. Strawberries and raspberries are especially good with the chocolate custard, but you may want to omit the chocolate if you use rhubarb or another sour fruit.*

1 Chop the mango flesh and divide among six flameproof dishes or ramekins set on a baking sheet.

2 Mix the cream, crème fraîche and vanilla pod in a large heatproof bowl. Place over a pan of simmering water. Heat for 10 minutes. Do not let the bowl touch the water. Remove the vanilla pod and stir in the chocolate, a few pieces at a time, until melted. When smooth, remove the bowl, but leave the pan of water over the heat.

3 Whisk the egg yolks and honey in a second heatproof bowl, then gradually pour in the chocolate cream, whisking constantly. Place over the pan of simmering water and stir constantly until the custard thickens enough to coat the back of a wooden spoon.

4 Remove from the heat and spoon the custard over the mangoes. Cool, then chill in the refrigerator until set.

5 Preheat the grill to high. Sprinkle 15ml/1 tbsp demerara sugar evenly over each dessert and spray with a little water. Grill briefly, until the sugar caramelizes. Chill before serving.

Energy 670kcal/2782kJ; Protein 5.2g; Carbohydrate 38.9g, of which sugars 38.4g; Fat 56g, of which saturates 34.6g; Cholesterol 261mg; Calcium 90mg; Fibre 1.8g; Sodium 31mg

Mississippi Mud Pie ✳

This is the ultimate in chocolate desserts – a deep pastry case, filled with chocolate custard and topped with a fluffy rum mousse and a smothering of whipped cream. It is perfect for a dinner party or special family meal.

SERVES SIX–EIGHT

1 To make the pastry, sift the flour into a bowl and rub or cut in the butter until the mixture resembles breadcrumbs. Stir in the egg yolks with enough chilled water to make a dough.

2 Roll out on a lightly floured surface and use to line a deep 23cm/9in flan tin (tart pan). Chill for 30 minutes. Preheat the oven to 190°C/375°F/Gas 5. Prick the pastry with a fork, line with foil and baking beans, then bake blind for 10 minutes. Remove the foil and beans, return to the oven and bake for 10 minutes more until the pastry is crisp and golden. Cool in the tin.

3 To make the custard filling, mix the egg yolks, cornflour and 30ml/2 tbsp of the sugar in a bowl. Heat the milk in a pan until almost boiling, then beat into the egg mixture. Return to the cleaned pan and stir over a low heat until the custard has thickened and is smooth. Pour half the custard into a bowl.

4 Melt the chocolate in a heatproof bowl set over a pan of hot water, then add to the custard in the bowl. Add the vanilla essence and mix well. Spread in the pastry case, cover closely with some baking parchment, cool, then chill until set.

5 Sprinkle the gelatine over the water in a small bowl, leave until spongy, then place over a pan of simmering water until all the gelatine has dissolved. Stir into the remaining custard, along with the rum. Whisk the egg whites until stiff peaks form, whisk in the remaining sugar, then quickly fold into the custard before it sets.

6 Spoon the mixture over the chocolate custard to cover completely. Chill until set, then remove from the tin. Spread cream over the top and decorate with chocolate curls.

3 eggs, separated

400ml/14fl oz/1²/₃ cups milk

150g/5oz plain (semisweet) chocolate, broken up

5ml/1 tsp vanilla essence (extract)

15ml/1 tbsp powdered gelatine

45ml/3 tbsp water

30ml/2 tbsp dark rum

175g/6fl oz/³/₄ cup double (heavy) cream, whipped

a few chocolate curls, to decorate (*see* Cook's Tip)

FOR THE PASTRY

150g/5oz/10 tbsp butter, diced

2 egg yolks

15–30ml/1–2 tbsp water

FROM THE STORECUPBOARD

250g/9oz/2¹/₄ cups plain (all-purpose) flour

20ml/4 tsp cornflour (cornstarch)

75g/3oz/6 tbsp caster (superfine) sugar

COOK'S TIP *To make chocolate curls, melt 115g/4oz plain (semisweet) chocolate. Pour on to a smooth surface and spread evenly with a palette knife. Leave to cool. Hold a large, sharp knife at a 45 degree angle to the chocolate and push it along the chocolate in short sawing movements to make curls. Lift off with the knife and leave to cool.*

Energy 827kcal/3454kJ; Protein 13g; Carbohydrate 83.5g, of which sugars 33.1g; Fat 50.2g, of which saturates 29.2g; Cholesterol 280mg; Calcium 200mg; Fibre 1.9g; Sodium 246mg

COOK'S TIP

An alternative way to make the toffee for this dessert is to place a 400g/14oz can of sweetened condensed milk in large pan, cover with water and bring to the boil. Boil for 4 hours, checking regularly to ensure the water never falls below the height of the can. Leave to cool for 15 minutes, then open the can and spread the toffee over the prepared base and arrange the sliced bananas and cream on top, as in the recipe.

115g/4oz/¹⁄₂ cup butter, diced

200g/7oz can skimmed, sweetened condensed milk

30ml/2 tbsp golden (light corn) syrup

2 small bananas, sliced

a little lemon juice

whipped cream, to decorate

5ml/1 tsp grated plain (semisweet) chocolate

FOR THE PASTRY

115g/4oz/¹⁄₂ cup butter, diced

FROM THE STORECUPBOARD

150g/5oz/1¹⁄₄ cups plain (all-purpose) flour

50g/2oz/¹⁄₄ cup caster (superfine) sugar

115g/4oz/¹⁄₂ cup light muscovado (brown) sugar

Boston Banoffee Pie ✳

This scrumptious pie is so easy to make. Simply press the wonderfully biscuity pastry into the tin, rather than rolling it out. Add the fudge-toffee filling and sliced banana topping and it'll prove irresistible.

SERVES SIX

1 Preheat the oven to 160°C/325°F/Gas 3. In a food processor, process the flour and diced butter until the mixture resembles breadcrumbs. Stir in the caster sugar and mix to form a soft, pliable dough.

2 Press into a 20cm/8in loose-based flan tin (tart pan). Bake for 30 minutes.

3 To make the filling, place the butter in a pan with the condensed milk, brown sugar and syrup. Heat gently, stirring, until the butter has melted and the sugar has completely dissolved.

4 Bring to a gentle boil and cook for 7–10 minutes, stirring constantly, until it thickens and turns a light caramel colour.

5 Pour the hot caramel filling into the pastry case and leave until completely cold.

6 Sprinkle the banana slices with lemon juice to prevent them from discolouring and arrange them in overlapping circles on top of the filling, leaving a gap in the centre. Pipe a swirl of cream in the centre and sprinkle with the grated chocolate.

Energy 608kcal/2547kJ; Protein 6.4g; Carbohydrate 78.5g, of which sugars 58.9g; Fat 32g, of which saturates 20.1g; Cholesterol 82mg; Calcium 169mg; Fibre 1.1g; Sodium 299mg

Meringue Layer Cake with Raspberries

This delicious dessert is made with a basic meringue mixture, and is the perfect way to enjoy raspberries, or any other soft fruit, depending on availability and personal preference.

SERVES TEN

1 Preheat the oven to 150°C/300°F/Gas 2. Line two baking sheets with non-stick baking parchment and draw two circles: one 23cm/9in in diameter and the other 20cm/8in. Fit a piping (icing) bag with a 1cm/^{1}/$_2$in star nozzle.

2 Whisk the egg whites until stiff peaks form, using an electric mixer. Keeping the machine running, add half of the sugar, 15ml/1 tbsp at a time. Using a metal spoon, carefully fold in the remaining sugar. Use most of the mixture to pipe inside the circles, then use the remaining meringue mixture to pipe nine miniature meringues on to the surrounding baking parchment.

3 Cook for 50–60 minutes, until lightly coloured and dry (the small ones will take less time). Peel off the parchment and cool.

4 Whip the cream until soft peaks form, sweeten with sugar and flavour with a few drops of vanilla essence or liqueur.

5 Lay the larger meringue on a serving dish. Spread with three-quarters of the cream and raspberries. Add the smaller meringue, spread with the remaining cream, and arrange the small meringues around the edge. Decorate the top with the remaining fruit and dust lightly with icing sugar.

4 egg whites

FOR THE FILLING

300ml/^{1}/$_2$ pint/1^1/$_4$ cups whipping cream

3–4 drops of good quality vanilla essence (extract) or 2.5ml/^{1}/$_2$ tsp liqueur, such as Kirsch or Crème de Framboise

about 450g/1lb/2^3/$_4$ cups raspberries

FROM THE STORECUPBOARD

225g/8oz/generous 1 cup caster (superfine) sugar, plus extra, to taste

icing (confectioners') sugar, for dusting

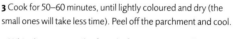

COOK'S TIPS

• Don't leave cooked meringues exposed to the air, as they will absorb moisture from the air, soften and "weep".

• Don't assemble the dessert too far ahead of serving, as the meringue will become soggy.

• If stored carefully in an airtight container, the meringues will keep well for several days.

• Making meringues is a great way of using up eggs that are not absolutely fresh.

Energy 298kcal/1252kJ; Protein 3.2g; Carbohydrate 39.5g, of which sugars 39.5g; Fat 15.3g, of which saturates 9.5g; Cholesterol 39mg; Calcium 55mg; Fibre 1.4g; Sodium 44mg

1 x 15–18cm/6–7in sponge cake (*see* p430)

225g/8oz raspberry jam

150ml/¹/₄ pint/²/₃ cup Irish whiskey

450g/1lb ripe fruit, such as pears and bananas

300ml/¹/₂ pint/1¹/₄ cups whipping cream

blanched almonds, glacé (candied) cherries and angelica, to decorate (optional)

FOR THE CUSTARD

450ml/³/₄ pint/scant 2 cups full-fat (whole) milk

1 vanilla pod (bean) or a few drops of vanilla essence (extract)

3 eggs

FROM THE STORECUPBOARD

25g/1oz/2 tbsp caster (superfine) sugar

Irish Whiskey Trifle ✳

This rich trifle is made with real sponge cake, fresh fruit and rich egg custard, but with Irish whiskey rather than the usual sherry flavouring. For family occasions you could use good-quality tinned fruit.

SERVES EIGHT

1 To make the custard, put the milk into a pan with the vanilla pod, if using, and bring almost to the boil. Remove from the heat. Whisk the eggs and sugar together lightly. Remove the vanilla pod from the milk. Gradually whisk the milk into the egg mixture.

2 Rinse out the pan, return the mixture to it and stir over low heat until it thickens; do not allow it to boil. Turn into a bowl and add the vanilla essence, if using. Cover with clear film (plastic wrap).

3 Halve the sponge cake horizontally, spread with the raspberry jam and make a sandwich. Cut into slices and use them to line the bottom and lower sides of a large serving bowl. Sprinkle with whiskey.

4 Peel and slice the fruit, then spread it out over the sponge. Pour the custard on top, cover with clear film to prevent a skin forming, and leave to cool. Chill until required. Before serving, whip the cream and spread it over the set custard. Decorate with the almonds, glacé cherries and angelica, if you like.

Energy 710kcal/2959kJ; Protein 12.1g; Carbohydrate 58g, of which sugars 42.6g; Fat 43.2g, of which saturates 14.4g; Cholesterol 171mg; Calcium 194mg; Fibre 2.3g; Sodium 336mg

Rhubarb and Ginger Cups ✳

Extremely quick and easy to whip together, this simple dessert uses ready-made rhubarb compote, but you could use home-made if you prefer. Alternatively, use whole-fruit apricot jam.

SERVES FOUR

1 Put the ginger biscuits in a strong, clean plastic bag and seal tightly. Bash the biscuits with a rolling pin until they are roughly crushed but not smashed to dust.

2 Set aside two tablespoons of crushed biscuits and divide the rest among four glasses.

3 Spoon the rhubarb compote on top of the crushed biscuits, then top with the cream. Place in the refrigerator and chill for about 30 minutes.

4 To serve, sprinkle the reserved crushed biscuits over the trifles and serve immediately.

12 gingernut biscuits (gingersnaps)

50ml/2fl oz/¹/₄ cup rhubarb compote

450ml/³/₄ pint/scant 2 cups extra thick double (heavy) cream

Energy 695kcal/2874kJ; Protein 3.6g; Carbohydrate 27.1g, of which sugars 14.1g; Fat 64.3g, of which saturates 39.4g; Cholesterol 154mg; Calcium 98mg; Fibre 0.6g; Sodium 124mg

Iced Raspberry Trifle ✳

This combination of sponge, sherried fruit, ice cream and mascarpone is sheer indulgence. The sponge and topping can be made a day in advance and the assembled trifle can be prepared an hour before serving.

SERVES EIGHT—TEN

115g/4oz/¹/₂ cup butter

2 eggs

115g/4oz/1 cup ground almonds

15ml/1 tbsp milk

TO FINISH

300g/11oz/scant 2 cups raspberries

50g/2oz/¹/₂ cup flaked (sliced) almonds, toasted

5ml/1 tsp almond essence (extract)

90ml/6 tbsp orange juice

200ml/7fl oz/scant 1 cup medium sherry

500g/1¹/₄lb/2¹/₂ cups mascarpone

150g/5oz/²/₃ cup Greek (US strained plain) yogurt

about 250ml/8fl oz/1 cup vanilla ice cream

about 250ml/8fl oz/1 cup raspberry ice cream

FROM THE STORECUPBOARD

115g/4oz/¹/₂ cup light muscovado (brown) sugar

75g/3oz/²/₃ cup self-raising (self-rising) flour

2.5ml/¹/₂ tsp baking powder

30ml/2 tbsp icing (confectioners') sugar

1 Preheat the oven to 180°C/350°F/Gas 4. Grease and line a 20cm/8in round cake tin. Put the butter, sugar, eggs, flour, baking powder, almonds and almond essence in a bowl and beat with an electric whisk for 2 minutes until creamy. Stir in the milk.

2 Spoon the mixture into the prepared tin, level the surface and bake for about 30 minutes or until just firm in the centre. Transfer to a wire rack and leave to cool.

3 Cut the sponge into chunky pieces and place these in the base of a 1.75 litre/3 pint/7¹/₂ cup glass serving dish. Scatter with half the raspberries and almonds.

4 Mix the orange juice with 90ml/6 tbsp of the sherry. Spoon over the sponge. Beat the mascarpone with the yogurt, icing sugar and remaining sherry. Put the trifle dish and the mascarpone in the refrigerator until you are ready to assemble the trifle.

5 To serve, scoop the ice cream and sorbet into the trifle dish. Reserve a few of the remaining raspberries and almonds, then scatter the rest over the ice cream. Spoon over the mascarpone mixture and scatter with the reserved raspberries and almonds. Chill the trifle for up to 1 hour before serving.

Energy 608kcal/2537kJ; Protein 17.2g; Carbohydrate 41.9g, of which sugars 33.7g; Fat 39.4g, of which saturates 18.1g; Cholesterol 134mg; Calcium 357mg; Fibre 2.8g; Sodium 269mg

Chocolate and Banana Fool ✳

Simple to make and utterly delicious, this is an ideal dessert for when you don't want to spend hours in kitchen, or for a sweet end to a mid-week meal. It can be made ahead and stored in the refrigerator overnight.

SERVES FOUR

1 Put the chocolate pieces in a heat-proof bowl and melt in the microwave on high power for 1–2 minutes. Stir, then set aside. If you do not have a microwave, put the chocolate in a heatproof bowl and place it over a small pan of gently simmering water and leave until melted, stirring frequently to remove any unmelted pieces.

2 Pour the custard into a bowl and gently fold in the melted chocolate to make a rippled effect.

3 Peel and slice the bananas and stir these into the chocolate and custard mixture. Spoon into four glasses. If you have time, chill for at least 30 minutes before serving.

115g/4oz plain (semisweet) chocolate, broken into small pieces

300ml/¹⁄₂ pint/1¹⁄₄ cups custard (see Cook's Tip)

2 bananas

COOK'S TIPS • You can either make your own custard (see page 500), make some from instant custard powder, following the intructions on the packet, or buy good-quality ready-made custard.

• Don't be tempted to use chocolate that contains less than 70 percent chocolate solids, or the flavour will be less good.

Lemon Posset ✳

This old-fashioned dessert combines lemon with soft whipped cream and sugar for a tangy, flavoursome and irresistible dessert. Serve the posset on its own, or with home-made shorbread biscuits for dunking.

SERVES FOUR

1 Pour the cream into a heavy pan. Add the sugar and heat gently until the sugar has dissolved, then bring to the boil, stirring constantly.

2 Add the lemon juice and rind, reserving a little of the rind for decoration, and stir constantly over a medium heat until the mixture thickens enough to coat the back of the spoon.

3 Pour the mixture into four heatproof serving glasses. Cool, then chill in the refrigerator until just set.

4 Serve the posset decorated with a few strands of lemon rind, and with a selection of dessert biscuits (cookies), if you like. Rich, buttery shortbread is ideal.

600ml/1 pint/2¹⁄₂ cups double (heavy) cream

grated rind and juice of 2 unwaxed lemons

FROM THE STORECUPBOARD

175g/6oz/scant 1 cup caster (superfine) sugar

COOK'S TIP To intensify the lemon flavour of this dessert even more, swirl a spoonful of lemon curd on the surface before serving.

Energy 268kcal/1127kJ; Protein 4.1g; Carbohydrate 42.1g, of which sugars 38.1g; Fat 9.6g, of which saturates 4.9g; Cholesterol 3mg; Calcium 81mg; Fibre 1.4g; Sodium 33mg

Energy 917kcal/3801kJ; Protein 2.7g; Carbohydrate 48.5g, of which sugars 48.5g; Fat 80.6g, of which saturates 50.1g; Cholesterol 206mg; Calcium 98mg; Fibre 0g; Sodium 36mg

Blackcurrant Fool ✳

The strong flavour and deep colour of this easily grown fruit makes it especially suitable for fools and ices, although this is an adaptable recipe which can be made using other soft fruits too. The fool can also be used to make an easy no-stir ice cream, if you prefer.

SERVES SIX

1 Put the blackcurrants into a small pan with 45ml/3 tbsp water, and cook over a low heat until soft. Remove from the heat, add the sugar according to taste, and stir until dissolved.

2 Leave to cool, then liquidize (blend) or sieve to make a purée. Set aside and cool. Add the lemon juice and stir well.

3 Whip the double cream until it is fairly stiff and, using a metal spoon, carefully fold it into the blackcurrant purée, losing as little volume as possible.

4 Turn the mixture into a single large serving dish or six individual serving glasses and leave to set. Chill in the refrigerator until ready to serve.

350g/12oz/3 cups
blackcurrants

5ml/1 tsp lemon juice

**300ml/^{1}/$_2$ pint/1^1/$_4$ cups
double (heavy) cream**

FROM THE STORECUPBOARD

**about 175g/6oz/scant
1 cup caster (superfine)
sugar**

VARIATION
To make blackcurrant ice cream, turn the completed fool into a freezerproof container. Cover and freeze (preferably at the lowest setting). Transfer from the freezer to the refrigerator 10–15 minutes before serving to allow the ice cream to soften. Serve with whipped cream and cookies, if you like.

COOK'S TIP
Fools are a very good way of using up a glut of seasonal fruit, especially if it has gone past its best and is a bit soft, since it is pulped up and combined with cream. Other fruits that work well include strawberries, raspberries, mangoes, gooseberries, peaches and rhubarb.

Energy 379kcal/1581kJ; Protein 1.5g; Carbohydrate 35.2g, of which sugars 35.2g; Fat 26.9g, of which saturates 16.7g; Cholesterol 69mg; Calcium 75mg; Fibre 2.1g; Sodium 15mg

Lemon Sorbet ✳

This is probably the most classic sorbet of all. Refreshingly tangy and yet deliciously smooth, it quite literally melts in the mouth. Try to buy unwaxed lemons for recipes such as this one where the lemon rind is used. The wax coating can adversely affect the flavour of the rind.

SERVES SIX

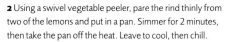

1 Put the sugar in a pan and pour in 300ml/^{1}/$_2$ pint/1^1/$_4$ cups water. Bring to the boil, stirring occasionally until the sugar has just dissolved.

2 Using a swivel vegetable peeler, pare the rind thinly from two of the lemons and put in a pan. Simmer for 2 minutes, then take the pan off the heat. Leave to cool, then chill.

3 Squeeze the juice from all the lemons and add it to the syrup. Strain the syrup into a shallow freezerproof container, reserving the rind. Freeze for 4 hours, until it is mushy.

4 Process the sorbet in a food processor until it is smooth. Lightly whisk the egg white with a fork until it is just frothy. Replace the sorbet in the container, beat in the egg white and return to the freezer for 4 hours, or until it is firm.

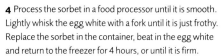

5 Cut the reserved lemon rind into fine shreds and cook in boiling water for 5 minutes. Drain, then place on a plate and sprinkle with sugar. Scoop the sorbet into bowls or glasses and decorate with the sugared lemon rind.

4 lemons, well scrubbed

1 egg white

FROM THE STORECUPBOARD

200g/7oz/1 cup caster (superfine) sugar, plus extra for coating rind to decorate

COOK'S TIP
Sorbets are especially delicious during the summer months, as they are refreshing and tangy without being too sweet. Lemon sorbet is great for cleansing the palate, and makes the ideal dessert after a spicy main meal. It is also extremely cheap and reasonably easy to make.

Energy 134kcal/570kJ; Protein 0.7g; Carbohydrate 34.9g, of which sugars 34.9g; Fat 0g, of which saturates 0g; Cholesterol 0mg; Calcium 18mg; Fibre 0g; Sodium 12mg

Classic Vanilla Ice Cream ✳

Nothing beats the comforting simplicity of vanilla ice cream, which can be served with all manner of hot desserts or with hot and cold sauces. Vanilla pods are well worth buying for the superb flavour they impart.

SERVES FOUR

1 Using a small knife slit the vanilla pod lengthways. Pour the milk into a heavy pan, add the vanilla pod and bring to the boil. Remove from the heat and leave for 15 minutes to infuse.

2 Lift the vanilla pod up. Holding it over the pan, scrape the seeds out of the pod with a small knife so that they fall into the milk. Set the vanilla pod aside and bring the milk back to the boil.

3 Whisk the egg yolks, sugar and cornflour in a bowl until the mixture is thick and foamy. Gradually pour on the hot milk, whisking constantly. Return the mixture to the pan and cook over a gentle heat, stirring all the time.

4 When the custard thickens and is smooth, pour it back into the bowl. Cool, then chill.

5 Whip the cream until it has thickened but falls from a spoon. Fold it into the custard and pour into a plastic tub or similar freezerproof container. Freeze for 6 hours, or until firm enough to scoop, beating twice with a fork, or in a food processor.

6 Scoop into dishes, bowls or bought cones and either eat it on its own or with a hot dessert.

1 vanilla pod

**300ml/¹/₂ pint/1¹/₄ cups
semi-skimmed (low-fat) milk**

4 egg yolks

**300ml/¹/₂ pint/1¹/₄ cups
double (heavy) cream**

FROM THE STORECUPBOARD

**75g/3oz/6 tbsp caster
(superfine) sugar**

**5ml/1 tsp cornflour
(cornstarch)**

COOK'S TIPS

• If you have an ice cream machine, follow the recipe up until step 5, then pour the mixture into an ice cream machine rather than a freezerproof container. Churn the mixture until thick, then transfer to a suitable container and freeze until it is required.

• Don't throw the vanilla pod away after use. Instead, rinse, dry and store in the sugar jar. After a week or so the sugar will take on the wonderful aroma and flavour of the vanilla and will be delicious sprinkled over summer fruits. Use it to sweeten whipped cream, custard, biscuits and shortbread.

• Home-made ice cream should be eaten within two weeks.

Energy 542kcal/2245kJ; Protein 6.8g; Carbohydrate 24.4g, of which sugars 24.4g; Fat 47.1g, of which saturates 27.4g; Cholesterol 309mg; Calcium 160mg; Fibre 0g; Sodium 59mg

4 egg yolks

300ml/¹/₂ pint/1¹/₄ cups semi-skimmed milk

250g/9oz dark (bittersweet) chocolate, broken into squares

25g/1oz/2 tbsp butter, diced

30ml/2 tbsp golden (light corn) syrup

90ml/6 tbsp single (light) cream or cream and milk mixed

300ml/¹/₂ pint/1¹/₄ cups whipping cream

wafer biscuits, to serve

FROM THE STORECUPBOARD

75g/3oz/6 tbsp caster (superfine) sugar

5ml/1 tsp cornflour (cornstarch)

Chocolate Ripple Ice Cream ✳

This creamy, dark chocolate ice cream, rippled with wonderful swirls of rich chocolate sauce, will stay deliciously soft even after freezing. It is perfect for every occasion and is sure to be popular.

SERVES FOUR–SIX

1 Put the yolks, sugar and cornflour in a bowl and whisk until thick and foamy. Pour the milk into a pan, bring it just to the boil, then gradually pour it on to the yolk mixture, whisking constantly.

2 Return the mixture to the pan and cook over a gentle heat, stirring constantly, until the custard thickens and is smooth. Pour it back into the bowl and stir in 150g/5oz of the chocolate, until melted. Cover closely, leave it to cool, then chill.

3 Put the remaining chocolate into a pan and add the butter. Spoon in the golden syrup. Heat gently, stirring, until the chocolate and butter have melted. Stir in the single cream or cream and milk mixture. Heat gently, stirring, until smooth, then leave to cool, stirring occasionally.

4 Whip the cream until it has thickened but falls from a spoon. Fold it into the custard and pour into a plastic tub or similar freezerproof container. Freeze for 5 hours, or until firm enough to scoop, beating twice with a fork, or in a food processor.

5 Add alternate spoonfuls of ice cream and chocolate sauce to a 1.5 litre/2¹/₂ pint/6¹/₄ cup plastic container. Freeze for 5–6 hours until firm. Serve with wafers.

Energy 900kcal/3749kJ; Protein 11g; Carbohydrate 74.9g, of which sugars 74.3g; Fat 63.9g, of which saturates 37.8g; Cholesterol 314mg; Calcium 211mg; Fibre 1.6g; Sodium 142mg

Cakes and Bakes

NOTHING BEATS A SLICE OF HOME-MADE CAKE OR
A CRUMBLY COOKIE AS A MID-MORNING SNACK
OR TEATIME TREAT, AND MANY ARE SURPRISINGLY
QUICK AND EASY TO MAKE. CHOOSE FROM EVERYDAY
CAKES, SUCH AS CARROT CAKE OR HONEY AND SPICE
BUNS, IRRESISTIBLE COOKIES, SUCH AS CHEWY
FLAPJACKS OR SHORTBREAD ROUNDS, OR WHY
NOT TRY YOUR HAND AT MAKING A RANGE OF
BREADS, INCLUDING QUICK WHOLEMEAL LOAVES,
PUMPERNICKEL OR ONION AND ROSEMARY FOCACCIA?

175g/6oz/³/₄ cup
soft butter

3 eggs, beaten

60ml/4 tbsp raspberry
or strawberry jam

150ml/¹/₄ pint/²/₃ cup
whipped cream or
crème fraîche

FROM THE STORECUPBOARD

175g/6oz/³/₄ cup caster
(superfine) sugar

175g/6oz/1¹/₂ cups
self-raising (self-rising)
flour, sifted

15–30ml/1–2 tbsp icing
(confectioners') sugar,
for dusting

Victoria Sandwich Cake ✳

Serve this richly flavoured sponge cake sandwiched together with your favourite jam or preserve.
For special occasions, fill the cake with prepared fresh fruit, such as raspberries, strawberries or sliced
peaches, as well as jam and whipped cream or chilled crème fraîche.

MAKES ONE 18CM/7IN CAKE

1 Preheat the oven to 180°C/350°F/Gas 4. Lightly grease and line the bottom of two 18cm/7in
shallow round cake tins (pans) with baking parchment.

2 Place the butter and caster sugar in a bowl and cream together until pale and fluffy. This can
be done by hand using a mixing spoon or with a hand-held electric mixer, if you have one, which is
far quicker and easier.

3 Add the eggs, a little at a time, beating well after each addition. Fold in half the flour, using a metal
spoon, then gently fold in the rest and mix to combine.

4 Divide the cake mixture between the two prepared cake tins and level the surfaces with the back
of a spoon.

5 Bake for 25–30 minutes, until the cakes have risen, feel just firm to the touch and are golden
brown. Turn out and cool on a wire rack.

6 When the cakes are cool, sandwich them with the jam and whipped cream or crème fraîche. Dust
the top of the cake with sifted icing sugar and serve cut into slices. Store the cake in the refrigerator
in an airtight container or wrapped in foil.

Energy 3577kcal/14948kJ; Protein 39.7g; Carbohydrate 377.4g, of which sugars 247.3g; Fat 223.1g, of which saturates 134g; Cholesterol 1101mg; Calcium 924mg; Fibre 5.4g; Sodium 1967mg

Carrot Cake ✳

Universally loved, this is one of the most irresistible cakes there is. Everyone has their own version; here poppyseeds add colour and crunch, and pineapple gives it moistness, while orange provides a tangy touch.

MAKES ONE LARGE LOAF

45ml/3 tbsp poppyseeds

3 eggs, beaten

**finely grated rind of
1 orange**

**225g/8oz raw
carrots, grated**

**75g/3oz/¹/₂ cup fresh or
canned pineapple, drained
and finely chopped**

**75g/3oz/³/₄ cup
walnut pieces**

**115g/4oz/¹/₂ cup butter,
melted and cooled**

FOR THE ICING

**150g/5oz/scant 1 cup
mascarpone**

**finely grated rind of
1 orange**

FROM THE STORECUPBOARD

**250g/9oz/2¹/₄ cups plain
(all-purpose) flour**

10ml/2 tsp baking powder

**5ml/1 tsp bicarbonate of
soda (baking soda)**

2.5ml/¹/₂ tsp salt

**5ml/1 tsp ground
cinnamon**

**225g/8oz/1¹/₃ cups soft
light brown sugar**

**30ml/2 tbsp icing
(confectioners')
sugar, sifted**

1 Preheat the oven to 180°C/350°F/Gas 4. Line the base of a 1.5 litre/2¹/₂ pint/6¹/₄ cup loaf tin (pan) with baking parchment. Grease the sides of the pan and dust with flour.

2 Sift together the flour, baking powder, bicarbonate of soda, salt and cinnamon into a bowl. Stir in the poppyseeds.

3 Mix together the brown sugar, eggs and orange rind in a separate bowl. Lightly squeeze the excess moisture from the grated carrots and stir the carrots into the egg mixture with the pineapple and walnut pieces. Gradually stir the sifted flour mixture into the egg mixture until well combined, then gently fold in the butter.

4 Spoon the mixture into the prepared pan, level the top and bake for 1–1¹/₄ hours, until risen and golden brown. (To check if the cake really is cooked in the centre, push a thin metal skewer right down into the middle of the cake. Pull it out immediately and feel if there is any sticky mixture clinging to the skewer. If it comes out clean the cake is done, if not, put it back for a further 10 minutes and test again.)

5 Remove the cake from the loaf tin and allow to cool on a wire rack. Remove the baking parchment when completely cold.

6 To make the icing, beat the mascarpone with the icing sugar and orange rind. Cover and chill until needed. When ready to serve, beat well, then spread thickly over the top of the cake. Cut into slices and eat.

Energy 3971kcal/16641kJ; Protein 76.3g; Carbohydrate 491.9g, of which sugars 294.7g; Fat 202.5g, of which saturates 84.5g; Cholesterol 879mg; Calcium 751mg; Fibre 17.6g; Sodium 992mg

Old-fashioned Treacle Cake ✳

The treacle gives a rich colour and a deep flavour to this easy-to-make cake, which is perfect for a mid-morning snack with a cup of tea or coffee.

MAKES ONE 20CM/8IN CAKE

1 Preheat the oven to 180°C/350°F/Gas 4. Butter a shallow 20–23cm/8–9in ovenproof flan dish or baking tin (pan).

2 Sift the flour and spice into a large mixing bowl. Add the butter and, with your fingertips, rub it into the flour until the mixture resembles fine crumbs. Alternatively you could do this in a food processor. Stir in the sugar and mixed dried fruit.

3 Beat the egg and, with a small whisk or a fork, stir in the treacle and then the milk. Stir the liquid into the flour to make a fairly stiff but moist consistency, adding a little extra milk if necessary.

4 Transfer the cake mixture to the prepared dish or tin with a spoon and level out the surface.

5 Bake the cake in the hot oven and cook for about 1 hour until it has risen, is firm to the touch and fully cooked through. To check if the cake is cooked, insert a small skewer in the centre – it should come out free of sticky mixture.

6 Leave the cooked treacle cake to cool completely. Serve it, cut into wedges, straight from the dish.

75g/3oz/6 tbsp butter, cut into small cubes

150g/5oz/1 cup mixed dried fruit

1 egg

15ml/1 tbsp black treacle (molasses)

100ml/3^1/$_2$ fl oz/ scant ^{1}/$_2$ cup milk

FROM THE STORECUPBOARD

250g/9oz/2 cups self-raising (self-rising) flour

2.5ml/^{1}/$_2$ tsp mixed (apple pie) spice

25g/1oz/2 tbsp caster (superfine) sugar

VARIATION *Vary the dried fruit you use in this cake – try using chopped ready-to-eat dried apricots and stem ginger, or a packet of luxury dried fruit.*

Energy 2089kcal/8805kJ; Protein 37.4g; Carbohydrate 343g, of which sugars 152.4g; Fat 72.8g, of which saturates 42.2g; Cholesterol 356mg; Calcium 720mg; Fibre 11.1g; Sodium 676mg

Overnight Cake ✳

This simple cake contains no added sugar – the sweetness comes from the dried fruit. It is at its most delicious eaten on the day it is made, its crust being crisp and flaky while the inside is soft and moist.

MAKES ONE THIN 23CM/9IN CAKE

1 Sift the flour and spices. Add the butter and rub in until the mixture resembles fine breadcrumbs. Stir in the dried fruit and enough milk to make a soft mix.

2 Mix the bicarbonate of soda with the vinegar and, as it froths, quickly stir it into the mixture. Cover the bowl and leave at room temperature for about 8 hours.

3 Preheat the oven to 180°C/350°F/Gas 4. Grease a shallow 23cm/9 in round cake tin (pan) and line its base with baking parchment. Spoon the cake mixture into the prepared tin and level the top.

4 Put into the hot oven and cook for about 1 hour or until firm to the touch and cooked through – a skewer inserted in the centre should come out free of sticky mixture. If the top starts to get too brown during cooking, cover it with baking parchment.

5 Leave in the tin to cool for 15–20 minutes, then turn out and cool completely on a wire rack. Serve with slices of crumbly white cheese, if you like.

115g/4oz/¹/₂ cup butter, cut into cubes

115g/4oz/²/₃ cup mixed dried fruit

300ml/¹/₂ pint/1¹/₄ cups milk

slices of crumbly white cheese, to serve (optional)

FROM THE STORECUPBOARD

225g/8oz/2 cups plain (all-purpose) flour

5ml/1 tsp ground cinnamon

5ml/1 tsp ground ginger

2.5ml/¹/₂ tsp bicarbonate of soda (baking soda)

15ml/1 tbsp vinegar

Energy 2069kcal/8681kJ; Protein 34.7g; Carbohydrate 267.9g, of which sugars 96.5g; Fat 103g, of which saturates 63.6g; Cholesterol 263mg; Calcium 780mg; Fibre 9.5g; Sodium 888mg

Walnut Cake ✳

This moist cake is made with a generous quantity of walnuts, flavoured with brandy and drenched in a delectable orange and cinnamon syrup.

SERVES TEN–TWELVE

1 Preheat the oven to 190°C/375°F/Gas 5. Grease a 35 x 23cm/ 14 x 9in roasting pan or baking dish that is at least 5cm/2in deep. Cream the butter in a mixing bowl until soft, then add 115g/4oz/generous 1/2 cup sugar and beat until light and fluffy.

2 Add the egg yolks one by one, beating the mixture after each addition. Stir in the brandy, cinnamon and walnuts using a spoon.

3 Sift the flour with the baking powder and set aside. Whisk the egg whites with a pinch of salt until they are stiff. Fold them into the creamed mixture, alternating with spoonfuls of flour until the whites and the flour have all been incorporated.

4 Spread the mixture evenly in the prepared pan or dish. It should be about 4cm/1 1/2 in deep. Bake for about 40 minutes, or until the top is golden and a skewer inserted in the cake comes out clean. Take the cake out of the oven and let it rest in the pan.

5 Mix the remaining sugar and 300ml/1/2 pint/1 1/4 cups water in a small pan. Heat gently, stirring, until the sugar has dissolved. Bring to the boil, lower the heat and add the brandy, orange rind and cinnamon sticks. Simmer for 10 minutes.

6 Slice the cake into 6cm/2 1/2 in diamond or square shapes while hot and strain the syrup over it. Let it stand for 10–20 minutes, until it has absorbed the syrup and is thoroughly soaked through.

150g/5oz/10 tbsp unsalted (sweet) butter

4 eggs, separated

60ml/4 tbsp brandy

300g/11oz/2³/₄ cups shelled walnuts, coarsely chopped

FOR THE SYRUP

30ml/2 tbsp brandy

2 or 3 strips of pared orange rind

FROM THE STORECUPBOARD

375g/13oz/generous 1³/₄ cups caster (superfine) sugar

2.5ml/¹/₂ tsp ground cinnamon

150g/5oz/1¹/₄ cups self-raising (self-rising) flour

5ml/1 tsp baking powder

a pinch of salt

2 cinnamon sticks

COOK'S TIP *The cake will stay moist for 2–3 days, provided it is tightly covered with clear film (plastic wrap). You do not need to store it in the refrigerator.*

Energy 563kcal/2,349kJ; Protein 8.5g; Carbohydrate 50.6g, of which sugars 39.2g; Fat 35.3g, of which saturates 10.1g; Cholesterol 108mg; Calcium 114mg; Fibre 1.5g; Sodium 177mg

Semolina Cake ✳

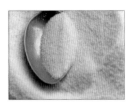

This simple cake takes very little time to make – about 20 minutes – and uses inexpensive storecupboard ingredients. It is perfect with coffee.

SERVES SIX–EIGHT

1 Put the sugar in a heavy pan, pour in the water and add the cinnamon stick. Bring to the boil, stirring until the sugar dissolves, then boil without stirring for about 4 minutes to make a syrup.

2 Meanwhile, heat the oil in a separate, heavy pan. When it is hot, add the semolina and stir until it turns light brown.

3 Lower the heat, add the almonds and pine nuts, and brown together for 2–3 minutes, stirring continuously. Take off the heat and set aside. Remove and discard the cinnamon stick.

4 Wearing an oven glove, gradually add the hot syrup to the semolina mixture, stirring continuously. It will probably spit at this point, so stand well away. Return to a gentle heat and stir until all the syrup has been absorbed and the mixture looks smooth.

5 Remove the pan from the heat, cover it with a clean dish towel and let it stand for 10 minutes. Scrape the mixture into a 20–23cm/ 8–9in round cake tin (pan), preferably fluted, and set it aside.

6 When it is cold, unmould it on to a serving platter and dust it with the ground cinnamon. Cut into slices and serve.

1 litre/1³/₄ pints/4 cups cold water

50g/2oz/¹/₂ cup blanched almonds

30ml/2 tbsp pine nuts

FROM THE STORECUPBOARD

500g/1¹/₄lb/2³/₄ cups caster (superfine) sugar

1 cinnamon stick

250ml/8fl oz/1 cup olive oil

350g/12oz/2 cups coarse semolina

5ml/1 tsp ground cinnamon

Energy 888kcal/3,731kJ; Protein 9.1g; Carbohydrate 133.1g, of which sugars 87.6g; Fat 39.1g, of which saturates 4.9g; Cholesterol 0mg; Calcium 75mg; Fibre 1.9g; Sodium 13mg

Honey and Spice Buns ✳

These golden little buns are fragrant with honey and cinnamon. Though they look more appetizing when cooked directly in a bun tin, they tend to rise higher (and are therefore lighter) when baked in paper cases.

MAKES EIGHTEEN

1 Preheat the oven to 200°C/400°F/Gas 6. Butter the holes of a bun tin (pan) or, alternatively, line them with paper cases.

2 Sift the flour into a large mixing bowl with the cinnamon and the bicarbonate of soda.

3 Beat the butter with the sugar until light and fluffy. Beat in the egg yolk, then gradually add the honey.

4 With a large metal spoon and a cutting action, fold in the flour mixture plus sufficient milk to make a soft mixture that will just drop off the spoon.

5 In a separate, clean bowl whisk the egg white until stiff peaks form. Using a large metal spoon, fold the egg white into the cake mixture.

6 Divide the mixture among the paper cases or the holes in the prepared tin. Put into the hot oven and cook for 15–20 minutes or until risen, firm to the touch and golden brown.

7 Sprinkle the tops lightly with caster sugar and leave to cool completely on a wire rack.

125g/4¹/₂oz/¹/₂ cup butter, softened

125g/4¹/₂oz/10 tbsp soft brown sugar

1 large (US extra large) egg, separated

125g/4¹/₂oz clear honey

about 60ml/4 tbsp milk

FROM THE STORECUPBOARD

250g/9oz/2 cups plain (all-purpose) flour

5ml/1 tsp ground cinnamon

5ml/1 tsp bicarbonate of soda (baking soda)

caster (superfine) sugar, for sprinkling

Energy 152kcal/639kJ; Protein 1.9g; Carbohydrate 23.6g, of which sugars 13g; Fat 6.3g, of which saturates 3.8g; Cholesterol 26mg; Calcium 30mg; Fibre 0.4g; Sodium 49mg

Apple and Cinnamon Muffins ✳

These fruity, spicy muffins are quick and easy to make and are perfect for serving for breakfast or tea, or for adding to a lunchbox for a tasty snack. The appetizing aroma as they bake is out of this world.

MAKES SIX

1 Preheat the oven to 200°C/400°F/Gas 6. Line a large muffin tin (pan) with six paper cases.

2 Put the egg, sugar, milk and melted butter in a large bowl, and beat with a spoon until thoroughly combined.

3 Sift in the flour, baking powder, salt and 2.5ml/^{1}/$_2$ tsp ground cinnamon. Add the chopped apple and mix roughly. Spoon the mixture into the prepared muffin cases.

4 To make the topping, mix the crushed sugar cubes with the remaining cinnamon. Sprinkle over the uncooked muffins.

5 Put the muffins in the centre of the preheated oven. Bake for 30–35 minutes until well risen and golden brown on top. Transfer the muffins to a wire rack to cool. Serve them warm or at room temperature.

1 egg, beaten

120ml/4fl oz/^{1}/$_2$ cup milk

50g/2oz/^{1}/$_4$ cup butter, melted

2 small eating apples, peeled, cored and finely chopped

FOR THE TOPPING

12 brown sugar cubes, coarsely crushed

FROM THE STORECUPBOARD

40g/1^1/$_2$oz/3 tbsp caster (superfine) sugar

150g/5oz/1^1/$_4$ cups plain (all-purpose) flour

7.5ml/1^1/$_2$ tsp baking powder

pinch of salt

7.5ml/1^1/$_2$ tsp ground cinnamon

Energy 236kcal/995kJ; Protein 4.3g; Carbohydrate 38.2g, of which sugars 19.1g; Fat 8.5g, of which saturates 4.9g; Cholesterol 51mg; Calcium 74mg; Fibre 1.2g; Sodium 73mg

Chocolate Chip Brownies ✳

These chunky chocolate brownies are moist, dark and deeply satisfying. They are delicious with a morning cup of coffee or as a dessert.

SERVES SIX

1 Preheat the oven to 180°C/350°F/Gas 4. Lightly grease a shallow 19cm/7^1/$_2$in square cake tin (pan). Melt the plain chocolate in a heatproof bowl over a pan of simmering water.

2 Beat together the oil, sugar, eggs and vanilla essence. Stir in the melted chocolate, then beat well until evenly mixed.

3 Sift the flour and cocoa powder into the bowl and fold in thoroughly. Stir in the chopped nuts and milk chocolate chips, then tip the mixture into the prepared tin and spread evenly to the edges.

4 Bake for about 30–35 minutes, until the top is firm and crusty. Cool in the tin before cutting into squares.

150g/5oz plain (semisweet) chocolate, chopped

2 eggs

5ml/1 tsp vanilla essence (extract)

60ml/4 tbsp cocoa powder (unsweetened)

75g/3oz/^{3}/$_4$ cup chopped walnuts

60ml/4 tbsp milk chocolate chips

FROM THE STORECUPBOARD

120ml/4fl oz/^{1}/$_2$ cup sunflower oil

215g/7^1/$_2$ oz/scant 1 cup light muscovado (brown) sugar

65g/2^1/$_2$ oz/scant ^{2}/$_3$ cup self-raising (self-rising) flour

COOK'S TIP
These brownies freeze well and can be stored in the freezer for up to 3 months in an airtight container or wrapped thoroughly in foil.

VARIATIONS
• To make white chocolate brownies, substitute white chocolate for the milk chocolate, and substitute additional flour for the cocoa powder (unsweetened).

• You could also use dark (bittersweet) chocolate in place of the milk chocolate, if you prefer.

• Try replacing the walnuts with chopped pecan nuts.

Energy 611kcal/2559kJ; Protein 8.7g; Carbohydrate 69.7g, of which sugars 59.9g; Fat 35g, of which saturates 9.9g; Cholesterol 66mg; Calcium 80mg; Fibre 2.9g; Sodium 124mg

Oat Chocolate Chip Cookies ✳

These crunchy cookies are easy enough for children to make and are sure to disappear as soon as they are baked.

MAKES ABOUT TWENTY

1 Cream the butter and sugar in a large bowl, until pale and fluffy. Add the lightly beaten eggs, milk and vanilla essence, and beat thoroughly.

2 Sift in the flour, baking powder and salt, and stir in until well mixed. Fold in the rolled oats, chocolate chips and chopped pecan nuts.

3 Chill the mixture in the refrigerator for at least 1 hour. Preheat the oven to 180°C/350°F/Gas 4. Grease two large baking trays.

4 Using two teaspoons, place mounds of the mixture well apart on the trays and flatten with a spoon or fork.

5 Bake the cookies for 10–12 minutes in the preheated oven until the edges are just colouring, then cool on wire racks.

115g/4oz/¹/₂ cup butter, plus extra for greasing

2 eggs, lightly beaten

45–60ml/3–4 tbsp milk

5ml/1 tsp vanilla essence (extract)

115g/4oz/generous 1 cup rolled oats

175g/6oz plain (semisweet) chocolate chips

115g/4oz/1 cup pecan nuts, chopped

FROM THE STORECUPBOARD

115g/4oz/¹/₂ cup soft dark brown sugar

150g/5oz/1¹/₄ cups plain (all-purpose) flour

5ml/1 tsp baking powder

pinch of salt

Energy 207kcal/864kJ; Protein 3.2g; Carbohydrate 22.1g, of which sugars 12g; Fat 12.4g, of which saturates 5g; Cholesterol 32mg; Calcium 30mg; Fibre 1.1g; Sodium 46mg

Milk Chocolate Crispy Cookies ✳

These little chocolate-coated cornflake cakes are always a hit with kids. They couldn't be easier to make – and are great for young aspiring cooks who want to get involved in the kitchen.

MAKES TEN

1 Line a large baking sheet with baking parchment.

2 Break the chocolate into a large, heatproof bowl and add the syrup. Set the bowl over a pan of gently simmering water and leave until melted, stirring frequently.

3 Put the cornflakes in a strong plastic bag and, using a rolling pin, lightly crush the cornflakes, breaking them into fairly small pieces but not into dust.

4 Remove the bowl from the heat and tip in the crushed cornflakes. Mix well, until the cornflakes are thoroughly coated in the chocolate mixture.

5 Place a 6.5cm/2¹/₂ in round cutter on the paper and put a spoonful of the chocolate mixture in the centre. Pack down firmly with the back of the spoon to make a thick cookie.

6 Gently ease away the cutter, using the spoon to help keep the mixture in place. Continue making cookies in this way until all the mixture has been used up. Chill for 1 hour.

7 Put a little icing sugar in a small bowl. Lift each cookie from the paper and roll the edges in the icing sugar to finish.

90g/3¹/₂ oz milk chocolate

15ml/1 tbsp golden (light corn) syrup

90g/3¹/₂ oz/4¹/₂ cups cornflakes

FROM THE STORECUPBOARD

icing (confectioners') sugar, for dusting

Energy 84kcal/355kJ; Protein 1.4g; Carbohydrate 14.2g, of which sugars 7.2g; Fat 2.8g, of which saturates 1.7g; Cholesterol 2mg; Calcium 21mg; Fibre 0.2g; Sodium 112mg

Shortbread Rounds ✳

There should always be a supply of shortbread in the cookie jar – it is so moreish. It should melt in the mouth and taste buttery but never greasy.

MAKES ABOUT TWENTY FOUR

1 Place the butter and sugar in a bowl and cream together until light, pale and fluffy. Sift together the flour, ground rice, or rice flour, and salt, and stir into the butter and sugar with a wooden spoon, until the mixture resembles fine breadcrumbs.

2 Working quickly, gather the dough together with your hand, then put it on a clean work surface. Knead lightly until it forms a ball. Lightly roll into a sausage shape, about 7.5cm/3in thick. Wrap in clear film (plastic wrap) and chill until firm.

3 Preheat the oven to 190°C/375°F/Gas 5. Grease two large baking sheets and line with baking parchment.

4 Pour the demerara sugar on to a sheet of baking parchment. Unwrap the dough and roll it in the sugar until evenly coated. Using a large knife, slice the roll into discs about 1cm/¹/₂in thick. Place the discs on to the prepared baking sheets, spacing them well apart. Bake for 20–25 minutes until very pale gold in colour.

5 Remove from the oven and sprinkle with golden caster sugar. Leave to cool on the baking sheet for 10 minutes before transferring to a wire rack to cool completely.

450g/1lb/2 cups butter

225g/8oz/scant 1¹/₂ cups ground rice or rice flour

FROM THE STORECUPBOARD

225g/8oz/generous 1 cup caster (superfine) sugar

450g/1lb/4 cups plain (all-purpose) flour

5ml/1 tsp salt

demerara (raw) sugar, to decorate

golden caster (superfine) sugar, for dusting

COOK'S TIP *The rice flour adds a toothsome grittiness and shortness to the dough, which is the quality that distinguishes home-made shortbread from the store-bought variety.*

Energy 275kcal/1147kJ; Protein 2.5g; Carbohydrate 32g, of which sugars 10.2g; Fat 15.7g, of which saturates 9.8g; Cholesterol 40mg; Calcium 37mg; Fibre 0.8g; Sodium 115mg

115g/4oz/¹/₂ cup unsalted (sweet) butter

90g/3¹/₂oz/generous ¹/₄ cup golden (light corn) syrup

1 large (US extra large) egg, beaten

150g/5oz preserved stem ginger in syrup, drained and coarsely chopped

FROM THE STORECUPBOARD

350g/12oz/3 cups self-raising (self-rising) flour

pinch of salt

200g/7oz/1 cup golden caster (superfine) sugar

15ml/1 tbsp ground ginger

5ml/1 tsp bicarbonate of soda (baking soda)

Ginger Cookies ✳

These are a supreme treat for ginger lovers – richly spiced cookies packed with chunks of succulent preserved stem ginger. They are sure to give a boost when your energy starts to flag.

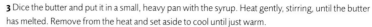

MAKES THIRTY SMALL OR TWENTY LARGE COOKIES

1 Preheat the oven to 160°C/325°F/Gas 3. Line three baking sheets with baking parchment or lightly greased greaseproof (waxed) paper.

2 Sift the flour into a large mixing bowl, add the salt, caster sugar, ground ginger and bicarbonate of soda and stir to combine.

3 Dice the butter and put it in a small, heavy pan with the syrup. Heat gently, stirring, until the butter has melted. Remove from the heat and set aside to cool until just warm.

4 Pour the butter mixture over the dry ingredients, then add the egg and two-thirds of the ginger. Mix thoroughly, then use your hands to bring the dough together.

5 Shape the dough into 20 large or 30 small balls, depending on the size you require. Place them, spaced well apart, on the baking sheets and gently flatten the balls.

6 Press a few pieces of the remaining preserved stem ginger into the top of each of the cookies. Bake for about 12–15 minutes, depending on the size of your cookies, until light golden in colour.

7 Remove from the oven and leave to cool for 1 minute on the baking sheets to firm up. Using a metal spatula, transfer the cookies to a wire rack to cool completely.

Energy 108kcal/454kJ; Protein 1.4g; Carbohydrate 18.9g, of which sugars 10g; Fat 3.5g, of which saturates 2.1g; Cholesterol 15mg; Calcium 24mg; Fibre 0.4g; Sodium 38mg

Chewy Flapjacks ✳

Flapjacks are about the easiest cookies to make and, with a little guidance, can be knocked up in minutes by even the youngest cooks. This chunky, chewy version is flavoured with orange rind.

MAKES EIGHTEEN

1 Preheat the oven to 180°C/350°F/Gas 4. Line the base and sides of a 28 x 20cm/11 x 8in shallow baking tin (pan) with baking parchment.

2 Put the butter, orange rind, syrup and sugar in a large pan and heat gently until the butter has melted.

3 Add the oats to the pan and stir to mix thoroughly. Tip the mixture into the tin and spread into the corners in an even layer.

4 Bake for 15–20 minutes until just beginning to colour around the edges. (The mixture will still be very soft but will harden as it cools.)

5 Leave to cool in the tin, then lift it out of the tin in one piece and cut into fingers.

250g/9oz/generous 1 cup unsalted (sweet) butter

finely grated rind of 1 large orange

225g/8oz/ ²/₃ cup golden (light corn) syrup

375g/13oz/3³/₄ cups rolled oats

FROM THE STORECUPBOARD

75g/3oz/ ¹/₃ cup light muscovado (brown) sugar

Energy 241kcal/1007kJ; Protein 2.7g; Carbohydrate 29.5g, of which sugars 14.3g; Fat 13.2g, of which saturates 7.2g; Cholesterol 30mg; Calcium 18mg; Fibre 1.4g; Sodium 125mg

Scones with Jam and Cream ✳

Scones, often known as biscuits in the US, are thought to originate from Scotland where they are still a popular part of afternoon tea served with jams, jellies and thick cream.

MAKES ABOUT EIGHT

1 Preheat the oven to 230°C/450°F/Gas 8. Sift the flour, baking powder, if using, and salt into a clean, dry mixing bowl. Add the diced butter and rub it into the flour with your fingertips until the mixture resembles fine, evenly textured breadcrumbs.

2 Whisk the lemon juice into the milk and leave for about 1 minute to thicken slightly, then pour into the flour mixture and mix to form a soft but pliable dough. The wetter the mixture, the lighter the resulting scone will be, but if they are too wet they will spread during baking and lose their shape.

3 Knead the dough lightly to form a ball, then roll it out on a floured surface to a thickness of at least 2.5cm/1in. Using a 5cm/2in pastry (cookie) cutter, and dipping it into flour each time, stamp out 12 scones. Place on a floured baking sheet. Re-roll any trimmings and cut out more scones if you can.

4 Brush the tops of the scones lightly with a little milk, then bake in the preheated oven for about 20 minutes, or until they have risen and are golden brown. Remove from the oven and wrap in a clean dish towel to keep them warm and soft until ready to serve. Eat with fruit jam and cream.

50g/2oz/¹⁄₄ cup butter, chilled and diced

15ml/1 tbsp lemon juice

about 400ml/14fl oz/ 1²⁄₃ cups milk, plus extra to glaze

fruit jam and clotted cream or whipped double (heavy) cream, to serve

FROM THE STORECUPBOARD

450g/1lb/4 cups self-raising (self-rising) flour, or 450g/1lb/4 cups plain (all-purpose) flour and 10ml/2 tsp baking powder

5ml/1 tsp salt

VARIATION *To make cheese scones, add 115g/4oz/1 cup of grated Cheddar cheese to the dough and knead it in well before rolling out on a lightly floured surface and cutting rounds.*

Energy 170kcal/720kJ; Protein 4.5g; Carbohydrate 29.9g, of which sugars 2.1g; Fat 4.4g, of which saturates 2.6g; Cholesterol 11mg; Calcium 172mg; Fibre 1.2g; Sodium 338mg

Scotch Pancakes ✳

Variously known as girdlecakes, griddlecakes and Scotch pancakes, these make a quick and easy breakfast, or teatime snack served with butter and drizzled with honey.

MAKES EIGHT–TEN

1 Lightly grease a griddle pan or heavy frying pan, then preheat it. Sift the flour, bicarbonate of soda and cream of tartar together into a mixing bowl. Add the diced butter and rub it into the flour with your fingertips until the mixture resembles fine, evenly textured breadcrumbs.

2 Make a well in the centre of the flour mixture, then stir in the egg. Add the milk a little at a time, stirring it in to check consistency. Add enough milk to give a thick consistency.

3 Cook the pancakes in batches. Drop 3 or 4 evenly sized spoonfuls of the mixture, spaced slightly apart, on the griddle or frying pan. Cook over a medium heat for 2–3 minutes, until bubbles rise to the surface and burst.

4 Turn the pancakes over and cook for a further 2–3 minutes, until golden underneath. Place the cooked pancakes between the folds of a clean dish towel while cooking the remaining batter. Serve warm, with butter and honey.

25g/1oz/2 tbsp butter, diced

1 egg, beaten

about 150ml/¹/₄ pint/ ²/₃ cup milk

a knob (pat) of butter and heather honey, to serve

FROM THE STORECUPBOARD

115g/4oz/1 cup plain (all-purpose) flour

5ml/1 tsp bicarbonate of soda (baking soda)

5ml/1 tsp cream of tartar

Energy 90kcal/379kJ; Protein 2.8g; Carbohydrate 12.1g, of which sugars 1.1g; Fat 3.8g, of which saturates 2.1g; Cholesterol 32mg; Calcium 47mg; Fibre 0.5g; Sodium 36mg

Apple Cakes ✳

These delicate little apple cakes can be rustled up in next to no time for eating hot off the bakestone, if you have one, or frying pan. The quantities have been kept small because they really must be eaten while still very fresh. To make more, simply double up on the measures.

MAKES EIGHT–TEN

1 Preheat the bakestone or heavy frying pan over low to medium heat. Sift the flour and salt into a mixing bowl. Add the butter and, with your fingertips, rub it into the flour until the mixture resembles fine breadcrumbs. Alternatively, whiz the ingredients in a food processor. Stir in the sugar.

2 Stir the grated apple into the flour mixture with enough milk to make a mixture than can be gathered into a ball of soft, moist dough. Work it slightly to make sure the flour is mixed in well.

3 Transfer to a lightly floured surface and roll out the dough to about 5mm/¹/₄in thick. With a 6–7.5cm/2¹/₂–3in cutter, cut out rounds, gathering up the offcuts and re-rolling to make more.

4 Smear a little butter on the hot bakestone or pan and cook the cakes, in batches, for about 4–5 minutes on each side or until golden brown and cooked through. Lift on to a wire rack and dust with caster sugar. Serve warm.

70g/2¹/₂oz/5 tbsp butter, cut into small cubes

1 small cooking apple, peeled, cored and grated

about 30ml/2 tbsp milk

FROM THE STORECUPBOARD

125g/4¹/₂oz/1 cup self-raising (self-rising) flour

small pinch of salt

50g/2oz/4 tbsp demerara (raw) or light muscovado (brown) sugar

caster (superfine) sugar, for dusting

Energy 121kcal/508kJ; Protein 1.4g; Carbohydrate 16.5g, of which sugars 6.9g; Fat 6g, of which saturates 3.7g; Cholesterol 15mg; Calcium 26mg; Fibre 0.6g; Sodium 45mg

VARIATIONS

• For a change, add a large pinch of ground cinnamon or mixed (apple pie) spice to the flour in step 2.

• Add a little vanilla extract to the egg before adding it to the flour mixture in in step 3.

• You could use half butter and half lard instead of just butter, if you like. This will give the cakes a lighter texture.

• The rolled-out dough could just as easily be cut into squares or triangles for a change.

Currant Cakes ✳

This recipe for buttery currant cakes is so simple to make – perfect for an impromptu afternoon snack. Serve them warm or cold, as they are, or buttered and sprinkled with a little cinnamon, if you like.

MAKES ABOUT SIXTEEN

125g/4¹/₂oz/¹/₂ cup butter, cut into small cubes

75g/3oz/¹/₂ cup currants

1 egg

45ml/3 tbsp milk

FROM THE STORECUPBOARD

250g/9oz/2 cups plain (all-purpose) flour

7.5ml/1¹/₂ tsp baking powder

small pinch of salt

100g/3³/₄oz/¹/₂ cup caster (superfine) sugar, plus extra for dusting

1 Heat the bakestone or a large, heavy frying pan over medium to low heat.

2 Sift the flour, baking powder and salt into a large mixing bowl. Then add the butter and, with your fingertips, rub it into the flour until the mixture resembles fine breadcrumbs. Alternatively, you can process the ingredients in a food processor. Stir in the sugar and currants.

3 Lightly beat the egg and with a round-end knife and a cutting action stir it into the flour mixture with enough milk to gather the mixture into a ball of soft dough.

4 Transfer to a lightly floured surface and roll out to about 5mm/¹/₄in thick. With a 6–7.5cm/2¹/₂ –3in cutter, cut out rounds, gathering up the offcuts and re-rolling to make more.

5 Smear a little butter or oil over the hot bakestone or pan and cook the cakes, in small batches, for about 4–5 minutes on each side or until they are slightly risen, golden brown and cooked through. Transfer to a wire rack, dust with caster sugar on both sides and leave to cool.

Energy 128kcal/540kJ; Protein 4.1g; Carbohydrate 22.8g, of which sugars 1.3g; Fat 2.9g, of which saturates 1.4g; Cholesterol 29mg; Calcium 66mg; Fibre 0.9g; Sodium 29mg

Rich Fruit Bread ✳

Stunning to look at and absolutely delicious to eat, this glazed dried fruit bread is perfect for any occasion. Simply leave it to cool in the tin and then slice and serve either on its own or spread with butter for a really decadent treat. It can also be made and given as a gift, wrapped in polythene and tied with a bow. This recipe makes two loaves, but you could halve the quantities and just make one loaf, if you prefer.

MAKES TWO 450G/1LB LOAVES

1 Grease two 450g/1lb loaf tins (pans) or a large baking tray. In a pan, bring the milk to just below boiling point. Add the butter and stir until melted. Pour into a large, heatproof bowl and leave until lukewarm.

2 Put the water and the 5ml/1 tsp sugar in a small bowl, sprinkle in the yeast and leave in a warm place for 15 minutes until frothy.

3 Add the egg to the milk mixture then add the yeast mixture, remaining sugar, salt and cardamom pods. Add half the flour and beat the mixture thoroughly.

4 Dust the fruit generously with flour, stir to mix and add to the mixture with sufficient flour to make a stiff dough that leaves the sides of the bowl clean.

5 Turn the dough on to a lightly floured surface and knead well until the dough feels firm and elastic. Put the dough in a bowl, cover with a damp dish towel and leave in a warm place to rise for 1 hour, or until doubled in size.

6 Turn the risen dough on to a lightly floured surface, knock down and knead again for 2–3 minutes.

7 Shape the dough into two loaves and place in the prepared tins or shape into rounds and put on the baking tray. Leave to rise again for 1 hour, or until nearly doubled in size.

8 Preheat the oven to 180°C/350°F/Gas 4. If you wish, brush the loaves with beaten egg to glaze.

9 Place in the preheated oven and bake for 30–40 minutes, until golden brown and the loaves sound hollow when knocked on the bottom.

10 Brush the cooked loaves with melted butter or dust with icing sugar and decorate with glacé cherries and nuts. Leave to cool on a wire rack, then serve in slices.

250ml/8fl oz/1 cup milk

115g/4oz/¹/₂ cup butter

120ml/4fl oz/¹/₂ cup warm water

2 x 7g/¹/₄oz packets easy-blend (rapid-rise) dried yeast

1 egg, lightly beaten

115g/4oz/¹/₂ cup candied peel, chopped

150g/5oz/1 cup raisins

beaten egg, to glaze (optional)

TO FINISH

melted butter or icing (confectioners') sugar

glacé (candied) cherries

nuts, such as almonds or mixed chopped nuts

FROM THE STORECUPBOARD

90g/3¹/₂oz/¹/₂ cup caster (superfine) sugar, plus 5ml/1 tsp

2.5ml/¹/₂ tsp salt

2.5ml/¹/₂ tsp cardamom pods, crushed

500g/1¹/₄lb/5 cups strong white bread flour

Energy 1889kcal/7972kJ; Protein 33.2g; Carbohydrate 333.5g, of which sugars 143g; Fat 56.3g, of which saturates 32.6g; Cholesterol 225mg; Calcium 658mg; Fibre 12g; Sodium 654mg

15g/¹/₂ oz fresh yeast

300ml/¹/₂ pint/1¹/₄ cups lukewarm water

60ml/4 tbsp lukewarm milk

FROM THE STORECUPBOARD

500g/1¹/₄ lb/5 cups strong white bread flour, plus extra for dusting

10ml/2 tsp salt

Split Tin ✳

As its name suggests, this homely loaf is so called because of the centre split. Infinitely versatile, it tastes vastly superior to store-bought bread, and contains no additives or preservatives.

MAKES ONE 900G/2LB LOAF

1 Lightly grease a 900g/2lb loaf tin. Sift the flour and salt together into a large bowl and make a well in the centre. Mix the yeast with half the lukewarm water in a jug, then stir in the remaining water.

2 Pour the yeast mixture into the centre of the flour and using your fingers, mix in a little flour. Gradually mix in more of the flour from around the edge of the bowl to form a thick, smooth batter.

3 Sprinkle a little more flour from around the edge over the batter and leave in a warm place to prove for about 20 minutes, until bubbles appear. Add the milk and remaining flour; mix to a firm dough.

4 Place the dough on a lightly floured surface and knead for about 10 minutes until smooth and elastic. Place in a lightly oiled bowl, cover with lightly oiled clear film (plastic wrap) and leave to rise, in a warm place, for 1–1¹/₄ hours, or until nearly doubled in bulk.

5 Knock back the dough and turn out on to a lightly floured surface. Shape it into a rectangle, the length of the tin. Roll up lengthways, tuck the ends under and place seam side down in the prepared tin. Cover and leave to rise, in a warm place, for about 20–30 minutes, or until nearly doubled in bulk.

6 Using a sharp knife, make one deep central slash the length of the bread; dust with flour. Leave in a warm place for 10–15 minutes.

7 Meanwhile, preheat the oven to 230°C/450°F/Gas 8. Bake for 15 minutes, then reduce the oven temperature to 200°C/400°F/Gas 6. Bake for 20–25 minutes more, or until the bread is golden and sounds hollow when tapped on the base. Turn out on to a wire rack to cool.

Energy 1888kcal/8008kJ; Protein 72g; Carbohydrate 387.2g, of which sugars 23.2g; Fat 16g, of which saturates 3.9g; Cholesterol 0mg; Calcium 1376mg; Fibre 16.8g; Sodium 4720mg

Quick Wholemeal Loaves ✳

This quick recipe couldn't be simpler to make – the dough requires no kneading and takes only a minute to mix. The bread freezes well, so make a batch and freeze what you don't need immediately.

MAKES THREE 21 X 11 X 6CM/8½ X 4½ X 2½ IN LOAVES

1 Thoroughly grease 3 loaf tins, each about 21 × 11 × 6cm/ 8½ × 4½ × 2½in and set aside in a warm place. Sift the flour and salt together in a large bowl and warm slightly to take off the chill.

2 Sprinkle the dried yeast over 150ml/¼ pint/⅔ cup of the water. After a couple of minutes stir in the muscovado sugar. Leave for 10 minutes, until frothy.

3 Make a well in the centre of the flour and whisk in the yeast mixture and remaining water. The dough should be slippery. Mix for about 1 minute, working the sides into the middle.

4 Divide the mixture among the prepared tins, cover with oiled clear film (plastic wrap) and leave to rise in a warm place, for about 30 minutes, or until the dough has risen by about a third to within 1cm/½ in of the top of the tins.

5 Meanwhile, preheat the oven to 200°C/400°F/Gas 6. Bake for 40 minutes, or until the loaves are crisp and sound hollow when tapped on the base. Turn out on to a wire rack to cool.

15ml/1 tbsp easy-blend (rapid-rise) dried yeast

1.2 litres/2 pints/5 cups warm water (35–38°C)

FROM THE STORECUPBOARD

1.4kg/3lb/12 cups wholemeal (wholewheat) bread flour

15ml/1 tbsp salt

15ml/1 tbsp muscovado (molasses) sugar

COOK'S TIPS

• Muscovado (molasses) sugar is a dark, moist unrefined cane sugar.

• The loaves should stay moist for a few days.

Energy 1466kcal/6235kJ; Protein 59.3g; Carbohydrate 303.4g, of which sugars 15g; Fat 10.3g, of which saturates 1.4g; Cholesterol 0mg; Calcium 180mg; Fibre 42g; Sodium 14mg

Rye Sourdough Bread ✳

This flavoursome loaf is easy to make, although you need to prepare the bread well in advance as the starter takes a few days to ferment.

MAKES TWO LOAVES

1 To make the sourdough starter, put the flour into a large bowl and stir in the yeast. Make a central well, stir in the water and mix together. Cover and leave at room temperature for 2 days.

2 To make the sponge, put the rye flour into a large bowl and mix in the sourdough starter and water. Cover tightly. Leave at room temperature for 8 hours.

3 Put the white bread flour into a large bowl and add the sponge mixture, yeast, water, caraway or dill seeds and salt. Mix to form a soft dough. Turn into a large, clean bowl, sprinkle the top with flour, cover with a clean dish towel and leave to rise in a warm place for about 2 hours, or until doubled in size.

4 Turn the dough on to a lightly floured surface and punch down. Knead for 3–4 minutes until smooth and elastic. Divide the dough in half, then shape each piece into a round loaf.

5 Sprinkle two baking sheets with corn meal. Place the loaves on the top and score each with a sharp knife. Cover and leave in a warm place to rise for 45 minutes, or until doubled in size.

6 Preheat the oven to 220°C/425°F/Gas 7. Fill a roasting pan with boiling water and place in the bottom of the oven. Bake the loaves for about 35 minutes until lightly browned and hollow-sounding when tapped on the bottom. Cool on a wire rack.

7g/¹⁄₄oz packet easy-blend (rapid-rise) dried yeast

250ml/8fl oz/1 cup lukewarm water

corn meal, for sprinkling

FOR THE STARTER

7g/¹⁄₄oz easy-blend (rapid-rise) dried yeast

250ml/8fl oz/1 cup lukewarm water

FOR THE SPONGE

250ml/8fl oz/1 cup lukewarm water

FROM THE STORECUPBOARD

250g/9oz/2¹⁄₄ cups unbleached strong white bread flour or a mixture of ³⁄₄ strong white bread flour and ¹⁄₄ wholemeal (whole-wheat) flour

200g/7oz/1³⁄₄ cups rye flour

1.6kg/3¹⁄₂lb/14 cups strong white bread flour

60ml/4 tbsp caraway or dill seeds

15ml/1 tbsp salt

Energy 3609kcal/15335kJ; Protein 98.8g; Carbohydrate 794.8g, of which sugars 14g; Fat 25.7g, of which saturates 3.8g; Cholesterol 0mg; Calcium 1462mg; Fibre 42g; Sodium 2981mg

Pumpernickel ✳

Made with chocolate or cocoa powder and treacle, this dark rye loaf is packed with flavour. It makes the perfect accompaniment to many dips or makes a delicious open sandwich spread with cream cheese.

MAKES TWO LOAVES

65g/2¹/₂oz cocoa powder (unsweetened)

7g/¹/₄oz packet easy-blend (rapid-rise) dried yeast

15ml/1 tbsp instant coffee powder

105ml/7 tbsp dark beer

90ml/6 tbsp treacle (molasses)

corn meal, for sprinkling

FROM THE STORECUPBOARD

200g/7oz/1³/₄ cups rye flour

300–400g/11–14oz/ 2³/₄–3¹/₂ cups strong white bread flour

5ml/1 tsp salt

2.5ml/¹/₂ tsp sugar

15ml/1 tbsp caraway seeds

15ml/1 tbsp vegetable oil

1 Place a bowl over a pan of water and heat the cocoa with 50ml/2fl oz/¹/₄ cup water. Stir to combine, then set aside. Combine the yeast, flours, salt, sugar, coffee and caraway seeds, if using.

2 Make a well in the flour mixture, then pour in the chocolate or cocoa, 175ml/6fl oz/³/₄ cup water, the beer, oil and treacle. Mix well to form a dough. Turn out on to a lightly floured surface and knead for about 10 minutes, or until smooth.

3 Place the dough in a lightly oiled bowl and turn the dough to coat in oil. Cover with a dish towel and leave to rise for 1¹/₂ hours, or until doubled in size.

4 Oil a baking sheet and sprinkle with corn meal. Turn the dough on to a lightly floured surface and punch down. Knead for 3–4 minutes, then divide the dough and shape into two round or oval loaves. Place the loaves on the baking sheet, cover with a clean dish towel and leave to rise in a warm place for 45 minutes, or until doubled in size.

5 Preheat the oven to 185°C/360°F/Gas 4¹/₂ . Bake the loaves for about 40 minutes, or until they sound hollow when tapped on the base. Leave to cool on a wire rack.

Energy 1276kcal/5400kJ; Protein 27.3g; Carbohydrate 246.4g, of which sugars 42.4g; Fat 24.3g, of which saturates 8.6g; Cholesterol 5mg; Calcium 395mg; Fibre 9.1g; Sodium 187mg

Bakestone Bread ✳

A loaf of bread that is cooked on the hob – watch it rise and marvel! Quick and very easy to make, the finished loaf has a distinctive appearance with a soft texture and scorched crust.

MAKES ONE LOAF

1 Put the flour into a large bowl and add the salt, sugar and yeast. Combine the milk with 150ml/^{1}/4 pint/^{2}/3 cup water and add the butter. Heat gently until the liquid is lukewarm, then stir into the flour and gather it together to make a dough ball.

2 Tip on to a lightly floured surface and knead until smooth, firm and elastic. Put the oil in a bowl and turn the dough in it until it is coated. Cover with cling film (plastic wrap) or a damp dish towel and leave to rise for 1^1/2 hours, or until just about doubled in size.

3 Tip on to a lightly floured surface and knead (gently this time) just until the dough becomes smooth. Using your hands or a rolling pin, press the dough into a rough circle measuring about 20cm/8in in diameter and 2cm/^{3}/4 in thick. Leave to stand for 15 minutes to allow the dough to relax.

4 Meanwhile, heat a bakestone or heavy frying pan over a medium heat. Using a wide spatula and your hands, lift the dough on to the surface and leave it to cook gently for 20 minutes.

5 Turn the bread over and cook the second side for 20 minutes. The top and bottom crusts should be firm and browned while the sides remain pale. Leave to cool on a wire rack.

7g/^{1}/4oz packet easy-blend (rapid-rise) dried yeast

150ml/1^1/4 pints/^{2}/3 cup milk

15g/^{1}/2oz/1 tbsp butter, cut into small pieces

FROM THE STORECUPBOARD

500g/1^1/4lb/4^1/4 cups plain (all-purpose) flour

5ml/1 tsp salt

5ml/1 tsp sugar

5ml/1 tsp oil

COOK'S TIP *Ensure you use standard plain (all-purpose) flour rather than strong white bread flour to make this bread, or it won't work.*

Energy 1928kcal/8179kJ; Protein 52.2g; Carbohydrate 399.8g, of which sugars 18.8g; Fat 24.4g, of which saturates 10.8g; Cholesterol 41mg; Calcium 885mg; Fibre 15.5g; Sodium 2136mg

7g/¹/₄oz packet easy-blend (rapid-rise) dried yeast

250ml/8fl oz/1 cup lukewarm water

FROM THE STORECUPBOARD

500g/1¹/₄lb/4¹/₂ cups strong white bread flour

15ml/1 tbsp salt

15ml/1 tbsp olive oil

Pitta Bread ✳

There are many different types of pitta bread, from flat examples, to those with distinct pockets and thicker cushions. The best pitta bread is always soft, tender and moist.

MAKES TWELVE

1 Combine the flour, yeast and salt. In a large bowl, mix together the oil and water, then stir in half of the flour mixture, stirring in the same direction, until the dough is stiff. Knead in the remaining flour.

2 Place the dough in a clean bowl, cover with a clean dish towel and leave in a warm place for at least 30 minutes and up to 2 hours.

3 Knead the dough for 10 minutes, or until smooth. Lightly oil the bowl, place the dough in it, cover again and leave to rise in a warm place for about 1 hour, or until doubled in size.

4 Divide the dough into 12 equal-size pieces. With lightly floured hands, flatten each piece, then roll out into a round measuring about 20cm/8in and about 5mm–1cm/¹/₄–¹/₂in thick. Keep the rolled breads covered with a clean dish towel while you make the remaining pittas so that they do not begin to dry out on the surface.

5 Heat a large, heavy frying pan over a medium-high heat. When smoking hot, gently lay one piece of flattened dough in the pan and cook for 15–20 seconds. Carefully turn it over and cook the second side for about 1 minute.

6 When large bubbles start to form on the bread, turn it over again. It should puff up. Using a clean dish towel, press on the bread where the bubbles have formed. Cook for 3 minutes, then remove the pitta from the pan. Repeat with the remaining dough until all the pittas have been cooked.

7 Wrap the pitta breads in a clean dish towel, stacking them as each one is cooked. Serve the pittas hot while they are soft and moist.

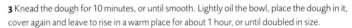

Energy 150kcal/638kJ; Protein 3.9g; Carbohydrate 32.4g, of which sugars 0.6g; Fat 1.5g, of which saturates 0.2g; Cholesterol 0mg; Calcium 59mg; Fibre 1.3g; Sodium 493mg

Onion and Rosemary Focaccia ✳

This bread is rich in olive oil and it has an aromatic topping of red onion, fresh rosemary and coarse salt. Serve it with a tomato and basil salad for a simple lunch, or with a bowl of tomato soup.

SERVES FOUR–FIVE

1 Sift the flour and salt into a bowl. Set aside. Cream the fresh yeast with the sugar, and stir in half the water. If using dried yeast, stir the sugar into the water and sprinkle the yeast over. Set aside in a warm place for 10 minutes, until frothy.

2 Add the yeast, the remaining water, 15ml/1 tbsp of the oil and the rosemary to the flour. Mix together to form a dough, then gather the dough into a ball and knead on a floured work surface for about 5 minutes, until smooth and elastic.

3 Place the dough in a lightly oiled bowl, cover with oiled clear film (plastic wrap) and leave to rise for 1–2 hours in a warm place, until doubled in size.

4 Lightly oil a baking sheet. Knead the dough to form a flat loaf that is about 30cm/12in round or square. Place on the baking sheet, cover with oiled polythene or clear film and leave to rise again in a warm place for a further 40–60 minutes.

5 Preheat the oven to 220°C/425°F/Gas 7. Toss the onion in 15ml/1 tbsp of the oil and scatter over the loaf with the rosemary and coarse salt. Bake for 15–20 minutes, until brown.

7g/¹/₄oz packet easy-blend (rapid-rise) dried yeast

2.5ml/¹/₂ tsp light muscovado (brown) sugar

250ml/8fl oz/1 cup lukewarm water

5ml/1 tsp very finely chopped fresh rosemary, plus 6–8 small sprigs

1 red onion, thinly sliced

FROM THE STORECUPBOARD

450g/1lb/4 cups strong white bread flour, plus extra for dusting

5ml/1 tsp salt

60ml/4 tbsp extra virgin olive oil, plus extra for greasing

coarse salt

VARIATION *You can add a range of toppings to the basic focaccia dough, including chopped, stoned (pitted) black or green olives, sprigs of oregano and diced sun-dried tomatoes.*

Energy 496kcal/2094kJ; Protein 11g; Carbohydrate 90.4g, of which sugars 3.8g; Fat 12.5g, of which saturates 1.8g; Cholesterol 0mg; Calcium 167mg; Fibre 4g; Sodium 496mg

1 baguette or bloomer loaf

FOR THE GARLIC AND
HERB BUTTER

**115g/4oz/¹/₂ cup unsalted
(sweet) butter, softened**

**5–6 large garlic cloves,
finely chopped or crushed**

**30–45ml/2–3 tbsp
chopped fresh herbs
(such as parsley, chervil
and a little tarragon)**

**15ml/1 tbsp chopped
fresh chives**

FROM THE STORECUPBOARD

**salt and ground black
pepper, to taste**

Garlic and Herb Bread ✳

This irresistible garlic bread includes plenty of fresh herbs. You can vary
the overall flavour according to the combination of herbs you choose.

SERVES THREE–FOUR

1 Preheat the oven to 200°C/400°F/Gas 6. Make the garlic and
herb butter by beating the butter with the garlic, herbs, chives
and seasoning to taste.

2 Cut the bread into 1cm/¹/₂in thick diagonal slices, but be sure
to leave them attached at the base so that the loaf stays intact.

3 Spread the garlic and herb butter between the slices evenly,
being careful not to detach them, and then spread any
remaining butter over the top of the loaf.

4 Wrap the loaf in foil, place in the preheated oven and bake for
20–25 minutes, until the butter is melted and the crust is golden
and crisp. Cut the loaf into slices to serve.

Energy 920kcal/3877kJ; Protein 22.1g; Carbohydrate 135.1g, of which sugars 7.2g; Fat 36.2g, of which saturates 20.8g; Cholesterol 82mg; Calcium 317mg; Fibre 6.3g; Sodium 1714mg

7g/¹/₄oz packet easy-blend (rapid-rise) dried yeast

50g/2oz/¹/₄ cup butter

250ml/8fl oz/1 cup lukewarm milk

1 egg, plus 1 yolk

poppy seeds and sesame seeds, for sprinkling

FROM THE STORECUPBOARD

450g/1lb/4 cups strong white bread flour

10ml/2 tsp salt

2.5ml/¹/₂ tsp caster (superfine) sugar

Shaped Dinner Rolls ✳

These professional-looking rolls are perfect for entertaining. You can make double the amount of dough and freeze half, tightly wrapped.

MAKES TWELVE ROLLS

1 Grease 2 baking sheets. Sift the flour and salt into a bowl and stir in the sugar and yeast. Add the butter and rub in until the mixture resembles breadcrumbs. Make a well in the centre. Add the milk and egg to the well and mix to a dough.

2 Knead on a lightly floured surface for 10 minutes, until smooth and elastic. Place in a lightly oiled bowl, cover with lightly oiled clear film (plastic wrap) and leave to rise in a warm place for 1 hour, or until doubled in size. Turn out on to a lightly floured surface, knock back and knead for 2–3 minutes. Divide the dough into 12 equal pieces and shape into rolls as described in steps 3–6.

3 To make plaits: divide each piece of dough into three equal pieces. Roll each piece to a sausage, pinch 3 strips together at one end, then plait them. Pinch the ends together and tuck under the plait.

4 To make trefoils: divide each piece of dough into three and roll into balls. Place the three balls together in a triangular shape.

5 To make batons: shape each piece of dough into an oblong and slash the surface of each with diagonal cuts just before baking.

6 To make knots: shape each piece of dough into a long roll and tie a knot, pulling the ends through.

7 Place the rolls on the baking sheets, spacing them well apart, cover with oiled clear film and leave to rise, in a warm place, for about 30 minutes, or until doubled in bulk.

8 Meanwhile, preheat the oven to 220°C/425°F/Gas 7. Mix the egg yolk with 15ml/1 tbsp water and brush over the rolls. Sprinkle some with poppy seeds and some with sesame seeds. Bake for about 15–18 minutes, until golden. Lift off the sheet and transfer to a wire rack to cool.

Energy 157kcal/665kJ; Protein 4.6g; Carbohydrate 32g, of which sugars 1.8g; Fat 2g, of which saturates 1g; Cholesterol 4mg; Calcium 86mg; Fibre 1.2g; Sodium 228mg

Soft Morning Rolls

These rolls are best served warm, as soon as they are baked as they tend to go stale quite quickly. They are perfect for breakfast with a fried egg and bacon, or spread with butter and your favourite jam.

MAKES 10 ROLLS

1 Grease 2 baking sheets. Sift the flour and salt together into a large bowl and make a well in the centre. Mix the yeast with the milk, then mix in the water. Add to the centre of the flour and mix together to form a soft dough.

2 Knead the dough lightly in the bowl, then cover with lightly oiled clear film and leave to rise, in a warm place, for 1 hour, or until doubled in bulk. Turn the dough out on to a lightly floured surface and knock back.

3 Divide the dough into 10 equal pieces. Knead lightly and, using a rolling pin, shape each piece to a flat oval 10 x 7.5cm/4 x 3in or a flat round 9cm/3½ in.

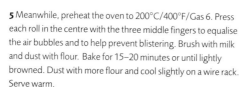

4 Transfer to the prepared baking sheets, spaced well apart, and cover with oiled clear film (plastic wrap). Leave to rise, in a warm place, for about 30 minutes.

5 Meanwhile, preheat the oven to 200°C/400°F/Gas 6. Press each roll in the centre with the three middle fingers to equalise the air bubbles and to help prevent blistering. Brush with milk and dust with flour. Bake for 15–20 minutes or until lightly browned. Dust with more flour and cool slightly on a wire rack. Serve warm.

20g/³/₄ oz fresh yeast

150ml/¹/₄ pint/²/₃ cup lukewarm milk

150ml/¹/₄ pint/²/₃ cup lukewarm water

30ml/2 tbsp milk, for glazing

FROM THE STORECUPBOARD

450g/1lb/4 cups plain (all-purpose) white flour, plus extra for dusting

10ml/2 tsp salt

COOK'S TIP
These rolls are ideal for serving with homemade beef burgers or sausages. If making hot dogs, shape the dough into long, thin rolls before baking.

Energy 160kcal/682kJ; Protein 4.7g; Carbohydrate 35.7g, of which sugars 1.4g; Fat 0.8g, of which saturates 0.3g; Cholesterol 1mg; Calcium 81mg; Fibre 1.4g; Sodium 401mg

Bagels ✳

These ring-shaped rolls are fantastic for breakfast spread with jam, or lunch topped with any number of foods, including cream cheese, cold meats, smoked salmon or fresh, chopped vegetables. The dough is first boiled to give it a chewy texture and then baked in the oven.

MAKES TEN–TWELVE

1 In a bowl, combine the yeast, salt and flour. Pour the lukewarm water into a separate large bowl.

2 Gradually add half the flour to the lukewarm water, beating until it forms a smooth, soft batter.

3 Knead the remaining flour into the batter until the mixture forms a fairly firm, smooth dough that is easy to handle without being too sticky.

4 On a lightly floured surface knead the dough by hand for 10–20 minutes or, if using a bread machine, 5–8 minutes, until shiny and smooth. If the dough is sticky, add a little more flour. (The dough should be much firmer than ordinary bread dough.)

5 Lightly oil a bowl. Place the dough in it and turn to coat it completely in oil. Cover with a clean dishtowel and leave in a warm place for about 40 minutes, or until doubled in size.

6 Turn the dough on to a lightly floured surface and punch down (knock back) with your fists. Knead for 3–4 minutes, or until smooth and elastic.

7 Divide the dough into 10–12 balls. Poke your thumb through each one then, working with your fingers, open the hole to form a bagel measuring 6–7.5cm/2¹/₂–3in diameter. Place on a floured board and leave to rise for 20 minutes, or until doubled in size.

8 Preheat the oven to 200°C/400°F/Gas 6. Bring 3–4 litres/5–7 pints/2¹/₂–3¹/₂ quarts water to the boil in a large pan and add the sugar. Lower the heat to a gentle boil. Lightly oil a baking sheet and sprinkle with corn meal. Beat the egg yolk with 15ml/1 tbsp water.

9 Add the bagels, one at a time, to the boiling water, until you have a single layer of bagels. Cook for 8 minutes, turning occasionally so that they cook evenly. Remove the bagels from the pan with a slotted spoon, drain and place on the prepared baking sheet.

10 Brush each bagel with the egg mixture. Bake for about 25–30 minutes, until well browned. Cool on a wire rack.

7g/¹/₄oz packet easy-blend (rapid-rise) dried yeast

250ml/8fl oz/1 cup lukewarm water

corn meal, for sprinkling

1 egg yolk

FROM THE STORECUPBOARD

25ml/1¹/₂ tbsp salt

500g/1¹/₄lb/4¹/₂ cups strong white bread flour

oil for greasing

30ml/2 tbsp sugar

VARIATIONS

• Add dried onions, garlic granules or poppy seeds to the bagel dough before boiling, or top the bagels with poppy seeds, sesame seeds, caraway seeds, dried onion or garlic granules before baking.

• For a healthier version, subsitute half the strong white flour for strong wholemeal (whole-wheat) bread flour.

Energy 188kcal/801kJ; Protein 5g; Carbohydrate 42g, of which sugars 3.9g; Fat 1.2g, of which saturates 0.3g; Cholesterol 20mg; Calcium 74mg; Fibre 1.6g; Sodium 985mg

Crumpets ✳

Home-made crumpets are less doughy and not as heavy as most supermarket versions. Serve them lightly toasted, oozing with butter.

MAKES ABOUT TWENTY CRUMPETS

1 Lightly grease a heavy frying pan and 4 8cm/3¹/₄ in pastry cutters or crumpet rings. Sift the flours and salt together into a bowl and make a well in the centre. Heat the milk and water mixture, oil and sugar until lukewarm. Mix the yeast with 150ml/¹/₄ pint/²/₃ cup of this liquid.

2 Add the yeast mixture and remaining liquid to the flour and beat for about 5 minutes, until smooth and elastic. Cover with lightly oiled clear film (plastic wrap) and leave to rise in a warm place for about 1¹/₂ hours, until bubbly. Stir the dissolved soda into the batter. Re-cover and leave to rise for 30 minutes.

3 Place the cutters or rings in the pan and warm, then pour in batter to 1cm/¹/₂ in deep. Cook for 6–7 minutes. The tops should be dry, with a mass of tiny holes. Remove the cutters or rings and turn the crumpets over. Cook for 1–2 minutes, or until pale golden. Repeat with remaining batter. Serve warm.

600ml/1 pint/2¹/₂ cups milk and water mixed

15g/¹/₂ oz fresh yeast

FROM THE STORECUPBOARD

225g/8oz/2 cups plain (all-purpose) flour

225g/8oz/2 cups strong white bread flour

10ml/2 tsp salt

30ml/2 tbsp sunflower or vegetable oil

15ml/1 tbsp caster (superfine) sugar

2.5ml/¹/₂ tsp bicarbonate of soda (baking soda), dissolved in 120ml/4fl oz/ ¹/₂ cup lukewarm water

English Muffins ✳

Perfect served warm, split open and buttered for afternoon tea; or try these favourites toasted, split and topped with ham and eggs for brunch.

MAKES NINE MUFFINS

1 Flour a non-stick baking sheet. Lightly grease a griddle. Sift the flour and salt into a large bowl and make a well in the centre. Blend 150ml/¹/₄ pint/²/₃ cup of the milk, sugar and yeast together. Stir in the remaining milk and butter or oil.

2 Add to the the flour and beat for 4–5 minutes, until smooth and elastic. Cover with oiled clear film (plastic wrap) and leave to rise in a warm place for 45–60 minutes, or until doubled in bulk.

3 Turn out on a floured surface and knock back. Roll out to 1cm/¹/₂ in thick. Using a 7.5cm/3in plain cutter, cut out 9 rounds. Dust with rice flour or semolina and place on the baking sheet. Cover and leave to rise in a warm place for about 20–30 minutes.

4 Warm the griddle over a medium heat. Cook the muffins slowly in batches for about 7 minutes on each side, or until golden brown. Transfer to a wire rack to cool.

350–375ml/12–13fl oz/ 1¹/₂–1²/₃ cups lukewarm milk

15g/¹/₂ oz fresh yeast

15ml/1 tbsp melted butter or olive oil

rice flour or semolina, for dusting

FROM THE STORECUPBOARD

450g/1lb/4 cups strong white bread flour

7.5ml/1¹/₂ tsp salt

2.5ml/¹/₂ tsp caster (superfine) sugar

COOK'S TIP *Muffins should be cut around the edge only and then torn apart. If toasting, toast the muffins first and then split them in half.*

Top: Energy 93kcal/393kJ; Protein 3g; Carbohydrate 16.5g, of which sugars 1g; Fat 2.1g, of which saturates 1g; Cholesterol 21mg; Calcium 48mg; Fibre 0.6g; Sodium 21mg

Above: Energy 201kcal/852kJ; Protein 6g; Carbohydrate 40.7g, of which sugars 2.6g; Fat 2.7g, of which saturates 1.4g; Cholesterol 6mg; Calcium 117mg; Fibre 1.5g; Sodium 356mg

Classic Preserves

Making jams, curds, marmalades, pickles, chutneys and relishes is a fantastic way to preserve seasonal vegetables and fruits for use later on in the year. Sweet preserves, such as Blackcurrant Jam or Lemon Curd, are delicious spread on toast or used to sandwich sponge cakes together, while savoury ones, such as Mango Chutney or Mixed Vegetable Pickle, make an ideal accompaniment to cheeses, curries and cold meats.

Blackberry and Apple Jam ✳

This simple recipe is ideal for the late summer and early autumn when a family day out blackberrying can supply the berries, and windfall apples are plentiful. Freeze any berries that you don't use immediately.

MAKES ABOUT 4.5KG/10LB

1 Remove any bad bruises from the cooking apples before weighing, then peel, core and cut them up roughly. Put into a large pan. Add half of the water, bring to the boil and simmer until the apples are soft.

2 Meanwhile pick over the blackberries, wash them gently and drain well.

3 Put the blackberries into a preserving pan with 300ml/¹/₂ pint/1¹/₄ cups water and cook gently until tender.

4 If you want a seedless jam, press the cooked berries through a sieve (strainer), then return to the rinsed preserving pan. Add the apples and the sugar to the berries.

5 Stir over a low heat until the sugar has completely dissolved, and then bring to the boil. Boil hard for about 15 minutes, or until setting point is reached (105°C/220°F) (*see* Cook's Tip).

6 Skim if necessary, then pour into warmed, sterilized jars. Cover, seal and store in a cool, dark place until required. The jam will store well for at least 6 months, if correctly stored.

1.3kg/3lb cooking apples

1.8kg/4lb/16 cups blackberries

FROM THE STORECUPBOARD

2.75kg/6lb/13¹/₂ cups sugar, warmed

> **COOK'S TIP** To test if jam or jelly has set, put a spoonful on to a cold saucer. Allow it to cool slightly, then push the surface with your finger. Setting point has been reached if a skin has formed and it wrinkles. If not, boil for a little longer and keep testing until it sets.

Raspberry Jam ✳

Universally popular, this delicious jam is perfect with scones and cream, on toast, or as a filling for a sponge cake. Raspberries are low in pectin and acid, so they will not set firmly – but a soft set is perfect for this jam.

MAKES ABOUT 3.1KG/7LB

1 Put 175g/6oz/1 cup of the raspberries into the preserving pan and crush them. Add the rest of the fruit and the lemon juice, and simmer until soft and pulpy.

2 Add the sugar and stir until dissolved, then bring back to the boil and boil hard until setting point is reached (105°C/220°F), testing after 3–4 minutes (*see* Cook's Tip).

3 Pour into warmed, sterilized jars. When cold, cover, seal and store in a cool, dark place until required. The jam will store well for 6 months.

1.8kg/4lb/10²/₃ cups firm raspberries

juice of 1 large lemon

FROM THE STORECUPBOARD

1.8kg/4lb/9 cups sugar, warmed

Top: Energy 11,740kcal/50,063kJ; Protein 33.9g; Carbohydrate 3081.3g, of which sugars 3081.3g; Fat 4.9g, of which saturates 0g; Cholesterol 0mg; Calcium 2.29g; Fibre 76.6g; Sodium 227mg

Above: Energy 7542kcal/32,220kJ; Protein 34.2g; Carbohydrate 1963.8g, of which sugars 1963.8g; Fat 5.4g, of which saturates 1.8g; Cholesterol 0mg; Calcium 1.40g; Fibre 45g; Sodium 162mg

Blackcurrant Jam ✳

This jam has a rich, fruity flavour and a wonderfully strong dark colour. It is rich in colour and taste and is ideal with scones for tea or spread on croissants for a continental-style breakfast.

MAKES ABOUT 1.3KG/3LB

1 Place the blackcurrants, orange rind and juice and water in a large heavy pan. Bring to the boil, reduce the heat and simmer for 30 minutes.

2 Add the warmed sugar to the pan and stir over a low heat until the sugar has dissolved.

3 Bring the mixture to the boil and cook for about 8 minutes, or until the jam reaches setting point (105°C/220°F).

4 Remove the pan from the heat and skim off any scum from the surface using a slotted spoon. Leave to cool for 5 minutes, then stir in the cassis, if using.

5 Pour the jam into warmed, sterilized jars and seal. Leave the jars to cool completely, then label and store in a cool, dark place.

1.3kg/3lb/12 cups blackcurrants

grated rind and juice of 1 orange

475ml/16fl oz/2 cups water

30ml/2 tbsp cassis (optional)

FROM THE STORECUPBOARD

1.3kg/3lb/6¹/₂ cups sugar, warmed

COOK'S TIP

• Before potting, it is essential to sterilize containers to destroy any micro-organisms. Check jars and bottles for cracks or damage, then wash in hot, soapy water, rinse and turn upside-down to drain. They may then be sterilized in one of two ways.

• To sterilize in the oven, stand the containers on a baking sheet lined with kitchen paper. Rest any lids on top. Place in a cold oven, then heat to 110°C/225°F/Gas ¹/₄ and bake for 30 minutes. Leave to cool slightly before filling.

• To sterilize in the microwave, half fill the glass containers with water and heat on full power until the water has boiled for one minute. Swirl the water inside them, then drain and leave to dry.

Energy 5504kcal/23503kJ; Protein 18.4g; Carbohydrate 1448.7g, of which sugars 1448.7g; Fat 0.1g, of which saturates 0g; Cholesterol 0mg; Calcium 1474mg; Fibre 46.9g; Sodium 122mg

Garden Jam ✳

This versatile mixed fruit jam uses a range of soft fruits, including blackcurrants, blackberries, raspberries and strawberries. You can use any combination, depending on what is available.

MAKES ABOUT 3.6KG/8LB

1 Put the blackcurrants into a large preserving pan and add 150ml/¹/₄ pint/²/₃ cup water. Bring to the boil and simmer until the berries are almost cooked. Add the rest of the fruit and simmer gently, stirring occasionally, for about 10 minutes, or until the fruit is just turning soft.

2 Add the warm sugar to the pan and stir over a gentle heat until it is completely dissolved.

3 Bring to the boil and boil hard until setting point is reached (105°C/220°F). To test, put a spoonful of jam on to a cold saucer. Cool slightly, then push the surface. It is ready if a skin has formed and it wrinkles to the touch. If not, boil for longer and keep testing, until it sets.

4 Remove any scum from the surface of the jam and pour into warmed, sterilized jars. Cover immediately, leave to cool, then label. Store in a cool, dark place for up to 6 months.

**450g/1lb/4 cups
blackcurrants
(stalks removed)**

**450g/1lb/4 cups
blackberries (or
whitecurrants
or redcurrants)**

**450g/1lb/2²/₃ cups
raspberries (or
loganberries)**

**450g/1lb/4 cups
strawberries**

FROM THE STORECUPBOARD

**1.8kg/4lb/9 cups
sugar, warmed**

Energy 7583kcal/32,328kJ; Protein 23.9g; Carbohydrate 1991.7g, of which sugars 1991.7g; Fat 1.4g, of which saturates 0g; Cholesterol 0mg; Calcium 1.44g; Fibre 31.1g; Sodium 203mg

Damson Jam ✳

Dark, plump damsons used only to be found growing in the wild, but today they are available commercially. They produce a deeply coloured and richly flavoured jam that makes a delicious treat spread on warm Scotch pancakes or toasted crumpets at teatime.

MAKES ABOUT 2KG/4¹/₂LB

1 Put the damsons in a preserving pan and pour in the water. Bring to the boil then reduce the heat and simmer gently until the damsons are soft.

2 Add the sugar to the pan and stir it in thoroughly. Bring the mixture to the boil.

3 Skim off the stones (pits) as they rise to the surface. Boil to setting point (105°C/220°F).

4 Remove from the heat, leave to cool for 10 minutes, then transfer to warmed, sterilized jam jars. Seal immediately to ensure the jar remains sterile. Leave to cool, then label with the name of the jam and the date. Store in a cool, dark place.

1kg/2¹/₄lb damsons or wild plums

1.4 litres/2¹/₄ pints/ 6 cups water

FROM THE STORECUPBOARD

1kg/2¹/₄lb/5 cups preserving or granulated white sugar, warmed

Energy 4300kcal/18360kJ; Protein 11g; Carbohydrate 1133g, of which sugars 1133g; Fat 1g, of which saturates 0g; Cholesterol 0mg; Calcium 660mg; Fibre 16g; Sodium 80mg

Sour Cherry Jam ✳

Stunning in colour and taste, this popular summer jam should be made when the sour cherries are in season. This recipe is for a runny conserve, which is delectable spooned on to fresh bread or drizzled over yogurt.

MAKES ABOUT 2KG/4½LB

1 Rinse and drain the cherries and put them into a large, heavy pan. Spoon the sugar over them, making sure they are all covered, and leave the cherries to weep overnight.

2 Place the pan over the heat and bring the liquid to the boil, stirring from time to time.

3 Add the lemon juice, reduce the heat, and simmer for about 25 minutes, or until the liquid thickens, bearing in mind that this will be a fairly liquid jam.

4 Leave the jam to cool in the pan and then spoon it into warmed, sterilized jars. Keep in a cool, dry place ready to enjoy with bread, or to spoon over milk and rice puddings. The jam will keep well for up to 6 months,

1kg/2¼lb/6 cups fresh sour cherries, stalks and stones (pits) removed

juice of 1 lemon

FROM THE STORECUPBOARD

1kg/2¼lb/5 cups sugar

VARIATION *If sour cherries are unavailable, you can use sweet ones instead, but you may need to increase the amount of lemon juice you add to prevent the end result from being too sweet.*

Energy 4420kcal/18840kJ; Protein 14g; Carbohydrate 1160g, of which sugars 1160g; Fat 1g, of which saturates 0g; Cholesterol 0mg; Calcium 660mg; Fibre 9g; Sodium 70mg

Dried Apricot Jam ✳

This richly flavoured jam can be made at any time of year, so even if you miss the short apricot season, you can still enjoy the delicious taste of sweet, tangy apricot jam all year round.

MAKES ABOUT 2KG/4¹/₂LB

1 Put the apricots in a bowl, pour over the apple juice and leave to soak overnight.

2 Pour the soaked apricots and juice into a preserving pan and add the lemon juice and rind. Bring to the boil, then lower the heat and simmer for 15–20 minutes until the apricots are soft.

3 Add the warmed sugar to the pan and bring to the boil, stirring until the sugar has completely dissolved. Boil for 15–20 minutes, or until setting point is reached (105°C/220°F).

4 Stir the chopped almonds into the jam and leave to stand for about 15 minutes, then pour the jam into warmed, sterilized jars. Seal, then leave to cool completely before labelling. Store in a cool, dark place.

675g/1¹/₂lb dried apricots

900ml/1¹/₂ pints/3³/₄ cups apple juice

juice and grated rind of 2 unwaxed lemons

50g/2oz/¹/₂ cup blanched almonds, coarsely chopped

FROM THE STORECUPBOARD

675g/1¹/₂lb/scant 3¹/₂ cups preserving or granulated sugar, warmed

Energy 4032kcal/17163kJ; Protein 40.9g; Carbohydrate 955.2g, of which sugars 953.8g; Fat 31.9g, of which saturates 2.2g; Cholesterol 0mg; Calcium 970mg; Fibre 46.2g; Sodium 142mg

Dried Fig Jam ✳

This delectable homemade winter jam is made with dried figs and pine nuts. Look for plump, succulent dried figs with a springy texture – available in some supermarkets, delicatessens and health food stores.

MAKES ENOUGH FOR THREE–FOUR 450G/1LB JAM JARS

1 Put the sugar and 600ml/1 pint/2¹/₂ cups water into a heavy pan and bring to the boil, stirring all the time, until the sugar has dissolved.

2 Lower the heat and simmer for 5–10 minutes, until the syrup begins to thicken. Stir in the lemon juice, aniseed and figs to the sugar syrup.

3 Bring to the boil once more, then lower the heat again and simmer for 15–20 minutes, until the figs are tender.

4 Add the pine nuts and simmer for a further 5 minutes. Leave to cool in the pan before spooning into sterilized jars and sealing. Stored in a cool, dry place, the jam will keep for up to 6 months.

juice of 1 lemon

5ml/1 tsp ground aniseed

about 700g/1lb 9oz dried figs, coarsely chopped

45–60ml/3–4 tbsp pine nuts

FROM THE STORECUPBOARD

450g/1lb/2¹/₄ cups sugar

Energy 869kcal/3693kJ; Protein 8.4g; Carbohydrate 197.5g, of which sugars 197.5g; Fat 10.5g, of which saturates 0.5g; Cholesterol 0mg; Calcium 492mg; Fibre 13.4g; Sodium 115mg

900g/2lb Seville (Temple) oranges

1.75 litres/3 pints/ 7¹/₂ cups water

FROM THE STORECUPBOARD

1.3kg/3lb/6¹/₂ cups sugar, warmed

Oxford Marmalade ✻

The characteristic caramel colour and rich flavour of a traditional Oxford marmalade is obtained by cutting the fruit coarsely and cooking it for several hours before adding the sugar.

MAKES ABOUT 2.25KG/5LB

1 Scrub the orange skins, then remove the rind using a vegetable peeler. Thickly slice the rind and put in a large pan.

2 Chop the fruit, reserving the pips (seeds), and add to the rind in the pan, along with the water. Tie the orange pips in a piece of muslin (cheesecloth) and add to the pan. Bring to the boil, then cover and simmer for 2 hours. Add more water during cooking to maintain the same volume. Remove the pan from the heat and leave overnight.

3 The next day, remove the muslin bag from the oranges, squeezing well, and return the pan to the heat. Bring to the boil, then cover and simmer for 1 hour.

4 Add the warmed sugar to the pan, then slowly bring the mixture to the boil, stirring until the sugar has dissolved completely. Increase the heat and boil rapidly for about 15 minutes, or until setting point is reached (105°C/220°F).

5 Remove the pan from the heat and skim off any scum from the surface. Leave to cool for about 10 minutes, stir, then pour into warmed, sterilized jars and seal. When cold, label, then store in a cool, dark place for up to 6 months.

Energy 5455kcal/23275kJ; Protein 16.4g; Carbohydrate 1435g, of which sugars 1435g; Fat 0.9g, of which saturates 0g; Cholesterol 0mg; Calcium 1112mg; Fibre 15.3g; Sodium 123mg

Lemon Curd ✳

This classic tangy, creamy curd is still one of the most popular of all the curds. It is delicious spread thickly over bread and also makes a wonderfully rich, zesty sauce spooned over fresh fruit tarts.

MAKES ABOUT 450G/1LB

3 lemons

115g/4oz/¹/₂ cup unsalted (sweet) butter, diced

2 large (US extra large) eggs

2 large egg yolks

FROM THE STORECUPBOARD

200g/7oz/1 cup caster (superfine) sugar

1 Wash the lemons, then finely grate the rind and place in a large heatproof bowl. Using a sharp knife, halve the lemons and squeeze the juice into the bowl. Set over a pan of gently simmering water and add the sugar and butter. Stir until the sugar has dissolved and the butter melted.

2 Put the eggs and yolks in a bowl and beat together with a fork. Pour the eggs through a sieve (strainer) into the lemon mixture, and whisk well until thoroughly combined.

3 Stir the mixture constantly over the heat until the lemon curd thickens and lightly coats the back of a wooden spoon.

4 Remove the pan from the heat and pour the curd into small, warmed, sterilized jars. Cover, seal and label. Store in a cool, dark place, ideally in the refrigerator. Use within 3 months. (Once opened, store in the refrigerator.)

COOK'S TIP
If you are really impatient when it comes to cooking, it is possible to cook the curd in a heavy pan directly over a low heat. However, you really need to watch it like a hawk to avoid the mixture curdling. If the curd looks as though it's beginning to curdle, plunge the base of the pan in cold water and beat vigorously.

VARIATION
Make the most of the short Seville (Temple) orange season by making a batch of orange curd as well as, or instead of, some Oxford marmalade. Using the same ingredients and method as the recipe for lemon curd, simply substitute the finely grated rind and juice of 2 Seville oranges for the 3 lemons. The result will be slightly sweeter than the lemon version.

Energy 1942kcal/8119kJ; Protein 22.5g; Carbohydrate 209.7g, of which sugars 209.7g; Fat 118.8g, of which saturates 66.8g; Cholesterol 1105mg; Calcium 242mg; Fibre 0g; Sodium 895mg

Spiced Apple Mincemeat ✳

This fruity mincemeat is traditionally used to fill little pies at Christmas but it can also be used as a filling for large tarts. To make a lighter mincemeat, add some extra grated apple just before using.

MAKES ABOUT 1.8KG/4LB

1 Put the apples, apricots, dried fruit, almonds, suet and sugar in a large, non-metallic bowl and stir together with a metal spoon until thoroughly combined.

2 Add the orange and lemon rind and juice, cinnamon, nutmeg, ginger and brandy and mix well. Cover the bowl with a clean dish towel, place in a cool place and leave to stand for 2 days, stirring occasionally.

3 Spoon the mincemeat into cool sterilized jars, pressing down well, and being very careful not to trap any air bubbles. Cover and seal.

4 Store the jars in a cool, dark place for at least 4 weeks before using. Once opened, store in the refrigerator and use within 4 weeks. Unopened, the mincemeat will keep for 1 year.

500g/1¼lb tart cooking apples, peeled, cored and finely diced

115g/4oz/½ cup ready-to-eat dried apricots, coarsely chopped

900g/2lb/5⅓ cups luxury dried mixed fruit

115g/4oz/1 cup whole blanched almonds, chopped

175g/6oz/1 cup shredded beef or vegetarian suet (chilled, grated shortening)

grated rind and juice of 1 orange

grated rind and juice of 1 lemon

120ml/4fl oz/½ cup brandy

FROM THE STORECUPBOARD

225g/8oz/generous 1 cup dark muscovado (molasses) sugar

5ml/1 tsp ground cinnamon

2.5ml/½ tsp freshly grated nutmeg

2.5ml/½ tsp ground ginger

COOK'S TIPS

• If, when opened, the mincemeat seems dry, pour a little extra brandy or orange juice into the jar and gently stir in. You may need to remove a spoonful or two of the mincemeat from the jar to do this.

• The flavour of mincemeat improves with age, so it is a good idea to make plenty in January, ready for the next Christmas.

Energy 6071kcal/25579kJ; Protein 52.2g; Carbohydrate 963.6g, of which sugars 939.7g; Fat 227.3g, of which saturates 92.4g; Cholesterol 144mg; Calcium 1156mg; Fibre 44.4g; Sodium 488mg

Poached Plums in Brandy ✳

Bottling plums in a spicy syrup is a great way to preserve the flavours of autumn and provide a store of instant desserts during the winter months. Serve them with whipped cream or vanilla ice cream.

MAKES ABOUT 900G/2LB

1 Put the brandy, lemon rind, sugar and cinnamon in a large pan and heat gently until the sugar dissolves.

2 Add the plums and poach for 15 minutes until soft. Remove the fruit and pack in sterilized jars.

3 Boil the syrup rapidly until reduced by a third, then strain over the plums to cover.

4 Seal the jars tightly. Label when cold and store for up to 6 months in a cool, dark place.

600ml/1 pint/2¹/₂ cups brandy

rind of 1 lemon, peeled in a long strip

900g/2lb plums

FROM THE STORECUPBOARD

350g/12oz/1³/₄ cups caster (superfine) sugar

1 cinnamon stick

VARIATION *Any member of the plum family can be preserved using this recipe. Try damsons or wild yellow plums as an alternative.*

Energy 3035kcal/12792kJ; Protein 7.1g; Carbohydrate 444.9g, of which sugars 444.9g; Fat 0.9g, of which saturates 0g; Cholesterol 0mg; Calcium 302mg; Fibre 14.4g; Sodium 39mg

COOK'S TIPS

• Make this delicious jam when tomatoes are in season, as they will be cheaper during this time.

• Do not be tempted to use canned tomatoes; they are too soft and will not produce the desired consistency or taste.

1kg/2¹/₄lb firm plum tomatoes

115g/4oz/1 cup whole blanched almonds

FROM THE STORECUPBOARD

500g/1¹/₄ lb/2¹/₂ cups sugar

8–10 whole cloves

Plum Tomato Jam ✳

This unusual summer jam is rarely available commercially, but it is well worth making at home. Made with slightly unripe or firm plum tomatoes, it is syrupy in consistency, and spooned, rather than spread, on to bread.

MAKES ENOUGH FOR TWO–THREE 450G/1LB JAM JARS

1 Skin the plum tomatoes. Submerge them for a few seconds in a bowl of boiling water, then plunge them straight away into a bowl of cold water. Remove them from the water one at a time and peel off the skins with your fingers or a small knife.

2 Place the skinned tomatoes in a heavy pan and cover with the sugar. Leave them to sit for a few hours, or overnight, to draw out some of the juices, then stir in 150ml/¹/₄ pint/²/₃ cup water. The tomatoes should be quite juicy – if not, stir in some more water, you may need up to 300ml/ ¹/₂ pint/1¹/₄ cups.

3 Place the pan over a low heat and stir gently with a wooden spoon for about 5 minutes, until the sugar has completely dissolved.

4 Bring the syrup to the boil and boil for a few minutes, skimming off any froth, then lower the heat and stir in the almonds and cloves.

5 Simmer gently for about 25 minutes, stirring from time to time to prevent the mixture from sticking to the bottom of the pan and burning, which would spoil the flavour.

6 Turn off the heat and leave the jam to cool in the pan before spooning into sterilized jars and sealing. Stored in a cool, dry place, it will keep for several months.

Energy 948kcal/4016kJ; Protein 11.3g; Carbohydrate 187.1g, of which sugars 186.1g; Fat 22.4g, of which saturates 2g; Cholesterol 0mg; Calcium 204mg; Fibre 6.2g; Sodium 45mg

Onion Confit *

This jam of caramelized onions in sweet-sour balsamic vinegar is an ideal accompaniment to cheese, bread and salads. You can make it with red, white or yellow onions, but yellow onions will produce the sweetest result.

MAKES ABOUT 500G/1¼ LB

1 Reserve 5ml/1 tsp of the oil, then heat the remaining oil with the butter in a large pan. Add the onions, cover and cook gently over a low heat for about 15 minutes, stirring occasionally.

2 Season the onions with salt and ground black pepper, then add the thyme, bay leaf and sugar. Cook slowly, uncovered, for a further 15–20 minutes until the onions are very soft and dark. Stir the onions occasionally during cooking to prevent them sticking or burning.

3 Add the prunes, vinegar, wine and 60ml/4 tbsp water to the pan and cook over a low heat, stirring frequently, for 20 minutes, or until most of the liquid has evaporated. Add a little more water and reduce the heat if it looks dry. Remove from the heat.

4 Adjust the seasoning if necessary, adding more sugar and/or vinegar to taste. Leave the confit to cool then stir in the remaining 5ml/1 tsp olive oil and serve.

15g/½ oz/1 tbsp butter

500g/1¼ lb onions, sliced

3–5 fresh thyme sprigs

1 fresh bay leaf

50g/2oz/¼ cup ready-to-eat prunes, chopped

120ml/4fl oz/½ cup red wine

FROM THE STORECUPBOARD

30ml/2 tbsp olive oil

30ml/2 tbsp light muscovado (brown) sugar, plus a little extra

30ml/2 tbsp balsamic vinegar, plus a little extra

salt and ground black pepper, to taste

Energy 678kcal/2827kJ; Protein 7.5g; Carbohydrate 87.9g, of which sugars 76.4g; Fat 35.5g, of which saturates 11g; Cholesterol 32mg; Calcium 161mg; Fibre 9.8g; Sodium 113mg

Apple and Sultana Chutney ✳

Use wine or cider vinegar for this chutney to give it a subtle and mellow flavour. For a mild chutney, add only a little cayenne, for a spicier one increase the quantity to taste. It is perfect with cheese and soda bread.

MAKES ABOUT 900G/2LB

350g/12oz cooking apples

115g/4oz/²/₃ cup sultanas (golden raisins)

50g/2oz onion

25g/1oz/¹/₄ cup almonds, blanched

red chillies (optional)

FROM THE STORECUPBOARD

5ml/1 tsp white peppercorns

2.5ml/¹/₂ tsp coriander seeds

175g/6oz/scant 1 cup sugar

10ml/2 tsp salt

5ml/1 tsp ground ginger

450ml/³/₄ pint/scant 2 cups cider vinegar

1.5ml/¹/₄ tsp cayenne pepper

1 Peel, core and chop the apples. Chop the sultanas, onion and almonds. Tie the peppercorns and coriander seeds in muslin (cheesecloth), using a long piece of string, and then tie to the handle of a preserving pan or stainless steel pan.

2 Put the sugar, salt, ground ginger and vinegar into the pan, with the cayenne pepper to taste. Heat gently, stirring, until the sugar has completely dissolved.

3 Add the chopped fruit. Bring to the boil and simmer for 1¹/₂–2 hours, or until most of the liquid has evaporated.

4 Spoon into warmed, sterilized jars and place one chilli in each jar, if using. Leave until completely cold, then cover, seal and label. Store in a cool, dark place. The chutney is best left for a month to mature before use and will keep for at least 6 months, if correctly stored.

Energy 1299kcal/5525kJ; Protein 10.9g; Carbohydrate 299.5g, of which sugars 297.7g; Fat 14.9g, of which saturates 1.1g; Cholesterol 0mg; Calcium 254mg; Fibre 10.4g; Sodium 3.97g

Pear and Walnut Chutney ✳

This chutney recipe is ideal for using up hard windfall pears. Its mellow flavour is excellent with cheese and oatcakes and also good with dishes made with grains, such as in pilaff or with tabbouleh.

MAKES ABOUT 1.8KG/4LB

1 Peel and core the fruit, then chop into 2.5cm/1in chunks. Peel and quarter the onions, then chop into pieces the same size. Place in a preserving pan with the vinegar.

2 Slowly bring to the boil, then reduce the heat and simmer for 40 minutes, until tender, stirring the mixture occasionally.

3 Meanwhile, put the sultanas in a small bowl, pour over the orange juice and leave to soak.

4 Add the sugar, sultanas, and orange rind and juice to the pan. Gently heat until the sugar has dissolved, then simmer for 30–40 minutes, or until the chutney is thick and no excess liquid remains, stirring frequently

5 Toast the walnuts in a non-stick pan for 5 minutes, until lightly coloured. Stir into the chutney with the cinnamon.

6 Spoon the chutney into warmed, sterilized jars, cover and seal. Store in a cool, dark place and leave to mature for at least 1 month. Use within 1 year.

1.2kg/2¹/₂lb firm pears

225g/8oz tart apples

225g/8oz onions

175g/6oz/generous 1 cup sultanas (golden raisins)

finely grated rind and juice of 1 orange

115g/4oz/1 cup walnuts, roughly chopped

FROM THE STORECUPBOARD

450ml/³/₄ pint/scant 2 cups cider vinegar

400g/14oz/2 cups sugar

2.5ml/¹/₂ tsp ground cinnamon

Energy 3501kcal/14797kJ; Protein 29.8g; Carbohydrate 705.3g, of which sugars 699.3g; Fat 81.4g, of which saturates 6.4g; Cholesterol 0mg; Calcium 603mg; Fibre 40.7g; Sodium 189mg

Mango Chutney *

The sweet, tangy flavour of this classic chutney complements the warm taste of Indian spices perfectly, but it is equally good scooped up on crispy fried poppadums, served with chargrilled chicken, turkey or duck breasts, with potato wedges and soured cream, or spread on cheese on toast.

MAKES ABOUT 1KG/2¹/₄ LB

1 Slice the mango flesh into medium-sized chunks and place in a large, non-metallic bowl. Sprinkle with salt and set aside.

2 Meanwhile, cut the apples into quarters, then remove and discard the cores and peel. Chop the flesh roughly.

3 Put the malt vinegar and sugar in a preserving pan and heat gently, stirring occasionally, until the sugar has dissolved.

4 Add the mangoes, apple, onion, garlic and ginger to the pan and slowly bring the mixture to the boil, stirring occasionally.

5 Reduce the heat and simmer gently for about 1 hour, stirring frequently towards the end of the cooking time, until it is reduced to a thick consistency and no excess liquid remains.

6 Spoon the chutney into warmed, sterilized jars, cover and seal. Store in a cool, dark place and allow to mature for at least 2 weeks before eating. Use within 1 year of making.

900g/2lb mangoes, halved, peeled and stoned (pitted)

225g/8oz cooking apples, peeled

1 onion, chopped

1 garlic clove, crushed

FROM THE STORECUPBOARD

2.5ml/¹/₂ tsp salt

300ml/¹/₂ pint/1¹/₄ cups distilled malt vinegar

200g/7oz/scant 1 cup demerara (raw) sugar

10ml/2 tsp ground ginger

COOK'S TIPS

• Once opened, store the chutney in the refrigerator and use within 3 months.

• When serving mango chutney with crispy poppadums, also offer a selection of other condiments such as salty lime pickle, finely chopped fresh onion salad and minty yogurt.

VARIATION To make a chutney with a fiery, spicy kick to serve with cheeses and cold meats, seed and finely slice two fresh green chillies and stir into the chutney with the garlic and ginger.

Energy 1401kcal/5997kJ; Protein 8.7g; Carbohydrate 360.7g, of which sugars 356.6g; Fat 2.2g, of which saturates 0.9g; Cholesterol 0mg; Calcium 238mg; Fibre 27.8g; Sodium 1019mg

Sour Mango Sambal ✳

This sour sambal can made with green mango, as here, or papaya. It is generally served in small quantities as a relish to accompany fried fish and shellfish, spicy grilled foods and fiery curries, but it can also be served on its own as a refreshing snack at any time of the day.

SERVES FOUR

1 In a small, heavy pan, dry-roast the shrimp paste until it is aromatic and crumbly.

2 Split the chillies in half lengthways and remove and discard the seeds, using the point of a sharp knife.

3 Using a mortar and pestle or food processor, grind the chillies with the salt to form a paste. Add the shrimp paste and sugar and pound into the spicy paste.

4 Peel and shred the mango, then add to the shrimp paste and moisten with the lime juice. Mix well and serve in little bowls.

5ml/1 tsp shrimp paste

4 fresh red chillies

1 green mango

juice of ¹/₂ lime

FROM THE STORECUPBOARD

7.5ml/1¹/₂ tsp salt

5ml/1 tsp sugar

Energy 34kcal/143kJ; Protein 1.7g; Carbohydrate 6.5g, of which sugars 6.4g; Fat 0.3g, of which saturates 0.1g; Cholesterol 6mg; Calcium 28mg; Fibre 1g; Sodium 794mg

6 large fresh corn on
the cob

¹/₂ small white cabbage,
weighing about
275g/10oz, very
finely shredded

2 small onions, halved
and very finely sliced

1 red (bell)
pepper, seeded
and finely chopped

FROM THE STORECUPBOARD

475ml/16fl oz/2 cups
distilled malt vinegar

200g/7oz/1 cup golden
granulated sugar

5ml/1 tsp salt

15ml/1 tbsp plain
(all-purpose) flour

5ml/1 tsp mild
mustard powder

2.5ml/¹/₂ tsp turmeric

Corn Relish ✳

When golden sweetcorn cobs are in season, try preserving their kernels
in this delicious relish. It has a lovely crunchy texture and a wonderfully
bright, appetizing appearance.

MAKES ABOUT 1KG/2¹/₄ LB

1 Put the corn in a pan of boiling water and cook for 2 minutes. Drain and, when cool enough to handle, use a sharp knife to strip the kernels from the cobs.

2 Put the corn kernels in a pan with the cabbage and onions. Reserve 30ml/2 tbsp of the vinegar, then add the rest to the pan with the sugar.

3 Slowly bring to the boil, stirring occasionally until the sugar dissolves. Simmer for 15 minutes. Add the red pepper and simmer for a further 10 minutes.

4 Blend the salt, flour, mustard and turmeric with the reserved vinegar to make a smooth paste. Stir the paste into the vegetable mixture and bring back to the boil. Simmer for 5 minutes, until the mixture has thickened.

5 Spoon the relish into warmed, sterilized jars, cover and seal. Store in a cool, dark place. Use within 6 months of making. Once opened, store in the refrigerator and use within 2 months.

Energy 1479kcal/6291kJ; Protein 20.3g; Carbohydrate 356.7g, of which sugars 275.1g; Fat 6.4g, of which saturates 1g; Cholesterol 0mg; Calcium 307mg; Fibre 15.5g; Sodium 3085mg

Lime Pickle ✳

This aromatic Indian pickle is often sold in jars at Asian stores and in supermarkets, but the flavour is better if you make it yourself. Hot, fiery and sour, it is best served as an accompaniment to fiery curries.

SERVES EIGHT–TEN

8–10 limes

3–4 garlic cloves, cut into thin sticks

25g/1oz fresh root ginger, peeled and cut into thin sticks

a handful of fresh or dried curry leaves

FROM THE STORECUPBOARD

30ml/2 tbsp salt

150ml/¼ pint/⅔ cup sesame or groundnut (peanut) oil

10–15ml/2–3 tsp brown mustard seeds

5ml/1 tsp coriander seeds

5ml/1 tsp cumin seeds

5ml/1 tsp fennel seeds

10ml/2 tsp ground turmeric

10ml/2 tsp hot chilli powder or paste

COOK'S TIPS

• *This pickle is delicious served with grilled or fried fish, and spicy stir-fried egg noodles.*

• *You can make it as fiery as you like by adding more chilli powder.*

• *Asian stores and markets are often the cheapest place to buy limes in bulk.*

1 Put the whole limes in a bowl. Cover with boiling water and leave to stand for 30 minutes.

2 Drain the limes and cut each into quarters. Rub them with salt and put them into a sealed sterilized jar. Leave the limes to cure in the salt for 1 week.

3 Heat the oil in a large frying pan and stir in the mustard seeds. When they begin to pop, stir in the garlic, ginger, spices and curry leaves. Cook gently for a few minutes to flavour the oil, then stir in the lime pieces and the juices from the jar.

4 Reduce the heat and simmer for about 45 minutes, stirring from time to time. Store the pickle in sterilized jars and keep in a cool place for 1–2 months.

Energy 96kcal/395kJ; Protein 0.3g; Carbohydrate 0.9g, of which sugars 0.6g; Fat 10.1g, of which saturates 1.5g; Cholesterol 0mg; Calcium 25mg; Fibre 0.2g; Sodium 1185mg

1kg/2¹/₄lb pickling onions

2–3 dried red chillies

5cm/2in piece fresh root ginger, sliced

2–3 blades mace

2–3 fresh bay leaves

FROM THE STORECUPBOARD

115g/4oz/¹/₂ cup salt

750ml/1¹/₄ pints/3 cups malt vinegar

15ml/1 tbsp sugar

15ml/1 tbsp coriander seeds

5ml/1 tsp brown mustard seeds

5ml/1 tsp allspice berries

5ml/1 tsp black peppercorns

English Pickled Onions ✳

These powerful pickles are traditionally served with a plate of cold meats and bread and cheese. They should be made with malt vinegar and stored for at least 6 weeks before eating.

MAKES ENOUGH FOR FOUR 450G/1LB JARS

1 To peel the onions, trim off the root ends, but leave the onion layers attached. Cut a thin slice off the top (neck) end of the onion. Place the onions in a bowl, then cover with boiling water. Leave to stand for 4 minutes, then drain. The skin should then be easy to peel using a small, sharp knife.

2 Place the peeled onions in a bowl and cover with cold water, then drain the water into a large pan. Add the salt and heat slightly to dissolve it, then cool before pouring the brine over the onions. Place a plate inside the top of the bowl and weigh it down slightly so that it keeps all the onions submerged in the brine. Leave to stand for 24 hours.

3 Meanwhile, place the vinegar in a large pan. Wrap all the remaining ingredients, except the bay leaves, in a piece of muslin (cheesecloth). Bring to the boil, simmer for about 5 minutes, then remove the pan from the heat. Set aside and leave to infuse overnight.

4 Drain the onions, rinse and pat dry. Pack them into sterilized 450g/1lb jars. Add some or all of the spice from the vinegar, except the ginger slices. The pickle will become hotter if you add the chillies. Pour the vinegar over to cover and add the bay leaves. Seal the jars with non-metallic lids and store in a cool, dark place for at least 6 weeks before eating.

Energy 109kcal/454kJ; Protein 3.1g; Carbohydrate 24.5g, of which sugars 18.6g; Fat 0.5g, of which saturates 0g; Cholesterol 0mg; Calcium 67mg; Fibre 3.6g; Sodium 8mg

Mixed Vegetable Pickle ✳

This fresh, salad-style pickle doesn't need lengthy storing so makes the perfect choice if you need a bowl of pickle immediately. However, it does not have good storing properties, so only make as much as you need.

MAKES ABOUT 450G/1LB

¹/₂ cauliflower head, cut into florets

2 carrots, sliced

2 celery sticks, thinly sliced

¹/₄–¹/₂ white cabbage, thinly sliced

115g/4oz/scant 1 cup runner (green) beans, cut into bitesize pieces

6 garlic cloves, sliced

1–4 fresh chillies, whole or sliced

5cm/2in piece fresh root ginger, sliced

1 red (bell) pepper, sliced

juice of 2 lemons

FROM THE STORECUPBOARD

2.5ml/¹/₂ tsp turmeric

105ml/7 tbsp white wine vinegar

15–30ml/1–2 tbsp sugar

60–90ml/4–6 tbsp olive oil

salt, to taste

COOK'S TIPS

• If you find the flavour of the chilli too hot, use only half a chilli and chop it into tiny pieces. Make sure you remove the seeds.

• Chop the vegetables into small bitesize pieces, and try to ensure they are all roughly the same size.

1 Toss the cauliflower, carrots, celery, cabbage, beans, garlic, chillies, ginger and pepper with salt and leave them to stand in a colander over a bowl for 4 hours.

2 Shake the vegetables well to remove any excess juices. Transfer the salted vegetables to a bowl.

3 Add the turmeric, vinegar, sugar to taste, oil and lemon juice. Toss to combine thoroughly, then add enough water to distribute the flavours.

4 Cover the bowl with clear film (plastic wrap) and leave to chill in the refrigerator for at least 1 hour, or until you are ready to serve the pickle.

Energy 776kcal/3211kJ; Protein 19.1g; Carbohydrate 42.5g, of which sugars 38.3g; Fat 59.6g, of which saturates 8.7g; Cholesterol 0mg; Calcium 302mg; Fibre 17.8g; Sodium 109mg

Pickled Turnips and Beetroot ✳

This delicious pickle is a Middle Eastern speciality, and it is a fantastic way to use these simple root vegetables. The turnips turn a rich red in their beetroot-spiked brine and look gorgeous stacked in the storecupboard.

MAKES ABOUT 1.6KG/3¹/₂ LB

1 Wash the turnips and beetroot, but do not peel them, then cut into slices about 5mm/¹/₄ in thick.

2 Put the salt and water in a bowl, stir and leave to stand until the salt has completely dissolved.

3 Sprinkle the beetroot with lemon juice and place in the bottom of four 1.2 litre/2 pint/5 cup sterilized jars.

4 Top with sliced turnip, packing them in very tightly, then pour over the brine, making sure that the vegetables are covered.

5 Seal the jars and leave in a cool, dark place for at least 7 days before serving.

1kg/2¹/₄lb young turnips

3–4 raw beetroot (beets)

about 1.5 litres/2¹/₂ pints/ 6¹/₄ cups water

juice of 1 lemon

FROM THE STORECUPBOARD

about 45ml/3 tbsp coarse sea salt

Energy 338kcal/1442kJ; Protein 14.1g; Carbohydrate 69.8g, of which sugars 66g; Fat 3.3g, of which saturates 0g; Cholesterol 0mg; Calcium 541mg; Fibre 29.7g; Sodium 4278mg

Pickled Red Cabbage ✳

This delicately spiced and vibrant-coloured pickle is an old-fashioned favourite to serve with bread and cheese for an informal lunch, or to use to accompany cold ham, duck or goose.

MAKES ABOUT 1–1.6KG/2¼–3½LB

1 Put the cabbage and onion in a bowl, add the salt and mix well until thoroughly combined. Tip the mixture into a colander over a bowl and leave to drain overnight.

2 The next day, rinse the salted vegetables, drain well and pat dry using kitchen paper.

3 Pour the vinegar into a large pan, add the sugar, spices and bay leaves and bring to the boil. Remove from the heat and leave to cool.

4 Core and chop the apples, then layer with the cabbage and onions in sterilized preserving jars. Pour over the cooled spiced vinegar. (If you prefer a milder pickle, strain out the spices first.) Seal the jars and store for 1 week before eating. Eat within 2 months. Once opened, store in the refrigerator.

675g/1½lb/6 cups red cabbage, shredded

1 large Spanish (Bermuda) onion, sliced

2.5cm/1in piece fresh root ginger

1 whole star anise

2 fresh bay leaves

4 eating apples

FROM THE STORECUPBOARD

30ml/2 tbsp salt

600ml/1 pint/2½ cups red wine vinegar

75g/3oz/6 tbsp light muscovado (brown) sugar

15ml/1 tbsp coriander seeds

3 cloves

Energy 674kcal/2868kJ; Protein 12g; Carbohydrate 161.4g, of which sugars 159.3g; Fat 2g, of which saturates 0g; Cholesterol 0mg; Calcium 405mg; Fibre 23g; Sodium 64mg

Pickled Mushrooms *

This method of preserving mushrooms is popular throughout Europe and it is a very good way to use a glut after a day's foraging. The pickled mushrooms are delicious served with chicken or grilled meat.

MAKES ABOUT 900G/2LB

1 Trim and wipe the mushrooms and cut any large ones in half.

2 Put the vinegar, salt, sugar and water in a pan and bring to the boil. Add the bay leaves, thyme, garlic, onion, chillies, coriander seeds, peppercorns and lemon rind and simmer for 2 minutes.

3 Add the mushrooms to the pan and simmer for 3–4 minutes. Drain the mushrooms through a sieve, retaining all the herbs and spices, then set aside for a few minutes more until the mushrooms are thoroughly drained.

4 Fill one large or two small cooled, sterilized jars with the mushrooms. Distribute the garlic, onion, herbs and spices evenly among the layers of mushrooms, then add enough olive oil to cover by at least 1cm/^{1}/$_2$in. You may need to use extra oil if you are making two jars.

5 Leave the pickle to settle, then tap the jars on the work surface to dispel any air bubbles. Seal the jars, then store in the refrigerator. Use within 2 weeks.

500g/1^1/$_4$lb/8 cups mixed mushrooms such as small ceps, chestnut mushrooms, shiitake and girolles

300ml/^{1}/$_2$ pint/1^1/$_4$ cups water

4–5 fresh bay leaves

8 large fresh thyme sprigs

15 garlic cloves, peeled, halved, with any green shoots removed

1 small red onion, halved and thinly sliced

2–3 small dried red chillies

a few strips of lemon rind

FROM THE STORECUPBOARD

300ml/^{1}/$_2$ pint/1^1/$_4$ cups white wine vinegar or cider vinegar

15ml/1 tbsp salt

5ml/1 tsp caster (superfine) sugar

5ml/1 tsp coriander seeds, lightly crushed

5ml/1 tsp black peppercorns

250–350ml/8–12fl oz/ 1–1^1/$_2$ cups extra virgin olive oil

VARIATION The pickle is very good made with cultivated mushrooms, but it is worth including a couple of ceps for their flavour.

Energy 931kcal/3844kJ; Protein 14.5g; Carbohydrate 11.6g, of which sugars 10g; Fat 92.3g, of which saturates 13.4g; Cholesterol 0mg; Calcium 52mg; Fibre 8.8g; Sodium 41mg

**20 small, ridged or knobbly
pickling (small) cucumbers**

**2 litres/3¹/₂ pints/8 cups
water**

**15–20 garlic
cloves, unpeeled**

2 bunches fresh dill

**30ml/2 tbsp mixed
pickling spice**

1 or 2 hot fresh chillies

FROM THE STORECUPBOARD

**175g/6oz/³/₄ cup coarse
sea salt**

15ml/1 tbsp dill seeds

COOK'S TIP
• *If you cannot find
ridged or knobbly pickling
cucumbers, use any small
cucumbers instead.*

• *Mixed pickling spices
can vary, so check what is
in them so you get your
preferred blend.*

Dill Pickles ✳

Redolent of garlic and piquant with fresh chilli, salty dill pickles can be eaten on their own or as an
accompaniment to a plate of assorted cheeses and cold meats.

MAKES ABOUT 900G/2LB

1 Scrub the cucumbers and rinse them well in cold water. Leave to dry. Put the measured water and
salt in a large pan and bring to the boil. Turn off the heat and leave to cool to room temperature.

2 Using the flat side of a knife blade or a mortar and pestle, lightly crush each garlic clove, breaking
the papery skin.

3 Pack the cucumbers tightly into one or two wide-necked, sterilized jars, layering them with the
garlic, fresh dill, dill seeds and pickling spice. Add one chilli to each jar.

4 Pour over the cooled brine, making sure that the cucumbers are completely covered. Tap the jars
on the work surface to dispel any trapped air bubbles.

5 Cover the jars with lids and then leave to stand at room temperature for 4–7 days before serving.
Store in the refrigerator.

Energy 45kcal/180kJ; Protein 3.1g; Carbohydrate 6.8g, of which sugars 6.3g; Fat 0.5g, of which saturates 0g; Cholesterol 0mg; Calcium 83mg; Fibre 2.7g; Sodium 5908mg

Back to Basics

MAKING YOUR OWN STOCKS, GRAVIES, SWEET
AND SAVOURY SAUCES AND PASTRIES WILL NOT ONLY
SAVE YOU MONEY, BUT IT WILL ALSO ENABLE YOU TO
PRODUCE DELICIOUS ACCOMPANIMENTS THAT ARE
EXACTLY TAILORED TO YOUR PERSONAL PREFERENCES.
FROM ONION GRAVY, CHOCOLATE FUDGE SAUCE
AND TOMATO KETCHUP TO MAYONNAISE, REAL
CUSTARD AND CHOUX PASTRY, HERE YOU WILL
FIND BASIC RECIPES THAT WILL TAKE YOUR
COOKING TO NEW HEIGHTS.

Basic Stocks and Gravies

A well-flavoured stock or gravy can really affect the final taste of a dish. Good-quality ready-made stocks and gravies – either cube, powders or liquid concentrate – are readily available, but stocks are easy and cheap to make. Always ask for the meat bones when buying from a butcher, and trimmings if you have fish prepared by the fishmonger, as these are perfect for making good stock. A chicken carcass from a roast makes excellent stock, particularly if you've packed it with herbs, onions, or other aromatics before roasting.

Beef Stock MAKES ABOUT 1 LITRE/1¾ PINTS/4 CUPS

900g/2lb beef bones

2 unpeeled onions, quartered

1 bouquet garni

2 large carrots, roughly chopped

> **COOK'S TIP**
> If you don't have time to make stock straight after eating fish or roasted meats, you can freeze the main ingredients – meat bones, fish trimmings or a cooked chicken carcass – until you are ready to make it at a later date.

1 Preheat the oven to 220°C/425°F/Gas 7. Put the bones in a roasting pan and roast for about 45 minutes, or until well browned.

2 Transfer the roasted bones to a large, heavy pan. Add the onion quarters, leaving the skins on, the bouquet garni and chopped carrots. Add 5ml/1 tsp salt and 5ml/1 tsp black peppercorns. Pour over about 1.7 litres/3 pints/7½ cups cold water and bring just to the boil.

3 Using a slotted spoon, skim off any scum on the surface of the stock. Reduce the heat and partially cover the pan. Simmer the stock on the lowest heat for about 3 hours, then set aside to cool.

4 Strain the stock into a large bowl and leave to cool completely, then remove any fat from the surface. Store the stock in the refrigerator for up to 3 days or freeze for up to 6 months.

Chicken Stock MAKES ABOUT 1 LITRE/1¾ PINTS/4 CUPS

1 large roast chicken carcass

2 unpeeled onions, quartered

3 bay leaves

2 large carrots, roughly chopped

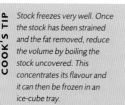

> **COOK'S TIP**
> Stock freezes very well. Once the stock has been strained and the fat removed, reduce the volume by boiling the stock uncovered. This concentrates its flavour and it can then be frozen in an ice-cube tray.

1 Put the chicken carcass and any loose bones and roasting juices into a heavy pan in which they fit snugly. Add the onion quarters, bay leaves and chopped carrots.

2 Add 2.5ml/½ tsp salt and 5ml/1 tsp black peppercorns to the pan, and pour over 1.7 litres/3 pints/7½ cups cold water. Bring to the boil.

3 Reduce the heat, partially cover the pan and cook on the lowest setting for 1½ hours. Using a large spoon, carefully turn the chicken in the stock and crush the carcass occasionally.

4 Leave the stock to cool slightly, then strain into a large bowl and leave to cool completely. When cool, remove any fat from the surface. Store the stock in the refrigerator for up to 2 days or freeze for up to 6 months.

Fish Stock

500g/1¼lb fish bones and trimmings, without heads and gills

1 bouquet garni

1 onion or 3–4 shallots, peeled and quartered

2 celery sticks, roughly chopped

1 Pack the fish bones and trimmings into a heavy pan and add the bouquet garni, quartered onion or shallots and celery. Add 2.5ml/¹/₂ tsp salt and 2.5ml/¹/₂ tsp peppercorns to the pan and pour over 1 litre/1³/₄ pints/4 cups water. Bring to the boil.

2 Reduce the heat, cover the pan and cook on the lowest setting for 30 minutes. Leave to cool, then strain into a bowl. Store in the refrigerator for up to 24 hours or freeze for up to 3 months.

Vegetable Stock MAKES ABOUT 1 LITRE/1¾ PINTS/4 CUPS

3 unpeeled onions, quartered

200g/7oz large open mushrooms

300–400g/11–14oz mixed vegetables, such as broccoli, carrots, celery, tomatoes and/or spring onions (scallions), roughly chopped

45ml/3 tbsp green or brown lentils

1 Place the onions in a heavy pan with the mushrooms, mixed vegetables and green or brown lentils.

2 Add 2.5ml/¹/₂ tsp salt, 10ml/2 tsp peppercorns and 1.7 litres/ 3 pints/7¹/₂ cups water to the pan. Bring to the boil, then reduce the heat and simmer, partially covered, for 50–60 minutes.

3 Leave the stock to cool slightly, then strain into a bowl and leave to cool. Store in the refrigerator for up to 24 hours or freeze for up to 6 months.

Thickened Gravy MAKES ABOUT 450ML/¾ PINT/2 CUPS

25g/1oz/¹/₄ cup plain (all-purpose) flour

450ml/³/₄ pint/scant 2 cups stock

45ml/3 tbsp port or sherry

1 Tilt the roasting pan slightly and spoon off almost all the fat, leaving the meat juices behind. Sprinkle the flour into the pan and heat gently for 1 minute, stirring constantly. Gradually add the stock, stirring all the time until thickened.

2 Add the port or sherry, season to taste with salt and freshly ground black pepper and simmer gently for 1–2 minutes.

Onion Gravy MAKES ABOUT 450ML/¾ PINT/2 CUPS

30ml/2 tbsp olive oil

25g/1oz/2 tbsp butter

8 onions, sliced

pinch of caster sugar

15ml/1 tbsp plain (all-purpose) flour

300ml/¹/₂ pint/1¹/₄ cups brown meat stock

1 Heat the oil and butter in a pan until foaming, then add the onions. Mix well, so the onions are coated in the butter mixture. Cover the pan and cook gently for 30 minutes, stirring frequently. Add the caster sugar and cook for a further 5 minutes; the onions will soften, caramelize and reduce.

2 Turn off the heat and stir in the flour. Gradually add the stock and return the pan to the heat. Bring the onion gravy to the boil, stirring all the time. Simmer for 2–3 minutes or until thickened, then season with salt and freshly ground black pepper to taste.

Basic Savoury Sauces

A good sauce can provide the finishing touch to a dish and is very easy to make yourself. This section contains many basic sauces, including a classic savoury white sauce, which can be served as a topping for vegetables or flavoured with additional ingredients such as cheese, herbs, onions or mushrooms, and a basic fresh tomato sauce, which is widely used for pasta dishes, pizza toppings and vegetable dishes. Also included are everyday condiments, tomato ketchup, mayonnaise, barbecue sauce, mushroom sauce and horseradish sauce, which can accompany all manner of dishes.

White Sauce MAKES ABOUT 300ML/½ PINT/1¼ CUPS

300ml/¹/₂ pint/1¹/₄ cups milk

15g/¹/₂oz/1 tbsp butter

15g/¹/₂oz/1 tbsp plain (all-purpose) flour

freshly grated nutmeg

salt and ground black pepper, to taste

1 Warm the milk in a small pan. In a separate pan, melt the butter over a gentle heat, then add the flour and cook, stirring, for 1 minute until the mixture forms a thick paste.

2 Remove the pan from the heat and gradually add the warmed milk, whisking continuously until smooth.

3 Return the pan to a gentle heat and cook, whisking, until the sauce boils, is smooth and thick.

4 Season to taste with salt and ground black pepper and plenty of nutmeg. Serve immediately.

Bread Sauce MAKES ABOUT 450ML/¾ PINT/SCANT 2 CUPS

1 onion

6 cloves

1 bay leaf

300ml/¹/₂ pint/1¹/₄ cups full-fat (whole) milk

150ml/¹/₄ pint/²/₃ cup single (light) cream

115g/4oz/2 cups fresh white breadcrumbs

knob (pat) of butter

salt and ground black pepper, to taste

1 Stud the onion all over with the cloves. Put the onion, bay leaf and milk in a pan and bring slowly to the boil.

2 Remove the pan from the heat and leave the milk mixture to stand for at least 30 minutes to allow the flavour of the onion and cloves to infuse (steep) into the milk.

3 Pour the milk through a sieve (strainer) into a large bowl and discard the clove-studded onion and the bay leaf.

4 Transfer the milk into a large, clean pan and add the single cream and breadcrumbs. Stir to combine.

5 Bring the mixture to the boil over a medium low heat, then reduce the heat and simmer gently for about 5 minutes, until the sauce thickens and becomes creamy.

6 Add in the butter while the sauce is hot and stir until it melts and is thoroughly combined. Season to taste with salt and ground black pepper and serve immediately.

Hollandaise Sauce

45ml/3 tbsp white wine or herb-infused vinegar

1 bay leaf

2 egg yolks

115g/4oz/½ cup butter, chilled

> **COOK'S TIP** *The sauce can be kept warm in a covered bowl set over the pan of hot water for up to 20 minutes. If the sauce is very thick, whisk in a few drops of hot water. If the sauce starts to separate, whisk in an ice cube.*

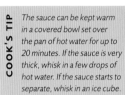

1 Put the vinegar in a pan with the bay leaf and add 5ml/1 tsp black peppercorns. Boil rapidly until reduced to 15ml/1 tbsp, then strain into a heatproof bowl.

2 Transfer the vinegar to a clean pan, add the egg yolks and a little salt and whisk lightly until thoroughly combined. Cut the chilled butter into small pieces and add to the pan.

3 Set the pan over a very low heat. Whisk continuously so that as the butter melts it is blended into the egg yolks. When all the butter has melted, continue whisking for about a minute until the sauce is thick and smooth.

4 Season the sauce with salt and ground black pepper to taste, adding a few extra drops of vinegar, if you like, to give a slightly tangy flavour. Serve warm.

Traditional Horseradish Sauce

45ml/3 tbsp freshly grated horseradish root

15ml/1 tbsp white wine vinegar

5ml/1 tsp sugar

pinch of salt

150ml/¹⁄₄ pint/²⁄₃ cup thick double (heavy) cream, for serving

1 Place the grated horseradish in a bowl, then add the white wine vinegar, granulated sugar and just a pinch of salt.

2 Stir the ingredients together until thoroughly combined.

3 Pour the mixture into a sterilized jar. It will keep in the refrigerator for up to 6 months.

4 A few hours before you intend to serve the sauce, stir the cream into the horseradish and leave to infuse.

Mayonnaise

1 egg yolk, at room temperature

15ml/1 tbsp lemon juice or white wine vinegar

5ml/1 tsp Dijon mustard

150ml/¼ pint/²⁄₃ cup olive oil

salt and ground white pepper, to taste

1 Put the egg yolk in a bowl with the lemon juice or vinegar, mustard and a little salt. Whisk together until combined.

2 Add the oil, drop by drop, whisking well between additions, until the mixture starts to thicken. After a few minutes, when the mixture is thickening slightly, add slightly more oil each time, whisking continuously until you have added all the oil and the sauce is thick and smooth.

3 Add salt and white pepper to taste, and add a few drops of lemon juice or vinegar if the mayonnaise is too bland. If the sauce is too thick, stir in a few drops of warm water. Cover with clear film (plastic wrap) and store in the refrigerator for up to 2 days.

Apple Sauce MAKES ABOUT 300ML/½ PINT/1¼ CUPS

450g/1lb Bramley apples (or other cooking apples)

30ml/2 tbsp cider or water

25g/1oz/2 tbsp soft brown sugar (or to taste)

25g/1oz/2 tbsp butter

1 Peel the apples, remove the cores and chop the apples into large chunks.

2 Put the apples, cider and sugar in a pan. Cook for 5–10 minutes, until soft.

3 Beat well with a wooden spoon or blend in a food processor depending on whether you like your apple sauce chunky or smooth. Beat in the butter and reheat, if necessary.

Fresh Tomato Sauce MAKES ABOUT 1 LITRE/1¾ PINTS/4 CUPS

1.3kg/3lb ripe tomatoes

120ml/4fl oz/¹/₂ cup garlic-infused olive oil

1 large onion, finely chopped

handful of basil leaves, torn, or 30ml/2 tbsp chopped fresh oregano

1 Put the tomatoes in a bowl, pour over boiling water to cover and leave to stand for about 1 minute until the skins split. Drain the tomatoes in a sieve (strainer) and peel using your fingers, then roughly chop the flesh.

2 Heat half the oil in a large, heavy pan. Add the onion and cook gently for about 3 minutes, or until softened but not browned. Add the tomatoes and the remaining oil and cook gently over a low heat, stirring, for 5 minutes or until the tomatoes are soft.

3 Add the herbs, cover the pan and cook gently for 20–25 minutes, stirring frequently, until the sauce is thick and pulpy. Season to taste with salt and freshly ground black pepper.

Tomato Ketchup MAKES ABOUT 1.3KG/3LB

2.25kg/5lb very ripe tomatoes

1 onion

6 cloves

4 allspice berries

6 black peppercorns

1 fresh rosemary sprig

25g/1oz fresh root ginger, sliced

1 celery heart

30ml/2 tbsp soft light brown sugar

65ml/4¹/₂ tbsp raspberry vinegar

3 garlic cloves, peeled

15ml/1 tbsp salt

1 Put the tomatoes in a bowl, pour over boiling water to cover and leave to stand for about 1 minute until the skins split.

2 Drain the tomatoes in a sieve (strainer) and peel using your fingers, then roughly chop the flesh and place in a large pan. Peel the onion, leaving the tip and root intact and stud it with the cloves.

3 Tie the onion with the allspice, peppercorns, rosemary and ginger into a double layer of muslin (cheesecloth) and add to the pan. Chop the celery, plus the leaves, and add to the pan with the sugar, raspberry vinegar, garlic and salt.

4 Bring the mixture to the boil over a fairly high heat, stirring occasionally. Reduce the heat and simmer for 1¹/₂–2 hours, stirring regularly, until reduced by half.

5 Purée the mixture in a food processor, then return to the pan, bring to the boil and simmer for 15 minutes. Bottle in clean, sterilized jars and store in the refrigerator. Use within 2 weeks.

Barbecue Sauce MAKES ABOUT 900ML/1½ PINTS/3¾ CUPS

30ml/2 tbsp olive oil

1 large onion, chopped

1 garlic clove, crushed

1 fresh red chilli, seeded and sliced

2 celery sticks, sliced

1 large carrot, sliced

1 medium cooking apple, quartered, cored, peeled and chopped

450g/1lb ripe tomatoes, quartered

2.5ml/¹/₂ tsp ground ginger

150ml/¹/₄ pint/²/₃ cup malt vinegar

1 bay leaf

4 whole cloves

4 black peppercorns

50g/2oz/¹/₄ cup soft light brown sugar

10ml/2 tsp English mustard

2.5ml/¹/₂ tsp salt

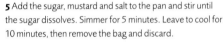

1 Heat the oil in a large heavy pan. Add the onion and cook over a low heat for 5 minutes.

2 Stir the garlic, chilli, celery and carrot into the onions and cook for about 5 minutes, stirring frequently, until the onion just begins to colour.

3 Add the apple, tomatoes, ground ginger and malt vinegar to the pan and stir to combine.

4 Put the bay leaf, cloves and peppercorns on a square of muslin (cheesecloth) and tie into a bag with fine string. Add to the pan and bring to the boil. Reduce the heat, cover and simmer for about 45 minutes, stirring occasionally.

5 Add the sugar, mustard and salt to the pan and stir until the sugar dissolves. Simmer for 5 minutes. Leave to cool for 10 minutes, then remove the bag and discard.

6 Press the mixture through a sieve (strainer) and return to the cleaned pan. Simmer for 10 minutes, or until thickened. Adjust the seasoning.

7 Pour the sauce into hot sterilized bottles or jars, then seal. Heat process, cool and, if using cork-topped bottles, dip the corks in wax. Store in a cool, dark place and use within 1 year. Once opened, store in the refrigerator and use within 2 months.

Mushroom Sauce MAKES 150ML/¹/₄ PINT/³/₄ CUP

mushrooms and salt (*see* Step 1)

3 garlic cloves, chopped

2 red chillies, seeded and chopped

5ml/1 tsp ground allspice

2.5ml/¹/₂ tsp freshly grated nutmeg

2.5ml/¹/₂ tsp ground ginger

300ml/¹/₂ pint/1¹/₄ cups red wine

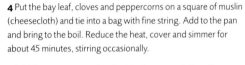
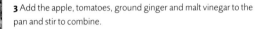
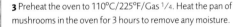
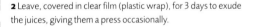
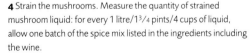
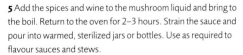

1 You will need 15ml/1 tbsp salt for every 450g/1lb mushrooms used. Roughly chop the mushrooms and place in a large ovenproof pan, sprinkling the salt on as you go.

2 Leave, covered in clear film (plastic wrap), for 3 days to exude the juices, giving them a press occasionally.

3 Preheat the oven to 110°C/225°F/Gas ¹/₄. Heat the pan of mushrooms in the oven for 3 hours to remove any moisture.

4 Strain the mushrooms. Measure the quantity of strained mushroom liquid: for every 1 litre/1³/₄ pints/4 cups of liquid, allow one batch of the spice mix listed in the ingredients including the wine.

5 Add the spices and wine to the mushroom liquid and bring to the boil. Return to the oven for 2–3 hours. Strain the sauce and pour into warmed, sterilized jars or bottles. Use as required to flavour sauces and stews.

Basic Sweet Sauces

From creamy custard to an elegant fruit coulis, sweet sauces can be used to uplift the simplest desserts to create a truly spectacular dish. They can be served as an accompaniment or make up an intrinsic part of a dish. Simple vanilla ice cream is taken to new levels when served with hot chocolate sauce or a fresh raspberry coulis, while a classic vanilla custard can be used as the base of a sweet soufflé. These sweet sauces rely on just a few basic ingredients and minimal effort, producing irresistible results.

Real Custard MAKES 300ML/½ PINT/1¼ CUPS

**300ml/¹/₂ pint/1¹/₄ cups
full-fat (whole) milk**

3 egg yolks

5ml/1 tsp cornflour (cornstarch)

**45ml/3 tbsp caster
(superfine) sugar**

> **COOK'S TIP**
> Adding a little cornflour (cornstarch) to the sauce during cooking helps to prevent it from curdling without affecting the flavour or consistency of the finished custard sauce.

1 Pour the milk into a double boiler or heavy pan and bring slowly to the boil over a very gentle heat.

2 Meanwhile, whisk the egg yolks with the cornflour and sugar until thoroughly mixed. Pour the boiled milk into the yolk mixture, whisking continuously until combined.

3 Pour the mixture back into the cleaned pan and cook over the lowest heat, stirring continuously with a wooden spoon, for 8–10 minutes, or until the mixture coats the back of the spoon.

4 Immediately pour the custard through a sieve (strainer) into a bowl or jug (pitcher) to prevent it from overcooking. Serve warm.

Butterscotch Sauce MAKES ABOUT 475ML/16FL OZ/2 CUPS

**200g/7oz/1 cup caster
(superfine) sugar**

**45ml/3 tbsp each cold water and
boiling water**

75g/3oz/6 tbsp butter

**150ml/¹/₄ pint/²/₃ cup double
(heavy) cream**

> **COOK'S TIP**
> Be very careful when making this sauce, as it involves handling hot sugar, which can give a nasty burn. You should always wear oven gloves.

1 Put the sugar and 45ml/3 tbsp cold water into a pan and heat very gently, without stirring, until all the sugar has dissolved.

2 Bring the mixture to a rolling boil. Boil until the sugar starts to turn golden, then quickly take the pan off the heat and immediately plunge the base into cold water, to prevent the sugar from overbrowning.

3 Standing as far back as possible, and protecting your hand with an oven glove, add the 45ml/3 tbsp boiling water to the caramel mixture, which will splutter and spit.

4 Add the butter and tilt the pan to mix the ingredients together. Leave to cool for 5 minutes.

5 Gradually stir in the cream and mix well until thoroughly combined. Pour into a jug (pitcher) and serve warm or cool.

Rich Chocolate Sauce MAKES ABOUT 250ML/8FL OZ/1 CUP

130g/4¹/₂oz caster
(superfine) sugar

175g/6oz plain (semisweet)
chocolate, broken into pieces

25g/1oz/2 tbsp unsalted
(sweet) butter

30ml/2 tbsp brandy or coffee
liqueur (optional)

1 Put the sugar in a small heavy pan with 120ml/4fl oz/¹/₂ cup water and heat gently until the sugar completely dissolves. Bring to the boil and boil for 1 minute.

2 Remove from the heat and stir in the chocolate and butter, stirring until the chocolate has melted and the sauce is smooth.

3 Stir in the brandy or coffee liqueur, if using, and serve warm.

Chocolate Fudge Sauce MAKES ABOUT 250ML/8FL OZ/1 CUP

175ml/6fl oz/³/₄ cup double
(heavy) cream

45ml/3 tbsp golden
(light corn) syrup

200g/7oz/scant 1 cup light
muscovado (brown) sugar

75g/3oz/¹/₂ cup plain (semisweet)
chocolate, finely chopped

1 Put the cream, golden syrup, sugar and a pinch of salt in a small pan. Heat gently, stirring, until the sugar has completely dissolved.

2 Add the chopped chocolate and stir until melted. Simmer the sauce for about 20 minutes, stirring occasionally, until thickened.

3 Use the sauce immediately. Alternatively, to keep the sauce warm until you are ready to use it, pour into a heatproof bowl, cover, and place over a pan of simmering water.

Summer Fruit Coulis MAKES ABOUT 250ML/8FL OZ/1 CUP

130g/4¹/₂oz raspberries,
washed and hulled

130g/4¹/₂oz strawberries,
washed and hulled

10–15ml/2–3 tsp icing
(confectioners')
sugar, sieved

15ml/1 tbsp orange liqueur
or Kirsch (optional)

1 Place the raspberries and strawberries in a food processor and process until smooth. Press the mixture through a fine strainer set over a bowl to remove the tiny seeds.

2 Return the strained fruit purée to the food processor or blender and add 10ml/2 tsp of the icing sugar with the orange liqueur or kirsch, if using, and process briefly until well combined.

3 Check the sweetness of the coulis, then add a little more icing sugar if necessary and process again to mix.

COOK'S TIP *Gently warm this delicious coulis and drizzle over vanilla ice cream for a luxurious dessert. You could also mix some cold coulis into natural (plain) yogurt.*

VARIATIONS *• To make raspberry and vanilla sauce: scrape the seeds from a vanilla pod (bean) and add to the food processor with 200g/7oz/1 cup raspberries and 30ml/2tbsp icing (confectioners') sugar. Process to a purée, adding water to thin, if necessary.*

• Substitute any soft summer berries, such as redcurrants, white currants or black currants for the raspberries or strawberries. Adjust the amount of sugar to taste.

Basic Pastries

There is a certain satisfaction to be gained from creating pies, tarts and desserts using pastry that you have made yourself, and most types are very easy to make at home. The exceptions to this general rule are puff and filo pastry, which, unless you are an expert with plenty of time to spare, are often better bought from a store. So try making shortcrust pastry to top sweet and savoury pies; sweet shortcrust pastry for special desserts; French flan pastry for making flans and tarts, or choux pastry for making éclairs or profiteroles.

Shortcrust Pastry FOR A 23CM/9IN PASTRY CASE

225g/8oz/2 cups plain (all-purpose) flour

1.5ml/¹/₄ tsp salt

115g/4oz/8 tbsp white vegetable fat (shortening)

45ml/3 tbsp iced water

1 Sift the flour and salt into a large bowl. Add the fat and rub it into the flour with your fingertips until the mixture resembles fine breadcrumbs and all the fat has been incorporated.

2 Sprinkle most of the iced water over the mixture. Use a flat-bladed knife or a fork to bring the mixture together, then use your hands to form the dough into a ball. If it is too dry to hold together, add a little more chilled water.

3 Wrap the pastry in clear film (plastic wrap) and chill in the refrigerator for 30 minutes.

4 Lightly knead the pastry on a floured surface, then roll to the desired shape and thickness using a floured rolling pin.

Rich Sweet Shortcrust Pastry FOR A 23CM/9IN PASTRY CASE

225g/8oz/2 cups plain (all-purpose) flour

15ml/1 tbsp caster (superfine) sugar

175g/6oz/³/₄ cup butter

1 egg yolk

30–45ml/2–3 tbsp iced water

1 Sift the flour into a large bowl and add the caster sugar. Add the butter and rub it into the dry ingredients with your fingertips until the mixture resembles fine breadcrumbs and all the butter has been incorporated.

2 Add the egg yolk and sprinkle most of the iced water over the mixture. Use a flat-bladed knife or a fork to bring the mixture together, then use your hands to form the dough into a ball. If it is too dry to hold together, add a little more chilled water.

3 Wrap the pastry in clear film (plastic wrap) and chill in the refrigerator for 30 minutes.

4 Lightly knead the pastry on a floured surface, then roll to the desired shape and thickness using a floured rolling pin.

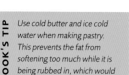

French Flan Pastry FOR A 23CM/9IN PASTRY CASE

200g/7oz/1³/₄ cups plain
(all-purpose) flour

2.5ml/¹/₂ tsp salt

115g/4oz/¹/₂ cup butter or
margarine, or half and half
of each, chilled

1 egg yolk

1.5ml/¹/₄ tsp lemon juice

30–45ml/2–3 tbsp
iced water

1 Sift the flour and salt into a large bowl. Add the butter and/or margarine and rub it into the flour with your fingertips until the mixture resembles fine breadcrumbs and all of the fat has been incorporated completely.

2 In a small bowl, mix the egg yolk, lemon juice and 30ml/2 tbsp iced water. Add to the flour mixture. Use a fork or flat-bladed knife to mix and moisten.

3 Press the dough into a rough ball. If the mixture is too dry to come together, add 15ml/1 tbsp more water. Turn on to a floured surface.

4 With the heel of your hand, push portions of dough away from you, smearing them on the surface. Continue in this way until the dough feels pliable and can easily be peeled off the surface.

5 Form the dough into a ball, wrap in clear film (plastic wrap) and chill for 30 minutes. Roll out on a floured surface to the desired thickness and shape.

Choux Pastry MAKES EIGHTEEN PROFITEROLES OR TWELVE ÉCLAIRS

115g/4oz/¹/₂ cup butter, cut into
small pieces

10ml/2 tsp caster (superfine)
sugar (optional)

1.5ml/¹/₄ tsp salt

250ml/8fl oz/1 cup of water

150g/5oz/1¹/₄ cups plain
(all-purpose) flour

4 eggs, beaten to mix

1 egg, beaten with 5ml/1 tsp cold
water, for glaze

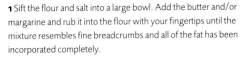

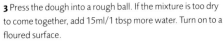

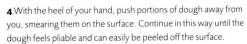

1 Preheat the oven to 220°C/425°F/Gas 7. Combine the butter, sugar, if using, salt and water in a large heavy pan. Bring to the boil over moderately high heat, stirring occasionally.

2 As soon as the mixture is boiling, remove the pan from the heat. Add the flour all at once and beat vigorously with a wooden spoon to mix the flour smoothly into the liquid.

3 Return the pan to moderate heat and cook, stirring, until the mixture will form a ball, pulling away from the sides of the pan. This will take about 1 minute. Remove from the heat again and allow to cool for 3–5 minutes.

4 Add a little of the beaten eggs and mix well to incorporate. Add a little more egg and beat in well. Continue beating in the eggs until the mixture becomes a smooth and shiny paste.

5 While still warm, shape choux puffs, éclairs, profiteroles or rings on a baking sheet lined with baking parchment.

6 Glaze with 1 egg beaten with 1 teaspoon of cold water. Put into the preheated oven, then reduce the heat to 200°C/400°F/Gas 6. Bake until puffed and golden brown and fill as desired.

Index

Acknowledgements

The Publishers would like to
thank the large team of contributors
to the book:

Recipe Writers: Pepita Aris,
Catherine Atkinson, Josephine
Bacon, Jane Baforth, Alex Barker,
Ghillie Basan, Judy Bastyra, Michelle
Berriedale-Johnson, Angela
Boggiano, Janet Brinkworth,
Georgina Campbell, Carla Capalbo,
Lesley Chamberlain, Kit Chan,
Jacqueline Clark, Maxine Clark,
Frances Cleary, Carole Clements,
Andi Clevely, Jan Cutler, Trish
Davies, Roz Denny, Patrizia
Diemling, Stephanie Donaldson,
Coralie Dorman, Matthew Drennan,
Sarah Edmonds, Joanna Farrow, Rafi
Fernandez, Maria Filippelli, Jenni
Fleetwood, Christine France, Silvano
Franco, Yasuko Fukuoka, Sarah
Gates, Shirley Gill, Brian Glover,
Nicola Graimes, Rosamund Grant,
Carole Handslip, Juliet Harbutt,
Rebekah Hassan, Shaun Hill, Simona
Hill, Deh-Ta Hsiung, Shehzad
Husain, Jessica Houdret, Christine
Ingram, Judy Jackson, Becky
Johnson, Bridget Jones, Manisha
Kanini, Sheila Kimberley, Soheila
Kimberley, Lucy Knox, Masaki Ko,
Elizabeth Lambert Ortez, Ruby Le

Bois, Clare Lewis, Sara Lewis, Patricia
Lousada, Gilly Love, Lesley Mackley,
Norma MacMillan, Sue Maggs,
Kathy Man, Sally Mansfield, Maggie
Mayhew, Norma Miller, Jane Milton,
Sallie Morris, Anna Mosesson, Janice
Murfitt, Annie Nichols, Suzannah
Olivier, Maggie Pannell, Katherine
Richmond, Keith Richmond, Rena
Salaman, Jennie Shapter, Anne
Sheasby, Ysanne Spevack, Marlena
Spieler, Jenny Stacey, Liz Trigg,
Christopher Trotter, Linda Tubby,
Sunil Vijayakar, Hilaire Walden, Laura
Washburn, Steven Wheeler, Jenny
White, Biddy White-Lennon, Kate
Whiteman, Rosemary Wilkinson,
Carolo Wilson, Elizabeth Wolf-
Cohen, Jeni Wright, Annette Yates

Home Economists: Eliza Baird,
Alex Barker, Julie Beresford, Sascha
Brodie, Jacqueline Clark, Fergal
Connolly, Joanne Craig, Stephanie
England, Joanna Farrow, Annabel
Ford, Christine France, Tonia George,
Carole Handslip, Kate Jay, Jill Jones,
Clare Lewis, Sara Lewis, Lucy
McKelvie, Emma MacIntosh,
Emma Patmore, Bridget Sargeson,
Jennie Shapter, Joy Skipper, Carole
Tennant, Linda Tubby, Sunil
Vijayakar, Jenny White

Photographers: Karl Adamson,
Edward Allwright, Peter Anderson,
David Armstrong, Tim Auty,
Caroline Barty, Steve Baxter,
Martin Brigdale, Nicki Dowey,
James Duncan, Gus Filgate,
John Freeman, Iain Garlick,
Michelle Garrett, Will Heap,
Peter Henley, John Heseltine,
Amanda Heywood, Ferguson
Hill, Janine Hosegood, David
Jordan, Andrea Jones, Maris
Kelly, Dave King, Don Last,
William Lingwood, Patrick
McLeary, Michael Michaels,
Steve Moss, Thomas Odulate,
Debby Patterson, Juliet Piddington,
Peter Reilly, Craig Robertson,
Simon Smith, Sam Stowell,
Polly Wreford

Stylists: Alison Austin, Shannon
Beare, Madeleine Brehaut,
Frances Cleary, Tessa Evelegh,
Marilyn Forbes, Annabel Ford,
Nicola Fowler, Michelle Garrett,
Carole Handslip, Jo Harris,
Cara Hobday, Kate Jay, Maria
Kelly, Lucy McKelvie, Marion
McLornan, Sarah O'Brien,
Marion Price, Jane Stevenson,
Helen Trent, Sophie Wheeler,
Judy Williams